James Purdy

James Purdy

Life of a Contrarian Writer

MICHAEL SNYDER

OXFORD
UNIVERSITY PRESS

OXFORD
UNIVERSITY PRESS

Oxford University Press is a department of the University of Oxford. It furthers
the University's objective of excellence in research, scholarship, and education
by publishing worldwide. Oxford is a registered trade mark of Oxford University
Press in the UK and certain other countries.

Published in the United States of America by Oxford University Press
198 Madison Avenue, New York, NY 10016, United States of America.

© Oxford University Press 2022

CIP data is on file at the Library of Congress

ISBN 978–0–19–760972–9

DOI: 10.1093/oso/9780197609729.001.0001

1 3 5 7 9 8 6 4 2

Printed by Sheridan Books, Inc., United States of America

Dedicated to
the memory of
Jorma Jules Sjoblom
(1919–2015)

Dennis Clay Moore
(1956–2020)

John Uecker
(1946–2022)

Contents

James Purdy

Introduction

The Mystery of James Purdy

"Get them by heart, and then between you and me we'll put them all in apple-pie order."

—James Purdy, *Jeremy's Version* (1970)

In October 1956, poet Dame Edith Sitwell sat in Montegufoni, the Sitwell family's Tuscan castle, transfixed by the stories of an unknown American writer. On a hunch, James Purdy had sent her his privately published collection. He had been struggling to get published, and earlier that year, a wealthy friend generously financed the printing of *Don't Call Me By My Right Name*. Purdy sent the slim volume, adorned with his Cocteauesque line drawings, to writers and critics with whom he thought his work would resonate.

Purdy mailed the book from New York, where he was visiting his older brother, Richard. He noticed a little post office near Richard's hotel. He rapped on the door but a man said, "We're closed!" Purdy looked so forlorn that the clerk let him in and examined his package to Italy. "What an address!" Purdy realized the clerk was Italian and seemed to know something of its destination. "This isn't tied properly," he remarked, and proceeded to retie it "beautifully." "Then he gave me a long look, said 'okay. Good luck.' Good luck, he said. He never knew how wonderful that was; I often wondered if that Post Office existed. Maybe it just appeared for that one day. Well, that changed everything" because, had Edith Sitwell not liked the book, "I would have given up and never become a real writer."[1]

Though Purdy received responses to his collection replete with praise from legends such as Langston Hughes, Tennessee Williams, Elizabeth Bishop, and Thornton Wilder, the grandest of all to reply was Sitwell. Many revered Dame Edith as a magnificent poet and tastemaker—a visionary in the tradition of great English eccentrics. She was a stern critic but also a strong champion of writers she found deserving but overlooked, some of them gay men, such as her brother, Osbert Sitwell, and Denton Welch. After finishing Purdy's collection, Sitwell felt compelled to write. Several stories were "superb; nothing short of masterpieces," possessing a "terrible, heart-breaking quality." She was so "deeply impressed by this book that, on the chance" Purdy had no British publisher, she had already written her London friend and publisher Victor Gollancz, advising him to acquire Purdy's book. She hoped Purdy would soon "have another work ready."[2]

Stunned, James was prompted to send Sitwell his novella *63: Dream Palace*, which another friend had paid to have privately published. In November, she responded that he was "really a great writer" and she was "quite overcome. What anguish, what heart-breaking truth! And what utter simplicity. The knife is turned and turned in one's heart. From the terrible first pages—(the first sentence is, in itself, a masterpiece) to the heart-rending last pages, there isn't a single false note." Sitwell judged *63: Dream Palace* equal to or perhaps "even greater" than the short stories and noted that her appreciation of the stories had only deepened since her first letter. She hoped they could meet when she would be in New York in early 1957. "You are truly a writer of genius," she declared.[3]

Through Sitwell's intervention, Victor Gollancz published *63: Dream Palace: A Novella and Nine Stories* in Great Britain in summer 1957, which led to New Directions publishing an expanded collection, *Color of Darkness*, in the United States late in the year. This in turn led to Farrar, Straus and Cudahy (later Farrar, Straus and Giroux) publishing four novels that established his reputation, beginning with *Malcolm* in 1959 and concluding with *Eustace Chisholm and the Works* in 1967. Sitwell reviewed his first British book in the *Times Literary Supplement*, again providing him with an invaluable introduction to the literary world. "Mr. Purdy is a superb writer, using all the fires of the heart and the crystallising powers of the brain." He was in the "very highest rank of contemporary American writers" and *63: Dream Palace* was "a masterpiece." Within two years, she was convinced that "in the future he will be regarded as the greatest American prose writer of our time." Going even further, Sitwell proclaimed: "I am convinced that in the future he will be known as one of the greatest writers produced in America during the last hundred years."[4]

Dame Edith's prediction never came to pass. Although Purdy's critical reputation quickly grew, it peaked in the 1960s, and he never enjoyed a bestseller. Among mainstream readers his name remains obscure. Nevertheless, his work has influenced a host of major writers and accrued a diverse cult following that includes many gay or queer readers. This influence has been both direct and indirect. For example, the minimalist aesthetic of Gordon Lish, an influential editor, writer, and teacher, was largely guided by Purdy's early stories. With Purdy in mind, Lish radically cut down Raymond Carver's early manuscripts, cocreating the neo-minimalist Carver style that became famous.[5] To Lish and several major figures like Jonathan Franzen, James Purdy was a visionary and an "authentic American genius," as Gore Vidal declared. Since Purdy's best work is on par with that of Melville and Faulkner, it is not surprising he was praised by the likes of Tennessee Williams, William Carlos Williams, and Joan Didion. Purdy's literary significance has long been much greater than his sales and public recognition suggest.

As is the case with many novelists, Purdy's work was personal, reflecting his own life experience. Through a unique alchemy, he transformed those raw life materials into powerful, symbolic works that critique American history, society, and culture—and especially, the family. To some degree, as scholar and critic Frank Baldanza wrote in 1974, Purdy's vision touches the "experience of every American family." Many critics failed to discern his work's social and political edge, but Purdy insisted: "All of my work is a criticism of the United States, implicit not explicit."[6] His dogged investigation of American origins, ancestry, and identity constitutes a larger project— an "exploration of the American soul," as he put it.[7] English critic Stephen D. Adams described his works as a "cumulative endeavor to chart the ancestry of the national psyche."[8] Gordon Lish said Purdy's work was regarded "as a sort of aberration, and reviewers attempt to account for him as such. But he is not an aberration at all. His work issues from the central American myths." Alluding to William Carlos Williams's book title, he added: "It is solidly in the American grain."[9] In Purdy's only television appearance, he told a Dutch audience: "You see, people say I don't like the United States. But I am the United States. You can only hate what you love, what you are a part of."[10] His work, Purdy wrote, was likened to an underground river "flowing undetected through the American landscape."[11] Archetypally, Purdy dramatizes crises of fate, identity, desire, and human nature, conveying a tragic sense of life couched in dark laughter.

In the 1960s, Purdy was familiar to aficionados of contemporary fiction, and his stories and novels were taught in colleges and even high schools. Purdy was praised by seminal critics including Brooks Atkinson, Ihab Hassan, Donald Pease, and R. W. B. Lewis, who rated Purdy alongside Ralph Ellison and Saul Bellow. In 1964, Susan Sontag declared "anything Purdy writes is a literary event of importance," and he was "indisputably one of the half dozen or so living American writers most worth taking seriously."[12] Although Purdy's name has since slipped under the radar of many critics and professors, Sontag underscored the "deservedly high place" he held "in contemporary letters." Philosopher of language and novelist George Steiner said Purdy is "a writer of remarkable talent" whose books "take one by the throat and shake one's bones loose."[13] His work embodies the "American language at its best." Experiencing its "honesty and sensual immediacy," its "power to make nerve and bone speak," its "sharpness, integrity," and "life-giving energy," the reader's "imagination emerges somehow dignified."[14]

By 1990, however, readership, reviews, and academic attention had waned. Overseas, scholars Richard Canning in England and Marie-Claude Profit in France rated him a major figure, and he had a cult readership in Italy, but at home, he was either unknown or his reputation was overshadowed by controversy. The question of what caused this falling off has been repeatedly asked, but never quite satisfactorily answered. Why did Purdy's works not become more popular during his lifetime? Why did he not become canonical instead of remaining a cult figure? Some have pointed to the diversity and uncategorizable nature of his work and the commensurate challenge of locating an apt critical approach to it; others point to the homophobia of many Cold War–era critics and publishers. In early stories like "Man and Wife," Purdy bravely represented homosexuality with sympathy. Opening doors for later writers, Purdy boldly pushed the envelope in subject matter and literary strategy, following the frankly homoerotic early stories of Tennessee Williams. He was the first literary writer to publish the word *motherfucker*—which was bowdlerized in his first book by its English publisher. Cambridge literary scholar Tony Tanner contended that Purdy had never been done justice by many leading contemporary critics, who "simply don't know how to read his work properly."[15] Six years after Purdy died, Jon Michaud assessed his oeuvre in the *New Yorker*: "Unsparing, ambiguous, violent, and largely indifferent to the reader's needs, Purdy's fiction seems likely to remain an acquired taste. But it is a taste worth acquiring."[16]

Part of the answer to Purdy's never receiving mainstream recognition lies not in the work, but in the man. Over several decades, upset with publishers, editors, reviewers, and sometimes friends and partisans, he made reckless remarks and took actions that ill-served him. Looking back on Purdy's career, composer Gerald Busby underscored a "big, important streak of self-destructiveness." He rarely agreed to sit for interviews and would not appear on American television. "He was precisely *not* playing the game. That delighted him." He knew his worth: he was a major writer and "they had to play his game." In the interviews he did give, he castigated major periodicals and critics of the East Coast publishing apparatus. Purdy would walk into "publishers' offices and go on tirades." Signed to numerous major houses, he would "alienate himself from each one." He could "push anyone's buttons, to get their attention," Busby said. Jorma Sjoblom, Purdy's lover and lifelong friend, said "he could be sharp in his criticism" and "alienated some people."[17] Running through publishers like fashion trends, Purdy vocalized his dissatisfaction with the recognition or promotion he received, which, at the best of times, was weighty. Over the decades, therefore, a growing list of editors and publishers crossed Purdy off their lists. A lot of people got back at him, Busby said. "He made enemies. They buried his books."[18]

James Purdy was a staunch individualist, not a team player. He would "not play ball with the team" of the establishment, his friend James Link wrote, refusing to review their books, swap blurbs, or join official guilds.[19] Instead, he identified with the individual fighter, attracted to images of bullfighters and boxers. In the 1940s he collected bullfight posters, and on his mantle and on the walls of his studio apartment on 236 Henry Street in Brooklyn Heights, he displayed several framed antique lithographs of boxers ready for fisticuffs. For a time, Purdy hung out in a New York gym where fighters trained, to listen to their talk. As a writer struggling to publish, battling baffled editors, homophobic reviewers, and stingy publishers, Purdy was a fighter. "Writing is like being a boxer," he said in late career. "If you don't want to get knocked down, you shouldn't be in the game."[20] In *Out with the Stars* (1993), Abner Blossom, based on composer Virgil Thomson, tells his protégé: "I am above else a soldier and a fighter. For an artist never surrenders, never has in his possession the white flag." He is the "fighting man forever. Battles are his life-blood and energy. Fight! Struggle! Engage in mortal hand-to-hand combat. And then soar upward!"[21] Or, as Ishmael Reed following Muhammed Ali put it: "writin' is fightin'." This was Purdy's credo as he put up his dukes to agents, publishers, reviewers, and eventually, the entire Eastern literary establishment.[22]

Thus, in one vein, his story is that of an uncompromising artist's quixotic battle with the publishing establishment, taking them on, on his own. Pyrrhic victories, among others, were won along the way. Numerous friends uttered these six words: "He was his own worst enemy." But from an alternate perspective, the fact that Purdy's works of integrity and vision failed to reach a sizable audience is a condemnation not of a temperamental artist, but of a conservative, cliquey New York publishing world and book review system that failed to take risks to promote his eccentric genius. From the start, Purdy's queer and transgressive content repelled and embarrassed some critics, and even some of his own publishers. Roger Straus, for example, refused to defend *Eustace Chisholm and the Works* after it was attacked in a homophobic hatchet job by another FSG author, Wilfrid Sheed.

Nonetheless, Purdy's loyal friends and admirers continued to spread the word, and interest in his writing and reissues of his books intermittently appeared. In 2005, Jonathan Franzen, celebrated author of *The Corrections*, nominated *Eustace Chisholm and the Works* for the Clifton Fadiman Award for Excellence in Fiction, bestowed upon an overlooked novel. In his award speech, Franzen declared: "Mr. Purdy's novel is so good that almost any novel you read immediately after it will seem at least a little bit posturing, or dishonest, or self-admiring, in comparison." For Franzen and many other readers, it was this dark, witty, and insightful novel about Daniel Haws—who ignores his Native ancestry and denies his love for another man—that hooked them. To Franzen, Purdy "has been and continues to be one of the most undervalued and underread writers in America."[23]

———

Writing a biography of James Purdy presents special challenges. He took pains to conceal his background throughout his career, tossing out red herrings about his past. He was reticent, even deceptive, in presenting basic facts, such as his birthdate. Even Jorma Sjoblom believed Purdy to have been nine years younger than he actually was. Purdy often claimed he was from Fremont, Ohio, but he was born in Hicksville and grew up in Findlay—forty miles from Fremont. His false claim was also a nod to Sherwood Anderson, whose *Winesburg, Ohio* was set nearby. Like Anderson, Purdy writes with compassion about the alienation and despair suffered by people in small communities who feel different, queer.[24] Purdy's evasiveness about these facts, his resistance to giving a chronology, and his rejection of past attempted biographers have thwarted a full-length biography until now.[25]

Purdy's friend Tom Zulick remarked: "As much as he was a radical in some ways creatively, he was also a classical Midwestern man with classical ideas and mores, but informed by his intellect and his experiences as a gay man." One pronounced theme running through Purdy's life is instability and isolation at different periods, including his upbringing; another is his position as an outsider. As a gay man from the Midwest born in the early twentieth century, he identified with marginalized peoples: Natives (he claimed faint Ojibwe/Anishinaabe ancestry), black people, and the poor. To African American critic Joseph T. Skerrett Jr., Purdy's work evidences his "emotional identification with the powerless, the stigmatized, and the frustrated." Purdy was "suspicious of power," and always responded to "the outsiders."[26] In the 1990s, Purdy was vexed by gay activists who asked, "When did you come out?" He rejoined, "I was born out."[27]

Delving into Purdy's contrarianism, this biography seeks to understand why he was rarely content with the treatment he received from agents, editors, publishers, and critics. Regardless of how much praise he received, it never sufficed. This led contemporaries and friends, such as writers Joyce Carol Oates and Paul Bowles respectively, to wonder what it was Purdy wanted. As he sought recognition and promoted his books, his efforts often seemed to squander the goodwill extended to him. "James Purdy didn't play the game of being a writer well," said editor Don Weise, and he gained a reputation as difficult, even irrational.[28] Purdy's laments always center on a figure who had betrayed or neglected him, who was supposed to love and support him. These feelings perhaps have deep roots in Purdy's early, troubled family dynamic—his oft-absent father, his parents' divorce, and his mother who turned the family home into a rooming house.

Even visionaries are shaped by their times. This biography considers his life and works over his long career in their Great Depression, World War II, Cold War, late modernist, and postmodern contexts. Purdy insisted on radical artistic freedom, and with his liberal-anticommunist political stance, he was able, even as a gay and challenging writer, to easily benefit from American cultural capital and the support of the US government. He was part of a network of writers, scholars, critics, and publishers who had been in the Office of Strategic Services (OSS), and/or affiliated with its successor, the Central Intelligence Agency (CIA), the Congress for Cultural Freedom (CCF) that was secretly financed by the CIA, or other agencies promoting the image of the United States abroad, such as the United States Information Agency. Circa 1960, even a writer critical of the nation, provided he was not "red" or too "pink," could be embraced by these bureaus as exemplifying American freedom of expression.

Purdy spent much time alone chasing his vision, but to meet him is to encounter his fascinating friends, who inspired him and became material for his narratives. Among them were Gertrude Abercrombie, a Chicago surrealist artist; Sam Steward, a Midwestern English professor and aspiring literary writer turned tattooist and pornographer; Chicago writer Wendell Wilcox, who, like Steward, was a friend and correspondent of Gertrude Stein and Alice B. Toklas; and two gifted musicians, singer and composer Richard Hundley and pianist and composer Robert Helps, who was Purdy's neighbor in Brooklyn Heights. Celebrity friends included Tennessee Williams, Virgil Thomson, Gloria Vanderbilt, and Ned Rorem; Edward Albee was a lifelong frenemy. At one party Albee invited him to at his large loft, after James arrived, Edward just stared at him. "I'm not sure Edward ever talked to him" that night, said John Uecker, actor, director, and Purdy's longtime friend and assistant.[29]

From the 1970s through his last years, Purdy attracted circles of younger friends and companions, and he exerted an enduring influence on a constellation of writers, composers, directors, actors, and artists. Some of them, like writer John Stewart Wynne, wrote well-received fan letters. Others, like John Uecker, met Purdy through mutual friends such as Virgil Thomson. Still others, like novelist Matthew Stadler, were enchanted after being assigned to review his work. These were mostly younger gay men, actors or writers who became intense admirers, often originally from the Midwest. Between Purdy and various combinations of acolytes was friendship, mentorship, brotherhood, and love; but also envy, rivalry, confusion, and, sometimes, hurt feelings. Some acolytes were excommunicated, some friends left of their own accord, but most who came into contact with James Purdy kept him in their minds and hearts for the rest of their lives.

James Purdy: Life of a Contrarian Writer both penetrates and celebrates mysteries of this enigmatic writer, while offering the first complete biography of him. In many cases, however, trying to solve a mystery just expands the scope of the mystery, or leads to more enigma. With so many participants gone, several puzzles of Purdy's life may never be solved—and probably ought not to be.

1

Hicksville, Ohio

"He was a stranger from Hicksville, Ohio."
—Mark Twain, *The Adventures of Huckleberry Finn* (1884)

James Purdy was born in Defiance County—appropriate for a fierce indi-
vidualist who would defy social norms and the literary establishment. In
his mother Vera's home village of Hicksville, James Otis Purdy arrived on
July 17, 1914. Lying in northwestern Ohio near the Indiana border, the
county and its seat, Defiance, were named after Fort Defiance, the base for
General "Mad" Anthony Wayne and troops during their 1794 war against
Shawnee, Delaware, Ojibwe, Ottawa, and other Natives who had repelled
Euro-American invaders of their homelands. Though descended mainly
from white settlers to the area, Purdy claimed a small strain of Ojibwe
(Anishinaabe) ancestry through his maternal great-grandmother.[1]

Growing up, James was struck by passed-down stories and memorials of
bloody Indian Wars and battles before and after Ohio achieved statehood in
1803. He heard tales of "Mad" Anthony Wayne being brought in by George
Washington to subjugate Natives who refused to cede land; of Blue Jacket
(Shawnee) and Little Turtle (Miami) leading the Native alliance in the 1790s
to battle escalating settler encroachments in what became western Ohio; of
St. Clair's Defeat, one of the worst losses ever inflicted on the American military by Natives; and of Wayne ordering all Indian villages and crops within
a fifty-mile radius of Fort Defiance to be destroyed. Although the Treaty of
Greeneville (1795) stipulated that whites could not settle in northwest Ohio,
the fort remained as a trading post in defiance of the treaty.

Vestiges and memory of an Indigenous presence was fresher in northwest
Ohio than in other parts of the state because it was north of the Greenville
Treaty line. Thus, in *Jeremy's Version* (1970), perhaps his most autobiographical novel, Hittisleigh, based on Hicksville, is "not entirely forgetful of Indian
battles and skirmishes and the War of 1812, with flowering forests and hills,

and valleys favored by yellow moonlight. This was where Wilders Fergus met and won the hand of Elvira."[2] Wilders Fergus is modeled on James's father, William Purdy: tall, handsome, serious, with blue eyes and dark, straight hair. Elvira Summerlad Fergus is based on his mother, Vera Otis Purdy: short, attractive, free-spirited, with round cheeks and light, curly hair. Like his father, James grew to be tall with expressive blue eyes that sparkled and laughed.

In 1817, the Treaty of Maumee Rapids was signed, forcing Natives to relinquish four million acres in northwest Ohio. In 1823, James's great-grandparents, Archibald and Margaret Purdy, moved from New York to north-central Ohio, near Mansfield, the seat of Richland County. They established a farm and raised a family of seven surviving children, suffering the loss of three boys. Born in Pennsylvania, Archibald Purdy had lived in Ontario County, New York, where he was in milling for several years before moving to Ohio.

James Purdy's ancestors were mostly English and Scottish Presbyterians; he had less Irish ancestry than he had believed.[3] As a boy, he nearly memorized the King James Bible while attending Presbyterian Sunday School and the works of Shakespeare at home. Purdy reflected, "I was brought up Calvinist in the Presbyterian Church. I'm grateful." Calvinist thought, stressing Martin Luther's doctrine of justification of faith alone, the grace of God, and predestination, influenced early American intellectual and literary culture. Hawthorne and Melville, two of Purdy's favorite American writers, grappled with Calvinism. Reading the King James Bible helped him greatly as a writer: its "beauty and outrageous stories" influenced his aesthetic. James Joyce is "like an old lady compared to the Old Testament. God, it's just full of everything. Terror! I don't know how lovely people read it without going mad," Purdy told Reed Woodhouse.[4]

With the 1831 Treaty of Wapakoneta, the remaining Natives in the region agreed under duress to give up their land. In 1833, James's grandfather, Boyd Wallace Purdy, was born on his father's farm. In 1856, Boyd Purdy attended progressive Oberlin College, which pioneered the integration of Negroes and coeducation for women. But he and his friends got in trouble for celebrating the election of a politician they had boosted with a raging bonfire and he left the college. Boyd later bought a farm in Richland County but sold it to enter livestock trading. He bought stock in Ohio, Indiana, and Illinois, then shipped it east and sold it in Buffalo, Albany, and New York City. For a decade, he made Buffalo his headquarters.[5] A Republican, Boyd Purdy was described as an "excellent citizen, genial and affable by nature."[6]

Around 1867, Boyd Purdy met Catherine (Kitty) Mason. Born in Niagara County, New York, in 1843, Kitty had been an orphan brought up by missionaries and was eventually adopted by Charles Mason of Lockport.[7] Two of her brothers operated tugboats in Brooklyn; one owned a house on Henry Street in Brooklyn Heights—the same street on which their great-nephew James lived eighty years later.[8] For over two years, Kitty had also attended Oberlin College and was among the second class to include women. In 1869, Boyd and Kitty married and went on to have eight children (three of whom died as infants). In 1870, the family settled in Wood County, Ohio, near Bowling Green. Boyd leased one thousand acres that he operated for four years, feeding livestock and shipping them east. He later purchased and farmed twenty-four acres and built an estate. White peach trees growing there offered sweet, flavorful fruit.[9]

In June 1877, James's father, Boyd William Purdy, was born. To avoid confusion with his father, he was called William. Nicknamed Will, he would exert his will to bring about progress and profit and could seem willful. As a student, he showed writing talent, winning a prize in school for best short composition among forty peers. On a different assignment, he did not receive a pleasing grade, so he asked the teacher "what ailed it. She said that it was 'too vivid.' Some of the class said if I wrote about a skunk you could smell him."[10] William had three older brothers—Andrew W. (Andy), Charles H., and Frank A.—and a younger sister, Cora Adelia.

Achieving higher class status, James Purdy's maternal line did not make their living off the land. His grandfather, George K. Otis, was born in 1844 and at age eighteen enlisted in the Union Army during the Civil War. After taking ill during the Battle of Franklin in late 1864, Otis served as military postmaster for several months in Kentucky before returning to battle. He again became ill and, after less than a year, was honorably discharged. Back home in Milford Township, Defiance County, George enrolled in business school.[11] Entering business, he acquired wealth early on, eventually building a showplace home in idyllic Hicksville. The grand Victorian George K. Otis residence, with turrets and even a small bowling alley upstairs, was emblazoned on a postcard. Otis was a friend and associate of Asa S. Bushnell, who became Ohio's fortieth governor in 1896. Like Bushnell, Otis sold farm machinery, among his many other enterprises.[12]

In 1845, James's maternal great-grandmother, Nancy Ann (Nettie) Shouf, was born in Ohio, one of fifteen children. "I knew my great-grandmother, and I remember her speech very clearly. In *The House of the Solitary Maggot*

Figure 1.1   Postcard of George K. Otis Residence, Hicksville, Ohio.

you might find her voice," Purdy later said.[13] Nettie grew up in Bryan, the Williams County seat, in the state's northwesternmost corner. Devoutly Presbyterian, Nettie was known for integrity and sociability.[14] James Purdy was told Nettie was one-eighth Ojibwe, a tribe once commonly found in northern Ohio territory. During his childhood, Purdy's maternal line spoke of their alleged Indian ancestry, piquing his interest.

On Valentine's Day, 1864, nineteen-year-old Nettie Shouf married Daniel S. Cowhick, twelve years her senior.[15] A Virginian, Cowhick moved to Ohio and became a miller in Bryan. In 1866, with a partner, he erected a steam flouring mill. In October, he and Nettie had a daughter, Minnie Mae Cowhick, Purdy's grandmother, later nicknamed "Cutie." Minnie's sister Maud was born two years later, but a son died in infancy. Daniel's business failed and the family moved around, settling in Hicksville in 1875 and returning there in 1879 after two moves.[16] Cowhick's itinerancy evinces his struggles to support his family. He went on an extended tour of the West without his wife and daughters, returning in 1882.[17] In August 1884, fifty-one-year-old Daniel Cowhick ended his pain, taking his life with a gun. Minnie, seventeen, was still in high school.

George K. Otis grew lonesome after his wife, the former Sarah Hilbert, died in 1883. Minnie Mae Cowhick, over two decades his junior, caught his eye while she was working as a copyist in Hicksville.[18] In April 1885, George, forty-one, married Minnie, eighteen, and the ceremony was held at Nettie's home, with a few friends present.[19] The next day, the newlyweds commenced a two-week tour of southern Ohio, and on their return, hosted a large reception at their splendid residence. The Hicksville Cornet Band tooted while up to a hundred guests ate, drank, and socialized on the spacious property. Afterward at Nettie's, "time was spent most happily in sallies of wit, humor, and in listening to vocal music" until late. The couple then spent several weeks enjoying Dayton, the Gem City, home of the Wright brothers and Orville Wright's classmate and friend, the black poet Paul Laurence Dunbar.[20]

In 1885, the year George Otis remarried, he stopped selling farm equipment and moved into general merchandising, speculation, then real estate. His varied enterprises, entailing a drug business and (like the Wright brothers) a printshop, sometimes failed and even lost great sums, but resiliently, he was always ready to start over with renewed vigor. Otis "always met his fellow-man with an encouraging word, a happy salutation and a hearty laugh, and none of the shadows, pains and disappointments of his own life were ever manifested to others." To his family he was "loving, considerate, patient and solicitous" for their comfort and success.[21] An elder of the Presbyterian Church, Otis was elected to political office several times, serving as clerk, treasurer, trustee, and justice of the peace in Milford Township, Hicksville Township, and Hicksville. In 1894, he was appointed a term as Hicksville postmaster by President Cleveland.[22] At some point after Minnie settled into her new home, Nettie sold hers and moved in with Minnie and George. Their home became to Nettie a "little kingdom, over which she ruled, a tender and loving sovereign, devoted to her children, yet always finding time in her busy life to share the joys and sorrows of her neighbors and friends."[23]

Vera Cowhick Otis, James's mother, was born in March 1887 at her parents' mansion on Cornelia and Main. Her middle name, Cowhick, was her mother's maiden name; Vera later extended this naming tradition to her son, James Otis Purdy. A spirited youth, vivacious and fun, Vera loved to sing and dreamed of a career in music. She also enjoyed painting china plates as a hobby. Young Vera went to see Ruby, a "black fortune teller, really a psychic," Purdy recalled. "You will have three sons and your middle son will become world famous," Ruby told her.[24]

Vera's brother, Lloyd Melville Otis, was born in 1888, the year after she was. He went to University of Michigan Medical College and graduated in 1913. A surgeon, Dr. Otis in 1915 established Otis Hospital in Celina, Ohio. In 1916, Nettie was a patient, and his mother Minnie Otis worked for him there

Figure 1.2 Otis family photo in front of the George K. Otis residence in Hicksville, Ohio. Front row second from left, Vera Otis (mother); center, George K. Otis (grandfather); top, third from left, Minnie Mae Otis (grandmother); top, second from right, Nettie Cowhick (great-grandmother). Courtesy of John Uecker, Purdy Estate.

for a time.[25] Dr. Lloyd Otis visited the Purdys in November 1918; having been commissioned a lieutenant in the medical corps, he was about to depart for Fort Oglethorpe, Georgia, a week before the Great War ended. Lloyd married Barbara de Audritsh and they had a son and daughter.[26] Their son, Purdy's cousin, James John Otis ("Dr. Jim"), became a doctor and joined his father's practice. (Dr. Jim's son, Jim Lloyd Otis, became a football hero, All-American for Ohio State, and in the 1970s, played pro for three NFL teams.)

Before William met Vera, in the late 1880s and 1890s, a natural gas and oil boom rocked northwestern Ohio, bringing frenzied growth and change. Invigorated were Findlay, where James would spent his later childhood and adolescence, and Wood County, his father's homeland. In the novel *Poor White*, Sherwood Anderson writes: "Over night, towns grew into cities. A madness took hold of the minds of the people. Villages like Lima and Findlay, Ohio" mushroomed to "small cities within a few weeks" and wealth seemed "to spurt from the very earth."[27] The boom attracted an influx of outsiders and led to increased lawlessness, but also spurred robust growth and, eventually, community development. In the "very heart of gas-land," Findlay was the headquarters of Ohio Oil Company, which by 1908 controlled half of all field production in Illinois, Indiana, and Ohio, and all that oil flowed to the refineries of John D. Rockefeller's Standard Oil Trust.[28] Between 1895 and 1903, Ohio was top producer of crude oil in the United States, before being surpassed by Texas and Oklahoma. In 1911, Ohio Oil again became independent when the Supreme Court broke up Standard Oil. The wells were extremely productive, but most involved in the industry, from wildcatters to tycoons, failed to understand this natural resource was in limited supply. So much gas was being flared in Findlay that it was called the City of Light, after Paris.[29]

Amid such flaming optimism, in 1897 William Purdy graduated from high school, and in the following year entered banking as a clerk at the Exchange Bank in Bowling Green. Will did not attend college, but was a great reader of James Fenimore Cooper's Leatherstocking Tales, Civil War history, and the King James Bible. He passed books and love of reading down to James. "I have always liked to read of the various Indian tales," William wrote James in 1961. "I liked *The Last of the Mohicans* and *The Deerslayer* although *The Pioneers* is rated best as it is famous as a picture of pioneer days in Northern New York."[30] At the turn of the century, Will's father, Boyd, was a rural mail carrier; among Will's siblings, Andy, Charles, and Cora were educators and Frank worked for the IRS.[31]

In 1901, William left his position in Bowling Green and started work at the Hicksville National bank sixty-five miles west. That year, electric lights reached the village, which also passed a law forbidding sale of beverages above 3.2 percent alcohol, to tamp down on the rowdiness that accompanied increased commerce.[32] William abstained, perhaps detrimental to his career, since he did not join colleagues in the "manly vices" of drinking and chewing, consistent with his service as treasurer for Hicksville Presbyterian Church.[33] Early on, Will seemed to make good contacts; in 1904, he joined the Masons and in 1905, invited by the Hon. W. G. Kopp, he attended an "entertainment given at the temple of justice in Defiance."[34] But in 1907, Dr. J. Scudder Hull, Frank Clemmer, and Will motored to Lima to attend horse races, and, after returning, attended to "matters pertaining to the races" in Hicksville, apparently acting as bookies.[35]

In late 1907 and early 1908, Will was quite ill.[36] In December it was reported "Mr. Purdy a short time ago became quite ill but recovered somewhat

Figure 1.3 Photo of William Purdy. Courtesy of the Purdy family.

and returned to his work in the bank and is now suffering a relapse."[37] In mid-January, he had been confined to his room for ten days without improvement. Late in the month, a "very severe attack of Rheumatism" confined him. He was hospitalized in Michigan and slowly recovered.[38]

Before his illness, Will had begun courting Vera Otis, almost a decade younger, a teenager when he commenced business in town. Will's sister, Cora, opinionated and willful like him, was protective. She felt he and Vera were ill-matched and stressed their contrasting temperaments. Vera was youthful and lively, while Will was formal in demeanor and clothing, favoring high collars and high shoes. Nevertheless, on Sunday afternoon, August 8, 1908, William and Vera, twenty-one, were married at George and Minnie's home, Vera's birthplace. Only relatives and a few close friends attended. Dr. Hull was best man, and Miss LaVerne Hart, an aunt, was bridesmaid. William, a "gentleman of high moral standing and social acquirements," had been accepted by the community, but the more popular

Figure 1.4 Portrait photo of Vera Purdy.
Courtesy of the Purdy family.

Vera was "highly accomplished and a favorite with the old as well as the young people who best know her."[39]

In 1909 the couple moved into a home near the George K. Otis manse. Vera Purdy, a sterling hostess, entertained the Home and Foreign Missionary Society of the Presbyterian Church at her and Will's "pleasant new home" and served delicious refreshments.[40] This neighborhood full of large trees is where James enjoyed his golden early childhood. As a boy, James played at grandmother Minnie's house, and the unique manse took hold of James's imagination, becoming a model for grand homes in his Midwestern novels.

During this period, Will and Vera had both bad luck and blessings. In December 1908, William was painfully wounded after catching a finger in a check puncher at the bank.[41] Also that month, only four months after his daughter's wedding, George Otis died at age sixty-five. In July 1909, William resigned from his position as assistant cashier at Hicksville National Bank and entered real estate—a far riskier profession.[42]

Setting up his headquarters on Main Street, Hicksville, USA, Will dealt in real estate requiring travel. In August 1910, William returned home after a month on the road through Michigan and Illinois on behalf of a real estate company, reporting fine crops and abundant fruit. He took in lectures at a Chautauqua held at Tecumseh, Michigan, named for the Shawnee leader.[43] Lengthy absences became increasingly typical, though on Thanksgiving 1909, Vera and William welcomed their first child, Richard.

If William was a staid businessman, Vera was a talented and ebullient young mother. In 1910, Vera, nearly twenty-three, sang "A Clean Heart" at a Woman's Christian Temperance Union meeting in Hicksville, and sang at another the next month.[44] (In the late twentieth century, when James hosted young gay men at his Brooklyn Heights apartment, he would quip: "it's like a WCTU meeting around here!") In the coming years, Vera kept performing at club meetings and events.[45] She was a member of the Order of the Eastern Star, a Masonic body open to both men and women.

Vera was a sometime protégée of two prodigies, though details are scant. One was lithesome Maude Adams, famous for playing Peter Pan on Broadway, whose father's family was from Ohio. Adams never married, preferring relationships with women. The second mentor, who trained Vera in singing, was actress and theater producer Amelia Bingham, who hailed from Hicksville. While Bingham went on to a successful career on Broadway from 1896 to 1926, family ties were strong, and she frequently returned to Hicksville, where she performed at Huber Opera House and visited the Defiance County Fair. Vera passed down her love of music and performance to Richard and James.[46]

As a young mother in Hicksville, Vera remained close with her mother and grandmother. Nettie and Minnie helped fill the gap when William was absent on business trips. In 1910, 1911, and 1912 the *Bryan Democrat* social page reported the same story: "Mrs. Nettie Cowhick, Mrs. Minnie Otis, Mrs. Will Purdy, and son Richard, of Hicksville" visited Vera's aunt, Mrs. L. V. Kenner (née Maud Cowhick) of Bryan, Ohio.[47] Nettie's father had established the *Democrat*, perhaps explaining the ample coverage of Nettie and family.[48] William, focused on flipping farmland, was absent from most such reports. In 1912, Vera and Richard, age two, traveled to Bowling Green "to visit Mr. Purdy's people for a week." They went on to Toledo, then joined William at Tecumseh, Michigan, for a longer visit. In December 1913, Will was with Vera, Richard, age four, and Minnie when visiting family in Toledo and Bryan over the holidays.[49]

William Purdy followed his ambition to become a successful financier and realize the American Dream. Three years after leaving banking, he had accumulated sufficient capital and the confidence of others and was poised to make a comeback. In 1912, in Columbus, Will, brother Frank, and three others incorporated the American State Bank of Hicksville, the village's second national bank, with capital of $75,000 (equivalent to over $1,960,000 in 2020).[50] On the corner of High and Maple Streets, they erected the American Building, Hicksville's only three-story business edifice, dubbed "the new Purdy block."[51] It was the most modern design in the county, and, four years after completion, remained the match of any building in a comparable Ohio town.[52]

In February 1913, Boyd W. Purdy died and was buried in Bowling Green. James therefore never met his grandfathers. "Purdy's microcosm—as far as hometown Ohio is concerned—is heavily matriarchal," Bowling Green professor Frank Baldanza has noted. More bad news followed in March as floods devastated Findlay, Dayton, and other cities, killing up to 470. After mourning his father, William kept bringing progress to Hicksville, developing the bank and the American Building. Renters included a dentist, an optometrist, and Maxwell Bros. clothing store. In June, the Post Office Department accepted his proposal to lease new quarters for a post office. In July, Hicksville contracted Will to establish, regulate, and maintain "two public water closets and two public toilet stations" for one year in the American Building. These "comfort stations," needed due to increased trade, promoted commerce and tourism.[53]

Business rivals accused Will of receiving special favor from the village and petitioned for an injunction. The mayor and city council retorted on the front page of the Tribune that "at no time, at no place" had "Mr. Purdy ever asked the Council for any favor or concession." On the contrary, he had spent his own money helping to construct and connect the new sewer line, though it was a public sewer any business on the street could tap into. Petitioners were motivated by selfishness. In 1914, Will with two others was appointed to the "County Board of complaints, to review tax assessments."[54]

Business was at first promising, but American Bank eventually ran into difficulty. Will's apparent early success as banker and entrepreneur was threatened by an accumulation of debts.[55] Before James was born, trouble was already brewing in his parents' marriage. Clashing temperaments, difference in age, and economic strain brought alienation. Exacerbating this, before James was born, Vera had given birth to a boy who died very young.[56]

Amid Will's frenzied activity, James Otis Purdy was born in Hicksville on July 17, 1914. His birthday was sandwiched between momentous events in Europe: the assassination of Archduke Franz Ferdinand on June 28 and the outbreak of World War I a month later.

Eight months later, grandmother Minnie Otis was married to widower Abner S. Nisley, who disappointed her. For one thing, he seemed to take an inordinate interest in his pretty stepdaughter, Vera. "Cutie" lived with Ab in Farmer Township until October 1918, when he sold his farm and they returned to Hicksville. Ab and Minnie thus held considerable savings then—a fact not lost on son-in-law William.

Will convinced Ab and Minnie, and his mother, Kitty, to loan him large sums. He ultimately lost most of this money in speculations that did not pan out. When James was a toddler, Will purchased 401 acres of farmland near Defiance for $60,000 (equivalent to about $1,424,600 in 2020).[57] The following month, he made "quite a considerable land deal," trading his American Building for 243 acres of rich Paulding County soil. The swap made William the owner of 645 acres total—a magnate. The consideration involved $100,000 worth of property (equivalent to around $2,374,400 in 2020). He had already disposed of most of his Hicksville properties, which included the Hicksville Handle Company. "It is not known just what Mr. Purdy will do," the *Fort Wayne News* reported.[58]

The Purdys were united in July 1916, when Will, Vera, Richie, age six, and James (then nicknamed Jimmie) visited the Bowling Green home of Kitty to celebrate James's second birthday. The following month, William ran for county treasurer; some claimed his interest in acquiring land was a conflict of interest, but he still won.[59]

In spring 1917, when James was nearly three, Will became secretary and general manager of Maumee Valley Manufacturing Company. This new enterprise bought a lumberyard and, boosted by the Chamber of Commerce, was supposedly "already overwhelmed with orders for auto hearses, showcases, and novelty furniture," some designed for banks, to be manufactured on a "much increased scale over its predecessor." In April, William bought a property on the corner of South and Main streets, where he planned to "remove the house and erect thereon a new residence." Since he was chosen as manager of the company, his family would continue to live in Hicksville. But five months later, Will resigned. In late 1918, the company had "not been operating up to its capacity," and soon disappeared, another of Will's disappointments.[60]

Figure 1.5 (Clockwise) Baby James, Grandmother
Catherine "Kitty" Purdy, Nettie Cowhick, Richard
Purdy, Minnie Mae Otis. Courtesy of John Uecker,
Purdy Estate.

In September 1918, William, his hair having turned prematurely gray
at age forty-one, received more bad news. The mayor of Hicksville filed a
lawsuit against him and five others who had been village councilmen until
1917. The case, which dragged out for three years, placed strain on Will,
souring him on the town. A report on the lawsuit predicted "some political
graveyards will be dug up before the question is finally disposed of."[61] The
petition stated that during 1914, the council offered street paving bonds for
sale totaling $48,000, to improve five streets. Because the Great War created
a "dull financial market," no bidders arose. As a result, the council passed
a resolution authorizing Will to act as agent, for which he received a commission of 5 percent or $2,400 (about $62,114 in 2020). Will sold the bonds
in Cleveland and received his cut.[62] The mayor, alleging the council had
no legal right to employ an agent, and noting the resolution and bids were

not advertised, sought the sum of $2,809 plus interest. When the council contracted Purdy, the streets were torn up and ready to be paved, the normal process of selling bonds having been expected. Expediting the contract was the need to complete the job before winter. The council said Hicksville lost no money in the process.

In 1919, when James was nearly five, a judge of the common pleas court absolved the ex-councilmen from responsibility, yet still held William, whom they contracted, to answer to the charge of receiving a commission. In 1920, the appellate court upheld the verdict, and in 1921, after another appeal, to Will's frustration, the Ohio Supreme Court ruled Will was liable for $2,309.[63] This seemed unfair, plus he had already spent the money on land. Will felt betrayed and bullied. This verdict is a major reason he decided to move his family two counties away.

2

A Day after the Fair

"There is something memorable in the experience to be had by going into a fair ground that stands at the edge of a Middle Western town on a night after the annual fair has been held. The sensation is one never to be forgotten. On all sides are ghosts, not of the dead, but of living people."

—Sherwood Anderson, *Winesburg, Ohio* (1919)

In April 1919, when James was not yet five, his family moved to Findlay, Ohio, the Hancock County seat, a small city about eighty miles from Hicksville. William Purdy would locate his business there, it was reported. He soon found work as an accountant. Vera did not particularly want to leave her picturesque hometown. James, too, later idealized the bucolic Hicksville of his early childhood. In contrast, Findlay was a boomtown after the boom, and the Purdys arrived a day after the fair, to use the idiom Purdy later borrowed for a title. At first, the family rented a house at 201 Lima Street, then a different house on Lima, before finally settling at 115 East Lima Street in 1925. James attended Lincoln Elementary School.[1]

A quintessentially Midwestern Main Street, Findlay offered an ice cream parlor, a candy kitchen, an Elks Lodge, and movie theaters. All seemed to be watched over by a copper John Hancock standing atop the grand Hancock County Courthouse built in 1880 during the oil and gas boom, and below him, a triad of female forms representing Law, Justice, and Mercy. The history of Findlay is saturated in the Indigenous and Americana. A Wyandot town that settlers called Indian Green formerly lay six miles west of Findlay; Wyandots tended maize along the Blanchard River and within present city limits. The city's origin was the site of Fort Findlay, which had aided troop movement north to Detroit in the War of 1812. Johnny Appleseed often passed through, and throughout the 1830s owned a nursery there. Late in

Figure 2.1 Postcard, "East Lima Street from South Main," with Purdy's house on right, second from front.

the century, thanks to the boom and industrialization, Findlay's population jumped from 4,630 residents in 1885 to 17,000 by 1900. Findlay College opened in 1886 amid industrial prosperity. But by the turn of the century, the "feverish pitch of oil development had declined" and by 1910, its peak had "long since passed." In the 1920s, horses were no longer commonly seen in town, replaced by automobiles that increasingly filled streets and curbs, necessitating traffic police at busy intersections, soon replaced by traffic lights. Findlay offered some urban amenities: at its peak, three electric inter-urban trolley lines could speed one to Toledo, Lima, and Bowling Green. Until 1932, in Findlay, one could hop on a streetcar, then connect to a train to go "just about anywhere and at any time on a railroad."[2]

In October 1919, Purdy's great-grandmother Nettie Cowhick died in Hicksville, and five-year-old James attended her memorable funeral. An Ojibwe woman wearing Native garb came to pay her respects. Family members found this odd or inappropriate and were scandalized; an attempt was made to usher her out. She persisted, declaring, "Nettie is one of us," Purdy related late in life.[3] Having Native blood in the early twentieth century was not often regarded as a source of pride among Americans, but rather a liability to conceal. Although William did not believe there was Indian ancestry in Vera's family line, Vera took an interest in genealogy and traced her ancestry to before the Revolutionary War, Purdy said.[4]

Figure 2.2 Purdy residence at 115 E. Lima Street, Findlay, Ohio, by Parker Sams. Courtesy of Parker Sams.

In April 1920, terror struck Hancock County. The "Palm Sunday outbreak," a series of ravaging tornados, struck the Midwest, killing hundreds. Tornados slammed townships over the county, destroying three hundred buildings including churches. Findlay, not directly hit, was damaged by forceful winds and rain.[5] In 1922, when James was eight, a storm toppled John Hancock from the courthouse, causing major damage. James also saw damaged Great War veterans in their thirties on his walk to school and back, some of them traumatized, disabled, or disfigured.

When the weather was fair, the Purdy family enjoyed diversions offered by Riverside Park, set along the Blanchard River, shaded by large maple and sycamore trees arching high overhead.[6] A fleet of boats transported folks between the park and Main Street bridge. Riverside Park offered a reservoir for swimming, boat rides, canoes, a petting zoo, mini cars and trains, a modest rollercoaster, moving pictures at the House of Mirth, a large auditorium, carnival games, and a carousel. The vibrant merry-go-round horses fascinated James. Marilyn Miller, a local talent who became a Broadway star, performed at Riverside with the Five Columbians, the Miller family vaudeville act that made Findlay their homebase.[7]

Residents of Findlay, predominantly white, "in outlook tended to be conservative," and at that time, did not yet significantly encourage pursuits of art, literature, and theater.[8] Fortunately, James and Richard found early mentors who did. One key mentor to James was Dr. Charles J. Ray of Gilboa, a village near Findlay, a family friend whom Vera fondly called "Doctie Ray." Ray was a bachelor, and probably a gay man; for decades, he lived with a much younger companion, Ed Scanland. Dr. Ray and Vera would go out foraging for remedial herbs, Purdy recalled.[9] Ray owned a library James found enchanting, and at age thirteen or fourteen, he borrowed eye-opening works such as Dr. R. von Krafft-Ebing's *Psychopathia Sexualis*, one of the earliest studies on homosexuality, and others by sexologist Dr. Havelock Ellis. "He had a splendid collection of books, mostly what people called belles lettres."[10] Dr. Ray often told Vera that James would become a writer.[11] Repeatedly, the doctor told a poignant story of a young couple's murder-suicide in an old, declining hotel in Gilboa. Dr. Ray was called to give medical aid to the murderer and the victim, his wife, but both died by the time he arrived. This tragic story stuck in James's memory.[12]

Another mentor was Nell Baker, a mutual friend of Dr. Ray and Vera, for whom James ran errands as a young boy. Like Dr. Ray, Nell Baker gave James books that were over his head. A strong woman, she was a head librarian and a journalist—the society editor for the *Morning Republican* and an editor of the *Courier*—and a charter member of the Symposium and Thursday Conversational club, spaces where women bonded over culture. Nell Baker died in 1936 in the home of Dr. Ray.[13]

A perennial outsider even as a boy, James began to identify with a constellation of oppressed and disenfranchised Americans. He became interested in the voices and stories of people of color. Findlay public schools were integrated, so seeing black classmates was not unusual. Although Findlay's population was predominantly white, there was a small black community.[14] In the early 1920s, James was enchanted by two elder black women who later influenced his dialogue. "I remember when I was a young boy, my mother didn't have time sometimes to make a dessert. She said, 'Go down the lane to Aunt Lucy and ask if she has something.' Aunt Lucy was about a hundred and lived in a shack with another black woman. They loved to talk to me." On his return, Vera would ask, "You were gone two hours for a cake?" He did not know much "then about racial prejudice. Those two black women seemed to me perfectly familiar. I found out who they were without knowing I'd found out."[15] Along with black people, Purdy also identified with the working class and he sometimes mixed with people of color on the "wrong" side of the river, such as migrant Mexican sugar beet pickers employed by Continental Sugar Company.[16]

The Purdy family expanded with the arrival of Robert Lloyd Purdy on July 11, 1921. When Richie, eleven, first saw his baby brother, he was told Robert came from heaven. After a few minutes of silence, he quipped: "Hurry up, baby, tell us all about heaven before you forget it."[17] Richie and Jamie, as James was now called, staying with their grandmother, were thrilled by the news, yet wished the new baby were a girl.[18] Growing up, Bob received a different set of influences than did his brothers and was more strait-laced. He was taken under the wing of John David Lindsey, a Presbyterian minister and family friend whose backyard adjoined theirs. Every Sunday, Bob would join Lindsey and son at church, Sunday dinner, followed by football in their common backyard. The minister became the namesake of Bob's son.[19]

James, at age eight or nine, began writing short pieces. A precocious child of wild imagination, he was already contemplating the color of darkness. "I wrote things as a child that my mother found very upsetting. They were for myself, these little stories" on yellow-ruled paper "about people we knew. She didn't know what to make of them. She found them peculiarly accurate."[20] Vera, chancing on "these outpourings," was bemused a child had written them. Teachers in the lower grades were likewise puzzled at his choice of composition.[21] His stories bothered them. His dark themes persisted in "anonymous letters" he enjoyed writing. One letter, not sent, was directed at their landlady, of whom Vera often complained. James mimicked things Vera said of people, but "when she saw it in black and white, she couldn't believe it. And she couldn't believe it was all being recorded by a . . . devil."[22] Purdy documented "terrible things" she said and imagined gorillas attacking and destroying the landlady. Vera found it and said, "My God, that's awful." But she held on to it, Purdy stressed.[23] Growing up in Findlay the son of a Civil War buff, James probably was familiar with the Nasby Letters penned by Findlay newspaper editor David R. Locke in the 1860s. In *The Jeffersonian* and in pamphlets supporting the Union, Locke created the persona of Petroleum V. Nasby, a "red-nosed, hard-drinking, self-seeking Copperhead" or "Peace Democrat," who defended the cause of the Confederacy. Purdy's letters, in satire and outrageousness, may have taken inspiration from the Nasby Letters, "masterpieces of ridicule." Regardless of influence, the visible effect of his writing on others left a deep impression, spurring him on. Even as a young boy, his stories got under people's skin.[24]

Richard loved the stories and called them "quite wonderful"—"because he was wicked!" James, encouraged, began self-publishing at age eleven or twelve. With a duplicator, an old, messy machine that used jelly, he printed five or six issues of *The Niocene*, a "little magazine." These were his "first published stories." He gave ten or so copies of each issue to his family and friends and even "sold some, too!"[25]

From the fall of 1925 through May 1928, James attended Donnell Junior High, named for an Ohio Oil president. Despite the recent modernization of Findlay public schools, Purdy said many teachers were disciplinarians and "beat the children, especially at Donnell Junior High," where "corporal punishment was practiced."[26] "I never enjoyed school," Purdy wrote, and "leave no grateful remembrance of it save for a few heroic schoolteachers and schoolfellows who must have been as miserable as I in this public conscription of brainwashing and straitjacket conformity."[27] Purdy recalled that the eighth grade boys were "very out of control" and on Halloween, they would gather at the home of their teacher and yell for her to come out. She and her sister were "outraged and a little afraid." But Al Fenstermaker Jr., a childhood friend and classmate from elementary through high school, said James was quiet and a good student.[28]

Piano was a consolation for school's unpleasantness. Richard, James, and Robert took piano lessons with Ada Lee Coe, a wonderful music teacher, songwriter, and poet. Another mentor, Coe operated a studio on Main Street, and for many years made annual trips to New York and Pittsburgh to continue her musical studies.[29] In 1926, James, not quite twelve, was one of many students who played piano at a recital at the Buckeye-Commercial Bank in Findlay.[30] James and his brothers loved to play Beethoven's "Moonlight Sonata," which projected through an open window, neighbors recalled.[31]

Along with music, three movie theaters offered escape and consolation. One film that made a deep impression was the original 1929 adaptation of Maugham's play *The Letter*, directed by Jean de Limur, set in an otherworldy Malaysia (filmed in a studio in Queens), centering on a femme fatale played by Jeanne Eagels. "I was brought up not on the theater, because we had no theater, but on the movies," Purdy later said.[32] He was forgetting the Marvin Theater on North Main, which for many years, was one of the largest playhouses in northwestern Ohio, where stars like Sarah Bernhardt performed until it burned down in 1930. In 1928, the "talkies" arrived at

Figure 2.3 James and Robert in goat wagon, Findlay, Ohio, 1927. Courtesy of the Purdy Family.

Harris Theater, which held exclusive rights to the Vitaphone in Findlay. Richard, with blonde hair and bright blue eyes, was then a handsome older teenager who exerted a profound influence, even if he liked to tease Jamie. An aspiring actor and gay youth, Richard felt stuck in this conservative Midwestern town. As for James, his first crush was on the iceman who delivered ice blocks to their home in those days before refrigeration.

The brothers were not especially close with their father, William, who was often away from home on business. As economic depression befell northwest Ohio in the 1920s with a decline in oil and gas production, Will Purdy performed skilled accounting and auditing work. For three years, he was a state bank examiner who traveled a great deal. His frequent absences from home slowly unraveled an already shaky marriage. Such a life entailed loneliness and seedy accommodations, but also a certain freedom. Dorothy Purdy said her father-in-law enjoyed telling stories of his time as bank inspector. One story, nephew David related, told of a banker who committed suicide ahead of an upcoming inspection that Will headed. Indeed, Albert De Fries, president of American State Bank at Gary, Indiana, was found dead at home in August 1930. His bank had been closed pending audit by the state banking department.[33] After a political change, William was replaced as bank examiner by a Democrat, so he re-entered real estate, buying and selling land not just in Ohio, but across Michigan, Indiana, Illinois, and Iowa. He worked for two firms, and when three firms merged into one, this formed a million dollars in capital; in its top year, that merger was the nation's largest dealer in farmland.[34] After shifting enterprises over the decades, Will stuck with real estate.

Although Findlay was an "overwhelmingly law-abiding" city, in January 1928, a gruesome murder made a searing impression on James, then thirteen. Findlay had never known this level of brutality; even in 1961, a city chronicle claimed few violent deaths had occurred across Findlay's history.[35] James knew the victim, knew or knew of the murderers, and knew a younger relative of one of the perpetrators, also a violent criminal.

Early on the evening of January 13, Samuel J. McMichael, almost seventy, was brutally killed by two youths. Purdy had believed that McMichael was killed by one of the many boys with whom he lived at his horseradish factory, and later suggested that McMichael desired the boys he employed. Funeral director John Renshler called him "queer" but extremely kind. Sam McMichael, gentle, benevolent, honest, but odd and naïve, made his living grinding and manufacturing horseradish in his one-room factory-home where he was slain. Sam was acquainted with his murderers—Arthur Brooker, twenty-two years old, and his half-brother, Delmar Haws, nineteen years old—and let them in. As he turned to close the door, Arthur struck him with a bottle of horseradish, which shattered, splattering blood and condiment. Arthur grabbed a milk bottle and bashed Sam with it until it broke. Someone struck Sam with a hand pump, puncturing his head. The killers dragged Sam's body a few feet to the doorway of his bedroom; his skull was crushed in three places, his head badly mutilated. The jagged end of the broken milk bottle was stabbed "in a crushed portion of his skull and twisted to make the deed all the more gruesome." James likely read of the "milk bottle murder" in the *Courier*, perhaps over breakfast.

Sam McMichael had been robbed two weeks before, and the murderers, fearing being identified, had returned to silence him forever. After the robbery, he told police he recognized the youths, one short and one tall.[36] For decades, Sam had been a peddler, operating a peanut and popcorn stand at the old courthouse, which James likely patronized, and many locals had been employed by Sam as boys or teenagers. He was a great reader of literature and could "recite poetry at great length" by the "leading poets of the world," and he could discuss a story he had read in detail.[37]

Bloody fingerprints led investigators to the culprits. Delmar Haws was arrested at the home of relatives in Columbus; Arthur Brooker was arrested in Lima, Ohio, after committing several robberies in Hancock County.[38] On May 7, after "persistent questioning," Brooker confessed and Haws "admitted his part in the killing."[39] The next day, while arraigned on a preliminary hearing in municipal court, Brooker pleaded guilty and Haws pleaded not guilty before the mayor. Five days later, however, in common pleas court, they reversed their pleas.[40] On the stand, Brooker admitted he beat McMichael to death in attempted robbery, but he claimed Sam had started him on a criminal career by teaching him to steal. Brooker and Haws were found guilty of first-degree murder, given life sentences, and imprisoned in June. In November 1929, Brooker and two other convicts went over a thirty-foot prison wall, and the body of Brooker, thought to have escaped after brutally mauling a guard, was found mortally wounded within 100 yards of the pen.[41] In its harrowing extremity, the murder broadly influenced Purdy's gothic horror novel, *Narrow Rooms*, focusing on four troubled young men prone to violent and bizarre homoerotic acts. He told Findlay journalist Parker Sams, "I based *Narrow Rooms* on the bits and pieces I could pick up."[42] Delmar's younger brother Daniel Haws, who was James's age, was also a delinquent and was placed in a boys' reformatory. He was surely part of the deep background of the character Daniel Haws in *Eustace Chisholm and the Works*.[43]

Happier memories derived from Purdy's job at Riverside Park's Green Mill Dance Hall, which had a major impact and appeared in his later fiction. "I was maybe fourteen years old," Purdy recalled. "All the town boys and girls went there. I earned 50 cents and didn't get home until one o'clock in the morning. My mother was a bit worried . . . I guess I felt free in the dance hall. 'Course they had good jazz orchestras—traveling, you know." The big bands of Glenn Miller and Tommy Dorsey swung for throngs of giddy dancers.[44]

James was a student at Findlay High School from the fall of 1928 to May 25, 1932. These were hard times for the approximately twenty thousand residents of Findlay. On October 29, 1929, when James was fifteen, the stock market crashed, signaling the beginning of the Great Depression nationally, though Ohio had already been coping with economic decline. "Tramps" would regularly walk up to the back door of his home, where compassionate Vera fed them. "They looked like hippies, but it was *real*." Toes stuck out of their shoes as in old cartoons and they "really stank." They had not eaten or combed their hair. "It was the real thing, so they were kind of beautiful because everything in their bodies meant exactly what it showed."[45] Amid the Great Depression, the State Legislature changed intangible tax laws, causing loss of revenue to the city and county; the schools suffered, and Findlay's low tax rate could no longer carry them. Teacher morale was low.[46] Purdy later wrote, "I found school intolerable all the way through. I don't think I ever learned anything." Teachers were mostly "very unhelpful and cold" and some "beat the children."[47] Not regarded as an elite student, James was placed on the "general" educational track, not "college prep" as Richard had been, nor "scientific" or "commercial." One useful class was typing.

Still, several teachers encouraged James and his writing.[48] The most important was Mildred Dietsch, a sophisticated English teacher who said he could become a writer. "I really loved her," Purdy later said.[49] Dietsch earned a BA from Western Reserve in Cleveland and a BS and MA from Ohio State.[50] During Purdy's senior year, she was completing a PhD. One of James's classmates recalled that sometimes, his English papers were read before the class as exemplary.[51] In the face of his parents' troubled marriage, James found an emotional outlet in poetry. He also began writing literary stories, including the first draft of "A Good Woman"—which later became his first bona fide publication. A neighbor recalled that James as a high schooler was a "good teller of tales," a real "yarn spinner," though "anemic looking."[52]

Like Richard, James was drawn to drama. Reading *Macbeth* in high school at fifteen left a deep impression. He "wondered why the other students weren't horrified" since the play was "dripping in blood. It's so awful, isn't it?" He listened to LPs of Dame Sybil Thorndike playing Lady Macbeth and became her admirer. Thorndike was known for Shakespearean repertoire and the role of Saint Joan, which Shaw wrote with her in mind. (Decades later, Purdy mailed her a book, and she became a fan.)

During James's high school years, not only did the Great Depression hit, but also his parents underwent a contentious divorce right in the middle of them. The depression and the divorce were related. In the late 1920s, William lost large sums he had borrowed, selling properties at a loss. Vera's brothers were upset that Will had lost their mother's money, and they let Vera know in no uncertain terms what they thought of him, putting greater strain on the marriage.[53] Moreover, Will and Vera continued to clash in temperament and outlook. Will remained somewhat stiff and Victorian or Edwardian in dress and outlook, while Vera took to heart new freedoms for women arriving in the 1920s. Vera, almost a decade younger, increasingly yearned for freedom from the husband who had been gone so often over the last nine years.

William and Vera were divorced on August 28, 1930, at the Hancock County Courthouse. Judge Duncan granted the divorce on grounds of "gross neglect of duty." Vera received custody and William was ordered to pay monthly child support of forty dollars, and eighty in arrears.[54] He also had to give her all family possessions. Will objected to the ruling, but his motion for a new trial was overruled by Duncan.[55] Will moved in with his sister and mother in Bowling Green. Purdy grappled with this calamitous event for nearly the rest of his life. In the 1970s, Purdy said on radio: "What a son or daughter always hopes for is there will be this ideal parent, who is a model, who is perfect, who has no clay feet, who will guide you and show you what to do. It's probably why we have God. Of course, all parents are not ideal; they're not models, they're flesh and blood, and the child usually has such an almost ferocious need to be loved and guided, that he is disillusioned early. This ideal father doesn't exist, and that leads to disillusionment and pain."[56]

William, surprised and hurt by Vera's divorcing him, "consoled himself by reading everything he could find on the Civil War," Purdy wrote. He must have pondered Lincoln's words, "A house divided against itself, cannot stand." Vera, to make ends meet, turned their family home at 115 Lima Street into a boarding house, to her sons' chagrin. The 1930 census recorded five boarders: three electricians, a stenographer, and a salesman. Purdy recalled: "Vera kept the wolf from the door by taking in roomers who were a questionable lot, to say the least. But Vera's cooking and the fact that she had clean sheets made the traveling salesmen very pleased to roost under her roof."[57] Vera was a superb cook and hostess, setting two tables, one for run-of-the-mill boarders, the second for family and "star boarders." In *Jeremy's Version*, to Jethro, the influx of "coarse, common" roomers resembles "an invasion of Mongolian warriors, or a plague of locusts."[58]

James felt worry and resentment over certain male boarders who flirted with, danced with, or were romantically involved with Vera. He did not approve of his mother having a "beau." Purdy later recalled: "Vera could hardly help the gents who spent the night there and attempted to have their way with her. Vera was stronger than many a male. She repulsed their advances, except perhaps one young man who fell in love with her golden curls and stole into her private domain."[59] When the house was full, James would sleep in a little sitting area in the staircase, where he could hear sounds emanating from under bedroom doors. He overheard his mother having sex with a boarder,

Figure 2.4 (Clockwise left to right) Richard Purdy, Vera Purdy, teenage James Purdy, unknown friend, Findlay, Ohio.

John Uecker said. Certain unconventional roomers were as, or more, interested in Richie and James as they were in Vera, Uecker suggested.[60] As a child, Robert sometimes had to sleep in the same room with a boarder.[61]

Aunt Cora Purdy was "engulfed by the scandals of the rooming house," Purdy recalled. She wondered how "such a pristine woman as Vera" could have "stooped to such a menial task as being landlady to traveling sales gents. But what well-to-do people don't know: poverty will soon change the moral character of someone hungry. Vera had no intention of going hungry in order to [please the] Presbyterian Minister who forgave her again and again from the pulpit for her misdemeanors in a rooming house."[62] Purdy felt stigmatized living with a single mother in a boarding house, with his father completely out of the picture. "Because my parents were divorced and we were very poor, our family was more or less looked down upon in Findlay," he said. "There were so many rich boys and girls in my class," the children of executives and management of Ohio Oil, forerunner of Marathon, who built lavish homes. "I began to develop a deep sense of inferiority. I found the town as a whole very smug and its values all tended toward wealth and outward respectability." Purdy later said that "enough people with a different outlook made up for the snobs."[63] One such person was Ruth Bowman, a stenographer who became a good friend of the family. In 1930, Ruth and Richard, both twenty, worked together at an Ohio Oil Company office, and at a Findlay radio station. If Ruth was "a bit wild," as Purdy recalled, she also sang hymns and joined church clubs.

During his senior year, Purdy was a member of the school's Book of the Month Club and participated in an event convening all clubs, each of which presented. James critiqued the *Review of Drama*. The Justamere club, exclusive to seniors, reviewed *She Stoops to Conquer*, Goldsmith's original and a rewrite. In 1932, the Justamere club discussed two Willa Cather novels and Negro Drama.[64] In April 1932, three months shy of eighteen, James won first prize in the annual Justamere party contest with a poem, "Expose," selected by a committee of six including Mildred Dietsch and Betty Crates, a "woman of great energy and enthusiasm." At the spring banquet, he was awarded a prize of three dollars, equivalent to $56.70 in 2020.[65]

As a mentor, Mildred Dietsch left an imprint. Although James was "openly laughed at by some of the tough boys for having written a poem," she strongly encouraged him to make plans to attend college. Money was tight, so James enrolled at the local state college in Bowling Green, where he could live with aunt Cora, his grandmother, and his dad. He started classes almost immediately, the summer after graduation.

3

The Nephew

From June 1932 through August 1935, Purdy studied at Bowling Green State Normal College, which was renamed Bowling Green State University shortly before he graduated. Bee Gee, or BG, as it is called, held its first classes in 1914 and became a college in 1929, with the goal of training teachers. By taking summer classes throughout, in just three years, James earned two degrees in the College of Education and Liberal Arts. The first was an AB in English, with a minor in history. The second, earned two months later, was a BS in education, with an English major and a French minor.

James did not live in a dorm or a fraternity house. Instead, he lived with his grandmother, Kitty, father, and Aunt Cora, in a white house at 135 Ridge Street. In 1925, Cora had bought out her brothers' interests in the property, so Will paid monthly rent.[1] James had already stayed there intermittently. Kitty soon passed away, in October 1932, and her memorial was held in their home.[2]

Somewhat of an outsider, Purdy mostly kept to himself in college. He wrote poems and stories, drew, and played the harmonica. Living off-campus with family made it harder to establish a social life. Outside of class, he saw his cohort at chapel, which was compulsory, but he did not seem to make many friends his age. Rather, he seemed to connect more with professors and neighbors. In 1971, Purdy told Frank Baldanza, a Bowling Green professor publishing on him: "I hope you won't dwell on my biography. My only biography is in my books. I never fitted in in Ohio any more than here. I was always a kind of outcast. I have no really friendly feelings toward that community."[3] The main characters of the story "Encore" (1959), a mother and collegiate son, are seemingly based on Vera and James. Merta frets over Gibbs, his lack of friends, and his habit of hanging out in a seedy Greek restaurant. "There are things wrong with Gibbs," she tells her brother, a doctor. "He's not popular at the college. He wasn't asked to join a fraternity, you know." Instead of frat brother Greeks, he mixes with Greeks. Merta worries Gibbs spends too much time with Spyro, a young modern artist, the restaurant owner's son. Gibbs even sits at length for a portrait by Spyro, hinting at a romantic

Figure 3.1 135 Ridge Street, Bowling Green, Ohio, 2009. Photograph by the author.

subtext. The college crowd did not hang out at the restaurant, so Gibbs "feels safe there from their criticism and can drink his coffee in peace." Vera by 1935 had moved to 417 West Sandusky Street in Findlay; although she still took in boarders, they were fewer than before. Later, Purdy rarely, if ever, mentioned Bowling Green, consistent with his silence on Hicksville and Findlay, but he nonetheless based at least two fictional towns on it.

During the spring semester of his first year, the very existence of his college was threatened. Although enrollment remained steady into the Great Depression, in 1933, the Ohio State Senate Welfare Commission proposed a plan to convert the college into a mental institution. Students, faculty, and administrators, alongside town residents, united to fight this, organizing a rally and march through downtown. A committee launched a letter-writing campaign to leaders throughout northwest Ohio, which helped convince the legislature that closing the school would be counterproductive. The measure was defeated by a 14–5 vote. Although the crisis was averted, the president noted damage was done, "which must be repaired." Students were urged to speak up about the "stability and permanency of the college in their home communities" and ensure "their local papers publish this fact. We invite and expect your cooperation."[4] Undergoing this crisis as a new student was doubtless demoralizing.

During his first year of studies, Purdy struggled, receiving middling grades. He was not gifted in the natural sciences, handed a D in botany and a C in geology and in zoology. He was an aesthete, not an athlete, getting Cs and Ds in gym. He received only a C in composition during his first summer semester, but raised it to a B in the fall, and got a B for the Bible. The only A grades he earned during his first year were in the yearlong introduction to literature sequence. In January 1933, he earned an A for a handwritten fifteen-page thesis, "Tragic America," which takes on contemporary US literature and cites then-recent publications, Louis Untermeyer's "A Letter to Poets" from *Saturday Review of Literature* and Ludwig Lewisohn's *Expression in America* (1932). For a young college student, it was eloquent and confident, and it hinted at a spiritual interest. He noted Henry Adams wrote of Christianity's failure: "Himself a lost soul, he could not lead the blind. The nihilism that preceded and followed the World War was not an 'answer to our questions'; neither is humanism nor any of the other 'isms' which have sprung up on all sides." Granted, the belief that satisfied the spiritual needs of Dante's day is not the same to fulfill the needs of today, "but neither is Christianity to pass into oblivion until there is a greater substitute or a remodeling of that philosophy to fit modern demands. It is belief in nothing that is destructive, which has dragged our literature and civilization away from its high idealism and given nothing in return." Theodore Dreiser, in whose work he found idealism, was "perhaps the only living novelist whose works have qualities of permanence." In concluding, Purdy agrees with Lewisohn, who reasoned the human spirit had "not known any long defeat. It will not now. And in any creative rebirth of the future, whether near or far, America will have her appropriate and splendid share." Purdy concluded: "It is with this last great hope in which I desire to believe, even though I have grave doubts for the future."[5]

Purdy's grades improved in his second and third years, when he increasingly connected with sympathetic professors and subjects that engaged him. In his second year, he earned As in yearlong courses in intermediate German and in modern European history, the latter with Frederick Nordmann, a mentor we will return to. He took two courses in American history, earning a B and an A. In a yearlong course in the French novel, he received a B and an A. He scored As in a yearlong Shakespeare course with Dr. Rea McCain, a recent New York University PhD who had taught him composition. McCain became another mentor, and during his third year, he took Chaucer and American literature courses with her, earning an A in each. McCain, a dynamic generalist who traveled extensively in Europe and wrote a travel column for the local newspaper, was the college's first and enduring English chair, directed plays, taught public speaking, and oversaw the debate teams.[6] In Purdy's third year, he took an introduction to philosophy course, earning an A, and did a year of classroom observation and student-teaching. In total, he took three courses in psychology—general, abnormal, and educational— and two in sociology, good training for a fiction writer. His overall GPA was 3.24, respectable but not suggesting brilliance.

Although Purdy later became a playwright, he never mentioned that he had acted. In the 1934–1935 academic year, James trod the boards repeatedly in a yearlong course in play production, again with Dr. McCain. His interest in acting was spurred by Richard, who co-organized Findlay's Little Theater Guild in 1933. On November 6, 1934, James performed in *The Old Soak* by Don Marquis, centering on a genial lush who battles Prohibition, which had ended eleven months earlier.[7] On January 24 and Valentine's Day, 1935, he played Charles in *Joan of Arc*, comprising brief scenes from Schiller's tragedy *Maid of Orleans*, adding original songs by students.[8] And in April 1935, James played two roles in the Bee Gee Players' production of Shakespeare's *The Merchant of Venice*: Tubal, a wealthy Venetian Jew, and Old Gobbo, father of Launcelot. The *Bee Gee News* rated the production excellent.[9]

One of Purdy's finest works, *The Nephew* (1960), is, among other things, a roman à clef reflecting Purdy's experiences in Bowling Green as a student, modeled on people he knew including family, neighbors, students, and professors. He borrowed a few names from real persons or invented names resembling those of models. For example, Boyd William and Cora Purdy, elderly siblings living on Ridge Street, had counterparts in Boyd and Alma Mason, on Crest Ridge Road. "Mason" is a tribute to his late grandmother Kitty's maiden name. The fictional college town, Rainbow Center, connotes Bowling Green, and indeed, a rainbow's center is literally green. Even the "intense high odor of mingled tomatoes, spices, and sugar" that grew pungent in late summer, emanating from the H. J. Heinz factory east of campus, lent *The Nephew* olfactory detail. The plant, where James worked one summer, was only two blocks away from the house where he lived. Alma is sickened by the "heavy burning fruit attar" but Boyd insists, "this whole town would be broke without ketchup." A chapter title, "An Odor of Ketchup," even riffs on Faulkner's "An Odor of Verbena." Purdy confirmed to Patricia Lear that Alma was based on his aunt, who lived in a town with a ketchup factory.[10] Aunt Cora, like Alma, had been an educator in another state and operated a small gift shop from her back porch. Cora had been an instructor and theorist of physical education at Indiana University after teaching in Boulder, Colorado.[11]

French professor Faye Laird was modeled on Professor Florence E. Baird, Cora's close friend, one of James's French professors, a neighbor, and a regular visitor. Alma feels Faye is just about the only person she could talk to in the neighborhood, "or indeed all of Rainbow Center, and the only woman perhaps she had anything in common." Florence and Cora were highly educated teachers who never married. In 1925, Baird began teaching Spanish and French at Bowling Green and sponsored the Foreign Language Club. Having earned degrees at BG and Ohio State University, where she also earned a master's, Baird did further graduate work in Mexico and Spain in the 1930s, including research in Madrid. Such study and travel likely influenced James to take similar journeys, along with the precedent of Hemingway.[12]

Professor Mannheim of the novel was based on Bernard Frederick Nordmann, history professor from 1931 through the mid-1950s, who lived adjacent to the Purdys in the 1930s.[13] Purdy's notebook for *The Nephew* even shows he originally named the character Nordmann.[14] A history minor, James took two yearlong classes with Nordmann, in ancient and mediaeval history and modern European history.[15] Born in Germany in 1888, Nordmann moved with family to the United States in 1906. He went to Stanford before earning a doctorate at University of Illinois, then taught at Eureka College and Ohio State before joining BG. Despite his accent, he was a popular teacher, though allegedly he took undue interest in favored coeds.[16] In *The Nephew*, Mannheim in his prime had "an almost abnormally intense gaze—it was his hair and eyes perhaps which had made him a kind of idol of the coeds in his history classes." He had a "magnetic physical presence" that, while "attracting the girls," was also "admired less than grudgingly by the boys."[17]

Purdy continued writing stories throughout college and began submitting them soon after graduation in the summer of 1935.[18] He learned how to deal with rejection. Most of the stories eventually published in *Color of Darkness* (1957) he wrote in his twenties, he said, but no one would publish them.[19] Stories were "always returned with angry, peevish, indignant rejections from the New York slick magazines" and "earned, if possible, even more hostile comments from the little magazines." Editors insisted he "would never be a published writer."[20] From 1935 through 1954, Purdy placed only two stories. But he believed in his gifts and kept writing and submitting.

To become a real writer, it seemed, he needed to venture out into the larger world beyond Ohio to gain more experience to write about. He set his sights on the ultimate Midwestern metropolis—Chicago, Sandburg's City of the Big Shoulders. Accepted for studies at the University of Chicago, James left the nest. After leaving home, Purdy tended to self-exile and "rarely went back to Ohio," according to Jorma Sjoblom.[21] Following his departure to Chicago and every place thereafter, he would sometimes seem nearly "missing in action" to his family, like Cliff Mason, the absent center of *The Nephew* who went MIA in Korea. Thus, in a sense, James was "the nephew." When Lear asked Purdy if he were Cliff Mason, he confirmed, "in a way, yes."[22]

4

Dream Palaces

In the late summer of 1935, twenty-one-year-old James Purdy said goodbye to family and friends in Ohio and traveled by rail to "stormy, husky, brawling" Chicago to begin graduate courses in English literature at the University of Chicago.[1] It is not known if he had any connections in the city, though his father had traveled there on business. "I thought Chicago was a pretty scary city. Very dehumanizing at the time," Purdy recalled.[2] "They tell me you are wicked and I believe them, for I have seen your painted women under the gas lamps luring the farm boys," poet Carl Sandburg writes in "Chicago." "And they tell me you are crooked and I answer: Yes, it is true I have seen the gunman kill and go free to kill again. / And they tell me you are brutal and my reply is: On the faces of women and children I have seen the marks of wanton hunger."[3] James took it all in during early explorations afoot. "It was the first big city I had ever known, and I was unprepared for its overwhelming confusion. It provided me with enough subject matter for the rest of my life."[4]

Purdy operated in a circumscribed area within which he encountered lively and diverse scenes of poverty and squalor, jazz and bohemia, and elevated realms of higher education. Scholar Paul W. Miller explains: "A relatively small section of South Chicago within walking distance of the university, extending from 63rd Street on the south"—or "Sixty-three Street" to Fenton Riddleway in *63: Dream Palace*—"55th Street on the north, State Street on the west, and Washington Park, Jackson Park, and Lake Michigan on the east," eventually became the principal setting, the microcosmos, of four works—*63: Dream Palace*; *Malcolm*; *Eustace Chisholm and the Works*; and *Gertrude of Stony Island Avenue*.[5]

In Hyde Park, James was exposed to intellectual circles and literary ideas thriving at the university and environs. Outside the academy, the Bee Hive Lounge was a celebrated multiracial jazz club on East 55th Street where bebop legends Charlie Parker and Max Roach gigged. Further south on State Street, the Stroll offered little speakeasies, chicken shacks, and jazz by and for black people. The Savoy Ballroom, the pride of the South Side, the world's largest when it opened, hosted stars like Dizzy Gillespie and Billie Holiday.

There were "jazz clubs up and down 63rd Street," said bassist Joe Levinson.[6] Writer, professor, and sexual revolutionary Sam Steward later recalled their mutual old "wonderful days in the ghetto-honkeytonk of South State street."[7]

Purdy quickly met and befriended three notable creatives in Chicago: painters Gertrude Abercrombie and Norman MacLeish and author Wendell Wilcox. In 1935, James met Gertrude, a bohemian artist and jazz aficionado born in 1909 who was just starting to gain recognition. She lived nearby at 57th Street and Harper, a few blocks east of the University and west of Stony Island Avenue. Purdy lived with "five or six 'funnies' in a 'pretty gay' house at the corner of 57th and Dorchester," she remembered.[8] In the mid-1930s, Abercrombie met Wilcox, the gay artist Karl Priebe, and Purdy, with whom she became close, lifelong friends.[9] James thought Gertrude was a "great seer of faces, as astonishing as Modigliani. Of course, she was a bruja. Very witchy!"[10] Composer Ned Rorem, then a gay bohemian teen living with liberal Quaker parents in Chicago, recalled that in the late 1930s, Gertrude, one of "many vanished painters, brought to the fore by the WPA" and its local

Figure 4.1 James Purdy kissing Gertrude Abercrombie in bed, undated, probably by Wendell Wilcox. Wendell Wilcox Papers, Department of Rare Books and Special Collections, Princeton University Library, box 16.

director, Norman MacLeish, were "toiling and giggling and drinking and dying within a bohemia that casually bisected that of my parents!"[11]

Abercrombie socialized with a small group of gay youths, "cute little fellows" in colorful velvets, in red shirts with gold fringe, whom she entertained.[12] She liked to "window shop" with them, and James would sometimes come along. Abercrombie was a self-described nymphomaniac; for her, window shopping meant cruising.[13] She led James on evening strolls through Washington Park, her favored cruising ground, and colorful streets, exploring this fast, intense, diverse milieu, so different from the small cities and farms of Ohio that he knew. James grew close to Gertrude and even accompanied her to have an illegal abortion.[14]

The influence of Gertrude Abercrombie and Wendell Wilcox on Purdy was deep and enduring. Gertrude said that she introduced James to Wilcox, a slim, clever Michigander born in 1906, who became the model for Purdy's sharp-tongued aspiring writer, Eustace Chisholm ("Ace").[15] But perhaps

Figure 4.2 James Purdy holding a drink and gesturing, undated, probably late 1930s, probably by Wendell Wilcox. Wendell Wilcox Papers, Department of Rare Books and Special Collections, Princeton University Library, box 16.

James actually met Wendell, another cruiser, in Jackson Park, which the older man favored—as in *63: Dream Palace*, when writer Parkhurst Cratty meets young Fenton Riddleway there. Sam Steward, among others, identified Cratty with Wilcox.[16] Perhaps "James was a hustler," as Purdy aficionado Dennis Moore insisted.[17] In 1939, Wilcox published "No One Ever Looks Up" in *Creative Writing*, with a woodcut by Abercrombie. Perhaps influenced by Wendell's meeting James, it is in any event a lost early gay story. A hungry youth with long blond bangs, as James had, feigning window shopping on a street corner, meets Bart, a gay, lonely older man. Acting like a new arrival, the youth complains that in the city, no one ever looks up, not caring if others are distressed or hungry. He seems to have trouble screwing up courage to ask the older man for money—or Bart is encouraged to believe this and is prompted to make the first move. "Why don't you ask me? I'm waiting to be asked," Bart finally says. Bart gives him a quarter, walks on, and the younger man grows peevish: Bart does not ask his name, and only gives him change to feel good about himself. So, Bart takes the youth out to eat and afterward, on their way to his house, they encounter two identically dressed boys with white flowers in lapels, "giggling and twisting" as they approached. After Bart takes the boy home, the youth again bemoans how no one notices anyone. But the older man figures the youth cannot see his own hunger, his desire for him. They end up in bed in the dark; the boy says Bart may caress his hair.

In real life, Wendell lived with Esther Wilcox, a librarian who supported her husband's career, unusual for the times. Nevertheless, Wendell's story was doubtless inspired by his pickups.[18] In *Eustace Chisholm*, Ace is the axis around which other characters revolve; Wilcox played a similar role, assisted by Esther. When Sam Steward, who later befriended Purdy, was "called on to defend this arrangement," he stressed Wendell was a genius, thus outside the "realm of ordinary morality and mores," and, given Esther's willingness, who were "lesser mortals to criticize such a way of life."[19]

Another artist friend was easygoing, older Norman Hillard MacLeish. Born in 1890, MacLeish was a watercolorist, heir to a department store fortune, and brother of Archibald MacLeish, the renowned poet, playwright, and Librarian of Congress. Their father had owned Carson, Pirie & Co. and was a key founder of the University of Chicago with John D. Rockefeller. Norman and Archibald grew up in a splendid mansion in Glencoe, a suburb, where Sandburg and Abercrombie visited.[20] A member of Chicago Society of Artists, MacLeish studied in Paris and at the Art Institute of Chicago.[21] A wealthy gay man prone to drink and hedonism, MacLeish was "financially totally irresponsible," Miller said.[22] Norman became the model for the decadent aristocrat Reuben Masterson, in *Eustace Chisholm and the Works*. As Rueben does for Amos, the department store heir fitted out James in nice outfits.[23]

Modernist Gertrude Stein was a touchstone to Purdy's Chicago circle, a friend of friends who visited the city in 1934 and 1935. But sadly, Purdy arrived a day after the fair, and never met this queer icon, leaving him still without a great champion. In 1933, at an outdoor art fair in Grant Park, Abercrombie met critic Llewellyn Jones, who had been literary editor for *Chicago Evening Post*. Mr. Jones introduced her to Chicago writer Thornton Wilder, known for his Pulitzer Prize–winning novel *The Bridge of San Luis Rey*, and they became friendly.[24] Through Wilder, Abercrombie and Wendell Wilcox met Stein when she and Alice B. Toklas visited Chicago during fall 1934 and early 1935 during their celebrated tour of the United States.[25] An art collector, Stein inspected Abercrombie's early paintings, and told her frankly, "paint more, and more neatly," which the younger Gertrude took to heart.[26] Wilcox, after graduating college in 1929, remained in Chicago hoping to become a writer. In November 1934, he imbibed Stein's lecture, "Poetry and Grammar" at the University of Chicago, and the following spring attended four more Stein lectures. When Abercrombie told Wilder of Wilcox's devotion, Wilder invited Wilcox to participate with select students in a series of ten conferences with Stein.[27] Wilcox thereby became a friend and correspondent with Stein, who helped find a publisher for his novel, *Everything Is Quite All Right* (1945).[28] In the 1930s, Wilcox struggled to publish, but found success during the 1940s, while James still struggled. Wilcox placed four stories in the *New Yorker* and *Harper's Bazaar*, then lucrative, and other stories in "little magazines."[29] Like "Ace" Chisholm, Wilcox was "always eliciting other people's stories" but "never told his own," Purdy said without naming Wendell.[30]

In April 1936, Wilder asked Stein: "Do you remember Gertrude Abercrombie, the painter with the thin sharp face and the disheveled hair and Wendell Wilcox the too-perfect story-writer? They are coming here for a home-made spaghetti dinner Wednesday night. Forgive me, but I can't like them. 'At most I have no tears' and golly what they ask is tears." In June, Wilder told Stein he had gone with Wendell and Gertrude to witness the preparation of Donald Vestal's marionette play, *Identity*, adapted from Stein and funded by the WPA. After seeing it, Abercrombie wrote Stein, excitedly telling of plans with the Wilcoxes to make a live-action film of *Identity*, with all acting, Wendell directing, and designer John Pratt doing sets, which was not developed.[31] Pratt and his lover, the African American dancer and choreographer Katherine Dunham, were also in Abercrombie's circle.[32]

Wendell's friendship with Stein and Toklas, and his success, spurred envy in Purdy. Likewise, Sam Steward's friendship and correspondence with them would soon rankle. In *Everybody's Autobiography* (1937), Stein wrote: "In America too the most interesting young men just then were nearer 30, Wendell Wilcox, Max White, Sam Steward and Paul Drus."[33] James, the younger writer, cherished Stein's "Melanctha" and grasped her influence on his early heroes, Ernest Hemingway, Sherwood Anderson, and Carl Van Vechten. "When I was taking a train home from Chicago, I read 'Melanctha' and I just loved the rhythm of the speech, and I thought, this is the way I want to write," Purdy later said. "What's behind Stein and Anderson, and my work is American speech."[34] A friend of Stein's, Van Vechten enthusiastically championed both her and Ronald Firbank, the English aesthetic novelist about whom Purdy was writing his master's thesis.

Wendell was a bee in Purdy's bonnet. Between them was a profound, sensitive dynamic, something deeper than friendship. Paul Miller, who interviewed Abercrombie and Wilcox, "assumed that Wilcox and Purdy were lovers," and their relationship was "compromised, or complicated, by Wilcox's marriage."[35] John Uecker surmised Purdy wanted "to be an artist with Wilcox—writers together as a team, living the bohemian life together!"[36] Purdy did not only go on to use Wilcox as a model for four characters, but startlingly, he "borrowed" Wilcox's titles of unpublished works for two of his own books, *Color of Darkness* (1957) and *Narrow Rooms* (1978). Wilcox's "Color of Darkness," 294 pages, is dated 1934, and his "Narrow Rooms," April 1935.[37] Purdy's expropriations were private messages to Wendell, who recognized himself in Purdy's works. Of *63: Dream Palace*, which was collected in *Color of Darkness*, Steward wrote, "Wendell said in a kind of mild outrage that it was Miriam and himself," and Sam had already "identified the characters easily." In 1964, James wrote Neely Orme: "Wendell has acknowledged [*Cabot Wright Begins*], and obliquely, me. Of course great Pride Esther can't."[38] After Purdy sent Wendell a manuscript of *Eustace Chisholm* in late 1966, Wilcox thanked him and added, "though I'm not going to go into more detail than I ever have, I feel I can add with safety (employing the outmoded language that Gertrude used so long ago) that I get the message." Perhaps James felt Wendell was never brave enough to accept himself and give himself over to loving men—specifically, Purdy.

Around this time, in an incident Purdy cherished, he was "recognized" as having Native ancestry. During two phone conversations, James told a story of when he was young in Chicago, locked out of his apartment, probably 5510 S. Cornell Avenue, in late 1936.[39] Waiting for the landlord, Purdy encountered an older chap, Ernesto Romero, who said he could get the door open. This achieved, Purdy invited him in. Ernesto kept staring, though, which made James uncomfortable. When James asked why, he declared: "You have Indian blood." Purdy asked how he knew. "Your cheekbones give you away. No white man has cheekbones like that." When Purdy joked that Romero did not "look so white" himself, he said he too had Native ancestry.[40] "I wouldn't have let a white man in. Didn't you know you had Indian blood?"

"I sort of knew."[41]

Figure 4.3 James Purdy smiling, undated, probably by Wendell Wilcox. Wendell Wilcox Papers, Department of Rare Books and Special Collections, Princeton University Library, box 16.

To make literary acquaintances, to receive letters from famous writers, and in some cases, to conduct research for his thesis on Firbank, Purdy reached out to many literary figures through the mail. From the winter of 1936 through the summer of 1937, probably consulting phone books at the public library, the aspiring writer mailed many letters from Chicago to famous authors, critics, and poets, garnering many responses. Purdy received replies from Sherwood Anderson on January 6, 1937, and February 2, 1938. In 1937, James had replies from Havelock Ellis (February 15); Lord Alfred Douglas, who had been beloved by Oscar Wilde (March 12); novelist Hamlin Garland, who wrote of Midwestern farmers (April 8); poets Robinson Jeffers (June 23) and Robert Frost (July 14); and *Main Street* author Sinclair Lewis (July 19). On July 7, social critic and editor H. L. Mencken wrote: "Every man, of course, shows some relation to other men, but if he really has anything to say, the differences are much more important than the resemblance." Replies also came from critics Burton Rascoe and Edmund Wilson (July 9). Purdy later told William Carlos Williams he used to write from Chicago when he was in high school—actually grad school—showing Purdy was perpetuating a narrative in which nine years were subtracted from his age.[42]

In spring 1937, Purdy earned his master's degree in English from the University of Chicago, having completed a forty-three-page thesis, dated December 1936, on Ronald Firbank, an author admired by Forster, Waugh, and the Sitwells. Like Edith Sitwell, Firbank was a classic English eccentric. To poet Wyndham Lewis, Firbank reincarnated "all the Nineties," blending the spirits of Oscar Wilde, Walter Pater, Aubrey Beardsley, and more.[43] Discussing Firbank's first novel, Purdy says the word *artificial* is "of the utmost importance in Firbank's art; it is the very heart of his work." Artificiality, and strange settings, characters, and style, represent "only the thin concealment of the despair and vacuity of his picture of the age, for behind this exaggerated picture is its model, the English bourgeoisie, with its exhaustion and emptiness, its petty trifling, its lack of values. *The Artificial Princess* becomes then not a fantasy but the most exaggerated and subtle of satires; not intellectual criticism of that society" but merely "delight in exaggeration or blurring of outlines," a literary strategy Purdy took to heart. Purdy thought Firbank's two "Negro novels," *Valmouth* and *Sorrow in Sunlight*, were his "great achievements," and he praised *Caprice*, but was quite critical of other books. Purdy assesses: "By pushing subjectivism to the limits" Firbank is the "perfect example of 'style without design': to him as an aesthete, manner, or style, was more important than substance." Likewise, in *Malcolm*, Madame

Girard declares: "texture is all, substance nothing."[44] Exploring the notion of gay sensibility, Edmund White writes: "Decadence, attracting figures such as Oscar Wilde and Ronald Firbank, was a movement characterized by exquisitely rendered surfaces, a concentration on detail rather than overall structure and the elevation of the doctrine of 'art for art's sake.' This was the 'artificial paradise' to which the outcast artist could escape, an illusory world in which the values that condemned eccentric behavior could be temporarily suspended or reversed."[45] Firbank was criticized for lacking values, but this is precisely what makes him interesting, Purdy reasoned. He did not possess the "values of a supreme artist or of a great writer," but the works hold "definite significance in their very absence of values," and represent a "more extreme expression of the spirit of the nihilism of the post-war intellectualism" than James Joyce. By valorizing the "trivial and the decayed," Firbank "inverted the values of Victorian literature" and "British civilization" as he saw it, showing his writing is "directed by a fine but disordered intelligence, 'sublime in laughter' at the waste land which it willfully creates." Firbank "sacrificed all to express nothing well, and indeed he expressed that nothing ness with something of genius for weaving invisible cobwebs in the air."[46] One reader called Purdy's eloquent thesis "an excellent piece of criticism."

In the summer of 1937, after his graduation, Purdy's address was 5707 Kenwood Avenue, Chicago, near the cross street of 57th Street, on which Abercrombie lived. Kenwood was associated with artistic enclaves and the Art Fair where Gertrude sold her work, leaning paintings against her ancient Rolls Royce. Purdy spent the summer writing feverishly, and not only stories. In July, he was finishing a novel manuscript, as a Findlay newspaper reported during a visit home. Vera admired her son's stylish new clothes and wondered where he had found them.[47]

Around this time, Purdy randomly met Ned Rorem, the teen scenester who knew Abercrombie and MacLeish. In February, Ned's friend told him of a queer pianist, Alfred R., who lived around the corner and would "do to you what you've never had done," so Ned called him for a date. "He did do something to me that I'd never had done, and there went another virginity!" Afterward, while Ned played pieces by Cyril Scott ("Lento" and "Lotus Land") on piano, "two figures who inhabited the shadows of his apartment wandered into the front room. One of these was James Purdy, whom I revisualize as being wraithlike and drastically blond with a troubled expression that would infiltrate his marvelous crazy prose in years to come."[48] Rorem observed: "Ever since Chicago, circa 1938 when his roommate corrupted me at my request," James and he had "gone to different schools together."[49]

Also in 1938, Purdy was introduced to Sam Steward by Wendell Wilcox, and they became close. Steward's circle overlapped with those of Wilcox and Abercrombie and included Charles Sebree, artist and playwright of the Chicago Negro Renaissance.[50] In Steward's infamous Stud File, in which copious copulations were catalogued, he recorded a single encounter with Purdy on a "Chicago" list, without detail.[51] When Sam met James, he had been reading Wilde's *The Picture of Dorian Gray*; his edition's frontispiece bore an image that looked "exactly like James," so within days, Sam began to deploy his "secret weapon," a "passive aggression" technique, and "pulled him into bed and gave him a blowjob." James made Sam "promise not to tell Wendell," a secret that he kept. This is intriguing, given the dynamic between Purdy and the married Wilcox.[52]

During fall 1938, Purdy did further graduate work in English at University of Chicago.[53] He wrote fiction, and after years of submitting, in January 1939, finally celebrated his first publication! "A Good Woman" appeared in the first issue of *Creative Writing*, a "tiny magazine in Chicago run by a conscientious objector," Robert Williams, and his wife, Margaret Williams.[54] The story focuses on a middle-aged woman in a small city much like Findlay, who has accrued a large debt at the local drugstore soda fountain, where she meets her friend for heart-to-hearts. The old proprietor, who finds her attractive, tries to persuade her to settle her account with some hugging and rubbing in the back room. Vera was likely the model. The title was likely borrowed from *A Good Woman* (1927), a novel by northern Ohioan Louis Bromfield.

In May 1939, Wilcox published "Not Ever Me," a dark story climaxing with a factory worker father killing his small daughter's cat out of resentment of her love of it. Recalling Poe's "The Black Cat," this story likely emboldened Purdy to explore similarly dark material and explosive conclusions. In this story and Purdy's "Why Can't They Tell You Why?" a parent who feels unloved terrifies a child by destroying, or trying to destroy, something the child prizes. Purdy's story, scholar Stephen D. Adams writes, is a "harrowing account" of chaos "in the wake of a father's disappearance," the latter becoming a Purdian theme.[55]

In March, James received a belated reply from Chicago poet Edgar Lee Masters, one of the many writers to whom he reached out.[56] Masters's *Spoon River Anthology* narrates the epitaphs of 212 residents of a rural Midwestern small town, sometimes with frankness that was startling. *Spoon River* and other key Midwestern works including Anderson's *Winesburg, Ohio*, Van Vechten's *The Tattooed Countess*, and Sinclair Lewis's *Main Street*, were formative influences. Purdy knew that authors such as Masters, Faulkner, and Thomas Wolfe—whose background had parallels to Purdy's, including growing up in a boarding house—caused hubbub in hometowns over characters modeled on real people, many still living. Purdy was on track to follow in their footsteps with his own startlingly original work that drew deeply from the well of his life. Like Wolfe, he sensed that you can't go home again, that he could never again live in Ohio.

5

The Running Sons

In the midst of World War II, in 1941, both James and Richard made life-altering moves. Late in the year, at age thirty-two, Richard left his job at Ohio Oil, bade friends and family adieu, and moved to New York to chase his dream of becoming a professional actor. In Findlay, he had been performing in the Little Theater Guild, radio plays, and civic and cultural programs.[1] In 1939, he had delivered a review and portrayal of Lillian Hellman's Broadway play *The Little Foxes*, starring Tallulah Bankhead, for a Quest club meeting, having just returned from New York, where he interviewed Bankhead, a camp icon.[2] In June 1941, Richard directed the Guild's production of *Moonset*, a "peace play," which earned first place in a WPA tournament.[3] For a few years after arriving in New York, Richard struggled to get roles, but by the late 1940s, he found success.

Like Richard, James made a major decision in 1941. From June 1940 through May 1941, in Chicago, he did editing and rewriting for Robert Williams, who had published him in *Creative Writing*. Williams revamped that little magazine into *New Horizons*, which aimed to give voice to "lonely men who search for God," but business failed.[4] On May 12, James, nearly twenty-seven, left his Chicago friends and enlisted in the US Army as a private. For a better assignment, it was preferable to enlist rather than wait to be drafted—which seemed inevitable, given the rising drumbeat of war. "I was a most unlikely soldier. I was going to be drafted, so I just joined up," Purdy later said. He was assigned to the Army Air Corps. His army record states his birth year as 1916; already he was chopping years from his birthdate.

For basic training, Purdy was stationed at Scott Field, in Belleville, Illinois, east of St. Louis. In the early 1940s, Scott Field was mainly an Army Air Corps technical training center specializing in communications, with a Radio School. Four mile-long concrete runways were under construction. Purdy recalled: "I was on KP [kitchen patrol] most of the time. They didn't know what to do with me. I just wasn't supposed to be a soldier." He bristled at constantly hearing his fellow soldiers' rough English. Although Purdy would later introduce the word *motherfucker* to literature, he thought, "If I ever get out of here, I don't ever want to hear that word [*fuck*] again." The army "nearly finished" him, but he was glad to have served.[5] Like his life in Chicago, service, though difficult, gave him both material and opportunity to write: "I wrote all the time in the Army, in my tent, in the library."[6] Purdy was amused by a brand name, Griesedieck Bros. Beer, that he saw on signs in the St. Louis area, and later burst into laughter reporting this to Norman MacLeish. Decades later, Norman recalled this when, dining with visiting St. Louis friends, he met a nice young member of the Griesediecks. With rare ribaldry, seventy-eight-year-old MacLeish declared: "I like to think of greasy dicks! But I'm glad my name isn't Griesedieck!"[7]

Serving in the Army Air Corps took Purdy for the first time to the Deep South. In late 1941, he was stationed at Keesler Field, near Biloxi, Mississippi, which offered basic and technical training.[8] Amid a Southern setting he had never before seen, heard, or smelled, taking in Spanish moss on live oak trees, and blooming magnolia trees, Private Purdy did typing and other office work in Personnel[9] and was trained in the Spanish language.[10] The government no doubt had plans for Purdy that involved Latin America.

Veterans later reported that at Keesler Field a "gang of gay friends" were regulars at the service club including a "campy MP" [military police] who swung his club, giggled, and called the men lined up for first-run movies "girls." At their table, a "swishy, giddy, gay" vibe prevailed, but they hewed to an unspoken taboo many followed against coupling with buddies and speaking openly about anyone's homosexuality.[11] At Scott and Keesler Fields, Purdy noticed other gay men, but mostly kept to himself, challenged by adjusting to GI life. He knew "a lot of boys were queer or gay"; he "just knew they were but they did their work properly," and he did his work the best he could, so "there was not a problem" and it did not bother him. It was hard to forge connections since men were "moved around so much that you never saw the boys you did basic training with again." Feeling "very uncomfortable," he did not form real friendships. He believed one in every ten men was gay, and some were "having sexual relations with men in town," but they were not a "threat to discipline because they were good soldiers." Purdy said he was friendly but otherwise "had nothing to do with any of them" since he had other problems. They did not "know anything about" him; the army was so large, people could get lost in it.[12] Discretion was key, since at the time, many soldiers were discharged for being homosexual, which meant they lost access to many privileges otherwise bestowed upon veterans.

On December 7, 1941, Japanese warplanes bombed Pearl Harbor and the United States was fully drawn into World War II. Despite this, on December 31, Purdy left the Army Air Corps, honorably discharged due to an unspecified physical disability.[13] A 1958 Bowling Green newspaper article stated Purdy had recurring "throat trouble" that first developed in the army, and surgery followed.[14] Thus, he did not have to go into combat as the country began sending soldiers overseas.

After recovering from surgery, Purdy served as personal assistant to Norman MacLeish from February through July 1942. He drove the gay painter through the Deep South, continuing southward to Mexico City, where he acted as interpreter. Moneyed MacLeish, about twenty-four years Purdy's senior, footed the bill, perhaps acting as a "sugar daddy." Twenty-five years later, MacLeish wrote to him: "I also frequently think of those happy times that we had, down the Mississippi Valley, through the Old South, and above all, in Mexico! You were very dear to me then, and I still feel that you are one of my best friends." He was very glad their friendship had "come to life again."[15] As war raged, the pair seemed to be on holiday, and they grew closer. In 1957, MacLeish professed: "I have known and loved you for a long time."[16] They enjoyed Cuernavaca, Acapulco, and Taxco.[17] Cuernavaca, a small city fifty miles south of Mexico City, offered beautiful flora, pleasant weather, and a large international community. It was common for wealthy North Americans and Europeans to vacation there. Norman later reminisced on "those evenings when we used to dine at the Restaurant San Angel, after which we would drive up onto the promontory overlooking La Ciudad with its lights spread out over the Valley, and because Mexico couldn't afford to play recordings of Bob Hope, etc., we had to content ourselves with the Music of Beethoven, Mozart, Sibelius, Debussy etc.!! Those were beautiful nights, and I have not forgotten them, nor will I—ever!" In Taxco, they stayed at "that nice Posada de la Mission" with a "gallery all around the building, and the bedrooms—as well as bathrooms—all had windows opening out upon it," MacLeish wrote. "And didn't the maid Concepcion peek in upon us taking showers in the bathroom?"

James and Norman shared some unforgettable experiences in Mexico City. They went to bullfights, where, comically, they could not avoid Hemingway. Every time they went, they "sat about four rows above Ernest Hemingway, and his then-wife, Martha Gellhorn," a fellow writer and war correspondent. "I have been asked why I did not make myself known to Hemingway. The reason was that he and my brother Archie [MacLeish] had just had a big falling out, and I feared that if I did, I'd get a good punch in the nose! And he looked as if he could deliver quite a Punch!"[18] Looking back, Norman was romantic and nostalgic, recalling the "Calla Lilies blooming on the roof of the Hotel Ontario in Mexico City on that memorable February night when the moon crossed the sky from east to west as that wacky old waiter dashed out with more and more—rum Collins's was it?"[19]

Like all good things, this idyllic trip eventually had to come to an end. James accepted the offer of a teaching job at a military school, meaning a very different pattern was in store. From fall 1942 through early 1943, James taught French and English at Greenbrier Military School in Lewisburg, West Virginia, a private boarding high school and junior college for boys and young men.[20] Purdy worked with youth from the West Virginian hills, absorbing their strong accents for his future work. Greenbrier Military School was probably a stifling atmosphere for a sensitive and artistic gay man; his employment was brief, and he is not found in the yearbook. The brevity may have been by design. The US Office of Education required anyone who was being sent to a Latin American nation as part of a teacher exchange to have held a "position of professorial rank in an institution of collegiate grade."[21] Since Greenbrier had a two-year college, it qualified, and Purdy didn't need to serve a full academic year. Two colleagues, Captains Snyder and Young, served as references; thus, no scandal caused his short tenure.[22]

From February 1943 through April 1944, Purdy worked for the US Office of Education, then part of the Federal Security Agency, in Washington, DC. He did not speak about these fourteen months in the capital serving as educationist and assistant specialist in inter-American education relations, grade P-2. Their program's goal was to demonstrate goodwill toward Latin America, promote the image of the United States, and monitor educational and political developments south of the border. The 1945 FSA manual stated the office was promoting development of "Inter-American understanding and cooperation" in education through student and teacher exchanges, language study, preparing and distributing exhibits and materials, and assisting Pan-American clubs and inter-American teacher-training programs. Funding came from the Interdepartmental Committee on Cooperation with the American Republics and the office of the Coordinator of Inter-American Affairs.[23] Purdy was groomed to participate in an exchange. In 1944, US Commissioner of Education John Studebaker said a priority of the Division of Inter-American Educational Relations was the "exchange of educational personnel" with Latin American countries in "co-operation with the Department of State, the Office of the Coordinator of Inter-American Affairs, and other government agencies"—such as the OSS and after 1947, the CIA—including "professorships, fellowships, and teacher exchanges." Addressing the future of the Office of Education, he proposed expansion of functions of the Department of State in "development of cultural and educational relations with other nations through the employment of educational and cultural attachés as members of our foreign missions." At one point, Purdy was the translator for a group of Latin American exchange students.

From February to December 1943, the agency gave Purdy an efficiency rating of "very good" (below "excellent"), with strengths in attention to detail, accuracy, industry, and cooperativeness, with no weaknesses. His rating slipped a bit over the next three months: at the end of March 1944, Purdy received overall rating of "good." He was rated "weak" in "ability to organize his work" but "excellent" in "effectiveness in meeting and dealing with others."[24] On April 24, 1944, Purdy resigned from his position of assistant educationist to do "private research and study in Mexico."[25] He gave 1120 East 55th Street, Chicago, as his address, where he spent a few months reconnecting with friends. He made plans to study Spanish at Universidad de las Américas Puebla. This was so he could meet another prerequisite to participate in a teacher exchange—"thorough knowledge of the language" of the country where he would be sent.

Purdy's studies at Universidad de las Américas Puebla were funded by the US government through the Division of Inter-American Educational Relations' partnerships with Mexican universities to assist US teachers.[26] The Veterans Administration added the two-year university to the list of schools where veterans could study with federal funding. Although Purdy did not care for the university, he again went to bullfights, which he liked. He later said the participants do not see bullfighting as a sport, but more an art akin to dance. "They see something spiritual in it—something like man's triumph over blind force."[27] Nevertheless, "they're terrible" but he kept going back. "I don't approve, but I couldn't help it. Until I saw a matador gored. That took some of the joy out of it."[28] While working in Mexico City, James met two Spanish exiles from Franco's dictatorship who took him under their wing and gave him a deeper view of bullfighting. He accompanied them to bullfights and on trips to the countryside where rancheros tested two-year-old bulls for bravery. Avid collectors of bullfight posters, the pair gave Purdy free samples. He ended up gathering one hundred posters including several by master craftsman Roberto Domingo, and one heralding the famous matador, Manolete, whom Purdy saw in Mexico and Spain. When Franco announced there would be no reprisals against those who had left during civil war, his friends returned to Madrid, but kept Purdy supplied with posters through the mail.

Living in Puebla, a colonial-era planned city in south-central Mexico, the state capital, and one of the largest cities in the country, Purdy became lonely. Tenderness and care toward his mother is suggested by a postcard sent August 15, 1944. "How is little Vera Cowhick today?" "I have worried about you so much, and don't want you to be troubled, as you will always be cared for by me. Varya." In at least two postcards, James calls her "Varya," apparently alluding to the character from Chekhov's *The Cherry Orchard* who holds her family together and frets over money. The postcard depicts a belltower of Puebla Cathedral. "I took this photograph I am writing on and a company here bought it. Isn't that strange? I may sell more of my photographs. Please let me know if you need anything and love to Chester. I'm so glad he can be with you." Chester Terpinski, who fled his native Poland during World War II, was a star boarder at Vera's house. He fell in love with the United States and married an American girl. Along with Vera, Chester was well liked by Bob and Dorothy Purdy.[29]

Perhaps the next day, he pledged, "I will write everyday as I know what it means to be lonely." He was doing very well in his work as translator and interpreter and expected to get a better job soon. "Won't that be fine so I can send you more each month." In September, he sent letters with money, and Vera was to keep all of it. "I don't want to sell the weights I left with you as I am returning to the States to work unless I get more money. I get a certificate in Spanish from University."[30]

While James was in Mexico, his younger brother Robert interrupted his studies at the University of Findlay, where he lettered in basketball, track, and tennis, to enlist in the US Navy. In 1944, during service, Bob married Dorothy in San Diego, where he was based, to the surprise of family and friends in Ohio. James, who remained lonely, wrapped up his Mexican jaunt and in late fall of 1944 returned to Chicago to continue his study of the Spanish language among friends. Through the spring of 1945, James took courses at the University of Chicago funded by the government. Since Purdy could choose the school, he preferred to return to the vibrant bohemian milieu of Abercrombie and the works over continuing to study Spanish among Spanish speakers.

Purdy's second period spent with Gertrude and her circle, like his first, had a profound effect. In Abercrombie, he found creative inspiration and a kindred spirit. Gertrude, her husband Bob Livingston, an attorney she married in 1940, and their little daughter Dinah, born in 1942, had moved into a tall Victorian house in Hyde Park near the university. Purdy was given a room there in exchange for babysitting.[31] Abercrombie remained in this house for the rest of her life, painting works there in magic realist style sometimes called surrealist; Dalí and especially Magritte were influences. Her friend, painter August Becker, wrote: "On the salon floor it was immense; a quite grand staircase spread gracefully down from its first landing. Servant quarters occupied the top floor, and backstairs led down to the kitchen" on the ground floor. Guests usually entered at the ground level, where there was an ample housekeeper's sitting room with a fireplace. Further back, the kitchen led to a rear garden.[32]

Thanks largely to Gertrude, James was steeped in both magic realist art and black culture. "There is magic everywhere if you stop and look and listen," Gertrude advised. "Everything is strange. I think it's a scream we're here at all . . . don't you?"[33] Her circle of Midwestern magic realist painters, some of whom were gay or queer, included handsome Karl Priebe; his boyfriend, Dudley Huppler; John Wilde; Ivan Albright; and brilliant but forgotten Julia Thecla. They influenced the development of Purdy's aesthetics as he marinated in their talk and work. Members of the magic realist group met at two salons: Priebe's home in Milwaukee, and Abercrombie's salon in Chicago, occurring while James lived there. He seems to have traveled to Milwaukee with Gertrude.[34]

Karl Priebe, also a friend of Billie Holiday, was enchanted by black culture. He painted portraits of Lady Day, blues icon Bessie Smith, and other black subjects, along with birds. He was born in the same year and month as Purdy, and shared many interests and contacts with him. Priebe's wide circle included the artists John Wilde and Carol Blanchard; jazz trumpeter Dizzy Gillespie; and poets Gwendolyn Brooks and Langston Hughes. By the 1930s, Tyler Friedman writes, a "slow erosion of racial barriers had reached such a degree in America's larger cities that a new cultural type emerged. This individual, classified as a 'hipster' by Norman Mailer in his essay 'The White Negro,' rejected the staid safety of white society for the untapped possibilities" of black culture. Such a crossover defined Karl Priebe's artistic identity.[35]

Long before the term "magical realism" became known in the United States as a literary genre, Purdy translated magic realist strategies from a visual medium to literary form. Early champions—Van Vechten, Sitwell, John Cowper Powys, and Tennessee Williams—recognized a quality of heightened realism in Purdy's early fiction as something new on the literary map.[36] Like the magic realism typified by Abercrombie's best paintings, that in Purdy's prose can evoke a dreamlike state in readers using a modernist strategy of defamiliarization: common situations are rendered strange and uncanny. In the work of both, the result is entrancing, unsettling, haunting.

Like these Midwestern painters, the bebop musicians who jammed and stayed at Abercrombie's home taught Purdy profound lessons in artistic creation through making use of one's native materials. Purdy evoked this lively atmosphere of her salon in fictional scenes of bebop hepcats, painters, and writers.[37] Purdy experienced lively parties and now, frequent jazz blowing sessions the Queen of Chicago hosted at her home on Saturdays or Sundays. Dorchester Avenue became a hotbed of bebop, the style revolutionizing jazz—an intense, harmonically complex idiom using bright tempos and key changes. Abercrombie's close friend, trumpeter Dizzy Gillespie, was an elite practitioner; he proclaimed Gertrude "*the* bop artist, bop in the sense that she has taken the essence of our music and transported it into another art form."[38] Legendary alto saxophonist Charlie Parker, "Bird," roosted there; his favorite painting was her *Design for Death*.[39] Gertrude socialized with many more legends including pianist Erroll Garner, trumpeter Miles Davis, percussionist Max Roach, singers Sarah Vaughan and Billie Holiday, and tenor saxophonist Sonny Rollins—and Purdy soaked it in. Hard-bop trumpeter Clifford Brown performed "Gertrude's Bounce," written by Richie Powell, in her honor while staying at her home.[40] There Purdy also interacted with future members of Modern Jazz Quartet: bassist Percy Heath and pianist John Lewis, members of Dizzy Gillespie's big band, who later found fame with the "ultimate cool synthesis of classical music with fugue-like jazz."[41] Lewis later became the model for a minor character, George Leeds, in *Malcolm*.

Purdy experienced unforgettable jazz moments, once accepting an invitation from Billie Holiday to sit on her ample lap. After James was settled on her lap, Billie remarked to MacLeish: "Oh, Norman, you brought me a *nice* boy tonight. Well, aren't you the cutest little blond thing."[42] Purdy later drew from Billie's sensuality and thirst for liquor for his character Melba in *Malcolm*, a popular singer and femme fatale.[43] Trumpeter and author Humphrey Littleton notes that Holiday "never had a bestselling record, never topped the most prestigious of jazz popularity polls, never broke successfully into movies and never rose, except sporadically, above the unspectacular, somewhat clandestine, life of a club singer." "In a world in which the catchy, the amusing and the ingratiating picked up the top prizes, her style was subtle, oblique, harsh and uncompromising. In other words, she was too good."[44] This appealed to Purdy.

At the salon, Purdy also became acquainted with the eccentric Marian Bomberger Bard Andreas, who styled herself as Miriam. Born in 1900, Miriam knew Wilcox and Abercrombie; the latter introduced her to James. To Paul Miller, Miriam was a "high-flying, heavy drinking, occasional painter, literary connoisseur, and amateur musician."[45] Miriam introduced James to Osborn Andreas, businessman and literary critic. Born in 1903 in Sterling, Illinois, to a prominent family, Osborn attended the University of Iowa, Cornell College in Iowa, and the University of Washington. In Cedar Rapids, Osborn and four brothers developed a multimillion-dollar feed and grain milling company, which they eventually sold to Cargill. Soft-spoken Osborn was an industrial engineer, cost accountant, and, in the late 1940s, agribusiness executive, but his real love was literature. He later published critical studies of Henry James and Joseph Conrad.

Osborn and Miriam were not married until 1946; however, since the 1920s, they were involved in each other's lives. A 1948 letter from Osborn to Professor Cox—not to be confused with the *Malcolm* character based on Wendell Wilcox—explains how Purdy could have met both long before their marriage. Edward G. Cox, who wrote a preface for Andreas's book on Henry James, had asked about his dedicatee. Osborn explained: "I met her at North Central College in Napierville, Illinois, when I was a sophomore, and we corresponded in the middle 1920s. I went to see her and we have been engaged to be married ever since. But meanwhile we have both been twice married and divorced—to and from two other people. . . . All four marriages were in some sense flights from each other, but the inevitable caught up with us at last." For Osborn, as with the *Malcolm* character Girard Girard, "marriage with her would be a continuous contest."[46] Osborn and Miriam were notorious squabblers. "Our relationship," Osborn observed, "has always been a complete mystery to all our friends, mutual and otherwise, and, above, all, to ourselves." Something archetypal about their antagonism begged a writer to dramatize it, "polarized opposites in temperament and sensibility, but equal in intelligence," doomed to be "eternally interested" in one another since neither could "finally pass judgment on the other." "We utterly exasperate each other more than half the time," but the "deepest insights and thoughts that come to me occur only because of my conflict with her."[47] John Uecker called their dynamic "emotional S/M. She was master."[48]

The day after Christmas 1944, Chicago received a crystalline gift from Tennessee Williams: *The Glass Menagerie* began its pre-Broadway tryout, in a ten-week run at the Civic Theatre. Amid trials and triumphs, the fragile play barely got to the New York stage intact. *Chicago Tribune* critic Claudia Cassidy was caught in the spell of a "tough little play" that was "vividly written, and in the main superbly acted." Laurette Taylor as Amanda Wingfield electrified audiences. Cassidy's review moved many to investigate; Purdy was one, beginning his lifelong relation with the plays, and, later, the playwright.[49]

James continued to write stories but failed to place them. As early as 1945, he believed he had written enough quality stories to comprise a collection. Continued rejection and harsh comments might have discouraged someone with less belief in his talent. New York editors and publishers, even the little magazines, rejected them with "astringent comments," Purdy noted.[50]

After completing the spring semester at the University of Chicago, during summer 1945, he returned to University of Puebla for a few more months of Spanish training. Purdy was next placed with a teaching position in Cuba, likely the culmination of a trajectory planned by the government. After receiving a telegram from the State Department, he embarked on September 13, 1945. "The government got me that job; it was sort of a teacher's agency, except it was the U.S. government," he explained. Naturally, "people said, 'Oh, you're a spy.'"

Within weeks of the Japanese surrender of September 2, 1945, Purdy was employed as a teacher at Ruston Academy in Vedado, a suburb in west Havana distinguished by high-ceilinged Cuban-style mansions. Bilingual and coeducational, Ruston, the premiere American school in Cuba, was founded by retired English teacher Hiram Hall Ruston and his sister, Martha Ruston, of Indiana. "It was a school for Cubans and Americans, and I taught English literature more or less," Purdy said, though the 1946 yearbook says his subject was history.[51] The school had trouble acquiring books, and Purdy was ashamed of some of the paperbacks they assigned, like *Dracula*. Novelist Edmundo Desnoes, his student there, recalled Purdy as "friendly and at the same time rigorous. Even while you lifted weights, there was something smiling and tense about you. The image is blurred but the mixture of sympathy and intolerance was there."[52] James found he did not care for Hiram Ruston, telling Vera in January 1946: "Mr. R. is very bad. I have gotten in contact with all the jobs." While he may have wanted to leave the position, he savored the sunshine and many aspects of life in Havana. He gazed on diverse, elaborate architecture, listened to mambo rhythms, and tasted "wonderful coffee to knock your hat off!"[53] He acquired a lifelong interest in Cuban literature.[54]

Purdy wrote a poem, "Cuban Mocking-Bird," on "the SINSONTE in his tree" evoking Havana's natural sights and sounds: "Sing in the ruined bougainvillea / Echo over the flame-tree / Pierce the top of the restrainèd sea / Make the hawk pause in his circle / And / Remind the palm trees that bow heavily over Roses, jasmine, orchids, cup-of-gold. Evening and morning / Morning and evening / The mocking-bird / Remembers ships, voices / And flies away from the sea and time."

Cuba was then a tourist mecca, reputedly licentious, attracting American celebrities and European aristocrats. Being gay in Cuba was risky, so discretion was the rule. In this predominantly Catholic society, homosexuality was forbidden by law, and those open about their non-heterosexual behavior were pariahs. One could find a few gay-friendly bars, and gay prostitution was a part of the sex industry that thrived in pre-Castro Cuba, catering to US tourists and servicemen. To David Breithaupt, Purdy recalled postwar Cuban "glory days" and "how dark and exotic the gay scene was."[55]

Purdy's posthumously published story "The Pupil" suggests there may have been mutual attraction between Purdy and a male student. A startling, homoerotic story set in a boys' prep school, "The Pupil" evokes fascination between a young male teacher-coach at his first teaching position and a teenage Cuban. Gonzalez, son of a deceased Cuban consul, is a budding artist who gazes at his Adonis-like teacher reverently, sketching him during class. This leads to the teacher posing nude on Gonzalez's request, the playing out of locker-room fantasies, and a shocking climax. In 1891, Henry James published "The Pupil," about an affectionate relationship between Pemberton, who tutors Morgan, an eleven-year-old student; the latent queer desire and even sadomasochism some modern critics detect in James's story beneath the teacher-pupil dynamic[56] is manifest in Purdy's story of the same name. Especially in the 1950s, such stark portrayal of taboo desire is subversive.

Cuba was stimulating, but Purdy stayed for only one school year, through June 1946. "I could have stayed on longer, but I didn't want to," he later remarked. Four señoritas gave their teacher a snapshot on the last day of school. One wrote on the back: "So that you remember 'Cubanitas.'" Hiram Ruston died shortly thereafter.

While James was in Havana, Richard was finding some acclaim as stage actor in New York. In September 1945, he starred in a psychological thriller, *Murder without Crime*, at Cherry Lane Theatre on 42nd Street. Burton Rascoe, drama critic for *New York World Telegram* and author of *Titans of Literature* (1932), declared: "Richard Purdy's melodramatic technique is unusually expert. He conveys, naturally and believably, the shifty, characterless personality of Stephen, his malleability in the hands of women, his craven fear of scenes of unpleasantness, his hysteria easily developed under the diabolic insinuations of Matthew, and his final crack-up." Richard's melodramatic technique is significant, as melodrama informed James's literary sensibility. To the *New York Post*, he was "most convincing as the weak young man who stuffs his mistress's body in the ottoman."[57] The *Brooklyn Eagle* praised Richard's acting as "sure, sharp, free," though regretted Richard was "not a tall young man" because uptown he would receive "fewer chances than he deserves." James was the tall brother.[58]

In spring 1946, while James was in Havana, his second publication finally appeared, the first since 1939. "You Reach for Your Hat" was placed in the respected journal *Prairie Schooner*, based at the University of Nebraska.[59] Derived from Findlay days, the story concerns gossip surrounding Jennie Esmond, whose husband died in the war, and her nighttime promenades that entail, scandalously, drinking in a bar with men, the saloon based on Findlay's The Mecca Bar, Parker Sams writes. Mamie seeks out her friend Jennie, and their conversation is one of many scenes in which Purdy depicts women's friendship. "You Reach for Your Hat" climaxes with Jennie's revelation of a lack of tender feelings—"I never loved him or anything he did to me"—toward her late veteran husband. Mamie is shattered, having wanted a "sweet memory talk," to allow her friend to unburden grief. But Jennie reveals Lafe "wasn't actually interested in woman's charm. No man really is."[60] She recalls his constant demands for cooking, her dependence, her lack of life outside marriage. Here and elsewhere, Purdy's perspective is sympathetic to women who struggle within patriarchy. The appeal of this story to women was underscored when, eleven years later, it was reprinted in *Mademoiselle*.

This second publication, however, failed to ignite further interest in his short stories. After war's end, Purdy began writing a novella, *63: Dream Palace*, drawing from Chicago experiences, and in the early 1950s, he finished a first draft. In 1946, *Story*, edited by Whit Burnett, accepted "Eventide" for publication, but three years later, they returned it, having decided not to publish it after all. "I don't think editors know what that does to a young writer. It is so devastating," Later, Burnett sent Purdy a congratulatory letter, after *Color of Darkness* came out, which he ignored.[61] Burnett had taught J. D. Salinger at Columbia, and in 1940, published his first story, "The Young Folks." Purdy eventually became rival to Salinger, whose work he loathed.

While Salinger became the darling of the *New Yorker*, in 1947, Purdy submitted "Eventide" to the *New Yorker* but, Purdy said, an editor rejected it with a discouraging comment: "You don't even know how to write." Fiction published in "those slick magazines has to go along with the ads—what's really important."[62] He was vindicated when "Eventide" was included in *Understanding Fiction*, a popular anthology assigned to students. The story is driven by dialogue in black vernacular between two sisters. Mahala rues to Plumy she has "lost" her son, Teeboy, who has left home and is not coming back. Teeboy left home to play saxophone professionally in his jazz band, which performs at the Music Box club and travels to other cities for gigs. Two black women Purdy had known as a boy, "Aunt Lucy" and her companion, guided the voices of Mahala and Plumy. "I shifted the locale to Chicago. But it is Findlay," he wrote Parker Sams. Teeboy has straightened his hair and is spending time in a mostly white neighborhood. This "loss" enables Mahala to empathize with her sister's deeper loss, seventeen years earlier, of her son, George Watson, at age four. Mahala, however, turns her living son into a frozen memory, as though he had died.[63]

Joseph Skerrett Jr., an African American critic, found "Eventide" convincing. He concluded it is "not a story about white experience done up in blackface. It is fully imagined in terms of a black situation." Dr. Skerrett concluded the "powerful and unusual images" of black characters found across Purdy's oeuvre had origin in his "intense emotional identification" with powerless, stigmatized, and frustrated people. Purdy's "most successful black characterizations are not effective because of sociological or even psychological accuracy as much as because they are emotionally convincing." Skerrett did "not know of another white American author" who had "created so satisfying a gallery of black portraits without resorting to history or sociology."[64]

In the summer of 1946, Purdy was offered a job at Lawrence College in Wisconsin. He decided to trade his somewhat itinerant lifestyle of the early 1940s for a more stable position in the upper Midwest. In July and early August, he visited family in Findlay, then took the train to Chicago to visit friends before traveling north to Appleton, Wisconsin—a predominantly white Midwestern college town with a thriving paper industry. Purdy had no clue how long he would stay.

6

The Professor

Beginning in the fall of 1946, the aspiring writer taught Spanish and Freshman Studies at Lawrence College, in downtown Appleton, a small city lying in the Fox River valley, southwest of Green Bay, north of Lake Winnebago. Appleton sits on the former homelands of the Menominee and the Winnebago; the Ojibwe, from whom Purdy claimed descent, lived in the northern part of what became Wisconsin. The government probably helped the veteran land this position. Postwar, Lawrence College, like other schools, needed more instructors. With returned veterans taking advantage of their G.I. Bill of Rights, enrollment jumped from below 600 to over 1,025 between fall 1945 and fall 1946. As a new faculty member, Purdy had to learn the ropes, plan lessons, and fulfill social duties. In October 1946, for example, he attended a reception and dinner at local homes in honor of a visiting Colombian lawyer and columnist.[1]

Along with teaching and service, Purdy wrote diligently. In Wisconsin, he composed or finished most of the stories later collected in *Color of Darkness*, but found it impossible to publish.[2] Teaching frustrated him and grading and meetings sapped time and energy. Wishing to devote himself fully to writing, he eked out time to write and edit during off-duty hours. Nonetheless, his submissions were rejected by several magazines, even after he was taken on as a client by a New York literary agent, Toni Strassman, who had worked for Viking and represented Texan writer William Goyen.

James remained in Appleton too because he felt obliged to keep sending money home to his mother, who struggled to make ends meet. Purdy's feeling of obligation to Vera is linked to his decision to slice several years off his actual age, even before he was an established writer. Some said that James fibbed so he would be perceived as a young, up-and-coming writer when he began to gain recognition—presumably preferable to the image of a middle-aged writer who had placed only two stories over fifteen years. Rejecting this, John Uecker said James sustained this deception to erase from his biography the nine and a half years he was employed by Lawrence College, because he felt trapped and obliged to send money home and was unable to devote himself fully to his true calling, his writing. On the rare occasions he later spoke of this period of his life, he usually claimed it lasted four years.[3]

Gertrude Abercrombie advised him to tell Vera to find herself a man.[4] But when she did, marrying an employed younger man, John K. Bauman, in October 1951, the family was not crazy about him. Bauman was a railroad worker, strong, and "kind of rough," who wore flannel shirts, white socks, and boots, altogether different from the three-piece suits and pocket watches of William Purdy. James did not care for Bauman, nor did Bob or Dorothy. A bit coarse, John rubbed Bob the wrong way, and family members wondered whether he treated Vera kindly.[5]

Despite Purdy's difficulty in gaining literary recognition, during most of his career at Lawrence, he enjoyed the support of college president, Dr. Nathan Marsh Pusey. Even though Purdy mostly taught Spanish, Pusey strongly encouraged his fiction writing. Known as the faculty's president, Pusey felt at home among them. Despite an administrative style deemed authoritarian, he took pains to cultivate his professors' respect and friendship. On Sunday evenings, he and his wife hosted small faculty groups for supper. The president attended all special lectures given by faculty members on campus and was "solicitous of new young faculty members."[6] Decades later, Purdy said he was moved by Pusey's encouragement. The president ran into Purdy outside a campus building, took him aside, and said he had heard good things about his writing. "You should try to spend more time on it. And less time in the classroom," Pusey advised. "James marveled at this comment" and over Pusey for having said it. In June 1948, Pusey commended Purdy's work to the college trustees.[7]

At Lawrence, James met a smart, handsome man who became a mainstay in his life. Born in April 1919 in Cleveland, Ohio, to Arvid (Alfred) and Siama (Wnorenorjie), Jorma Jules Sjoblom was a tall, slim, Finnish-American professor of chemistry.[8] He had studied at Western Reserve University and done his graduate work in physical and inorganic chemistry at the University of Minnesota, in Minneapolis. Jorma and James were close neighbors. "We were advised to rent bachelor quarters at South House, close to campus," Sjoblom explained. "We had separate rooms, but they happened to be right across the hallway, so we got acquainted." They shared meals at a dormitory dining room on campus.[9] James and Jorma hit it off, quickly becoming good friends and romantic partners. "We were lovers, but sexual intimacy was not the most important part of our friendship. Fate brought us together." At Lawrence, except for a few "sympathetic friends," colleagues were not aware of the "deep feeling" between them. Oddly, even to Jorma, James misrepresented himself as much younger than he was. Jorma believed that he was four years older than James, when in reality, James was nearly five years older than Jorma.[10]

James and Jorma operated in their Cold War context. Sjoblom, as a chemist at Lawrence specializing in phosphorescent dyes, which are used in security printing of international banknotes, doubtless assisted the secretive Institute of Paper Chemistry (IPC), which created partnerships between Lawrence College, the local paper industry, and government intelligence. Collaboration between the OSS and Lawrence led to the counterfeiting of enemy banknotes and passports. Westbrook Steele, a "dynamic fundraiser" who was brought in to help reorganize Lawrence, cofounded IPC in 1929 and was its executive director. Steele was friendly with the acting chief of OSS counterespionage, who was searching for bright young men with foreign language skills.[11]

A good friend of Purdy and Sjoblom was Dr. John Bucklew, a professor of psychology hired in 1947, who was apparently a gay man. Bucklew researched and published on subjects including the effects of marital dominance on children, language behavior, retrograde amnesia, and phenomenology, and he coauthored *Empirical Foundation of Psychology*.[12] For two and a half years, Bucklew did military psychology work for the government, in Africa, Europe, and stateside.[13] Such links between academia and military work were typical of several colleagues James knew in the postwar and Cold War periods.

Bucklew loved Purdy's anonymous anomalous letters and satirical news bulletins "for immediate release" that he wrote as a professor. James also made humorous tape recordings spoofing people and situations at Lawrence. After Purdy became an established writer, Bucklew wrote that he had liked almost everything Purdy had written, "clear back to the Brooks lectures tape recordings" Purdy had made "while living the life of Raskolnikov" in the attic of Gabe Jones, a professor of art history. (Raskolnikov, the murderous but conflicted protagonist of Dostoevsky's proto-existentialist novel, *Crime and Punishment*, lived in cramped poverty.) Charlie Brooks, a target of Purdy's satire, was a professor of art and architecture from 1946 to 1974. "None of these things was ever really obscene," Bucklew wrote. "They dealt with obscene materials but were extremely funny. You felt put upon by outrageous implications that you didn't want to accept but couldn't really deny. All you can do is laugh."[14] Purdy was inspired to create outrageous art aimed, at least initially, toward a specialized audience of friends.

Within his first year at Lawrence, Purdy was given opportunity to hone his Spanish skills in Spain. Before boarding a ship, James enjoyed visiting his brother Richard in New York at his room at the Hotel Wentworth near the Times Square theater area and meeting "the prologue player & his wife & Luis the bellhop."[15] On March 20, 1947, at age thirty-two, Purdy began his voyage to Madrid, stopping in Santa Maria Island in the Azores, and Lisbon, Portugal. He spent five months abroad studying and sightseeing, perhaps also doing translation work.[16] At that time, one could "live in cheap hotels for nothing."[17] He "fell in love" with Spain, and Cervantes' story "Rinconete and Cortadillo," about two young runaways in Seville, "made a deep impression." Reading it as a gay story, Purdy saw himself "only too clearly as the runaways."[18] He spent time in Spain "wandering around on no money—you didn't need money then."[19] His love of Spanish culture deepened and he took in bullfights. The greatest thing was the women, who were "completely feminine and completely women, and seem to have sprung right out of the earth," Purdy wrote John Cowper Powys. "They have no tricks except those of their sex. I think this is because the men are so virile still. Or maybe the men are virile because the women are so womanly."[20]

Purdy knew a young Spaniard who was enraged by those running Spain— "the Fascists. He really felt like killing all of them." Dictator Federico Franco, who was friendly with fascists, declared Catholicism the official national religion and supported the Church. "Being an American," James could "only listen spellbound," feeling he had "no right to say anything in return." He did not know "most Spaniards were very critical of their church." He was passing a church when his friend walked out. "You see that church? That's my church! It doesn't belong to any of those politicians." "I learned in Spain to keep my mouth shut," Purdy reflected.[21]

In late July, to "Richie" he wrote on a postcard picturing the grand Royal Palace of Madrid. It was hot, but he liked Spain and Spaniards very much; he was headed to Barcelona that night. He sent thanks for sending one of his stories to *Harper's*. On August 2, he wrote on a postcard depicting Iglesia de Santa Maria that he was enjoying San Sebastián, a port city on the Bay of Biscay in the Basque Country, and would return to Madrid August 10. "You'd like this old city. We'll talk so much when I return."[22] Spain was not all pleasure. "I used to get upset when I lived in Spain because I was communicating with Spaniards, but it was in a language that was not my own. I started getting ill because of it."[23] James departed Madrid on August 25, and arrived in New York two days later.

While James was in Spain in July, his grandmother Minnie Mabel Otis died at age eighty and was buried in Hicksville, in Forest Home Cemetery. A decade earlier, the once grand but diminished manse where she had lived with George K. Otis was sold "for $1 and natural love and affection." In the late 1920s, the third floor, with cupola and mansard roofs, was removed.[24] James recalled Minnie fondly over decades to come, and a bounty of stories from her and her mother, Nettie Cowhick, informed a subset of his work.

After Purdy's return to Wisconsin, in 1948, there was a flurry of news from Chicago friends, whom he periodically visited. In January 1948, Osborn S. Andreas married Marian (Miriam) Bomberger.[25] In February, Osborn wrote Professor Cox from their honeymoon in Paris: "Alice B. Toklas came over for lunch the other day and stayed four hours," discussing Ford, Pound, Hemingway, and Wilder. "Since Stein died, Toklas has become Stein in everything but genius, a diminutive edition but assuming full authority." The next

Figure 6.1 Photo of actor Richard Purdy in Pirandello's *Henry IV* with Great Dane, New York, 1949. Courtesy of Purdy family.

week, the newlyweds were going on a "ten-day cruise from Cannes over to Tunis, stopping also at Naples, Genoa, Milan and Malta."[26] Correspondence from Harold Knapik, Chicago chef and composer, in Paris, to his wife, Virginia Knapik, in Rome, also sheds light on Purdy people and their relations to one another and to Toklas. On a Saturday in 1953, Harold had a surprise visit from Miriam Andreas that shocked him. He told her that Virginia was in Rome; they talked of Chicago and Osborn. She was "completely off her nut" because "she had not done anything in her life and now insists that she is a painter," having been inspired by a Cézanne show. "She looks very old and her legs are swollen and her conversation is impossible." Harold offered the only liquor in the house, which she consumed while he played piano and she spoke along old themes of how wonderful Frank Sandiford and Gertrude Abercrombie are and how creative and tricky a businessman Osborn is. She was still thirsty, so they went out to the café Voltaire, where he had a beer, she three martinis, and they closed the place. Marian wanted to keep drinking; Harold balked and put her in a cab, hoping she would return to her hotel, since she had an early flight to Spain. He simply could not bring himself "to haul her around the Paris streets," feeling that "in some way it would be contaminating them." He concluded his "original premise that she had destroyed herself for money" was "only too true" and she could not enjoy it. Her sudden appearance recollected all the difficulties they had in Chicago. Harold and Virginia Knapik, as it turned out, were undercover CIA. Another unusual thing about them is that they were first cousins—his brother was married to her sister.[27]

Like Osborn, Gertrude Abercrombie also remarried in 1948. Abercrombie divorced Bob Livingston, having decided her life was too conventional, and, on New Year's Eve, she married memoirist and jazz critic Frank Sandiford, seven years her junior. Sandiford had owned a record store, mixed in jazz clubs like The Bee Hive, and was hip to the scene. Through him, Gertrude expanded her circle of musicians, both local and touring. Jam sessions at their house were legendary. Artist August Becker said Gertrude quaffed cheap red wine; alcohol and "its effect on outsized sexual appetites" was an "important dimension in her life and all their lives in the 1950s," and most parties ended drunkenly. Scenesters held "very few preconceived attitudes as to whom one might end up in bed with" since no hard line was drawn between straight and queer. Many cliques were either gay or straight, but at Gertrude and Frank's, all were "quite mixed up." Gertrude's husbands had "homosexual appetites," Becker notes, Livingston's "perhaps not as demanding" as Sandiford's, though neither was stereotypically gay.[28] Yet even amid this free sexuality, there was much "clandestine activity," the sexual ethic of the circle being "perhaps singular, even in Chicago." Purdy did not much care for Sandiford, the former high society burglar, or "second-story man," as he dubbed himself, later satirizing him in *Malcolm*.

In Wisconsin, Purdy reconnected with artists John Wilde and Karl Priebe, magic realists he had met in Chicago. On breaks away from campus, Purdy could occasionally be found "prowling the dark side" with them in Milwaukee or during mutual visits to Chicago.[29] Jorma Sjoblom shared that a gay underground was active during this homophobic period in Wisconsin and other Midwestern locales, in which certain bars and campus men's rooms became known as cruising grounds for gay men. In Appleton, the Hotel Conway was known as a place one could find a partner to give or receive oral sex; a music professor and a speech professor were frank about their rendezvous, Sjoblom said.[30]

After three years at Lawrence College, in 1949 Purdy was promoted to assistant professor of Spanish.[31] A third Spanish instructor, Elizabeth Burbridge, was hired, joining him and Kathleen Joyce.[32] Professor Purdy became known for his collection of large bullfighting posters, some of which he hung in his classrooms. In 1951, a picture of James with one of a hundred posters accompanied a profile of him in the Appleton *Post-Crescent*. He admitted he still did not really understand bullfighting. "It's as complicated as music or ballet, and it takes years of study and attendance to be an aficionado." Cruel and barbaric, yes, but fascinating. Students were not liable to doze under the blazing colors of the posters, he remarked.[33]

Along with his classroom decor, Purdy's home decor was memorable. On the white walls of one apartment, he executed large, flowing freehand charcoal drawings, which was striking to visitors, Jorma recalled. At another point, the word spread to Bowling Green that Purdy had painted his Appleton apartment walls black.[34]

Toward the end of the 1940s, he was actively writing and submitting stories through his agent, Toni Strassman. Before Christmas 1948, Purdy was working on a story about Cuba. In January 1949, she reported that *Story* magazine "had a new lease on life," so perhaps Whit Burnett would finally publish Purdy's stories that he had bought, but no such luck. After "Send In a Younger Man" was rejected several times, Strassman returned it, and it remains unpublished. Purdy had expressed interest in playwriting, but she advised, "Don't write a play: it's a heartbreaking experience." Although

Tennessee Williams and Lillian Hellman later encouraged the opposite, arguably, she was prophetic in that Purdy's many plays remain neglected and little-produced.[35]

Two years after Richard Purdy trod the boards with Maurice Evans in a transcontinental tour of *Hamlet* that ran from December 1946 through spring 1947, the tragedy was staged at Lawrence in March 1949, directed by Ted Cloak, lead professor and director in the theater department. *Hamlet* was taught in Freshman Studies by Purdy and others, and by the time it was performed, every student knew it. All students and faculty participated, so a community shared an authentic intellectual experience, "one of the most exciting things" President Pusey ever saw in education.[36] This *Hamlet* experience likely reminded James of Richard's success, which he may have contrasted with his own obscurity. If James lived "the life of Raskolnikov" during the late 1940s, Richard debuted on Broadway in a revival of *Crime and Punishment* as Zametoff, a young detective, in December 1947 and January 1948. Dick shared the National Theatre stage with the English legend John Gielgud and fellow Buckeye, Lillian Gish, the First Lady of American Cinema. In summer 1949, James returned to Findlay to visit family.

Purdy also had reason to be envious of Warren Beck, a novelist-professor from Indiana who spent his summers teaching creative writing at Breadloaf in Vermont.[37] A World War I veteran, Faulkner scholar, and respected longtime professor at Lawrence, Beck published novels, including the acclaimed *Final Score*, and story collections in the 1940s and 1950s. In 1960, Bucklew described Beck in the faculty lounge: "He is a big, paunchy aunty now who waddles about his business amiably. He looks at one blandly, deigns to discuss himself and his affairs briefly, then turns to reading his mail with complete disinterest in whomever he is talking at," just like the "rest of Lawrence's great ones," all "self-important nonentities."[38] When Purdy was later asked about Beck and Lawrence by a writer preparing an article for *The Nation*, he said he had read his stories to Beck, who encouraged him, but advised against having them privately published and against leaving teaching to devote himself to writing. Warren Beck "made no effort to place the stories" and "could have done so, had he cared. We are no longer friendly or in communication."[39] After Dr. Beck died in 1986, Purdy wrote a story inspired by him, "Dr. Dieck and Company," published posthumously.

During the 1950s, Purdy became better known to students and faculty. In 1950, he spoke on a panel organized by Students for Democratic Action, opposing US aid to Spain under Franco. Purdy said no aid should be given to a regime that had "shown itself incompetent to improve Spain industrially, agriculturally, or socially." Franco had kept Spain in a state of perpetual terror, he told sixty-five students. He advised the Spanish Club, which hosted a fiesta in the Beta Theta Pi House in May. In 1951, at a Sunday dinner meeting, he spoke to Junior Pilgrim fellows at First Congregational Church.[40]

In June 1950, communist North Korea, supported by Russia and China, invaded South Korea, beginning a short but disastrous war. Concern over communism spreading and its threat to the nation took hold in the heartland. A year later, Pusey announced an Air Force Reserve Officers Training Corps would arrive on campus and participation would be mandatory for virtually all men entering college in fall 1952.

Meanwhile in Paris, in June, the Congress for Cultural Freedom (CCF) was formed and established its headquarters. Among many writers and critics, Tennessee Williams, Carson McCullers, and James T. Farrell attended its first meeting in Frankfurt. Purdy would indirectly benefit from the CCF and similar agencies. Planned in 1949, the CCF was committed to waging a cultural Cold War, peddling soft power, operating through many offices in Europe and globally, awarding prizes, organizing concerts, festivals, and readings; publishing and translating books; and publishing or funding journals aligned with the Non-Communist Left (NCL). In *Finks: How the CIA Tricked the World's Best Writers*, Joel Whitney explains the CCF was "the CIA's new propaganda front, its attempt to offset the use of culture by the Soviets to lure intellectuals to the fringe benefits of communism—which included government funding for the arts."[41] From 1950 through 1967, the CIA funneled tens of millions of dollars into the CCF and similar projects such as the United States Information Service (later Agency). Formed in 1953, the USIS maintained a list of anticommunist and pro-American books to distribute at American embassies and Information Resource Centers globally. Being a favored or non-blacklisted author helped sell books.[42] CCF funding was largely controlled by Cord Meyer, head of the CIA's International Organizations Division, who oversaw the agency's "greatest single concentration of covert political and propaganda activities," Saunders writes. Meyer, an elitist Ivy Leaguer, was part of an early CIA that was surprisingly literary and modernist. Meyer followed in the footsteps of James Jesus Angleton, legendary counterintelligence chief, who introduced Ezra Pound to Yale, founded poetry magazines, and was the nexus of "the P source"—Professor— comprising Ivy League links.

In the early 1950s, Richard Purdy's acting career exploded into a new medium, television, where he played forty-four roles between 1949 and 1955.[43] In 1951, when Dick appeared on a mystery program, *Ellery Queen*, a critic wrote, "Richard Purdy's face will be quickly recalled. He is one of TV's busiest actors."[44] Television's early producers and sponsors brought high culture to the masses. A highlight was *Studio One*, a live drama program. Among his many roles there, in 1949, Richard played a modern man who believes he is Henry IV, Holy Roman Emperor, in Pirandello's *Henry IV*; in 1950 he was Chillingworth in an adaptation of Hawthorne's *The Scarlet Letter*; and in 1951, he played scheming Sicinius in Shakespeare's *Coriolanus*.[45] He costarred with Maria Riva, daughter of Marlene Dietrich, in an episode, "The Angelic Avengers" (1951), and in an episode of *You Are There*, "The Conspiracy of Catherine the Great" (1954). William Purdy visited Richard and accompanied him to the TV studio, where Dietrich was visiting her daughter backstage. "Marlene took a shine to our father," James said, and after she and her daughter left, Will turned to Richard and asked, "who was that lady who was talking to me?"[46] In 1952, for *Kraft Television Theater*, Dick played Jacob Marley in "A Christmas Carol." He did not foreswear theater roles and in December 1951 played an "eerie visitor from the Other World" in a comedy, *Fancy Meeting You Again*, at Locust Street Theatre in Philadelphia. The *Inquirer* praised an "excellent cast" and mentioned him.[47] Although James did not own a television set in Wisconsin, he must have learned from family of Richard's success, perhaps feeling a renewed pang to be recognized as a writer.[48]

Appleton, Wisconsin, was the hometown of Senator Joseph McCarthy, who launched his anticommunist crusade in 1950, enjoying widespread support over the Fox Valley. Fortunately, President Pusey stood up for academic freedom, receiving national attention for his clashes with McCarthy. Pusey fought McCarthyism by refusing to ban *The Communist Manifesto* from the curriculum, a move that impressed the faculty.[49] Before McCarthy's reelection campaign in 1952, Pusey joined the Wisconsin Citizens' Committee on McCarthy's Record, which published a pamphlet exposing the senator's abuses of power. Pusey's stand took courage, since some industrialist trustees strongly supported McCarthy. McCarthy lashed out at Pusey, calling him an intolerant phony, hypocrite, and "a rabid anti, anti-Communist." McCarthy's vitriol undermined the college president's credibility in the area among many supporters. When Pusey was appointed as Harvard's president in the summer of 1953, McCarthy sniped, "Harvard's loss is Wisconsin's gain."[50] After the announcement, which drew reporters from *Time* and *Life* to Appleton, students and faculty gathered in front of the president's office and serenaded the Puseys by torchlight.[51]

In the summer of 1952, Purdy traveled in Europe, enjoying sites in France, Spain, and Italy, embarking June 6.[52] In Paris, he stayed near La Tour Eiffel in the 7th Arrondissement, an upscale area, and met Esther Wilcox and Sam Steward in a trendy café in St-Germain-des-Pres on the Left Bank, associated with writers and painters. Purdy read in French Jean Paul Sartre's new work on Jean Genet, icon of transgressive writing, whose works Purdy admired. In a postcard to Wendell and Esther Wilcox, he called *Saint Genet* "nearly 600 pages of madness" and wondered if Sartre had not gone mad. "The book is a crazy quilt of repetition. His last play showed signs of madness. I think everyone who can stand it should read it, but of course that limits the audience to about 3 people."[53]

James went on to Rome, joining Steward there. Since the end of World War II, throngs of Americans had flocked to Rome, with writers and artists leading the way. Since 1948, Tennessee Williams was a regular visitor, and gay creatives like Samuel Barber, Gore Vidal, Paul Cadmus, and James Merrill were "resident or semi-resident at this time," creating an "artistic community of young, dynamic English-speaking homosexually active expatriates," Justin Spring writes. Sam and James met for breakfast one morning, and James recalled their "fine walks around old Rome."[54] On August 25, Purdy sent a postcard to the Wilcoxes saying he was in a pension on Via Palermo in Monti, central Rome, and liked the city "best of any place yet." Monti is full of palazzos, churches, and archeological sites including the Colosseum. He headed to Florence next. He had visited Spain, "but didn't enjoy it so much this time." He found "the Italians are sweeter than the Spanish," and he was enjoying speaking Italian.[55] He returned to Appleton for the fall 1952 semester.

Purdy later said he started writing full-time in 1953, but this couldn't have been the case because he was still teaching.[56] Nevertheless, he wrote stories and continued writing a novella. He ironically lived on Eldorado Street, as Appleton was hardly his city of gold. He plotted Chicago visits and in January wrote Abercrombie cryptically: "I have heard from the horse's mouth where you go / Fridays & but I am not jealous; I hope you stock your / pleasure and ask no more than that. / When can I come to call on you & will you be cold / as usual, / love / james / i still know you" [*sic*]. He tantalizingly added: "i am writing a new book in which you kill a man by hiding him," seemingly referring to Claire and Fenton Riddleway in *63: Dream Palace.*[57]

On June 12, 1953, James and Jorma went to Europe, setting sail on the *Nieuw Amsterdam* from New York to Southampton, England. Purdy spent time in Paris alone, possibly doing translation work, and visited Italy and Spain.[58] He received a "strange compliment in Spain" when a young man approached him, started chatting in Spanish and asked, "What part of Spain are you from?" Surprised, Purdy said he was not Spanish. "I know you're not a Spaniard, but your Spanish is very good." Sjoblom went further north, to his ancestral Finland, to study chemical labs. Afterward, Jorma met up with James in London. They met up with John Bucklew, who was going to study phenomenological psychology at Collège de France, Paris, on a Ford Fellowship for the 1953–1954 year.[59]

Back in Lawrence in September, Purdy continued to serve the community in sometimes amusing ways. Earlier in the year, Purdy and Ellen Stone, Dean of Women, had judged a costume contest. Attended by 150 students, faculty, and townies, the Beaux Arts Ball was held at the Worcester Art Center on campus. Five rooms were filled with genre spoofs and dancing. One winning couple dressed as Martian spaceships, reflecting the current UFO craze. Another dressed as William Tell and his apple.[60] In October, he and three others judged a homecoming decoration contest. In five fraternity houses and ten dorms, he assessed variations on a theme of "prophesying doom" to Knox College, their "grid opponent." "Freshman girls" participated in a "pajama parade" and skit competition. That year, one group performed a minstrel show number in blackface, covered by the local newspaper, while another billed themselves as Saki Sippers, offering a Japanese-styled performance. No letters are available to gauge Purdy's response to such appropriations by the school's almost entirely white student body.[61]

Purdy never taught any black students at Lawrence because none were enrolled during his tenure. Back in 1949, while visiting, Dr. George Kelsey of the National Council of Churches called out the college for having no Negro students, finding this "rather peculiar" since Lawrence had 800 or 900 students and a Christian background. Reportedly, the last time an African American was enrolled was in the 1920s. Kelsey's challenge led to clubs and editorials asking for Negroes to be recruited or, as one student put it, "secured." A dean defended the college, claiming only six had made inquiries over twenty years, and none had formally applied. Relatively high application fees were one reason attributed, an institutional barrier to working class students. Despite the controversy, no black students enrolled until over a decade later.[62]

In 1954, Douglas M. Knight became Lawrence's president. At age thirty-two, he was then the youngest college president in the country, and was hired from the faculty at Yale, where he earned three degrees in English.[63] Although President Knight made contributions, he was not sympathetic to faculty but rather condescending toward what he deemed their "distempers of the mind." Of all the constituents he "had to serve and (if possible) to lead, the faculty were the most complex, the most unrelenting and at the same time the most changeable in their views." Faculty dissent was "a favorite parlor game—but I never could play it as casually as it often deserved." He claimed to be confronted with "almost consistent negativism of a minority who were as difficult" with colleagues as they were with him, referring to "baiting tactics of equally young faculty" agitated by low salaries. Lawrence was "poor; but its reputation went beyond its modest resources." To Knight's credit, he doubled faculty salaries, but it is unknown if this was done while Purdy was on staff.[64]

Knight was a literature specialist, but unlike Pusey, he did not support Purdy or his writing. Purdy satirized Knight's surveillance of faculty in a Firbankian news bulletin. "Appleton, Wisconsin, Oct. 30. The annual loyalty awards for safety, security, and free-espionage were awarded today by President Knight" to "Deaconess Anne Perfect Jones, Archbishop E. Grim Waring, and Liaison Officer M. Schumann. Each received a solid gold replica of the Lawrence listening-ear."[65] Sjoblom reflected, "James and I were not terribly pleased with Lawrence College campus affairs or interested in faculty affairs, either." In fact, they were "both fed up." Travel provided escape. "The beautiful thing about teaching at a four-year liberal arts college is you have the whole summer to yourself."[66]

In the summer of 1954, Purdy returned to Paris, where he had friends such as Bucklew, who was wrapping up his Ford Fellowship. He planned to spend those months not traveling but writing.[67] During the 1954–1955 school year, Purdy still taught at Lawrence, but he was increasingly throwing himself into writing. On April 6, 1955, Purdy wrote the Wilcoxes on Jorma's birthday; he gave "Finn Sjoblom" a Roman coin from the era of Hadrian. "I have been through a hell morning writing on my little novel. Sometimes I wonder why I do it, but then I know I will go on forever doing it. Forever that is until it is never." After finally finishing 63: Dream Palace, he knew it had value, but he had great trouble getting it published.[68]

In summer 1955, Purdy's third publication appeared in the fifth issue of the *Black Mountain Review*, his first in over nine years. "Sound of Talking" is a grim story of aging, disability, and failed communication in a married couple. "It was a godsend, because I couldn't get anything published," he told novelist Bradford Morrow. Linked with experimental Black Mountain College in North Carolina, the *Black Mountain Review* was edited by poet Robert Creeley, who, in an essay, discussed different kinds of contributors. Some "simply appear with no previous or necessarily continuing sense of relationship, like James Purdy." To be among the first in the country to publish Purdy was "surely a pleasure." Creeley responded to Purdy's manuscripts and books with thoughtful and appreciative responses and suggestions.[69]

That summer, Purdy visited Vera in Findlay and saw his brothers and other family. Unforgettable were Vera's delicacies and elaborate table settings entailing fingerbowls and multiple forks. His nephew David remembered James was "very soft-spoken, almost whisper-like when he talked." A teasing remark James made to Dave, who was then around eight, made an enduring impression. Dave found the decor at his grandmother's house to be unusual, intriguing—so different from how Vera's own parents had adorned their home. There were fascinating statues and in frames lining the staircase were images of "naked women or something"; Dorothy suggested "cupids, with arrows." David agreed, "Cupids or something, but I'd never seen anything like that. There was a bunch of them in one picture, maybe seven or eight" nude or scantily clad women. David was playfully walking up and down the steps, accompanied by his uncle, and he looked over, struck by these risqué pictures. "I'm fascinated. We didn't have anything like that at our house." David and Uncle Jim "stopped and looked at those." Later, at the dinner table, he was surprised when his uncle said, "David was taking an interest in the *picture* on the steps."

"I was *not!*"

"But I was! So I lied; I was totally mortified, so I lied like a fool." Dave never forgot how his Uncle Jim had prompted him to lie and he "always felt bad" about it later.[70]

James and Richard were linguistically playful and inventive, and even Bob sometimes got in on the act, Dave recalled. They would "make up their own little language," often alluding to "Bokie Truefeather." Whether this was someone real or entirely fictitious, Dave never knew. Even when his brothers were not around, the coach might randomly reply to his wife asking about his day, "I ran into Bokie Truefeathie" (*sic*).[71]

For the 1955–1956 school year, Purdy took a leave of absence from Lawrence College. As the fall semester began, it was reported that James Purdy of the Spanish department would study abroad that winter.[72] Instead, he went to Chicago and found a cheap apartment. Jorma Sjoblom completed his PhD by dint of laboratory work done at Lawrence, and he and James celebrated at Chicago's Palmer House hotel, where Jorma met some of James's old friends.[73]

In the fall of 1955, Osborn Andreas and his ex-wife Miriam focused on supporting Purdy and his writing.[74] He was trying to complete *63: Dream Palace* "in Chicago, living in terrible rooms." He typed the manuscript on a tiny toylike typewriter, writing at all hours. "My friend, Mrs. Marian Andreas, lived in a penthouse. She said I could live in the top room, and that's where I finally finished it."[75] In May 1954, Osborn Andreas was married to artist and sculptor Margot Beman, and they had two sons.[76] Nevertheless, Osborn remained involved with Miriam, who, like Madame Girard in *Malcolm*, kept her ex-husband's last name. In the fall of 1955, Richard Purdy was in town and Abercrombie was commissioned to paint his portrait, probably by Miriam. August Becker gossips that Guy Cardin, a brilliant, handsome youth, was a lover to both Miriam and Gertrude. A "clever dandy," Cardin was "extremely well read, intellectual" but lacked "visible means of support." When Becker first knew Cardin, he was "kept by Dana Stone, a well-off gentleman of the Near North Side who as a teen used to procure sexual companions for his mother's society bridge partners," and some said Dana had "never quite given up his sex trafficking," despite other interests. Cardin later lived with Miriam in her North Shore penthouse "under the auspices of Osborn Andreas," who remained "totally responsible for her." Cardin was later found dead in his underwear on a Chicago rooftop; Becker wondered whether the rooftop had been Miriam's. "That would explain it to some extent."[77] This raises questions about the nature of relationships and patronage among James, Gertrude, Osborn, and Miriam.

In May, Purdy's artwork was shown in Lawrence College's Worcester Art Center. In a trancelike state, he executed a series of continuous-line drawings of faces that might be compared to those of Cocteau or Picasso. In August, it was reported that Purdy had spent his leave in Chicago, not just writing fiction, but also creating art projects.[78]

Feeling burnt out by rejection over the years, James took matters in his own hands, with help from friends. Using one of his line drawings for the cover, Purdy privately published 600 copies of *Don't Call Me by My Right Name and Other Stories*, financed by Osborn Andreas. Later that year, Jorma Sjoblom borrowed money to finance publication of 500 copies of *63: Dream Palace*. "I was so overwhelmed by that story that I decided I'll get the story printed," Sjoblom said.[79] Both books were published through William-Frederick, a New York subsidy press. With personalized cover letters, Purdy mailed inscribed copies to writers, critics, and others with whom he felt an affinity. Had these two books not been published by friends, Purdy said, "I would have been unheard of forever. I couldn't have gone on because of all the rejections. I probably would have written, but it would have all been left in bureau drawers."[80]

Early in 1956, Purdy's sharp tongue caused a permanent break in his long-time friendship with Wendell and Esther Wilcox, when, at a lively dinner party at Gertrude's, he insulted them.[81] Wendell, responding to a remark by Purdy, said he sounded like a communist.[82] This was a dirty word in the 1950s, and James, no fan of communism, took offense. He lashed out with something like, "At least I'm not married and go suck cock in the park every night."[83] James tried to apologize to Esther on multiple occasions, but she would not accept it. Wendell would have preferred to continue knowing James.[84] In 1969, Purdy had a copy of a Spoken Arts LP recording of him reading *63: Dream Palace* mailed to the Wilcoxes, who then were living in Chapel Hill. James and Wendell had been corresponding intermittently, but this gift ended it.

When Es opened the package and found the record it seemed to revive most of what she went through the evening of the scene at Gertrude's. I thought that the depth of this reaction had diminished but I guess it has not. So I thought it best to send the record back to the shop. I think it best that we stop writing each other since I realize now that she is merely repressing extremely painful emotions when she is reminded of you. You I am sure will understand the power of such emotions for if you had not been under the influence of such a power, the evening at Gertrude's would never have occurred. Emotions are there or they are not. They go or they don't and there is little one can do about them consciously. Es doesn't want me to break off, nor did she . . . want me to send back the record. I don't want to either. You realize that. Otherwise I would not have responded at all. I am very sad about it, but I am sure it is the best thing.[85]

James reported to Abercrombie: "She never forgave me . . . for what I said that night *chez toi*. It's always bad to lose your temper, but I think they had it coming. I've never met such snobs as they are. Only they don't have anything to be snobs with. Oh well, they had to do what they did."[86]

Purdy, hungry for recognition, seemingly resented Wendell's literary success thus far. He certainly resented what he saw as his hypocrisy. Facing a lack of momentum, he dashed off a series of increasingly frustrated letters to Toni Strassman. He raked her over the coals for failing to get his stories placed, despite receiving glowing endorsements from notable writers and critics to whom he had sent his two private books.[87] He would not have to wait long for a path to success to open, however. His gamble of mailing his books to carefully curated recipients was about to pay off.

7

James Purdy Begins

Purdy resigned his position at Lawrence College in August 1956. His announcement was seemingly sudden, since, as late as August 3, the *Post-Crescent* reported he would return in September. Jorma said that "he was going to concentrate on his writing, which was very excellent." Opportunity first knocked in 1955. Dr. Sjoblom, after scanning *Wall Street Journal* want ads, landed a position with Air Products in Pennsylvania researching cryogenics. In February, Jorma accepted the offer and resigned "very suddenly" from Lawrence. "I extended an invitation to James to come stay with me in Allentown, Pennsylvania." Air Products manufactured oxygen and other gases in tonnage quantities for industry, including steel companies around the Lehigh Valley. The plant was located in the village of Emmaus, adjacent to Allentown, so Jorma daily took "the road to Emmaus," central to the New Testament story in which a resurrected Jesus Christ was not recognized by his disciples until later. Moreover, Jorma had borrowed money from the Bank of Emmaus to finance the publishing of *63: Dream Palace*. James, who loosely identified as Christian though was not a churchgoer, was struck by this biblical name. Indeed, failure to recognize others is a central Purdian theme.[1]

Family and hometown newspaper readers, however, were told that throat trouble forced him to quit.[2] Christine Purdy thought Uncle Jim stopped teaching because of throat polyps. In 1957, his father William asked, "How is your throat? I hope it is causing no trouble." In 1958, the Bowling Green *Sentinel-Tribune* stated Purdy "took up writing professionally when physical misfortune overtook him in losing his voice. A language teacher, he found prolonged use of his voice in the classroom became impossible, although he is now able to use it in ordinary conversation." In 1962, Will wrote: "We think you should feel quite encouraged as few people have had to change their occupations like you have due to the loss of your voice."[3] For many years, of course, James had longed to quit teaching to write. This may have been a cover story to justify abandoning his academic career, as Jorma never mentioned throat trouble as a factor in Purdy's resignation from Lawrence. In the fall of 1956, Purdy moved in with Jorma.[4]

Before formally resigning, in the summer of 1956, James traveled to Paris, his third trip there within four years, where he wrote and practiced French. On the way, he stopped in Chicago to visit friends including Gertrude Abercrombie and Sam Steward.[5] He and John Bucklew, who supported his decision, even patronized Steward's tattoo shop on South State Street, where Purdy got a small anchor, a classic design seen on navy men.[6] Six months later, Steward praised the finesse, delicacy, polish, and penetrating sentences of 63: Dream Palace, which he read with the "same awe that struck" him on reading the stories, and congratulated James on his good fortune, feeling like Emerson saluting Whitman "at the beginning of a great career." He also sent a copy to the "Kinsey group" of sexologists with whom he had collaborated. A few months later, Sam offered "Jaime" a critique, suggesting that if he wanted to reach a wide audience, he ought to add characterization and sensory prose. "Don't curl your pretty patrician lip and think me canaille."[7] Steward, who tattooed as Phil Sparrow, would later appear in Malcolm as the tattooist Professor Robinolte. From Chicago, Purdy then stopped in New York to see Richard, and while there, mailed his story collection to Edith Sitwell in Italy.[8]

After his return from Paris, at first, James lived with Jorma at 2640 South 4th Street, a remote spot on the far southern edge of Allentown abutting thick woodlands. But even in this relative isolation, they could not be open about their relationship.[9] They became "acquainted with local ethnicities," most immediately, the Pennsylvania Dutch. They did some cooking, but "often had to go to restaurants."[10] As writer Edmund White explains, in that era, it was "extremely rare to find a gay couple who lived openly as lovers, who'd acknowledged their homosexuality to their parents and friends and colleagues, who had a sense that they constituted a real romantic pair capable of being faithful to one another or if not sexually exclusive, at least committed in some sense for the long haul."[11]

Despite any difficulties he felt being part of a gay couple in a new town in the 1950s, Purdy felt authentic. For years, he had yearned to focus on writing. Twenty years later, he reflected: "writing for me is real life, or a more real life. I used to be a teacher, trafficking in other men's books, but I decided that I simply had to start living my own life, that I had to start writing. Teaching and then trying to write during your spare time were impossible. Although I must confess that I miss the security of a dependable income and sometimes regret my impetuosity in resigning a life-sinecure; still, if I hadn't, I would never have found the time to write my books."[12] He usually found academia "stultifying and oppressive." Too often, English professors looked for cues from "essentially disreputable literary powers" in New York when they should look "to themselves, because the really good critical minds are not in New York," nor are they "in the hire of the New York newspapers—at all."[13] In the 1990s, he avowed he would "rather wash dishes or scrub floors than teach."[14]

That autumn of 1956, Purdy reaped a harvest of correspondence from recipients of *Don't Call Me by My Right Name and Other Stories* and *63: Dream Palace*. This bounty vindicated his talent and risky decision to leave his teaching position.

Modernist poet William Carlos Williams wrote in September. Since he had suffered a stroke five years earlier, reading was difficult, so he depended on his wife, Florence Williams. She read aloud the first three stories, which they both enjoyed, and they planned to finish. Williams was frank in praise and criticism: "You have a rather lumpy style but at least there's no redundancy and the perception and feeling makes the stories notable to a receptive mind. They're downright good if at times somewhat crude—you certainly have a telling insight into the mind of the Negro," which he found "fascinating and moving." Williams wrote a week later, anticipating Purdy's novella. W. C. Williams permitted Purdy to quote from letters as blurbs.[15] In 1960, he pledged himself an "attentive reader" of anything Purdy might publish following "that memorable book of short stories" and he wrote a blurb to help promote *The Nephew*.[16]

Chicago writer Nelson Algren, a friend of Gertrude Abercombie who caused controversy with tough urban novels like *Walk on the Wild Side* and *The Man with the Golden Arm*, thanked him for the collection. "Your people come sharply alive. Hope the next book will be hardcover, and as honest as this one."[17] Thornton Wilder also wrote from Chicago with "many thanks" for the stories; he read them with "much admiration," finding them "filled with remarkable insights," especially "Eventide" and "Sound of Talking." "The short story is a form which I have never found satisfactory—but you are very accomplished in it." He hoped Purdy would soon apply his "many gifts to longer works."[18] Though Wilder knew Abercrombie, Wilcox, and Steward, he seems not to have met Purdy. Such enthusiasm from a figure both nationally acclaimed and central to members of his circle was satisfying.

The most magnificent reply was from Dame Edith Sitwell. In late October, Purdy's fate was forever changed. Although Purdy mailed the book to Sitwell, her discovery of it was a "minor mystery that was never solved," her secretary and biographer Elizabeth Salter states. Edith fell asleep one afternoon at

Castello di Montegufoni with "windows shuttered and doors closed against draughts and intruders as was her custom," but when she awoke, a book was lying on her bed that "had not been there when she went to sleep." Her memory may have failed her, though, since she was drinking a lot of wine in those days and had recently bloodied her face after a bad fall.[19] Reading "Eventide" first, Sitwell believed she had "stumbled on a great Negro writer," Salter writes.[20] On October 20, 1956, Sitwell wrote from Montegufoni: "I do not know whether it was you, or whether it was your publishers, who sent me your *Don't Call Me by My Right Name*. But I owe a debt of gratitude to you and to them." Rating several stories as "nothing short of masterpieces," she had taken the liberty of advising her London publisher, Victor Gollancz, to acquire it.[21] At her loneliest, Edith found that Purdy's stories, with their "great compassion, insight, and mastery of language," provided much consolation, biographer Geoffrey Elborn writes. She could "identify with the mood," and was "overjoyed to have discovered a new writer in whom she sincerely believed."[22]

Stunned, James then sent *63: Dream Palace*. Sitwell read it twice within two days of its arrival. According to Purdy, after reading its devastating ending capped with an obscenity, Sitwell swooned, and declared: "My former life has come to an end!"[23] On November 26, Sitwell marveled: "What a *wonderful* book! It is a masterpiece from every point of view." She was "quite overcome. What anguish, what heart-breaking truth!" He was "truly a writer of genius." She had already written to Gollancz about the short stories and would alert him to the novella, which she found equally great. Believing *63: Dream Palace* and the stories ought to be bound together in one volume, she recommended her agents including David Higham and said she would write to them. She thought poet "Stephen Spender's *Encounter* might be a good place" for his stories in England.[24] As is now known, *Encounter* was secretly funded by the CIA. As soon as Spender returned to England, Edith wrote him about the stories.[25] She spread the word to friends. To Portuguese poet and BBC Radio presenter Alberto de Lacerda, she acclaimed Purdy as a "much greater writer than Faulkner." She could not think of "any living prose writer of short stories and short novels who can come anywhere near him. He is really wonderful."[26] With this all set in motion, within months, Gollancz accepted the works for publication.

Sitwell's lyrical responses to his books nearly had an "unhinging effect" on Purdy. Reading her letters over and again, he could scarcely believe Sitwell had written them, since the works she extolled were the "very same works, unchanged in any particular" that American publishers had rejected with "bitter denunciation, contempt, and derision." Andreas and Sjoblom were deeply moved by Sitwell's praise, but not as surprised since they believed in him "more consciously" than he believed in himself. Years of "rejection and persecution" by the US publishing industry had forced him to live in "a kind of half-world," he reflected. "In my inmost soul I thought I was a writer of vision and talent, but in the daytime real world of publishers and editors, I felt I did not exist, was nothing."[27] On Purdy's forty-third birthday, Sitwell wrote: "I am certain as I can be of anything that you will, in the course of time, be given the Nobel Prize." He replied, "The person who should win the Nobel Prize, my dear Edith, is *you*! So many poets not fit to tie your shoelaces have won it."[28] Sitwell's correspondence showed "extraordinary kindness and devotion to those she believed in," and "warrior-like courage in defending them," Purdy wrote Elborn.[29] A fighter, Purdy admired those who fought for their convictions.

Many literati found Purdy's use of black vernacular in "Eventide" authentic, and like Sitwell, a number of them initially assumed him to be black, including novelist and photographer Carl Van Vechten, poet Langston Hughes, and British novelist Angus Wilson. A longtime supporter and friend of black creatives, Van Vechten's misapprehension is corroborated by his letter of November 1956: "I wish you would read *Giovanni's Room* by another Negro friend of mine, James Baldwin." Set in Paris, Baldwin's novel was groundbreaking in its frank depiction of gay and bisexual life. Before meeting Purdy, "Carlo" solicited more information and a photo, and in December, he wrote: "I don't mind TOO MUCH your NOT being a Negro. The reasons your Washington [DC] friends think you ARE is doubtless because you make frequent references to matters like 'passing' but doubtless you do it to tease or terrify." In early 1957, Van Vechten stated, "Whether you are white or colored doesn't make too much difference to me, but I am a little prejudiced in favor of COLOR!"[30] When Purdy first arrived at his Park Avenue West apartment on December 18, Van Vechten seemed to hold out hope that James had a smidgen of African "blood" because Carlo "seemed surprised when he saw James," Jorma said. Tall, white-haired Van Vechten looked him up and down and quipped, "I don't think you have a drop."[31] During the evening, Van Vechten photographed the couple. Purdy was "one of the last writers Van Vechten championed seriously and continually," and he even arranged for Purdy's early papers to be accepted into Yale's Beinecke Rare Book and Manuscript Library.[32]

A week before Sitwell responded to the novella, Van Vechten wrote: "63: Dream Palace is NOW MY Dream Palace. The pranks of Fenton Riddleway, the exasperating behavior of the greatwoman, the huddled belligerency of Claire, the unholy purposes of Parkhurst, all fascinate and bewilder me. Somehow I felt as tho I were watching sexuality on TV or watching orchestral instruments enjoying orgasm with one another. I pray that your books will never end and then they do, quite unexpectedly with the word 'motherfucker.' I would like to attend a wedding with you, on some bleak day, each carrying tiny cages of white rats in lieu of a prayer book. This would be HEAVEN. Hell would be attending a football game in evening clothes. I want to send some of your wet-dream palaces around and I find your publisher ridiculously slow in shipping. We must think of a better plan." Carlo made it clear he intended to help Purdy find a good publisher. Seemingly referring to James, Van Vechten added a limerick exemplfying camp aesthetics:

> Said a morbid and dissolute youth
> I think Beauty is greater than Truth,
> But by Beauty I mean
> The obscure, the obscene,
> The diseased, the decayed, the uncouth.[33]

Such a response from this legend was thrilling. James in turn began to shower Carlo with new poems, satires, and stories, signed and dedicated to him.

Purdy later declared that Edith Sitwell rescued him from certain obscurity, which is an attractive myth. But even if Sitwell had never encountered the work, Van Vechten would have helped him to get published in New York—just as he had helped Ronald Firbank, Langston Hughes, Nella Larsen, and many others. Though a bit long in the tooth, Carlo yet held influence on New York publishing. Van Vechten scholar Bruce Kellner even asserts that he was "largely responsible for publicizing James Purdy's work" by sending "several copies" of the two private books to his friends.[34] After Purdy was published in England, he told Van Vechten he did not think he would be published in America. Where did you get that idea, Carlo wondered. "You already have been, and you are sure to be in the future."[35] Van Vechten continued to photograph all notable Negroes who were willing, along with a few whites, such as Purdy and handsome Sjoblom. According to iconic poet Langston Hughes, who witnessed the behind-the-scenes help Van Vechten gave Purdy in speaking with magazine editors and publishers, Carlo was the

Figure 7.1 James Otis Purdy standing over Jorma Jules
Sjoblom by Carl Van Vechten, December 18, 1956.
Carl Van Vechten Papers. Yale Collection of American
Literature, Beinecke Rare Book and Manuscript Library.
Courtesy of Edward M. Burns, the Carl Van Vechten Trust.

main mover who launched Purdy's career—not Sitwell. "James Purdy is a
recent example of Van Vechten discovery and interest from manuscript to
final printed page," Hughes later wrote in tribute to his patron and friend.[36]
Kellner affirms that Sitwell became "James Purdy's leading defender, after
CVV."[37]

Langston Hughes also wrote in November to thank Purdy for an inscribed
collection. Hughes too believed Purdy was black then, not just because of
"Eventide," but also due to the story title, "Color of Darkness."[38] Hughes gave
Purdy's stories thoughtful appreciation: "Your episodes are concise and your
people so vividly presented that the reader feels he is looking at them then
and there—but a sort of outside view like a passerby—who keeps on down
the street wondering about the why—but remembering them all the while.

Figure 7.2 James Purdy by Carl Van Vechten, March 15, 1957. Carl Van Vechten Papers, Yale Collection of American Literature, Beinecke Rare Book and Manuscript Library. Courtesy of Edward M. Burns, The Carl Van Vechten Trust.

Which makes a reader want to know more about most of the folks, maybe in the extended form of the novel. What DID happen to the Kleins? And Teeboy with that white girl's arm around her neck? And Ethel after that? And the guy with the beard? (As if enough hadn't happened to them already, huh?). But they could (or the method could) still be spun out like a spider web in various directions interestingly."[39] Such a response from Hughes, especially to "Eventide," let Purdy know he was on the right track. In January 1957, the poet provided an endorsement: "James Purdy's characters and situations linger in the memory long after one has finished reading his stories. He is an effective writer of unaffected prose."[40]

In September, Brooks Atkinson, the noted drama critic for the *New York Times*, wrote to say he enjoyed the stories Purdy had sent, which seemed to him "original in their approach to life, sympathetic in their characterization and honestly written." Great actors also sent their praises. Sir Laurence Olivier wrote from St. James's Theatre in December, thanking Purdy for his kindness. "Dame Sybil Thorndike has forwarded me your book, which I know I shall enjoy reading immensely." Gollancz had suggested mailing a copy to Thorndike. Purdy subsequently learned Sitwell was snobby about actors. "Frankly, what *does* it matter what Thorndyke [*sic*] or Laurence Olivier think of your book? The opinion of neither bears the *very slightest* weight in literary circles or among ordinary readers. Their opinion might have a little weight for middlebrow books for suburban readers, but not for books of importance. They are both very nice people and good actors, but they have nothing to do with the world of letters. . . . If you are going to ask Dame Sybil, Sir Laurence Olivier, and, perhaps, the President of the Royal Academy to give their opinion, it invalidates the statements of people whose opinion does count." Asking "people who are not eminent writers" to give opinion "lowers your dignity."[41]

Another actress who became a fan was Lillian Gish, the Ohio native who had shared a stage with Richard Purdy. She sent "a thousand thanks" for the collection, sent on Van Vechten's recommendation. "I have enjoyed immensely the vivid way you paint with words." "Don't Call Me by My Right Name" paints a "frightening, ugly, but unfortunately true picture." Ahead of her time, Lois is a career woman who resists a patriarchal society that belittles her. She has married at an older age than average in the 1950s, after she was well-established. Like Abercrombie, she had "always been known socially and professionally" under her "own name." She detests her new name, Klein, and increasingly was using her maiden name. *Klein* means small in German, suggesting diminishment. During a party, Lois finally says since she does not like the name, she wants Frank, her husband, to change his name—and thus her name—underscoring patriarchal power. Horrifyingly, Frank hits Lois at the party and out on the sidewalk. According to Uecker, the couple was based on Frank Sandiford and Gertrude, who may have been pressured to change her name, but Lois was also influenced by Miriam Andreas.[42] In 1957, *New Directions in Prose and Poetry* published what became one of Purdy's best-known stories.

October commenced a long friendship between two gay geniuses from the heartland. Purdy thanked Virgil Thomson—legendary composer, critic, and Stein collaborator—for his "kind and generous words" about the stories. Thomson found them "delightful (for there *can* be delight in grimness [and in good workmanship])."[43] Shortly before Christmas, Thomson said his words could used for a blurb. He enjoyed both books and hoped there would be "lots more."[44]

Late in October, Purdy told Strassman he was "writing a novel called *Malcolm*."[45] He later said he "wrote *Malcolm* for a friend," Jorma Sjoblom, who gave him love and a place to live. James drafted chapters during the day while Jorma was at work. In 2009, Jorma vividly recalled his delight on reading each new section or chapter after returning home, how he rolled on the floor with laughter, and looked forward to each new episode after a hard day's work at Air Products. The story was "awful too, I mean it was awful because it was true." Jorma's depth of appreciation inspired James to outdo himself the next day.[46] James was grateful for how Jorma understood what he was doing in *Malcolm*, which is unconventional and episodic. Malcolm is a blank-faced cypher, a teenager adrift, looking for his missing father, who meets fascinating, eccentric, and often treacherous adults—slightly reminiscent of Truman Capote's *Other Voices, Other Rooms* (1948).

James drew from a range of Chicago experiences, creating versions of Wendell Wilcox, Gertrude Abercrombie, and others. After it was published, August Becker wrote: "it is not Gertrude and Frank and Miriam and Osborn [Andreas], etc that have got under my skin, but Eloisa and Jerome and the Girards. It's not every one that can tell you that, I suppose."[47] Jorma had observed most of them firsthand by Purdy's side. In *Malcolm*, the bohemian artist Eloisa Brace is clearly based on Abercrombie, down to her habit of saying "OK" a lot, and Jerome Brace, her ex-con husband, is based on the omnisexual Frank Sandiford, who in 1953 published a prison memoir, *Next Time Is for Life*, in pulp paperback under the pen name Paul Warren. In his memoir, soon after the narrator is released from jail, he feels the urge to start burglarizing again, as though deep down, he wants to return to jail. Likewise, pederastic Jerome published a prison memoir, *They Could Have Me Back*. "Is that you naked on the cover?" Malcolm asks.[48] Jorma Sjoblom made sporadic comments on *Malcolm*, but mainly, his desire to keep reading in itself was catalytic. This notion of writing for a small but tuned-in audience came to shape Purdy's persistent method of creation.

For *Malcolm*, along with Chicago friends, James also drew inspiration from particular jazz musicians he met while living at or visiting Gertrude's house. "Quiet, gracious, and dignified" John Lewis, of Dizzy Gillespie's band and then the Modern Jazz Quartet, was the model for George Leeds, "the piano player with the quartet" in *Malcolm*. After sharing a bed with

Malcolm after one of Eloise's parties, on the next morning, the pianist poetically avers in reply to his questions: "You see, Malcolm, I just stick to the piano. And the rest of the world and the people, too, even nice people like you, well, I just let them go, if you don't mind me saying so."[49] The Clifford Brown & Max Roach Quintet, who gigged at the Bee Hive Lounge, recorded the tune "Gertrude's Bounce," written by their pianist Richie Powell, who was inspired by her walk. In *Malcolm*, Purdy pays homage to trumpeter Clifford Brown, whom friends called "Brownie," with a character who is also nicknamed Brownie: Gus, who had been married to Melba, the nightclub singer. Although he still loves Melba, he zips around the city on his motorcycle trawling for "contemporaries" for her companionship, Malcolm being, fatally, one of them. Both Brownies died young. Clifford Brown and Richie Powell died in a car accident in June 1956, and Gus expires mysteriously at the Turkish Bath and bordello where he had taken Malcolm to further "mature him up" after he was tattooed at Robinolte's Tattoo Palace.[50]

While he composed *Malcolm*, more missives from luminaries filled Purdy's mailbox, many of them from women, showing his intuitions had been right. In November, no less than feminist-existentialist Simone de Beauvoir sent thanks for the stories from Paris. "I like them very much and it is nice of you to have sent the book."[51] Poet Elizabeth Bishop wrote from Rio de Janeiro: all the stories were "very good" and "touching" but "Eventide" was the best, as it seemed "the realest." "Please believe I'll be on the lookout for more of your work."[52] "Eventide" was singled out for praise by several recipients including Alice B. Toklas, who thanked him for the collection. Later, though, Toklas became miffed when James seemed overanxious to secure an endorsement and later told Sam, "James Purdy bores me."[53] Nevertheless, Toklas later changed her mind and "came to admire him a great deal," Steward writes, and *The Nephew* was her favorite, a fact that Steward's biographer Justin Spring overlooks, falsely casting both Steward and Toklas as basically indifferent to his work.[54] In 1974, Purdy explained to Steward that Van Vechten had asked him to send books directly to Toklas, which he should not have done. Then Victor Gollancz asked him to write her to solicit a blurb, "which was even worse protocol." "I would know better today. Mr. Gollancz was a terrible man."[55]

Not every recipient liked everything, but nevertheless still found much to admire. Poet Marianne Moore wrote from Brooklyn to say she liked "not all of the content" of the stories but she liked the "manner of them; that is the way to write. And that title!" She came to regard Purdy as a "master of the American vernacular."[56] In the 1950s, Chester Page, an aspiring concert pianist and book collector from Georgia, became a Brooklyn Heights resident and befriended Moore. During his first visit to the poet, she mentioned James Purdy, and in January 1958, when Page and his mother visited, she again spoke of Purdy and the novella he had sent. Moore had liked the stories, but did not care for 63: Dream Palace. "I imagine Miss Moore almost fainted away" at the obscenity, Page remarked, laughing.[57] She meant to return the novella, but accidentally mailed the similar-looking story collection instead. Purdy scolded her with a "terrible" letter, "shocked at her lack of appreciation. He asked if she were trying to ruin his career," Page writes. After Moore realized she had mailed the wrong book, she wrote again, asking James to return it because "she had liked that one." Purdy was grateful for that response.[58]

James had lived in Allentown only a few months, but toward the end of November 1956, he and Jorma moved from the edge of the woods to the heart of the city: 439 Walnut Street, apartment 6. Thoroughly urban, they were close to St. John's Lutheran Church, with its magnificent stained glass windows, and the old post office at 5th and Hamilton Streets. "I live here in the Negro slums and enjoy it," Purdy told John Cowper Powys. To Van Vechten, "the emperor of central park west," he said, "I live in the Negro and Puertorican district." He sent Carlo a poem called "Vendrá" in early 1957: "at night under the caving roof / (heard, a rat or perhaps a squirrel) / in the window a vigil light / on the wall an old bandera: a flag / These are all reminds them of Puerto Rico, / they sit there with guitar and sing . or with dominos. Sometimes they cry." Then the observed spies the observer: "Quién es? who is? Who is out there / who is watching me in my *not* native land? [. . .] who is watching me / who is watching / in the night in the dawn in the afternoon without joy or hope or ease, / who is watching / in a land where no one watches. who is it holds a finger still on the guitar / and gives a silence without breath?"[59] As in Chicago, James was inspired by his multicultural surroundings.

Allentown, prospering from a silk industry, breweries, and manufacturing Mack trucks and transistors, offered trolleys and other big-city amenities. Nevertheless, it lacked culture, Sjoblom recalled. By 1956, Allentown was a major retail and entertainment hub and department stores including Hess Brothers, where James shopped, spurred a thriving area in the Central Business District, a ten-minute walk from their apartment. James would walk to The Brass Rail for a tasty Philly cheesesteak. Several cinemas and theaters lined Hamilton Street nearby.[60] James completed the first draft of *Malcolm* in a few months on Walnut Street. He did not believe anyone would ever publish it, however. It needed an ending, for one thing.[61]

A gripping exchange unfolded between Purdy and a real Malcolm—critic Malcolm Cowley—leading to an impasse. Novelist and advisor to Viking Press, Cowley was known for *Exile's Return*, a memoir and commentary on 1920s Lost Generation writers. In November 1956, Cowley said he enjoyed the Purdy collection Strassman had submitted. At Viking, the stories were "read with a good deal of interest—I might almost say excitement," but he raised questions about *63: Dream Palace* and recommended adding scenes to it. Looming was the "problem of bad language. You don't know how much trouble the simple word 'fuck' can make for publishers—and not only in Boston!" (Contemporaneously, Cowley, working with Jack Kerouac, eliminated an entire gay scene from *On the Road*.) Cowley thought they needed more high-quality stories to round out a book and asked Purdy if he had "any other *good* material that could be used," which no doubt annoyed.[62]

Purdy refused to change the obscene but thematically appropriate word, which apparently had never appeared before in literary fiction. In December, Purdy apprised Strassman he had told Cowley, and therefore Viking, his answer was no. He would not "fundamentally alter the book for them. The word *motherfucker* must remain, and the other so-called obscene words."[63] Purdy held fast to integrity, foregoing the chance of a major publishing contract. Cowley persuaded Viking not to publish what became *Color of Darkness* over the vigorous protest of Pascal Covici, Purdy said. Romanian Jewish-American editor Covici convinced John Steinbeck to sign with Viking and was his editor for forty years, and worked with Saul Bellow and Arthur Miller.[64] Cowley admitted that Purdy was a genius, but a "primitive genius."[65] Purdy was bitter for many years; in 1963, he replied with poison pen to a Viking employee: "Either you are extremely stupid, or like most Madison Avenue people, both stupid and immoral, or you would never approach me to help a publishing house like Viking Press, asking me to praise" a forthcoming book. He "had to be published in England" because Viking, led by "pious stuffed-shirt old expatriate humbug" Cowley and "timid late ignorant" Thomas Guinzburg, barred him from their "hallowed list." "I will hate Viking Press and Malcolm Cowley as long as I live, and it is impossible for me to believe you could do anything honest, decent or in the interests of American literature. I am giving the advance proofs which you have the brazen gall to send me to a neighbor's dog to relive himself on."[66]

In early December, Sitwell wrote a rapturous review of the privately published *63: Dream Palace*, intending to place it in the London *Times* Books of the Year feature, and sent a copy to Purdy. He replied: "I was quite annihilated by your wonderful review . . . I feel like a man who has come out of Plato's cave and looked at the sun! I do want to be worthy of your tribute, Dame Edith, and I will spend the rest of my life writing in the hope that I may. . . . You are, needless to say, my patron saint."[67] She affirmed, "That you have a very great career before you is inevitable. You are a very great writer indeed." Osbert Sitwell was also reading Purdy with "immense admiration." Yet she felt "distress and righteous anger" after Leonard Russell of the *Sunday Times* rejected her piece on *63: Dream Palace* because he feared the newspaper would be criticized for promoting an obscene book, as they had when Graham Greene recommended Nabokov's *Lolita* as one of three best books of 1955 and controversy and a two-year ban of the book ensued.[68]

Sitwell's praise was thrilling but it intensified feelings of frustration that his career was not progressing even while earning such recognition. In December, Purdy complained to Toni Strassman about her inadequate representation, and he was not always reasonable. On the subject of obscenity in *63: Dream Palace*, he wrote: "You say consider the publishers' point of view. I say fuck the publishers." "I dare say" without Sitwell's interest, "none of you would be concerned with my work today." He was so vexed by his agent, he wanted to break ties. In December, he wrote: "As soon as you feel it possible, I want you to cease being my agent. I would rather go on alone here in the United States, as I did before, than have someone as vague and irritable and as condescending as you deal with my work." In her defense, Strassman wrote, "Jim, *please*, —believe me and my faith in you and my ability to look after your best interests . . . You have no idea how I've worked for you." After this threat, for various reasons, his stories started being accepted in prestigious magazines.[69]

James was also frustrated with New Directions Books, who became interested in publishing him after learning his first book was accepted for publication in Britain by Victor Gollancz. In late December, he wrote Robert MacGregor, known for editing Ezra Pound, apologizing for an "immensely rude" letter he'd sent; he had been "under terrible pressure, working all day," and preparing writing for publication at night. Purdy felt remorse since Bob MacGregor was one of the first to encourage his writing, and his praise gave him the "confidence to choose the title" of *Color of Darkness*.[70]

Purdy informed Strassman that Osborn Andreas was "turning over his being my advisor to Mr. Lincoln Kirstein," patron of the arts and director of the New York City Ballet, who held Purdy's "full confidence."[71] Kirstein sent Purdy's collection to the Parisian agent, Madame Jenny Bradley, a well-known figure in the Franco-American literary business. Jenny and her novelist husband, William A. Bradley, hosted a literary salon at their home on the Île Saint-Louis and placed many manuscripts by famous American writers with Gallimard, which became Purdy's French press. Kirstein said Purdy's work was "quite wonderful," Edith relayed, seconding him.[72]

On December 16, Tennessee Williams, riding high on success, thanked Purdy for the books. He was reading both but admitted he was a "very slow reader." Finding both books "fresh" and "original," Williams wrote: "I would very much like to meet you and discuss your book with you." Williams "fell in love with the fiction of James Purdy after reading *63: Dream Palace*," Peter Theroux noted in *Vanity Fair*. Immediately, Tennessee encouraged James to write drama since the novella showed "a sense of drama which should make you write a very exciting play." Williams planned to finish reading the novella flying from Florida to New York. Williams suggested they might meet while he was staying there.[73] Purdy told Powys: "Williams wrote me a long letter and asked me to meet him in New York, but I was afraid to go to see him and anyhow when he wrote I didn't have the money for such a trip and was hiding in the mountains in Pennsylvania." Van Vechten had told Purdy to send his books to Sandy Campbell and Donald Windham. Campbell, a handsome actor, bibliophile, and partner of Windham, a novelist, told Purdy their friend Tennessee should have a look at *63: Dream Palace*, to which Windham's *Dog Star* (1950) seems a precedent. Donald and Sandy had James over for a drink at their place in New York on December 18; the next month, Williams asked Campbell: "Tell me something about him, what's he like? When I go north again, I would love to meet him." He thought Purdy's novella was "just about the freshest writing since *Dog Star*."[74] James and Jorma were invited to "a wealthy man's townhouse for dinner with Tennessee Williams," Sjoblom recalled. Guests had to climb several flights of steps; this was difficult for Jorma, who had "stiff legs" from his 1940s bout with tuberculosis of the knee. With kindness, Williams put his arm around Jorma and helped him up the steps. Tennessee praised Purdy's dialogue and characterization and kept encouraging him to write drama.[75]

The day after Christmas 1956, William Purdy responded supportively to his son's confession of frustration and money woes. "Do not get discouraged, as I surely know from bitter experience how hard the way seems at times. As long as I have any money you can be sure I will not forget you. I am enclosing a check for your use." Richard was "having a pretty hard time too." Will wanted to visit James "for a day or two right after the new year."[76]

The *Evergreen Review*, a hip journal published by Grove, printed one of Purdy's new stories, "Cutting Edge," in its debut issue, in 1957. It had distinguished neighbors: an essay by Sartre, a story by Beckett, and an interview with early jazz drummer, Baby Dodds. Founded by maverick editor Barney Rosset, the son of a rich banker, *Evergreen Review* would, starting with its next issue, feature San Francisco and Beat Generation poets and writers. Purdy's "Cutting Edge," fitting that mood of youthful rebellion, has long appealed to young readers. It tells of a young artist who has been living in New York City, tensely visiting his parents in his hometown. They, especially his mother, fixate on his new beard, fiercely objecting to it. In a Midwestern novel, *Going All the Way*, Dan Wakefield writes that "having a beard in the summer of 1954 was like running around without any clothes on or passing out copies of the Communist Manifesto or reading a dirty book in a crowded bus. It was asking for trouble." The conflict dredges up old domestic issues that arose in the protagonist's childhood, such as father's dalliances with servants. Partly autobiographical, "Cutting Edge" became one of Purdy's best-known stories, reprinted several times. Being published in alternative magazines like *Black Mountain Review* and *Evergreen Review* gave Purdy credibility with the Beats and their successors, the 1960s counterculture, though Purdy was not a partisan of either. Purdy later characterized their audience as "a kind of un-stuffy reader who likes my writing."

In February 1957, Purdy received his first published review—of *Don't Call Me by My Right Name*. It was rare for a privately published book to be reviewed by a major journal like *Commonweal*, which had a Catholic orientation. Anthony Baily compared it with Whitehill's *Able Baker and Others*, finding the latter to be lackluster. Evidence of the sorry "state of fiction in this country," Whitehill had won five awards and the blessing of Maxwell Geismar, while the much more gifted Purdy had struggled to publish two stories and had submitted a blurbless paperback accompanied only by the author's "witty, tremulous drawings." When Baily first read "Sound of Talking" in *Black Mountain Review*, he realized that it was precisely "this kind of discovery" that "vindicates all the 'avant-garde' nonsense that is printed." The result is "lucid, strong and extraordinarily evocative. His prose has demotic rhythms; the lilt of natural, American speech; and the characters spring forth like crops from fertile soil." Purdy's dialogue "goes deep," his stories are original, and, in sum, Baily could not think of "a recent first book of short stories of equal stature and merit."[77] Especially as the first published commentary, this was deeply perceptive criticism.

Norman Mailer, another recipient of a personalized package, wrote a postcard in February saying he had finished 63: *Dream Palace* and thought it showed "most definite talent." He would contact Theodore Purdy (no relation) at Coward-McCann to tell them so. Four months earlier, Mailer had written to say the story "Don't Call Me by My Right Name" was "very good up to a point," but "its physical violence" left him flat. Violence was interesting as a subject, but it was difficult to say something new since something in its nature "defies contemplation." Nonetheless, if Purdy wrote a novel, Mailer would send the manuscript to his publisher and say it merited attention based on the story he read.[78]

Though Purdy still did not yet have a commercial book, it is clear that he was now fairly well known to the cognoscenti. In its March 1957 issue, *Mademoiselle* recycled Purdy's first publication, "You Reach for Your Hat," as "You Reach for Your Wraps." Their reason, Purdy later said, was "no lady reaches for her hat. The editors had never lived in America."[79] Purdy was paid $400 (about $3,735 in 2020). Under the editorship of Betsy Blackwell and Cyrilly Abels, *Mademoiselle* became known for fine contemporary writing. Managing editor Abels played a major role shifting its reputation solely from a fashion magazine for young women to an important vessel for work by young, talented writers, publishing Truman Capote, Carson McCullers, Katherine Anne Porter, James Baldwin, Flannery O'Connor, and Sylvia Plath. In 1960, the story was anthologized in *40 Best Stories from Mademoiselle*.[80]

On St. Patrick's Day, 1957, Purdy finally met Dame Edith Sitwell in person. He traveled to the luxurious St. Regis Hotel in Manhattan to see her, as she insisted that she was unwilling to leave America without seeing her protégé. James presented her with camellias.[81] Purdy told Elborn he was "dreadfully poor" then, so he had to borrow money and clothing to travel into the city from Allentown. He was "somewhat apprehensive about meeting her," he admitted in a review of her autobiography for *Life* magazine, but knew from their correspondence she was "formidable only to critics and other paid fools." Van Vechten had joked: "Do not be afraid of Dame Edith except in appearance. She is nine ft tall and quite broad and looks like the leaning tower of Pisa if it were straight, but she is usually affable and ALWAYS will be with you."[82] Actor Alec Guinness described her as striking: "immensely tall, although slightly stooped," her "long, oval face was chalk-white, the mouth small, thin and straight, the arched eyebrows like faint pencil lines querying the tiny eyes."[83] Purdy recalled that Sitwell donned a "dark long beautiful gown and a kind of headdress," and resembled a "queen of mourning but of great vitality, wit, and dynamism." For *Life* he reflected: "Although the press has harped on about her 'eccentricity,'—a term she defined as being unafraid of the opinions and vagaries of the crowds—I found nothing affected or odd about her except, of course, she was more human, more animated, and kinder than most other people." Her costume and advocacies were "no more arbitrary or chosen to attract attention than was Thoreau's decision to live at Walden Pond."[84] James felt at ease immediately, as though he had "known her always." Sitwell asked if everything was going well with the forthcoming Gollancz publication.

"Well, Dame Edith, there was just one thing," Purdy began.

"Not *motherfucker!*" Dame Edith declaimed, overheard by an astonished waiter, whose mouth hung open as he nearly dropped his tray.[85]

Like Purdy, Sitwell had found recognition "only slowly and painfully," but amid early struggles she was not so fortunate as he, never having found a champion, she told him. While this was not entirely true, she was in an anxious period, and at this time, James was one of few who, albeit unknowingly, helped her "survive emotionally" and face "another round" of exhausting readings she was doing with her brother, Osbert.[86] Geoffrey Elborn added that Sitwell could be "rather snide about some writers she championed," such as Carson McCullers, but she never said an unkind word about James behind his back or waned in her support.[87] To James, Edith was the kindest, most generous, and largest-hearted person he had ever met, excepting some members of his own family. This New York rendezvous proved to be their only meeting. Two days before seeing Sitwell, he visited his other major champion, Carl Van Vechten, and sat for photographs.

Again the recipient of praise from Britain, Purdy received a note from Noël Coward, the famous playwright and composer, saying he had enjoyed the stories very much. "You can capture a mood, you know how to tell a story and your characterization is good. I hope you will go on writing because you obviously have talent." Coward did not publicly acknowledge it, but many knew him to be gay, sometimes exuding a high-camp sensibility. Purdy claimed that Coward and Powys were two writers Sitwell had criticized, but who "came to be her great admirers partly because all three of them found they liked my books so much."[88]

Unlike Coward, the English writer Angus Wilson was openly gay, which was then quite rare. Known for dark, comedic stories in *The Wrong Set* (1949) and a satirical novel, *Anglo-Saxon Attitudes* (1956), Wilson wrote in May expressing "great admiration" for both books Purdy had sent at the recommendation of Rudolf Burkhardt, editor of the homophile magazine, *Der Kreis*.[89] "You Reach for Your Hat" was "one of the most moving" stories he knew and the novella is a "small masterpiece." Within a year, Wilson recommended Purdy for a Guggenheim grant.[90] With Sitwell and Powys, Wilson completed a triad of major British champions.

As for Purdy's emerging American reputation, when *The New Yorker* ran "About Jessie Mae" in its May issue, it marked a milestone in Purdy's career. After decades of struggle, he was appearing in the New York "slicks." For decades, however, Purdy expressed rancor over editor William Maxwell's excessive cutting of "About Jessie Mae," including most of the ending. Maxwell, he believed, "personally butchered the story, cutting it so close to the bone that the *New Yorker* version is unintelligible."[91] Purdy exaggerates, but he has a point, especially regarding the ending: five lines of dialogue and two sentences, the denouement, were omitted, making the story end abruptly. *Paris Review* interviewer Annette Grant replied to a similar complaint from John Cheever directed at editor William Shawn. "It's the classic story about what *The New Yorker* is rumored to do: remove the last paragraph and you've got a typical *New Yorker* ending."[92] Yet at earlier points in "About Jessie Mae," Maxwell's edits streamline a story that was sometimes fussy with detail.[93]

The story of the edits is more complex than Purdy depicted and he approved the editorial changes at each step. On March 14, Maxwell sent Strassman the "preliminary editing" of the story that arrived under the title "It's Not Everybody That Can Tell You," which they thought "ought to work out for the New Yorker with a little more fixing, of a kind that the author alone can do." Purdy approved initial changes made on March 17 and sent revisions the next day. Five days later, he sent another revised manuscript and did the additional requested "fixing," such as specifying the setting and ages of the characters. "In general, Mr. Purdy's humor is very successful," Maxwell told Strassman, but they objected to a "tendency to overwriting in the passages between the dialogue." Maxwell advised Strassman "usually a little more editing" is done "before a story gets into print, but that he will in any case have a chance to see it, in proof, and object to anything that does not seem right to him." Four days later, Purdy mailed revisions, saying if they were not satisfactory, he would be glad to try again. Maxwell thought Purdy's revisions would "do the trick." He then sent the final proof for Purdy to check. Katharine White, the fiction editor, wondered if Naples, Florida, was the "right place for these people. It is all right for Jessie Mae," but she recalled Naples as a "place of huge houses along the ocean, where very rich people live, and no town behind them, to speak of. If this is true, wouldn't Tallahassee be more likely?" More than any editor besides Ross, Katharine White gave shape to *The New Yorker* and "set it on course," William Shawn said. White was "always reaching out toward writers who were not characteristic of the magazine," like Purdy.[94] The choice of Florida as setting was arbitrary, as it was for "Cutting Edge," probably only chosen as acceptable to New York editors. Founding the magazine in 1925, editor-in-chief Harold Ross declared that the *New Yorker* would not be "edited for the old lady in Dubuque." Acceptable settings included the East Coast, Hollywood, Florida, and Paris—places where its ideal readers lived or traveled—but nothing Midwestern, please, as noted by William Maxwell, himself an Illinois native and a fiction writer.[95] Writing on April 25, Purdy enclosed the final proof and agreed with changes. "Thank you for your sympathetic reading of my stories, and for your kindness and interest."

In a complaint that later became thematic, Purdy said the *New Yorker* editors treated "About Jesse Mae" with a lack of understanding of American speech; for example, they did not know that "funning" is a verb. By that, he means Midwestern speech, the Ohio speech he heard growing up and read in predecessors like Sherwood Anderson. In a 1965 article on Purdy in the *Times Literary Supplement*, William J. Weatherby, a British journalist making his career in the United States who was a friend of James Baldwin, appreciates the influence of Ohio on Purdy's writing style. It results from "just as much private discipline and practice as Hemingway's more famous style" and is "just as truly regional as Hemingway's, rooted in the flat, frame-house Ohio that he grew up in, as Hemingway's was rooted in Oak Park, Illinois, and the Michigan woods." Very few American writers maintained such a style, but somehow Purdy had resisted the "brainwashing of modern communication and retained his native rhythms and Ohio vocabulary" and manners. "You make every word count in Ohio—or you did when James Purdy was growing up there."[96]

Surprisingly, "About Jessie Mae" was his only story ever placed in *The New Yorker*. Purdy told scholar Celia Simon-Ross that William Maxwell or his assistants rejected all the stories that were later collected in *Color of*

Darkness and more published later. Purdy's rejections partly resulted from policy set by Harold Ross. Amid this editorial process, Maxwell rejected other submissions including *63: Dream Palace*: "it just isn't our kind of surrealism." Nevertheless, he claimed to have "enjoyed it," as he had enjoyed the other pieces, and looked forward to more. "Enjoy" seems odd diction to apply to this grim story. In retrospect, there was zero chance *The New Yorker*, with its glitzy ads, would have published this story of urban squalor centering on two poor white Appalachians in Chicago, suggesting Strassman's lack of acumen as an agent. She had run into William Shawn and mentioned the novella and that New Directions planned to publish it; he asked her to send it in. She realized offending words could not "be printed in a magazine, so naturally blanks or substitutions would have to be used." Maxwell also rejected "Everything Under the Sun," Purdy's stunning story of conflict between an older and a younger man, confronting male same-sex desire. There was much to admire, "but it isn't right for The New Yorker."[97] At some point Purdy soured on the magazine. In 1963 he told William Peden it had the "worst influence" on the contemporary American story.[98]

As she had promised upon her first encounter with his work, Edith Sitwell had persuaded Victor Gollancz to read Purdy's two privately published books. Purdy later joked to novelist Matthew Stadler: "She commanded the British Empire to publish me. She felt she was Queen Elizabeth. If she decided a book should be published, there was nothing they could do but publish it. But that era has passed."[99] Sitwell relayed that Gollancz said it was the "saddest book he knows." She agreed. "I can't think, sometimes, how you bear the spiritual agonies you undergo."[100] Victor Gollancz was impressed enough to publish *63: Dream Palace: A Novella and Nine Stories* in Great Britain in the summer of 1957. Gollancz, however, replaced the novella's last word, *motherfucker*, with *little bugger*, distressing James and Edith. Sitwell was incensed Gollancz had the "effrontery" to bowdlerize the text without consulting her or the author. Although Gollancz was known for progressive work, he was also known to censor manuscripts, including those by George Orwell, most overtly *Down and Out in Paris and London* (1933).[101] In an afterword to a 1980s reissue of that book, Gollancz claimed Orwell's words were "doubtless of a kind that no publisher could have printed at that time without risking gaol; and even if he had decided to risk it, no printer would have abetted him." The publisher quoted from a poem circulated by Gerald Gould: "Once aboard the lugger / Straight from the quarter-deck the fiat falls: / You may say bloody but may not say bugger, / You may say bottom but may not say balls."[102] Gollancz in the 1950s therefore believed it was daring to print *bugger* [sodomite], which was a word "not normally printed over here."[103]

In Britain, *63: Dream Palace: A Novella and Nine Stories* was "both praised and damned" but was "reviewed everywhere" establishing Purdy's "name as a serious writer." Purdy's British book inspired praise by British novelist John Cowper Powys, with whom James maintained a hearty correspondence, that was used in promotional copy. In an evaluation Purdy cherished, Powys attested: "Purdy is the best kind of original genius of his day. His insight into the diabolic cruelties and horrors that lurk all the time under our conventional skin is as startling as his insight into the angelic tenderness and protectiveness that also exist in the same hiding-place. Few there be that recognize either of these things. But Purdy reveals them." Purdy's prose "has about it the simplified concentration we get in the Greek tragedies, especially in Sophocles and Euripides." Poet James Michie in *London Magazine*, while holding some reservations about the novella, said the best stories are "extraordinarily powerful" and "observed as if through the unblinking eye of a tiger or a child"—Sitwell was "rather jealous" Michie thought of that line. She sent the review to Purdy, commenting that, although part of the review was "idiotic," much of it is "really splendid" since Michie recognized Purdy was "a man of genius." The London *Times* reviewer thought the short stories lacked substance but "the novella shows true creative power" and the critic had "nothing negative" to say about it. Though Purdy was seemingly "obsessed by the macabre," his ability to evoke it was unquestionable. "Cruelty and tenderness mean more to Mr. Purdy than they do to most writers." Late in the year, Angus Wilson chose the collection as one of his three favorite books of 1957, hailing it as "the most original fiction of the year" in *The Observer*.[104]

But in a review for the *Observer* published on June 30, critic Tom Hopkinson offered a lengthy dissenting opinion. The novella is a "scorched, aborted masterpiece. It has no form, or rather the author forgets the form with which he started" as he "dived deeper into darkness and disintegration." The protagonist and story "disintegrate and collapse together." Hey, he still called it a masterpiece. Hopkinson saw Purdy as perverse, his power deriving from an "intensity of feeling" aroused only by horror. "Torture alone arouses him to love; and he paints the life of the damned in such a lurid glow, it seems more real," more intense than the lives of those "whose emotions have not been cauterized, who can laugh as well as shudder." The short stories were "more literary," some reading like "experiments in technique." Only "Why Can't They Tell You Why?" was a complete success. Most stories and the novella are "strongly homosexual." Explicitly, in that flashes of "appalling pity, sly betrayal or outrage are almost entirely between men." Implicitly, since women loom as "monstrous mother figures whom guilty, over-sensitive boy-men struggle impotently to appease. If a man kisses a woman, it is to conceal his loathing and sidestep, if possible, her ill-concealed violence and destructiveness." Without denying Purdy's power, he hoped the distinguished Powys was unduly pessimistic when he called this "narrow, demoniac talent" the "best kind of original genius of our day" in his blurb.[105] Purdy thought it was written by "one of the little followers of the very pale conservative critic V. S. Pritchett."[106] He felt the nasty review was literally dictated by Pritchett, "one of the worst influences on criticism."[107] He told Strassman he was upset the *Observer* had called the book homosexual—"whatever in the hell they mean by that. Terms like that are so terribly unfair, like calling a book Jewish or colored or communist or any of those other words that are not descriptive of a thing like a book, and have no right in criticism. There are certainly lots of mean people in the world!"[108] Retrospectively, Purdy felt this review inaugurated a homophobic pattern; when his first book was published, among "very fine reviews, came a vicious homophobic attack on me and my book in the London *Observer*, pointing the way to the same kind of attacks on me in the *New York Times* book review."[109]

Powys passionately defended Purdy in a letter airing "astonishment and indignation." "Homosexuality—nothing! O how easy it is for the Mr. Tom Hopkinsons of this world to apply the particular term of abuse fashionable in their age, and most popular among normal 'Heteros,' whether they wish to abuse Sappho because she invented the most effective metre for expressive emption, or to abuse Catullus for believing in eternal sleep!" Responding, Hopkinson doubled down on his claim Purdy's work is "strongly homosexual" and said concentration on this "aspect of life has a limiting effect on his sympathies, and therefore on his authority. He writes of half of the human race with manifest loathing." Powys concluded: "Homosexual, heterosexual—*nothing*! Do you, or don't you, try to dig down to the heart of life upon this Planet Earth along with Homer and Shakespeare and Milton and Dante, as Mr. James Purdy struggles to do?"[110]

Purdy was fortunate to have such passionate apologists. Purdy thanked Powys for rising to the occasion, calling his rebuttal "spirited and noble." Hopkinson, "consciously or unconsciously, uses the word homosexual (God knows *what* that means!) to explain away his own guilty fear of the things I tried to portray! If we use his word *homosexual*, then Hamlet, Don Quixote,

Oedipus Rex, the Iliad, Moby Dick, Leaves of Grass, Bouvard et Pecuchet, The Way of All Flesh,—all, all are merely homosexual and therefore *nothing*! What drivel! The fact is that the Freudians and their ilk are all at heart little petty bourgeois idiots who are as ashamed of common humanity as they are of themselves. They are horrified of the human, and with Freud are trying to get rid of it. And they seem to be succeeding." The self-described Calvinist continued: "They would like to get rid of suffering, effort, love, and pain, so that they could all be these adjusted automata, sitting around having refined and happy thoughts. Well I believe in original sin, if not theologically, at least in FACT!" In October, Purdy wrote to Powys: "How very thrilling is your discussion of those words *homo* and *hetero*. I really am very queer, I suppose, in that I have NEVER believed in any of those terms. (I don't believe in words like Jew or Negro or any of them.) The main thing is to care about everybody you can, and begin where you are, and I let those words just bounce around and come out where they will. It would be a terrible world, though, with only ONE sex in it. There just has to be, somehow, the male and the female, and nobody can be satisfied with just the one, some part of him will cry out." He did not like "our modern world at all," a world that always pigeonholes people, "dividing them up, judging, criticizing, spoiling.... Why cannot people accept one another as they came into the world and as they were meant to be?" Purdy was grateful for Powys's yearlong friendship; sadly, they never met in person.[111]

Edith Sitwell's *Times Literary Supplement* review appeared unsigned five days after Powys's rebuttal of Hopkinson. Sitwell placed Purdy in the "very highest ranks of contemporary American writers" and declared, "Mr. Purdy is a superb writer, using all the fires of the heart and the crystallising powers of the brain." The novella *63: Dream Palace* is "a masterpiece" from beginning to end.[112] Such lavish praise inspired many to seek him out; but it also caused contemporaries like Edward Albee to seethe in envy. Albee confessed Purdy "received public praise of a fulsomeness—the extravagance of enthusiasm— that may have sown envy and maggoty urgings toward revenge in the hearts of many."[113]

Van Vechten was, like his protégé, overcome by Sitwell's hosannas. Carlo wrote Purdy: "Naturally I cried a good deal after reading Dame Edith on 63 Dream Palace! What a woman! What a review! It is only one in a thousand years that any writer is blessed with such a Godmother, and please do not forget that you have a saintly Godfather too! How lucky you are, kid. Pee your pants, no longer! Spread your wings and fly into all the desolate corners of the world and tell the millions how happy (or unhappy) you are. In other words, create and write and convince the world of your greatness!"[114]

In the midst of this tremendous response to Purdy's early work, James and Jorma traveled to New York. Richard Purdy entertained them at his hotel and cooked them a tasty meal. While James was breaking into a literary career, sadly, his brother's personal troubles sabotaged his acting career. In July 1957, Richard toured with a production of Cole Porter's *Can-Can*. He was also part of the original "smash hit" Broadway production, which ran for almost 900 performances.[115] Each night, social drinking followed the show. Richard also formed a bad habit of turning to the bottle to cope with stage fright and the intense grind of the tour, and his alcoholism got the better of him.[116] This was his final curtain call on the national stage.

In late 1957, William Purdy, tall, blue-eyed, now white-haired, traveled East for a few days to visit with James and Jorma—and to New York to retrieve Richard, accompanied by them. A teetotaler, William "fussed" when he found a whiskey bottle stashed in Richard's room, Jorma said. Will surely did not know James and Jorma were a couple. Tail between his legs, Richard returned to his hometown of Findlay, Ohio.[117] James said when Richard returned home, Vera did not recognize him at first.

Dick moved in with Vera and father-in-law, John Bauman, and began seeking help for alcoholism. In February 1958, Will sent Dick an inspiring letter full of good advice, and sent a copy to James. Will advised him to taper off drinking, smoke less to improve appetite, walk a lot, and get plenty of fresh air. "Much depends on your will power to regain your old time strength and ambition to succeed." He quoted from memory Longfellow's "Rainy Day": "Be still sad heart and cease repining, / Behind the cloud is the Sun still shining; / Thy fate is the common fate of all, / Into each life some rain must fall, / Some days must be dark and dreary." He urged his son: "Remember that I still have faith, respect, and love for you. RUB OUT ERRORS OF THE PAST: GET A NEW GRIP ON LIFE: WORK, STRIVE, STRUGGLE, and ACHIEVE SUCCESS. This letter is from one who has been robbed, betrayed, libeled, scorned, belittled but is sure of his own character and who just never knows the words—Quit, Retreat, or Surrender."[118] James may have found his father's words to Richard inspiring in tough times, and he inherited this plucky spirit of endurance and self-belief. Unfortunately, these words seemed to have little effect upon Richard. In May, Will wrote saying both he and Vera were "at a loss to know what to do about that fellow R.W.P., but we will try to do anything in reason to see that he recovers his old standing."

In July, Will reported he had gone to Findlay and "dictated a release of all claims on the leasehold of the room" Richard had "occupied for the last ten years" in New York, which Richard signed. Vera and Will even sought help from Dr. Charles Ray in Gilboa. Will noticed a hopeful improvement. "He seems well, was clean and neat; showed no trace of his usual condition. In May 1959 he hoped Richard would get it together soon since he could not afford to pay another three thousand dollars, "all for his own bad conduct."[119] In summer 1959, Dick told James he and the family were investigating alcoholics' hospitals.[120] In 1960, in a sign of recovery, Dick was a guest speaker at a meeting of the Fort Findlay Playhouse, reading short selections, including one by his brother.[121]

In an undated, possibly unsent letter, James extended his true feelings about Richard's illness. "Richard, we love you, but it is high time you faced the facts. You are completely dependent on alcohol. You look terrible. You are making no effort to get work. You simply are no longer yourself. . . . Your physical as well as mental health is terrible. You repeat yourself like some senile old man. Don't talk to me about being the WCTU. You have let extravagance, liquor, dissipation, and utter irresponsibility wreck your career. You have tortured Mama and Papa for years with your drinking. Isn't it about time you woke up and became a MAN? I am ASHAMED of you! By God, what you need is a MAN to knock the hell out of you. I want you to get out of that stinking room. Put that God dam whiskey bottle away, get your hair cut so you don't look like some God damned fairy, and GO GET A JOB." "For years you've lived high and handsome, spending money like water. NOW GOD DAMN YOU WAKE UP. GET YOUR LAZY ASS OUT OF THAT STINKING HOLE OF DRINK AND IDELNESS AND BE A MAN. You NEED someone to knock you down. We have all been too kind and patient with you. You are mentally a complete bore. Don't tell me I know. We love you and are willing to stand by you, but you have to make the effort." "There's nothing wrong with you but drinking, laziness, and idleness. Get back your pride! And go to work. Quit living in the past." This masculinist rhetoric is surprising, but it seems James felt desperate measures were called for.[122]

In mid-July 1957, in Allentown, Purdy reflected on the strangeness of his British success as he plugged away in obscurity and poverty. "Jack, I live here in the Negro slums and enjoy it, but I seem to have heard from only you from that far-off land ENGLAND, and I simply cannot believe they published me and that I am ESTABLISHED. I cannot even believe sometimes Dame Edith is REAL! I am alone here and nobody even knows I write. THIS IS NOT

A COMPLAINT. Jack, for your friendship and kindness and encouragement I can never thank you."[123] He began his letter to Powys with a short phrase from Homer in ancient Greek since Powys was working on a book on the epic poet. Jim admitted his Greek script was "a bit on the amateur side. What I need is a Greek teacher!" Interested in ancient Greek tragedy, within a year, Purdy was studying ancient Greek with a young Greek man from the local Greek Orthodox Cathedral.[124]

Amid such mounting praise of his writing, change was brewing. In the summer of 1957, Jorma found a better job at the New York University College of Engineering, doing lab research in propellants and lasers. This enabled him and James to move to New York City and pursue Purdy's dream of being a professional fiction writer. Around the beginning of August, they packed their meager possessions, to prepare for the move. Van Vechten had been enticing Purdy to move to the Big Apple. Soon, they would rub elbows with the literati, hopefully winning over even more to sing his praises. A move to New York was the right move at the right time.

8

Success Story

In early August 1957, Purdy and Sjoblom moved into Apartment 2B at 138 West 70th Street in Manhattan, just west of Central Park. They were struck by an odd building across the street designed in Egyptian revival Art Deco style. The Pythian Temple, gathering place for Pythian lodge members, was luxuriously decorated in brightly colored glazed terracotta ornaments depicting figures from antiquity. Part of the building was leased to Decca Records as a recording studio, where Buddy Holly, Sammy Davis Jr., and Billie Holiday all recorded in the 1950s. In November 1956, Paul Robeson, concert singer, civil rights activist, and communist sympathizer, spoke at The Temple, at a meeting of the National Council of the American-Soviet Friendship Association, soon after Soviet suppression of the Hungarian revolt; he and others were pelted with eggs and garbage by right-wing protestors. Relishing the lively neighborhood, on August 10, he wrote Powys: "Here I am in an entirely different world. It is just as much a 'melting pot' as ever, and I don't think they will ever get everybody 'melted' down here, which is good."[1]

James loved to explore the city, sometimes walking around all day. "I had to buy a new pair of shoes at once because I am such a walker," he told Powys. One night in August, though not prone to drink, James wandered into a tavern on 86th Street where all spoke German and were most friendly. "A great Tom cat" who "seemed to be in charge of the entire tavern" leapt onto the stool next to him, "purred and talked."[2] A lover of animals and birds, Purdy began to haunt the Central Park Zoo, having "silent conversations" with younger gorillas who were interested in his buttons, hat, and sacks of groceries. The coati was also a favorite.[3] "I am really rather mad about animals and whenever the weather permits. . . . I *communicate* with special favorites," Purdy told Powys.[4]

In September, he explored "this old and terrible city a bit more." He was visiting a famous boxing gym where many great pugilists had trained: Stillman's Gym. They let him "sit there and hear the pugs talk," and the grubby gym was "just great, old and crumbling," like something out of Jack London. St. Nicholas Arena had great matches, and "the talk is just wonderful, but a bit out of my price range." At that time, Purdy planned to write a story about a boxer.[5]

Almost immediately, James and Jorma regularly socialized with Carl Van Vechten, who resided nearby on Central Park West. For decades, he and his wife, the Russian-born silent film star Fania Marinoff, regularly hosted multiracial gatherings and parties, and he downed cocktails and photographed guests. James and "Carlo" began to rapid-fire notes and letters back and forth, replete with poems and bon mots. Purdy recalled that Van Vechten's friendship, enthusiasm for his writing, and "encouragement in the harsh years to follow" helped make his "stay in the megalopolis half-endurable at least."[6] On August 14, Purdy told Powys: "I went to see Carl Van Vechten last week, and he spoke of you, and we had a nice evening together talking and talking until Morning." Purdy entered an aesthetic, decadent world. Coleman Dowell, a young writer who joined Van Vechten's circle early that year, evoked the rococo drawing room: "The day of our meeting in January 1957 was dark and the chandelier was blazing. Coruscant in its light were seagreen *peau de soie*, china cats, portraits, the marzipan colors of impressionist paintings; on a large table under the source of light were boxes: of silver, cloisonné, sandalwood, studded with turquoise or lapis lazuli, or intricately inlaid. Later I was to be offered from those boxes candied ginger, crystallized violets and rose buds, and other sweetmeats to rival the delights of Konfituerenburg in *The Nutcracker*."[7] Among others, Van Vechten introduced James and Jorma to the novelist and essayist James Baldwin, with whom the couple dined out at least twice. "We liked him right away," Sjoblom recalled.[8] Discussing *63: Dream Palace*, Baldwin told Purdy, "I wish I had written that."[9]

On August 23, Van Vechten visited James and Jorma at their apartment, enjoying coffee and cheesecake, and he loved Purdy's "savoir faire and the strewed evidence" of "nonchalance." "Prince Sjoblom was superb yesterday and wore his panache with an air, but his hair is too short and that bothered me."[10] They were visiting regularly. At the end of the month, Carlo wrote: "Dearest Jaime, yesterday with you and Jorma Jules was beeswax and heaven I enjoyed and appreciated the golden seconds." The couple confirmed they would visit the following Tuesday. "You and Jorma Jules are certainly mes copains favoris and stick around pals!"[11]

Not all was sweetness and light in Purdy's new Manhattan life, however. His championing by Sitwell and Powys rankled some critics, who tried to undermine such highfalutin praise in a backlash. In September, chameleonlike Dwight Macdonald, then associate editor of *Encounter*, delivered a nasty attack on the British collection. He castigated it as the "latest avantgarde march to the rear. A *fiasco d'estime*, issued under the proper auspices: New Directions is the American publisher and the book is dedicated to Dame Edith Sitwell, dealer in premature laurel wreaths (wholesale only). The title novella is a kind of low-key nightmare in which the prose is as flat as the action is bizarre. One might think it a mannerist exercise were not the author obviously sincere. As it is, the effect is of a fantasy, full of violence, sadism, and homosexuality, reported to his analyst by an inarticulate neurotic. Joyce, Eliot, Hemingway, and others of the old-class avant-garde were also 'difficult' at first reading, because they were establishing new idioms which later became everyday language. But Mr. Purdy is unable to break out of his private world, which is to say he is not talented, the ability to communicate to others one's own world being one mark of talent. His work is typical of the present avantgarde," a false label since it "doesn't clear the way for the main army to follow but rather settles down snugly in permanent little camps off to the side which will never be on the main line of march."[12]

Macdonald's masculinist objection to Sitwell's praise and the "sadism" and "homosexuality" he finds therein reveals his prejudices. Sitwell thought that poet and editor Stephen Spender "must have been away when that ass insulted us in *Encounter*. He is *always* attending Conferences and Congresses and what have you! He would not have allowed this."[13] Purdy relished Sitwell's "barbs at a very conservative would-be Marxist critic . . . whom we called 'Goat-Beard' who styled himself a revolutionary although he drinks martinis and writes for the arch-conservative *New Yorker*." Edith continued to write James about twice monthly for eight years.[14]

Purdy was already breaking into foreign language markets. He told Powys that *Color of Darkness*, to be published by New Directions Books in a few months in the United States, was also going "to be published in GERMANY in German translation, by a firm called Rowohlt, in Hamburg. I was *astounded*! And the Swedish firm Bonnier have taken out an option on it!"[15] Rowohlt continued to publish Purdy through 1970 and Purdy's books were translated into numerous European languages. Some translations may have been sponsored by the Congress for Cultural Freedom or United States Information Agency, which, during the 1950s and 1960s, actively sponsored translations of American authors of the noncommunist left.

In addition to holding political views that the US government could back, Purdy expressed antiracist views supporting civil rights. In April, Carlo replied, "How any people can consider the color of their skin a matter of superiority is certainly cracked as you submit."[16] On September 9, Van Vechten was "very happy" about Purdy's "manifestations against the Governor of Arkansas and hope indeed that he CROKES" [*sic*]. Orval Faubus refused to comply with the US Supreme Court decision in *Brown v. Board of Education* integrating schools; instead, he called out the Arkansas National Guard to stop black students from entering Little Rock's Central High School.

As Purdy became more comfortable in Van Vechten's circle, he revealed new facets of his personality. Carlo wrote: "Dearest Jaime, You are your old self again this AM, full of the old nick as usual. The Pseudo-heterosexual disguise is a delight! Yesterday you hauled out a new personality. Miss Marinoff said after you had gone, 'I had no idea Mr. Purdy was so handsome! What beautiful eyes he has.' I noticed your eyes and also your snow-white legs." Yale bibliographer Donald Gallup was also impressed by Purdy's "all-around majesty," he reported, congratulating James on his "beauty and charm." In an undated postcard, he apprised Purdy: "Attending the party awarded Brooks Atkinson, by the stars of the stage last night, I talked at length with Lillian Hellman and she confided in me that her feeling for your work is most enthusiastic. She asked if I thought you would be able to write a play and I averred that you were able to do ANYTHING." Everyone was there, from Marilyn Monroe to Laurence Olivier.[17] Time and again Van Vechten advocated for Purdy's work and tried to insinuate him in his cultural circles. On October 14, 1957, Purdy wrote a clever, sexy poem called "Love" and sent it to Carlo.

> Love, you are a Banana without a peel,
> An old movie with an unending reel:
> You are a pussy cat with steady cream,
> And the spread-eagle with the million dollar scream.[18]

Purdy truly got his audience, preferring vintage oddballs like Van Vechten to academics or Beats. Carlo seemed almost enough, though Purdy might have been more proactive in making literary contacts. In March 1958, Purdy told Powys, "I can't get interested in these literary people in New York, and I have abandoned them completely, except Carl Van Vechten, who is at heart a rogue."[19]

At Van Vechten's, Purdy met Coleman Dowell, a songwriter, author, and playwright. An extremely talented but forgotten novelist, Dowell sought Van Vechten's blessing in a planned adaptation of *The Tattooed Countess*. Even before Dowell had read Purdy's stories, Purdy was "touched with magic" because Dame Edith had championed him. Prior to meeting Purdy, Dowell thus anticipated "nuances," an "offbeat beauty," and a "sense of turbans and pearls." Instead he found "the uncompromising bleakness of his own 'Daddy Wolf.' And a certain defensiveness about his work that could easily pass for pettiness." Dowell claimed that he had never met a "more perfect embodiment of Middle America, nor of Waspishness." In conversation, Dowell referred to the horrific ending of "Why Can't They Tell You Why?" in which a mistreated child spews black cords from his mouth, and asked the author, "*How* could you do it?" Dowell thought his remark may have elicited lifelong enmity, which, through their sporadic correspondence, was "never far from the surface."[20] Nevertheless, they became "pretty good friends."[21] Dowell became jealous of attention Carlo paid to Purdy. Hayworth writes, "For unsubstantiated reasons, Dowell felt that his favored position in Van Vechten's circle was being usurped." Dowell was also jealous of Purdy's attentions to his companion and patron, Dr. Bertram Slaff, a tall psychiatrist. Van Vechten wrote Dowell, saying that Purdy wondered, "Does Bert Slaff know that he is destined to be captured by vampires?" Dowell, resenting "Mr. Purdy's excessive interest in Bert's future," warned: "That young man should be advised that, if there are any vampires in the picture, I have priority, a sharp tooth and (for rivals) a silver bullet! Also a sharpened stake, wolf's bane, hen's bane and garlic—so there!" Dowell thereupon began to write short fictions and plays with an "experimental nature" like "those Van Vechten admired by James Purdy." Later, Dowell parodied Purdy's style, along with their mutual bête noire, Susan Sontag, in his novel *Mrs. October Was Here*. Purdy got under his skin.[22]

In early October 1957, Jorma and James positioned a small telescope to watch the USSR's Sputnik fly over Manhattan. They were also talking about Purdy's "Success Story," as a header read within William DuBois's book column for the *New York Times*. Purdy had visited the newspaper offices to sit for the interview. Slender and soft-spoken, he bore an "astounding resemblance to the young, clean-shaven Hawthorne (if you can imagine Hawthorne in loafers and gabardine)." The struggling writer was finally going to be published in the United States later that year by New Directions Books, after having been rejected by all the major New York magazines and publishers—including New Directions themselves. The public learned how Purdy, with help from friends, self-published two books and mailed copies to writers and critics, and caught the eye of Sitwell, leading to British publication and stoking interest among US publishers. Purdy made "contacts abroad thanks to a gift of tongues, which enabled him to earn travel expenses as an interpreter in Latin America, France, and Spain."[23] This account elides the government training and funding he received and emphasizes his self-made literary career.

On Sunday, October 27, Purdy and Sjoblom took in a fascinating performance at Carnegie Hall by Paul Swan, a dancer, actor, portraitist, and sculptor, then seventy-three years old. A worshipper of ancient Greek culture and gods, Swan was known for his decades of dance and dramatic performances. With long hair and fingernails, bisexual Swan wore thick stage makeup on and off stage. Raised in Illinois and Nebraska, he found fame in the early twentieth century. During Swan's Sunday shows, sophisticated Forrest Frazier, his handsome young secretary, opened the door for a small group composed mostly of elderly followers.[24] "Paul Swan, it is whispered, is really a man of 80, although he appears to be quite young. Only very old people were in the audience of this small concert hall." A gong was struck and one smelled strong incense. "The lights were extinguished and when they came on a nearly naked man came dancing over the small stage." At the end, Swan, dressed in Asian cap and adorned with many jewels, gave a lecture on individualism and the Greeks. Underneath Swan's "strange and often outlandish behavior," one sensed "a genuine man. And if he is 80 his dancing is remarkable for its vigor if nothing else."[25] Dowell was less charitable; he recalled evenings with Van Vechten "refraining from laughter" at Swan's recitals, "where dancer and audience practice an extreme form of masochism."[26] This event led to an unusual relationship between Swan and Purdy that was the genesis of Purdy's novel *I Am Elijah Thrush* (1972).

Paul Swan wrote two days later with lavish praise of Purdy's two privately published books, which James possibly gave him at the recital. "I have spent all day immersed in the artistry of your stories. So varied in mood and characters, so smooth in the unfolding and so original in theme and observation." They all bore the "same high imprint of a supreme artist."[27] The mail was not fast enough for Swan since he phoned actor Sandy Campbell, the partner of novelist Donald Windham, requesting Purdy's phone number, having "spent the day, apparently in ecstasy," reading his books, and wanted to tell James "how much he liked them." Two days later, he told Purdy, "I hope you will be present to stimulate my muse Sunday! I've needed an incentive for more than two years. But a mentality as rich and fertile as yours will serve to bring out the utmost of my capacities. We both are destined to be in solitude except upon rare occasions. I do not think our separate talents will neutralize each other. Do you?"[28] Over the next five years, Swan sent James and Jorma several free tickets and "half a dozen times" they attended his recitals at Carnegie Hall, which were "out of this world," Jorma recalled. He also sent invitations to dinner. Swan was "an important element in our Manhattan life."[29]

In the early 1960s, Purdy perpetrated a prank, or forged fantasy, intervening in Swan's reality. Purdy developed a pattern of turning reality into story almost immediately by transforming people who interested him into characters he would write about in anonymous letters and news releases, which sometimes evolved into poems, stories, even novels. From 1961 through 1965, Swan developed a bizarre relationship with a nearly deaf boy from Albany, whom the boy's grandmother brought to a recital when he was eleven. Swan, hard of hearing, sympathized and, after the show, lavished extra attention on him, "gesturing, making clucking noises, and pointing out items around the studio. The boy responded. Several other visits were arranged, and by the time the boy returned home they were able to communicate." Swan found the boy attractive, and his disability heightened his allure, as though it were a mark of the divine. Swan believed he discovered certain taps and clucks that the boy could understand. They invented a private code and were "able to 'speak' on the phone." Friends and family, however, grew concerned over Swan, watching warily as he became increasingly obsessed with the handsome youth. Swan's handsome pianist, Richard Nealy, recalled Swan being on the phone for hours on end, clicking and clucking, and he wondered whether someone was actually on the line.[30] Purdy would call Swan, pretending to be the boy he called "the Bird of Heaven," and would tap and utter code words. Purdy and Swan "developed a language together," Uecker said, but "Paul thought the Bird of Heaven is a real person on the phone."[31] Semi-obsessed, Purdy wrote a series of satires and fake news bulletins on Paul Swan that preceded his novel.[32]

In December 1957, New Directions Books published *Color of Darkness*, Purdy's first American commercial book. Reading Purdy's private books, founding publisher James Laughlin had been "immediately struck by his directness and lack of decoration in the style. He puts it down hard and rough; he's not one of the sweet lispers."[33] The collection used all material from the British *63: Dream Palace: A Novella and Nine Stories*, adding "Color of Darkness" and "You May Safely Gaze." Purdy later said he thought the title should have remained *63: Dream Palace*. But such a numerical title presents trouble for cataloging, and what is more, American publishers "thought it referred to an unnatural sexual position."[34] Purdy told the publisher the book was "very handsome," the jacket "perfect!" and the binding "very stunning," preferring it to the English edition. Tennessee Williams provided a blurb, which read in full: "It isn't enough to write well, you must also have a distinctly personal attitude and the temerity and power to project it, and I don't think that a new writer since Paul Bowles has shown these organic qualities so impressively as James Purdy in *Color of Darkness*. He may shock and offend some partisans of the well-trodden paths in fiction but he will surely enchant the reader who values a new experience in our very new times."[35]

That Purdy was published by New Directions is peculiar because they had rejected some of these stories before and major publishers were competing with that smaller house to acquire the book. Alfred Knopf "wanted to publish *Color of Darkness* also, but somehow, New Directions outbid them," Purdy told Powys.[36] But Laughlin enjoyed supplementary income: in 1953, Laughlin received an initial grant for $500,000 from the Ford Foundation, which was often used as a front or conduit for CIA money, to edit and publish abroad *Perspectives USA*, a journal promoting American culture that targeted the noncommunist left in France, England, and Italy. Laughlin stressed the aim of *Perspectives USA* was not "so much to *defeat* the leftist intellectuals in dialectical combat as to *lure* them away from their positions by aesthetic and rational persuasion" and "promote peace by increasing respect for America's non-materialistic achievements among intellectuals abroad."[37] To this same end, Laughlin likely continued to receive help from the Ford Foundation and/or CIA for New Directions Books and *New Directions in Prose and Poetry* (*NDPP*) during the 1950s and early 1960s. Purdy later acknowledged that Laughlin helped to keep him afloat by assiduously publishing shorter works—poetry, stories, and plays—in *NDPP*, a haven for adventurous work like his.[38] However, within a couple of years of signing with New Directions, Purdy was bitterly complaining at his treatment.

His American debut was "greeted on the whole by respectful acclaim," Purdy recalled. Early on, *Color of Darkness* earned very positive reviews in the *New York Times* by William Peden, who became a consistent supporter, and in the *New York Herald Tribune* by poet and critic Winfield Townley Scott, who compared the book favorably to Gertrude Stein's *Three Lives* and Sherwood Anderson's *Winesburg, Ohio*.[39] Even *Time* magazine, that bastion of middle-class sensibility, gave the book a generally positive write-up. The anonymous *Time* reviewer concluded that although the stories are all strange and grotesque, "caught in them, like the tremble of a bird in cupped hands, is the undeniable flutter of life." Purdy's "purpose is to reveal the horror underlying the humor . . . the canker that lies at the heart of comedy." The reviewer, who interviewed Purdy three times over the phone, wrote that Purdy did not want to be considered morbid and argued that "despair in art shows concern."[40]

One important story on homosexuality that reappeared in *Color of Darkness* but was never placed in a magazine was "Man and Wife," in which Purdy critiques institutionalized homophobia. In it, Lafe, a working-class gay man, has failed to accept his desire. He is married and tries his best to be a "normal" man, but because of his queerness and wayward looks at young male coworkers, he is fired from his factory job. He confesses his lack of normalcy and manliness to his wife, Peaches Maud, who refuses to hear such "mental talk." We sense integrity in this man victimized by homophobia when he tells his wife he will support her, whatever may happen. Allowing him to retain dignity, Purdy critiques widespread Cold War homophobia, during which a worker could lose a job over mere suspicion of homosexuality, with no ramifications for the employer. Purdy obliquely comments on Executive Order 10405, signed by Eisenhower in 1953, which allowed the government to fire employees over homosexuality. (Purdy and Van Vechten mocked Eisenhower in correspondence.) In the 1950s, communism was linked with homosexuality as deviancy by Senator McCarthy and other red-baiters. Gays and lesbians, who felt forced into the closet, were seen as security risks, regarded as easily blackmailed by spies, for example. Gender and sexuality conformity were a social mandate, and Purdy shows their harm in this poignant story.[41]

One remark he most appreciated and thought "one of the finest appraisals" of his work came in a letter from acclaimed fiction writer Katherine Anne Porter, who found Purdy's style "as fluid and natural as a man thinking to himself in the dark, yet controlled, coherent, with an innate sense of form, and great powers of concentration. All the stories are very short, but the impression is one of a long story." Purdy possesses the "priceless gift of compassion," and although he "knows the worst, no doubt," he also knows "something else very good, very real, and he is loyal to that without question. I believe in this talent and hope it may thrive."[42] In February 1958, Porter wrote from Connecticut, pledging support. There was "not much to add to the Hallelujah Chorus that greeted" *Color of Darkness*; "but surely you must feel now that nothing stands between you and whatever you wish to do."

She predicted, "Now, I expect you may have anything you want in the way of grants, fellowships, residences, etc., if you have any need for that kind of aid. They are meant for such as you, and if they will help, you may as well have them. I am on the Board at Yaddo, if you would like to go there for a work period. The Guggenheim Fellowships still give occasionally a grant to an artist" and "the National Institute of Arts and Letters has a yearly round of grants, $1000 dollars each." She thought Purdy was then a high candidate for "any and all benefits." He had become a cachet writer. "Let me again wish you well with all my heart—for it is in a mysterious way a matter of the heart's joy to see a new good gift growing and taking hold and making its way—and to hope it will now be made possible for you to work without too many obstacles and energy wasting occupations."[43]

As Porter predicted, following the release of *Color of Darkness*, Purdy was showered in awards in 1958. Sitwell wrote: "I have never—and I mean never—known any writer to be acclaimed at his true worth so quickly! It is such a joy to me."[44] In April, he won a $1,500 National Institute of Arts and Letters Award.[45] He also received an American Academy of Arts and Letters award to live in Rome for a year beginning October 1958, with free residence and a $1,750 stipend, which for some reason he never took up.[46] In May, he won a John Simon Guggenheim Memorial Foundation Fellowship Award for creative writing. "I must watch myself or when I get that Guggenheim money I will turn into a very lazy no-account person!" he joked to Powys.[47] Another kind of award was the validation that arrived in August from playwright and novelist Samuel Beckett: "Thank you very much for *Color of Darkness*. I think it is very fine and I look forward to your next work."[48]

Though still emerging, Purdy had already drawn so many important letters from literary stars like Porter that Van Vechten thought his papers should be archived at the Beinecke Library at Yale University, where he and Purdy worked with librarian Donald Gallup. At the time, Purdy was honored, but about twenty-five years later, he was less positive when corresponding with friend and bookdealer, Robert A. Wilson, who had been a companion of Van Vechten. "Carlo took advantage of my naiveté—for instance he persuaded me to give him the original typescript of *63: Dream Palace*. He then gave it as a gift to the Beinecke Rare Book Room! I didn't know then that such things had financial value!"[49]

He told Powys he had been "doing a lot of silent kind of meditation and prayer, and God knows I need it—who doesn't—because I have promised Miss Lillian Hellman that I will try my hand at writing a play for Broadway!

After I told her I would do it, I was HORRIFIED at what I had promised,—almost as horrified as if I had told her I would erect a new skyscraper with my own two hands! Well the fat is in the fire and I am writing a play called *Madonna*, together with my novel *Malcolm*." In April, *Publishers Weekly* announced: "Impressed by his stories in *Color of Darkness*, Lillian Hellman and Lester Osterman, a producing team, have given James Purdy an advance to write a play."[50] *Madonna* focused on a possessive mother, "a kind of sacred WHORE type, who has had so many lovers she actually DOES NOT remember who is the father of her son, 15 years old; he is passionately concerned with finding out who his father is, and the *Madonna* is just as passionately lost in the remembrance or non-remembrance of her past lovers, all of whom could have been and are fit to have been, she feels, the Father of Anybody."[51] He was considering the Ozarks as a setting. Purdy may have been thinking of his mother Vera being courted by roomers at their home. In any event, akin to Malcolm, here was another fifteen-year-old looking for his father. A month later, he was under pressure to finish his play, and then had to "entirely rewrite, and *change* my novel *Malcolm*."

In March, prodigy director Elia Kazan showed interest in filming *63: Dream Palace*. "A very off thing is now going on: the movies are interested in making a film out of *63: Dream Palace*," Purdy told Powys. "I cannot believe this! But a famous Hollywood director talked to me *a very little bit* about it, asking little queer questions here and there of me. I was too astonished to say much to him."[52] Kazan had worked with Tennessee Williams on *A Streetcar Named Desire* (1951) and *Baby Doll* (1956), and directed *On the Waterfront* and an adaptation of Steinbeck's *East of Eden* with James Dean (1955). Alas, in April, director John Stix relayed that Kazan thought *63: Dream Palace* "too special," thus not suited for cinema audiences.[53]

New York offered cultural opportunities unavailable in Allentown and Appleton. In April, Purdy met Kenneth Rexroth at the Five Spot jazz club in the East Village, where the poet was reading. Rexroth, who had called Purdy's first collection "one of the best first books of short stories" he had read, was fusing poetry and jazz, accompanied by the Pepper Adams Quartet, featuring trumpeter Donald Byrd.[54] In June, Purdy went to an exhibition of Van Vechten's photographs of African Americans at the Museum of the City of New York, covering nearly three decades. "All the great American Negroes had been photographed by him, and all their faces watching you from the walls were quite impressive," he told Powys.[55]

In June 1958, "Home by Dark," an awkward exchange between an orphaned boy and his grandfather, appeared in *Harper's Bazaar*, a major women's magazine. In 1956, Van Vechten had talked to his friend, baroness Eleanor Perenyi, the features editor there, and she asked to see Purdy's collection.[56] *Harper's Bazaar* was in this period publishing fiction by Capote, McCullers, Isherwood, and Porter.[57] "Home by Dark" also appeared that month in *London Magazine*.

Also in June, "You May Safely Gaze" appeared in an obscure magazine, *High*, "the man's home companion" based in Canton, Ohio. The story addresses repressed male same-sex desire and anxiety over same ("gaze" may even pun on "gays"), but also depicts women's lusty interest in men's muscular bodies. The issue featured Playboyesque cheesecake, fiction, and articles. "You May Safely Gaze" had been rejected by *New Yorker*, which found the outrageous ending—in which the tight swimsuits of two exhibitionist bodybuilders, flexing for an enraptured beach crowd, simultaneously rip wide open at the crotch—was not right for them. Ahead of its time, "Gaze" was reprinted in *The Other Persuasion: An Anthology of Short Fiction about Gay Men and Women* in 1977, and later in *The Signet Classic Book of Contemporary American Short Stories*.[58] *High* also reprinted "Cutting Edge" in its November 1958 issue. Perhaps placement in a "men's magazine" was meant to make him appear less effete, more in keeping with acceptable Cold War masculinity. The caption above "Cutting Edge" reads: "He was trying to assert himself—she to stifle his manhood." In the 1950s, maternal and other feminine threats to normative American masculinity was a popular topic, as criticism of "Momism" abounded in public discourse. These two placements in *High* were never included in bibliographies such as Jay Ladd's *James Purdy: A Bibliography* (1999) or that appending *The Complete Short Stories of James Purdy* (2013).

Purdy's streak continued in July, as "Night and Day" debuted in a major slick for men, *Esquire*. Demonstrating the value of story-writing in that period, Purdy was paid $600—(equivalent to $5,378 in 2020).[59] A soap opera, "Night and Day" tells of a young mother whose husband is absent and missing. After having caved in somewhat to sexual pressure from "Grandy," her father-in-law, she finally and totally rejects his manipulations. Although "Night and Day" was tersely rejected by William Maxwell for the *New Yorker* in 1957, Rust Hills, the new fiction editor at *Esquire*, aimed to restore the magazine's literary identity by publishing "Bernard Malamud, James Purdy,

Italo Calvino—serious writers who would give something more than the pulp fiction most other magazines published."[60]

In the same issue of *Esquire*, Dorothy Parker, usually parsimonious with praise, lauded *Color of Darkness* in her column: "here is a striking new American talent, sure and sharp and powerful."[61] In June, Parker wrote to Purdy to say "how deeply and proudly" she appreciated his letter and books he had sent. "Night and Day" was "stunning." She had suffered a "hellish" slipped disk, delaying response. "I know how busy you are (Lillian Hellman says you are writing a play, which is the best news I have heard in a long, long time) but if you ever have any vacant half-hours, I don't think you know how glad I would be if you would come see me." She shared her quaint phone number, Butterfield 8-7500. He was "really thrilled" Dorothy was impressed because "she didn't like anything. But my publishers didn't care."[62]

Carl Van Vechten, who had introduced Purdy to Parker, soon connected him with Paul Bowles, the expatriate writer and composer who said Purdy's prose is the "closest to a classical American colloquial" that we have. Usually living in Tangier, Morocco, Bowles was in New York in September 1958 working with an opera production and ran into Van Vechten, who asked Paul if there was anyone he wanted to meet while in town. Bowles had just read *Color of Darkness* in Lisbon, sent by Laughlin, and was impressed, so he uttered "James Purdy." "Come Wednesday at seven," responded Van Vechten immediately. Purdy later remarked: "I was at the beginning of my own career as a writer, and was a bit nervous at meeting so mysterious and legendary a figure as Mr. Bowles. My apprehension was put at an end when I met him. He seemed like a quiet, very dignified and kind man, perhaps like a doctor of medicine." Bowles in turn found Purdy "a reticent and unassuming man" whom he "instantly liked." Van Vechten took photographs.[63]

In July 1958, Robert Giroux, editor-in-chief at Farrar, Straus & Cudahy, wrote Purdy directly after having finished *Color of Darkness*. "I have to tell you what an excellent book I think it is—the best first book of stories by an American writer since *A Curtain of Green*" (1941) by Eudora Welty. "I shall be very much interested to read your next book. I suppose your publishing plans for future work are settled, but in the event that you are free to discuss them, we would be proud to have your work appear under our imprint." Purdy underplayed his excitement at being solicited by a major US publisher after years of pursuit. It was "very kind indeed" of Giroux to write and he was "very much pleased" he had enjoyed *Darkness*. He was busy working on a novel and a play, but would keep Giroux's "kind offer in mind." In the meantime, Purdy recommended his new pieces in *Harper's Bazaar* and *Esquire*.[64]

Purdy later confessed he took drastic measures to prevent New Directions from publishing *Malcolm*, wanting some place bigger. Purdy later accused Laughlin of having caused him "great misery" through "long refusal to release *Malcolm* to a publisher who could actually sell" his books.[65] He told novelist Matthew Stadler: "I was obliged by contract to offer them my next book, and Laughlin wanted it, but I told him if he published [*Malcolm*] I would kill myself. I wanted a new publisher. He didn't know if I would actually do it, so he gave up and I sold the book to Farrar Straus." Stadler was astonished: "you told him you'd kill yourself?" Purdy replied: "If you can't exaggerate, you're reduced to idiocy."[66]

Four months after Robert Giroux wrote Purdy saying that Farrar, Straus would be proud to publish him, James Laughlin and Robert MacGregor of New Directions Books visited Giroux in his apartment. MacGregor later told Purdy they visited Giroux to gain his interest in "taking over" Purdy's novels since the novels "might be better published by a larger house." Independently, MacGregor and Laughlin had "already surveyed all the publishers in this country and decided that Bob [Giroux] and Farrar, Straus would be the very best" for Purdy and his development. "Surely this is one of the most generous things one publisher has ever done both in relation to an author and to another publisher," McGregor ventured. He was under the impression that Giroux did not yet know Purdy's work then since he accepted the copy of *Color of Darkness* they brought, was impressed by their enthusiasm and by statements and articles on Purdy they gave him, and promised to read it rapidly. "We've always been so very happy that this move worked out so well for you, for [FSC], and in fact for our continued publication of your stories." Did Giroux pretend to the New Directions publishers that he had not already read Purdy's work and reached out to him?

Purdy had a different account, which he later shared with Roger Straus: "I came to you at the very insistent and daily persistent urging of Mr. Robert Giroux, in 1958, who did all in his power to get me away from New Directions, promising me just short of the sun and moon." Purdy arrived with a "brilliant reputation, earned in England and Europe."[67] In any event, he signed a contract with Farrar, Straus & Cudahy for four novels, beginning with *Malcolm*, which had been rejected by Malcolm Cowley at Viking and other publishers.[68] The twin engines powering the press were Straus and Giroux, but Straus was in the captain's seat. Unlike his partner Straus, who was vulgar, self-indulgent, scrappy, and chintzy with staff and many authors, Giroux was a Jesuit-trained liberal, intellectual, and quietly, a gay man. Editor Robert Gottlieb wrote that Giroux was a "modest, passionately literary man whose homosexuality was known and disregarded; he shared his life with the same man for more than half a century, until they died."[69] Giroux, who worked with T. S. Eliot, Flannery O'Connor, Robert Lowell, and Jack Kerouac, was known for his taste, care, integrity, and a passion for opera. "Giroux treated James with awe," Uecker said, and Purdy was pleased with his reception.[70]

Despite his many story placements over 1958, which now included "The Lesson" in the first issue of *Texas Quarterly*, edited by Harry Ransom, Purdy still felt he was not being properly represented. On December 8, Purdy wrote Toni Strassman angrily, done with her. "I would like to tell you now and tell you for the final time that I do not wish you to represent me in any future dealings in any way with any publisher." He itemized her failings, resenting that she never showed she thought he was an "unusual writer." He did not think she was able to judge the quality of his work. "If you want to cause trouble, by not completely withdrawing as my agent, I have the facts, and I have the people to back me. I am not going to allow you to ruin my career. I am also aware of the things you are saying behind my back." (What she was allegedly saying is unknown.) On December 17, he sent a telegram and a letter, threatening legal action. "If you want trouble, I am ready to give it to you, in a way you have never known possible. Withdraw as my agent: I owe you nothing." This is heavy-handed, but apparently he had lost all faith. "You have been paid. But what you want is to either be my agent or destroy my career." He threatened to remove any right she had to represent him, even on *Color of Darkness*, if she could not "collect what ND rightfully" owed him. "You have in every case been remiss, idle, negligent, and unaware of your responsibilities." Strassman refused and continued to represent him.[71]

More supportive was his loyal friend John Cowper Powys, who wrote to tell Purdy his work would endure. It was the "greatest thing anybody ever said" to him. He was so encouraged because he was finally finishing *Malcolm*. Through the ordeal of rewriting and revision, his "guts and brains had been pulled out through" his eyes. "I have been pulled through the eye of the needle!" He was reading Lord Byron's letters: he preferred the bisexual poet "as a human being," a letter-writer, than as a poet. "There is nothing better than to read about someone who was noble enough to suffer, and to admit it, and that is how he wins the heart."[72]

———

Beginning in late 1958, James and Jorma lived at a new address: 236 Henry Street, Apartment 8, in Brooklyn Heights. They had viewed the West Side apartment as temporary. Noting Purdy's "indecision at ever settling down, a young man in publishing insisted" that he view an available room in an old mansion. Brooklyn Heights in this period was considered a "suburb of Greenwich Village, a quiet bedroom community where writers lived in reasonably priced apartments near a pleasant" walkway with view of the water. W. E. B. Du Bois had a place nearby; Jorma and James glimpsed him standing by the window.[73] They lived near the Promenade or Esplanade, which offered excellent views of Lower Manhattan and New York Harbor and had a gay reputation. Around the corner on Montague Street was Lassen & Hennigs, Purdy's favorite delicatessen, where he would order whitefish and pike or a turkey sandwich.[74] Also on Montague was Sam Colton's bookstore that he ran with his wife, Sylvia, where James was a customer and later inscribed books to them and gave them tickets to an adaptation of his work.[75] John Strausbaugh writes that on approaching Purdy's building, from two blocks away, he knew he had spotted the place. A brooding "behemoth of a red-brick Victorian mansion, complete with mansard roof and gables and even guttering gaslights out front, it could be home to many of his characters, the big old house unmoored in time where they fret and pace and go mad" and "shoot their lovers and then hang themselves from the rafter in the attic."[76]

Rumor had it the house was haunted. The mansion, he was told, was built by a sea captain around 1875 and as late as the early 1950s, "old-time residents recalled seeing the surviving sisters of the captain, now extremely venerable, taking their supper by candlelight, attended by elegantly attired black servants," Purdy later wrote. After the sisters died, the house was sold and divided into at least eleven "whittled-down units, thus destroying some of the essential grandeur of the house, but allowing the beautiful hand-carved staircase to remain mostly unscathed." His favorite feature was big windows facing south and east. Pausing from writing, he could look out on an "endless procession of human beings of every ethnic origin imaginable, see the southern sky with its panorama of clouds, and look down on the shrubs of holly, spirea, honeysuckle and rose of Sharon."[77]

Brooklyn Heights possessed a rich gay literary legacy. Walt Whitman, the American poet most precious to Purdy, who celebrated "adhesive love" among men, had lived in the neighborhood and hand set the first edition of *Leaves of Grass* there. Purdy lived down the street from the storied St. George Hotel, at Henry and Clark Streets, a "notorious gay rendezvous point up through the 1960s," and below the hotel was the Clark Street subway station, with a "cruisy reputation." A native of northern Ohio like Purdy, poet

Figure 8.1 Purdy's residence at 236 Henry Street, Brooklyn Heights, 2019. Photo by the author.

Hart Crane, the muse of Tennessee Williams and other gay writers, lived at the St. George for short periods in the 1920s. In Crane's cosmology, queer love, Whitman, and Brooklyn were tightly interwoven, as they became for many others. In Brooklyn Heights, the inveterate cruiser Crane had several places from which he could choose to cruise. For future generations of LGBTQ people, Brooklyn Heights "now held a special luster." In the early 1940s, February House on 7 Middah Street was an artist and writer commune that attracted LGBTQ writers, poets, and composers including Carson McCullers, W. H. Auden, Paul and Jane Bowles, Aaron Copland, and Virgil Thomson. Lincoln Kirstein helped turn it into a commune.[78]

From Purdy's new perch, he maintained his publishing streak, perhaps with a little help from behind the scenes. *Commentary*, a Jewish-American intellectual journal focusing on politics, religion, and socio-cultural issues, ran "Encore" in March 1959, a short story that drew from his college days. Again Purdy struck gold in October, as *Commentary* published "Mrs. Benson," a dialogue between an alienated mother and daughter set in Paris. *Commentary*, subsidized by the American Jewish Committee, was linked to the American Committee for Cultural Freedom (ACCF), which in 1954 created an "editorial command center" for Congress for Cultural Freedom magazines that were CIA-backed, such as *Encounter*, and acted as a "clearing-house service" furnishing material for *Commentary* and *Partisan Review*. The ACCF basically offered "literary agency services at large" and told members if they wrote pieces aligned with "broader aims of fending off critiques" of the United States, and if they were a member or friend of ACCF, the committee would help them publish in multiple markets, which Purdy was enjoying. The ACCF was funded by foundations that were CIA fronts (e.g., Farfield, Asia), or were used to channel CIA money, such as the Ford.[79] "Encore" received an even wider audience when it was reprinted in *Prize Stories 1960: The O. Henry Awards*, introduced by Wallace Stegner.

From the early days of Farrar, Straus, Roger Straus, a veteran of Naval Intelligence, lent a hand to the Central Intelligence Agency for at least a decade, providing cover to operatives in Italy.[80] This explained the publisher's extensive reach in European literature in translation. Straus had a dedicated telephone line in his office for his CIA contact. It was his "patriotic duty" to do all he could—and federal subsidies were persuasive.[81] Straus operated the books committee of Eisenhower's People to People program, countering communist propaganda globally. Also involved in the program was the United States Information Agency, which pitched books they funded to Straus.[82]

On March 15, 1959, Purdy told his editor Giroux he was working on a "new novel called *The Nephews*." The pluralized title is interesting considering that, in gay lingo, *uncle* and *nephew* convey the dynamic of a type of multigenerational couple. In the story, Alma Mason sets out to write a "memorial" of her nephew, Cliff, who is at first described as MIA in the Korean War. In the process, Alma learns how little she knew not only the nephew, but also the neighbors. For example, Cliff spent a lot of time at the home of Willard Baker, an older gay man, and his young live-in companion, Vernon Miller, a figurative nephew who is fascinated by Cliff. Willard Baker was based on Purdy's Bowling Green neighbor Clifford Schrader, the son of a doctor who, like Baker, had been an urban house detective. The topic of same-sex love and desire was edgy for a novel published nine years before the Stonewall Inn protest. It was also risky, given the neglect and criticism Gore Vidal and James Baldwin suffered after publishing their gay novels, *The City and the Pillar* (1948) and *Giovanni's Room* (1956). Purdy's notebooks show that, in early drafts, characters such as Perry Miller (later changed to Vernon) are less ambiguous in their view that Cliff was homosexual than they would be in the final version: Perry even insinuates that Cliff tried to be a "gold digger."

James was not only remembering, but contemplating how memory shapes our sense of identity. A notebook shows he studied chapters of William James's *Principles of Psychology* (1890), and Pick's *Memory and Its Doctors* (1888).[83] He also employed warm-up exercises of freewriting and poetry to get juices flowing for novel drafting. Maybe it was "gibberish but the books come out of it." On drawing characters from his neighbors, his family, and places in Ohio, he reflected, "Who else have you got but what happened to you / and who you knew—they are the ones."[84]

In his notebook, Purdy recorded the routine he kept from September 1958 through August 1959. "7:30–8:30 Breakfast / 8:30–11:30—The Nephews / 11:30–12:00—Mail / 12:00–1:30 Lunch / 1:30–3:30—Play [writing] / 3:30–5:30—Shopping, Recreation / 5:30–7:30—Sublies [meaning *sublime* in French, this seems to denote dinner] / 7:30–8:30 Short Stories." In June 1959, he managed to complete the first draft of *The Nephew*, and a revised, incomplete typescript was dated August.[85] Though Purdy was busy writing and not very social in 1959, through Sitwell, he befriended the Filipino poet José Garcia Villa.[86]

Clearly his priority was on long-form writing. In April 1959, the *New Yorker* thought it seemed "like a long time since" they had seen a Purdy story. "I'd be grateful if you'd tell him we asked about him," editor Newman wrote Strassman, who was still representing him. "We'd like to have him in the magazine again." Learning Purdy had just finished a novel, Newman asked if they could see a copy of the manuscript or advance proof "in the hope that we might be able to excerpt something."[87] Nevertheless, the *New Yorker* never published anything else by Purdy.

In summer 1959, "Everything under the Sun," a story exploring the love and power dynamic between an older and younger man cohabitating in a big city, was published by *Partisan Review*, a leftist intellectual journal. Sam Steward wrote, "'the joy of recognition' was almost too strong; it rattled me."[88] Its placement was prestigious since "no young novelist, whether successful elsewhere or not, could feel secure about his status as a serious writer until he had been favorably reviewed, or better still published," in *Partisan Review*, wrote *Commentary* editor Norman Podhoretz.[89] Philip Rahv, co-founder of the journal, was close to Roger Straus, with whom he trawled for sexual adventure.[90] An unofficial Congress for Cultural Freedom magazine partially funded by the CIA, the *Partisan Review* benefited from the CCF gifting subscriptions to individuals overseas. Purdy's next British publisher, Secker & Warburg distributed *Partisan Review* in England; in 1952, Warburg joined the British Society for Cultural Freedom, which produced *Encounter*, an affiliate of the CCF, but he was unaware of any secret CIA funding.[91]

In August, Purdy sent "Sermon," his unsettling monologue of God, to Giroux. Sitwell had earlier described it as a "terrible monologue," but eventually found it "a very great work. I think it frightened me so much, when I read it first, that I was stunned."[92] Van Vechten also found it stunning. *New Directions in Prose and Poetry* wished to publish it, but were willing to let someone else publish first if they would pay a fair price. Rejected by *Playboy*, which never published Purdy, "Sermon" finally appeared in *NDPP*. Showing a cordial author-editor relationship, Purdy met Giroux at Lüchow's German restaurant in East Village in Manhattan. "What a grand room that is!" He thought it wonderful they saw Djuna Barnes there and hoped Bob might sometime introduce him to this lesbian novelist.

Also in August, John Farrar, president of FSC, wrote Purdy, saying he had read their forthcoming *Malcolm* "with enormous admiration and amazement." It carried him back to his beloved Laurence Sterne, and "in a way," Norman Douglas's Firbankian *South Wind* (1917). "I don't know when I have had a better time with a novel. I laughed out loud constantly, but it was brave of you to call it a 'comic' book. Its tragic and bitter overtones will stay with me long after the brilliant wit." He asked to let him know when he would visit the office: "I would like so much to see you." Purdy was "quite delighted" since it was "so rewarding to meet with a reader who feels as the author hoped his reader would feel!" Purdy looked forward to meeting Farrar.[93] Later that month, Purdy told FSC that John Stix, who had directed on Broadway and assisted Elia Kazan, was anxious to see *Malcolm* for "consideration for a film."[94]

Malcolm was still searching for a home in Britain since Gollancz had rejected it as "unintelligible." Victor Gollancz, "for all his posturing, was very money-conscious and hypocritical, and sentimental and false," Purdy later accused.[95] Secker & Warburg next considered it. Fred Warburg sent *Malcolm*, which was in a final draft or proof, to Angus Wilson, who surprisingly gave it a "very hostile report indeed." Since Wilson was Purdy's "principal backer in this country apart from Sitwell," Warburg "turned it down without more ado," he later explained to Roger Straus. In May 1959, Angus Wilson wrote Purdy saying he did not think *Malcolm* would go over well with British readers, which must have been a blow.[96] Sitwell reassured him in June: "Do not worry, James, about *Malcolm*. I *had* to tell you of the difficulties, as your friend and your profound admirer." Her agent David Higham was "*sure* it would find its publisher," and, she reminded him, "You are most truly a man of genius."[97] After FSC published *Malcolm* in America, however, "Angus decided he might have made a mistake" and Secker & Warburg reconsidered it. When Fred and his wife, Pamela de Bayou, read it, they were delighted, "difficult at first sight though the book was," and Wilson reversed his original judgment. In the meantime, *Malcolm* had been rejected by six other British publishers. Fredric Warburg understood the queer subtext of *Malcolm* but now he was keen to publish. He did not want to repeat the mistake he had made with Gore Vidal's *The Judgment of Paris* (1952), when he deferred to colleagues' concerns about its eroticism and turned it down. Thus for British publication, Purdy followed in George Orwell's footsteps from Gollancz to Secker & Warburg.[98]

When *Malcolm* was published by Farrar, Straus & Cudahy in September 1959, it had been a long journey. Purdy later claimed twelve publishers rejected *Malcolm* and FSC picked it up only "rather reluctantly" as they were "afraid of it."[99] Labeled a "comic novel" by its publisher, *Malcolm* evokes laughter that "sounds a little like the beginning of a death rattle," major critic R. W. B. Lewis wrote in a positive review for the *New York Herald Tribune Book Review*. Placing *Malcolm* in the "fine old comic picaresque tradition" and calling it a "work of baffling, perverse and very real distinction," Lewis, a Yale professor, hailed Purdy as a "writer of exceptional talent, who must be acknowledged in the company of Saul Bellow and Ralph Ellison—with whom, for all his uniqueness, Mr. Purdy has much in common."[100] Purdy's themes are the great ones: Malcolm is a "familiar American fictional hero. Like Melville's Billy Budd, he is a helplessly godlike young man. He is passive, beguiling and nearly mindless; the object of a constant and furious yearning; at once an inspiration and a disaster for his new acquaintances. And his story turns on the question that has most agitated Mr. Purdy's ablest contemporaries," which is "how to come alive—how to experience the sheer sensation of existing—in a deadening modern world, when, to paraphrase one of Purdy's characters, people refuse to keep their hands off one's soul." In a 1962 chapter for the edited collection *A Time of Harvest: American Literature 1910-1960*, Lewis compared *Malcolm* to *Invisible Man*: "Both Purdy and Ellison (in their exceedingly different ways) introduce their comically ill-equipped young heroes," their title characters, "to individuals and situations that are clearly representative of the great sources of power and control in our epoch," thereby creating modern allegories illuminating these greater forces impinging on the individual trying to come alive.[101] In *Malcolm*, observe Fate (Professor Cox, astrologer, modeled on Wendell Wilcox), Death (Estel Blanc, mortician), Art (Kermit Raphaelson, Eloisa Brace), Money (Girard, Madame Girard), and finally, Sex (Melba the diva). Therefore "something large and comprehensive" is latent in this "hectic little book," only seen from "below the water-surface, the layers of habit and of reason." What Purdy sees "with his disturbingly unfamiliar eyes is a crucial portion of the truth about ourselves," recorded with "uncommon and inimitable fidelity."[102]

In September, veteran critic Granville Hicks called *Malcolm* opaque in the *Saturday Review*, not his cup of tea.[103] It was not an attack, since Hicks called *Color of Darkness* "grimly impressive" and said Purdy's "disciplined style is enough to entitle him to respect, and his grotesque characters are brilliantly conceived." Hicks found *Malcolm* to be fantasy rather than comedy, its intentions nebulous. "It leaves me cold." Purdy fired off a scorched-earth letter to the editor printed in the *Saturday Review*, captioned "Purdy's Purge," ridiculing the periodical as indifferent to real literature, and recalling Hicks had been a communist. "Mr. Hicks, basing himself on the proletarian reality of the 1930s—to which he has been a fairly weak-kneed (*sic*) apostate—would naturally not be temperamentally capable of evaluating *Malcolm* as a work of literature." Purdy concluded: "As to Granville Hicks and his ilk, sitting their chairs of retirement and spouting guff about 'reality,' the quicker they leave the literary scene, the better."[104] If the editors considered Purdy's response ill-advised, they did not show it, since they later gave *The Nephew* a positive review by William Peden.[105] "Purdy's Purge" underscores his basically liberal anticommunist views embracing individual artistic freedom. In a 1971 letter, Purdy continued to vent: "There is probably nobody more disgusting than a fashionable weathercock pink like Granville Hicks, who was radical as long as it paid off to be, then he became quite respectable, but still as stupid and dull as ditchwater."[106] Purdy told interviewer Fred Barron: "So many critics grew up in the 1930s, in Marxism, which is one of the worst disciplines for a literary critic" because it is a formula that "cripples the brain and your sense of values." Purdy opposed all nostrums. "You can't apply a formula to a work of art" that is "new and will resist it." The "old Marxist mossbacks always condemned" his books for not being socially relevant. "But they are." It was hard to please such hidebound "political people," he told French interviewer Marie-Claude Profit.[107] Purdy's politics were liberal, but ultimately he was not partisan and was widely accepting, quoting the credo of the Roman comic dramatist, Terence: "Homo sum, humani nihil a me alienum puto": I am human; therefore nothing human is alien to me.

Though Hicks irritated Purdy, Hellman celebrated him. In late September, Lillian Hellman proposed Purdy for an Academy of Arts and Letters award, seconded by Dorothy Parker and Glenway Wescott, an openly gay poet and novelist who had been part of the 1920s expatriate scene, but he did not win it this time.[108] Hellman also gave a blurb for *Malcolm* that was used in advertising: "I have admired Mr. Purdy from his earliest stories. '*Malcolm*' is a brilliantly comic book. Mr. Purdy is his own man, and that's a wonderful thing for a writer to be."[109]

In October, Purdy revealed to columnist Lee Segal aspects of his technique and how he found ideas. Once he had a story, he liked to "strip it of it ready meanings, down to the basic human thing itself." One must never study people any more than "go out to love them or frame them or condescend to them. It's best just to relax, keep your senses awake and, in the words of Henry James, let nothing be wasted on you." Living in New York gave him opportunity to mingle with strangers, which stimulated his writing; preserving anonymity allowed him to listen better. Often, a chance remark from an unknown person provided inspiration for part or all of a story. He sometimes even phoned people whose stories appeared in newspapers.[110]

In late November 1959, he revised *The Nephew* based on praise and criticism from Giroux of the first two hundred pages of his draft. Giroux wanted to discuss "several problems that should not be lost sight of. Particularly toning down the suspense or mystery aspects of 'What was Cliff *really* like?' I'm sure this is not the point of the book, but there's a chance this could run away with it. Your theme, as I take it, is 'What is Alma like?' and we learn (so does she, in a dim way) through Cliff's disappearance." Give the town a name and decide whether the school is a university or a small college, since this matters.[111] Purdy was fortunate to work with such a sensitive editor and friend.[112]

Throughout the winter, Giroux annotated *The Nephew* and Purdy revised. In December, FSC called Purdy into the office: they thought *The Nephew* "very remarkable." If he would make a few minor changes—such as, removing a character who was electrocuted by falling into telephone wires, which the publisher had determined was implausible—they wanted to publish. Purdy had told Powys *The Nephew* would be dedicated to him, but Giroux asked if the book could be co-dedicated to him. Bob "pleaded very hard, which was rather queer for an editor. Then he said, You know I have gone through hell and high water to get your books published."

In the December 1959 *Esquire*, Dorothy Parker hailed *Malcolm* as the "most prodigiously funny book to streak across these heavy-hanging times."[113] This was a crucial review: only after Parker raved over *Malcolm* was it noticed, Purdy maintained.[114] *Malcolm*, Parker wrote, was one of the "major miracles of ink and paper": its varied characters would last her through the years, all "loud with life" and "perfectly outrageous." Praising Purdy's "unique quality of mercy," she concluded: "I have no claim, the Lord knows, to be counted among the special nor have I the voice to shout hosannas or the eyes to see into the future. I do not know how James Purdy will be rated, come the next century. I know only that I believe he is a writer of the highest rank in originality, insight and power, and if, in the Two Thousands, there is a grain of consciousness left among my dust, I will still believe it."[115]

While working on his own writing, Purdy delved deeper into the work of a favorite writer, Herman Melville. He deemed *Mardi* a "very queer book" and Melville was "certainly a very peculiar man even for an American writer," he told Powys. Purdy greatly admired Melville because he "went his own way and was ignored by society," he later said. Melville's books were "almost, perhaps, the only literature that can still be read from either the nineteenth or twentieth century. At least I go on rereading them and finding new things about them." He added that Jean Genet is a "very, very fine writer," and later placed *Our Lady of the Flowers* on a top-ten list, and admired stories by Jean-Paul Sartre. Among American writers, he also admired Nathaniel Hawthorne, Sherwood Anderson, and certain works by Edgar Allan Poe, Stephen Crane ("George's Mother"), Theodore Dreiser (*An American Tragedy*), Willa Cather ("Paul's Case"), and William Faulkner ("A Rose for Emily" and *Absalom, Absalom!*).[116]

Amid work on the novel, he completed a peculiar story, "Daddy Wolf," a monologue partly based on "the 'confession' of one of the petty criminals" he heard "at the Night Court" in New York, he later said. The language he heard was "that good rich American talk, as it seems only the old American stock is arrested, the Jews and Italians and Poles not so often arrested, but the Negroes and the Americans from the South are often on trial for things like vagrancy, street-walking, stealing apples, striking men in saloons, or exposing oneself in public." The parlance of these men, the police who arrested them, and the judges who admonished them were of great interest, giving him material.[117] He thought *Encounter* would publish it, he told Powys, which seems naïve. They rejected it, limning as it does poverty and squalor, presenting a negative image of America and thus counteracting the loose agenda of that CIA-financed magazine. In late 1960, Purdy sent Powys a copy of "Daddy Wolf," which was published in *New World Writing*. It had "horrified the publishers, the old farts, nearly all of them. I am tired of grown up people being horrified, but if they weren't, maybe there would be no point in us being writers."[118]

In December 1959, writer Italo Calvino, during a tour of the United States, visited Purdy at home. Calvino was on the editorial staff at Giulio Einaudi Editore in Turin, which would publish a translation of *Color of Darkness* in 1960. Disillusioned by the Soviet invasion of Hungary in 1957, Calvino had left the Italian Communist Party. While he still endorsed principles of global communism, he never joined another party. The US government saw a propaganda opportunity here, and floated Ford Foundation money for Italo to tour New York City and the country. Despite stringent domestic restrictions against non-citizens holding communist views, he stayed for six months during 1959 and 1960, four of them in New York. Before meeting Purdy, Calvino mingled at parties with several New York patrons, critics, and publishers who worked with Purdy including Barney Rosset, James Laughlin, and Sheila Cudahy, vice president of Farrar, Straus, and Cudahy. Calvino dined at the apartment of author and critic Giuseppe Prezzolini and met aristocrats including a Hungarian count and Cudahy, whom he described as a Catholic widow of the Marquis Pellegrini, with whom she had run Cudahy Pellegrini press. Calvino did not hear good reports on Purdy, however, which indicates that right from the start James might have benefited from stronger support from his publisher. In Calvino's limited experience, Purdy was not being discussed by the literati nor did he appear on their lists of best living writers. Likewise, Norman Mailer did not mention Purdy in his frank essay on his (male) literary competition, "Evaluations: Quick and Expensive Comments on the Talent in the Room," collected in *Advertisements for Myself* (1959). Calvino writes: "N.B. Opinions on Purdy and particularly on *Malcolm* are negative even in the Farrar Straus environment. I have not found anyone who had a good word to say about Purdy; on the other hand, yesterday evening they were unanimous in lauding [Bernard] Malamud as the great new writer; an interesting verdict coming from Catholics. Consequently, in this year's planning [of Einaudi's translations of American books], I would say to promote Malamud more than Purdy." He never met Farrar, Straus, or Giroux, however. Like Straus, Malamud, Mailer, and Salinger, a writer he admired, "seventy-five percent of the publishing world is Jewish. Ninety per cent of the theater is Jewish," Calvino reckoned. At Prezzolini's place, after "days of meeting only Jews, this mixing with reactionary Catholics" was a "not unpleasant distraction," the communist remarked.[119]

Calvino's conclusions oddly support Purdy's emerging feeling that Jewish writers were being privileged and his later theory that he was unsupported and later undermined by Farrar, Straus. In *Making It*, Podhoretz writes that by the 1950s, the "New York literary world" had acquired an identity popularly called an "Establishment," later known as the New York Intellectuals. Not the first, Podhoretz used a metaphor of a Jewish family to describe this establishment. Not all "core members" were Jewish; "nevertheless, the term 'Jewish' can be allowed to stand by clear majority rule and by various peculiarities of temper." In the 1960s, thanks to rising prominence in publishing during the previous decade, Jews enjoyed a "newly chic status," Podhoretz writes.[120]

After visiting Purdy's home on Henry Street, Calvino wrote in his diary that Purdy is a

> very pathetic character, middle-aged, big and fat [*sic*] and gentle, fair and reddish in complexion, and clean-shaven: he dresses soberly, and is like [poet Carlo Emilio] Gadda without the hysteria, and exudes sweetness. If he is homosexual, he is so with great tact and melancholy. At the foot of his bed is weight-lifting equipment; above it, a nineteenth-century English print of a boxer. There is a reproduction of a Crucifixion by Rouault, and scattered all around are theology books. We discuss the sad state of American literature, which is stifled by commercial demands: if you don't write as the "New Yorker" demands, you don't get published. Purdy published his first book of short stories at his own expense [*sic*], then he was discovered in England by Edith Sitwell, and subsequently Farrar Straus published his work, but he does not even know Mrs. Cudahy, and the critics don't understand him, though [*Malcolm*] is, very slowly, managing to sell. There are no magazines that publish short stories, no groups of writers, or at least he does not belong to any group. He gives me a list of good novels, but they are nearly all unpublished works which have not been able to find a publisher. Good literature in America is clandestine, lies in unknown authors' drawers, and only occasionally someone emerges from the gloom breaking through the leaden cloak of commercial production.

Calvino would have liked to have talked about socialism and capitalism with Purdy, but he would not have understood, since "no one here suspects that socialism exists, capitalism wraps itself round and permeates everything, and its antithesis is nothing but a meagre, childish claim to a spiritual dimension, devoid of any coherent line or prospects." Calvino seemed to disfavor Purdy's skewed individualism.[121]

Even so, Italo Calvino grew to esteem Purdy's writing. Calvino had planned to publish a book from his American travel notes but when he saw the proofs, he canceled the book, perhaps because of how critical he seems. In the fall of 1961, Calvino was training a young literary critic, Guido Davico Bonino, to take over his position as director of Einaudi. Bonino said that although Calvino was "very critical of American literature" being published in those years, he said, "little prized in his own country but in my opinion a real writer is James Purdy," who was "certainly influenced by Poe, a homosexual who speaks of separation as an obsession, but with a gently dazed sweetness all his own." Einaudi had published *63: Palazzo del Songo* but it "sold very poorly: let's hope they let us continue with him." While Calvino and Bonino were with Giulio Einaudi, they published seven more Purdy books in translation, though they waited until 1965 to publish *Malcolm*.[122]

Closer to the earth amid such rarefied literary discourse, Purdy during the early 1960s sustained a long, weird correspondence with Neely Orme, an insurance agent and former cotton buyer of Marvell, Arkansas, whom Purdy met in Chicago.[123] Their correspondence shows that Purdy now held ambivalence or even hostility to some of his old Chicago friends. Neely was a mutual friend of Osborn and Miriam Andreas and lived with Maud, seemingly his wife, though Purdy calls her Neely's mother. In March 1960, Purdy wrote: "I never hear from Miriam-Marian or her epic former spouse O.A." James promised to come to Arkansas when he could but *The Nephew* had "to be finished to perfection. It is killing me. . . . Every word has to be right. I hope you will continue to write me, and be good to me." He scolded and pleaded with Neely: "Why can't you be better and kinder to me. Why can't you appreciate my tireless efforts to make you beautiful and interesting and important [with imaginative fake news releases and anonymous letters]. Think of all those millions of unanswered words I have sent over the mule paths beyond Memphis. . . . Neely, you are important, you are beautiful, you are real."[124] In 1962, Miriam Andreas wrote from Bell Hill Farm, Cobden, Illinois, saying that Orme had stayed with her, but he made too many phone calls and acted "fresh, smart, babyish & unlikeable & although he doesn't know it, he can't come here again." She was returning to "the Chicago place."[125] In 1964, Purdy lashed out at Neely, Osborn, and especially Miriam in resentment:

> You and Miriam must be said to shed crocodile shit in your noble fear I might earn some money. There you both are protected on your fat asses, she hasn't lifted a finger to do anything for 40 years, kept by a crook, who wanted her drunk, wanted her irresponsible, wanted her cruel so he might feel he was alive.
>
> You cant admire such people. If she's the smartest woman you ever knew, I feel sorry for you. / She's smart like a lynx or a wolf. / She wouldn't give a penny to a starving roger. / You should give up the gin and clear your brain by having men exercise you up to your adam's apple then down to your corns / Yours, with a chiding tongue, / JAMES / All of Miriam's values are rotten, to be rich and show off, to have read right books and flash to have right this that. She is quite plebianly a shitty snob, but with such insane feelings of inferiority she could never be the Big American Flash she would like to be. She represents everything rotten in America today. Her charm is that she has totally failed to be Miss America Slob. This makes her human as if a turd aspired to be a dove.
>
> You <u>fool</u>![126]

Despite his criticism of Neely, James visited the Ormes in Arkansas at least once.

Purdy's creative friends responded to *Malcolm* with moving letters from around the world. In January 1960, Paul Bowles wrote a poignant letter from Tangier about his wife, writer Jane Bowles, who had suffered a stroke: "*Malcolm* is the first complete book that Jane has read,—and the only one—since her illness three years ago. It took her three and a half months, exactly, to complete the reading, but the fact that she was actually able to do it is a miracle. The other day I noticed that she was depressed, but said nothing; a little later she said sadly: 'Malcolm's dead.' She lived in the book during the time she was reading it; she says it is one of the great books of the century." Now that Jane had finished it, Paul could reread it.[127]

Virgil Thomson wrote: "Your *Malcolm* has made me infinitely happy. It seems to leave a residue also. I find myself remembering it all the time."[128] A delighted Purdy replied quickly, sharing his unlisted phone number. Purdy had first met Thomson through Van Vechten; those two seemed to know everyone and were skilled at matching talents and personalities for collaborations and friendships.[129] In more pleasing news about the novel, Gallimard purchased *Malcolm* for a French translation and "paid a very fine sum," so he would be "eating regularly at least until summer!" He was living simply and cooking nearly all his own meals.[130]

In March, Purdy's financial situation was greatly improved when he was awarded a Ford Foundation grant of $7,500 to produce drama. He would work with the Actors Studio, it was reported.[131] Norman Holmes Pearson, Yale professor of English and American Studies, and CIA liaison-recruiter, reached out: "The news of the Ford award coincided with the full moon. This is divine lunacy, and may it touch us all in time. Congratulations! I couldn't be more pleased." Pearson's allusion to "divine lunacy" is intriguing, hinting that strings were pulled from high places, perhaps with his involvement. As noted, the Ford Foundation was used to channel CIA funding, and "at times, it seemed the Ford Foundation was simply an extension of government in the area of international cultural propaganda," Frances Stonor Saunders writes. Pearson was "an OSS-CIA *incunabula*" who trained future OSS and CIA officers at Yale whom he recruited. His confidant and most famous protégé was the modernist literary man and CIA officer, James Jesus Angleton.[132] During Pearson's work for the OSS in London during World War II, he became friends with Purdy's champion, Edith Sitwell, and her writer brothers, Osbert and Sacheverell, and was a good friend of former OSS colleague, Archibald MacLeish, brother of Norman.[133] Pearson was therefore ideally disposed and positioned to support Purdy behind the scenes. For example, in April, Pearson replied to Purdy: "Of course I'll write to Mr. Richardson of Lippincott, and hope he will." Stewart (Sandy) Richardson was an editor at J. B. Lippincott and coedited the journal *New World Writing*, published in mass-market paperback format by Lippincott. It is unknown what Purdy had requested, but later that year, "Daddy Wolf" appeared in *New World Writing*. In December, Pearson sent his appreciation for the story: "I always admire the way you feel things through your ears. If the snow melts some February day, why come to New Haven anyway. Or we can meet in some steamroom in New York where it's sure to. Affectionately, Norman." Also in 1960, J. B. Lippincott published *Paradigms for Psychopathology* by Purdy's friend, Dr. John Bucklew, who acknowledged help from James Purdy of the Spanish department.[134] Finally, in mid-1961, Lippincott reissued *Color of Darkness* in a quality paperback series.

In 1960, Purdy hit a peak of critical acclaim and he continued to be showered with an embarrassment of riches. He informed Powys of the Ford

Foundation grant to pursue his writing, and he was most grateful to them and to Powys for recommending him. He was offered a second Guggenheim fellowship, but when the Guggenheims learned of the Ford Foundation grant, they asked him "to relinquish their fellowship," as they felt, he gathered, that with two, he would "be apt to become a plutocrat and take to doing nothing at all!" He was also named a finalist for the 1960 National Book Award for *Malcolm*, something he apparently later forgot, since in 1967 he told FSG that he rejected an invitation to attend an National Book Award luncheon because he had never been nominated, as though he did not exist. "I regard these yearly invitations to sit down with my enemies as utterly revolting, and *I want them stopped*." In 1960 he also received a Rockefeller Foundation grant. Like the Ford Foundation, there were close connections between the funds and the US government including the CIA, and the Rockefellers had granted large subsidies to the Congress for Cultural Freedom. Both foundations were integral parts of "America's Cold War machinery," Saunders writes. Regardless of the source, these grants meant that Purdy could relax about money and focus without distraction on writing.[135]

In March 1960, another recent Ford Foundation recipient, James Baldwin, reappeared in New York after living in Paris. He reached out to Purdy. "Dear Jim, Back in the zoo, and feeling very strange. Up to my neck in work. Will give you a call after the weekend, or you call me. . . . Looking forward to seeing you."[136]

In April, the American writer and poet Conrad Aiken accepted three poems for the journal *Botteghe Oscure*, which was based in Rome, directed by a princess (American-born Marguerite Caetani), and edited by poet Giorgio Bassani. "Vendrá," "An Ode to Godwin Dwight," and "Merry-go-round Horses and Carousel" were Purdy's first published poems. Purdy writes: "Merry-go-round horses' eyes are jewels / and when they look at you they have only that one look: / *Come into the Enchantment*."[137] Purdy first sent them to Van Vechten in 1957 along with a signed postcard of dance photographer and World War II veteran Dwight Godwin (his actual name) in military uniform.[138] In "Ode," Purdy writes: "your eyes show strain, though beauty, / as though perhaps you cheated at cards / or in the silence of a very quiet room / struck a boy with a knife / your high reticulate brow / shows a tempest of conflicting thoughts." It is unclear whether Purdy was stationed with Godwin, who was part of the invasion of the Philippines.

In May 1960, *Malcolm* was published in Britain by Secker & Warburg. A few months earlier, Purdy enjoyed meeting Fredric Warburg and his wife,

Pamela de Bayou, in New York.[139] Purdy's change in publisher better aligned with the Cold War climate. Victor Gollancz was a communist-sympathizer, while Purdy's new publisher, Secker & Warburg, was both anticommunist and antifascist, thus amenable to the Congress for Cultural Freedom, which paid them to print *Encounter*. Secker & Warburg tended to publish works by authors of the anti-Stalinist left. Reviewing the British edition, David Daiches, the distinguished Scottish and Jewish critic, called *Malcolm* stunning, a "splendid mixture of farce and realism." Daiches, who had encountered "nothing like it in modern fiction," noted Purdy's literary strategy of defamiliarization, how he gazes at common aspects of American society with "such disturbing steadiness that the familiar becomes bizarre under his (and our) eyes and the real turns into the fantastic." It was moreover "a very funny book." The *Times* of London said "Purdy writes like an angel, with accuracy, wit, and freshness, but a fallen angel, versed in the sinful ways of man."[140]

Purdy had seemingly not been back to Ohio to see family for years. For William Purdy's eighty-third birthday in June, Purdy sent a dozen red roses. Will replied with thanks, sharing that "the Real Estate boys and the Chamber of Commerce" threw him a birthday party with some small gifts. Apparently having trouble with vision and memory, he had not been able to drive his car for a few months, but hoped to resume soon since he couldn't "attend to this kind of work without a car." His grandson David recalled that a year or two before, while he was riding his bike around his hometown, Berea, he spied a familiar green Ford and pedaled up to it. "Papa?" Will was trying to visit, but got lost. "Follow me!" William hoped the new book he was writing would bring "much success" financially and professionally.[141]

The wolf, Daddy or otherwise, was no longer at the door. The wolf, in fact, had not been seen in a while. At the start of the 1960s, Purdy, acclaimed by copious writers and critics, was receiving abundant help and encouragement from several parties.

9

Threshold of Assent

In October 1960, Farrar, Straus & Cudahy published *The Nephew*, a special work that became a favorite of many Purdy aficionados. Purdy dedicated it to John Cowper Powys and Robert Giroux. The novel, telling of Aunt Alma Mason's quest to create a memorial to her nephew, Cliff Mason, marked a development, showing his ability to write a Midwestern realism, but one laced with strangeness and dark humor. After reading an advance copy, Carl Van Vechten told Donald Gallup it is "completely different from his past work in subject matter and is quite an extraordinary performance. Written, as usual, with enormous skill."[1] The book was also written with love—especially for his father and Aunt Cora. Poet Thom Gunn later wrote that at the close of *The Nephew*, through "the widening of her sympathies," Alma learns "we love only as we can, not necessarily as we want to, and most often our love is indirect, hidden, perhaps even unrecognized for what it is." The novel "is itself Purdy's act of love, and one of great strength and permanence."[2]

To William Carlos Williams, who provided lengthy blurbs, Purdy had "such a way of biting into the bare core of our lives," that great Russian writers such as Gorky "could not have done better."[3] So profoundly had he captured the essence of the American town, that Williams was moved to say: "Rainbow City"—Rainbow Center is setting of *The Nephew*—"where I grew up and practiced medicine for 42 years—is proud of you. You have squeezed us in a ball, tenderly, heart and soul, and laid us bare with complete understanding. If we like ourselves, we must be satisfied and if we do not like ourselves, we must acknowledge that we have been treated fairly." Williams was "much affected by a fine piece of writing."[4] Purdy was "overjoyed and proud" that "America's greatest living poet" felt what he "had hoped so much others would feel."[5]

As Purdy worked on his play, *Madonna*, felicitous responses to *The Nephew* filled his mailbox.[6] In September, drama critic Brooks Atkinson, "flattered to receive" an inscribed *Nephew*, was "delighted" with it as soon as he began reading. "I can't tell you how much I admire it," he wrote. "It is thoroughly original, always under control" and apparently "owes nothing to what anyone else is writing today."[7] Paul Bowles read an advance copy as soon as it arrived and was "completely delighted." Purdy had "done something quite new." Ivy Compton-Burnett had "done it for the English, but nobody has done it for the Americans until this book." *The Nephew* emerges "wholly fresh,—a new thing. I loved *Malcolm*, but it was a tour de force and therefore unique. This has nothing of the tour de force about it, and is therefore more brilliant."[8]

Readers struggled to articulate the oddly moving quality of *The Nephew*. Poet James Merrill, who was openly gay, found *The Nephew* "very strange and beautiful." He concluded a note to Purdy: "When I reached the end I felt I had a prism in my hands." He asked if James would like to come out to visit him at his home in southeastern Connecticut for a few days. Purdy first met Merrill and his partner, writer and artist David Jackson, in late 1959.[9] Novelist and poet Robert Penn Warren, a major literary figure, wrote with thanks for an inscribed copy. Disagreeing with Bowles, he wrote, "It is a glittering tour de force, but also a great deal more, with sharp stabs of reality throughout, a strong and impressive book." He was "happy to see it so well appreciated by the press."[10]

While *The Nephew* at first appears to be familiar Midwestern realism, it emerges as odd and funny, bursting into moments of Purdian outrageousness. One example is deranged Mrs. Laird's racist, xenophobic rant ("shoot to kill!") as she watches television, winding down with a patriotic salute to the flag. Part of the black humor movement, Terry Southern praised *The Nephew* in his review for *The Nation*, referring to another scene as a "genuine surprise" exemplifying the difference between "the creative and the merely literary."[11] Purdy was sometimes lumped in with black humorists by critics, which he did not appreciate—refusing to join any club that would have him as a member. Nonetheless, Purdy could appreciate such writing. In 1959, he thanked Southern for sending *The Magic Christian*; he "laughed out loud through it, and what could be better than that." Jim wanted to see Terry if he ever came to New York. Purdy agreed to recommend Southern for "any of the Foundations, etc.—feel free to use my name—though I wonder if it will impress *them*." In 1962, Purdy wrote "as strong of a recommendation as [he] dared" for Southern to the Guggenheim foundation.[12] Within a couple of years, then, he went from just receiving these prestigious fellowships to also recommending them for others.

Along with Southern's positive review, Webster Schott lauded Purdy and *The Nephew* in the *Kansas City Star*. "Without a doubt," Purdy was one of the "most conspicuous literary talents to appear in the United States since the end of World War II" and *The Nephew* is a "beautifully executed contemporary tragedy." It is "not a vast all-encompassing work of art" since Purdy is a "miniaturist" who makes "small paintings, with carefully defined limits and ambitions." This definition was interesting, given the influence of Abercrombie, who executed many miniature works. But Purdy's characters move with the "vitality of their life-size sources, and to be appraised, his skills must be contrasted with those of only the greatest miniaturists in literature—Anderson, Chekhov, Flaubert." *The Nephew* was "by far the finest thing" he had written, "one of the best novels of the year and perhaps years to come."[13] Yet there was no consensus: novelist Herbert Gold in *The New Republic* thought the plot was a "mere excuse for a curious parody of a Norman Rockwell illustration or an Edgar Lee Masters poem."

Back in Ohio, Vera was "so excited" and happy over the "wonderful publicity" *The Nephew* had received and the praise it was earning from critics. She felt encouraged about Richard, who was living with her and John Bauman in their Findlay home, because he was working long hours at his new job and did not have time to drink. Richard was planning to talk to the local head of Alcoholics Anonymous. She hoped he would become healthy enough to be "self-supporting and get a place of his own" so she "wouldn't have so much extra work and could rest more" and noted, "I have carried a heavy burden these past few years. Maybe it will all work out some day." In the meantime she credited James, "Your good letters and love have given me great comfort and help and my heart is grateful even greater than you know."[14]

Esquire continued to support Purdy and paid well. In its October 1960 issue, *Esquire* published a dark story of suffering, "Goodnight Sweetheart," selected by Rust Hills. It tells of a teacher who was raped and her clothes stolen in an act of revenge, who turns to a former student for shelter. Purdy finished the story in April, and *Esquire* accepted it in May, paying him $750 (about $5,675 in 2020). FSC, which was now serving as his agent for stories, took 10 percent.[15] This seems an unusual arrangement, but Purdy didn't want Strassman to represent his new stories and had no other agent lined up. Just a few months later, Hills was already reaching out to Roger Straus since he felt "a little out of touch with James Purdy" and wondered if he had stories available. If Purdy was working on a novel, *Esquire* wanted a chance at some form of prepublication. "I know you always think of us in regard to Purdy, but I just want to let you know that I was thinking of him too. Is there anything?"[16] He was in an enviable spot.

While the *Esquire* issue was on the newsstands, Purdy was sick in bed with what he thought was sciatic flu. He also had conjunctivitis in one eye and looked like he had been in a fight.[17] Within a month, though, he was feeling better and writing a "new book about a man who got out of the penitentiary and fell in love with two women at the age of 42." He took many walks and returned to the night court to hear the speech cadences of "petty criminals on trial."[18] In the cold of December, he contended with a temporary failure of light and heat in his building.[19]

Purdy's public profile was rising. In October, Nolan Miller, editor of the *Antioch Review*, wrote FSC asking for biographical data on Purdy, as he was planning a feature. He had "the feeling the excitement being generated by James Purdy, the expectancy of each new work, is significant. There's been nothing like it since a figure of such size as Hemingway." Giroux replied his office was the "best place to send mail to Mr. Purdy, who comes in regularly."[20]

In November, the as-yet-unknown writer Joan Didion praised *The Nephew* in William F. Buckley's *National Review*. Although Didion is some-what critical of what she saw as conventionality in this Midwestern novel, she concludes Purdy transcends this limitation. *The Nephew* is a "sure, spell-binding, chillingly good little novel, an uncanny triumph of matter over mind. Like Mr. Purdy's far more surrealist *63: Dream Palace*, *The Nephew* compels by the sheer brilliance of its telling."[21]

Since Purdy tended to model the characters of *The Nephew* upon local persons in Bowling Green, Ohio, the book became a *succès de scandale* in his father's hometown. Besides William Purdy and Aunt Cora Purdy, these included a handful of neighbors including two professors; when some read the novel, they were upset or disturbed by their presumed portrayal. Its set-ting, the college town of Rainbow Center, was a "near reflection" of Bowling Green.[22] Gradual awareness of the novel's contents rocked the town as copies were passed around and friends and neighbors debated which character was based on whom.[23] Bowling Green State University professors later recalled that "local anger" erupted over similarities between "fictional characters and real persons": "Bowling Green residents, especially at the time the novel was published, thought that all of the characters were patterned after local per-sons; many in Bowling Green were upset with the Purdy novel, even though others recognized that he wrote well."[24] Within a month of its publication, already "quite a demand" for *The Nephew* had grown locally, William shared. In February 1961, Will, still in real estate, asked his son for a signed copy to give to the manager of City Loan Company. Will was proud the novel was publicized in the *New York Times* and elsewhere. Yet it is not clear he ever read a James Purdy book, perhaps fearing what he might find.[25] In March, in the BGSU Union, the Books and Coffee club discussed Purdy's work, especially *The Nephew* and whether it was "brilliantly written." Introduced by Dr. Edgar Daniels, the novel was "criticized from many points of view." Because Purdy had lived in BG, he could write with realism derived from experience, which was not appreciated by all. Knowing that a small town's odor of ketchup is "a reality, rather than a figment of the author's imagination, seemed to color the objectiveness of those criticizing the novel."[26]

Purdy based Professor Mannheim, the perennial subject of small-town scandal and rumor, on his former neighbor, Dr. Frederick Nordmann, who taught him history over the course of four semesters. In *The Nephew*, Alma Mason recalls overhearing Mannheim's first wife in tears, telling Cliff: "You must never repeat what I have told you about the professor," which aroused in her suspicion of "indiscretions with co-eds."[27] Mrs. Van Tassel tells Alma of how she, long ago, accidentally discovered Mannheim, who was married, with a coed *in flagrante delicto* in a dark cemetery. After Mannheim's first wife died, he married a former student and lived quietly.[28] Likewise, in Bowling Green, after Dr. Nordmann's first wife Agnes died, in 1937 he was married to a former student over a dozen years his junior, Marjorie I. McKee, an elementary education major.

Professor Mannheim had one staunch defender, Faye Laird, modeled on another neighbor of the Purdys and a close friend of Cora's, Florence Baird, a Spanish professor. Purdy's portrayal of "midget-faced" Faye Laird was unflattering to Flo Baird, however. Laird's hopes for marriage having been thwarted by her mother, she carries on a secret affair with the much-younger Vernon Miller, who is apparently "kept" by an older man, Willard Baker. Like Faye Laird, "Miss Baird" (as she was known, though a professor) lived with and cared for her increasingly dependent mother, Ida Baird; Purdy regretted how Flo Baird's personal life was thwarted by her devotion to her mother. A Bowling Green resident was told Baird was "furious about the portrayal of her." Florence Baird retired in 1968 and that year, she sent Purdy a Christmas card with a handwritten note, suggesting she no longer held hard feelings.[29] In the novel, Faye tells Alma that Mrs. Barrington, the meddling "old monarch" who overlooks the town from her Victorian manse, tried to get Mannheim fired long ago on charges of "moral turpitude" that were never proven, just because he wrote a number of articles on Marx. Mrs. Barrington is partially modeled on Mrs. Belle Case Harrington, who wrote hymns and articles for women's magazines, who likewise lived in a splendid Victorian home directly south across the street with huge trumpet vines on trellises.[30]

Although Nordmann was more conservative than his fictional analog, he nevertheless understood being stigmatized just as well as Mannheim, but not for being Marxist during the Cold War. During the mid-1940s, as a German native, Nordmann had his career put in limbo during World War II. Purdy, opposed to Red Scare rhetoric, updates the story to the early 1950s, when left-wing academics were limited or fired because of unfavorable political views. To Faye, no one in Rainbow Center had "treated him as he deserves to be treated, as a scholar deserves to be treated. Certainly the college never had the decency to promote him, despite his achievements."[31] Purdy's story addresses an archetypal urge to scapegoat the other.

In *The Nephew*, the reader learns that Cliff Mason had once dissuaded Professor Mannheim from thoughts of suicide. On July 22, 1961, nine months after *The Nephew* was published, Frederick Nordmann hanged himself in the garage of his home, where his body was discovered by his wife. A close friend of professors Diane Pretzer and Wally Pretzer said Dr. Nordmann "felt that Purdy had so ruined his reputation that he committed suicide not long after expressing his utter dismay" to a professor of mathematics. In 1990, a BG resident wrote, "the second Mrs. Nordmann tried to prevent the library's circulation of the book."[32] Eerily, in the novel, Alma tells Mrs. Van Tassel, "Professor Mannheim doesn't look very strong or well," and if he "doesn't take care of himself, he won't be with us much longer, I fear." When Dr. Nordmann took his life, he had been ailing from heart trouble for several months and had been increasingly ill and despondent, but the novel and the controversy surrounding it in town contributed to his dark state of mind.[33] It is not known whether Purdy ever knew about his former professor's suicide.

Katherine Anne Porter, although she wished Purdy well, wrote in January to express displeasure that her private words praising *Color of Darkness* were being used for an ad for *The Nephew* and were slated to appear on the British jacket. Her personal policy was that only her published reviews could be used for blurbs. She confirmed that *Color of Darkness* is a "splendid collection." "I said so then and say it again, but not, please, for the dustjacket of the book as I did not intend it so." Porter was unhappy his publishers had failed to ask permission to use her "privately expressed opinion" as a blurb. "I simply detest this whole business, and will not take part in it, and I want you to please call them at once and tell them unequivocally that they must not use my name or word on any cover" or ad without her "express permission." Porter offered the younger writer food for thought: although she believed she had been blessed with the best press any contemporary writer had received, it did not seem to help her sales much, which were small but steady, "just long life with honor, which is what we all really want, isn't it?" "It's been a good life, with no tracks in it. I wish you not only as well, but better!" Two days later, she wrote: "My life for all these years has amounted to a state of siege on this jacket business." The day before, a friend showed her the jacket of *Malcolm* using the words she had written of *Color of Darkness*. Just between the two of them, she confessed she was not a fan of *Malcolm*. "All good short story writers have the devil of a time getting published and we have to help each other; but they mustn't take a paragraph written for one book and attach it to another as if it were written for *that* occasion," she chided. "Forgive me," she asked. "I am going to read *The Nephew* and I expect to be entirely convinced" but in the meantime, "we have this sad little episode." Purdy intervened to remove her words from the British *Nephew*. This was "a most disturbing collision," Purdy told Giroux, explaining that Porter agreed to allow her quotation to stand on the forthcoming Lippincott reissue of *Color of Darkness*, but not on any other edition or work—adding that Yale had ordered 350 copies of this edition for fall courses.[34] Ironically, Porter's words of praise would reappear on Purdy book jackets.

In March 1961, Secker & Warburg published *The Nephew* in Britain and issued *Colour of Darkness* with a preface by Edith Sitwell, restoring the word *motherfucker* that resoundingly concludes *63: Dream Palace*, which Gollancz had replaced with *little bugger*. Fred Warburg thought *The Nephew* was his best book. Angus Wilson offered a dust jacket blurb: "Mr. James Purdy is one of the few novelists whose progress really excites me. After the baroque elaboration of his earlier work, he has found in *The Nephew* a magnificent simplicity. But let no one be deceived. This simple-seeming story of the innocence of old age is a complex, reverberating work with a subtle dialogue that constantly makes the reader turn his head as the second meanings overtake him."[35] Edith Sitwell, astonished by the quality of writing and moved to tears by Purdy's "compassion and insight into poor human nature," wrote that it was "great in the same way Balzac was great,—yet without his hatred." She declared: "If *The Nephew* is not acclaimed a masterpiece, it will be a disgrace both to England and America."[36] For the *Observer*, English critic John Davenport reviewed *Colour of Darkness* and *The Nephew*, which was his "best book," a "modest masterpiece." Even when he dives "deep into the waters of perversity he never drowns in them." He is a "moralist, but a compassionate one; he is too wise to preach." As for *63: Dream Palace*, the Dostoevskian novella was "on its way to becoming a modern classic."[37] Purdy was "open-mouthed with astonishment" at this beautiful review.[38]

Despite cold weather, James, sometimes with Jorma, would climb up to the roof of their building to stargaze. With tensions between the United States and Cuba and its ally Russia soaring, Purdy remarked that he had been "sure we would have all been blown up by now by the Russians, but here we are looking up at the constellations in their nightly progress," he wrote Powys.[39] Within days, New Yorkers were hit by bone-chilling snowstorms. On February 6, Purdy was "snowed in under 18 inches of snow, eating canned salmon and Finnish bread, and not going out." New York was "paralyzed— the worst weather since 1881—since Walt Whitman!"[40]

After the snow relented, in March, Purdy saw Ionesco's *Rhinoceros* on Broadway. Despite finding it boring, he made a useful connection to critic Theodore Solotaroff, who sent Purdy some of his work, which Purdy complimented as "quite heroic."[41] Purdy was also writing plays; by late March, he had written an as-yet untitled short play that a producer was interested in staging. "It only lasts an hour," he told Powys, "but he said that was all any audience could stand, they would all go home and get drunk after it was over."[42] In September, Purdy wrote a play called *Professor McGowan and the Lemonade*, which was never produced or published.

In March, in a form of intellectual teasing or trolling, Purdy again sent his books to the Austrian-American émigré psychoanalyst Dr. Edmund Bergler (1899–1962), with whom he had a vigorous correspondence. A prolific author and critic of Dr. Alfred Kinsey, Dr. Bergler called homosexuality a perversion and denied the existence of bisexuality.[43] In 1956, he published *Homosexuality: Disease or Way of Life?*, concluding it was a disease that could be cured, one that reflected misogyny in the subject. Bergler's etiology of homosexuality was not biological, social, or Oedipal, but rather the product of an unsolved masochistic conflict with the mother during earliest infancy. Later in 1956, after reading stories in *Don't Call Me by My Right Name* with interest, Bergler wrote: "They show that you are familiar with basic masochistic motivations and pseudo-aggressive defenses in people." Bergler was concerned, though: "You are making unnecessary troubles for yourself by being too outspoken in some of your stories. Besides insisting on tragic themes exclusively, you avoid innuendos. Very captivating is the deep sympathy you show for your dramatis personae. Wishing you success."[44] After reading *The Nephew*, Bergler criticized Purdy's "morbid *literary* preoccupation with homosexuality" and warned he was "moving in the wrong direction." Bergler apprised Purdy of the "real aim of homosexuals: suffering." Bergler specialized in masochism, which he regarded the basic neurosis. In his next novel, *Cabot Wright Begins*, Purdy satirizes Dr. Bergler with the character Dr. Bugleford, who endorses compulsory heterosexuality and "fun" marriage for all.

Purdy plunged into this new book, an urban shocker after the relative Midwestern calm of *The Nephew*. He described the project to Powys: "Here it is June already, and we had no spring, we plunged from winter to summer. I have begun a new novel called *Cabot Wright Begins*, which concerns a well-known young rapist, who ravished nearly 300 women before he was caught. My publisher is somewhat sad I have chosen this, but gradually he has grown used to the idea, and now he is enthusiastic about what he has read. I never can believe I will finish any of the books I begin, they are so hard for me to do, and then step by step, day by day, somehow they are all written, perhaps done by a force hidden in the keys or the wood of the writing table."[45] In October, Paul Bowles wrote, "anxious to see your rape-novel, or anything else you write."[46]

In the meantime, his earlier work was getting renewed attention. In June of 1961, Lippincott published a quality paperback edition of *Color of Darkness* with an introduction by Sitwell in their Keystone Short Stories series. A full-page ad announcing the new series appeared in the summer issue of *Paris Review* and another full-page ad offered mail-order tickets for Gene Andrewski's future production of *Malcolm and Others by James Purdy* at the Poetry Center. Andrewski was a friend and supporter who in the summer of 1959 had visited Edith Sitwell several times at the Sesame Club in London where she stayed and they spoke warmly of Purdy.[47] Andrewski worked for the CIA-embedded and -funded *Paris Review*, for which he served as a managing editor and advertising director. Terry Southern, who was friends in Paris with the founders of *Paris Review*, later wrote a comical letter to Fayette Hickox, assistant to George Plimpton, pretending to think Mr. Hickox was a woman. Southern writes: "For many years, one of our senior staffers (like several of our staffers), a certain Gene Andrewski, functioned as a top operative in Paris with both the KGB *and* the CIA, using the Review Office and literary activities as his 'cover.' "[48] Although Southern is hyperbolic, Peter Matthiessen, a *Paris Review* editor who was an undercover CIA officer, later admitted he created the *Paris Review* as cover.[49] The *Paris Review* website states Matthiessen had been "sent to Paris by the newly created CIA. Recruited into the agency" by Norman Holmes Pearson, Matthiessen "agreed to the assignment largely for the opportunity it afforded him to pursue a career in writing."[50] Purdy inscribed copies of his books to Andrewski with "heart-felt thanks in friendship and with affectionate wishes."[51] Writer Elga Liverman Duval hosted a party for Purdy and this *Color of Darkness* reissue.[52] Duval was friends with figures of the 1950s New York art scene, such as Willem de Kooning and glass sculptor Adolph Gottlieb, and was married to the painter and stained glass sculptor Jean-Jacques Duval.

The New Leader, a liberal anticommunist journal covertly supported by the CIA, ran a homophobic takedown of *Color of Darkness* in its June issue.[53] Critic Alfred Sundel's invective is disturbing; he uses the word "faggot" seven times in one paragraph in facetiously summing up *63: Dream Palace*. Myron Kolatch, the new executive editor of *New Leader*, clearly had no problem with hate speech. Novelist and public intellectual Gore Vidal, in an essay on Tennessee Williams, explains: "During the forties and fifties the anti-fag battalions were everywhere on the march. From the high lands of *Partisan Review* to the middle ground of *Time* magazine, envenomed attacks on real and suspected fags never let up"; from 1945 to 1961, "*Time* attacked with unusual ferocity everything produced or published by Tennessee Williams."[54] Likewise, Sundel claims "Purdy's world is close to Capote's—a very special one of hopelessly effeminate male imagination."[55]

As for the author he was compared to, Truman Capote, in July 1961, in Palamós, Catalonia, he replied to his friend Andrew Lyndon that he had not read anything by James Purdy except, several years before, the story collection, which he found "interesting but unsuccessful." This phrase, Capote claimed, was Purdy's own assessment of an unspecified novel by the British Hispanist Gerald Brenan, who was an admirer of Purdy's work and corresponded with him.[56] Purdy had been friendly with the gay Southern novelist Donald Windham, but Donald had told Capote that Purdy was a "real little bitch." "Is he?" Capote asked Lyndon. "No, I guess he couldn't be or you wouldn't like him."[57] Ironically, twelve years earlier, Tennessee Williams wrote Windham from Naples after having a brief falling out with Capote over a "rather vicious anecdote" delivered by Capote. Tennessee, however, reversed his decision and would rejoin Truman and his lover. "Tell me! What do you think Truman is, a bitch or not?" the playwright wondered. "I can never quite make up my mind about it."[58] Donald Windham may have been upset because although Purdy had enjoyed his story collection, *The Warm*

Country (1960), he did not publicly endorse it. Van Vechten wrote Windham's partner, Sandy Campbell, saying that "Purdy DID receive *The Warm Country* and loved it. Purdy by nature is not generous and it is quite different for him to want letters about his own books and to be able to think that others may want letters about theirs. I am enthusiastic about Purdy, as you know, but it is difficult for me to write him about them and I never do until the time arrives when I HAVE to say something. Probably this is because his understood demand brings about a tension."[59]

That summer, Purdy was suffering "deep-seated depression over writing a new novel, and all the sunshine in the world isn't going to help."[60] He wrote Powys: "I am enjoying summer and trees and being outdoors all the time as much as I can with the 'contract' for my new novel hanging over my head; I never feel I will live through another book, they are too horrible! Still, I manage to." But in the fall, James said his drafting of *Cabot Wright Begins* was "going ahead, and since I have such a small audience, I am not taking any pains to spare that audience's sensibilities this time at all, if I ever did before. I am writing it exactly as I please and to the lowest hell with America." He was "very pleased" he had the roof to go up to, since he was growing tired of his room that he shared with Jorma, a "Finnish chemist, who is almost certainly an alchemist to boot." Purdy had been rising at 5 A.M. "to see Venus, now observable at that hour," and his favorite constellation, Orion; "his belt of three stars at the present time is very clear. Saturn and Jupiter are also beautiful earlier in the evening." Purdy spent most evenings on the roof of "this old house looking out to sea and to the sky."[61]

Purdy suggested some weariness with his living arrangement, and indeed, the studio apartment allowed no privacy, as it was basically one big room apart from the small bathroom. James and Jorma continued to share it, but it seemed to be more Purdy's place, as opposed to their previous residences. In 1959, Sjoblom got a job at Technical Research Group (TRG) on Long Island, doing research and development in solid state physics. For over a year, he commuted from Brooklyn to Melville on the Long Island Rail Road. He made new friends in Long Island and started going to bars. Meanwhile, as Purdy increasingly focused on his writing career and drafted *Cabot Wright* with intensity, he had less time to spend with Jorma, who began to feel like a "distraction." Around early 1962, Jorma moved out of Henry Street and relocated to Huntington. This way, Jorma could cease his taxing commute and Purdy could write in isolation, Jorma said. Ultimately, this was Purdy's decision. But they remained close and for a long while, Jorma still saw James "quite regularly, once a week." Jorma later met a "gypsy cab driver" from the Bronx and fell in love.[62]

Purdy was starting to receive significant royalty checks and sent some money home. In October, Vera told her son she was proud of his success and thanked him for a generous check. She said William had visited briefly, but he lived in the past and it was hard to communicate with him about the problem of Richard's alcoholism. In the previous year, she relayed, Richard drank a quart a day. He had gone to The Phoenix coffee shop to get a job, willing to do "anything for a dollar so he can buy whiskey." Both parents felt there was no sense in giving him money, as he would not use it well. "Richard acts like we owed him a living." It was placing a big strain on Vera's health. "Sunday we drove over to Hicksville & picked up Aunt LaVerne and then drove on to Butler, Indiana to spend the day with Bertha & Harold Bevington." Disturbingly, after dinner, Vera had "a terrible heart attack" but stabilized and did not mention being hospitalized. For Christmas, James sent his dad an azalea plant. Richard visited William and Cora in Bowling Green and Florence Baird came over to share Christmas dinner—which James would have enjoyed, Will wrote.[63]

Early in 1961, Will had not heard from Richard except for a thank-you letter for Christmas gifts. "Every time they get some new Doctor who is going to do wonders and nothing happens." William was afraid Richard might "make some legal offense" and cause "lots of trouble." Vera insisted Dick must not "go to any institution where he is confined and where he cannot get alcoholic stimulants."[64] In October, Will said Richard still drank "plenty of Whiskey" and he had taken Richard's case to his own doctor. After Christmas, Will told James he had "paid $445 for Richard in the past few weeks" since Vera "feared he might be arrested." Two banks wanted money that Richie had borrowed. A business, Fort Findlay House, held a claim that would "cause criminal trouble if neglected too long." But he got everything cleared up. Hearing this kind of news rankled James, who was trying to focus on his writing career.[65]

In October 1961, Oklahoma City native Gene Andrewski's dramatization and direction of *Malcolm and Others by James Purdy* debuted at the Poetry Center, at the YM-YWHA (Young Men's and Young Women's Hebrew Association), 92nd Street, an institution that was the site of many readings by famous poets and writers. A famous married couple, Zachary Scott and Ruth Ford, starred in the dramatized readings from short stories and *Malcolm* and Purdy himself played the Narrator. Ruth Ford, a model and actress of the stage and screen, declared that *63: Dream Palace* was the most extraordinary story she had ever read.[66] Ruth Ford also had an important role as a salonnière. For over four decades, she hosted in her Dakota apartment notable guests like William Faulkner, Tennessee Williams, Truman Capote, Edward Albee, and now, James Purdy.[67] Zachary Scott was known for film roles such as Joan Crawford's love interest in *Mildred Pierce* (1945) and various scoundrels. Ruth and Zachary were regulars at the gatherings at Van Vechten's apartment, where, near the entranceway, Carlo offered to guests a tall stack of copies of *Malcolm*, which Avon issued in mass-market paperback in 1960. James probably first met the acting couple there. After the show wrapped up, Purdy wrote the couple a "sweet letter." Ruth replied: "Even with all the trials and tribulations, it was a wonderful experience for us. All the hard work was a challenge and the fact that it turned out so well was very rewarding." Also starring were Betty Field, who had racked up copious Broadway and film credits, and Eli Wallach, a character-actor. Zachary Scott was the monologist of "Daddy Wolf"; Field and Wallach were "Man and Wife," and Philip Andrus was Malcolm.

In November, Purdy informed FSC that the esteemed agent Audrey Wood was going to handle his one-act play, "Children Is All," for production purposes. The longtime agent of Tennessee Williams, Wood became legendary in the theater world.[68] James was taken out to dinner by Wood's assistant Jack Phelps, who later became Purdy's manager after he struck out on his own. In February, Purdy finished revising "Children Is All," which centers on Edna Cartwright, a fifty-year-old Midwestern mother awaiting her son's arrival after release from prison. In reality, he breaks out of prison and is shot while escaping; when he arrives home, she does not recognize him, even as he dies in her arms. Years later, John Uecker pointed out to Purdy how Vera's failure to recognize Richard when he returned to Findlay from New York in 1957 was mirrored by the mother in the play.[69]

Although his new novel was not yet complete, Purdy wrote Bob Giroux, saying Tracy Brigden, fiction editor of *Mademoiselle*, was "most anxious to see the manuscript of *Cabot Wright Begins*, as she feels she would like to publish parts of it, before it appears in book form." Purdy said *Cabot* was "going ahead quite steadily but slowly." He added a postscript: "I am in some financial difficulties and if *Mademoiselle* would buy sections of *Cabot Wright*," this would help. Neither this nor any serialization transpired. It is hard to imagine a satirical novel about people wanting to write and publish a book about a serial rapist appearing in a women's "slick."[70] By 1962, Purdy was "over halfway through the first draft" of *Cabot Wright Begins*, he told Terry Southern, whose outrageous novels arguably inspired Purdy's no-holds-barred satire.[71]

In late 1961, Angus Wilson visited Purdy in New York with his younger partner, Tony Garrett. When they met, Angus was apparently surprised by Purdy's pallor; Purdy later remarked that when Wilson and Sitwell came to America, each had been "under the assumption" that he "was black."[72] Novelist Margaret Drabble writes: "Purdy offered them a break from the cocktail-party circuit by taking them to an old ale house near the Bowery, some off-limit drinking places, and the Night Court." Angus and Tony seemed "deeply absorbed in these proceedings," Purdy wrote.[73]

Purdy's work was reaching international audiences beyond Britain. It was even the topic of a broadcast by an American propaganda outlet. In February 1962, Radio Free Europe devoted a half-hour program to his work, broadcast from Munich to Prague in Czech. "*Malcolm* was discussed in detail, and also translated in part, and the other books commented on," Purdy told Straus. The broadcaster was Egon Hostovský, Jewish-Czech novelist, a past exile of fascism and "refugee from the present communist regime."[74] In May, the American journalist and historian Carleton Beals, a Latin American specialist, wrote saying he was pleased Purdy "had cracked TV in Cuba" with a recent story adaptation. Humberto Arenal, a friend of Purdy's friend and former student in Cuba, writer Edmundo Desnoes, translated "Don't Call Me by My Right Name."[75] "That speaks well for the Cubans is less well for the U.S.," Beals wrote (*sic*).[76]

In March, William thanked James for sending the Danish translation of *Malcolm*. "We were glad that you had it published, although we could not read it." Despite Will's advanced age, he still came to "the Office most every business day" and still hoped to "make good money" that year. "I use none for myself except the simplest needs." In June 1962, William told James that Richard, who was "living on the River Road west of Cleveland," was appearing in two programs at the Zoo Park theater in Toledo and his picture was in the *Toledo Times*. "I do not know how well it pays. He claims that he is getting along with very little or no liquor. He is meeting every week with Alcoholics Anonymous, he states in his letters." Will was still active in his eighties, though he no longer drove and his hearing and vision were diminishing. He shared a tragic detail, perhaps feeling James might appreciate its dramatic potential: "Business has been hurt by the Wall Street collapse. I am getting some appraisals: one goes to court where a Gas Company serving a farm home completely destroyed the home, killing a small child. It will be hotly contested in a damage suit."[77]

Despite his acting gig, Richard was still borrowing heavily from his parents. In November, James sent Vera forty dollars on Richard's behalf. Will, along with buying Richard a "fine new blue suit," had sent to him $442 at various times over the past year. "It is a disgrace and a foolish way to spend money; I am bothered to know what to do. It is easy to talk about an asylum but very nearly impossible to obtain any results. He is not insane, not dangerous, harms no one but himself and is rated as an alcoholic." James was thoughtful in sending regular birthday presents to his father, such as books, soap, Spermaceti candles, and an old English Sovereign coin of gold.[78]

In March 1962, writer and actor James Leo Herlihy reached out to Purdy in appreciation of his work. Like Purdy, Herlihy was a gay Midwestern writer who moved to New York. Herlihy was staying in Key West and shared that the film made from his first novel, *All Fall Down* (1960), adapted by playwright William Inge, starring Warren Beatty, Eva Marie Saint, and Karl Malden, was in theaters. [79] Herlihy would become better known for his second novel, *Midnight Cowboy* (1965), especially after its adaptation directed by John Schlesinger appeared in 1969. Purdy was "so delighted" to receive a letter from Herlihy: "I look forward very much to meeting you, for I do admire your work and hope to read more and more of it." Purdy heard from producer Sidney Eden that Herlihy was considering "doing the stage adaptation of *Malcolm*," which "thrilled and delighted" him. "I *do* hope you will! You are the ideal one, Jamie, for it! Wonderful news about your film." Herlihy, like his friend, Tennessee Williams, was energized by Purdy's work and he asked his close friend, writer Anaïs Nin, if she knew *63: Dream Palace*, which he had just read in paperback: "Brilliant, beautiful, terrifying. He does a splendid, illuminated realism that comes out surrealistic." After Purdy and Herlihy later met in person, Herlihy replied: "I did *not* notice there were cannibals there when we met. But this is one of my serious troubles these days. I do not always notice when cannibals are present and feel that this is just the kind of thing I will need some of your help with!"[80]

In June, John Bucklew wrote from Lawrence College. Several weeks before, art professor Charles Brooks, a past target of Purdy's tape recoded satire, called him one evening, "completely crocked as usual" and "wanted Purdy's phone number which he said he couldn't get." A former student of Brooks's who was "greatly impressed" with Purdy's writing was with him. "I've become tired of watching people become fonder of you as you grow more famous, but probably not half as much as you are."[81] In October, Bucklew thanked Purdy for the planned dedication in Purdy's second collection, *Children Is All*, but repeated, "Aren't you uneasy over becoming identified with psychologists, the current *betes noires* of the literary world?" He liked "Everything under the Sun" and re-read "Daddy Wolf" and "Sermon," which, along with "The Lesson," he thought were "real gems" of Purdy's "special brand of humor." Bucklew was glad that Purdy "began the book with one of them. They are such a delightful mixture of satire relieved by a kind of Mack Sennett buffoonery and good nature." He added: "I liked the touch of humor in the dedication to Bruce [Ross] and myself. Thanks for *what*? the reader will wonder."[82] Dr. Bruce Ross was another Lawrence friend and colleague; he went on to join the psychology faculty at Brown University and The Catholic University of America while maintaining a correspondence with "Jim." In 1970, Purdy wrote Bucklew a "fine recommendation" for a Guggenheim research grant.[83]

Although they had been acquainted for years, Purdy visited Virgil Thomson at his rooms on the ninth floor of the famous bohemian Chelsea Hotel, perhaps for the first time, in late June. James wrote Virgil: "I enjoyed my evening with you extremely well. The company was fine. What a delicious repast!"[84] Of the Chelsea Hotel, Thomson said: "Everybody's lived here at one time or another—usually when they were young but not famous." Residents included Tennessee Williams, Thomas Wolfe, Dylan Thomas, Arthur Miller, Edgar Lee Masters, who was Thomson's next door neighbor, and Gore Vidal.[85] Thomson, who was an incredible cook and host, enjoyed one of the hotel's best suites, where he remained for nearly fifty years. As Purdy entered and settled in, he took in three large, high-ceilinged rooms decorated with etched-glass panels and carved-wood trim, richly hued hand-molded tiles, a fireplace, and a bay window offering a breathtaking view of the city. Inside was a baby grand piano, and walls were lined with custom shelves stuffed with first editions by friends like Capote, Williams, and Purdy, and adorned with paintings by friends.[86]

In their August 1962 issue, *Cosmopolitan* published Purdy's apocalyptic short play, "Cracks." Ceaselessly talking, cosmically indestructible Nera was based on Vera Purdy in old age.[87] Once sociable and charming, Vera was now seen as a "reclusive old woman" or, to the kids on the block, the "neighborhood witch," according to Dan Cryer, who mowed her lawn. Very few in Findlay realized she was the mother of a "celebrated novelist."[88] Earlier in the year, Purdy wrote FSC, begging them to "send the *Cosmopolitan* check at once as I need the money badly." He received a check for a thousand dollars in late March (about $8,693 in 2020).[89]

Unfortunately, James Leo Herlihy would not get to adapt *Malcolm*, and in November 1962 it was reported that William Archibald was adapting *Malcolm* to the Broadway stage. Archibald wrote plays and screenplays after achieving success as a dancer, choreographer, and Broadway actor; he and Truman Capote adapted Henry James's *The Turn of the Screw* to a screenplay for *The Innocents* (1961). Other adaptations were raised as possibilities. James Oliver of James Brown Associates sent *Malcolm* to George Cukor, a famous Hollywood director and a gay man. Cukor found it "charming and witty, unexpected, lovely, implicitly fine, first rate, fresh, remarkable, so funny. Remarkable talent." But he had "grave misgivings as to it as a mo pix. A distinguished mo pix, yes, yes, but successful, no."[90] Purdy later said Cukor wanted him to come to Hollywood to work on screenplays.[91]

According to connoisseurs and *Esquire*, Purdy was "in"—even if he later insisted he never was. The July 1963 issue of *Esquire* included a famous colorful "power chart" accompanying "The Structure of the American Literary Establishment" by Rust Hills. A lava-lamp-like blob of orange-red color denoted "The Hot Center": Purdy and FSC stablemates (Flannery O'Connor, Bernard Malamud, Robert Lowell) and publishers and editors (Farrar, Giroux, but not Straus) made it in. Further evidencing his vogue, Purdy continued to saturate the women's "slicks" with drama, publishing "Children Is All" in the November *Mademoiselle*, his second placement there.[92] He was unhappy with the play's bland presentation in this issue, however. His name was absent from the cover, and no illustrations accompanied the text, which was buried in ads. Purdy complained to FSC, but Straus thought Candy Donadio had acted as his agent at the time. Candida Donadio of Russell & Volkening sat "at the center of the hot center" of *Esquire*'s chart.[93]

Purdy later informed Straus that his new agent was Jack Phelps, whom FSC privately thought was a dud. "When MCA went out of business, Miss Audrey Wood's assistant," Phelps, did not follow Wood to her new firm. That might have been a red flag. Since Phelps did "all the actual work" on "Cracks" and "Children Is All," Wood, Phelps, and Purdy agreed he should continue to represent Purdy on those properties. Phelps was also handling *Color of Darkness* and *Children Is All* "for TV, etc." An in-house annotation on a copy of Roger Straus's response said, "Ech! Bad move, I think, but NOT our business."[94]

On November 15, New Directions published *Children Is All*, collecting ten stories and two recent short plays. The odd book and play title is taken from Edna's colloquial phrase, "children is all," as she indicates the source of disturbing noise near her home at the margin of town and country— kids lighting firecrackers on Independence Day eve. Given the title phrase's link to patriotic ritual, the book's dedication to a former military psychologist (Bucklew), the author's support from Harold and Virginia Knapik and Norman Holmes Pearson, and his propensity for embedding puns or in-jokes within titles (e.g., *Eustace Chisholm*/Useless Jism), it was probably no accident that the crooked title phrase has the initials "CIA." The title page layout even encourages one to read "CIA" vertically. Purdy would have pre-ferred that FSC publish *Children Is All* instead of New Directions, but he was under contract. He later raged against James Laughlin: "By forcing me against my will to give you *Children Is All*, you again showed all in the literary world that you did not care about the author and his deep feelings, but only yourself and your vanity as a rich man and publisher."[95]

The collection received mostly positive responses. Virgil Thomson could not express the joy with which he read the stories and reread the plays col-lected in *Children Is All*, which New Directions sent to him ahead of publica-tion, and he wanted James to sign it, inviting him to a gathering where guests included the Knapiks and the cultural attaché, John L. Brown.[96] The queer novelist Alfred Chester offered a blurb: "Using gentility and restraint like a pair of swords, Purdy slits open a world so horrible and funny that who can doubt for a moment that it is ours? These stories are the surest and best things he's done so far, and they leave me with the feeling of having been to a quiet tea party in Babylon or Sodom."[97] In *Saturday Review*, the major critic Ihab Hassan wrote: "The uncanny technical skill of Purdy brings his material to terrible life because it is backed by an authentic vision of love, anguish, and incongruity." The vision blurs at times, but so seldomly that "we can rejoice again in the possession of this new book by one of America's best writers." Contrastingly, in *Commonweal*, while novelist Richard Horchler praised "Daddy Wolf" and "Encore," he panned the plays and found the volume on the whole "weak and faltering."[98] Although the collection included characters modeled on his mother, as with his father, it is not clear that Vera ever read his books. At one point, Dorothy Purdy asked James if Vera had read his latest book. He said something to the effect of, "she wouldn't understand it, or wouldn't appreciate it."[99]

Edith Sitwell wrote an intensely glowing review of *Children Is All*. "I think it undoubted that James Purdy will come to be recognized as one of the greatest living writers of fiction in our language. Perhaps the word 'fiction' is wrong: for these works are not the production of imagination alone. They are the raw material of life itself, shaped by a great artist. He pierces down to the most secret places of the heart, then brings those secret places into the light of the all-seeing, the compassionate sun, that, like the fire of Christ, loves all that lives." Sitwell continues: "Even when he touches our raw nerves," his touch is "that of a healer, because he teaches us compassion, teaches us to be ourselves. 'Judge not, that ye be not judged.'" Sometimes, evoking anguish, he speaks in a "desolate whisper. But he does more with that whisper than most novelists do by yelling at the tops of their voices—and more with a few sentences than other novelists with several pages. There is never a sentence too much, a word too much." *Children Is All* is a "sublime work of pity and tenderness" that only a great writer could have produced.[100]

Sam Steward, commenting on Purdy's earliest work, had expressed excited praise but also reservations about the starkness of his minimalism, but now he offered only praise. In contemplating the best pieces and their effect on him, Steward "wondered what your secret is, and how you do it because your method and technique really can't be analyzed anymore—pure magic, done with mysterious glands which all my training as a critic in the classroom can't unravel or understand." Even Sitwell seemed somewhat at a loss to explain it in her poetic praise. "I guess it's just genius, that's all," and one must "make a little helpless gesture of defeat" trying "to see How It's Done."[101]

James hopefully found moments of happiness and satisfaction as he basked in the glow of such acclaim in the early 1960s. Sitwell's sumptuous praise was both blessing and curse, however. Some critics waxed skeptical, knowing Dame Edith had a track record of taking gay male writers and artists under her richly plumaged wing, while certain other writers were deeply envious of her hymns of praise. They went out of their way to take down the author's works.

10

The Mourner Below

The 1960s were a period of great artistic growth and recognition for James Purdy, the writer. Personally, however, it was a decade full of painful losses, of many family members, friends, and champions, making him quite forlorn by the late 1960s.

On December 14, 1962, Vera Otis Purdy Bauman died at age seventy-five years of a heart ailment. Shocked by his mother's death, James traveled to Ohio for her funeral. Jorma Sjoblom drove him as far as his own parents' house in Cleveland to spend the night; then, James took a westbound train toward Hicksville.[1] The funeral occurred in the former George K. Otis residence, Vera's childhood home where she was born and married, long since converted to a funeral home. Vera's second husband, John Bauman, commented: "Some people are lucky to have one or two good friends in a life. That little lady had hundreds of them."[2] Vera was predeceased by her sister, Della, and a brother, Dr. Judson Otis, a dentist. "I was heartbroken. I am very alone in the world," Purdy told Powys.[3] After Vera's funeral, John Bauman "took all the money and moved out," Purdy later learned. Bauman died in 1965 on March 17—Vera's birthday—and was buried in Hicksville alongside Vera.[4]

Perhaps some small consolation was a new friendship begun in 1963, when the unpublished writer and critic Bettina Schwarzschild mailed Purdy her first letter in what became a long correspondence. A Jewish housewife and mother of two, Schwarzschild as a girl and her family had been among the last Jews to escape Germany before the Holocaust. After reading *Color of Darkness*, and learning how Purdy's friends had printed and distributed the predecessors of the book, she wrote Purdy: "Your writing hurts to the quick and I don't think I'll ever recover from the pain. It's as though your characters received a blow over their heads by reality and have been stunned ever since." She thanked him for the courage of his vision and that of his friends. She went on to publish critical articles on Purdy's works that apply archetypal and psychoanalytic theory.[5]

To target commercial writing and publishing, during this period Purdy shifted the focus of his satire in *Cabot Wright Begins* to five characters who are trying to write and publish a profitable book about the serial rapist. The emphasis changed from Cabot alone to the "*meaning* Cabot Wright has for the semi-illiterate car-salesman from Chicago, 'Bernie' Gladhart and his money-hungry wife, Carrie Moore." In Purdy's new framework, Cabot tells his story to Bernie, who misunderstands, and Cabot is "caught up in the pleasure of lying and misleading" him. Later, Zoe Bickle, the ghostwriter wife of failed novelist Curt Bickle, arrives to help Gladhart write a bestseller, nearly becoming the main character, and the quintet is completed by the declining New York publisher Princeton Keith, who hungers for a big score. By December 1962, he had begun the second draft using this approach and sent Robert Giroux the opener: "Nobody knows how the arteries and nerves of the man sitting next to you make him see you and the world that surrounds you both." Editor Hal Vursell, like Giroux, a gay man, penciled in the margin: "Wonderful beginning: in fact, *classic!*" Purdy became quite fond of Vursell, one of FSG's great editors, a "dapper, slim, and devastatingly witty man" sporting a Clark Gable mustache. In May 1963, Purdy reported the novel was "now going forward in the final version."[6]

As Purdy completed *Cabot Wright Begins*, he also composed "Tecmessa Starr," a one-act play about a black woman who murdered her six husbands, he told John Cowper Powys.[7] Little did he know that his longtime epistolary friend and champion had less than four months left. In June 1963, John Cowper Powys died at age ninety without personally meeting James.

Jack Phelps clumsily took up the business relationship with Giroux. In January 1963, Phelps wrote that Purdy had "allowed" him to review the contract for *Cabot Wright Begins* dated June 1961, and he was "more than surprised" by what he found. Although the contract was signed, Phelps thought the $2,000 advance should be renegotiated to $4,000 because of Purdy's enhanced status. Giroux issued a stinging rebuke. Phelps "should have had more expert advice." "I resent your saying 'It is not a good contract for Jim' as much as you would resent my saying 'Jack Phelps is not a good agent for Jim.' As Jim can tell you, I have given him more help on contracts and terms than any agent" ever did. He resented Phelps's letter "not only as Jim's publisher, but as his friend." Was it Phelps's intention to damage their friendship by "creating bad feelings where only the best of feelings existed before"? Giroux was unsparing, calling his interpretations "stupid." He accused Phelps of horning in and trying to take credit for the groundwork FSG did in working with foreign publishers on translations and for negotiating serial rights. When Jim signed the contract, the $2,000 advance was the "highest he had received from any publisher in any country." Giroux was "very proud of the fact that, through our belief in Jim's talent, the publication of *Malcolm* in this country marked a turning-point in his career, and started a big increase in his earning-power as an author." Then, in 1963, in walks a "Johnny-come-lately" saying the "advance wasn't big enough." Since any confidence Giroux may have held in Phelps was rendered "non-existent" by his letter, he was "much more interested in whether Jim himself thinks this advance is too little" since when FSC proposed it in 1961, Jim said he was "very pleased." That was the "sole reason for us agreeing to it."[8] Known as a sensitive aesthete, here Giroux showed his assertive side in shutting down Phelps.

Giroux and Straus nevertheless decided to give Purdy an added bonus advance. In February, Giroux was "awfully glad" Purdy had finished the final chapter of *Cabot Wright Begins* and a new opening chapter. As soon as he received those, he intended to "sit down and re-read the entire script." It seemed "very hopeful for Fall publication," he was very happy to report. Giroux enclosed a check for the advance plus a bonus advance that he and Straus had "agreed should be paid" considering his present situation. "I am glad we had talked about this last Sunday." Giroux had not heard from Jack Phelps after his stinging response.[9]

William wrote from Ohio to relate his difficulties. For Richard he had paid out over six thousand dollars in the last seven years, and "of course it did him more harm than good, as he never uses the money well." And for the first time in more than a half-century in real estate, Will had "actually lost a small amount of money" in 1962. In June 1963, anticipating his eighty-fifth birthday, he admitted that, unable to drive and "pretty deaf," he was missing most good deals because he could not "follow up and contact the prospective buyers." In August, Will offered better news: Richard seemed to be "quitting his bad drinking habit." In Findlay, a minister and his wife had taken a "great interest in him" and William hoped it would help. "He is different looking and acting than he has been for the past six years. Of course he has no money."[10] The next month, however, Will shared that Richard was still drinking and running up debts; he had checked out of the Murphy Hotel and William had to pay his bill.[11] In many letters, Will sent his "best regards to Jo," Jorma Sjoblom, although he had moved out. Dorothy Purdy and her children, David, and Christine, recalled that "Papa Purdy" remained immaculately well dressed in his old age, rarely seen in anything but a three-piece suit in outmoded cut, complete with pocket watch. As late as the 1960s, William frowned on females wearing pants. One day, Will pulled up unexpectedly at the Robert Purdy residence in Berea. Chrissy told her mom, who, like her, was wearing pants, that he had arrived; Dorothy thought she was joking. Dorothy asked Christine to entertain her grandfather while she changed. As she opened the door, Papa Purdy declared, "You're dressed like a boy!"

In April 1963, James visited Yale University in New Haven to read and talk to students; such a distinguished occasion was something new for him as a writer. Norman Holmes Pearson, who probably invited him, was not surprised to find him "so involved with the students." "Your evening at the Elizabethan Club was a splendid success. And naturally, too, I was disappointed not to be able to be alone with you and to say how very much indeed I admired *Children Is All* and how happy I am about your continued growth as a writer."[12] Novelist Robert Penn Warren, a professor of English at Yale, had written in February, asking permission to add "Daddy Wolf" to the revised edition of *An Approach to Literature.* "*Children Is All* is very powerful and 'Daddy Wolf' is the most powerful thing in it, a kind of masterpiece." Warren heard Purdy was coming to New Haven and asked when he would be in town. "Perhaps then I can have the session I have been promising myself." Four days later, he added that "Daddy Wolf," a "terrific story," was not the only one at that level of quality. "In fact," the two collections were among the "most powerful books published for some years."[13] Along with Warren and Pearson, R. W. B. Lewis was surely there as well.

In May, Purdy was again honored with a grant from the Guggenheim Memorial Foundation, technically his third, but the second time he got to keep the money.[14] Roger Straus wrote a letter of recommendation: few American writers were "more serious, more talented, and more deserving of financial help" than Purdy. From the start, Purdy had adhered to "non-compromising standards and he has devoted all his time *exclusively* to writing. The sacrifice which this entails since he is wholly dependent on his own earnings, is a measure of his devotion to his art."[15] It is almost scary how he never stopped writing once he devoted himself to it.

In 1963, Purdy met Richard Hundley, a singer and budding composer in his early thirties who soon became a close friend and collaborator. Hundley hailed from Cincinnati and, like Purdy, had experienced his parents' divorce in youth. For a few years, flamboyant Hundley sang in the Metropolitan Opera chorus but "was fired for always coming late," Purdy said.[16] Hundley was first introduced to Purdy's work, then to the man, by an intriguing couple—Harold and Virginia Knapik, undercover CIA agents. In Paris, Virginia had worked at the American Embassy; Harold's cover was he was writing a book on musical counterpoint. In 1962, Virgil Thomson sent Richard Hundley to Harold Knapik for musical study. "Harold was a composer, who, like James, had benefitted from Chicago businessman Osborn Andreas's largesse (in different ways)," Hundley remarked.[17] Harold told Richard that his friend had written a wonderful book called *Malcolm*, and soon afterward, when Hundley went in for a lesson, he saw a tall stack of paperbacks emblazoned by a vibrant, jazzy illustration featuring a saxophone, a woman wearing a red bikini, and Malcolm in a lavender shirt and jacket on a golden bench.[18] Handing him a copy, Harold said: "This man comes from the same place as you do—Ohio. This is a delightful novel; you should read it. If you like it, tell me." A few days later, Hundley brought *Malcolm* on a long subway ride to Coney Island and its beach. He immediately became captivated by its story, so mesmerized that when he finally looked up, he had traveled two stops past his destination.[19] When Hundley went to his next lesson, he told Knapik that he loved and was overcome by this extraordinary book. "The author would love to hear that," Harold replied, and afterward arranged for James and Richard to visit over dinner at his home. Purdy and Hundley "took each other up immediately with enthusiasm" and began speaking every day, Hundley said.[20] By 1964, Hundley and Purdy had become close friends and cross-influences.[21]

Hundley encouraged James to keep writing poetry and in increased quantity. Purdy said that without Richard insisting that his verse was as important as his fiction and plays, he would not have continued. Early in their relationship, Purdy began to send poems and then began to send "pages of automatic writing" that he did in the morning as warm-ups for writing fiction. "These were the most imaginative, wonderful things I had ever read. I began to circle whole batches of lines and words, and they all turned out to be the very poems that were published in *The Running Sun* [1971], which I began to set to music. He didn't think they were poems, but he then realized they were so imaginative, that they were really the poems."[22] James and Richard became sustained collaborators, and James Purdy's name is known to many in the art-song world because of Hudley's adaptations, especially "Come Ready and See Me." Standout recordings were made by tenor Paul Sperry and soprano Bethany Beardslee.

A break between the Knapiks and Richard Hundley came in 1965, however, when Virginia Knapik passed judgment on Hundley's personal life, and Hundley had to halt his lessons with Harold Knapik. "Virginia (Fear-Fairy) Knapik said he could not give lessons to paederasts while she was paying the big bills for Harold's experimental cooking," Purdy later explained to Gertrude Abercrombie. (A paederast, to be clear, is a man who has sex with a boy.)[23] In response, Purdy had a "terrible falling out with Virginia Knapik—a bitch," Hundley recalled.[24] Purdy lampooned Virginia as "Virge the Splurge" in anonymous letters and news releases, believing she and Harold were spendthrift of funds granted to them by Osborn; later, he learned that her splurging was underwritten by the CIA. Purdy wrote a satire on "Mr. and Mrs. Knapik, Frauds," fabricating a quotation from "Thompson" (sic), suggesting that Harold's CIA cover was thin; cooking was Harold's real forte and he later published a fancy cookbook.[25] "Mr. Knapik's compositions look impressive owing to the expensively printed form in which they appear, but careful study soon reveals he is more at home in the kitchen than on the podium or at the piano, and his symphony should be performed with pots, pans, heavy iron skillets, and deep-fat containers rather than any known musical instruments."[26]

In August 1963, Secker & Warburg published *Children Is All* in Britain. Purdy was appalled, however, when he saw their "flea-bitten sordid fire-sale edition," the jacket "fifth-rate, ugly, unimaginative, idiotic, badly copied from the New Directions publication (which is imaginative and good). Your edition could only have been approved by someone completely indifferent to taste and completely uninterested in my book." He issued an ultimatum: "If you intend to promote this book in the same shoddy unimaginative cheap way you have printed it, this, of course, is the end of any connection I will have with your publishing firm." The collection generally received praise from British critics, including a very positive review by the author Jocelyn Brooke in *The Listener*, who said these "startlingly effective" stories were by a "true original" of great versatility.[27]

Also in August, an unknown young playwright, Terrence McNally, then in a relationship with a famous playwright, Edward Albee, wrote John Farrar of Farrar, Straus & Giroux, thanking him for introducing him to Purdy's work. "Another reason this has been a good summer has something to do with you. Remember sending me three James Purdy books? They were *Malcolm*, *The Nephew* and *Color of Darkness*. And oh! What books those are, John. So beautiful, so terrifying, so sad. And wise, so very wise. I certainly can't think of any other books *like* them and would be hard-pressed to name many books as good. The Purdy fans must be in legions by now and I am a late-comer to their ranks. But thank you, thank you, for making me aware, even at this late a date, of a talent, an *instinct*, so pure that beside it I can feel the presence of an angel. A rather dark angel, to be sure, but such a glistening, shining one!" Farrar sent a copy of McNally's letter to Purdy. "It is perhaps young and emotional, but it is from a man of great talent. I imagine you have no idea of how many of these young people there are (not all writers by a long shot) who feel very much the same about you."[28] That it was Farrar and not Albee who introduced Purdy's work to McNally is surprising, given that Albee later adapted *Malcolm* to the Broadway stage.

Passionate about Purdy, Terrence McNally wrote a strong adaptation of *Malcolm* dated summer 1964 that was never produced, and oddly, Purdy and his circle were never aware of it. McNally's *The Play of Malcolm* begins with characters declaiming Purdy quotations from Webster Schott's feature in *The Nation*. After that, his adaptation is faithful to the novel, unlike Albee's, though it has a postmodern metadramatic quality in which characters describe themselves to the audience. Intriguingly, Albee, after his beautiful boyfriend broke up with him in early 1964 after they had been together since 1959, acquired the rights to adapt *Malcolm* and in 1965 wrote a vastly inferior adaptation.[29] Even though Albee was riding a crest of success, McNally's deep affection for Purdy's work exacerbated Albee's confessed feelings of envy toward Purdy and the praise he had received—making all of this quite personal.[30] McNally's and Albee's friend, Robert Heide, explains: "Edward did not like the idea of then-lover Terrence competing with him in the playwriting department, and their relationship ended." McNally later admitted "it seems absurd that the author of 'Who's Afraid of Virginia Woolf?' would be competitive with" a young man "trying to write his first play," but "Edward had his limitations."[31] Albee did not support McNally since he was "withholding, remote, ungenerous." They had a "very unhappy, angry, bitter breakup. I mean, I left him and he was not amused." For years afterward, they did not speak.[32] It is strange to discover *Malcolm* in the middle of this and helps to explain Albee's subsequent bizarre handling of Purdy's novel.

Edward Albee, probably accompanied by McNally, went to see a performance of *Color of Darkness: An Evening in the World of James Purdy*, which opened on Monday, September 30, 1963.[33] Produced by Margaret Barker, who had acted onstage, for her Harvest Productions, and directed by William Francisco, who taught at the Yale School of Drama, it was done off-Broadway at the Writers Stage Theater at East 4th Street.[34] Ned Rorem, who wrote incidental music for the production, wrote in his diary: "Not the least effective element of *Color of Darkness*, which opened Monday at the Fourth Street Theater, is the music which plays almost constantly, even during intermission when the taped saxophone wails into the washrooms." Rorem noted that his "date" was model, actor, and heiress Gloria Vanderbilt, a fact the newspaper "duly noted" while failing to mention his "artistic contribution."[35] Through Van Vechten, Vanderbilt had become a Purdy fan. The first part was five stories adapted by Ellen Violett.[36] Barker insisted: "We were absolutely determined to put Mr. Purdy on the stage, not Miss Violett. We would stick to his own story line, his own characters, and his own very sparse dialogue."[37] "Cracks" culminated the evening, featuring Eleanor Phelps.[38] Facing external obstacles including a newspaper strike, the program had a short run, through November 3.

Color of Darkness: An Evening in the World of James Purdy received both negative and positive reviews. The *New York Times* theater critic Lewis Funke noted that Purdy was considered "one of the few writers who matter on the American scene," and he praised the performances of Eleanor Phelps as loquacious Nera, Doris Roberts as Jennie in "You Reach for Your Hat," Ann Hegira as Merta, the worried mother in "Encore," and Kevin Mitchell, both as her son and Cade in "Everything Under the Sun." "The unhappy fact," though, was that Purdy's stories had simply not been well adapted "from the written page to the spoken word." Atmosphere was not enough; "there must also be drama on a stage" that connects with an audience. This review was dispiriting, but the program was praised by the *Wall Street Journal*, which called it an "off-Broadway production that's on target." Concurring were Candice Womble of *New York Amsterdam News* (a black newspaper), an AP reviewer, and the actor Leonard Harris.[39] Purdy was later critical of Bill Francisco's direction.[40]

Purdy received support from Gloria Vanderbilt as he attracted more distinguished fans. On November 17, when Purdy gave a reading at the YM-YWHA, Vanderbilt and Ned Rorem attended, and afterward Ned, James, and Jorma went to a dinner party for Purdy hosted by Vanderbilt at her swanky apartment. Jorma recalled meeting Gloria's husband, director Sidney Lumet, and the singer Johnnie Ray, who had hits in the 1950s including a number-one single, "Cry." Also present that night was the English actress, Hermione Gingold, who was known for her eccentric, campy style. Gingold, who appeared in the movies *Gigi* (1958) and *The Music Man* (1962), became a friend of Purdy's and later starred in a radio adaptation of *I Am Elijah Thrush*.[41]

Earlier in the month, Purdy thanked Thomson for a lovely evening at his home: "everything was superb." He reciprocated by inviting Virgil to dine at Gage and Tollner in downtown Brooklyn.[42] Gage and Tollner was in a four-story Italianate brownstone featuring gas lamps and a romantic atmosphere. Someone without Purdy's knowledge gave copies of *Malcolm* to the elegant black men who waited there, and "they became fans of that book and others by me," Purdy later wrote. Purdy cultivated friendships with them.[43]

Ahead of the 1964 World's Fair, during the fall of 1963, New York police began to crack down on homosexuals in Brooklyn Heights despite the Heights being a longtime bohemian enclave tolerant of gays and lesbians.[44] A December 1963 *Times* article headlined "Growth of Overt Homosexuality in City Provokes Widespread Concern" noted the State Liquor Authority had revoked the license of Tony Bonner's Heights Supper Club on 80 Montague Street, one of three "homosexual haunts" repeatedly raided by police. The city's "most sensitive open secret—the presence of what is probably the greatest homosexual population in the world and its increasing openness—has become the subject of growing concern of psychiatrists, religious leaders and the police."[45] Purdy satirized such oppressive homophobic policing in his current project, *Cabot Wright Begins*.

On November 22, President John F. Kennedy was killed in Dallas. Uncannily, Purdy had written a poem in 1957 titled "Memoirs of an Assassin" containing the line "it's raining in Dallas, / Goodbye dear and goodluck." It was raining that morning before the sun came out, prompting secret servicemen to remove the bubbletop from Kennedy's limousine. On the National Day of Mourning, Bob Purdy and family visited Cora and William in Bowling Green where they owned no TV or radio. Cora said they had thought the assassination was a hoax until they saw the story corroborated in a second newspaper, their niece Christine said. Wanting animal companionship, Will and Cora used to "coax the squirrels into the house, until somebody got bit."[46]

On Monday, February 24, 1964, William Boyd Purdy died at age eighty-eight after a short stay in a nursing home. The realtor, accountant, and former banker had a heart attack while walking home from his office, as he had done thousands of times before. His funeral was held at First Presbyterian Church, and he was buried in Oak Grove Cemetery nestled on the Bowling Green State University campus. FSG sent flowers. "The country's gone," Purdy later remarked. "I went back for my father's funeral and I was horrified because where he had lived [as a boy], out on a farm, there were all these cement buildings."[47] In a large car with family members, James was seated next to sixth grader Christine Purdy, who always remembered her uncle saying to her, "I don't like funerals." Purdy repeated, "I don't like funerals, and, I'm never coming back." Chrissy was "taken aback" by this: "It kind of hurt my feelings, honestly." As a "little kid," she thought to herself, "this is my uncle. You're not coming back, but we're not all dead here. There are living people here, too." Dorothy remarked, "Why would he say that to a little kid?" Christine replied, "Maybe it was his way of dealing with hurt and emotion." Purdy's inheritance was substantial; from his father's estate, which included three local properties and a green 1956 Ford four-door sedan, Purdy inherited $6,652 (about $55,320 in 2020), but he did not receive the check until 1966.[48] His father's death followed soon after that of another uncle, Vera's brother, Dr. Lloyd Otis.

His parents both now gone, in March, Purdy made his first known anti-American comments in the press. He told *Wilson Library Bulletin*: "I regard American civilization as a totalitarian machine, very similar to Russia . . . the only way for an individual to cope with it is to ignore it as much as possible."[49] He told Webster Schott of *The Nation* that all of his work is an implicit criticism of the United States. "This is a culture based on money and competition, is inhuman, terrified of life, sexual and other, obsessed with homosexuality and brutality. Our entire moral life is pestiferous and we live in a completely immoral atmosphere . . . the human being under capitalism is a stilted, depressed, sick creature . . . we toil and enjoy and live for all the wrong reasons, and our national life is a nightmare of noise, ugliness, filth and confusion." He concluded, "I don't believe America has any future." Schott wrote memorably: "Intensely private and as fixed in focus as a dime-store telescope, Purdy's work thus far constitutes the most arresting description of dissociation and human transgression to be found in American literature. It cannot be accounted for except in terms of naïve genius and personal torment of the kind that would drive a man to self-destruction if he couldn't write." Purdy explained: "I am not even writing novels. I am writing *me*. I go on writing to tell myself at least what I have been through."[50]

Purdy had been through a lot and remained bereft after his losses, his sadness only temporarily dissipated by attending Virgil Thomson's gatherings and receiving a visit from Virgil to his flat.[51] Despite having such a witty and well-connected friend, he was chronically sad and depressed. To Neely Orme, his friend in Arkansas, he wrote: "You are not as lonesome as I am.

I have nobody. My one brother is a hopeless alcoholic, and the other brother is a Babbitt. Anyway they live a million miles away. Jorma Jules lives a million miles away. . . . I appreciated your phone call, and I love you." (Sjoblom lived on Long Island.) At times, the weight of melancholy crushed his spirit. "I really want to die. I don't think I ever wanted to live. It's all too hard and I am too crippled."[52]

At FSG and elsewhere, Purdy had gained a reputation for being hard to please. In April, Paula Diamond, in charge of subsidiary rights at FSG, wrote a memo addressing points made by Purdy's agent relating to the publication of *Cabot Wright*. "We're going to have to work very carefully and very thoroughly all along the line. And we might as well get used to the fact that Purdy is irrational and insatiable in his demands, so although we can't hope to satisfy him, maybe we can keep his complaints minimal."[53]

Regardless of any troubles Purdy caused his publishers, his works were receiving another round of international marketing, thanks to the US government. Virgil Thomson's friend, John L. Brown, cultural attaché to Mexico, of the Foreign Service and the United States Information Service, wrote Roger Straus about his Mexican James Purdy promotion. Also a poet and critic, John L. Brown esteemed Purdy as "one of the top Americans writing." Straus had sent Brown galleys for *Cabot Wright* to assist with his programming.[54] "The James Purdy programs are shaping up nicely," Brown told Straus. The first, held in the Benjamin Franklin Library in Mexico City, was a talk on James Purdy by novelist and critic Luis Guillermo Piazza, who devoted a column in *Excelsior* to Purdy. That talk, Brown said, would be the basis of a TV show to be presented on Televisión Universitaria later in the month.[55] In 1962 and 1963, Editorial Sudamericana in Buenos Aires published Spanish translations of *Malcolm* and *The Nephew* (*El Sobrino*), and the long-standing Editorial Seix Barral in Barcelona published *Color de Oscuridad*. Four years after this Purdy promotion, the Mexican literary publisher Joaquin Morítz published *Comienza Cabot Wright*. Straus shared Brown's letters with Purdy, who responded that his books were "very well known in Cuba—more so than in Mexico," and Havanan radio and TV had "devoted a good many hours to dramatizations" of his work. Purdy asked if Straus could arrange to send two copies of *Cabot Wright Begins* to the Cuban novelist Edmundo Desnoes, a "good friend" and former student in Havana who wanted to review it. Cuba then boasted a "very bright literary group," Purdy wrote.[56]

Fred Warburg of Secker & Warburg wrote Purdy's agent with more good news. Phelps had requested that Purdy's advance be raised to $3,500, a "very high figure," claiming that Purdy "needed the money very badly indeed." Since Secker & Warburg had the "highest regard for James and his work" and wished to remain his publisher, they took pains to meet the request. Warburg made it clear they, or any London publisher, could not have met this figure without the "support of a paperback house" so was happy to report Penguin had accepted the book with a "sizable advance."[57]

In October 1964, Farrar, Straus & Giroux finally published *Cabot Wright Begins*. Giroux officially replaced Cudahy in their company name only the month before, so it was one of the very first FSG books. Focusing on Cabot Wright, a well-heeled Yale graduate of Wall Street and serial rapist, and five people hustling to write and publish a book on him, the novel lampoons New York publishing, American society, and Americans' sexual mores. In an endorsement for FSG, Paul Bowles hailed it as "a delight all the way through." Purdy "succeeded better than anyone around at the moment in recreating the USA and presenting it simultaneously as his own invention and as a faithful reflection of reality—not an easy feat."[58] Regarding the genesis of the unusual story, Purdy said a "crazy ex-convict" he knew (Frank Sandiford) was "always going to write a story about a rapist," and became obsessed with the idea. "I got so sick of hearing about it, and I knew he would never write about it because he is not a writer, so I wrote it for him!"[59] In its satirical focus, Purdy brilliantly anticipates Capote's "non-fiction novel" *In Cold Blood* (called *Indelible Smudge* about Cabot), serialized in the *New Yorker* in 1965, and even Bret Easton Ellis's yuppie predator in *American Psycho* (1991). Since Capote was researching *In Cold Blood* throughout the early 1960s while living in Brooklyn Heights, and shared mutual friends like Donald Windham, Purdy caught wind of his project. Purdy's satire centering on those seeking to profit from writing about a rapist was ironically dedicated to two women, one of whom, Bettina Schwarzschild, focused on writing about Purdy. Witty and obscure Jeanette Druce, whom Purdy met through Paul Swan, was an existentialist, playwright, and the widow of British actor Herbert Druce.

Veteran critic Orville Prescott wrote a hatchet job of a review of *Cabot Wright Begins* in the *New York Times*, which was predictable, or even inevitable, since Prescott is lampooned in the book as Doyley Pepscout. Van Vechten replied to the black novelist Henry Van Dyke: "Purdy roasts Prescott in the Times in his book and naturally he gets roasted back. BUT the Herald Tribune devoted a page of high praise to Cabot Wright last Sunday. . . . Remember that Purdy only gets what he asks for. Don't be too naïve about reviews. Everybody gets bad ones."[60] Prescott had negatively reviewed *Malcolm*, but he then praised Purdy's "precise, firm and beautifully controlled prose style." Prescott, never letting on he is parodied, claims the novel fails as satire because, for satire to be effective, the satirist must believe in "better standards of human conduct," which allegedly Purdy does not—a homophobic assumption. "That is one reason why writers who believe, or affect to believe while at their typewriters, that life is totally absurd never seem very significant [and seem] less worthy of serious attention when they combine their ineffectual satire with obsessive concentration on perverted and criminal sexual activities. What they may intend as healthy ribaldry is all too often the sick outpouring of a confused, adolescent and distraught mind." *Cabot* is "as wretched a waste of small talent and of a reader's time as any novel published in recent years." Prescott did his best to thwart potential readers. *Cabot Wright Begins* is "no more disgusting than several other books published this year, but it is duller. In fact, a drearier bore than this pretentious novel would be exceedingly hard to find." *Cabot* was so bad, it seemed not worth reviewing, but he wanted to make a special point of exposing the alleged fatuousness of "a small coterie of critics" and readers "who consider themselves a cultural elite." He closed by iterating his condemnation of the novel's "failure as satire and its noxious and noisome atmosphere."[61]

Mr. Prescott's condemnation actually drove curious readers to seek out the novel. *Esquire* had relegated Prescott and the *New York Times Book Review* to Squaresville on their "power chart" mapping the structure of the literary establishment. "If Orville Prescott in the *Times* reviews a book unfavorably," Hills wrote, "most of the people on this chart will probably think a little better of it."[62] Indeed, FSG took advantage of the dreadful review, running an ad asking of his father, "Why is a certain New York literary critic so outraged by *Cabot Wright Begins*? Could it be that he believes he bears an uncanny resemblance to Doyley Pepscout . . .?"[63] The critic's son, Peter S. Prescott, protested to John Farrar, since for the first time criticism of his father had "exceeded all bounds of propriety and responsibility." Peter hoped Farrar would call Orville, apparently a friend, to say "whatever he can find it in his heart to say." Farrar replied, "Since you are in publishing yourself, I am sure you have learned that an editor's first loyalty is to his author. You apply the words 'literary assassination' to our ad, yet the author, my colleagues, and many readers felt the words could apply to the review," which required an answer. "We had an obligation to defend our author, just as I understand your wish to defend your father. In the end, all I can say is that I wish the review had not been written in the language and tone in which it was and, similarly, that the ad had not been published." He was "sincerely sorry if it offended."[64]

In the *Herald Tribune Book Week*, Theodore Solotaroff gave *Cabot Wright Begins* a glowing review memorably titled "A Stud Farm for Horselaughs." " 'Make it new,' Ezra Pound advised. Many try, few succeed. One who has, in a quiet but unmistakable way, is James Purdy." *Cabot* is a "brilliantly controlled spoof," a "rich, resonant, and deadly accurate satire on American values, as good as anything we have had since the work of Nathanael West."[65] Ten days later, Purdy had a friendly lunch with Solotaroff and enjoyed his company. Although Purdy did not wish to "run the risk of being a bore or irritating," or seeming insensible to the critic's "good review" while at lunch, he followed up in a letter to disagree with Ted's criticism that Mr. Warburton's "explosion is not prepared for" at the conclusion. One of the main themes is "bifurcation of character, and 'the double,'" Purdy explained. What some critics called overwriting was to his mind necessary to present the "final distortion of bifurcation," and Giroux agreed.[66]

By 1964, Purdy was already regularly criticizing New York critics. In October, the front cover of *Books*, a news sheet published in New York, featured Purdy and *Cabot Wright Begins*. "Its outraged and outrageous look at contemporary society is irreverent, merciless, and extremely funny," its satire comparable to that of the film *Dr. Strangelove*. Purdy attacked the critics, especially the so-called New York Intellectuals, and publishers in a way that later became familiar: "The critics—the so-called squares, such as [Alfred] Kazin, [Malcolm] Cowley, [Dwight] Macdonald, [Irving] Howe, [Norman] Podhoretz, [Arthur] Mizener—have, to my mind, no understanding or sensitivity to imaginative literature; they base their evaluation of writing on sociological categories which are now, and always have been, illegitimate. Great organs of culture like the *New Yorker* tell me I have no reason to exist because I am not sophisticated in a cultured Jewish–*New Yorker* way." Purdy continued his jeremiad: "The *New Yorker* heresy which controls most successful American writing says: 'Never express any emotion in any color that cannot be read with the calm with which, say, George Edwards of WQXR reads Helena Rubinstein ads.' The fact that I caught an inner truth about people I have known in America and presented it in a language which is American has prevented my being accepted and indeed published." He claimed that "had Malcolm Cowley and the New York establishment had their way," he never "would have been published in the United States in the first place. This is important to remember when we hear these great noble liberal critics testify to their love of God; they are the same ones who tell us how they love the Negro but won't bus their children because the kiddies might miss TV or a hot lunch." Purdy was already skewering privileged liberals. He continued: "I don't exist in America. The *New York Times*, following the weathercocks, decided that John Updike was a great writer and that I was just a footnote to the period. Unfortunately, I am not a Negro or Jewish, a beatnik or a Roman Catholic or a communist. This is a tiny civilization."[67] Here and elsewhere, Purdy did not share details of his background or past career. Out of the thousands of authors approached by the Gale firm that publishes literary reference works, only Purdy refused to furnish information. "I am opposed to giving out biographies of myself." Robert Cromie remarked, "He may be the only shy writer in the world."[68]

In October, Susan Sontag, a fellow FSG author, praised Purdy's black comedy in the *New York Times Book Review*. *Cabot Wright Begins*, in many ways Purdy's "most ambitious" novel, "might be loosely described as a bravura work of satire—a satire on pornographic fantasy, a satire on New York literary life, a satire on affluent eccentric mid-century America. Except that satire is perhaps too narrow a term to convey the kind of comedy that Purdy writes, comedy in the tradition that includes both *Candide* and *The Goon Show*," Spike Milligan's BBC radio program. She taxonomized three Purdys: the "satirist and fantasist"; the "gentle naturalist of American, particularly small-town American, life"; and the "writer of vignettes or sketches, which give us a horrifying snapshot image of helpless people destroying each other." Thus, Purdy could be respectively compared to Nathanael West, Wright Morris, and Carson McCullers. Purdy's "most impressive gift" was for "dark comedy," the "rhetoric of exaggeration"; he had a "marvelously inventive gift for parody." Yet Purdy lacked the "gift for great realistic writing; his work lacks the body, the vigor, the unselfconsciousness that realistic writing requires," Sontag thought. Realistic fiction also requires that Purdy "transcend his rather limited vocabulary of character, in which such types as innocent young men, predatory middle-aged women, and saintly half-cracked old people appear with insistent regularity." Ultimately, *Cabot* is not a realistic novel, though it is "surely, a powerful vision of a very real America. And it is a very American book, too." One of Purdy's best, *Cabot Wright Begins* is a "fluent, immensely readable, personal and strong work by a writer from whom everyone who cares about literature has expected, and will continue to expect, a great deal. Anything Purdy writes is a literary event of importance. He is, to my mind, indisputably one of the half-dozen or so living

American writers worth taking seriously. Any reservations about his work I have suggested should be understood to assume the deservedly high place he now holds in American letters."[69]

Despite receiving high praise from a trendy critic, James found fault with Sontag's review. He was upset about her criticism of his characterization and that she said *The Nephew* steered "dangerously close to sentimentality." Years later, he said he did not like or dislike Sontag, but "her comments about my work are irrelevant, because she doesn't have the soul and background to enter into my world. She's irrelevant and typical of the period." Purdy became semi-obsessed with Sontag, satirizing her in bulletins and poems. "She's camp. She's Hippy. She's Jewish. She's 'in.' (The New York Times front page Book Section) She's Susan! Buy her! She's unreadable."[70] Sontag was a close friend and sometime lover of Roger Straus, and, like other authors who yearned for such a powerful and devoted protector, Purdy grew envious of her success, which was linked to her relationship with Straus, who enabled her career. He felt like a perennial misfit and outsider, whereas Sontag's books received a level of editorial and marketing care that no other FSG author approached.[71]

Below Sontag's review on the same page of the *New York Times Book Review* was a positive review of *With Shuddering Fall*, the first novel by Joyce Carol Oates, who was then twenty-six years old. Soon, in *The Kenyon Review*, Oates disagreed with Sontag, panning Purdy's new novel and wondering at his high literary status. An "inspired parody of a novel" that is really a padded-out "pamphlet celebrating the evidently endless possibilities of literary American horror," *Cabot Wright Begins* aims "to demonstrate the sterility of modern America by achieving metaphoric sterility as art." "At its best, Purdy's satire is as biting as it is strident. . . . At its worst, however, Purdy's satire is noisy and tedious and inexplicably commonplace." His anger, "like any writer's, is justified only if transformed into an art that can arouse in its audience similar feelings. Writing evokes worlds; it does not simply state its intentions." She compared him to Nathanael West, but Purdy was "nowhere near" that satirical level. At the outset of her discussion of Purdy (she also criticized Ken Kesey's new novel and praised Jean Stafford's stories) she quotes Purdy as saying, "our entire moral life is pestiferous; we live in an immoral atmosphere," and she concludes with an attempted takedown. Purdy remained a "fascinating writer not because of his writing—which has certainly been better than it is here, although not spectacularly better—but because of his extraordinary reputation: '. . . James Purdy will come to be recognized as one of the greatest living writers of fiction in our language,' says Dame Edith Sitwell. And without writing fiction: surely this is possible only in modern, 'pestiferous' America!" Oates, who quotes the critic Dwight Macdonald, continues the pattern he established in 1957 of jabbing at an allegedly overinflated raft of Sitwellian praise.

Beyond satire, *Cabot Wright Begins* is early postmodern metafiction—writing about writing—but nearly everyone overlooked that aspect, Purdy said. Tony Tanner, in *City of Words: American Fiction 1950–1970*, states that Purdy's "extraordinary and original" oeuvre addresses "problems involved in the very fiction-making process itself." In "Beyond Omniscience: Notes toward a Future for the Novel" (1967), *TriQuarterly* editor Charles Newman wrote: "As in Nabokov, a writer whom Purdy at his fleeting best most resembles," the protagonist's struggle "to overcome his environment is merely a refraction of the narrator struggling to overcome language itself." In this light, "Cabot Wright" can be heard as a slurring of "cannot write." Amid discourse on the death of the novel, Purdy certified that "if a novel is to mean anything in our day, it must have as its central proposition the question of its own existence."[72] Despite Purdy's groundbreaking achievement in postmodern literature, as Matthew Stadler notes, Purdy was excluded from discussion by "the postmodern team" of white male heterosexual writers including John Barth, Robert Coover, William H. Gass, Donald Barthelme, and Thomas Pynchon, and their literary analysts. An exception is John Hawkes, who in a 1964 interview included Purdy on his list of writers exemplifying his notion of the avant-garde along with West, O'Connor, and Heller.[73] This omission is "all the more glaring because Purdy's absence" is not due to ignorance. Purdy was "a major force in American letters; even within this narrow corridor of influence, Purdy's work had been offered as an exemplary case of postmodern fiction by Ihab Hassan," whom Barth credited with inventing this critical frame, Stadler writes. Hassan, one of the most insightful and creative theorists of post-war and postmodern American literature, contributed to our culture's understanding of postmodernity. Of all the factors that marginalized Purdy's work, "this neglect by writers whose professed hopes for the novel were consonant with Purdy's achievement is among the most discouraging."[74]

Purdy lost his first and most fervent literary champion when Dame Edith Sitwell died on December 9. In Purdy's *Life* magazine review of Sitwell's autobiography, he called her the "greatest literary personality of an age" who in her final book confirmed "how lively and fearless, how entertaining and moving, how rich and incomparable she could be."[75] Purdy believed she "never faltered in her belief" in him. "I was always at a loss that I could give her so little in return except my devotion and love. Without her, I doubt that my work might ever have been published at all, for American publishers and reviewers are among the most benighted in the world, the most indifferent to works of the imagination and style." Along with letters, Edith sent messages to him through celebrated visitors. Sitwell feared Purdy would be "reduced to silence" by attacks on 63: Dream Palace that "stemmed from the V. S. Pritchett circuit. She was therefore greatly pleased when Malcolm and especially The Nephew received such good press in Great Britain and America." Purdy mourned her death as "a great personal loss to me. But her encouragement and belief in me has kept me writing in a world of coarse and short-sighted men and rank commercialism and shoddy vulgarity. She touched many lives and remains a vital force in letters."[76]

Soon after Purdy's greatest British champion passed, so did his greatest American booster. On Christmas Eve 1964, Carl Van Vechten died at age eighty-four. The intensity of their early correspondence could not have been sustained, but they remained good friends. In a tribute poem, "Carl Van Vechten," Purdy imagined his heaven: "A great wide-eyed, white-haired Child / innocent of death and pain, / seated at the head of a long pink table / presiding over a perpetual birthday party in his honor."[77] Within two years, James Purdy had lost both his parents, two uncles, and his two greatest champions.

He also seemed to be having money problems, despite his advances and royalties. In January 1965, Purdy asked Giroux if he would serve as reference in his application for a grant-in-aid from the Merrill Foundation, overseen by poet James Merrill. "In case you may be somewhat surprised at my again asking for additional economic assistance, I am heavily in debt from past years, and nearly everything I make this year and perhaps next must go to meet these debts."[78] Given all the grants and fellowships he had accrued, this would be somewhat surprising. Worries over money exacerbated his already troubled emotional state. "I am sick with my nerves," he wrote Neely Orme. "I would drink but I can't tolerate it, so suffer with headaches. I've been sick with my nerves my whole life and wouldn't care if I died. I think I will start having a Swedish masseur give me treatments. Nothing relieves the awful pressure." Cabot Wright wasn't selling, "but my publisher says Be Glad at least you Belong to the Future. What I need Neely is a present. I am so tired of being poor."[79]

If Purdy was unhappy with sales and his income, hopefully he derived some satisfaction from the critical esteem he was earning. In February, an illustrated feature by Douglas M. Davis in the *National Observer* covered the Black Humor literary movement, discussing Terry Southern, William S. Burroughs, John Barth, J. P. Donleavy, Joseph Heller, and James Purdy, who seemed to many to be "the brightest star in the new galaxy," having demonstrated talent in "almost every kind of fiction, from the novel of manners (*The Nephew*) to the darkly symbolic (*Malcolm*) to bizarre farce (*Cabot Wright Begins*)." Unsparingly, Purdy dwells on the "most hopeless and pitiable of characters, putting them into the most sordid and brutal of situations," some oddly comic. Purdy told Davis: "The American public's fear of emotion and analysis, its gregariousness, and its passionate love of cliches are both the reason why I am not read and the subject of my work." Purdy read a little Greek and Latin each day, then went out "spying on the universe." At age fifty, Purdy told Davis he was forty-one.[80]

Purdy's outrageous new novel was getting attention around the country. Chicago writer Studs Terkel, who interviewed guests on WBAI, told Osborn Andreas he wanted to help promote *Cabot Wright Begins*, an example of Purdy's rippling Chicago connections. Roger Straus replied to Purdy: "How can I possibly forget anyone named Studs Terkel?"[81] In June, Purdy granted permission for Studs to read from *Cabot* during an on-air book review.

Along with his new fiction, Purdy's poetry was gaining attention among his peers. Purdy was beginning to share his poems with FSG in hopes of a future poetry book and word was spreading about his quirky verse. In March, Purdy told Bob Giroux that Maurice Sendak, illustrator and author of the successful children's book *Where the Wild Things Are* (1963), was "very much interested in illustrating" Purdy's planned "book of verses" and had been phoning Purdy. Purdy wanted Giroux to send Sendak copies of the whimsical poems he had sent FSG.[82] Sadly, this collaboration between two gay geniuses did not transpire.

Through Van Vechten's circle, Purdy became friends with a young black writer, Henry Van Dyke, author of *Ladies of the Rachmaninoff Eyes*. On the jacket of this Stein-related novel, Purdy offered a rare endorsement: "In the age of the official zombie, Mr. Van Dyke is a rarity, for he has written a charming and incisive, witty and entertaining book. He has loads of talent." An ad quoted Purdy: "Readers whose palates are not tolerant of the hard-tack of mournful novels written by college professors will welcome the taste of Mr. Van Dyke's digestible and delicious confection." Privately, Purdy told

Giroux, who sent proofs, that he thought the book "very fine—the first half. Then he spoiled it all—ruined and threw away Maurice LeFleur as a character. Aunt Harry could *never* have revealed Sargeant's homosexuality in the manner she did. The murder of Peacock is bad. Ending ditto. Anyhow Mr. Van Dyke has **lots** of talent, and can write. I loved all the beginning."[83] Virgil Thomson thanked Purdy for sending him a copy. Van Dyke in his second novel, *Blood of Strawberries* (1969), irreverently based characters on Van Vechten and Fania Marinoff, as Coleman Dowell would do in *Island People* (1976) and Purdy would do in *Out with the Stars* (1993).[84]

Purdy's downcast mood dominated an appearance at Columbia University's Harkness Theatre in May, which was covered by critic and sportswriter Dick Schaap in the *Herald Tribune Book Week* supplement. His lecture was billed as "The Writer without a Public," but he just read from *Cabot Wright Begins*, "Daddy Wolf," and "Sermon." Schaap described Purdy as soft-spoken, "gentle and shy and immediately likeable, with light thinning hair and a pleasing smile." "Deliberately vague about his past" in Ohio and Chicago, Purdy lived alone, devoting "almost all of his time to his writing." Purdy felt pessimistic, claiming he was not respected or read. Although 150 people came out, Purdy thought "they didn't like my reading because they didn't like my book." He did not like to speak publicly and rarely sat for interviews or mixed with "literary crowds." Schaap thought 90 percent of the crowd had read *Cabot Wright* already and wanted to hear Purdy discuss himself and his literary problems and techniques. "But Purdy refused to accept this logical explanation. He thought the audience disliked him." Replying to a question that interrupted his reading, Purdy said the theme of all his books was the "alienation of the individual from a culture that is no longer human." When asked what society needs, Purdy said: "Each human being should be treated as a human being. And that has never happened, as far as I know. We're treated as dangerous objects. That's what *Cabot Wright* is about, and that's why nobody reads it."[85] Purdy seemed to refuse the success he was having, if modest. He did much better in July, when interviewed on *The Arlene Francis Show* on WOR radio and he felt it was possibly the best interview he had yet done. The host, an actress known as a panelist on the television show *What's My Line*, had "even read the book."[86]

Eight months after its US release, *Cabot Wright Begins* was published by Secker & Warburg in Britain. On May 30, 1965, in the *Observer*, Angus Wilson said it was his funniest novel and admirable as a departure from previous work. Purdy's talent had developed with each book, and *Cabot*, his "splendidly unfair assault on the United States, has its own strange pity. Mrs. and Mrs. Warburton are enchanting monsters born from an unholy union of [Ronald] Firbank with [humorist S. J.] Perelman." If Purdy sympathizes with Zoe Bickel's declaration, "I won't be a writer in a place and time like the present," the paradox is that "the more Purdy loathes 'the American way of life,' and more particularly its presentation in New York, the more his creative energies seem to boil and bubble over." If anyone was "still thinking to set the world on fire with 'the great American novel,' he may rest assured that Mr. Purdy will be ready to put out his blaze with the great American debunk." "Few modern novelists enjoy what they write as much as Mr. Purdy does. Indeed, one of the real dangers he runs—and does not wholly avoid in *Cabot Wright Begins*—is playing his own horror game with such zest that the reader is left now and again feeling an embarrassed intruder."[87]

Along similar lines, another English reviewer, P. N. Furbank, a literary biographer and critic for *Encounter*, called the "high-camp black humor" of *Cabot Wright Begins* "one of the most authentic things in American writing today." Extraordinary is the "speed and precision, the zestful ferocity with which, in a sentence or brief exchange of dialogue, he compasses extremes of absurdity and violence." Furbank memorably stated: "What Purdy is doing in this novel, one might say, is to translate the act of swearing into actuality. He is saying "F--- America" (with all the ambiguity that is involved in swearing, that is, the invoking of what is most desired or revered to express hostility) in the person of a hero who does literally that." If *Cabot Wright Begins* "is not the great anti-American novel, it is because, fundamentally, he is enjoying himself too much," so "his ghosts and monsters are annihilated too easily."[88] Befitting the loose agenda of *Encounter*, Furbank highlighted Purdy's individualism and freedom to lambaste the venal society he saw surrounding him. Nonetheless, *Partisan Review* and *National Review* panned the novel from the left and right in the spring of 1965.[89]

Purdy's money problems were solved temporarily when Avon issued a paperback of *Cabot Wright Begins* in November, having given him a sizable advance of $17,500. The paperback did not sell as well as expected, however, despite its sensational subject; sales estimates made in 1965 and 1966 were overstated. During 1968, Avon shipped a thousand copies, but in 1969, Avon's manager told FSG, "I must, in all honesty, state that it is not very likely that we will be able to 'earn out' the remaining $13,000 of the advance."[90] The provocative cover featured a painting of a newspaper clipping with a picture of Cabot and the headline, "Rapist Released," stamped with a lipstick kiss.

The copy reads, "Girls! He's back!" Purdy told Straus he found it "atrocious. If they want to public to think it is a dirty book, they should hire a competent dirty artist, instead of the jejune imitation of [Bruce Jay Friedman's 1964 black humor novel A] *Mother's Kisses* or whatever that trash was." He called it a "cynical and shameless insult to a writer like myself. I cannot overlook it."[91]

In spring and summer 1965, Purdy took stock of his career, asking FSG to reissue *Color of Darkness* in hardcover with the Sitwell preface and also to compile a "James Purdy Reader." Purdy told Giroux: "the hardcover edition of the book as published by New Directions, is 'cribbed' and electrotyped from the original private editions." To Laughlin, Purdy had highly praised the physical book on publication, but now it was an "ugly book, along Scotch Presbyterian miser lines," resembling "Aunt Netty's Cook Book." These projects did not come to fruition. Purdy became frustrated, even angry with James Laughlin and Bob MacGregor at New Directions for not selling the rights to his two collections to FSG. Laughlin was willing to license the stories but would not relinquish rights. Enraged, Purdy fired off a series of scolding missives. In July, MacGregor, after combing through New Directions files, wrote a detailed, seemingly reasonable, four-page single-spaced typed letter responding to Purdy's condemnation, which had inflicted "gashes" on him and Laughlin. Piecing together evidence from correspondence, MacGregor thought he proved the publisher had gone above and beyond in enthusiasm and promotion, back to their encouragement when Purdy submitted "Don't Call Me by My Right Name" in 1953, which they published in 1957. Bob attested he could only be "amazed at how much everyone here was doing" for Purdy all along. The number of free promotional copies sent to tastemakers and writers, often at Purdy's request, but often on their own steam, was "almost overwhelming." Laughlin had made a list of one hundred people who should receive free copies of *Color of Darkness*. No other writer on their list, "or any writer on any publisher's list—was promoted with so many free copies of books of short stories." Surely, MacGregor thought, Purdy might be satisfied.

But that was impossible. Purdy wanted FSG to control the stories and would do whatever it took to make this happen. He responded with acid tongue:

I am sorry about your hurt feelings. For years I crawled through dirt to get published, and have always suffered from every kind of poverty, and lack of the necessities. If you think these terrible experiences are going to make me weep over your sensitive feelings, you are quite mistaken. My writing is a matter of life and death, and neither you nor James Laughlin is a writer, or has ever been acquainted with poverty. If you think you can continue this persecution of me (and I can just see you shaking your heads as you apply the standard clichés of psychoanalysis here) by holding back my just ownership of the rights to my books you are quite mistaken. You will either return the rights or you can devote the rest of your lives to hearing from me. Jay with his wealth and his power can use the grossly unfair methods of the publishing world to keep my books while neither you nor he do a thing in the way or promotion or advertising. Fortunately I now have the ear of responsible and decent-thinking persons, who believe I should have full rights to my books. If you and J. want to go on with your pious declarations of concern for my well-being while gouging and bullying me out of what is mine, very well. But you are in then for a hot summer, and I intend to spend all my energy, all my time, all my talent in bringing home to you the injustice you are doing. I will never rest until you return to me my rightful ownership of my books. Never, never, never![92]

Such tirades contributed to Purdy's reputation among some gay creatives as a "bitch." Nine days later, Purdy made his point again, this time to Laughlin:

You are obviously unaware that by retaining rights to my books, you are causing me to lose income and prestige. . . .

Only a very wealthy man out of touch with reality and with a total lack of comprehension of a writer could behave as you do. You pretend to care about my welfare. You care nothing about it. You have never visited me or showed any of the concern for my existence as has Robert Giroux. It may be too late to avoid a tragedy, but I do not see how. You will understand that by tragedy I do not mean of course anything pertaining to you. You are too cold, too selfish, too rich to know tragedy.

I mean a tragedy.

Either you return the rights to me, by ceding them to [FSG], or you must be convicted by literary conscience as a man who for vain personal reasons for years has held an author to him against the author's will in the most degrading relationship I have ever experienced, depriving the author of needed income, and causing him great personal anguish. You are the most odious person in my life. You are wealthy and powerful, but the conscience of the decent literary community will convict you and you will remain in literary history, known by that conviction. Nothing will wash it away, and your previous good actions will remain soiled by it. This is the serious consequences of your stubborn, selfish, and coldly egomaniacal course.[93]

Purdy's histrionics did not sway New Directions this time.

Giroux and FSG increasingly promoted Purdy's poetry and planned a collection. These whimsical poems can be seen as his escape into childhood memory prompted by the loss of his parents. In July, Giroux wrote Webster Schott, serving as editor of *Focus/Midwest*, who accepted "Seven Poems" untitled and brief: "Since the book's complete contents and title have not been settled, I suggest you say something like, "these poems are from a work in progress by Mr. Purdy which now bears the tentative title *Poems for Children Away from Home*. It will eventually be published by Farrar, Straus & Giroux." In September, James told Straus his good friend, Richard Hundley, was at the MacDowell Colony, and relayed that Howard Moss, poetry editor of the *New Yorker*, liked Purdy's work and was "interested in seeing some of the nonsense poems" Giroux had been disseminating. Roger Straus approached Moss, a closeted gay, alcoholic poet, saying Purdy had "from time to time been writing poetry which we call nonsense verse. One of these days we are going to do a book of them. In the meantime I thought you might be interested in seeing them. I will of course be much interested in your reaction." Moss replied he was happy to get to read Purdy's poems but did not think there was "anything here" for the magazine. "Children's poems—and I'd say these are—somehow never seem to fit in to the *New Yorker*, though why I don't know, when you think of Carroll and Lear."[94]

If his poetry was prompted in part by the loss of his parents, as a novelist, Purdy, though beclouded by grief, found an artistic silver lining in that he felt the death of his parents liberated him to write about anything.[95] So in 1964 and 1965, he drafted a work even more outrageous than *Cabot Wright Begins*, drawing from his early years in Chicago. Composing what became *Eustace Chisholm and the Works*, in September 1965, Purdy told Abercrombie: "You will like my new book—the one I'm writing right now—it has the old real you in it—describes your first abortion and your gay life before you married those dumb men. You must be *you* again. You're too great for men. Come back, Gertrude, come back! You can! I LOVE YOU!" Gertrude had separated from her second husband, Frank Sandiford, who had recently taken up with a younger woman he met while relaxing at the Yaddo retreat, having conned Saul Bellow into recommending him. Writing this new novel was taxing and creating the violent climax was most painful. One morning, he could not arise from bed and had to go to hospital, he later said.[96]

In March 1965 and in February 1966, Purdy appeared at a celebrated Manhattan salon at "the Crane apartment" at 820 Fifth Avenue overlooking Central Park Zoo. His champions like Edith Sitwell, Virgil Thomson, and Tennessee Williams had been visitors and recipients of patronage. At Louise Crane's Tuesday Afternoon Class, he read to an invited group of ladies in a gold salon called The Big Room, lavish with paintings and sculpture, Chester Page writes. For each visit, he was paid one hundred dollars (about $820 in 2020). The first reading likely focused on *Cabot Wright* and the second from work-in-progress *Eustace Chisholm and the Works*. One wonders what these refined ladies including poet Marianne Moore thought of this new, edgy material.[97]

Although *The Nephew* had scandalized his father and aunt's hometown of Bowling Green, Ohio, the state university was now eager to offer him a job. While James was visiting Neely Orme in Marvell, Arkansas, he got a postcard from Aunt Cora saying "someone in authority" at BGSU was trying to contact him about a teaching position. "He wanted your telephone no. but I was not sure of that so gave him your address and I said that you had a new book, now with the publisher or printer. He spoke highly of your writings. I think they pay pretty well here. Probably better than in the East." But Purdy had no interest in teaching Spanish or any subject at Bowling Green—nor anywhere, if he could help it.[98]

Joseph Skerrett Jr., a young black professor, responded to a second letter from Purdy in September. Skerrett, then early in his career at Trenton Junior College, was pleased to receive it and doubly pleased to hear Purdy had enjoyed his essay on Purdy's works. "It is very assuring, at least to the *beginning* critic, to find that he and the author do not hold diametrically opposed opinions of the author's hard work." *Malcolm* was being taught in a course on the novel at Skerrett's college.[99]

Purdy completed *Eustace Chisholm and the Works* in January 1966. He asked Giroux for three sets of galley proofs because Jorma Sjoblom and Peter L. Redmond, who became a co-dedicatee with Edward Albee, had promised help with proofreading. Peter Redmond was a neighbor, friend, correspondent, and patron who knew Paul Swan and Bettina Schwarzschild.[100]

Most people would choose to take a rest after completing such an intense novel, the writing of which had taken a toll. But, as Purdy joked, there is no peace for the wicked.[101] He did not seem to pause for a moment but straightaway began drafting a semiautobiographical novel about his up-bringing in Ohio. Material was flowing freely. "I am getting rather deep into *Sleepers In Moon-Crowned Valleys*; this book seems to have a rather large structure, and may have to come out in two volumes," he predicted.[102]

11

Maggoty Urgings

In January 1965, the famous playwright Edward Albee was adapting to the stage the Purdy novel that his ex-boyfriend, Terrence McNally, had adapted fruitlessly the previous summer. Ned Rorem heard about this and wrote Purdy, expressing interest in composing music for *Malcolm* in hopes that Purdy might champion him. This was an unlikely bid, since William Flanagan was not only Albee's official composer, as Rorem noted, but also his former romantic partner. "But it goes without saying that I'd also love to do it if *you* want me!"[1] Ned wanted to see James again soon. Rorem had privately recorded that he felt Flanagan's music lacked direction, so it was not theatrical.[2] Rorem could have written better music for *Malcolm*, being familiar with its Chicago milieu, and some of his songs had a jazz flavor. But the best score would have been written by a jazz composer.

In June 1965, Bill Flanagan wrote Albee, who was in Europe, saying he had seen Purdy at a party hosted by the poet Frank O'Hara. This is notable since no other link has been established between Purdy and this gay literary legend. When Flanagan told Purdy that Albee was in the midst of adapting *Malcolm*, he "seemed astonished. I hear he's awfully broke, and that may have explained the look of sudden cheer on his face."[3] Thirteen months later, O'Hara died tragically following an accident on the beach at Fire Island Pines.

In October, Rorem saw doom on the horizon for Albee's *Malcolm*. He reckoned "the Candide theme (Herlihy's *Midnight Cowboy*, Genet's *Querelle de Brest* or Southern's *Candy* versus Britten's *Billy Budd*, Bernstein's *Candide* or the Purdy-Albee *Malcolm*) makes good reading but bad theater. The beautiful but dumb cipher-hero plunging down a narrow path causing distress and destruction to intelligent victims—whom he ignores as victims—is inherently undramatic, being anticlimactic."[4]

In retrospect, Albee's *Malcolm* was built to fail. Albee removed central characters, including a black undertaker (Estel Blanc) and his transgender, racially ambiguous singer and dancer (Cora Naldi), turned two other black characters white, replaced a little person (Kermit Raphaelson) with the world's oldest man, and removed the tattoo parlor. In so doing, Albee penned a lackluster adaptation that sometimes missed Purdy's themes. Albee, who was known for being controlling with productions, strangely disengaged from that of *Malcolm*, even with the knowledge that director Alan Schneider was unenthusiastic about Albee's take on the novel. This behavior is irrational.[5]

Purdy had little say over Albee's choices and was only allowed to offer him feedback toward the end of the process. Albee, who had planned to finish the play in August 1965 and begin rehearsals in October, was still completing revisions at the close of 1965. Therefore, by the time Albee sent the script to Purdy, there was hardly time to make any significant changes.[6]

A huge disappointment, Edward Albee's adaptation of *Malcolm* was a flop, closing after only seven performances on Broadway. "Of all Albee's plays, *Malcolm* is probably the one with the fewest admirers, the easiest to categorize as a mistake," biographer Mel Gussow assesses.[7] Its premiere on January 11, 1966, followed twenty half-price preview shows at the overly capacious Schubert Theater. Just as dreamy teenager Malcolm was destined to die prematurely in Purdy's novel, so was his namesake play destined to fail, it seemed. This outcome was particularly painful for Purdy and his admirers, since had such an adaptation been a success, it would have boosted Purdy's career significantly. As it happened, the play diminished the reputation of the novel, sullying it, and Purdy generally, with failure. Albee, on the other hand, though floundering between the huge success of *Who's Afraid of Virginia Woolf* (1962) on Broadway and its film adaptation in 1966, survived the *Malcolm* debacle totally unscathed.

Albee's *Malcolm* was panned by critics across the board, though some found things to admire, such as the clean modernist set design. But not one critic liked Albee's insipid script, not even those who had liked Purdy's novel. After low ticket sales and half-empty houses, Albee's producers, Clinton Wilder and Richard Barr, "decided not to risk further loss," it was reported. To observers, however, it seemed not credible that a playwright of Albee's caliber could have taken such a fall. In the aftermath, critic Richard L. Coe broke down the financials, concluding something was "grievous wrong" when "any play by a leading playwright, no matter how poorly received, is unable to survive better than this. Who says economics has nothing to do with art?" Coe reasoned tickets should have been offered again at a half-price scale to keep the show running rather than canceling it after seven performances. The rapid shutdown was weird and confounding.[8]

Albee, contending with demons of paranoia and alcoholism, viewed Purdy as a genius, a rival, and a threat. Possessing a "prickly personality marked by malice,"[9] Albee was neurotically envious of the cornucopia of praise Purdy had received. Arguably, Albee adapted *Malcolm* in bad faith, making changes detrimental to scenes and characters that sapped energy and muddied meaning. The critical consensus was the play seemed meaningless, and Albee seemed content with that. This was less an adaptation than a hostile take-over. Albee sought to take down Purdy and thwart McNally, who had wanted to adapt *Malcolm*, by co-opting, defacing, and legally co-owning rights to Purdy's signature work. Albee could then control and horde *Malcolm* as a "property." After this botched production, Malcolm became a "merger" and Purdy could not greenlight any adaptations without Albee's approval. The merger placed *Malcolm* in the middle of two mad geniuses. Editor and publisher Don Weise, who worked with both, commented: "When you put Edward Albee and James Purdy together, it's like an *explosion*."[10]

Matthew Cowles played *Malcolm* in his debut role. When Purdy met him in his dressing room, he thought Cowles had really turned into Malcolm. So he gave him a copy of *Cabot Wright Begins* "to save him," Purdy told Giroux.[11] Privately, Purdy thought Cowles had "much of the naiveté and innocence—very good—but lacks the 'divine' or 'princely' aura implicit in the meaning. Doesn't suggest deeper meaning" but "anyhow Matthew Cowles was fine." Veteran actress Estelle Parsons played Laureen Raphaelson, who leaves her husband Kermit, in the novel an artist and a little person. "Laureen was well played by Estelle Parsons," Purdy noted privately, but of Kermit, "no old man can replace a midget." As for Alan Schneider, he had directed the American premieres of *Virginia Woolf*, *Tiny Alice*, Albee's adaptation of McCullers's *Ballad of the Sad Café*, and *Waiting for Godot*.

Nevertheless, Albee's *Malcolm* was abysmal. Mel Gussow wrote that Albee's adaptation was "artificial and undramatic and the production failed on basic levels." The *New Yorker* trounced it.[12] *Time* condemned it: Albee "finds all his vintage wines in another man's cellar. The trouble is that these wine bottles are now empty, and the wind whistles over them all evening in a low, monotonous, deadly moan." Indeed, Albee emptied out of the novel much excitement and significance. *Choice*, published by the American Library Association, reviewed the play unfavorably, but stressed Purdy's novel is "clever and well written," and, unlike Albee's take, "Purdy's use of irony, humor, and improbable situations is fresh and expansive."[13] Fourteen months later, Albee claimed to believe it was "a good play, a better play than the critics said it was. Something went very wrong with the production," which "sort of got out of my control."[14] Privately, Purdy thought it lacked the "visual splendor necessary to convey the background of the novel." The mise en scène was "not splendid enough. Everybody economizes where I am concerned."

In the late 1960s, Purdy said publicly he liked Albee's adaptation, but he didn't, as his personal notes on the script show. "Albee's concept of Malcolm" was "very different" from his. Omissions of the "midget" who denies his difference, the black undertaker, and tattoo palace are "not just omissions of a dramatic exigency but show a radically different concept."[15] Albee claimed he could not find anyone to play "the midget, or dwarf, so he changed it to a one hundred and twenty-year-old man, and that doesn't work at all," Purdy told storywriter Patricia Lear. John Uecker said that the actor Michael Dunn, who had been in Albee's adaptation of *The Ballad of the Sad Café*, "hated the script and refused to do it," so Albee changed the part "out of spite."[16] Changing characters is like adding the "wrong thing in the soup after it's perfect, and then you can't drink it."[17] Privately, Purdy was no humbler: "Albee removed two crucial characters, the colored undertaker and Kermit as a midget and artist. Like removing Hamlet's ghost father and the Queen from *Hamlet*. Can't work as *Malcolm* without these." In notes for an article intended for *Life* magazine, he said the lack of a midget was "a death blow." In 2000, Purdy was forthright: it was "terrible. Awful. I like Edward Albee, though. I'm glad he did it. It had moments, but I don't know that anyone could put *Malcolm* on the stage."[18] In his notes, he said the actor playing Mr. Cox was "dreadful" and "wretched!" He was gutted by how things turned out: "I hate the stage and the theater—Broadway is just for the clank of jewels, wigs, manufactured cunts. Awful institution should be bombed."[19] In 2004, to novelist Martin Goodman, Purdy said Albee "didn't understand the book at all. When the great gold curtain went up there was just the bench. When the great gold curtain came down there was silence. Then the great gold curtain went up and there was the boy on the bench. That was the only good thing. He should have stopped there and told the audience to go home." After that, according to Purdy's notes on the playscript, "none of this worked dramatically or visually—Dead."[20]

Jarringly, Albee removed the blackness from Purdy's story, including nearly all the jazz. Estel Blanc is central, "essential to book or play." Purdy stated plainly in his article draft: "Edward Albee's recent dramatization of my book excludes carefully and thoroughly all the Negro elements (I can only guess why)."[21] Albee's script gestures only once at the modern jazz that Purdy had heard at Abercrombie's salons. Purdy told Marie-Claude Profit, "it was not my work. It was rather gloomy. He cut out all the humor. And he changed all the blacks to whites and the musical score instead of being jazz was sort of avant-garde music of many years ago. It had a very ambitious score." Purdy wrote privately: "Mr. Flanagan's musical score was distinguished, but doesn't convey all the shades of the novel—it is sparse like everything else in the production."[22] Estel Blanc says he is "puzzled" by Malcolm's "coolness, detachment, and lack of receptivity." After Estel suggests it may be because of his prejudice toward his occupation or "racial strain," Malcolm offends by saying he likes him and is "willing to just forget you were an undertaker or a mortician or a . . . a . . . Abyssinian, or anything!" Estel Blanc, a man with "dark" skin tone whose surname ironically means "white," tells teenage Malcolm to "come back in twenty years, and we shall understand one another." Privately, Purdy toyed with an outrageous idea. Ruth White is a "good actress but not Madame Girard," he mused, "perhaps a man could play Madame Girard more effectively." This in turn led him to expand the idea that, had blacks not become so establishment, "Malcolm should be played entirely by a Negro male cast."[23] Purdy complained privately: "Albee ignored fact that nearly half the characters in Malcolm are colored. He made it all white." Albee whitewashed Gus and his ex-wife, the popular nightclub singer, Melba. Purdy does not specify Melba's race, but she had been married to a black man at a time when that was rare, if not illegal, and her character was influenced by the jazz legend, Billie Holiday.[24] In Albee's version, white actors played Gus and Melba. Purdy thought Gus was played by "a good actor but not dreamy enough" and "should have been colored." Pair a weak script with a lifeless set and a set of distracting treadmills that never quite worked right—"you get on them and suddenly you've forgotten all your lines," an actor said—and you have a surefire recipe for disaster! The director did not even meet the cast until the day before Thanksgiving 1965.[25]

Albee kidnapped Purdy's "golden boy," Malcolm, and stupefied and neutered him for purposes of his own, writing a play that was "dull from start to finish," as the Library Journal called the book published of Albee's play. Albee's apparent purpose was to inflict harm upon both Purdy and his admirer, Terrence McNally. In Albee's 1980 foreword to the Dream Palaces omnibus that was also appended to three separate paperback reissues, he curiously remarks that Purdy "received public praise of a fulsomeness—the extravagance of enthusiasm—that may have sown envy and maggoty urgings

toward revenge in the hearts of many." Albee's use of the passive voice is revealing; this is only what he decided to confess in print.

Albee was willing to have one of his plays bomb to take down Purdy a
peg. Critic Robert Brustein gives the game away in the *New Republic*: Albee's
"declared intention was to attract readers to Purdy's writings, but he seems
to have precisely the opposite effect."[26] Purdy gathered a sense of this. His
essay "*Malcolm*, Mr. Cough Syrup, and the American People," published by
the *Harvard Advocate* in March 1966, skewers masculinist critics, particularly Stanley Kauffmann (Mr. Cough Syrup), who reviewed Albee's *Malcolm*
for the *New York Times*, liking the costumes and sets but panning Albee's
play. Just eleven days after Kauffmann's review of *Malcolm* appeared, the
critic published his infamous article "Homosexual Drama and Its Disguises"
in the *Times*, which begins: "A recent Broadway production raises again the
subject of the homosexual dramatist." Notoriously, Kauffmann claimed that,
because of society's censure of homosexuality, gay playwrights had been
staging gay dramas in drag. Posing as progressive, in reality Kauffmann liked
to take down gay writers; for example, he was nearly alone in his scathing
criticism of Capote's *In Cold Blood* and he sneered at Donald Windham's *Two
People*.[27] In Purdy's notes, he wrote: "Imagine old pious professional heterosexual 'normal' Kauffmann, petty middle-class freak off [the] couch of psychoanalysis. He pinches women on his TV show to indicate he had graduated
into heterosexuality. Verdict: a repressed fellator, hates women *and* men."
Although Purdy's piece in the *Harvard Advocate* had the goal of exposing
the limitations of types of East Coast critics, Purdy also did damage control
when he clarifies: "The amusing thing about it all is that the Broadway drama
critics nearly all pretended to think highly of my novel *Malcolm*. Some of
them called it a 'classic,' pointed out that it had been translated into 15 foreign
languages, and was read in colleges and universities. They even said it was
readable. It was the play *Malcolm*, they argued, which was bad-bad, and also
very homosexual."

Albee's producer Richard Barr confessed: "Edward wrote that play with a
sword instead of a pen and we overproduced it."[28] In a dark place, seething
with envy, Albee plunged his sword into his rival. Purdy intuited the truth: "As
a matter of fact, I never believed *Malcolm* was on Broadway, and I don't now,
and it probably never was."

In his draft of an article intended for *Life*, Purdy suggests he grew suspicious of Albee's character. Albee altered some characters "in line with his
own concept of 'evil.' None of the characters in my novel are 'evil' in the sense

that they have planned to 'corrupt' the 15 year old here. They simply have no values by which to live." Albee, for dramatic purposes, "or because he reads life this way," made two characters, "Eloisa Brace, the jazz queen [and artist], and Jerome Brace, the burglar, actively evil, in that they sell Malcolm to an irresponsible person who causes his death, while in the original story, the characters are too unaware of the meaning of life to know they are harmful by default. Evil in the novel is gratuitous—people harm because they are not sufficiently alive to care about others, while in Mr. Albee's play, people are purposely harmful and conniving."[29]

Albee's play of *Malcolm* was published by Atheneum, with Purdy's name on the cover along with the playwright's, much to the chagrin of FSG, which felt violated. A January 1966 in-house note from Giroux stated their quarrel was "not with Atheneum but with (1) Purdy and (2) Albee." Contractually, Purdy had granted FSG exclusive right to publish and authorize publication of *Malcolm* in book form. If Purdy had granted any publishing rights, it was only through reference to the Dramatist Guild contract, but Albee never even asked for a quitclaim. "Too bad Phelps is such a dope," Giroux wrote. "Does anybody know William Morris well enough to get information from him?"[30]

In fall of 1967, Purdy complained to Giroux that Jack Phelps had "left all the proposed movie adaptations, plays, etc. in such a bang-up mess," he hardly knew "where to turn." Because *Malcolm* was legally a "merger" with Albee's adaptation, Purdy "thought it best to turn this over to a lawyer, rather than bother" Giroux with it. "I have also asked Edward Albee to dissolve the 'merger', so that '*Malcolm*' will be returned as a 'property' entirely to me."[31] Purdy began his missive to Albee: "May I ask you a favor . . . would you consider releasing the 'merger' of your play '*Malcolm*' from my novel, or whatever the legal jargon is."[32] Albee replied quickly: "Considering the obligation that we both have to the unfortunate investors who put their ill-gotten money into the stage production of *Malcolm*, I don't think we can release *Malcolm* in the way you suggest."[33] If the men were angry, they did not show it since Albee invited Purdy to have champagne at his place on Christmas 1967 and said it would be fine if James brought his doctor friend along (likely Dr. Sjoblom). As late as 2005, in reply to Purdy, Albee refused to budge on relinquishing *Malcolm*. "The rights are merged and will stay so."[34]

After the debacle on Broadway, Purdy for a long time soured on the idea of adapting *Malcolm* into a movie, which was related to Albee now having 50 percent ownership. He considered the proposal of Chicago theater producer Bob Sickinger, who wanted to adapt *Malcolm* into a film, but ultimately concluded he did not want a film made, much to the producer's disappointment. He wanted to concentrate all his time on *Sleepers in Moon-Crowned Valleys*.

Albee had final thoughts about the debacle of his *Malcolm*. He fled New York and was taking an extended trip throughout Europe. The failure did not faze him; in fact, he felt fine. He pretended to feel "guilty and uneasy" about how well he felt. "Indeed, why was I not going into a decline? Why was I *not* sleepless, disoriented, and given to feelings of worthlessness and subject to writers-block?" On the contrary, *A Delicate Balance* flowed out of him after the regenerative violence of taking down Purdy and limiting McNally. "Maybe I shall have a collapse, months from now. Maybe I *will* fall apart and become a stone, or rage." This seems improbable, given that in this same letter, he reported meeting Richard Burton and Elizabeth Taylor in Rome to discuss them starring in the film of *Virginia Woolf.* "Right now, though, I am of good mind, am working, resting, and—at most—mildly curious to know, when the time comes, whether or not the commercial failure of *Malcolm* was a true statement of its artistic value, as well. Otherwise, I couldn't care less about it. Had it not been an adaptation!!!! Well now!!!)."[35] Albee's coldness, not even mentioning Purdy, is stunning. The photo by Alix Jeffry on the dust jacket for the book of the play says it all. Sitting on the left, blending in the background, Purdy is in a casual jacket and tie, speaking amiably with Schneider, center. In sharp focus, dark Albee dons an immaculate tuxedo, his hair apparently recently styled by a professional. He is glaring at Purdy.

As for Purdy, he closed a letter of January 21, 1966, to Straus: "I'm recovering from Armageddon at the Shubert! Let's have the Mafia sprit away the next adapter."

———

Adding to Purdy's worry, a homophobic backlash review against *Cabot Wright Begins* was collected in hardcover. In the chapter "The Correction of Opinion" from *Standards* (1966), Stanley Edgar Hyman delivers a savage hatchet job on Purdy, in which the critic calls Purdy a boring and terrible writer. In turn, Purdy called Hyman "shit-face."[36] From 1961 to 1965, Hyman was literary critic for *The New Leader*, a magazine that ran Alfred Sundel's homophobic attack on Purdy in 1961 and Hyman's denunciation of *Cabot Wright Begins* in late 1964.[37] In his introduction, Hyman proclaims that his collection is the record of an "experiment in regularly confronting the literature of our time with a hard eye, insisting on standards of excellence at a time of general cultural debasement." Raised an Orthodox Jew, Hyman became a staff writer for the *New Yorker* in 1940 under the editorship of William Shawn, and then a professor at Bennington College, despite having no graduate degree. Although Hyman was an important critic, he is better known as the husband of writer Shirley Jackson. Though Stanley Hyman was a rampant philanderer, he strongly supported Jackson's literary career, so in his original review, arguably he was gunning down her competition. Both Jackson and Purdy were highly praised in the early 1960s and dealt in strange, dark subjects, their stories sometimes climaxing in shock. Jackson died young in August 1965.

Moving past the Broadway fiasco, to avoid cabin fever, James got out of New York to speak on college campuses. In April 1966, he gave readings at Lafayette College in Pennsylvania and at Wesleyan University in Connecticut; *Malcolm* was taught at both, and Lafayette professors said it was received well. He enjoyed the students at Wesleyan, but those at Lafayette "were much brighter and more alert." He said the best audience he ever had was at Bennington College, however.[38] Whether he interacted with Stanley Edgar Hyman there is unknown.

In 1966, Purdy revised and rewrote parts of *Eustace Chisholm and the Works*. In the heat of July, he sweated over revisions. Needing to rewrite about thirty-five pages of the gruesome conclusion, he devoted all his time to finishing it. "The book seems as terrible in subject matter as this weather, and I am making it for that reason as formally polished as possible."

At last, with a sense of relief and triumph, on July 13, four days before he turned fifty-two, Purdy personally delivered the complete revised first draft to his editor, Robert Giroux.[39]

12

The Sun at Noon

Farrar, Straus & Giroux supported Purdy during the editing and publication process of his novels. Purdy was in a good situation with FSG, especially with Robert Giroux as editor, which he did not always seem to appreciate.

In September 1966, Purdy told Bob Giroux he was pleased with the responses that he and Hal Vursell had given to his revised draft of *Eustace Chisholm and the Works*. Some of the direction of Giroux's thought worried him, though, since he seemed too concerned about "placating a kind of critic, which will be impossible in any sense." Giroux felt scenes involving the wealthy heir, Reuben Masterson (based on Norman MacLeish), and "Ace" Chisholm (based on Wendell Wilcox) could be reduced profitably, and he wanted to abbreviate the title to *The Works*, which Purdy rejected as "arcane and affected." Moreover, Giroux wanted Eustace to become a bit more likable. Purdy countered that Eustace was "quite important by reason of his scurrility, incapability of love, and spiritual deadness—he is part of the Depression, while Amos and Daniel are beyond and outside of it." Purdy struggled to revise the story to introduce Amos Ratcliffe earlier. He asserted he had given everything up for his writing and did not write the novel "to please anybody in the critical world of New York," insisting "we cannot pare down the scurrility and horror of the character" to "please those who can never be pleased." Giroux replied quickly. Purdy had misunderstood; he agreed it is "impossible to placate them anyway." He and James both did not know nor care what critics wanted in a book, since only two critics interested him—himself and Purdy. "I know that you can make this fine novel a better book, and that is all that interests me." The only change Giroux now suggested was to make "stronger and more central" the relationship between Amos and Daniel, which in his view, the book was mostly about. If they were both satisfied in the final round, then "bugger the critics. Of course, where this will leave Warburg," he did not know. Giroux was curious what his reaction would be.[1]

The editorial decisions touched off a war of words between American and English publishers. In late September, Giroux sent Fred Warburg an angry letter. Fred had read an early typescript draft of *Eustace Chisholm* with "extraordinary interest" as he told Purdy, but made no immediate commitment for Secker & Warburg to publish because he felt the typescript was "in pretty bad shape." The story had "caused a rather intense depression" in him and a second reader. The novel seemed pointless, not written with the "economy and wit of earlier books" but rather "full of a rather unpleasant and juvenile pornography and to contain at the end a scene of sadistic murder which is most revolting in every way." He supposed they could "sell a few thousand," but unless he and the reader were crazy, which was "always possible," there was no way the novel would receive good reviews or benefit Purdy's reputation at all. Warburg said Giroux might hold a different view of the novel and he wanted to hear it in confidence; meanwhile, he would not commit to publishing a book he deemed "a disaster."[2]

Warburg told Giroux that his reply was "real slashing and I feel my back is covered from weals from your whip. In defense of myself I would say that I had no desire to see Purdy's novel before you operated on it, merely a typescript when the editorial agony had been completed." This shows the important role played by Giroux, who had declared, "it happens to be Purdy's best book." Warburg countered: "I am both surprised and not surprised at this statement but since I am dealing with an editor whom I knew to be gifted with second sight into Purdy's entrails, a gift which must at times be a source of sadness to you, I accept this statement with only the tiniest grain of salt." This punning use of "entrails" alludes to the biblically named Daniel's ghastly disembowelment at the climax, after he is thrown, or throws himself, to a lion, Captain Stadger—but is not saved. "Since I have written nothing to Purdy or Phelps yet, I will follow your advice by writing immediately and selecting from the list of powerful adjectives you have provided me with in your final paragraph to keep him in the mood of comparative sanity. If I do this effectively, it should be helpful to you rather than not."[3] Revealing of his editorial relationship with Purdy, Giroux replied: "The key phrase is 'difficult at first sight though the book was.' You refer to *Malcolm*, but the words apply to *Eustace* and indeed every Purdy book. I should not have written in anger and I regret it, but the anger arose from the fact that Purdy is being extremely difficult about editorial changes, and I am fearful that two cooks may spoil the broth. *Eustace* contains his strongest characters and one of his best stories; it is very American, very violent, very shocking. We may not succeed in eradicating the flaws; any kind of advice from any other quarter, whether praise or adverse criticism, is going to complicate matters."[4] At times, Purdy had to be handled with kid gloves.

Fred Warburg then wrote Purdy, saying the manuscript seemed "far from being in final shape as you must know, and I have no doubt that you will find Bob Giroux a fast, patient, and brilliant editor. At the moment there are various difficulties in the novel which I know will be ironed out before you go into proof" and he would not sign a contract until this was done. He wanted to see a later draft, expressing concern about "strong pornographic and sadistic elements" that could stymie publication. Jack Phelps jumped: he and his lawyers construed Warburg's response as a rejection of *Eustace*. He also wrote Giroux, concerned about editorial changes. As usual, Phelps stirred up confusion and, sometimes, hard feelings. Why Purdy did not sell better in the early years when he was eliciting so much high praise is partially attributable to mediocre or poor agents in Strassman and Phelps, respectively.[5] After all these words, Secker & Warburg turned down *Eustace Chisholm*, and instead Jonathan Cape published it in 1968.

Even as Giroux vigorously defended his prose, Purdy grew anxious over some aspects of his editing. Having thought it over, he was "really quite upset" he planned to excise so much from the opening. "I really prefer the book the way I presented it to you in the first place, for I do not see any conflict in the slow, rather than dramatic introduction of Amos. However, as you say, it is perhaps advisable for the book to go to the printer. . . . I felt in your other corrections, frankly, that you had soft-pedaled far too many things. Otherwise, of course, it is a very fine piece of editing."

The other thing worrying Purdy was what he characterized as Giroux's "general gloom" about the novel's chance of any kind of success. "Frankly, I have reached a crisis in my career. Unless *Eustace* can be made to have some sort of decent 'commercial' success, I do not see how I can continue to write for formal publication. In other words, the people who have kept me from starving to death since 1954, are quite prepared to simply publish the rest of my work, the way they began, 'privately.' I have found living in New York, and putting up with all the irritations and deprivations of publishing, **unendurable**. I do not think I can stand much more. It may very well be that with *Eustace*, I simply bow out and resume my career as privately existing and privately publishing."[6] In November, Giroux explained to Phelps that he was one-third finished with the revisions of *Eustace*, but it was "very slow work." Giroux maintained the "essential character of the book is not changed"; revisions were "clarifications and simplifications—polishing, really. This procedure James and I have followed on all his books beginning with *Malcolm*, and it is no different with the new novel." No character or event was changed.[7]

On December 18, 1966, James's aunt, Cora Purdy, died in Bowling Green. "I remember how much you used to hear from her," Norman MacLeish wrote with condolences. "And I always had an idea that she was almost more of a mother to you than your own mother."[8] "Aunt Cora was a wonderful woman," Purdy wrote his cousin, Frank Purdy. Her "devotion to family" was "a kind of religion." Purdy said he left New York to attend her funeral but did not make it; he injured his back and "slipped a disc, and have had a bad time with it since."[9] Exercises and walking helped, but back problems would recur in April 1967.[10] With this loss, James received another sizable inheritance. In October 1967, Cora's estate issued him a check of $4,632 (about $36,860 in 2020). So between June 1966 and October 1967, Purdy inherited $11,285 ($92,180).[11] Given that his books never sold in large numbers, these inheritances provided a cushion of financial comfort and helped him to write whatever he pleased. But even when he had money, Purdy would "cry poormouth."

With Cora and other departed family members—the Sleepers—in mind, in early 1967, Purdy continued drafting the manuscript that became *Jeremy's Version*, using the working title *Sleepers in Moon-Crowned Valleys*, which became the series title for several associated novels partly inspired by stories he heard from his grandmothers.[12] "I had lots of trouble with *Jeremy*," Purdy told the French scholar Marie-Claude Profit. "It was very difficult to write. The structure is so difficult. I couldn't tell it straight, because you're going way back in time—about seventy years. So in order to do that, I had to have a narrator who is based in the present" to provide proper distance. "And that I found very difficult, to hold all the narrators together. It's like driving lots of horses with just one driver."[13] As a child, James had listened to his grandmothers' bottomless store of recollections of small towns, hamlets, and "sinister cities." "When death had silenced the narrators," Purdy began to recall, as if "prompted by the dead, these stories" beyond his own recollection. *Jeremy's Version, The House of the Solitary Maggot, Mourners Below, On Glory's Course*, and *In the Hollow of His Hand* are the "pieced-together, often broken fragments" of his ancestors' lives. "I grew up in a family of matriarchs. I even knew my great grandmother"—all "inveterate story-tellers."[14] Critic Vince Aletti said these novels are "steeped in American Gothic, a grotesque and glorious territory all his own. Going back to memories of the Ohio country towns he grew up in during the 1920s [and early 1930s], Purdy strews a mythic landscape with grandiose, 25-room mansions, vaguely scandalous boarding houses, and sweetshops." "My family was real to me. I'm from a small Ohio town. And that was real. And then everything since then has been unreal," he told artist Stephen Varble during an interview.[15]

Comparing the names of principals in *Jeremy's Version* with those of Purdy's family members underscores its biographical underpinnings. In the fictional Fergus family, the estranged parents are named Elvira and Wilders (Vera and William). The novel's three brothers are named Rick, Jethro, and Rory (Richard, James, and Robert). The young "starter," narrator Jeremy Cready in the novel's present, whose "version" of the past we read, bears many parallels to and is compared to young Jethro Fergus and both names somewhat resemble "James Purdy." Just as Jeremy fashions a text from the stories of elders, so does his creator. In the novel, Elvira Summerlad's mother and grandmother are Melissa and Annette (Minnie and Nancy Ann/Nettie). Like Purdy's great-grandmother Nancy Ann Cowhick, Annette is also said to have Native American ancestry.

In January 1967, Purdy, emerging from the past, tried to relax with Jorma Sjoblom at gay-friendly Fire Island off the south shore of Long Island. When Norman MacLeish learned of this, he invited Purdy and his "friend Joe Sjöblom" to visit him and Ed in Naples, Florida. Norman made multiple invitations, gave enticing descriptions of the ambience, and even offered financial support to subsidize the trip.[16]

Through the early 1960s, Purdy had received direct and indirect support from American cultural Cold War efforts, but now such sources of funding were starting to diminish. Around this time, the Congress for Cultural Freedom was exposed as basically a front for CIA propaganda. *Ramparts*, *The Nation*, and then the mainstream media reported that *Encounter* was backed by the CIA, and federal agencies had infiltrated student groups and various publications. The CCF was allowed to die off as President Lyndon B. Johnson de-emphasized cultural Cold War efforts, refusing to fund leftist intellectuals and writers like Purdy who, though nominally anticommunist, criticized US military engagement in Vietnam. Previously generous wells of funding benefiting creatives of the noncommunist left dried up. The era in which serious writers like Purdy could dip in such government troughs was over.

Purdy was "sort of involved" in protesting the Vietnam War.[17] In 1967, he wrote a statement for *Authors Take Sides on Vietnam* opposing the war, but he also used the opportunity to skewer America's anesthetic consumer culture, harkening back to *Cabot Wright Begins*. Gore Vidal, in "Rabbit's Own Burrow," criticized John Updike's support of the war, citing his statement in *Authors Take Sides* that expressed offense at a "cheerful thought" that Purdy contributed: "Vietnam is atrocious for the dead and maimed innocent, but it's probably sadder to be a live American with only the Madison Avenue Glibbers for a homeland and a God." Acidly, Vidal wrote: "Rabbit will go to his final burrow without ever realizing the accuracy of Purdy's take on the society in which Updike was to spend his life trying to find a nice place for himself among his fellow Glibbers." Purdy also loved to hate "Mother Updike," as he called him.[18]

Reassuring Purdy after his anxiety over some of Giroux's edits of *Eustace Chisholm and the Works* and its chances for success, John Farrar, Roger Straus, and Robert Giroux each reached out in appreciation of the book after reading galley proofs. In January 1967, Hal Vursell was "enormously impressed again by its power and originality." "It is chilling, wonderful, and terrible. In short, I love it, and my hat is off to you." In March, Straus called *Eustace Chisholm* "a marvelous novel, and all of us, as you know, are pleased and proud." They would publish it "with all the energy at our command, and hope to be able to give the book the success—in every sense—that it deserves." In May, Farrar, increasingly less active in the firm since the early 1950s, called it "a masterpiece." Farrar had "always been proud to be associated" with Purdy's books and now he was "prouder than ever." "Your technical perfection is matched by your wit, your uncompromising savagery and your uncanny wisdom."[19]

On May 22, 1967, FSG published *Eustace Chisholm and the Works*, a dark classic ironically emerging just before the Summer of Love. Set in Chicago during the Depression, *Eustace* became the favorite of many Purdy readers and was lauded by great American composers. Virgil Thomson declared: "oh, how grand!" It was absorbing, "full of great scenes," and "fulfilling at the end. I shall now begin it all over again savoring every detail and reality." He wished to meet up again. Thomson's former protégé Ned Rorem wrote to say he was "overwhelmed" by the "best so-called fiction" he had read in an age. "Everything pleased me: the horror and pity of love, the revival of my own adolescent Chicago years, the extreme sexuality of at least three of your characters (I literally lusted)," and above all, "your musical ear." Rorem was sorry to have missed the book party given for *Eustace Chisholm* and invited James to accompany him in July to Lincoln Center to hear the premiere of his *Sun*, which adapted eight poems by various poets. A composer before he was a fiction writer, Paul Bowles offered: "I found it exciting to read; it seemed to go back to the world of *Dream Palace*, which I've always loved. And the subliminal pornography is deft. And as always, I'm delighted with the way you tell a story, a way which can come only from inhabiting the invented cosmos, knowing one's way around in it, as it were, with one's eyes shut. It's the thing I admire in Jane [Bowles]'s work, too."[20]

Explicitly presenting both male same-sex love and desire and a lethally sadomasochistic relationship, *Eustace Chisholm* drew controversy and was widely reviewed, sharply dividing the critics. Responses ranged from rapturous to scathing. Editor and critic Ross Wetzsteon wrote in *Book Week*: "Through an extraordinary act of courage and insight, Purdy seems to have achieved a kind of self-liberation—and has written far and away his finest novel" in which he sounds his "first authentic note of love, hope and compassion." In *Life* magazine, Angus Wilson called it a "remarkable achievement" by a "master of the horrible, the wildly funny, and the very sad."[21] Webster Schott offered a blurb: "James Purdy is a genius, a misanthrope, the hatchet man of love. There is no writer like him in America. The next century awaits him with its honors." After the book's British issue in spring of 1968, George Steiner reviewed it "brilliantly" for *The Sunday Times*, praising Purdy's integrity and the sharp, affirmative energy of his artistry, which manifests the "American language at its best."[22]

Despite earning such high praise, *Eustace Chisholm and the Works* "outraged the anesthetic, hypocritical, preppy, and stagnant New York literary establishment," which often responded with rank homophobia. Purdy later complained of critics' failure to find value in the story of Daniel Hawes, a young man who is "really an Indian chief" but takes no interest in his ancestry, who cannot "reconcile the fact that after nothing but sexual relations with women, he suddenly realizes he's in love" with Amos Ratcliffe. "He can't face that in himself." Daniel's problem is universal: "We can't face what is most ourselves, what is deepest in ourselves. Like Macduff, in Macbeth, who was from his mother's womb untimely ripped, we want to rip out the really delicate beautiful things in us so that we will be acceptable to society." Purdy's book was ahead of its time even in merely representing homosexual desire as something to accept; as Mike Wallace remarked of a controversial project he worked on: "This was 1967. People weren't talking openly about homosexuality."[23]

The Catholic novelist and critic Wilfrid Sheed, a fellow FSG author, executed a homophobic hatchet job of *Eustace Chisholm* in the *New York Times* headlined "An Alleged Love Story."[24] He likened Purdy to "a down-at-heel Iris Murdoch, working seedier equations" and remarked that though the publisher claimed the novel is about love, "we have only the author's word that it is there at all." Sheed simply could not recognize love between men. He criticized Purdy's style as often clumsy and concluded the novel "has overall interest only if it is viewed as a work of black nihilism." He conceded that the gruesome sadomasochistic ending involving Captain Stadger and Daniel Haws, while being a "purple feast," is "also a risky, serious piece of writing" that is "possibly the best writing Purdy has done."

The *Times* editor's choice of Wilfrid Sheed as reviewer was bound to result in a pan. Already in May 1965, Sheed had broadcast his homophobic views in "Heterosexual Backlash," his review in *Commonweal* of two rivaling plays by gay playwrights—whom he did not even name, as though out of discretion. He berated Terrence McNally's professional playwrighting debut, the Albee-ish *And Things That Go Bump in the Night*, and Charles Nolte's *Do Not Pass Go*, which was produced by McNally's embittered ex-boyfriend, Edward Albee, and his team of producers Barr and Wilder and director Schneider. Though Sheed called McNally's *Things* a "bad play," he said it was good sign that it was the "most overtly homosexual play" ever brought to Broadway, because this would encourage plays that presented homosexuality more honestly, and not via heterosexual "transvestism" (*sic*) that spread "half-truths and falsehoods" about straights—against which a "heterosexual backlash" was beginning to form. Sheed concluded perhaps there was "something to be said for having the homosexual sensibility asserted openly in one play rather than sneaked into twenty. It would, if nothing else, leave a cleaner smell." Eight months later, Stanley Kauffmann's much better known screed, "Homosexual Drama and Its Disguises," repeated many of Sheed's arguments. Sheed even quotes Kauffmann at the outset of his *Eustace Chisholm* review, saying that Purdy had acted upon Kauffmann's request for homosexual frankness "in spades."[25]

Because Sheed was also an FSG author, Purdy felt not only angry at the *Times*, but also betrayed by his publisher. Purdy later concluded: "That little synthetic prick Wilfrid Sheed of course was told to go ahead and try to destroy the book in the *New York Times*—the editor then was the horrible Wasp Francis Brown, who hated anything that resembled writing."[26] Purdy mocked Sheed in a brief published poem, "Whenever You Pee," and a decade later, called him a "paid hatchet man for the New York establishment" who penned a "disgraceful and totally unprofessional" review. When Sheed wrote "homosexual," he meant "if you are a homosexual or write about homosexuality, you are *ipso facto* deprived of any basic true judgment or vision. Now no one would dare say because you're a Jew or black your vision is impaired. They would not dare say that. So I am glad to see gays are now marching against critics and newspapermen who say, in effect, because you're gay your vision and your lifestyle are not correct and we cannot respect you."[27]

Mr. Sheed's review and its fallout haunted Purdy. He wanted Roger Straus to step in to defend *Eustace* by taking out an ad, as FSG had done after Orville Prescott's attack on *Cabot Wright Begins*.[28] Purdy believed Straus did nothing because Sheed was an acclaimed FSG author; moreover, he suspected that Straus, who may not have actually read the complete proofs, was privately dismayed that he had published such a shocking, violent, and flagrantly homosexual book, and wanted to bury it. Although Straus was libertine in his personal life, he wanted his press to be respectable and was therefore prudish about sexual content, taking exception to books he considered "dirty," said a later FSG president, Jonathan Galassi. In conversation before the novel's publication, Straus told professor and critic Warren French that *Eustace Chisholm* "poses difficulties because it is about homosexuality," and French, after reading the novel, wrote him to say this was a "drastic oversimplification." Straus may have chosen not to stand by the book.[29]

Adding insult to injury, later in the year, Chicago writer Nelson Algren gave *Eustace* a wiseacre drubbing in *Critic*, dismissing it as a "fifth-rate *avant-garde* soap opera." Algren, who knew Gertrude Abercrombie and shared friends with her, had encouraged Purdy's early work but now made vicious homophobic swipes. "What makes the book such a deadly bore, what makes the reader's mind boggle, is that the author is unaware of anything preposterous about men who believe so firmly in both prayer and faggotry that they can go from sex to penitence without getting off their knees." Much later, Purdy remarked that this was one of the "most savage attacks" he received, rank with dehumanizing homophobia.[30]

It did not help his mood that his original admirers and champions were quickly passing away. In May, the great Langston Hughes died, followed the next month by Dorothy Parker, who bequeathed her estate to Martin Luther King Jr. Fortunately, Purdy's work was earning new fans. Christopher Isherwood, from his home in Santa Monica that he shared with Don Bachardy, phoned James "out of the blue one afternoon" to say he was "so knocked out by *Eustace Chisholm and the Works* that he felt compelled to congratulate the author." The writers had never met.[31]

Gertrude Abercrombie was alive but not well. Purdy's depiction of her as Maureen O'Dell was in some ways unflattering, but art critic Donna Seaman reads it as betrayal. Years before publication, however, Purdy had told Gertrude she was the model for a character, even specifying that her backstreet abortion that he accompanied her to was depicted. She did not object but boasted of being the model for multiple Purdy characters. Seaman writes that the novel "features a bawdier, boozier, and more embattled and despairing version of the artist, Maureen O'Dell, a character Abercrombie, no matter how resilient and well-armored she was, had to find excruciatingly painful to confront," especially given her recent divorce from Frank Sandiford and the death of her first husband, Bob Livingston. Gertrude's health and spirits were poor when "her longtime friend betrayed her," Seaman charges, "albeit, it must be said, in a novel of graphic intensity that courageously addresses the suffering of homosexuals at a time in which they were subjected to vicious prejudice, resulting in debilitating shame and necessary secrecy."[32] If Nelson Algren likewise felt that Purdy had betrayed their mutual friend Abercrombie, then perhaps he wrote his scathing review in part to avenge this slight.

In June, Purdy's worries were eased when he was notified he would win a Rockefeller Foundation award of $5,000 for work in imaginative writing, effective July 1967. He wanted this second Rockefeller grant to be kept secret and not announced, possibly because the "convergence between the Rockefeller billions and the US government" in cultural Cold War projects "exceeded even that of the Ford Foundation" and was becoming increasingly known. "One cannot apply for this award, but one is recommended for it. I don't know who recommended me. Probably somebody from the Great Beyond, and certainly nobody from Manhattan Island!" Giroux's handwritten annotation clarifies that Purdy "was recommended by [Southern novelist] Walker Percy—and I've told him this."[33] Straus congratulated Purdy, calling the Rockefeller "well deserved," and sent a positive review from Paris of Le Satyre [Cabot Wright Begins], published by Gallimard, who issued translations of six Purdy titles during the 1960s. In July, Purdy thanked Giroux for the review of Eustace Chisholm in America magazine, published by the Jesuits, which compared Purdy to Gertrude Stein and Sherwood Anderson, and concluded that ultimately, Purdy communicates a "deep moral revulsion at man's predilection for violence and hate." Purdy noted: "What a difference from Grandma Sheed."[34]

In August, "Scrap of Paper," which tells of the relationship and power struggle between a wealthy older white woman and her black servant, appeared in the hipster journal Evergreen Review. Purdy was delighted that his longtime friend, the British film director Anthony Harvey (A Lion in Winter), enjoyed this story rich in tart dialogue. It had been rejected for two years: "Nobody in New York wanted it. Not surprising when you think that creatures like Susan Sontag and 'critics' like Eliot Schapiro Fremont-Smith are taken seriously." Harvey had spoken with a critic who had read *Eustace Chisholm* and thought Amos was, as the critic said, "in love with a 'nigger.'" That's typical, Purdy wrote angrily: "They can't read, and even if they could read, would not understand anything. The whole world has always been run, I guess, by idiots, madmen, criminals, and fools. The surprising thing is it somehow survives. Maybe the bomb will change that." No one but the "silent ones" liked *Eustace*. "One must have the hide of a rhinoceros and the staying power of a whole jungle to survive as a writer. Only bad writers are recognized. In the past, only Christian writers and white writers were taken seriously. Today to be a Christian writer, like myself, is sure oblivion. However, people who don't ever make themselves heard, go on liking me, and one must write for them, they are all that matter."[35]

Black Sparrow Press published "Scrap of Paper" plus eleven of Purdy's poems in a limited edition, *An Oyster Is a Wealthy Beast*, gratefully dedicated to his friend and benefactor, Andreas Brown of Gotham Book Mart.[36] Operated by John Martin, Black Sparrow was known for publishing Paul Bowles, Charles Bukowski, and John Fante. As had become typical, *New Directions in Prose and Poetry* reprinted "Scrap of Paper" in 1968.[37] John Martin wanted Bob Giroux to know that he believed Purdy while with FSG had become "our greatest living prose writer. *The Nephew* is as monumental a classic as, for example, Faulkner's *The Wild Palms*. And *Eustace Chisholm* is simply the finest novel published during the past decade."[38]

Purdy stewed over FSG's failure to address the Sheed obloquy and what he perceived as the failure of *Eustace Chisholm and the Works*. On August 6, Purdy wrote Roger Straus a long, emphatic letter of which he composed multiple drafts, like other communiqués to Straus and Giroux in this period. Because of the "very spectacular failure of *Eustace Chisholm* so far as sales are concerned," he would have to rearrange his life. For the past decade, he had "struggled to survive economically." He had established "some sort of international name," but could not attribute this to any publisher. Things had become "quite desperate," and, he claimed, he was "planning to leave New York in the near future." He believed his books had all sold in paperback and Avon had been cheating him. "Your failure to make the *New York Times* do anything about their disgraceful smear of me shows me again that while you enjoy having a 'name' writer, you have neither the force nor will to defend me, or stand up for me." Purdy later told Straus that FSG had not only failed to promote his "books and reputation," but were also "guilty of allowing" them to "suffer gross defamation at the hands" of FSG's own writers. His agent had tried to convince FSG to "take action to have some sort of public apology and some decent kind of statement on your part, of regret, a statement of defending me and my work and character, [but] as usual where my interests are concerned, and my future and livelihood are at stake, [FSG] were content to do absolutely nothing. To sit on your hands, and look the other way." He had come to FSG at the urgent persistence of Robert Giroux, who did all he could to get him away from New Directions, promising "just short of the sun and moon. None of these promises were ever remotely fulfilled. I came to you, in 1958, with a brilliant reputation, earned in England and Europe. You have added nothing to my reputation. Instead you have stood by while it was besmirched and stained. Only my books, indifferently promoted by you, have continued to gain me readers and fame. Your wretched promotion of me, your poor salesmanship, and your refusal to keep me properly informed on subsidiary rights (the Avon affair stinks to heaven, if there is a heaven over New York) and finally, your persistent and passionate preferential treatment of other authors as against your lukewarm support of me, all these things made me want to leave your firm."[39]

Purdy later ratcheted up his accusation, claiming that according to rumor, Sheed's hatchet job was an inside job meant to boost Susan Sontag. He told Roger Straus that many persons in publishing circles were "convinced that the Wilfrid Sheed defamation of my character originated with persons in [FSG] who wished that another author who was to have a book shortly appear might profit from my book being hatcheted. (*Her* book of course made the front page of the *Times*, and was heralded by all your artillery, which was of course denied to me.)"[40] It was well known that "Roger's loyalty to her was unquestioned," stirring up envy in other authors, biographer Benjamin Moser writes. In February 1968, Purdy told FSG if they could get Sontag on the front page of the *Times*, they could "damned well get" him on it, too. "My books have been known throughout the world for over 10 years, yet I can be burned and massacred by some shitty little hack like Sheed, and not a hand is raised in my defense. I've been treated like dirt by the *Times* for years, and no real defense from you is forthcoming. You can build a fire under them if you want to, but you don't want to."[41]

Purdy's theory perhaps overreaches. For example, contrasting one of his claims, on August 18, 1967 the *Times* gave Susan Sontag's *Death Kit* a negative review. Nevertheless, watching a newer FSG author receive the success he craved, Purdy could not help but feel slighted.[42] Purdy continued, "the fact is that [FSG] all stood idly by when the Sheed defamation appeared, and did nothing to restore my name and the dignity and decency of my personal life, and my years of hard work and accomplishment. . . . What are publishers for, if not to defend an author when so criminally attacked. The answer is you were never my publisher of course. You printed the books and sat on your hands." This was all, of course, insulting to Roger Straus and especially Bob Giroux, who had poured so much of himself into editing Purdy's novel manuscripts. Giroux surely regretted that Straus made his championing of Sontag so blatant, stirring up such problems, and later grumbled, "Susan is the real editor in chief of FSG."[43]

FSG always had the highest regard for his work and would continue to do so, Straus stressed. He made himself clear: "To charge that we had a part in arranging for a bad review" is "simply absurd. We regretted the review and deplored it as much as you did, and we suffered from it too."[44] Later, Purdy dropped his insinuations of sabotage, but for decades, deeply resented that Straus never stepped up to the plate to defend *Eustace Chisholm*.[45]

Although Purdy said he had resolved to leave FSG, still he discussed the possibility of them publishing his next novel. As to *Sleepers in Moon-Crowned Valleys*, he told Straus, FSG could not publish it "until some reckoning" was made. Purdy saw "no excuse for the abysmal, tragic, wholesale failure" of *Eustace Chisholm and the Works*. New Directions would have done just as well. He added he was no longer able to afford an agent, so Phelps would not be handling future books.[46] Straus countered their respective estimates of the "sale, publication of, and reception" of *Eustace* were quite different. He was sorry James felt it was a failure, since from where he sat, its record was "very creditable (stupid reviews apart)." It had sold nearly six thousand copies and counting, and it had been contracted by a new paperback house, Bantam, for an advance of $7,000 and had been contracted for England by Jonathan Cape, for Purdy's biggest advance yet. Straus was not taking credit for that, but he saw a different picture than did Purdy. Signs were favorable for translations; Straus heard that the Rockefeller grant Giroux recommended had gone through. The promo and advertising budget came to $6,900, roughly one dollar per copy sold. He thought this was evidence of their "faith in the book," if not already indicated by the "genuine advance enthusiasm which all of your friends here communicated." They were as disappointed with the reviews as Purdy was, especially Sheed's, but experience convinced him there was "no way to deal with unfair and unintelligent reviews except by silence.

The reviews fade away; the book remains." Reassuring him that "we continue to have faith in and admiration for your genius," he advised, "don't go before giving yourself plenty of time to make sure that you will be satisfied with the alternatives" to living in New York.

Despite Purdy's venomous letter, he quickly and lengthily replied to Straus hoping they could work out an agreement for *Sleepers*. Purdy laid out a narrative explaining his need for more money. "Since 1955, when I decided to sink or swim and to devote myself solely to writing (I hate teaching and it prevents my finishing books), my yearly income has been approximately $1,890. From 1955 until 1960, my income from writing was practically nothing (I had no other employment then either), and during this period I spent all my own money, then borrowed, and am at present over $10,000 in debt. As I don't believe the Great American Public is ever going to shell out for my books, my problem for the next three years is to find grants from foundations which will enable me to finish *Sleepers*. I don't want and don't expect some large advance from any publisher, which would only saddle me with indebtedness when there is no indication the Public is ever going to support me. However, I have been happy with things at FSG," despite poor sales, and Giroux is "especially fine and brilliant, very understanding, and we work well together. Nonetheless, at the rate I have been going, my only future is a room in the Poor House."[47] Purdy was offered a contract for *Sleepers in Moon-Crowned Valleys* to be signed by August 22 with an advance of $7,000: $1,000 on signing, $3,000 on delivery of rough draft, and $3,000 on delivery and acceptance of final draft. It had Jack Phelps's name on it. Purdy said he was pleased about the contract.[48] Hal Vursell said he, along with colleagues, had been "greatly distressed" about Purdy's unhappiness about *Eustace*, so Purdy's "understanding and generous telegram and letter" made him very happy. "I would hate, repeat hate, any one else to publish you, so high is my regard for your work."

Still Purdy was holding grudges and revisiting battles despite such high praise his work often received from his publisher and many critics. In September, Paul Bowles reported to James Leo Herlihy: "A letter today from James Purdy makes me feel he is not in a very good way. He feels *Eustace Chisholm* was a failure. And he adds the reason is that he is not Jewish or Negro or a 'taker of LSD.' What can you gather from that?"[49] Purdy's feelings of suspicion and misgivings over FSG were not over; he thought he found a new piece of evidence backing rumors. In late September, Purdy wrote Giroux, enclosing a letter and note from Webster Schott. "You will see on the first letter, unsigned by him, that he refers to Sheed. . . . Without trying to purvey 'alarming rumors' you must be aware of the persistent rumor (probably a dirty lie) that the Sheed review plan was cooked up right in the office of [FSG] by some unknown 'somebody.' . . . As a publisher, you may not understand the horror, and shock of my being treated this way by the New York *Times*. None of your other writers are treated so. Why am I? I think it is because I am a Christian and have talent, and will stick to this." In Purdy's mind, things reached a head. Two days later, he telegrammed Straus: "Wish to be released from contract with you for 'sleepers in moon crowned valleys' my complete confidence shaken in your firm do not wish to continue with you i cannot write for a publisher i have lost faith in. Jack phelps will communicate with you do not communicate with me" (*sic*).[50]

On October 10, however, Purdy told Giroux he was glad to continue with him as his editor, replying to Giroux "man to man, and not writer to publisher." First, "the *Times* condemned me over and above the book as a homosexual, the most damning epithet this petty cheap society can use to harm one of its non-conforming members. What should have been done then immediately was to have demanded an apology of the Times, and if Mr. [Francis] Brown would not do so, an apology should have been demanded of the publisher himself." "Since you brought up the name of Miss Sontag, I must tell you that I cannot agree with you that she is an 'admirer,' since when she was 'in' she gave *Cabot* a very condescending review [*sic*] in the Times, and never recommended it again (Her review was actually a damnation of me, if you would read it carefully). Furthermore, to be completely frank, I feel she owes her entire 'fame' to Roger Straus and his pushing of her." Indeed, Straus "made Susan's career possible," publishing and promoting all her books and "keeping her alive, professionally, finanicially, and sometimes physically," Moser writes. "I cannot see that she has written anything even of minor importance. Yet she is discussed, spotlighted, 'in,' while I am treated like a diseased rat." Purdy found it ironic that Susan Sontag in part made her fame from her essay "Notes on Camp," which appropriates dated gay slang while de-emphasizing the gayness of camp aesthetics. While Sontag thrived, many gay writers struggled to earn recognition.[51] "I am not an anti-Semite, since I am a Christian, but my entire neglect is owing in large part to the Jewish propaganda machine which celebrates writers like Malamud and others, while hardly admitting I exist." "To again be brutally frank, I cannot think that Roger Straus is either friend or admirer of me, and his type of world is so far removed from mine, I'm sure I would fit in with the reindeer-drovers in

Lapland better. Nonetheless I am a name, I long ago declared unconditional war to be heard, and heard I will be. The cheap vulgarians, millionaires, and pimps who run New York will not stop me, and I will just go on fighting my own battles, since in the end nobody can do this but myself. As to Jack Phelps, he has no testicles. We will leave him in charge of contracts and signing his name. Where blood is to flow, I want to be in charge," Purdy wrote sadistically. "Meanwhile I admire you as an editor, but I will continue to fight my own battles to be heard, since nobody else has showed up to do it for me since Edith died."[52]

In October, chaos continued to reign as Jack Phelps apprised Purdy that he was "going out of the agency business." Purdy asked him to return to him all contracts and documents, strongly feeling Jack should not be positioned "to collect further monies on any contracts which you helped draw up on the past, to wit," those for *Sleepers* in the United States and Britain, and *Eustace*. Purdy stressed that Phelps withdrew at an inopportune moment when "important matters were being discussed" with FSG, leaving Purdy in the lurch. Meanwhile Purdy informed Giroux that Phelps was no longer his "representative in any capacity." By November 1967, Purdy was partly assuaged by Giroux and Straus, and FSG was acting as his agent.[53]

Purdy lost another old friend and supporter when Osborn Andreas was found dead in the living room of his home in Chicago, shot twice in the head, in October. Osborn was under federal indictment with five others for conspiring to rig the price of Pentron Electronics stock, facing up to twelve years in prison and a $25,000 fine.[54] (In *Malcolm*, Girard Girard, modeled on Osborn, is criticized by Mr. Cox as a "common manipulator of the stock market."[55]) The alleged rigging took place in early 1966, after Andreas had resigned as director and parted ways with Pentron, but he apparently remained a key player in skullduggery.[56] Their fraud cost "suckers," including Gertrude Abercrombie and Miriam Andreas, up to two million dollars. Police declared Osborn's death to be suicide. Associates said he had been despondent over financial affairs.[57] Statistically, it is extremely unlikely, however, that he could have shot himself in the temple after shooting himself in the forehead. More probably, he was murdered by the mafia, given the "widespread reports of criminal syndicate activity in stock transactions" that were circulating.[58] In June, US Attorney Robert Morgenthau refused to comment on "reports of murder, blackmail, underworld connections or threats in connection with the alleged stock rigging," even after others involved in the investigation were found shot to death or went missing. One who was shot,

Alan Robert Rosenberg, was an associate of the notorious Felix Alderisio (Milwaukee Phil), a "plunger" in stocks under investigation and "Underboss" to the Chicago Outfit Boss, Sam Giancana.[59] "Osborn wiped out a lot of us," Abercrombie rued to Purdy. Bud Fallon, a failed writer and friend of Nelson Algren who lived in her house, said it was "surely a good subject for you. The whole mess." Miriam Andreas had to take a proofreading job, and they were "damned mad at being wiped out." She and Miriam's anger seemed to overrule their sadness at losing Osborn.[60]

While Purdy worked on his new book, his earlier works, which tended to model a character on Miriam, continued to draw interest, despite his complaints that they had been poorly published. On the evening of October 14, radio WBAI broadcast Purdy's "own special reading—over an hour in length—of *63: Dream Palace*" from New York.[61] In November, he read at City College, selecting an excerpt from *Eustace Chisholm* about "Amos and his father and the Ku Klux Klan, then skipped to the 'pay day' abortion chapter." He said the reading went quite well, but "one young girl became so upset, she had to leave. There were quite a few Negroes in the audience, and they seemed to 'get' it the most," Purdy told Giroux.[62]

In the fall of 1967, Purdy wrote three drafts of "Mr. Evening," a Jamesian gothic tale of collection and possession that was published the following fall in *Harper's Bazaar*. Purdy urged Virgil Thomson to pick it up: " 'Mr. Evening' has something for you, I feel."[63] James was delighted to learn Virgil had liked it and a set of poems. "I have always been grateful for your comments, and your kindness. I would invite you here, but my room is a kind of lair, and is nearly uninhabitable. I would like to see you very much too. I hear your fine music on my radio frequently, and enjoy it greatly."[64] The mononymic English novelist Bryher, who had been a close friend of Edith Sitwell, was most impressed and brought "Mr. Evening" to her friend, Norman Holmes Pearson.[65] Pearson wrote saying the tale is "absolutely first-class—believe me! One of your absolute best, maybe *the* best—but I don't like comparisons. It's Hawthorne and Poe and Purdy. And the ambiguity is rich and right." When *New Directions* reprinted the story in 1969, Purdy asked Laughlin to send review copies of the issue to George Steiner, literary critic Cleanth Brooks, Robert Penn Warren, and City College of New York professor and critic Leo Hamalian; the latter three had anthologized his stories.[66]

Despite having his work sent to professors, during this period Purdy felt hostile toward most academics and insisted that no one besides Bettina Schwarzschild should write a book on his work. In 1968, Schwarzschild's

The Not-Right House: Essays on James Purdy was published in the Literary Frontiers Series from University of Missouri Press, directed by William Peden, who consistently praised Purdy in reviews. Purdy thought this first book dedicated to his work was the "most brilliant and perceptive thing written" on him since Powys and Sitwell, but a later champion of Purdy, editor and novelist Gordon Lish, found her "benighted."[67] Attempting to foil a book project in the works, Purdy used outrageous humor as he twice warned Donald Gallup, Yale librarian, that "fat, pursy, sneaking and disreputable Henry Chupack of C.W. Post College" was writing a book for "vanity publisher Twayne attacking me and my work." Purdy had asked FSG and New Directions to deny permission to Chupack and another scholar to quote from his works. Still, "be wary" lest he "get into the collection of letters, etc. at Yale by proxy. However, as he is as lazy as he is criminal and shifty, I doubt the old thing will appear at Yale; he is said to be bloated with disease, and may soon end his days on Long Island. But should you see a fat and bloated cat in the library" it may be Chupack, and it "would be doing humanity a favor to send it at once to the mercy chamber. Use your strongest cyanide."[68] After Chupack's book *James Purdy* (1975) was published in Twayne's United States Authors Series, Purdy dismissed it as a "terrible book by an idiot." Feeling that homosexuality was "one of modern society's more urgent problems," Chupack misreads *Eustace Chisholm and the Works*, claiming that Purdy aims to expose the "hopeless nature of homosexual love in a world without God" and the "hellish and frustrating life that homosexuality involves." In one howler, he takes Carl Van Vechten to be a "Negro novelist." Showing his inaptitude as a critic of Purdy, as late as 1975 he wondered whether creating a novel almost totally concerned with homosexuality was "not inflating an aspect of human experience that is at best only an abnormal sexual experience."[69]

After many years of struggling with alcoholism, Richard Purdy died on December 22, 1967. James's mother and Aunt Cora had died in the month of December, "so it was another very sad Christmas," he told Giroux. Richard had begun to help James on "some details of Sleepers In Moon-Crowned Valleys." Purdy shared with Giroux his brother's decline: "He died in utter squalor. There was nothing we could do to save him. Both my father and mother really died of grief over him."[70] Richard died "in a flophouse in Toledo," he told Richard Hundley.[71] Perhaps feeling bitterness toward his departed brother, and adhering to his avowal to his niece Christine that he would not return for more funerals, James did not attend his brother's funeral in Findlay on Christmas Eve, which was attended by family and friends, many from his theater group. Richard's niece and nephew recalled him as a nice and generous uncle. "I really loved him," David said.[72] Richard joined the Sleepers in Moon-Crowned Valleys in Union Cemetery, Hicksville, nearby Vera. James wrote to his cousin, Frank Purdy: "Richard had lots of bad luck the last few years, as he got to drinking and it mastered him. It grieved us all, especially of course his mother and father. Aunt Cora was very upset over it. There doesn't seem to be anything you can do for it. It was awful to see him go downhill."

James still had his younger brother, Robert, but they were not close. A few years later, James told Sam Steward: "All my people are dead now, but a younger brother, who doesn't like my books."[73] Bob and Dorothy would always call James around Christmas time, but they and their children did not visit him in Brooklyn Heights. In 1976, Purdy said on air, "everyone feels isolated." As you age, "the family falls away; they die" and you become "isolated from your roots" and "you stumble through the world as an outcast because life is constantly changing; you're constantly having to part with one gift after another from your family, until you are quite alone." Purdy was a "true inheritor" and never lost his roots. He could not write the books without "memory of those speech patterns and cadences." "So actually, I don't really write the books. I'm just an instrument." His interlocutor mentioned "ancestor worship." Purdy laughed and said, "it's not worship, it's just inheritance."[74]

In December, Purdy was delighted with the cover of the Bantam paperback edition of *Eustace Chisholm and the Works*. Its bold cover featured a painting of a handsome young man in the nude with arms crossed, shadow concealing his lower body, with caption reading: "THE SENSATIONAL NOVEL OF PERVERSE LOVE." Purdy was becoming known as a "homosexual writer" in some circles, about which he felt slight ambivalence. He wrote Roger Straus in February: "I was a bit surprised to see an ad in the *Evergreen Review* of the Trojan Book Service, which is evidently a 'homosexual book club' (!)" offering *Eustace* as a bonus. "It doesn't bother me, and I am not fussy as long as it sells books, but did you know about it?" Straus did not know specifics, only that Peter Clark in sales had sold books to " 'some clubs' that were hustling them" for FSG. "I too caught it and was a little embarrassed. Shall we stop servicing them?" Purdy replied, "as to 'homosexual book clubs,' I think we will have to bow to the inevitable, and let all of them have *Eustace*." The Bantam edition was carried by "all the pornographic stores on 42nd Street, and is said to be selling well." West 42nd Street and Times Square were then notorious for their seedy, sleazy vibe. He thought *Eustace Chisholm* would "survive professional homosexuals" since it "survived already the prissy little prudes that run the New York Times." He had "no objection at all."[75] He did strongly object, however, to dramatizations of the book, stung as he was by the Broadway disaster of Albee's *Malcolm*.

Though he was then leery of dramatizations of his work, he was not opposed to their appearing in non-print formats. Spoken Arts of New York released a boxed set of Purdy reading *63: Dream Palace* on four vinyl discs, directed by Dr. Arthur Klein, its president, whom Purdy found "very sympathetic and understanding." Jorma Sjoblom, who had financed the private printing of the novella, was underwriting the recording. Gotham Book Mart distributed it. In 1970, Spoken Arts released *Eventide and Other Stories*. Both recordings were praised by *Antioch Review*, then under the editorship of Nolan Miller, an author, professor at Antioch College in Yellow Springs, Ohio, and an enduring supporter.[76]

Drawing from early memory, Purdy was rapidly composing material that was growing wider in scope. In January 1968, Purdy informed Giroux he was "somewhat staggered by the amount of material and narrative" in *Sleepers in Moon-Crowned Valleys* and would need to break it into three volumes. At that point, he envisioned each volume dealing with the same characters, seen from a slightly different focus. As it turned out, each novel would be set in a similar rural small-town locale, but each had a different cast—most based largely on family members and locals. Purdy found it hard to know what to keep and what to cut. "In this book, I have so much to handle, I have trouble deciding just where to start." By October, he decided the title of the first volume was *Jeremy's Version*. He hoped to have the rough draft to FSG by Thanksgiving.[77]

During this period, Purdy increasingly chafed against the East Coast literary establishment, which seemed ever more Jewish to him as it showed less and less interest in his work. In April, Giroux thanked Purdy for sending Truman Capote's *Playboy* interview, which he found interesting for many reasons, not least of which was his reference to Purdy's work. For many years, the interviewer prompted, US literature was dominated by Southern writers, but, as Capote had noted elsewhere, over the last decade, a "large percentage of the more talented American writers are urban Jewish intellectuals." How did Capote feel about this "shift in ethnic, geographic and literary emphasis?" It had brought about the rise of "the Jewish Mafia in American letters, a clique of New York–oriented writers and critics who control much of the literary scene through the influence of the quarterlies and intellectual magazines. All these publications are Jewish-dominated and this particular coterie employs them to make or break writers by advancing or withholding attention. I don't think there's any conscious, sinister conspiracy on their part—just a determination to see that members of their particular clique rise to the top." Malamud, Bellow, Roth, Singer, and Mailer are "fine writers, but they're not the *only* writers in the country, as the Jewish literary Mafia would have us believe." Capote rattled off many "excellent writers" including gay authors— Purdy, Windham, and Herlihy—whose names were not well known because the "Jewish Mafia" had "systematically frozen them out of the literary scene." Capote was "not against any particular group adhering to its own literary values and advancing its own favored authors"; he only objected when a "particular group gets a stranglehold on American criticism and squeezes out anybody who doesn't conform to its own standards." He claimed that "everyone in the literary world" knew this but never writes about it. Many gay writers especially felt frozen out. Gore Vidal remarked that for many New York critics and editors, there was room for only one "O.K. *goy*" on lists of important writers of his generation. In 1965, Philip Roth attacked Albee's "ghastly pansy rhetoric and repartee" in a review of *Tiny Alice*, to him a "homosexual daydream."[78] And in 1970, Joseph Epstein wished "homosexuality off the face of the earth."[79]

Although Capote's diatribe strongly suggests antisemitism, there was a kernel of truth to it. This is well evidenced by Jewish critics, such as Norman Mailer, in an essay-review of Norman Podhoretz's *Making It* for *Partisan Review* (1968), and Richard Kostelanetz's *The End of Intelligent Writing: Literary Politics in America* (1974). Kostelanetz shows that Lionel Trilling and the *New York Review of Books* were, respectively, the de facto leader, and one of the representative organs, along with *Partisan Review* and *Commentary*, of what he calls the "New York literary mob" that dominated the US scene in the 1960s. Mailer assessed "no major critic and no major novelist had developed" from their specific influence. Some critics, like Macdonald, Kazin, and Howe, were first-rate, but failed to "grow over the years," and "no schools of criticism developed from them, no seminal ideas, no ferments." They were "guardians rather than catalysts."[80] Likewise, Kostelanetz charges that the New York Intellectuals never produced a coherent body of theory and their cliquishness damaged US literature, often preventing innovative fiction and criticism from being published. He quantitatively establishes that the *New York Review of Books* was "corrupt" in the 1960s since its editors heavily promoted their own interests with Random

House and Vintage in selecting books and reviewers. This clubbiness became so evident that some lampooned the periodical as *The New York Review of Each Other's Books*.[81] This bias promoted careers of this Cold War group of mostly Jewish anticommunist liberals, such as Fiedler, Sontag, Roth, and Mailer himself.[82] Purdy subsequently attacked the "New York literary establishment" in several interviews. Purdy's younger friend Tom Zulick opined that while Purdy in his criticism of the book world could sound antisemitic, "he was not really antisemitic."[83] The fact Purdy sent books to George Steiner, the son of Viennese Jews, and cultivated relationships with Jewish writers and critics like Bettina Schwarzschild and Theodore Solotaroff reinforces this.

A long friendship began, somewhat shakily, between Purdy and a Jewish editor and writer who soon became quite influential, Gordon Lish. When Lish found Purdy's work by accident when he was fifteen or sixteen, he was "completely bowled over."[84] In the spring of 1968, Lish, working for the Education Development Corporation of Palo Alto, California, was assembling a book and record anthology, *New Sounds in American Fiction*. A recording of actor Ken Lynch reading "Daddy Wolf" was made and Lish wished to add an interview, but Purdy's fee was $250, which became a hassle given the budget. Lish nevertheless remained a diehard advocate. In July, Purdy thanked him for praise and for generating interest in his work. Purdy was glad Gordon had liked *Eustace Chisholm* and "Mr. Evening." He later wrote: "Your book and the recording are very good. Congratulations! You should feel proud. What is your next project?" Purdy was glad Lish had "omitted all the holy wart hogs of the New York Establishment."[85] He sent material from *Jeremy's Version* and Lish offered comments. "I do appreciate your saying what you said, believe me, about Jeremy. I'm on the last section now. It's hell to write." He wanted to see Lish when he was done.[86]

In April, Purdy found diversion in seeing Tennessee Williams's Southern Gothic, *The Seven Descents of Myrtle* at the Ethel Barrymore Theatre. Estelle Parsons, who acted in *Malcolm*, shone in the title role. Although Purdy found the play wonderful, critics were harsh, and it closed after a month. José Quintero was drinking excessively, Williams said, and did not direct Parsons advantageously.[87] Purdy liked "so very much" the story of Lot, a neurotic, tubercular youth who is secretly a transvestite, and Myrtle, a former showgirl and occasional sex worker, that he wondered if James Laughlin would publish it with New Directions Books—which he did.[88] As for Purdy's mutual admirer Tennessee, he was in a "state of panic and confusion." Before the play opened, a sense of impending doom loomed overhead.[89]

Roger Straus reached out to Purdy in September, a year after Purdy had expressed a total loss of faith and a wish to break with them. "I know Bob Giroux is in touch with you but I need to write you this personal note to say that all of us here are very, very much on your side. We want it to work out for you and for us together."[90] In November, Purdy wrote a friendly letter to Giroux, "very excited" that his editor had published a fine article in *Films in Review* on Mack Sennett, the director and actor of silent film comedies. Purdy thought that Sennett had influenced his work.[91]

In what must have been a shock, in December, Purdy informed Straus: "Owing to the fact that my novel *Sleepers In Moon-Crowned Valleys* is based on persons still living, and because it seems sure that these persons would strenuously object to such a novel being published at the present time, I am forced to abandon the writing of the book. I am therefore asking you to cancel the contract which was originally drawn up." Of course, Purdy had scant relatives this could apply to. Publication "would create serious difficulties for all who are concerned in the contract," and he therefore advised him it was "impossible for the work to be published without incurring serious risks to all those concerned." He did not offer apology or details. But this was only part of a ruse to shake Phelps and rid him from making any more money from his work. On the same day, he wrote Giroux: "Here is a copy of the letter I have sent to Roger. You will notice that this is slightly different tack, and if you do not approve of it, I will change it to suit you. I thought this might convince the agent [Phelps] more than our first plan. Let me know what you think." Purdy added that "if another book were mentioned, to be contracted for, *Jeremy's Version*, that is, he would smell a rat." In handwriting: "Of course I want you and only you to publish *Jeremy's Version* and of course Jonathan Cape, in England. 'Moon-Crown' itself is never mentioned until the final or perhaps penultimate volume," so they could pretend the work called *Sleepers in Moon-Crowned Valleys*, of which *Jeremy's Version* was actually the first volume, had been abandoned. The same day, he added a letter addressed to Straus and Giroux, apologizing for "having written you such intemperate letters, and hope you can overlook them." He had been under "too much pressure" and "economic hardship."

A few days later, Purdy told Straus he was finishing *Jeremy* and wished to submit it within the next few weeks. "As you have not drawn up a contract for *Jeremy's Version*, would you please do so at your earliest convenience." He no longer had an agent, so *Jeremy's Version* must be contracted between FSG and him, he specified. On December 9, FSG canceled the contract for *Sleepers in Moon-Crowned Valleys*. The thousand dollars he had received on signing would be deducted against future earnings of other books. To sever any Phelps claim, they pretended *Sleepers* was a totally different manuscript from *Jeremy's Version*.[92] On January 24, 1969, Giroux said he was happy to send contracts. "It was a pleasure to read the draft you brought in. The two families, Fergus and Summerlad, are marvelous tribes and the Elvira-Winifred tussle is a battle of titans. The book is rich in promise as a novel of and very much 'with' America."[93]

Purdy seemed capricious with would-be adaptors of his work. Director and producer Joseph Hardy was interested in filming *63: Dream Palace*; Purdy told Straus he was impressed by Hardy and he should do it.[94] On the other hand, he told Straus to apprise Hershel Williams he did not think *Eustace Chisholm* was "suitable for adapting by anybody," and gratuitously, that he did not believe Williams was capable of adapting it. This disappointed Williams, who said Purdy had encouraged him to pursue it at length. Then Purdy did a 180 turn on Hardy, writing James Laughlin: "Now another thing that will make everyone, I am afraid, ill with disgust and frustration. But it's better now than later. I think we must drop the Joseph Hardy plans to adapt *Dream Palace*. In fact, I think we must drop any plans and refuse all offers on the part of anybody to adapt any of my work for any media." Purdy had heard that Hardy planned to use Bill Francisco, the director who "ruined" his stories off-Broadway, who would "certainly fail in a film." He claimed to have turned down several offers in past months that he regarded as unserious.[95]

Purdy was likewise capricious with FSG, suddenly asking them for a much larger advance after it seemed he was about to sign a new contract with them. Behind the scenes, Doubleday had lured Purdy with a generous offer that he was now trying to get FSG to match. In late January 1969, Purdy asked Giroux if he could raise the total advance "to say $15,000. I realize this may sound steep, but my own financial situation is terrible. I have now been with your firm for 10 years. I feel that unless you can make more hefty support of me, I must go to work, and when I work I doubt I can do much writing." He meant teaching. "I realize the public does not buy me, but on the other hand," FSG controlled four books, with "all subsidiary rights in paperback, foreign, etc., and I do not think the advance proposed is excessive. I am heavily in debt." The Ingram Merrill Foundation granted Purdy money applied for in 1965, but it had "already been spent in debts."[96] Giroux replied, saying he had spoken with Roger about the possibility of increasing his advance and he suggested FSG add a clause to the present contract, stipulating that in the case of a major book club selection, they would then make Purdy an additional payment against royalties, making the total advance $15,000. "As you will recall, Jim, when we originally Contracted, I made every effort to get the advance increased to the present level," Giroux wrote. "I know how severe your financial problem is and I think it would be a serious hindrance to your work to interrupt it with other commitments. At lunch the other day with Harry Ford of the Merrill Foundation, I urged them to continue their generous help; I also spoke to Dr. Freund of the Rockefeller Foundation about you."[97] FSG continued to make serious efforts to assist Purdy through their wide connections.

In February, Purdy thanked Giroux for his good words to foundations. Even so, he was "greatly disappointed" in Giroux's response. It was unsatisfactory that FSG proposed to make the $15,000 advance contingent on "the whims of Book Clubs, notorious" for overlooking meritorious works. "You certainly cannot be unaware of the fact that other publishing firms have been wooing me for a long time. I prefer to stay with you because I am certain that you are the finest, the best, and the only editor for me. However, I was published in England and gained international renown without any editor so much as dotting an *i* or crossing a *t*. All these years FSG have taken no real financial risk or responsibility for me, while I have suffered all kinds of risk and economic privation, living on a salary beneath that of your scrubwomen and typists. If you cannot see your way to advance me the very modest, and completely fair advance of $15,000, I think it would be best for all of us that I leave you and go with more responsible and enthusiastic publishers. I hope you will reconsider."[98]

Giroux laid down the line:

I don't blame you for wanting more money—who doesn't? and I wish we could give you fifteen thousand dollars, but it is not possible except in the manner Roger suggested. We have a contract for your novel, on which we paid a thousand dollars when you signed it. This contract will not be cancelled of course until you sign the replacement contract now in your possession (which we drew up, at your request, in order to help solve the problem you wrote us about). Since the replacement contract does not bear either your signature or ours, it is at the moment no contract at all. If you sign the new contract, we will pay you the three thousand dollars now due. If you do not wish to sign, we can abide by the old contract. *Can* abide, but you know very well, Jim, that I do not subscribe to the legalistic school of publishing. I have been happy to work with you and publish your books because I admire and believe in your writing. So do Hal and Roger and Mike [Michael di Capua] and all your friends here. But if you can get fifteen or twenty-five or fifty thousand dollars elsewhere (and from reading the papers you'd think that a quarter or half million dollars elsewhere was fairly common), I certainly don't want to be the cause of preventing you from getting it. More power to you. My only suggestion is that you get competent and friendly help from an agent who is not only respected in the publishing business but who understands your very special point of view. I'm only sorry that you chose this particular moment to bring up the matter of money, when it appeared that we had no contract at all. We do have a contract, and as soon as your new publisher repays the advance of one thousand dollars already credited against it, we will release the publishing rights to your new novel. . . . Wishing you all success, wherever you may go, and assuring you that we would like nothing better than to proceed under our present contract, I am, Yours ever, Robert Giroux.

Purdy returned his personal check of $1,000 and Roger Straus said he hoped this meant Purdy had placed the novel with another publisher at a higher advance. "We are certainly in no hurry for the return of the advance if your arrangements are still pending." "It is a privilege and a pleasure to be the publisher of such a distinguished author. Bob Giroux and all our staff join me in wishing you every success in your new relationship. We sincerely hope you will find the rewards your talents have always merited."[99]

The stress of this sustained wheeling and dealing with his agent and publisher was eased by the hospitality and letters of Virgil Thomson. In April, Purdy sent many thanks to Virgil Thomson for sending his eponymous memoir. James found it "not only entertaining" but also "full of facts and anecdotes one loves to know!" Thomson was a "master of the clean sentence—now a rarity!" He added, "Your parties are always fine, and I enjoyed the last one immensely."[100] In the 1960s, Thomson enjoyed the company of a younger coterie of gay artists and writers including Albee, Vidal, and, when in New York, Christopher Isherwood and his partner, Don Bachardy. Through Ned Rorem and poet Kenneth Koch, Thomson met and mixed with the pansexual painter Larry Rivers; Larry's friend and sometime lover, poet Frank O'Hara; O'Hara's partner, television writer Joe LeSueur; and O'Hara's blond boyfriend, aspiring writer J. J. Mitchell.[101] In May 1969, Purdy thanked Thomson for a "happy evening, a delicious dinner" and "wonderful company." Purdy found Thomson's secretary Jay Sullivan, a rugged but polite Southerner, "very handsome, and the architect said many fine things." The architect was doubtless Philip Johnson, a rich and famous gay modernist who was a regular with his sister. Tennessee Williams, Peggy Guggenheim, and Leonard Bernstein all appeared at Thomson's soirées in this era. Purdy sent two copies of *Eustace* for Virgil to "bestow on visitors."[102]

At Thomson's apartment, James appeared to enjoy moments of pleasure and bonhomie. Otherwise he seemed to devote so much of his time unhappily in conflict with people, like Farrar, Straus, and Giroux, who seemed to have his interests as a writer in mind, both artistically and commercially, or in struggles to whip recalcitrant *Jeremy* into shape.

13

Sleepers in Moon-Crowned Valleys

Purdy was not bluffing with Farrar, Straus & Giroux, and in the spring of 1969 he moved to Doubleday. Because he distrusted Roger Straus and desired to have his talent recognized in the form of a higher dollar figure, he left the esteemed house that published his first four novels. Ameliorating this situation were emerging friendships and more income. Travel provided diversion from his stress over publication and recognition.

Going to Doubleday meant trading off for a large commercial house that did not devote as much care and energy to him in the manner he had become accustomed to at Farrar, Straus & Giroux. Unlike FSG, Doubleday was not esteemed as a literary publisher and offered no editor with Robert Giroux's acumen. Certainly they wanted to sign James Purdy in part to raise their literary status. In 1963, Purdy had basked in the "red hot center" of *Esquire*'s literary power chart, whereas Doubleday, America's largest publisher, was stuck in Squaresville, "not a factor in the structure of the literary establishment." One cannot help wondering whether Straus's being Jewish factored in Purdy's choice to leave FSG for a house run by WASPs. "Roger Straus is Shylock, Simon Legree, and Caliban in one," he told his friend and champion, Angus Wilson.[1]

Purdy maintained a correspondence with this gay British writer, saying he often recalled the visit that Angus and his partner Tony Garrett had paid. In June 1969, he thanked Angus Wilson for connecting him with his friend, Ian Chappell, with whom he had supper at a Mexican place in Brooklyn Heights before sitting on the promenade to take in Wall Street and Manhattan across the river. He wanted to read Wilson's biography of Charles Dickens and had not yet seen his *Collected Stories*, but planned to buy it immediately and talk it up. He claimed to be sorry he could not leave New York for good: he never seemed to earn enough money to leave, but it cost "too much to stay!"

Supported by his large Doubleday advance, however, he was able to escape from New York, at least temporarily. In the summer of 1969, Purdy took an extended vacation at Massachusetts resorts. From the end of June through July, while queer patrons of the Stonewall Inn rioted against police persecution, Purdy tried to relax oceanside at Oak Bluffs, a town on the island of Martha's Vineyard. Known for its colorful "gingerbread cottages," Oak Bluffs historically attracted black tourists, which interested him.[2] But even there he could not stop worrying over FSG. He complained he had not heard from Roger Straus and asked again about Avon paperback sales numbers and what FSG intended to do about all his book rights, which he was demanding to have returned. Roger assured Jim that his reply was either waiting in his mailbox in Brooklyn or on its way to Massachusetts, but he included a copy, adding:

> I did not, of course, answer part two of your question of July 16 as I assumed it was self-evident, but let me now do it. We published four of your novels, Jim, with pride and pleasure, and not only have we *always* kept them in print but in several instances we put them into Noonday editions at your request even when we knew that we would have only very modest sales because of the competition of the mass paperback edition. We have also arranged license for many foreign editions of your books both in cloth and in paper, and we continue to "police" these contracts to arrange new editions. . . . We shall always take pride in having published those books of yours, and we shall certainly wish to keep them in print, promote, sell, distribute and publicize them as best we can. I should like to think that this is the way you would want us to handle your work, leaving all of the business aspects to one side.

Straus was known for his devotion to authors, but Purdy rejected the house's guidance and care. In July, his new agent Gilbert Parker, vice president at Curtis Brown, Ltd., was in place. Bantam told him they had 245,000 copies of *Eustace Chisholm* in print and had reprinted it six times since March 1968. Since Bantam had been "so much more successful" than Avon, Purdy hoped Straus would "take all care and thought in transferring" all paperback rights from Avon to Bantam, if possible.[3]

In August, Purdy stayed in Truro, south of Provincetown on Cape Cod, which he called "whippoorwill-land." It is not clear if he was alone the whole time, but Jorma Sjoblom probably drove him, since he owned a car and James did not drive. Purdy's magnanimous older friend Edward Hefter, a rich global investor he had met in Chicago, gave James thousands of dollars to go to Provincetown, John Uecker said. He liked it so much that he returned the next summer, telling his neighbor and friend, author Paula Fox, that he was "crazy about Provincetown," a "beautiful retreat" with "lots of room," plentiful "good restaurants *en todas partes*," and "*hundreds* of whippoorwills!"[4]

Purdy enjoyed another windfall when Metro-Goldwyn-Mayer purchased the option rights to *Cabot Wright Begins*.[5] In 1972, Purdy said MGM bought it cheaply, but the sum the studio paid for it seemed like a great deal of money at the time.[6] In 1997 he recalled: "I had twenty dollars in the bank, then I had this check for $75,000! [adjusting for inflation] They looked at me at the bank, then they looked at the check, and said, 'You can't draw any of this money for two weeks.'" MGM participated in the Cold War "militant liberty" program beginning in the mid-1950s, collaborating with the government to promote a positive national image, to embed pro-American, anticommunist messages into American movies. Such coordination continued into the 1960s, which may have influenced MGM to shelve *Cabot Wright Begins*, due to its blatant criticism of American society and culture and its focus on a serial rapist.[7] It is possible MGM purchased the film rights to ensure a movie was never made. Regardless, the option money gave Purdy more financial security.

In late November, Gilbert Parker wrote a revealing postscript to Giroux: the situation was unusual because of "management upheaval at MGM." The MGM attorney informed Curtis Brown, off-record, that MGM was being "extremely tough about the assignments" in hopes the "deal may collapse, which would save them the $15,000 option price." That figure was a tremendous sum to Purdy ($107,448 in 2020). MGM was "willing to sign the contract and make the option payment even though the new management has no plans at the moment to actually make the film," but if they could "find a way to avoid signing the papers with a semblance of honor," they would. "Because we find ourselves on the brink of losing Jim Purdy $15,000, we are particularly grateful for your response to the pressure we've exercised on his behalf," Parker wrote. Giroux thanked him for the explanation: "it makes the whole problem somewhat academic."[8] MGM never made the movie, but Purdy got paid.[9] Purdy stated frankly he was only interested in the contract for the money. In January 1970, Purdy's agent phoned to say MGM had "met the down-payment on their filming" of *Cabot*, he told Giroux. "I hope they get around to paying the second installment too. I haven't decided where to hide in case they do make the film."[10]

Purdy received much advice from writer friends but doesn't seem to have yet often reciprocated. But now, corresponding with Sam Steward regularly, Purdy encouraged Sam's idea to write a pornographic novel under the pen name Phil Andros (lover of man). These books, which were often fantasies of tough hustlers, brought Sam much attention and some money. Purdy's way of encouraging Sam was a series of teasing "anonymous letters" and naughty fake press releases that mentioned Purdy's friend and neighbor, composer Robert Helps ("Babe Helps"), and narrated darkly erotic activities inside Sam's "Invisible House." During the 1970s, Purdy also urged Steward to write his memoirs.[11] Despite Purdy's sustained support, James was not always treated well in return by Sam, who seemed envious of Purdy's talent and success, and relished fabricating sexual gossip.

Robert Helps became a very close friend to James beginning in the mid-1960s. A handsome piano prodigy, Bob lived a few blocks away on Montague Street. For years, James would have dinner at Bob's almost weekly and they enjoyed strolling on the promenade together. Mutual friend Michael Tillotson said James, a "ferocious social critic," and Bob, an "astonishingly good pianist" who wore long hair and a beard, were "outliers and non-conformists." For a professor educated at Columbia and Berkeley, Helps led an unconventional, "unexpected life" that was kind of wild. Between 1963 and 1967, Helps lived in Brooklyn Heights, giving concerts and recording an album for RCA. From 1967 to 1978, Helps divided his time between Brooklyn and the Bay Area, becoming a professor at San Francisco Conservatory of Music, and then, artist in residence at University of California Berkeley.[12] James and "Babe" shared a quirky sense of humor and enjoyed transforming the world into a mutual fantasy, writing zany press releases and other cracked communiqués. Gerald Busby, a composer and a good cook, introduced them. Gerald prepared food for parties that Bob Helps hosted where renowned singers and composers like Aaron Copland and Virgil Thomson mingled. Helps was also a fine cook and Purdy's mutual friend, drama professor Barry Horwitz, recalled a dinner party he attended at which a visiting Copland, Thomson, and Purdy were the other guests: "the BABE made a fabulous Babe Dinner at his tiny studio." Guests "crammed in" around a baby grand piano, into a tiny booth and "dined on Babe's wonderful fare—usually a roast leg of lamb." James was "in fine fiddle" and they exchanged stories, but Virgil as usual was "kind of competitive" and, compared to the others, "James was kind of quiet." "James loved Bob because he was so brilliantly gifted, but also so brilliantly neurotic," Horwitz recalled, noting that Helps had a delicate disposition prone to nervous breakdowns and stage fright.[13]

Helps had a neurotic mother who was always on the lookout for UFOs and aliens, chronicling this in letters to her son. "This was gold for James. They connected on the basis of those letters," Busby said. James answered the letters in the persona of Babe Helps (aka "Babe Helps with the Chocolate Drop Eyes" or "Babe Heaps"). "Bob's personality, his genius as a musician, were just made for James. James could express anything he wanted. Bob loved it. He was the perfect friend for James." For some time, there was almost daily contact between them. James would visit and read Mrs. Helps's wacky letters. "James was always looking for a spontaneous way of connecting to someone through story. He would find the most fecund bed of a story." In the 1970s, James typed countless "anonymous anomalous letters" for and about Bob, many involving soprano Martha Jean Hakes ("Madame Hakes"), Helps's student and collaborator. Typical of this Purdian genre, they made comic accusations of outrageous sexual transgressions committed by the recipient. For a writer who at times seemed beset by loneliness and anger, this friendship was clearly treasured.[14]

A rivalry focused on James then developed between Robert Helps and Richard Hundley, whose musical and personal styles were so different. Hundley's compositions are fairly simple and melodic while Helps's are more complex and avant-garde (he had been the protégé of serialist composer Roger Sessions). Pianist and composer Joseph Fennimore, who knew Purdy and his composer friends, said "maybe in some ways Bob seemed closer" to James "than even Richard Hundley." To James, each composer would trash the other's work. Bob, with his academic credentials, "fed James snideries about Hundley's music from assorted composers and James passed them back to Richard," the gist being that "Richard was not, as he bitterly recounted, 'a *real* composer.' (No degrees.) Richard, no slouch in invective, would intelligently lambast Bob's music to James," who would spill this to Bob. All was "grist for James's mill as he figured out the lay of the land" of the period's "pettily vicious" composer politics.[15]

Alongside the challenging *Sleepers in Moon-Crowned Valleys*, Purdy continued to seek outlets for his poetry and short stories. One story in particular courted controversy among the literati. In 1970, Black Sparrow published *On the Rebound: A Story & Nine Poems* in an edition of three hundred, with Purdy drawings, dedicated to publisher John Martin. This comical tale of race, power, and revenge in New York literary salons had been rejected by *Esquire*, *Harper's Bazaar*, and *Playboy*. The fictional Thursday salon of the heiress Georgina Comstock seems partly derived from the long-standing salon held by the acting couple Geraldine Page and Rip Torn in their Chelsea, Manhattan, brownstone. Guests included James Baldwin, Tennessee Williams, Truman Capote, Edward Albee, and Terry Southern.

Baldwin wrote of Geraldine Page admiringly in a 1962 magazine feature calling her "Bird of Light" and photos show Torn, Page, and Baldwin
clowning at a gathering in 1963, the year when "Torn Page," as they were
collectively known, married and started holding a regular salon.[16] In "On the
Rebound," Rupert Douthwaite, a George Plimpton type, tells a few American
writers that Georgia caused her own downfall when she verbally "attacked"
Burleigh, a famous black novelist who came to be regarded as the nation's
"greatest Black," in front of "everybody who matters on the literary scene."
With Burleigh's profile and "angry smile," he seems inspired by Baldwin. In
several iterations, Georgia told Burleigh she "would never kiss a black ass
if it meant" that she and her "Thursdays were to be ground to powder." The
scandal resulting from this gaffe finished Georgia and her salon, and Rupert
took over with his own. But, Rupert insists, he never dreamt that she would
actually agree when he told her that, to get her salon back, all she needed to do
was to give Burleigh "the token kiss" she had sworn she never would.[17] This
leads to a conclusion even more outrageous than expected. While Geraldine
Page, known for playing Tennessee Williams heroines, is not known to have
insulted James Baldwin, Rip Torn certainly did during the London production of Baldwin's play, *Blues for Mister Charlie*, which he had coaxed the
writer to finish. To appease British censors, Baldwin had made changes to the
script's violent words that Rip Torn had defended, and upon learning this,
the actor angrily insulted Baldwin and the director, causing his firing.[18] To
Gordon Lish, now fiction editor at *Esquire*, "On the Rebound" was "stunning
business—but for reasons that have nothing to do with anything," he would
not publish it. He added: "Now if you want to know what I'd really like to do,
that's to have a Purdy story in the manner of 'Daddy Wolf' or 'Why Can't
They Tell You Why?' or 'Don't Call Me By My Right Name' or etc. etc. Would
it be appropriate to commission a story? To offer a guarantee or some such?
Hell, I don't really know how these things work. . . . All I know is that I MUST
have a Purdy story sooner than later, that I must have the best of Purdy while
I'm here to do something about it." Purdy could not have been pleased to be
told he had done better work a decade before. Lish combed through *Jeremy's
Version*, trying to find a suitable excerpt to publish, which did not transpire.
Throughout 1969, Lish continued to request a story.[19]

   After June 16, 1970, Purdy was again in Truro, near Provincetown, enjoying
close access to the beach. He put the money that MGM had sent him, minus
the agent's fee, "away for cloudbursts. It didn't seem real." (A month before,
Purdy inquired into opening an account with Wellfleet Savings Bank in Cape

Cod.) British *Vogue* "must have smelled the money," for they were planning "a 'big' article" on him. Brian Robertson, a "very bright" British writer who liked all of his books, had been visiting for several days asking questions. Robertson had penned a "very favorable and judicious review" of *Eustace Chisholm* for the *Spectator*. Although he was enjoying the retreat, he was also working hard. He told Paula Fox on June 20 that he was nearly finished reviewing galleys of *Jeremy's Version*: "Several days I thought I was dying, and once I *was* dead, but now I've done about all I can." He did not really stop to rest, however, since within a few days of finishing his review, Purdy was already drafting "volume two of *Sleepers In Moon-Crowned Valleys*," as he told Bob Giroux, which he now thought would comprise four novels. He asked for the proofs of volume one to be sent to friends.[20]

In July, Virgil Thomson shared: "I stayed up all night with Jeremy. It is very real and grand, and a thriller. And now I am practically a relative of everybody in it. Wonderful!"[21] James was so happy. "Did you know there is more? I am on the second volume, or it is on me." He hoped to see Virgil in the fall, and later wrote: "I love your parties, and *you*. Everything is superlative, and your guests are as delicious as the food."[22] Among these guests was Gloria Vanderbilt, who in August sent to James "with love and admiration" a copy of *Gloria Vanderbilt Book of Collage*.[23]

In October, Doubleday published *Jeremy's Version*, dedicated to "William, Cora, and Richard" Purdy. The month before, Purdy, recently returned to New York from Cape Cod, sat for interviews timed to promote his new book.[24] Paul Bowles offered an encomium: "Until *Jeremy* my favorite Purdy was *The Nephew*; now I prefer the new one. I think it's the richest of all in material and treatment. The era and the region are miraculously evoked, principally in the dialogue, the nearest thing to a classical American colloquial I know."[25] Novelist Guy Davenport praised it in a long, perceptive review for the *New York Times*. Atlantan critic Frank Daniel acclaimed it as "probably the ripest, richest" fruit of this "extraordinary talent."[26] James R. Lindroth concluded his review for *America*: "As one of the most talented novelists of the sixties, Purdy, with this novel, promises to become one of the most significant voices of the seventies." *Newsweek* strongly disagreed. Its reviewer, novelist Geoffrey Wolff, confused Purdy with his narrators, who deploy idiom and colloquial language, and concluded Purdy had trouble writing proper English.[27]

After Jonathan Cape published *Jeremy's Version* in Britain in the summer of 1971, Purdy complained of reviewers, especially British, who misunderstood his use of American speech that he had heard growing up. He vented to Frank Baldanza, a professor at Bowling Green State University who, although specializing in the modern British novel, also wrote on American authors. Despite Purdy's professed aversion to academia, he trusted Baldanza and appreciated his critical work. "I have just been reading horrible reviews of *Jeremy* in the British press. The English reviewers have always been as stupid as the American ones. Sometimes stupider." Despite receiving a brief negative review in *The Guardian* and a mixed review in the *Times* of London, the book garnered mostly good reviews in England, such as that in *The Sunday Times* by literary critic and crime writer Julian Symons, who called it "a family saga that might have been sired by William Faulkner out of Mrs. Henry Wood," the latter the pen name of the nineteenth-century novelist Ellen Wood. The fact that Symons had been a sharp and sustained critic of Edith Sitwell's poetry made his positive review seem all the more significant.[28] The *Times Literary Supplement* gave it a mixed review but conceded that the novel could be read as "the working of American legends, which have attained mythical weight, and American history" into a "grand tragi-comedy."[29] The reviewers, Purdy told Baldanza, "made me tired in their criticizing the 'melodrama' of *Jeremy*, and the archaic queer style. This is because they do not know the people I based my work on. This is the way the characters were. The reviewers are blaming me—they ought to blame God. Reviewing is a joke. They only like the ordinary, the jejune. Whatever I do is wrong, according to them." Purdy appreciated that Baldanza accepted his vision "without the himming and hawing and gagging and posturing of the bourgeois 'reviewers.' Everything has gotten a million times worse since *Cabot Wright Begins* was published."[30]

Purdy also singled out Jewish reviewers, as they seemed to resent and not understand American English, he thought. "There are of course fine critics who are Jewish, but the New York ones, and some of the British ones, suffer from never having heard any authentic idiomatic language. (This is Mrs. Schwarzschild's trouble, but she is aware of it.) So they brand my language as clownish, ungrammatical, inept, corny, etc. One of the worst attackers was old Stanley Edgar Hyman. Another is Lionel Trilling, who condemned Sherwood Anderson's characters as 'subhuman.' He meant by that he had never met anybody outside a Columbia University classroom. That's why they admire Nabokov so much, the Kazins, Trillings, and the rest. Nabokov has no relationship with native American culture any more than [Alfred] Kazin or Trilling do. They feel at home with his marrow-less, bloodless, papier-mache intellect."[31] In 1977, Purdy declared to an interviewer: "I am what they call Middle-American, Christian and white, and I write American speech. That means death."[32]

The warrant underlying Purdy's claim about native American speech raises questions of voice, dialect, and authenticity. Gerald Rosen, a novelist and professor who wrote his dissertation on Purdy and befriended him, was concerned about these notions of "real American language." If, as Purdy claimed, New Yorkers spoke an "artificial language, a kind of show-biz patios," where did this leave Rosen, since this was the speech he had grown up with? "Why was his language the true American language? Why not mine? I was an American, too. Where did the authority come from to declare which was the 'real American language'?"[33]

Esquire in its November 1970 issue published "Short Visits with Five Writers and One Friend" by an obscure author recently hired to write a fiction column, Barton Midwood. Midwood was "quite a piece of work," one of the only people whose presence editor Harold Hayes found vexing enough to shut his office door. Grace Paley and Purdy had both published in *Esquire*, and Lish wanted to publish them again. Midwood's article was series of a flat profiles that, while not unkind to Paley, made Purdy appear a "surly simpleton."[34] "Anti-Semitism constitutes a problem for him," Midwood writes ambiguously. Midwood quotes Purdy saying "the Russian soul is anti-Semitic" and Dostoevsky was profoundly antisemitic, citing *Diary of a Writer*. Textual evidence backs Purdy's view there and in other works, but Midwood tried to catch him out: "When asked to comment on that chapter in the *Diary*" in which Dostoevsky defends himself against charges of anti-Semitism, "Purdy said that he had not read it." Midwood also presents dialogue between himself and his friend, Maurice, who is not otherwise identified and not present during Midwood's interview with Purdy, discussing Purdy's ideas, improbably casting him as a Luddite with pastoral vision, someone doubtless into nudist camps. Purdy said Midwood chose all topics, none of which he wanted to discuss. "I know nothing about Russia or her treatment of religious groups. The quote he puts in my mouth came from a Russian and a Polish friend of mine." On October 11, Purdy told Lish he had "never read a more irresponsible vicious" interview. "I am not quoted correctly, words are put into my mouth I never said, and the whole intent is to belittle and denigrate me. Why did you send such a pipsqueak Spiro Agnew–Senator Joseph McCarthy here? You told me this man admired my work. He has read almost nothing of what I have written, and understood nothing. . . . No responsible magazine would have printed such a gutter defamation."[35]

Lish tried to assuage Purdy, explaining their policy was to let writers have free expression, not omitting opinions that editors disfavored. *Esquire* wanted to "promote a free forum of ideas," even if it led to discomfort of an editor, as it had. Lish had thought Midwood would find Purdy and his work "as worthy of admiration" as he did. Purdy did not want to reply in a published letter. "When the hack you sent arrived, he sniffed around, supercilious about everything, and never asked anything about the real me or my work. All he wanted to talk about was his interest, his opinions. . . . He was all primed before he came here to prove me stupid, uninformed, and an idiot, because I did not share his little 'liberal' Madison Avenue opinions of the hour." It was a lost opportunity for promotion, perhaps underscoring his hurt about the reception of his new book. *Jeremy's Version* was not as widely reviewed as *Eustace Chisholm*, and Purdy had seen only two reviews of *Jeremy's Version* so far. "I'm the wrong race, color, religion, and I guess sex to interest the old foaming-at-the mouth New York. The whole country makes me sick. Do you think it's going under? I don't think it has enough energy or guts to have the revolution they talk about."

Nonetheless, Purdy did not take out all his anger on Gordon Lish. He wrote to him on October 17: "I very much value your kind and courteous letter, and please do always remember I appreciate you and your friendship." Purdy sent him an inscribed *Jeremy's Version*. Lish in turn thought Purdy "would like seeing some of the Raymond Carver stories" he was taking for *Esquire*, which he had solicited and carved, omitting high percentages of sentences, and writing new ones, co-creating the Carver style. As editor, Lish was using Purdy's early "marrow of form" aesthetic as his main template. Thanks to Lish's heavy editing inspired by Purdy, Raymond Carver by the 1980s became known as the major voice in the new minimalism following postmodernism, which became the dominant aesthetic. "Lish reworked and returned them, using as his model the disorienting, unemotive stories of James Purdy," explains *New Yorker* staff writer D. T. Max.[36] Of "Neighbors," author Carol Polsgrove writes, "On some pages [Lish] took out entire paragraphs, giving the story a flat, ironic style characteristic of a writer he particularly liked, James Purdy."[37] Throughout 1970, Lish begged for a story. "Please, Jim, do consider a short story. They are such lovely, frightening events in your so gifted hands." In February 1971, Lish said he was rereading stories in *Color of Darkness* for "the eighth or better time, and if they aren't among the greatest in the language then I don't know the first damn thing about prose fiction. Which is a goddamn lie."[38]

Perhaps starting to appreciate what he had lost, and regretting his curtness, Purdy sought reconciliation with Roger Straus, whose press held on to subsidiary rights for the four novels they published. "I very much appreciate your and Lila's good efforts in effecting the change from Avon. I am very much in your debt. I always very much regret the violence and harsh words which came from me when I left Farrar Straus and Giroux. Please forgive me." Purdy's trouble, he wrote, was always he "never had a competent agent." So he had been "forced to do all the overseeing, and it has been too difficult." Purdy was quite pleased with how Bantam distributed and sold his books. They had "purchased *Jeremy* at a very good price, and they have done remarkably well with *Eustace*, and are doing quite well with *Color of Darkness*."[39]

Purdy's friendship with Robert Helps led to a performance of his *The Running Sun* poems, adapted into a song-cycle by Helps, featuring singer Bethany Beardslee. Purdy was surprised by the praise that two composers in the audience gave his poems, jazz clarinetist Benny Goodman and Morton Gould. He claimed both Doubleday and New Directions wanted to publish the poems, but he did not know if he cared "to give them to the world." Purdy doubted anyone "in the fart-brigade" of New York would understand what he was doing, he wrote his friend, Bill Weatherby, author, literary critic, and senior editor at FSG. "It's bad enough to have one's novels puked upon by the alternating rectums of Wilfrid Sheed and John Leonard." He was halfway through the first draft of *The House of the Solitary Maggot*, the second installment in the *Sleepers* series, but he had "no editor over there [at Doubleday] at all" since it seemed his editor Stewart (Sandy) Richardson was euphoric over everything but him and his work. "When I appear he puts on an asbestos napkin and I realize he doesn't even read my books: they're just sent to the cracker factory for printing."[40]

A play of *The Nephew* opened, presented by Studio Arena Theater in Buffalo. Ned Rorem, commissioned to write incidental music, after finally reading the novel, told Purdy it was a "perfect book" and perhaps "one day could make an opera." On March 24, Rorem wrote in his diary: "*The Nephew*, play based on motionless Purdy novel, opens in Buffalo with my music, composed (for flute, viola, cello) in three days, mailed upstate, recorded there and superimposed onto the production without further ado. Exactly, I've always felt, as these things should be done." If he liked it, they would consider bringing it to New York, Purdy told Lish. The play was not well received.

Purdy wrote consoling notes to Guy Du Brock, the director and adaptor, and, at his suggestion, Margaret Hamilton, who played the lead character Alma. Best known for playing the Wicked Witch of the West in *The Wizard of Oz*, Hamilton was stung by the reviews and Purdy did his best to cheer her up.[41]

Over Easter, James and Jorma traveled to Key West to see Edward G. Hefter, a financier and philanthropist who was a mutual friend of Tennessee Williams. In 1969, Hefter had offered to cover round-trip tickets and lodging in his downstairs apartment, and even to help Purdy purchase a house in Key West if he liked it there.[42] (A decade later, he asked James: "Have you sent Tenn all your works? He said he wanted to read everything you wrote."[43]) Ed and James went back to early Chicago days. Hefter, who had lived in San Francisco and Manhattan, helped Purdy a great deal. He tipped Purdy to invest his MGM loot in specific stocks, telling him when to buy and sell. Heeding Hefter's advice, Purdy thrived. "He made James independent," John Uecker said.[44] In *Garments the Living Wear* (1989), Edward Hefter's analog, Edward Hennings, is called an "international manipulator of the stock market" who keeps "everything secret." Late in the story, Des Cantrell overhears Hennings talking on the phone, and relays Edward is "some kind of international con-man and secret agent to boot!"[45] Purdy "didn't fall head over heels" in love with Key West and "this disappointed Ed." It did not offer "nearly enough trees, flowers, birds, or walkable avenues" and he didn't care for the restaurants or the people.[46] In late 1971, he asked Hefter to comment on the situation of Jorma Sjoblom, who had lost his job, but had not saved much money, and was perhaps receiving assistance from James. Hefter was surprised since Jorma's habits seemed moderate; he thought the economy would pick up soon.[47] In January 1972, Hefter, who had been sending copies of *Jeremy's Version* to friends, invited Purdy to return to Key West. "I could find you a small apartment nearby, and you could accept it as my guest."[48] To Abercrombie, Purdy later shared: "He helped me out of some difficulties a few years back. I [first] met him on the street. You warned me against him at a big ball [in Chicago]. Remember? You said that man is danger. It might as well have been in 1880. Time is a big ocean." Back then and presently, Hefter hankered for young hunks and was sugar daddy to some. "No, my predilections do not run *exclusively* to teenagers although I must admit when one arrived at second childhood it helps to keep me *feeling* a bit younger to have some contacts with the younger set," Hefter wrote in 1962.[49]

In May, Purdy wrote Sam Steward in Berkeley, relieved to hear from him again, having heard "vague and terrible rumors." Since the Wilcoxes cut him off, Sam was his "last link" to Chicago, besides Gertrude Abercrombie and Miriam Andreas. Stewart sent welcome praise of his newest novel. "Damme, baby—*Jeremy's Version* is absolute wonderful—and I thank you for it. I was completely absorbed in it—a wild dark thing, like an early twentieth century *Wuthering Heights*—and can hardly wait for the next volume, and after reading it, I was more than ashamed to send you a copy of mine; you have the greater talent by far, and are really turning into (or have already become) one of the major American novelists! I am really proud to be called your friend, believe me. And whether it pleases you (I doubt it), it gratified me that there is a little mark of me on you, on your right arm, just above your right elbow. Alas, that I was not the expert that I became later—but just the same, where you go, I go, and I love it." Sam had jettisoned tattooing and was focusing on writing pornographic novels. "Believe me, old friend—I value our knowing each other more than anything, and hope it will go on and on and on. And you are the last link with Chicago and the wonderful days in the ghetto-honkeytonk of South State Street."[50]

14

Elijah Thrush

In the spring of 1971, Purdy conjured *I Am Elijah Thrush*, his allegorical fantasy originally inspired by Paul Swan. This surreal short novel explores race, power, identity, parasitism, and art in dazzling prose. An octogenarian oil heiress, Millicent Frayne, who pines for a ninety-year-old mime, poet, and pederast, Elijah Thrush, engage in an extended power struggle. "When shall we be married?" she asks. "When hell freezes its oldest star boarders," is the queer thespian's reply. Caught in between is the narrator, Albert Peggs, a young black man from the South who was hired by Millicent to write her memoir and spy on Elijah. This description only begins to scratch the surface of the strangeness. Opulent and camp, *I Am Elijah Thrush* bears the strong influence of Ronald Firbank, the subject of Purdy's master's thesis, and the "decadent movement" he was part of. Atypically, Purdy wrote *Elijah* in longhand in a notebook because it felt like a more personal book. In June, he sent the first two pages to Sandy Richardson at Doubleday, who found them wonderful. James considered Sandy an old friend and had co-dedicated *Malcolm* to him—but Purdy's emerging difficulties with Doubleday placed strain on their relationship.[1]

Not just Swan was an inspiration, but also Purdy's friend, John Carlis, a black poet, painter, and designer whom Purdy sent to Van Vechten to be photographed; Carlis was a model for narrator, Albert Peggs.[2] In May, Jorma Sjoblom gave his feedback on the new work. The beginning reminded him "so much of the torrid Mother's Day we spent with John Carlis in the divine Fairmont Hotel. The sensuous as well as psychic qualities are that intense. And it is such a highly visual novel."[3] Built by the International Peace Mission of Father Divine, a charismatic black leader who claimed to be God, the Divine Fairmont was an integrated first-class hotel in Jersey City, where Carlis lived for a time. Purdy later told Abercrombie that the novella, "narrated by a black youth," was "in a way based on John Carlis and Mrs. Stark," but set in New York.[4] Inez Cunningham Stark, a model for rapacious Millicent DeFrayne—along with Miriam Andreas and perhaps even Gloria Vanderbilt—was a Chicago Gold Coast socialite, poet, critic, and patron.

Stark, a reader for *Poetry* and president of the Renaissance Society at the University of Chicago, believed that Negroes could write "serious literature." To this end, during the 1940s and early 1950s she led Wednesday evening workshops: Carlis was a student in her Chicago Poets' class, along with poet Gwendolyn Brooks.[5] In 1968, Carlis told an interviewer he had a "Chicago friend, a white writer" named James Purdy whose *Malcolm* quite interested him. Carlis had long wanted to write, but felt he needed more life experience. Purdy said, "you've got to write about things you really know about. That you've really lived through," so Carlis began writing of his childhood.[6] In 1976, Purdy occasionally ran into Carlis, a friend of Chicago artist John Pratt, but thought he had become "too difficult to know any more."[7]

In June, Purdy wrote Gordon Lish bitterly; he should pick up *New Directions in Prose and Poetry* 23 and read "On the Rebound," which he had rejected. "You would also reject my short novel *I Am Elijah Thrush* if it were sent to you," he challenged, "so quit playing that you are master in your own house, or that you are with a serious magazine. If you were a serious magazine you would have published 'On the Rebound' and countless other work by me, but *Esquire* has always been a fraud, and a frost. Whatever good has got into its pages was sheer astrology. I don't mind frauds, but when they try to pretend they have my best interests at heart, it's time for the vigilantes to come."[8]

Rather than cut his friend off, Lish later in the month said he had perused the second installment of *Elijah Thrush* and was totally convinced that Purdy was "writing the great American novella. Jim, thus far, it's an absolute masterpiece, perfection, stunning in every respect." "What an inspired piece of work, what genius!" Lish ranked Purdy's novella on par with his early stories, which, he iterated, are "among the best in the language." Lish needed it for *Esquire*, and though printing one hundred pages presented "enormous problems," he was ready to tackle them and "fight like hell to have what" he must have. "Well, Jim, feel good, feel very good: we're going to stick it in their ear, we're going to force their attention."[9]

Within a month, Purdy mailed Lish corrected manuscript pages. As was Lish's wont, he tried to change the title. Purdy wrote: "No, no, no, no, no, no, NO! The title must be I AM ELIJAH THRUSH." Purdy likened this to when *Mademoiselle* editors, who had "never lived in America," changed "You Reach for Your Hat" to "You Reach for Your Wraps," because "no lady reaches for her hat." "Don't follow their example. My title has 100 different meanings, the one you have chosen is like 'You Reach for Your Wraps': morgue-rotting death. DONT DO IT!"[10]

In July, Purdy told Robert Giroux he had just finished the rough draft and shared some of its backstory. "I would like to have you read the rough draft *as a friend* if you would care to." Lish and Murray McCain, Purdy's friend who worked at Bantam, were enthusiastic, he shared. James also invited him to come to Brooklyn for dinner, perhaps with FSG editors Michael DiCapua or Hal Vursell, suggesting an Arab restaurant that McCain, Virgil Thomson, and he had enjoyed together recently.[11]

Having written this unusual novel, Purdy regretted his decision to leave FSG. Later in July, Purdy was "extremely pleased" to have seen Giroux on a recent night and hoped to see him again soon. "As you know—I am writing this to you as a friend, and not as my publisher, I am very unhappy with Doubleday, but I doubt any change can be made, for it seems too late. Furthermore, I do not know whether Roger [Straus] would in any case, wish me to return. As you know, I do not think he and I were ever too fond of one another. My leaving FSG was owing entirely to my needing money desperately, and only Doubleday would come through with it." Richardson and Doubleday, however, seemed "entirely uninterested in literary concerns, and I think I bore them. They have no real time for me, and do not seem interested in my literary reputation." They had no idea what to do with *Elijah Thrush*. If Giroux thought FSG could publish it, maybe Purdy could tell Doubleday they were not a good fit and deny them it. Purdy said they had options on two remaining books in the *Sleepers* series, but they had "no real option" on *Elijah*. Purdy did not know how to proceed. "I would not want to come back if there would be unpleasantness or resentment on the part of anybody at SG [*sic*], but only you know this." *I am Elijah Thrush* was one of his most important books and needed "serious presentation as an important literary work." Purdy urged Giroux to regard this and the manuscript as confidential, between friends.

Giroux appreciated Purdy's candor and sympathized: "The trouble here is not Roger, who actually supported me in my admiration for your work from *Malcolm* on, or any individual." Rather, his contract with Doubleday and options would make this a "one-shot publication, and no publisher really likes to do that." He should ask for another editor; surely there were "newer editors who would leap at the chance of being associated with your work." It was possible that Richardson, once he learned of *Esquire* paying "so handsomely" for *Elijah*, might view its "book possibilities now with a fresh eye" as "confirmation of the book's worth may jolt him and Doubleday" out of inertia. Giroux suggested the "ploy" of waiting for *Esquire* galleys, and resubmitting it in that form: "There's something about printed matter, as against typescript." Giroux was certain *Elijah* would be published success-fully. "It is too funny and well written not to be." At least Doubleday paid him $8,000 for *I Am Elijah Thrush*.[12] On July 31, Purdy dramatically read the first, lyrical chapter of his forthcoming novel on radio WBAI, which was twice rebroadcast.

In August, Purdy thanked Richardson for his kind note along with the "Royalty, or rather non-Royalty statement" for *Jeremy's Version*, which was "very disappointing." But he knew it took a long time for one of his books "to make its name." *Malcolm* was "ignored and pooh-poohed by the *New York Times*," but "now it is taught even in high school." It did "make life hard ec-onomically, and without that money from Hollywood," which taxes had reduced to nearly nothing, he would have to go to work. "Perhaps *Elijah Thrush* will make more of a stir, for all the *wrong* reasons." Meanwhile, he was working on volume two of *Sleepers*. "I wish I were rich, and I would pub-lish everything privately! I don't want to meet the public, I don't want to be reviewed!"[13]

During this period, James and composer Richard Hundley grew even closer as friends and companions. They enjoyed walks through the Brooklyn Botanical Gardens and going to the Metropolitan Opera. "James was a truly rare bird," Hundley said. "He was something out of this world." For years, he and James would luncheon together at Casa di Pre, a cozy Italian restaurant in Manhattan near Richard's apartment. James might come home with him, go directly to the piano, and begin improvising. One time, Hundley asked, "Jimmy, can you make snow?" Purdy went into a sort of trance state and pianistically simulated snow. When Hundley looked outside, it had begun snowing: "James was a sort of witch!" "He always said the artist must be free of shame."[14] During the 1970s their collaboration was fruitful. In 1971, Hundley set Purdy's poems to music. "We had a concert of them at LaMaMa Experimental Theater" in East Village, James told Gertrude Abercrombie.[15] In July 1971, during Festival of the Arts at Ram Island Arts Center in Maine, Hundley's "Vocal Quartets" premiered, adapting three Purdy poems. Their originality, melded with the "extraordinary feeling and mood" evoked by Hundley through "his style and elegance of vocal line," made "these works immediately accessible."[16]

"For Richard Hundley," in 1971 Purdy published *The Running Sun*, a limited edition of sixteen poems including the title poem alluding to Native Americans. Its illustrations are by Paul Waner, a Kansan artist and singer, the brother of Hundley's lover, singer David Waner. In Hundley's copy, Purdy inscribed: "These poems were written in Maine, Cape Cod, and dusty screeching Brooklyn. Richard Hundley made me write them, as I was afraid, if not ashamed of them. They were my night children, my bastards! And they kept emerging. I can't stop writing my poems. I write more poems than prose perhaps and my prose is in many ways poems. My prose is against the canon of the day, my poems equally so. . . . The so-called poets of our day would not approve of them partly because they insist on writing dead-lawyer prose. I published these poems at my own expense. Why submit them to a publisher who would cheat me or to reviewers who would never understand them?"[17]

In December, Giroux was delighted to receive an inscribed new edition of *Malcolm*. "I found myself starting to read it all over again, and I realized once more that it remains one of the best written books on which I have ever had the honor and pleasure of working as an editor." Given that Giroux edited Flannery O'Connor, William Gaddis, and Thomas Merton, this is high praise indeed.[18]

Esquire in its December issue published an abridged *I Am Elijah Thrush*. Purdy initially told Frank Baldanza to "beware" since it was "all cut up," as the manuscript marked by Lish amply shows.[19] Yet in his next letter, he urged him to get the issue "at once, before it goes off the stands, and read the abridgement" albeit it was "cut and tampered with in places." Lish collected this version of the novel in *All Our Secrets Are the Same: New Fiction from Esquire* (1976). *Sleepers in Moon-Crowned Valleys* might "turn out to be as many as five or six volumes." These were hard times for visionary writers. "I may have to go back to teaching, as nobody buys hardcover books. I don't know what to do."[20] Bantam reprinted the first volume, *Jeremy's Version*, in paperback with a cover painting of an attractive Edwardian mother flanked by two brooding brothers in outline.

In 1972, Purdy spoke freely to critic Irving Malin for a reference work, *Contemporary Novelists*. "As I see it, my work is an exploration of the American soul conveyed in a style based on the rhythms and accents of American speech." Despite his trouble being published or appreciated in New York, Purdy believed his work was the "most American of any writer writing today." The message of "American culture—commercial culture, that is—is that man can be adjusted, that loudness and numbers are reality, and that to be 'in' is to exist." His work was "furthest from this definition of 'reality.' All individual thought and feeling have been silenced or 'doped' in America today, and to be oneself is tantamount to non-existence." He discerned no difference between Russia and America since both were "hideous failures, both enemies of the soul, both devourers of nature, and undisciplined disciplinarians who wallow in the unnatural." In the United States, anything that makes money is sacred; consumers were "easily persuaded to move from their old crumbling Puritan ethic to belief in things like sexual deviation and coprophilia, provided and only provided these bring in money and notoriety. The one crime is to be oneself, unless it is a 'self' approved and created by the commercial forces. Beneath this vast structure of madness, money, and anesthetic prostitution, is my own body of work."[21]

For *Fiction: The Universal Elements* (1972), a short story anthology for classrooms that included "Cutting Edge," Purdy again discussed his work, which he described as cutting "against the grain." "To explore what is 'inside' will always be unpopular or taboo so far as any 'establishment' is concerned." Likewise, his style, "based on the rhythm and idiom of common American speech," from his "own small-town Ohio background, jarred and still jars on the ears of the spokesman-salesman for blue-skim homogenized prose à la New York City." The public, "devourers of bestseller fiction, demand now as always candy-wrapped lies." They applaud anything, as long as they are not required to feel since anesthesia is "the boon they have always asked of the writers applauded by the New York book trade." The advantages, however, of having no public were considerable: he had only to please himself, and since he had never been in, he need not fear being out.[22]

Although they had fallen out decades earlier, Purdy still felt something of the loss of Esther Wilcox in January 1972. In Chicago, James had shared a strong bond with Wendell Wilcox, and he and Esther served as models for characters. Long ago, it seemed Purdy wanted to be with Wendell as a team, but he already had Esther, who cared for him like a mother. Abercrombie wrote to tell him the news, saying: "Wendell is of course out of his mind. . . . I guess he'll be strapped for money now. And really for everything."[23] A few months later, Purdy reflected on their aging and her feeling sad and lonely as their mutual friends died. "Everyone is dead or gone—the same thing. I have some admirers but they are too young to know me. Ghosts are everywhere, real ghosts."[24]

In February, James and Jorma visited the Southern port city of Charleston, South Carolina, on a secret getaway, his "South Carolina hegira." He bought flowers from some older black women who spoke to him, just for the experience, and as he walked away, they resumed speaking in what he guessed was Gullah. "I enjoyed our trip, your fine performance as driver and companion," he wrote Sjoblom.[25] "Williamsburg was almost the best. Also the deer at Jamestown. It was a phantom I suppose, perhaps Paul Swan," who had died on February 1. He told Sam Steward: "I've not seen any place quite like [Charleston], anywhere, but I doubt I would be happy living there. I can't start all over again. But perhaps if I found an apartment in San Francisco, I could spend half the year there and half here." James had friends who kept "hounding" him to come to San Francisco.[26] For all his denigrating of New York literary critics, he never seemed to seriously consider a permanent move.[27]

In March, he was struggling to build *The House of the Solitary Maggot* amid heavy New York snowfall.[28] On April 2, Purdy attended the premiere of Tennessee Williams's *Small Craft Warnings* off-Broadway. For Williams it represented a minor comeback. Set in a seamy beach bar, it is populated by marginal losers, users, and fragile people depending on the kindness of strangers. Despite the drama being set on the West Coast, it feels informed by the lifestyle of Key West "Conchs" that Williams had witnessed at Sloppy Joe's and other taverns. Cherry Davis played Violet, but at some point, Candy Darling, the transgender Warhol Superstar, took over, and Tennessee himself took over the role of Doc, a drunken abortionist. *Small Craft Warnings* was perhaps the first time Williams dramatized overtly gay characters.[29]

Doubleday published *I Am Elijah Thrush* on May 12, 1972. It should have been an occasion for pride but Purdy thought Doubleday was uninterested, so, "in a real sense, it was never published."[30] Sam Steward sent him fulsome praise, for which Purdy was deeply grateful. "I loved your letter, and loved you for liking Elijah Thrush. You know it's all based on real people, at least on Paul Swan (Elijah) who was nearly 100 and died just before the book was published." Sam's letter cheered him up enormously when he was feeling blue: "as you say we aren't getting especially younger, and when I went over my address book the other day I felt I was visiting twenty or thirty cemeteries."[31]

In May, Paul Bowles extended his appreciation from Tangier. "Each new book you write is an event. *Elijah Thrush* has caused a good deal of argument and discussion here." Artist and art critic Maurice Grosser, Virgil Thomson's partner, believed it was allegory, but could not "decide about whom or what." Bowles was "content to enjoy it as I did *Malcolm*, without assigning ultimate meanings to the characters. I've read it three times; one thing which has struck me is that each time, I had the impression that I was reading it for the first time . . . rather that I was reading a different version. And that I find strange. I shall have to continue and see what happens on a fourth attempt."[32]

Purdy, like Melville, did not set out to write allegories or symbolist works, but afterward, he could see that he had. "I never actually say to myself: I'm going to write an allegory of this or that . . . but I see these things too, later."[33] Applicable to Melville and Purdy, the closeted gay critic F. O. Matthiessen wrote in *American Renaissance*: "Here again we have a token of the unconscious working of the creative mind."[34] Purdy's fire of imagination in *Elijah Thrush* also resembles that of Nathaniel Hawthorne since both authors project the inner life into "intricate symbols and archetypal patterns of experience," British critic Stephen D. Adams writes in his critical study *James Purdy* (1976). However, Purdy's "concern for the fate of the human heart" in a hostile culture in this novel "is not expressed in such an unremittingly tragic view of life." The baroque humor and wit of the novel's surface, which recall Oscar Wilde and Ronald Firbank, blend with "darker tones to produce that tension of comedy and pathos" that are hallmarks.[35]

After reading *I am Elijah Thrush*, Norman MacLeish declared "James Purdy will be remembered and classed among the greats ones long after he has gone!" He and his partner Ed lived in Florida but summered in Maine, where he invited Purdy to come north to visit.[36] Although MacLeish had apparently not seen Purdy in decades, he wrote: "I have thought of you so often, and I still think of you as one of my best friends," and a year later, "I have always—and still do—love you!"[37]

Purdy mailed *I Am Elijah Thrush* to the tenor saxophonist and composer Sonny Rollins in Brooklyn, who had replied affirmatively to a note from him offering to send books. "I hope you will enjoy reading *Elijah Thrush*. . . . I admire you very much indeed."[38] Purdy recalled a night on the subway, when he was "so delighted" to observe, about a car's length away, a black woman, "very tastefully dressed with heels," reading *Elijah Thrush* with a "bemused expression." He had a large but silent audience, he told Matthew Stadler. "I don't have a public, but I have an audience," which is preferable. "An audience comes to you and through you. A public is invented by strange forces and quickly loses interest, due to the whim of destiny. But my audience finds me."[39]

Purdy didn't need to visit MacLeish in Maine since surprisingly, he was given a house of his own there. In late 1969, a friend left him a house in a tiny town, he told Giroux. It was "pretty close to moose and wolves and bear, but I suppose I could get used to them too."[40] During June through August 1972, he lived at Mt. Desert, on an island. Jorma drove him there, taking a ferry from Stonington, Maine, to reach the island. In June, with Jorma at the wheel, he traveled from there to Bangor, then south to Portsmouth, New Hampshire, and Lowell, Massachusetts.[41] Jorma was his companion and chauffeur, as Purdy did not have a car or driver's license. Back in Mt. Desert, Purdy was surrounded by white cedars, yews, balsam firs; the air "breathable and the quiet overwhelming." He told Gertrude, "New York makes me sick in the summer with its red-hot fumes and *no air!*" Maine was beautiful, but he missed his "young men friends." He had trouble relaxing despite the pleasant ambience. "I am very sad and lonesome somehow but keep working. Still, nothing seems to be right. I feel I am asleep because so many loved ones are gone. Richard's death was a terrible blow to me. I needed him to go on."[42] Though his older brother had died five years ago, and had caused his family grief, still he was much missed. But he liked Maine, "all woods and little mountains and birds." He found a witch hazel tree; nearby were a pet crow, pet raven, pet owl, chipmunks, raccoons, blacklegged foxes, eagles, wildflowers, and a "loon that screams murder on Echo Lake." At times, these Maine trips were restorative; he thrilled to sounds of nature he missed in the city. "There are lots of easy small mountains to climb here, and I do this each day," he wrote Paula Fox. "The view is wonderful."[43]

In late July, Purdy, usually defiant about his outsider status, felt depressed over his treatment by the New York establishment. The *New York Times* gave *I Am Elijah Thrush* a negative review by literary critic Lawrence Graver and the *New Yorker* ran a mixed review that said "Mr. Purdy astonishes us with the vividness and fluency he imparts to an extremely fanciful story," even if the novel has "bad moments."[44] "What they really wish to do is take the bread out of my mouth," he complained to Sandy Richardson. "No, kill me." *Elijah Thrush*, which he said he began writing back in 1959, is "a *major* statement from me about our world. It is not minor, and not deserving of this shameful treatment. It is also *new* in style, treatment, etc." He hoped Doubleday would protest to the *Times* and place good ads. "My readers do not know a new book by me has been published!" Discrimination against him at the *Times* began with the "ascendancy" of John Leonard, who was promoted to daily book reviewer at the *New York Times Book Review*, he said. In August, James told Sandy Richardson he had "asked the Black-legged fox to put a curse on John Leonard. You will hear." *The Nephew, Children Is All*, and *Cabot Wright Begins* received "very respectful treatment (Before Leonard). Even Susan Sontag (then a darling of the Times) said I was one of the six American writers worth taking seriously." But when Leonard and Sheed arrived, they unleashed "their vendetta." Echoing his words to FSG after the Sheed imbroglio, "Surely Doubleday might find some way to partly counteract such gross unfairness."

He was writing lots of poems but *Solitary Maggot* was a "hell book to write." Nevertheless, he had already produced over three thousand pages to be "boiled down."[45] Throughout the summer, he "tried to tame thousands of manuscript pages of *The House of the Solitary Maggot*."[46] He assured Gordon Lish he was working on a story for *Esquire*, but was vague: "one day I hope to send you the story of your dreams." In July, Purdy said he was writing for Lish every day, "but the demons do not always bring a story in for you. Thousands of passages, pages, about Elsie, Wendell, Gertrude, Herman, and a story called 'Narrow Rooms.' But still in the shell."[47]

Jonathan Cape published *I Am Elijah Thrush* in Britain in October 1972. In the Sunday *Telegraph*, novelist Francis King noted when he last reviewed Purdy, he had called him a genius, not a word he often used. When his earlier review appeared, King, a gay man, worried he had overstated Purdy's case, but after imbibing *Elijah*, could "only repeat his original judgment." The *Times Literary Supplement* called it an "American *Satyricon*" and "an American parable." It was as if this "dark exotic jewel" set in a "fairy-tale city of New York" had been "fathered by Cocteau on F. Scott Fitzgerald." Otherwise, however, the book tended to receive very negative reviews in England, some taking offense to its characters' bizarre hankerings. *The Listener* called it "muddle-headed and rather obscene" while the *Spectator*'s reviewer, Auberon Waugh, son of novelist Evelyn Waugh, said the novel "should be read by all aspiring novelists as a terrible example." If Doubleday were on top of things, they would have removed the last four words from the phrase just quoted and used it as a blurb.[48]

This only exacerbated his frustration. In October, Purdy railed against publishers to his publisher/friend. "You are my friend, but you are also my publisher, and a wide gulf therefore separates us," James told Sandy Richardson. Doubleday had not properly stood by him with *Elijah Thrush*. "It is a great blow to my morale and pride that you have never advertised *this extremely important book* (The only important work of the imagination published since *Jeremy's Version*.) However, I am garnering my energy and strength to go on with my own writing. I have found one cannot win with American capitalism in any of its forms. America is rotten to the core, and

I am not going to Europe as its representative."[49] Ironically, in November, Purdy was interviewed for Voice of America radio, the government's international radio organ, controlled by the United States Information Agency.[50]

In late 1972, Purdy was interviewed for Andy Warhol's *Interview* magazine by the queer street artist and designer Stephen Varble. Varble offered high praise: "James Purdy is one of the heroes of modern literature, and perhaps the greatest writer of fiction in America today." His works are "charged with divine comedy and human possibility. They are visionary even when they go in the disguise of ordinary subject matter." Varble spoke with authority on the visionary, since he strolled New York streets in large, elaborate costumes made from a cornucopia of fabrics and found objects. Varble led underground gallery tours through SoHo and enacted "protest performances in banks, Fifth Avenue stores, and in the street."[51] Noting Varble was, like Elijah, a mime, Purdy believed he was "creating a kind of art form of his own—where that will lead, I don't know." After this interview, Purdy and Varble became friends.[52] Purdy liked to bring people in his life together, and introduced Stephen Varble to Bob Helps.

Directed by Stephen Varble, on Saturday, January 13, 1973, a dramatic reading of the first forty pages of *I Am Elijah Thrush* was broadcast on Pacifica radio WBAI, lasting nearly ninety minutes. Varble played Thrush's assistant, Eugene Bellamy; Robert (Bob) Christian, a young black actor, was Albert Peggs, the narrator; and Purdy's friend Dame Hermione Gingold was "very fine" as mighty Millicent Frayne. James himself was Elijah Thrush, after the Australian actor Cyril Richard backed out at the last minute. Purdy said Cyril Richard, deeming *Elijah Thrush* "too immoral," thought he would lose his reputation. "Since I have no reputation I couldn't fear losing mine."[53] The dramatization was produced by Varble's partner, artist Geoffrey Hendricks. Purdy's close friend Bob Helps composed piano music that was played by Joe Fennimore.[54] This was a performance to remember, a gathering of Purdy partisans voicing a strange and special work.

15

Solitary Confinement

The ensemble radio performance of *I Am Elijah Thrush* was a bright moment, but during the early 1970s, Purdy often felt isolated and lonely in his second-floor Henry Street perch, gazing out the window. On July 17, 1973, Purdy turned sixty, but "I might as well be 100 years old or 150," he told Frank Baldanza. Everyone close to him was "dead or sick or gone, or isolated, or something." The only people he knew were "very young men, and a few older women" who were "married and quite busy." He still claimed a lack of money kept him "living in this awful noisy filthy city."[1] Purdy's oppressive sense of isolation, relieved by visits from young men who attended to him, set upon him as he toiled on *The House of the Solitary Maggot*. He translated this feeling and scenario into powerful literature there and especially *In a Shallow Grave*.

In 1973, Purdy fought loneliness by traveling South with Jorma Sjoblom for a speaking engagement at the Boatwright Literary Festival in Richmond, Virginia. Jorma, after losing his research job, had left New York for Baltimore to pursue a new career as a librarian. James traveled to Baltimore and stayed with Jorma, who drove them the rest of the way. In this somewhat rare appearance, Purdy read from *Solitary Maggot* and briefly lectured. He was invited by an admirer, Professor [Robert] Jere Real of Lynchburg College, who during the 1970s brought in major American gay authors to speak: Tennessee Williams, Gore Vidal, Truman Capote, and Edward Albee. Purdy was not as familiar to the faculty. Jere Real grew up in Jackson, Mississippi, neighboring Eudora Welty and met Purdy in New York through their mutual friend, publisher Frank Hollman. The three had lunch in Greenwich Village at an Italian place Purdy favored. Real found Purdy "very nice, soft-spoken, and genteel" and this persona seemed "at odds with what he wrote." Jere Real interviewed James for *Blueboy*, a gay magazine akin to *Playboy*, with cultured articles and interviews accompanying beefcake photography.[2]

Mostly Purdy was in New York writing. He told Sandy Richardson that he was "on the right track now with *The House of The Solitary Maggot*," and was "going right ahead with it." In March, he completed two-thirds of the novel in rough draft. He was also trying to get Doubleday to promote his books more,

Figure 15.1 View out Purdy's window at 236 Henry Street, Brooklyn Heights, New York. Photo by the author.

both as a publisher and as a bookseller. He was concerned about the publicity department, having connected to a Mrs. Thomas in publicity at last, who, he believed, had been "unaware there is a James Purdy" or that Doubleday published him.[3] He asked Richardson if the Bantam paperback of *I Am Elijah Thrush* could be "more prominently displayed" in Doubleday bookstores. Its cover featured an open-shirted, chiseled Albert Peggs, clutching his belt buckle, leaning in front of a design of large comedy and tragedy masks, and at top: "THE OUTRAGEOUS NOVEL OF LOVE AND PERVERSITY." Doubleday, he charged, had not done right by him with *Jeremy's Version* or *Elijah Thrush*. "In the case of *Elijah* the only publicity you gave me was when, so to speak, I put a gun in your faces, and a grudging ad was placed in the *shitty Times*. I realize your influence and power are limited, but your survival does not depend on my books; mine does, and Doubleday is not helping me to survive, but sink." Purdy still signed such scolding letters amiably.[4]

Purdy attended some parties at Virgil Thomson's, but extended regrets for missing others.[5] Gerald Busby, who scored Robert Altman's film, *Three Sisters*, met James at a party and was fascinated: "It was as though he was writing in your presence." Purdy, highly intuitive, rapidly gained a "sense of everyone" in the room, and started "writing a story about them right then and there." Purdy's intuition seemed nearly supernatural. He later told scholar Richard Canning: "they say I'm psychic. This young man who helps me—my director, off-Broadway, John Uecker—will ask me what I get about a person. I just tell him whatever comes into my mouth and it turns out to be true."[6]

In April 1973, Joyce Carol Oates wrote out of the clear blue sky. She responded to "Writing from Inner-Compulsion," his statement to Observations of American Writers in observance of International Book Year 1972, which was reprinted in periodicals. "It's puzzling to me that you should think you are not widely known—in fact you are very well known. Perhaps you are comparing yourself to someone who is extraordinarily famous, like Capote?—Roth? But these writers, though 'famous,' are not necessarily read with as much attention, or taught by as many professors of English, as your works. I think you may have somewhat prematurely judged the reality of 'Purdy' in our culture. Tony Tanner, whom I know, thinks very highly of your work, and he is extremely influential; and what about Gordon Lish (who continually rejects my fiction)? And here at the University [of Windsor, in Ontario] is my good friend Gene McNamara who admires your work very much." In 1962, McNamara, who categorized Purdy as a postmodern novelist, was one of the first critics to use the term, though he did not clearly define attributes of the postmodern novel. "This may be the most objective letter you will ever receive, because I write as someone who cannot respond to your fiction—though I respond to the fact that you write, that you are writing from an 'inner compulsion' which I think we all share. Because I cannot quite get into your fiction I don't review it—I don't feel that I should attempt it— and when I decline, a reviewer likely to give you a more positive, sympathetic notice will probably be assigned the book." But Oates was not quite accurate about not reviewing his fiction, since in 1965, she had savaged *Cabot Wright Begins* in the *Kenyon Review*.[7] And Purdy later listed Oates among "nonentities," claiming she had "reviewed *I Am Elijah Thrush* unfavorably. She threw up her hands and said she didn't know what it meant."[8] "Though I suppose you dislike me (or the incredible 'image' of me that seems to have floated free of me, of my own self) you might want to consider what it would be like if 'Purdy' were suddenly 'well-known.' You would probably feel the same mingled bewilderment and embarrassment and irritation that I feel— and a growing sense of helplessness, as the 'image' becomes utilized by other people," she wrote pointedly. Should Purdy become famous, he would "look back with nostalgia upon simpler days." As Purdy had pointed out, there is a certain advantage in being an outsider on the margins.

Purdy replied to Oates: "I appreciate what you say in your letter too much not to wish to thank you for it, and I am grateful to you for wanting to write it. I have no personal ill-will toward you whatsoever. I have been disturbed at times over what some people have said you said about me, but I did not know if you had really said those things. I don't think I have ever wanted great public acclaim, but one can only resent it when such powerful newspapers as the New York Times make it a point to tell their readers not to buy my books, and take the bread out of one's mouth."[9]

In May, *Esquire* published Purdy's mock dialogue, "Q & A," excerpted from the short play "Wedding Finger." It took aim at Manhattan, the location of the *Times* and the epicenter of American book publishing. In the play, the questioner is Saint Stephen and the interviewee is Prince Antelope from Haiti, who can merge his soul with beasts. The prince has come to marry the Island of Manhattan and tow it away, as prophesied and directed by the Forces, and "through divine soul-breath and soul-principle, we, Manhattan and I, will soon sail away into an unknown ocean which is above the atmo[sphere]." This short piece fulfilled Purdy's fantasy.

Purdy missed having an attentive editor as he had in Robert Giroux. He had been "quite disturbed" that Sandy Richardson had not been able to give "more time, attention, and guidance" to *The House of the Solitary Maggot*, making thus far "only a very few comments." This *House* was "extremely difficult" to erect, making great demands on him. Richardson's "seeming tenuous hold" on his aesthetic goals for this novel and his "lack of any encouragement and guidance" had forced him to "let other people read it, encourage, and respond." Acknowledging Richardson's increased duties at Doubleday, Purdy followed Giroux's advice, suggesting that perhaps there was an assistant editor under his supervision who could relieve him of some responsibility toward the novel. James handed over the typescript at a luncheon Sandy invited him to share, but he came away thoroughly disappointed. For one thing, his editor swilled "many martinis" and a glass of wine. "This luncheon was to be concerned with the book, but he spent the entire hour talking about *Deep Throat*, saying I should go see it. But I wasn't interested in pornography. I came away feeling utterly devastated. I felt like I'd been beaten to a pulp. He never even read the typescript. I made that book with no help."[10]

Contrastingly, in June, he shared a felicitous lunch with Robert Giroux and FSG senior editor William J. Weatherby (Bill). "When next I saw Bob," Bill wrote, "we expressed exactly the same reaction to that lunch with you—what an enjoyable occasion it was!" Weatherby, an author and critic from England, in 1965 had praised Purdy's novels in a *Times Literary Supplement* piece, "The Choler of Despair." He was particularly pleased because he admired both Purdy and FSG and was thus delighted there was no ill will on either side over Purdy's departure. "You both have the cause of literature at heart, which is a great deal to have in common these days. I have worked for a cross-section of American publishers and FSG is the only one I have found that doesn't pay merely lip-service to literature but is truly serious." That last comment did nothing to assuage Purdy's remorse about going over to "Doubledip."[11]

In August, Purdy complained to Bill Weatherby about Richardson. Sandy spent "most of his time at Hyannis port with Rose Kennedy, helping her write *her* book," *Times to Remember*, for which Kennedy was paid $1.525 million. He did not want to assign another editor to Purdy, "being a real dog in the manger. It's a dreadful impasse *and* experience. They are a horrible pub-lisher."[12] In November, Purdy told Sandy's assistant: "I have been treated with little short of contempt with regard to the writing of this book. He has never discussed the book with me in any detail. He has not said ten words about it. I feel that now the book is going into production, there can be little in the way of 'editorial comment' which would be helpful to me. I do not feel I have been treated with professional respect, and I am deeply offended." He had "*never* been so unhappy with any publisher."[13] After Purdy corrected the final galleys, neither Richardson nor anyone in his office reviewed them; rather, they "went straight to Mr. Rounds," the proofreader, "who though excellent, is after all not an *editor*." Richardson had only given real attention to the novel "in its final form" when Doubleday president Samuel S. Vaughan interceded on Purdy's request. But even then, Richardson's attention was "hurried, un-helpful, and vague."[14]

From July through September 1973, Purdy revised and corrected his new novel, which he dedicated to Minnie Mae Otis. Purdy reflected: "One story my grandmother told me was *House of the Solitary Maggot*. When I began to rewrite that, I thought I'd take out the section where he blows the eyes out of the boy, picks them up and puts them in his mouth. I thought, 'I won't have that.' Then I dreamed my grandmother told me, 'You put that back. I told you that, and you're going to write the story the way I told you.' My mother used to scold her, saying: 'You shouldn't tell him those things. He's already so strange. He's too young to hear terrible stories.'"[15] Paul Bowles, who selected an ex-cerpt from it for publication in *Antaeus*, praised the novel's "American vision and speech and power." Personally editing Purdy's manuscript, however, Bowles expressed dissatisfaction with idiosyncrasies in Purdy's sentences in a letter to Daniel Halpern, editor of *Antaeus*.[16]

Once again feeling let down by his book publisher, Purdy turned back to a magazine editor he had previously felt wronged by. In February 1974, he appreciated Gordon Lish's sympathy and support. "You are a good friend—I appreciate your words more than you can know. I am deeply *depressed*. I feel I should only publish privately. The obscene creatures that run the New York publishing world sicken me more and more.[17]

On Monday, April Fool's Day, 1974, Purdy's Lawrence University friend John Bucklew died unexpectedly after a short illness at age fifty-nine. A tribute stated that the psychologist was "the symbol of a near perfect integration of research and instruction. He was what every college would like to have—an active, respected scholar in close contact with students." In 1975 and 1976, the university sponsored a John Bucklew Memorial Lecture Series.[18] Bucklew had felt trapped and unhappy at Lawrence, and given the date and lack of details of his death, he may have taken his own life.

For an endorsement requested by Doubleday on Purdy's recommendation, in June, Sam Steward offered a long, allusive response to the galley proof of *The House of the Solitary Maggot*. "It is brilliantly conceived and stylishly executed—on an odd balance, where everything is turned just a little sideways or titled into another dimension—a dark and somber Wuthering Heights climate of clouds and mist, with the Castle of Otranto standing just beyond the grey chopped waters of the lake, and the dim palace of Xanadu far in the distance." It is at once tender and grim, a "macabre yet wildly humorous creation, having touches of the Grand Guignol interspersed with vividly perceptive observations about man and his state." He was "impressed tremendously" and believed it "may be indeed his best work to date." James was "deeply moved" by Sam's "beautiful letter" and Doubleday was "thrilled and appreciative."[19]

Though Purdy was never asked to sit for a *Playboy* interview like Truman Capote, Gore Vidal, or Tennessee Williams, he surprised many "stuffed shirts" when he was interviewed for the July 1974 issue of *Penthouse*, filling five pages of this men's magazine that featured more explicit erotica than *Playboy*. He was treated very respectfully. Interviewer Fred Barron declared: "more than any other modern writer, Purdy is the chronicler of the American soul." *The House of the Solitary Maggot* was a "profound tragedy of classical proportions that stands above current fiction like *Oedipus Rex* above a bedroom farce" and was his most important work. Purdy, with the "distinguished, cordial formality of a Southern gentleman, and in the mildest of tones, proceeds to say the most devastating things. If he were not speaking the truth, his words would be horrifying; but he is, so they are catastrophic." A screenwriter, Barron submitted his interview to "all the so-called respectable magazines," who refused it. "The only place that would print it was an unrespectable magazine." Purdy said he would not be offended: "what do we care where it appears, if our point of view and our opinions can be heard?"[20]

In the interview, Purdy laid bare all his criticisms of the country, American culture, and the media. "Everything in America is sold. If they can't sell you, you don't exist. We're a nation of anesthetic whores. . . . America is really over, everything is collapsing, and all that remains is the memories of great things like Lincoln and Melville. Everything is meretricious." Soon before the Watergate scandal broke, Purdy said "the government is a fraud and a murderer on a mass scale." The press is "completely megalomaniacal" and the "greatest of whores. It thinks and says it is the safeguard of liberty, when it really has prostituted and sold everything. It has never disseminated the truth."[21] Purdy remarked that his actual return from books was very low. He earned almost all of his living by "handouts or foundations or by other sources." New Yorkers, with superior attitudes, were always asking him to "sign something to defend a Russian writer who is being mistreated," which, while true, "look how the Americans mistreat their own writers. I mean, how dare they bewail the tyranny of Russia when we have the same thing over here. The only difference is that in America, they'll only publish and praise what is tenth-rate, whereas in Russia, they only publish and praise what follows the party line." He recklessly proclaimed "it would be very good if the *New York Times* went out of business along with *Newsweek, Time,* and the *New York Review of Books*." On freedom, both a Cold War and countercultural buzzword, Purdy stated: "There is no freedom except that which you achieve for yourself through your work. Freedom can't be given to you like chewing gum." The only people who are free are "those who have no allegiance to anything but themselves and their invisible spiritual world. Prayer, fasting, withdrawal are almost the only methods to live through the tyranny and poisoned insanity given to us by our government and our media."[22] In this country, "no one has any memory"—the United States of Amnesia, Gore Vidal called it. "All that exists is what's being shoved up or down at the moment. It can't really be called capitalism anymore. I don't know what it is. Capitalism was a kind of simpleminded fraud, but what's going on now is something much more vicious. Capitalism has even turned against itself." But if you are a writer, "you really have only your memory which—in our culture—is what they want to destroy." "Memory is the soul: it's the psyche. There really is only the soul for a writer. And America—the America we have now—wants to destroy the soul and body both."[23] "Everything is memory," he said two years later. "Even as it happens, the event becomes instantly memory, and this is the only reality, however dubious and unreliable."[24]

Purdy was an equal-opportunity offender. When Barron asked if he considered himself a gay writer, Purdy said "No. I'm just a monster. Gay writers are too conservative for me. Actually, I think the only really gay writer was Hemingway. 'Gay' has become a household word now, so it's meaningless."[25] The interview created "quite a sensation" and "offended many stuffed shirts," to Purdy's satisfaction.[26]

On October 4, 1974, Purdy's Midwestern Gothic family saga *The House of the Solitary Maggot* was published to little fanfare, even at the Doubleday office. Purdy was "heartbroken on the day of publication of The Maggot," because not only did Sandy Richardson break their "luncheon appointment," but also no one in the office even knew it was publication day, and Purdy was "grossly insulted" by Sandy's assistant then and on successive days.[27] While Doubleday did not seem to appreciate the novel, Robert Giroux said it was not only "worthy successor to *Jeremy's Version*, but one of the best books" Purdy had written.[28] Nevertheless, the manuscript was declined by Jonathan Cape in England.[29] In 1976, Purdy denigrated "the moulting immigrant Tom Maschler," the head of Cape, as the worst British publisher.[30]

The *New York Times* did not even review his new work, much to Purdy's chagrin. Late in life, Purdy complained that the gay author "Edmund White wouldn't review *Solitary Maggot*, saying he didn't care for Southern Gothic writing; which is nonsense, since I come from the Midwest and lived for so long in Brooklyn. As a result, the book wasn't reviewed in *The New York Times*, and was pretty much overlooked by the mainstream."[31] This was unprecedented for his books since Purdy was "considered a major writer."[32] Editor "John Leonard gave *Solitary Maggot* to Edmund White, which they never should have done because he's only interested in homosexuality," Purdy fumed. White "wrote a letter saying he hates James Purdy, I hate Southern writers, I don't want to review it. They never found another reviewer." In 2020, White explained: "I didn't review the solitary maggot because I had resolved after my twenties never to review a new novel negatively." According to Matthew Stadler, his mentor novelist Guy Davenport, who had positively reviewed *Jeremy's Version* for the *Times*, said John Leonard asked him to re-view *Solitary Maggot*, but he did not care for it, so declined. Guy Davenport told Leonard that the novel was not worth reviewing, perhaps trying to shield it from a bad review from a less sympathetic reviewer.[33] In August, Purdy wrote to Richardson's assistant suggesting Sandy Richardson write to Mr. Leonard, "enclosing a quotation from Dr. Tony Tanner, and telling him that Doubleday considers this a major literary work, and a literary event. Of course I never remember the *Times* ever being aware of anything but the sound of dollar bills falling." Decades later, Purdy still seethed. "He hated me. Oh God, John Leonard. Oh, it was terrible how the *Times* treated me. My most important book they never reviewed. . . . Why? There's nothing gay in it."[34] Conveniently, he overlooked that he had just stated in a national maga-zine he hoped the *Times* went out of business. Likewise, the other periodicals published in New York that he wished doom upon—*Time*, *Newsweek*, and the *New York Review of Books*—also ignored his novel though they had reviewed his work in the past. New York gave him the high hat, refusing to enter Purdy's *House*.

Yet Purdy was well aware he had written a novel that would challenge readers, one that begins, "Do not disturb!" While writing *The House of the Solitary Maggot*, he expressed this to his friend and neighbor, novelist Paula Fox: "It seems very wild, and there is no pity or care given to any reader, the reader is ordered out on the first page, and then pelted with rocks for the rest of the book; at the last page if there is still a reader hanging on he is thrown off the precipice and curses from the deepest hell hurled at him."[35]

Nonetheless, outside of New York, some reviews were ecstatic. On the West Coast, the *Los Angeles Times* gave *Solitary Maggot* a glowing review by critic James Martin, who was inspired and likened Purdy to Tennessee Williams. "Purdy's moon-crowned valleys are the jerkwater burghs of the Midwest: forlorn and forgotten hamlets where the milk train doesn't stop an-ymore, but where archetypal families—big, brawling clans" are "summoned from slumber to play parts in a metamorphic allegory. Purdy unearths their remains, rattles their closeted skeletons, and chronicles the decline and fall, the riving of the fabric of their lives; their ultimate, utter extirpation." His "feverish vision sets the pages ablaze," and "ghastly goings-on" are etched upon the reader's subconscious.[36] Elliott Anderson, executive editor of *TriQuarterly*, declared in the *Chicago Tribune* that brooding Aiken Cusworth was the most powerful fictional character in literature since Heathcliff in

Emily Brontë's *Wuthering Heights*. Tony Tanner at University of Cambridge, who had assessed Purdy at length in his book *City of Words: American Fiction 1950–1970*, gave an endorsement: this stunning novel has "an awesome cumulative power" at once "unreal and overwhelmingly too real—inducing an odd feeling"—one cannot believe it, but "knows it is true." Literary critic Warren French concluded "one can only be awed" by the novel in his review for *The Great Lakes Review*.[37]

In August, Purdy was "more than appalled" to learn that Doubleday had allowed *Jeremy's Version* and *I Am Elijah Thrush* to go out of print without alerting him. "You did not wish me to have an agent, but I feel only an agent can deal with the many failings which Doubleday are guilty of. I do not see how I can continue with you as a publisher, and unless these abuses are changed, I will have to ask you to excuse me from fulfilling the three-book contract." Since Sandy Richardson's attentions were diffused, James felt "completely isolated, unknown, and 'anonymous' in so large a corporation as Doubleday." They might rally and take action to promote his new book—but he doubted it. He believed his books only sold at all because of his "considerable reputation," not due to Doubleday's efforts. "I have never seen a worse publicity department. What does it do?" He concluded: "I do not see how I can continue with you under these circumstances, and should like you to consider the matter carefully. P.S. if *Jeremy's Version* is not back in print by the time *The House Of The Solitary Maggot* appears, I will consider this in itself grounds to break my contract with Doubleday." Purdy later said he was "so distracted by Richardson's drinking," he could not continue working with his old friend.[38]

In October, Purdy returned to Brooklyn Heights after several weeks vacationing in Maine.[39] He picked up his assault by letter on Richardson: "I am torn between my friendship for you and my extremely strong feelings that because of your important position, you cannot perform the editorial and promotional tasks necessary for my survival as a writer." After scolding him, he conceded, "Of course you have done many fine things for me at Doubleday, and before that, and I am grateful, and you are one of my oldest and most valued friends. But it is my life and profession which are at stake here, and friendship for you cannot blind me to the fact that I need an editor who can give me time, encouragement, and real editorial cooperation. After all, I am not earning a *living* from my writing, and I do not think you *really* understand or appreciate that, and I do not think you understand my sacrifices. I am a name you like to have on your list, but you are not willing to give me the time and nurture which my books and I require to survive. That is why real changes must be made, or I must leave, and not fulfill my contract."[40]

Richardson replied with a phone call, which relieved Purdy that "something tangible and forthright" would be done to promote his new book, an excerpt of which appeared in *TriQuarterly*. Purdy brought up window displays: several small bookstores, such as Robert A. Wilson's Phoenix Bookshop in Greenwich Village and Andreas Brown's Gotham Book Mart in Midtown Manhattan, had placed displays for *The House of the Solitary Maggot*. Both booksellers supported and followed his career and carried his small-press limited editions. Purdy regarded his friend, Wilson, as "one of the most civilized of men" and "one of the very few book dealers who is literate and who cares about serious writers."[41] While Purdy counted on their support, Doubleday stores, as usual, had "done *nothing* to display *The Maggot*." But as the storywriter David Means remarked: "When you write a long, strange book, and call it *House of the Solitary Maggot*, you can't shoot for the stars."[42]

James asked that *Solitary Maggot* be sent to Betty Allen, the great black mezzo-soprano, who, like Purdy, was born and raised in northern Ohio. She was going on a State Department tour of South America and would be singing songs by Richard Hundley adapted from Purdy's poems in *The Running Sun*. Betty Allen would read from Purdy's text after singing each song.[43] Allen collaborated with Rorem, Bernstein, and Copland and made her debut in *Four Saints in Three Acts* by Thomson and Stein. She appeared to support Purdy's earlier work as well in her capacity as executive director of the Harlem School for the Arts, putting on Joseph Fennimore's short opera adaptation of "Eventide" in three different seasons.[44]

With Gordon Lish as fiction editor, *Esquire* maintained its support of Purdy, publishing "Summer Tidings" in its December 1974 issue. The story contains a subtext of transgressive love, that of Galway, a Jamaican gardener, for Rupert, a white boy from a wealthy family who is celebrating his thirteenth birthday. Even amid the permissive climate of 1974, it seems the story should have raised controversy. Although some readers have overlooked the pedophilia, Lish later said the Jamaican gardener's longing for the boy was not only crystal-clear, but was also his "raison d'etre for publishing." He said he edited the story to make this more pronounced, believing its publication would cause "a shitstorm." Lish improved the title, as was his wont; Purdy's was "Summer Testament."[45] In March, Purdy protested he had worked on the story for over a year, and it was already one of his best as submitted—so he had "no desire to change it" for Lish. He was unhappy, noting that material Lish had already published in *Esquire* had been "cut in such a way that its artistic integrity" had been abused. "I do not see any need to send you anything in the future, and I will instruct Doubleday not to send you anything."[46] Purdy changed his mind, but remained dissatisfied. In October, he wrote: "You have also got so you correct my prose in order to suit the New York style, and you omitted crucial sentences from 'Summer Tidings,' which explain why the Jamaican gardener is so emotionally overwrought." Three days later, he added: "Of course I have appreciated your championing of my work, and I respect and admire your abilities and devotion. But you have become increasingly wanton and shears-happy with regard to my prose and my very structure. It is an occupational hazard with editors. You change things that cannot be changed because the changes destroy both the style and meaning." To the editor called "Captain Fiction" he commanded: "You *cannot* change my prose, unless I have misspelled a word, or contradicted myself." Purdy was annoyed Lish seemed unable to appreciate his writing's evolution, as Tony Tanner had.[47] Then, the next day, Purdy personally took his story to *Vogue* offices after he "riled" Gordon. Purdy said of course he would prefer *Esquire* to publish it and thought Leo Lerman would understand if Lish really wanted it. Besides, Purdy could not imagine *Vogue* actually publishing it since they had "rejected everything" he had ever written. Despite Lish's skillful editing, Purdy still carped to Frank Baldanza the story was "tampered with by the stupid editor." But soon, Purdy was fairly reconciled to Lish's edit. He told Steward of his new story in *Esquire*: "they have tampered with it here and there, but I guess it is about the way I wrote it, and when it comes out in book form, it will be all as I said it." Its republication in *Candles of Your Eyes* (1987) maintained most of the Lish edits, restoring certain phrases Lish had cut. Though it did not generate the controversy Lish had hoped for, "Summer Tidings" was reprinted four times.

On a roll, Purdy wrote an astounding story, "Some of These Days," but Lish rejected it, saying the narrator did not talk like a convict. Purdy rejoined: "Have you ever heard convicts talk? Are there such things as convicts? And don't you know that prisoners are like everybody else, and come from every walk of life, and in prison and out talk like everybody else."[48] Ironically, the story's unlearned, marginal voice recalls "Daddy Wolf," a Lish favorite. He told Baldanza that James Laughlin at New Directions would publish it, but *Penthouse* might beat him to it. Although owner and publisher Bob Guccioni thought it was too "homosexual," the young editors liked it very much.[49] "Some of my best stories, recent stories, such as 'Some of These Days' about the young man who was in prison and tries to find his landlord—languish without publication. People would not publish that story on the grounds that it was homosexual. Now from one point of view it is about homosexuality, but I think the real theme of this story transcends any kind of sexual orientation." The story can be read as an allegory of man's futile search for God or just meaning amid urban squalor. To James Martin, "Some of These Days" is "as trenchant a condemnation of dehumanizing city life" as Herlihy's *Midnight Cowboy*.[50]

On December 1, James told Sandy Richardson he enjoyed their meeting and the "luncheon was very fine." Purdy felt "very much gratified" the editor "thought so highly" of the finished product of *The House of the Solitary Maggot*. Ten days later, James thanked Sandy for writing the *New York Times* about their lack of a review—still, nothing was quite right. Richardson had promised to promote *Solitary Maggot* as "a *major* work," which had not happened. "My friends have put the greatest pressure on me to leave Doubleday as they are convinced you are destroying my reputation by such indifferent promotion. I have also gone to Brown, Ltd., for it is obvious that I cannot survive without an agent to speak up for me. I cannot tell you how distressed I have been over the way Doubleday has mismanaged everything with regard to this book."[51]

Bantam broke with him as his paperback publisher, refusing to bring *Solitary Maggot* into paperback "because it wasn't mentioned in the *New York Times*." The "tyranny of the *Times*" ensured it "never had support. If they ignored it, you were dead." Critic Irving Malin, a consistent supporter, praised it in *New Republic* but Purdy disagreed with assessments of his work as Gothic, Southern or otherwise, nor did he think of his characters as "grotesque." His roots went "back to Twain and Cooper, and of course Sherwood Anderson and Gertrude Stein."[52] Anderson, of course, literally wrote "The Book of the Grotesque," the opening chapter of his famous *Winesburg, Ohio*.

In early 1975, Ned Rorem wrote Paul Bowles: "I told James Purdy what you wrote about his thoughtfulness, and he was pleased, especially since he admires you so much. Coincidentally, both his and my new books have been almost entirely ignored by the press, as well as by our respective publishers, and we feel paranoid; your words thus come as a balm."[53] Paul's words provided solace to James, who lacked peace as his latest book was overlooked by critics and the market. But Purdy was a fighter and was not about to throw in the towel. He was reaching for new heights as he composed *In a Shallow Grave*.

16

Lighting Out

In the mid-1970s, Purdy longed for escape, whether it was delving deep into the past, indulging in recreational anonymous letters, or, like Huckleberry Finn, lighting out for the West. In mid-to-late 1974, he drafted *In a Shallow Grave*, a rich Southern Gothic story of love and healing, imbued with religious allegory. It centers on Garnet Montrose, a grotesquely injured Vietnam veteran who appears to be turned inside out, his relation to the past, and his search for assistance, brotherhood, and love. The English literary critic Stephen D. Adams was reminded of one of Purdy's favorite books, Unamuno's *The Tragic Sense of Life* (1912), which locates "man's essential being in the antagonism between the soul's yearning for immortality and a timeless love, and the body's premonitions of death and dissolution."[1] Refracting relationships between Purdy and young men who played roles in his life including John Uecker, the short novel is considered a classic.

In February 1975, Purdy, recollecting his youth, purchased vintage sheet music of the 1930s tune "On the Alamo" by Gus Kahn and Isham Jones. He annotated: "This song is sung by one of the characters in *In a Shallow Grave*," and was "sung by the real person" on whom Montrose is based, surely himself, but he wrote: "In real life a young soldier who had served in Vietnam." The lyrics reflect Garnet's nocturnal rambling: "Lonely through the long weary day, / Lonely in the gloaming I stray, / And in fancy / I am down where / Someone's waiting for me. / Down there where I long to be roaming, / Noonlight tells me love's dream is o'er, / Moonlight finds me wandering once more." By February 20, Purdy completed *In a Shallow Grave*, originally intending to publish it with seven stories published in magazines.

A veteran, Purdy wrote a lot of himself into Garnet Montrose, though he himself had remained stateside and never seen combat. Scenes occur in a "ruined dance hall in a small Virginia seacoast town, where songs such as 'On the Alamo' would have been played," Purdy wrote on the sheet.[2] The dancehall was personal, as Purdy doubtless heard the tune at the Green Mill Dance Hall in Findlay. Discussing the "provenance of the book," Purdy claimed he "used to be visited by returning servicemen from Vietnam who always had horror stories to relate either about themselves or their friends. Mutilation in this last war was quite a commonplace occurrence." More universally, in Montrose, Purdy created an archetypal outcast. To interviewer Chris Huizenga, Purdy recalled lines from Handel's *Messiah*, which are taken from the Book of Isaiah: "'He was despised and rejected of men; a man of sorrows, and acquainted with grief.' Of course, that gives it all away."[3] The verse continues, "and we hid as it were *our* faces from him; he was despised, and we esteemed him not." "But he *was* wounded for our transgressions, *he was* bruised for our iniquities: the chastisement of our peace *was* upon him; and with his stripes we are healed." Stephen D. Adams sees the story's movement as affirmative, "assembling the shattered constituents of a human being in a process of healing." Garnet learns even the "deepest love can never attain its object or arrest it from the flux of time." At the end, Garnet is reunited with the Widow Rance, or Georgina, the childhood sweetheart he had courted prior to being mutilated in war and to whom he sends a series of letters. But this is not quite a happy ending since he longs for Daventry, who is sacrificed in a hurricane, driven into a pine tree in a kind of crucifixion. Garnet remarks, "the droll thing about getting what you long for is the longing was better, longing pains more, but it's more what you want. I had just walked away from Georgina leaving her under the ruined polka-dot moon and the orchestras doing 'On the Alamo' for the twentieth time."[4] Such longing is a "longing for the impossible, a longing, in fact, for God," Adams writes.[5]

On Sunday, March 3, Purdy arrived at Notre Dame University in Indiana in time to attend the opening ceremony of the Sophomore Literary Festival, featuring a reading by Joseph Brodsky. Tennessee Williams had been scheduled as headliner but had to cancel. Throughout the week, Purdy attended classes and lectures, and mixed with fellow authors including James T. Farrell, a Chicago writer who had been an early supporter, poet Lawrence Ferlinghetti of City Lights Books, Robert Bly, and Tillie Olson. The next night, Purdy read from *The House of the Solitary Maggot* and other work to an appreciative audience who laughed in the right places.[6]

California was an escape route Purdy was planning to take. In May, he told Sam Steward he was coming to San Francisco on July 8 and might stay through October. He had friends in Berkeley and San Francisco, but wanted a place of his own. He planned to stay in a hotel first and await what lodging friends might find. If he liked it out West, he "might stay for quite a while." James flew out with Bob Helps, who had his own house in the hills that summer, but did not stay with him. Helps had "hounded" Purdy to go West, "so he better find me a good room. He has told me the West was made for me and I am a fool to be East. So he will be on trial more than California."[7]

In July and August, Purdy stayed at an apartment at 2425 Durant Avenue, near the intersection of Telegraph and Durant Avenues in Berkeley.[8] His first night at the Palace Hotel was paid for by a Los Angeles patron, and a professor told Purdy that "an anonymous patron" would soon be funding him for a while, he told Paula Fox, wondering "if this can be true." The University of California campus and its library was close by and a couple blocks north was People's Park, synonymous with 1960s protest. Bob Helps connected James with the flat and showed him around the neighborhood, but Bob was "not well," James informed Fox. Bob introduced James to Barry David Horwitz, a professor of drama and theater at St. Mary's College of California who became a friend. They would often sip coffee and meet people at the Mediterranean Café on Telegraph, an "old hippie hangout" that became their "office." Coming from New York, the weather there, "even when it is bad it is paradise, and when it is good it's too good for me."[9]

That summer, Purdy often visited Barry Horwitz's house on 2724 College Avenue, in the old Elmwood District. Professor Horwitz owned the two-family house with his friend and former lover, Dr. Larry Abramson, whom Purdy called Doctie A, and had Michael Tillotson, a young classicist and friend of Bob Helps, sharing his flat.[10] Tillotson had recently moved in with a bunch of cats, inspiring Purdy to dub the property "Puss Meadows." In the summer of 1975, Tillotson had recently withdrawn from an academic career track after completing oral exams at Stanford University. "James Purdy appeared as if on cue," Tillotson said. "For the next three years, I felt that I was living in a James Purdy story." With a shared sense of humor and interests including works by Pliny the Elder, they were fast friends. Tillotson and Horwitz had wildly opposed personalities—"almost a comedy team," Tillotson recalled. Purdy improvised a meta-life about his Berkeley friends in "anonymous letters" and press releases that Tillotson calls "fantasy impromptus." Horwitz was B.D., so James dubbed Tillotson D.B.—the Damask Beauty. Around intimates, Purdy could be "outrageous, often provocative."[11]

Stephen D. Adams, working on a monograph on Purdy, came to America in 1975 and visited with his subject in Berkeley. Bob Helps invited Adams, who was staying at a "fleabag hotel" in San Francisco, to stay at his house in Berkeley, where he gave impromptu piano concerts. Adams later learned that James was "a little piqued" by their rapport. Purdy and Helps were both "gracious, hospitable and perhaps intrigued by a hitherto unknown species, a 'live' Purdy scholar." Berkeley and San Francisco were wild, buzzing with countercultures. "James didn't fit in with this really, but was amused by it," Adams writes. Purdy dressed conservatively, and his demeanor betrayed an "old-fashioned gentility—an outward disguise for his sense of humor and delight in testing people's attitudes." On Adams's first day in Berkeley, he met James and Bob, who took him on a "long walk on a—very—gay beach."[12] The following year, Adams published *James Purdy*, which its subject deemed excellent.[13]

While in Berkeley, James reunited with Sam and relished their visits. James and friends including Bob and Barry drove out to Sam's modest apartment in the back of a house adorned with rose bushes—the Invisible House of Purdy's anonymous letters. Michael Tillotson, who visited him with James on another occasion, said Steward was "like a character in a Purdy novel"—which he was. Horwitz disliked Steward, who showed off a framed napkin he said came from Hitler's bunker. He called Steward a chilling, vampiric, "self-important man we laughed about behind his back," with whom Purdy had an "ambivalent relationship." Sam was a "little martinet. We all knew he was jealous of James's infamy or fame. Sam wasn't nice or astute." They visited Sam a few times, and Sam in turn came over for at least one dinner.

Purdy and friends attended a dinner party for Richard Bridgman, an English professor at UC Berkeley and a friend of Horwitz. Bridgman, author of *Gertrude Stein in Pieces* (1970), was intrigued by Sam Steward's relationship with Stein and Alice B. Toklas. Sam "did his bit, told his stories, claimed he was a soldier in World War II," said Horwitz, but afterward, Bridgman seemed "highly skeptical" of Steward. During this period, Steward was writing less pornography and focusing on a memoir of Gertrude Stein and Alice B. Toklas. Sam was withdrawing from the gay community into a "lair of decadent isolation."[14]

Purdy's friends and two noted composers met Imogen Cunningham, the famous art photographer, and she took a portrait of Bob Helps. She shared dinner with Purdy, Helps, Aaron Copland, a visiting Virgil Thomson, Bridgman, Stewart, and Horwitz, and the evening was "very gay."[15] Purdy inscribed a copy of *The House of the Solitary Maggot* to Cunningham, who died the following year, calling her portrait of Helps "wonderful."[16]

The reunion of Purdy and Steward revived old memories of Wendell Wilcox. In August, Sam phoned Wendell and said James was in the Bay Area, Wendell told Gertrude Abercrombie. "Sam almost never calls or writes and

I had an uncanny feeling that James was listening to the conversation. It didn't seem too natural. I asked him for a description of how I looked [in a photo] and it was far more restrained than S's usually very caustic descriptions of people." Over the decades Wendell remained in James's thoughts.[17]

Sam Steward introduced Purdy to a transgressive young couple, Jim Kane and Ike Barnes, and their sadomasochistic lifestyle. Caring friends, Kane and Barnes routinely checked in on Steward. Purdy later mailed them a copy of *The House of the Solitary Maggot*. According to cultural anthropologist Gayle Rubin, Jim Kane, formerly a Roman Catholic priest, was a "central and charismatic figure in the classic period of gay male leather," an "icon of impeccable leather style." Rubin explains the home Kane shared with "his slave, Ike Barnes," aka the Pink Alley Playhouse, became a "major nexus of the international social and sexual circuits of gay SM, welcoming a steady stream of visiting leather luminaries."[18] A few months later, Purdy asked Steward: "If I return to California, do you think Master Kane would torture Ike good and proper if we paid them another visit? You might inquire, if you feel such an inquiry can be made through the mail." And in January 1976, he asked whether Ike had received the book. "Is he being tortured in the hell-chamber? I would like to know more about how he is branded and whipped and screw-ironed. It is more interesting now from a distance and a later time, so keep me posted." James opened up: "I miss you very much, Invisible House master, and of course miss that enchanted city" along with "Sweet Puss Horwitz and wicked Doctie A." He complained that 1975 was the worst financial year yet; the outlook was "very glum unless something breaks."[19]

By August, he was venturing into San Francisco alone. But their subways, though cleaner than New York's and "truly beautiful," were hard to negotiate and not as useful as hoped, he told Fox. It was "run by a computer, and you have to be taught how to get in and out. A stranger could stand before its immaculate gates forever, and never gain entrance." In Berkeley, "they gave a big party" for Purdy, inviting Professor Mark Schorer, a distinguished literary critic and biographer of Sinclair Lewis; his wife, Ruth; the head of the university library; and others. Purdy's arm got a workout signing stacks of books brought by guests. That summer, Purdy also mixed with his admirers, Christopher Isherwood and Don Bachardy, who sketched him, but he found them repellant. "I do not like old Bacardi or his daddy lover," he told Steward. "They *bored me*. He did a drawing of me where I look like Bette Davis. I hated it. Burn yours, or wipe on it. He doesn't see anything, old vile catamite that he is."[20]

He was interviewed by a gay rights activist for an underground newspaper but found the interviewer held the "same kind of closed-off mentality as the Marxists or the other Holy Groups that run everything, only he was of course a pederast, an official one, pious and waving banners." One remark Purdy made seemed a "totally new concept to his brain": "Everybody suffers, everybody is in hell, and everybody is hurting other people, so how can there be any group that monopolizes all the suffering to themselves." He reminded Purdy of the "queer priest who had seduced [his friend] George McKay as a child, an evil old fraud," who did not think *The House of the Solitary Maggot* was good or interesting because "the brothers did not have sex with one another."[21]

Several people wanted James to stay on in California, but he did not know "what to do about it," he wrote Paula Fox. There was "no real reason" to keep living in New York, "but I don't know there is even as much reason to stay here, I keep wondering about the earthquake too. It certainly would solve all problems." He returned in September and the next month, he told Sam Steward he missed him very much. "It all seems dreamlandy long away and gone. I do suppose I was there, though."[22] Four months later, Purdy told Abercrombie he liked California and might return. "Things are in a funny flux here." He added, "I live alone, but lovers visit."[23] Gerald Busby said that James while in his fifties "gave up practicing sex per se." He hired young hustlers but would only talk to them and "would not have sex with them." The topic of sex was just "another way to get into the personality of the person. All that energy went into his writing. All of his sexuality was turned into a vehicle for getting to know someone." Busby, himself highly sexed, did not find James "sexually attractive in any way," however. "Anybody would be put off—he was too smart, too crazy, too weird. These were major distractions." Conversely, when it came to friends and acquaintances, "the more neurotic, the more James was interested."[24] He said eccentrics were the true originals. "People are inclined to call them eccentrics," Purdy said in interview, but they are "just themselves. They're not dwarfed. They don't care, in the best sense, what other people think."[25]

One of Purdy's closest young admirers at this time was the aspiring writer John Stewart Wynne, who first reached out with a "fan letter" in 1974. Wynne, a gay man from Indiana, shared Midwestern roots, part of his appeal and their bond. They became close friends during the late 1970s. "I went with James everywhere," Wynne said, who lived nearby in Columbia Heights. For a time, they shared a meal every day. They met for breakfast nearly every morning at The Promenade Restaurant, with its thick gold drapes, vinyl booths, chandeliers against walls, and glass globes hanging over tables.[26] Sometimes they visited Lüchow's on East 14th Street in the East Village, where James savored German boysenberry pancakes. To Wynne, entering Lüchow's with its tall curtains was like stepping onstage of a Wagnerian opera at the Met. In June 1975, Purdy told Fox that he and George McKay went there and enjoyed "big German flaming pancakes" as a reward after "too sensitive" George was sickened by the violent conclusion of the film adaptation of Nathanael West's *The Day of the Locust* and almost fainted in the theater. "But the *Locust* pursued us: a Vietnam veteran in the bar got mad and threatened to mash the place to bits." Another favorite spot to many in his coterie was The Brasserie, a French restaurant beneath the swanky Four Seasons restaurant in the Seagram Building on East 53rd Street. One could order desserts sent down from Four Seasons; Wynne and Purdy, who had a sweet tooth, savored Swiss chocolate cake. Douglas Turnbaugh confirms Purdy loved pastries, "particularly rich chocolate confections." During this period, Wynne also met James a few times a week for dinner. Wynne accompanied him to parties at Lincoln Center and at Virgil's and found that Purdy knew many opera singers.[27]

In October, Purdy attended "Music by Joseph Fennimore" at Carnegie Recital Hall including performances of two Purdy adaptations, short operas of "Eventide" and "Don't Call Me by My Right Name," reviewed by the *New York Times*. "Name," in which "a drunken couple argue senselessly at the end of a party, was mordantly entertaining, droll on the surface but with a rueful undercurrent." Mr. Fennimore noted a "white opera company a decade or so later" wanted to do "Eventide," and he "could see with a word or two changed, how this could work," but "Jimmy said no. It must stay black."[28]

Feeling desperate after Doubleday had failed him "so bitterly," Purdy signed with a new publisher, Arbor House, an independent chosen by his agent. Arbor House was begun in 1969 by Donald Fine, who had been vice president of Dell and a cofounder of Delacorte. In December 1975, they published *In a Shallow Grave*, a stunning novel with spiritual resonance set in rural Virginia near the ocean. Purdy said Arbor House was then "very energetic and aggressive, and I need that!" This edition was dedicated to Edward Hefter, Robert Helps, and George Andrew McKay. Speaking with a slight Scottish accent, McKay was a friend who taught at Bishop Ford High in Brooklyn, where he assigned Purdy's work to students.[29] Virgil Thomson, who "loved American speech, gave a little party" for *In a Shallow Grave*, and "in his high-pitched voice," he wondered, "Where did you get that lingo?" Purdy did not talk like that, Virgil said. "But I hear like that," he responded.[30]

Unlike his previous novel, his new book was not left out of the *Times*. In February 1976, Purdy was relieved that novelist Jerome Charyn gave his novel a positive review in the *New York Times Book Review*, finding it "funny, sad, and touching." *In a Shallow Grave* is a "modern Book of Revelation, filled with prophesies, visions, and demonic landscapes."[31] Critic James Martin analyzed the novel at length in a positive review for the *Los Angeles Times*. In *The New Leader*, leftist writer Hope Hale Davis offered an overview of his novels and their critical reception, arguing that his new novel refutes "once and for all the theory that Purdy's work asserts 'the impossibility of giving and receiving love.' True, the love in Purdy is likely to be concealed or distorted, misdirected and unrequited; when openly expressed it may be too passionate for the health of the object. . . . Yet there is always a quest for love, and it does not invariably fail." Back in Ohio, literary critic John A. Weigel hailed the book in the *Cincinnati Enquirer*: "May this wonderful little novel survive the vulgarisms of our time! We need such miracles. Stories used to charm and heal while telling the truth. Perhaps they will again."[32]

For the edition of *In a Shallow Grave* published in 1978 by W. H. Allen, his new British publisher, actor John Uecker replaced Hefter as the first of three co-dedicatees. Uecker said it was "heavy" having such a profound work dedicated to him. In the 1970s, John Uecker was "a beautiful young man with long, darkish brown hair," recalled Philip F. Clark, an English professor at City College who attended a writing workshop put on by Purdy and Uecker in the basement of St. Ann's School in Brooklyn Heights. To writer Edmund White, John Uecker was a "Brando lookalike" who had an affair with his beloved roommate and muse, actor Keith McDermott.[33] Purdy was introduced to Uecker by Virgil Thomson in the early-to-mid-1970s. Before meeting Purdy, Uecker was already a young friend of Edward Albee and a guest at his gay parties in Manhattan and Montauk in the early 1970s. Uecker would smoke marijuana with Albee and admitted that he once "rolled around with him" in bed.[34] Albee's boyfriend, Stefan Karsaba, who moved in with Uecker at Edward's request, introduced Uecker to Purdy's work by giving him *Malcolm* to read: "That's how I got hooked." Addicted to Purdy's work, reading book after book, John felt compelled to meet the author. Uecker learned that Purdy was a friend of Thomson and a sometime guest at his parties. So John's friend J. J. Mitchell, a handsome blond writer who had been the last boyfriend of the late Frank O'Hara, took him to a few parties at Thomson's. Thomson had socialized with O'Hara, Mitchell, and O'Hara's longterm partner, Joe LeSueur. The third time was the charm.[35] Once, after Uecker arrived and mentioned his interest in Purdy, Virgil called James at 5:30 and imperiously demanded, "I want you to come to dinner right away." Purdy apologized, saying he had another engagement. "Well, cancel it! Cancel it!" Another time, Virgil called and said, "Now look here. There's a young man who likes your books and I'm having him to dinner *two weeks* from today, so you gotta come." This did the trick, the dinner meeting was felicitous, and John was soon invited to dine out with Virgil and James.

John Uecker then became a devotee of not just the work, but also the man. Uecker became his "most avid fan," who waited for him and did his bidding, Gerald Busby said. Purdy "loved that. John Uecker was a very good looking man." Horwitz more critically said John would "do anything to ingratiate himself." He "could be a character in Purdy" and James became somewhat like Garnet Montrose, the wounded veteran needing care in his novel. "There was manipulation both ways. Maybe he brought sensuality into James's life."[36] Attending events together, they grew closer. Their closeness raises the unavoidable question of whether they were lovers. Busby thought that in a sense, their early relationship was about sex, but it was "more an allure, an unqualified attraction." Even so, Busby "wouldn't be surprised if they had sex." There "may have been a sexual or sensual connection."[37] On Valentine's Day 1976, Purdy made early reference to Uecker in correspondence; he was looking for an old stethoscope since an old doctor appears in his manuscript, *Narrow Rooms*, and he wanted to get it right, he told Sam Steward. "I will listen to the heart chest and kidneys of my close friend Gold Puss Uker, who has volunteered" (*sic*). Philip F. Clark said that John "knew James in a way others didn't." Very protectively, he looked out for James, like his "younger righthand guard." Clark saw Uecker at readings James gave at the Gotham Book Mart. "James would invite everyone" to their writing workshop and then "John would weed them out." Purdy later wrote: "A young actor of remarkable talent and insight, John Uecker, a friend and assistant of Tennessee Williams, urged me to write more plays for the theatre." Uecker was "sort of helping" Tenn because "he wasn't very well," Purdy said. Tennessee Williams began to attend James's off-Broadway one-acts and stressed to John: "You've got to tell James to write full-length plays."[38]

So in 1976, Purdy wrote *A Day After the Fair*, a violent tragedy in five scenes dedicated to John Uecker.[39] Cameron Northouse told Purdy his plays are "almost revenge tragedies," particularly this one. "It's been called a Jacobean play," Purdy replied, but he did not understand how he came to write it. He had studied clowns and knew some circus clowns and street jugglers, he claimed. In June, he told Gertrude Abercrombie that *A Day After the Fair* might be mounted off-Broadway that winter. He spent two days with director John Stix and more with the "leading man." Stix found the play "very unusual and original," Purdy said, but "they always find excuses not to do something original." *Fair* is "too much against the American stage" to produce. Tom O'Horgan, who directed off-off-Broadway before finding fame with *Hair* and *Jesus Christ Superstar*, found it "very remarkable" and "wanted to do it," but didn't try "very hard to put it on."[40] In 1977, Purdy remarked, "if there were a real dynamic theater, I might want to write for it, but I don't think there is any in America. The theater, like everything else, is a way of making money and really, appealing to an audience that is not interested in the theater. So the only theater that seems vital is the off-off-off Broadway, and one could probably write something for them." He could not "imagine bothering to write a play for modern American commercial theater." Even if "one wrote a good play, it would have no chance for success because there is no real critical approach to the theatre; everything is just money and manipulation."[41]

In late 1975, Purdy commenced a new manuscript, yet untitled, about Torrence Reardon, a singer who retires at age thirty-one, returns home, and becomes involved with a youth named Lakes, who wanted to imitate his career. He described other characters, like Elsie Avery and her husband, Karl Avery, who had murdered Elsie's brother. "You can see it is as impossible a subject as I could find," he told Sam Steward. In January, he revealed the title of his new novel, *Narrow Rooms*, about "a popular singer who gave it all up and came back to a tiny town and ruined everybody's life all over again, his own being beyond ruin." This vision of the story, which was abandoned, seems informed by the fall and aftermath of Richard Purdy's stage career. Through 1976, Purdy worked on this first vision of *Narrow Rooms*, which is only tangentially linked to the gothic horror it would become after multiple rewrites.[42]

In April 1976, Adrian Hall staged *Eustace Chisholm and the Works* at the Trinity Square Repertory Theater in Providence, Rhode Island. As artistic director, Hall had wanted to adapt it for several years, but Purdy resisted, feeling the novel's episodic structure would not be suitable for the stage. Purdy saw a Hall production that impressed him, however, and then believed Hall could achieve what had seemed unlikely, if not impossible.[43] Some reacted strongly to the play's onstage male nudity and homosexuality, a graphic depiction of

Maureen's abortion, and torturing acts of Captain Stadger. A reporter said that, despite shock, it was "in many ways, one of the best things Trinity have done"; another called it Hall's masterpiece.[44] Huizenga hailed it as "stunningly forceful, compassionate drama." Hall's adaptation conveyed the characters' desolation via "brittle direction" and "masterful *mise en scène*."[45] The production "attacked the sensibilities of the audience, stunned and horrified them," theater professor Valleri J. Hohman writes. After that season, the Trinity board fired Hall, but he was in a position where he could fire the board that fired him and then hire a new, more sympathetic one.

In mid-June, Purdy flew West for his second Californian summer. He told Gertrude Abercrombie in Chicago: "I would stop off [to visit] on the way to Berkeley, but I got a free ticket and am so hard up I shouldn't go to California, but I stand to make some money going there. My board & room will be mostly free." He gave his address as care of Barry Horwitz on College Avenue. At "Puss Meadows," lavish in redwood, James enjoyed his own wing. Michael Tillotson, who was a frequent visitor, remarked: "The Sixties hadn't ended. People floated around; it was a different world." Barry Horwitz states he was "always sweet" to Purdy and "did his bidding," attempting to be present and available as much as possible. James was "reasonable, but a bit autocratic," yet Barry "understood his way." On July 11, Barry found a new table for Purdy that was better suited for typing. After a morning's work, Purdy often enjoyed a siesta. Despite Horwitz's best efforts, Purdy was hard to satisfy. At the start of July, he told Sam Steward that he was "somehow not getting settled" and was even thinking of returning to New York, "though that is certainly frying pan to hot blazes, but still this is a little too difficult for me, and also boring." Purdy had apparently become fairly set in his ways. James visited Sam in August.[46]

Barry Horwitz recalled pleasant meals with Purdy and friends at Brennan's in west Berkeley, which attracted working-class Joes for Irish coffee and buffet-style fare. In the 1970s, Brennan's had an "off kilter-ambience" attracting a diverse clientele, and Purdy became fond of the place. "Let's go look at the Bokies," he proposed, using his term for good-looking, probably straight working-class males, which recalls he and his brothers' past jesting reference to a certain "Bokie Truefeather." They would request a table allowing a good view of men perched at the bar. In 1991, he joked to Sam Steward, "I was told there is an underground passage for Blue Collar young men between Brennan's Restaurant and the Invisible House!"[47] Purdy enjoyed Berkeley and San Francisco in part because they were cool compared to New York, which was "a furnace or a water blister most of the year."[48] He also found San Francisco culturally freer and more open than New York.

That summer, *Antioch Review* published "Short Papa." Dedicated to Barry Horwitz, the story is drawn from Purdy's youth, reflecting the years when his folks remained married but Will was itinerant, often absent, and had lost family money in bad investments. Like Will, Short Papa is "tall and lean," his nickname referring to his short sentences in jail rather than his height. The boy's mother says: "Father or no father, after what that man has done to us. . . . I'll feed him but I won't take him in, and you give him my message, hear?"

Michael Tillotson, a self-described preppie who went to Andover and Yale and was an out-of-work academic, grew closer to Purdy that summer. Michael was alluring, "decayed gentry, a type James loved," and James "fell for him," Horwitz said. Tillotson said he spent much time with Purdy while he was finishing *Narrow Rooms* and "read some of the drafts" awestruck as "words, scenes," sprang "fully out of his head like Athena" from Zeus's skull. He was "encouraging, maybe excessively encouraging" of this extreme story and so became a co-dedicatee of *Narrow Rooms*, which James gleefully called a "terrible book."

In early summer 1976, Purdy took Tillotson to meet Tennessee Williams at the Clift Hotel in San Francisco. Tenn was in town to oversee a production of *The Two-Character Play*, which was to alternate with *The Glass Menagerie* at the Showcase.[49] Tillotson said that meeting this legend did not seem strange because he was already steeped in Purdy's enchanted world. At the historical redwood-paneled bar, they met Tennessee, donning a planter hat, accompanied by a friend from Georgia. Williams made "admiring remarks" about Purdy's work and they engaged in literary gossip. Afterward, they visited a bookstore, where both writers checked shelves for their works. Williams invited them for a nightcap at his room in the luxurious St. Frances Hotel on Union Square. "I felt like Malcolm," said Tillotson, a "very slow developer" and "far too innocent in this world." He was treated like an "innocent abroad" though he saw himself more as an observer. Purdy likewise regarded him as a sympathetic Malcolm-like figure, "both worldly and innocent."[50]

Tillotson's experience with Purdy was an extraordinary chapter. Always Purdy turned "reality into fantasy," bringing a "phantasmagoric quality" to everything. It is all in how you look at life, so put on your "Purdy spectacles"—"it's like an acid trip." Purdy usually scorned drugs, but while in the Bay Area, "if a joint was passed, he would take a few tokes." It almost got him and his host in hot water. Tillotson told of a "wonderful incident" in which he was driving and Purdy was a passenger in the backseat with a young man. They were crossing a bridge to reach San Francisco, finishing a joint, and Purdy puffed, not trying to conceal it while talking and gesturing. The next thing he knew, they were being pulled over by a motorcycle policeman, and Tillotson swallowed the reefer. A young black cop asked Purdy to step out of the car. "James's eyes were just twinkling" as though he had conjured up the scenario. The cop told Tillotson, "I know what you are doing," but he let them go with a verbal warning. Purdy was "thrilled by the whole episode" but the eyes of the "kid in back" were "popping like saucers." Tillotson soon underwent life changes removing him from Purdy circles, mostly comprising gay men, to whom he seemed to suddenly vanish—also like Malcolm.

By the end of September, Purdy had returned to New York and was not happy about it. Edith Sitwell's biographer Geoffrey Elborn had been in New York while James was in California, a pity because Purdy could have made Elborn's stay "more bearable, although it is a monstrous and difficult and very uncomfortable city. I really hate it." His flat was "quite a terrible looking room" into which he admitted almost no one.[51] Purdy told Brooklyn-born writer Robert R. (Bob) Fox, who ran Carpenter Press in Ohio, that living down the street was a "multi-millionaire's daughter, who dresses like a dope pusher and abuses policemen as pigs daily, what greater slave to conformity can you think of? I suppose everything is always a fake anyhow. The main thing is to hide most of the time and keep working."[52]

Around March 1977, Purdy discarded the first version of *Narrow Rooms* and began rewriting "really from scratch." He hoped to complete it by the end of the year.[53] "The first time, I realized I was on the wrong track and I didn't think I would ever be able to finish this book," he admitted. After he completed the second version in August, the story was "still not right." With the third draft Purdy "really began to get into the subject," and in September, he rewrote that draft in Berkeley. It was a "very difficult book to write" and he had "terrible problems" with it, he told Matthew Stadler. "I thought I couldn't finish it, that maybe my career was over. I then went to Berkeley and it just came out. I'd worked very hard on the beginning, but maybe I was just afraid of the book."[54]

In 1977, Purdy's bloody one-act play "True" was published in *New Directions in Prose and Poetry*.[55] Ewen demands of his younger brother, Chester: "Did you see another man stab a man." Ewen had stabbed a man in a bar toilet for mocking Chester and his own care for him. Then, perplexingly,

Chester uses the murder weapon to stab Ewen repeatedly in the throat, then stabs himself. Ewen, somehow still able to speak after being stabbed in the throat "again and again," then stabs his younger brother vehemently without difficulty. John Uecker, who later played Ewen, the older brother, said he was "*both* of the boys in the story *True*," Purdy told Virgil Thomson. "He also says he misses seeing you."[56] *True* is a lesser, confounding work that would shock and horrify its audience, but to what end is not clear.

The Gertrude Abercrombie Retrospective Exhibition was held at Hyde Park Art Center from January 28 to March 5, 1977. Though invited, Purdy did not attend, but he contributed a poem and an homage for the catalog. Gertrude had asked James to lend her portrait of him for the show, but he did not accede. When Abercrombie was interviewed about a month before she died on July 3, she felt rejected by James, whose friendship had "meant so much" and "sustained her for so long." "It wouldn't have hurt him to lend it to me."[57] Purdy knew she had been ill and perhaps feared his portrait might never be returned. Purdy's poem casts Gertrude as the fearless, powerful "Woman in the Vale" who alone braves ice, wind, rain, and cold, "to defy them all." His homage begins: "Gertrude is a poet of American landscapes and faces," a creator of portraits as astonishing as Modigliani. Gertrude's world is "berserk, cloudy, enchanted, sad, both fluid and frozen, and funny. She is a *bruja*, of course." Identifying with Gertrude, he said her "American vision will take some time to be fully understood and appreciated." Contrasting Purdy's pithiness, Wendell Wilcox wrote a lengthy reflection and analysis of her paintings.[58]

Though Gertrude's productive life was over, Purdy's working day then involved getting up early, around 5:30, and completing his "hard work" by 10:00 A.M. He would become interested in a particular person, group, or story he had heard. Suddenly, he saw this as material he could develop. "Usually, however, the only stories I can work with are the ones that at first blush, I think are totally impossible and I think I can never write because they just bristle with all kinds of impossibilities. And those, in the end, are the only stories that I can write." During the rest of the day, he researched, checked information, and answered letters. Sometimes he perused manuscripts, preparing them for publication. Then, he would see "lots of people" since "a writer's life depends on people." The ones he enjoyed were "different and unusual, sensitive," and "not part of the media."[59]

By mid-July 1977, Purdy was back in Berkeley for his third summer, again staying with Barry Horwitz and Dr. Abramson.[60] It was a timely escape since on July 13, a blackout struck nearly all of New York City, looting and vandalism ensued citywide, and parts of Brooklyn were set ablaze; and on July 31, the Son of Sam committed another random murder, this time in Brooklyn.

When interviewer Cameron Northouse visited him in Berkeley, he was primed for another broadscale attack on American civilization. He railed against government aid to arts and publishing, saying books were "pushed by money with special influence and special political coteries," for whom "political hacks" and "monied spokesmen" worked. Publishing had become "a kind of cartel."[61] Government support of arts, especially to writers, is "evil." He suspected many authors featured on front pages of "these literary reviews are, one might say, CIA-approved writers" and our government is in many ways "very oppressive." If government gives money to writers, it then tries to control them. "Governments never like writers or artists" unless they are propagandists. Thus, "government has a bad influence on the arts." Media and government shove "down our throats" the greatness of certain composers and writers. Major newspaper reviews' championing of particular books betrays political overtones; government grants privilege some writers while ostracizing others. Rewards and attention are about who is "respectable politically, not who is really a good writer." There was already "too much government influence."[62] Though he did not say so, he spoke from authority since he had benefited from Cold War government programs and agencies. Anticipating the Reagan 1980s, Purdy worried that the country was "slipping into another very dead period like the 1950s." Things were growing conservative again, with Americans cherishing "creature comforts" and television. He did not "feel any vitality in the world of art."[63]

In such a stifling cultural climate, Purdy felt his career had come full circle. As in the early 1950s, his new works were "too 'far out' for the publishers," some of whom found the plays horrifying.[64] "I'm right back where I started when I began my career: I am now publishing my own book privately, which I think contains some of my best work. But no publisher was interested in publishing it and so my friends published it for me." In August 1977, Five Trees Press of North Beach, San Francisco, printed *A Day After the Fair: A Collection of Plays and Short Stories.* Ever the individualist, Purdy stated: "the lesson—if there is one—is that one has to depend on himself and on those who understand his work, which will be a very small number of people. And you shouldn't expect too much. You should expect everything from yourself, and not very much from other people, and nothing from society. Because if you do, you're going to be very disillusioned."[65] Dedicated to Abercrombie and Miriam Andreas, *A Day After the Fair* joined seven stories and two short plays, "Wedding Finger" and "True," to the title play, which was also published in *Texas Arts Journal*. Purdy continued to "amaze, delight, and above all, entertain," James Martin wrote in his review for the *Los Angeles Times*. "Mr. Evening" is a "tale worthy of Poe," but only Purdy could have written the "romping, hilarious 'Lily's Party,' whose climactic pie-throwing orgy borrows from Mack Sennett to parody Fielding and Lawrence." When Gordon Lish rejected "Lily's Party" in 1973, Purdy was "amazed" at his "lack of perception." Everyone who had read it saw it as "a parody or satire on pornographic art, except I guess you." Purdy listed five "acclaimed" stories of his that had been rejected by *Esquire* (prior to Lish's tenure) "on the grounds they were either indecent or offensive to taste" and included quotations from rejection slips.[66] Purdy's dialogue distinguished him among contemporaries, critic Jim O'Brien wrote in the *Chicago Daily News*. Brilliant prose results from combining the "street language of modern America" with the wit of Wilde, Firbank, and the Elizabethans.[67] Tillotson took copies of *Fair* to sell to bookstores throughout the Bay Area.

In September, Purdy gave a reading from *A Day After the Fair* at Paperback Traffic on Polk Street in San Francisco's Castro neighborhood. Central to the burgeoning LGBTQ culture, the store was operated by a gay couple and owned by the parents of comedian Margaret Cho, who described the neighborhood as full of "old hippies, ex-druggies, burn-outs from the '60s, drag queens, Chinese people, and Koreans. To say it was a melting pot—that's the least of it." Paperback Traffic was the first bookshop in the Castro to carry significant gay content. They held readings for authors and poets such as Thom Gunn and Armistead Maupin. Gunn was a great admirer of Purdy, and Maupin attended Purdy's reading.[68]

Purdy finally completed *Narrow Rooms* in Berkeley after four rewrites.[69] In August, he finished the first full typescript of *Narrow Rooms*. Looking back, he did not know how he "ever wrote that, it was so violent." After finishing, he said he "got so sick" he "had to go to the hospital," a claim he also made after completing *Eustace Chisholm and the Works*, but nothing more is known of this sickness. *Narrow Rooms* was a story that had brewed for decades, with its deep roots in the 1928 "milk bottle murder" in Findlay.[70] Considering Purdy's environment while he finished *Narrow Rooms*, one might conjecture his exposure to gay and SM subcultures influenced scenes of physical domination and punishment found therein. Friends from the period say James was not a night owl, though, nor did he express interest in gay bars or the gay scene. "None of us were drinking, really. We were kind of old-fashioned," Horwitz said. Tillotson said James did not pursue a gay lifestyle in Berkeley, but spent time writing; for fun, they went out to dinner or coffee. John Uecker could not recall James ever going to a gay bar.[71] Barry even thought James seemed "not open to the gay world at all," though in Purdy's first summer in California, Steward had taken Purdy to the infamous dungeon of Ike Barnes and Jim Kane. If sexagenarian Purdy in California was sexually active, observed, or even participated in sadomasochism, as has been rumored, there is no documentation.[72]

In late September, Purdy returned to Brooklyn Heights.[73] Over the holidays, he and John Wynne spent an evening at Richard Hundley's unconventional apartment at Westbeth Artist Housing, where James read his poem "The Running Sun" as Richard tried to set it to music. It was a snowy night, so returning to Brooklyn was "a trip."[74] James gave his young friend an inscribed copy of *The Running Sun*. On Christmas, he joined a small group of friends for dinner at the Art-Deco Russian Tea Room, accompanied by the English critic Stephen D. Adams, who was in town.[75]

In January 1978, Purdy replied to Thom Gunn, the gay English poet who lived in San Francisco. After Gunn sent Purdy a fan letter, Purdy thanked him and hoped they could meet. Purdy reported he was trying to find "some kind of work to keep the wolf from the door" since his publisher did not pay him a "living wage." He shipped an inscribed copy of *Narrow Rooms* to Gunn, who was "very honored" and glad to have a second copy to reread and one to loan out.[76] Gunn's San Franciscan friend Jack Collins wrote Purdy, saying Gunn was "delighted with the tonal variations" across his books. Gunn heard echoes of the Jacobeans in *Eustace Chisholm and the Works*, yet also felt Purdy's writing was "purely American and purely modern." Thom Gunn had been reading Purdy's works from the beginning "continuously for several months now," with "great enjoyment, admiration, and anger" that his books did not enjoy wider circulation. Gunn wrote his friend, critic Tony Tanner: "I have been reading all of James Purdy. I find *The Nephew* fantastic, almost like Jane Austen." He likened *Jeremy's Version* to Charlotte Brontë. "He dares to be melodramatic and gothic, and mostly it all comes off. And I love his weird mannerisms."[77] After Gunn finished reading all of Purdy's books, he was inspired to start writing poems again for the first time in two years. In December, Purdy wrote the poet, again hoping to meet him but not sure when he would return to California.[78]

Somewhat randomly, in February 1978, Purdy found himself a visiting artist-in-residence at the University of Tulsa, he apprised Alec Wilder, another composer friend.[79] In December, he had been deliberating the offer since he liked the people at the university but worried: "I will languish in that dreary place." He found the weather in Oklahoma was "not so severe as New York. The sunsets and sunrises are beautiful, not like back home." The "air is good and the sun shines," he told Paula Fox.[80] Both the university's literary magazine, *Nimrod*, and *New Directions in Prose and Poetry* published "How I Became a Shadow," an odd story of Mexican cockfighters, doubtless informed by Purdy's having lived in Mexico. He made informal remarks to faculty and students that were collected in a piece, "Notes on Recognition," published in *Nimrod*. Modern life is about recognition. "We are all waiting for someone to recognize us, but they won't. It's too difficult, or too painful, or too embarrassing. So they turn away. They say all the polite expected things; they say all the flippant cruel things—all the words we speak because we are not recognized and because we are avoiding recognizing someone else."[81]

Purdy was invited to speak at evangelistic Oral Roberts University in Tulsa, but he thought maybe they had the wrong writer. "Excuse me, have you read my books?" he asked. Indignantly, they said yes. "I thought it must be a mistake. I went, and the first book I saw them reading was *I Am Elijah Thrush*." They read his work as religious allegory, akin to *Pilgrim's Progress* or Spenser's *The Faerie Queen* and *Elijah Thrush* was their favorite. "As I laughed, they stuffed three hundred dollars in my pocket. I thought, Religion must pay 'round here."[82]

The timing was serendipitous. James was thinking and talking about Jesus during the late 1970s, encouraged by Thomas Zulick, a burgeoning writer awestruck by Purdy's work who became "very close to him." In 1978, Purdy told Professor Jere Real that "God's kingdom, or Jesus' kingdom, is for everybody. It's not reserved for pious heterosexual hypocrites" like Anita Bryant, former Miss Oklahoma, singer, and orange juice spokeswoman, who in the 1970s became a vocal opponent of gay rights. "After all, Jesus was one of the first social radicals. He didn't appeal to the 'respectable' people of his time" but rather he "ministered largely to outcasts."[83] In 1978, Tom Zulick, a former Marine Officer, moved to New York from Pennsylvania and became a freelance writer. After he published a piece on New York writers for *The Brooklyn Paper*, Purdy reached out and "struck up a conversation." They became good friends, walking together on the Promenade after meeting at Henry Street, and sharing meals and conversations about Purdy's characters, "Christ, and love." James walked with an unhurried rhythm, Zulick said, a sliding gait that reminded him of John Wayne's. Tom was a seeker who offered something unique to Purdy in New York. A key "thing about James" was his "real spiritual core" and Zulick "helped him focus, or focused with him, on his spiritual life in some way," though not having intended to do so. Perhaps it was the "Midwestern ethos" of Purdy's work, but it became clear the "very essence" of Purdy was "a sort of piety, you can call it a Calvinistic piety." Perhaps Purdy was a "closet spiritualist who created characters who are very complicated, and yet good. There was goodness in him, and a goodness in the crazy characters he created." He possessed a "keen sense of what is right and wrong" and was scornful of the "ways in which human beings could rationalize" wrongdoing.

Generously, Purdy helped Tom Zulick secure a job at Andreas Brown's Gotham Book Mart in Midtown Manhattan. Truman Capote would come in, calling out greetings to the elderly founder Miss Frances Steloff. Tom waited on David Bowie who was dressed as an English schoolboy. James Purdy was celebrated there: *Narrow Rooms* got a big window display. Once Purdy took Tom to the apartment of Tennessee Williams, who signed their books. Zulick called Purdy his uncle, "Tío Jamie," noting that Purdy's Spanish was still very good. Zulick, then discovering himself, says he was straight, but Purdy wanted him to be "someone other than who" he was. James and George McKay would ask him, "Are you a werewolf or not?"[84] John Uecker claimed that Zulick, during a visit to Purdy, emerged from the bathroom naked, then proceeded to read aloud from *Eustace Chisholm*.[85] Richard Hundley remarked, "James loved to hear works he was working on read aloud. James told me about one boy, who was very beautiful, who asked if there wasn't something he could do for James." "Well, you look rather warm, why don't you take your clothes off?" Purdy suggested. So the clothes came off and "the young man read to James, *nude*. But there was no sexual activity. But this was how much these young people who came into James's life felt they were connected. They felt James was writing their life story."[86]

James helped Tom Zulick find his path. After much soul-searching, he decided to attend seminary in Philadelphia. James was not surprised and respected his choice, Zulick said (alternatively, Uecker says Purdy directed Tom to the seminary). Their friendship tapered after Tom left New York, but the two stayed in touch. Although Zulick insisted that Purdy had never discussed the specifics of his Ohio upbringing, Zulick ended up working for the Lutherans in Purdy's hometown, Findlay, and then his father's hometown, Bowling Green. Even stranger, as part of his duties as regional gift planner,

Zulick routinely entered Purdy's childhood home on 115 East Lima Street, which had become the office of Lutheran Social Services of Central Ohio.

On April 15, 1978, Arbor House published *Narrow Rooms*, a gothic horror that centers on the torrid, violent dynamic between four young men in rural West Virginia. Roy Sturtevant, called "the renderer" due to his grandfather's occupation of rendering animal fat into products, holds power over the other three. Although one Arbor House editor embraced it, Purdy's agent believed the publisher did not support Purdy's dark tale, which was "viciously reviewed," and they did not issue it in paperback. "Yet it had a wide circulation." Founding publisher Donald Fine struggled to find someone to host a release party for *Narrow Rooms*, which may be related to the extreme nature of the novel but also suggests Purdy had alienated many in New York publishing. Author and reporter Lucy Freeman agreed to host in her apartment overlooking Central Park, said Wynne.[87] Later that year, Fine sold Arbor House to Hearst Corporation. He remained president until 1983, but Arbor House would publish no more Purdy titles after *Narrow Rooms*.[88]

Gore Vidal provided a remarkable encomium: "Over the past quarter century, James Purdy has created an American language which was always there but never noticed until he began that series of prose works whose most recent manifestation is *Narrow Rooms*, a dark and splendid affair by an authentic American genius." And late in the year, Vidal feted Purdy over lunch at the Plaza Hotel in Midtown Manhattan. To Purdy, Vidal was "one of the few civilized people" remaining.[89] Like Vidal, he did not see *Narrow Rooms* as a "gay novel." He told interviewer Allen Frame: "I don't think those men are conscious they're homosexual. I think that would come as a sort of amazement to them. They're so busy loving and hating one another they don't know it has a name."[90] In May, *Penthouse* published a shocking excerpt from *Narrow Rooms* they titled "Crucifiction," paying a handsome sum, Purdy told Lish, who had become an editor at Knopf.[91] This windfall allowed him to decline a residency offered by the University of Tulsa, who wanted him back. In May, he returned to Ohio and read successfully from *Narrow Rooms* at Miami University.[92]

Though delighted by Vidal's attention and praise, James was jolted when the feminist author Katha Pollitt panned *Narrow Rooms* in the *New York Times*. It "drove him through the roof," John Wynne said. Pollitt derided the novel as a "tale of love among the bondage-and-discipline crowd in, of all places, West Virginia." Pollitt does not know why editor Harvey Shapiro assigned the review to her, since she did not previously know Purdy's work (but became familiar with them since she judged his earlier work superior). *Narrow Rooms*, though focused on "physical passion," is strangely disembodied, lacking distinct characterization and sense of place, Pollitt said.[93] In the *Antioch Review*, Purdy acidly responded to the review. *Narrow Rooms* was "sneeringly hatcheted by a well-known hack who writes for the largest New York book review; the book was condemned on the grounds that it would appeal only to homosexuals of the S. and M. cult (though *Narrow Rooms* was described by Mr. Gore Vidal as the work of 'an authentic genius')." In other words, Pollitt, not to mention the editor who chose her, has a "mind indistinguishable from that of Anita Bryant." His books were not "grotesque, depressing, homosexual," or any of the other adjectives "hurled at them." His books had reached and were reaching a "large audience," despite attempts of the "American establishment and publishing empires to gag and bind" him and bury his works.[94] A few years later, in a piece aptly titled "James Purdy's Fighting Words," Purdy complained to Christopher Cox of the *Soho News* that the *Times* had run a vicious review: "It was by some cunt named Katha Pollitt. She's what I consider a hitwoman. You see, I'm not considered a 'respectable writer.' "[95]

His British publisher, W. H. Allen, was "shocked" by *Narrow Rooms* and "immediately turned it down," Purdy told Geoffrey Elborn. "I have been so shabbily treated in England, that I believe this now ends my publishing career there." His first book had been "censored and mutilated (Dame Edith's word was stronger)" by Gollancz, and no British publisher had ever championed his work. They seemed "even more Jewish and commercial" than their New York counterparts, "and that is saying a great deal."[96] *Narrow Rooms* was finally published in England in 1980, by Black Sheep Books of Surrey. Purdy informed his bibliographer Jay Ladd that the British edition is the "only correct text of the novel. The American was full of errors."[97] This edition was dedicated to Michael Tillotson and Stephen D. Adams. In 1977, Adams was working on *The Homosexual as Hero in Contemporary Fiction* (1980), which includes a chapter analyzing *Narrow Rooms* and *Eustace Chisholm and the Works*: "Purdy neither proselytises for homosexuality nor depicts it as an 'affliction.' He simply accords it the same power to damn or to save as any other kind of love." Adams said he wrote that book "as a sort of testament to someone I had loved and admired," his partner, the actor and gay activist Michael Turner-Holden, who on September 23, was brutally murdered in a pub. "James helped me through a time of grief and—perhaps in light of my personal tragedy, I was touched to find he had dedicated an edition of *Narrow Rooms* to me."[98]

From June through October 1978, Purdy returned to Provincetown, Cape Cod, well known for its theater scene and gay culture.[99] He had stayed in nearby Truro earlier in the decade. Purdy asked John Wynne to accompany him, and his young friend stayed through July. "I was kind of like a kid at a candy shop," he recalled. Wynne and Purdy were "inseparable during that period," said Wynne's partner, Harold Dennis Schmidt, then an assistant literary agent at ICM whom friends called Dennis. They stayed at Sam Graybill's guesthouse, which attracted a robust gay clientele, and Purdy had his own private cottage. They enjoyed each other's company, discussing writing and sharing laughs. But Purdy was often beset by darkness, obsessing on Katha Pollitt's disdainful review. Purdy wrote Pollitt anonymous letters, made prank phone calls, and wrote "terrible things" about her in graffito on Provincetown walls and on a monument, Wynne said.[100] In 2020, Pollitt did not remember "menacing letters, prank phone calls, or that sort of thing" from that period beyond the prank calls women typically received back then. She did, however, bring up Purdy's insult in his interview: "I thought about writing a letter to the *Soho News*—because I'm quite sure they would not have printed a comparable racial or anti-gay slur, but women, then as now, are fair game. But I let it go."[101]

Under this dark cloud, James moreover had a tough time in Provincetown, feeling old and misplaced in 1970s gay culture. "It's for young people, not for me," he complained. Handsome Wynne was smoothly mixing with other gay men, while Purdy seemed to envy his youth. He was also worried over money and declared: "I'm financially ruined!" He suspected, probably correctly, that Graybill overcharged him. He was often bitter and the number of enemies "the man had was incredible," Wynne remarked. Yet, James could rise above all that "for a while and become witty, a real joy to be with. But then a cloud might descend because of some slight. James would fester. He didn't know how to deal with it." He was impulsive and made "poor business decisions." Wynne saw him as a "lone voice railing against the establishment." Even on summer vacation, Purdy went to the post office every morning to mail letters to editors and critics, plus whimsical anonymous letters to friends. He wrote an angry letter and would mail it almost immediately: "He would leap before he looked." Even when Wynne and Purdy were enjoying the Provincetown library or bookstore, James's mood might darken if he saw a book by a writer on his enemies list. At the store, James would tear pages from such a book and was never caught. This was both funny and crazy, Wynne remarked. Thankfully, the "bluebird of happiness" appeared when the film rights to *In a Shallow Grave* were sold and Purdy relaxed a bit.[102]

At close hand, Wynne observed Purdy's "very disciplined" habits as a writer. In the morning, he wrote fanciful anonymous letters to limber up for the real writing, which in Provincetown would come after lunch. He worked for at least a few hours in the afternoon and shared work in progress with Wynne, who assisted with manuscripts including *Narrow Rooms*. In New York, on any evening, there might be a party, dinner, or play rehearsal. In Provincetown, they might walk out to Captain Jack's Wharf, where Tennessee Williams wrote plays and "got lucky in love," as John Waters put it.[103]

Purdy worked on short plays including "Now," which he intended as a companion to "True." "Now" presents two men who love one another in squalid urban environs, one of whom is ill, recalling Herlihy's *Midnight Cowboy*. When John's friend Dennis Schmidt came to visit one weekend, he was paid to retype Purdy's annotated typescripts since Purdy knew he was an expert typist. Wynne and Schmidt thought recent short plays including "Now" were not great, but rather seemed "slapdash, thrown together," like the anonymous letters, as though Purdy decided to write a play, but lacked true inspiration, Wynne said.[104] Their lack of enthusiasm rankled Purdy for a time, but they regarded their relationship with him as genuine and honest. "We wouldn't lie and say they were wonderful," Schmidt said. They "couldn't give false praise," while others who approached James had "hidden motivations." Within a month, Purdy and Wynne were getting on better.[105] "We've never had a big falling out," Schmidt said. "There wasn't a big blowout over Purdy's writing." That year, John Stewart Wynne made a splash with "The Sighting," a homoerotic Midwestern chapbook-story entailing both UFOs and Bela Lugosi, launching his literary career. Wynne said he stopped seeing Purdy partly because "it wasn't just a friendship James wanted." "I couldn't give James what he wanted in the end. I needed to start my own writing."[106]

Through Purdy's involvement with play productions, he made new friends and contacts; he enjoyed working with thespians.[107] He fell in love with theater anew as he watched his work "interpreted by flesh and blood people" including his "special friend" John Uecker.[108] Attended by Wynne and Purdy, on June 30 and July 1, 1978, "True" debuted at Westbeth Theatre Center's first summer festival, starring Edward C. Gierke and John Uecker. Purdy called it successful. Uecker said Gierke was "like an angel" but a misfit angel who had trouble functioning in the ordinary world. Though Ed Gierke was "a divine boy," he got a bit carried away in his role as Chester. "He really stabbed me," Uecker said. "I was cut." New London Press of Dallas later published *Two Plays* soaked in blood: "A Day After the Fair" and "True."[109]

In November, a short play, "Clearing in the Forest," set in a large farmhouse near an ocean, premiered at the Ensemble Studio Theater in Hell's Kitchen in New York. Like "True," it is another stabby play climaxing in sudden violence, which seemed to hint at Purdy's mental strain. He regarded his plays as "more incandescent than the novels—direct conflagrations in front of the spectator—like Roman candles going off without any preparation." Someone had remarked that they are "like the scenes in *Oedipus* when he gouges his eyes out. There is no old-fashioned preparations with maids coming in to dust the room, for we don't have time for exposition any more. We could be blown up at any moment!"[110] Uecker was Burk, Gierke was Gil, John Stix directed, and Todd Waring was stage manager. Tennessee Williams came to see "Clearing in the Forest," which influenced his postapocalyptic microplay, *The Chalky White Substance*, written in 1980 and dedicated to Purdy. Going out to dinner with Purdy and Williams and watching them interact, John Uecker thought he was "in the company of two gods. I didn't think anyone else existed."

Jack Collins wrote in July, reflecting on the unique affective resonance of Purdy's work. He enclosed his poignant manifesto on *Narrow Rooms* for the *San Francisco Sentinel*, a gay newspaper. "What Purdy's characters accomplish in their brief but intense lives is the overthrow of our culture's basic unit: The American family." The "liberated inhabitants" of narrow rooms, cells and wards, labeled deviates, "have emerged to form relationships with one another" that are "not romantic, but mythic, not conventional, but revolutionary." Purdy had achieved nothing less than replacing "the Holy Family at the heart of our civilization with the Four Horsemen of the Apocalypse."[111] Purdy's work had a profound impact that changed Jack's whole life. Voices in the novels made him feel "so antsy" that his "life began to seem very unsatisfactory." Now, his life was beginning again. "For that you are responsible in no small measure, and I thank you." A few months later, he added, "now I am so alive that I feel filled with joy and pain."[112]

On Friday, November 23, 1979, while visiting New York, Collins joined Thom Gunn and Purdy during their sole meeting. After sharing lunch, the poet recorded in his diary that Purdy was "nice, 'soft-spoken,' but keeps getting round to his persecution by critics & publishers." To a friend, Gunn added: "He's bats, but I still think he writes—and still writes—the best short stories of anybody living."[113]

Purdy confounded not only the straights and squares, but also the gay literary culture rapidly emerging in the wake of gay liberation. As early as 1977, Purdy declared, "I believe in things like gay rights" and he was glad to see gays "marching against" homophobic "critics and newspapermen," he told Northouse.[114] But in a gay magazine, he told Jere Real: "I've had some trouble with some of the gay press too. Some of them say I'm not 'gay enough' in my writing. By that, they mean I don't always say 'gay is best' and always have happy endings. *Narrow Rooms* may be treated as a gay novel—certainly I deal with the subject head on in it—but it ends tragically. But that's because that is the way I see the human condition." "We often reject the real part of ourselves. We too often cannot love it, and we only value that part, that tinsel part of ourselves, that is given to use by society. To me, some of the professional gays are guilty of the same point of view as the straight people. They have this petty bourgeois view of life" and think being gay is the solution. Some say "gay is better, that to be gay solves everything. However, I believe life is tragic. It's my view that nothing ever solves anything. Oh yes, life is full of joys, but it is essentially tragic because man is imperfect. He can't find solutions by his very nature." Stephen Adams notes that Purdy's vision shares affinities with Unamuno's *Tragic View of Life* since each uniquely articulates the sense that the "dialectic of faith and doubt itself," rooted in "the paradox of suffering," offers an authentic way of being.[115]

In 1979, Purdy drafted *Mourners Below*, a Midwestern novel he envisioned as the third installment in the *Sleepers in Moon-Crowned Valleys* series. Duane Bledsoe, a lonesome youth living with his father, Eugene, is haunted by the ghosts of his two brothers who died in war overseas and is tempted by Estelle Dumont, one of Purdy's "irresistible, devouring women," as critic Julia M. Klein put it in the *New Republic*.[116] Much unspoken desire lies between Duane and his handsome tutor, Duke La Roche, who lives alone in a large, crumbling mansion. Their bond is intensified in their mutual love of Aileen, Duane's absent mother.[117]

In January, Purdy attended the New York premiere of Tennessee Williams's *A Lovely Sunday for Creve Coeur* [heartbreak] at the Hudson Guild Theater, starring Shirley Knight, a play in two scenes set in 1930s St. Louis—the same setting as *The Glass Menagerie*. In turn, Tennessee was at the Herbert Berghof Studio Theater in September, when the HB Playwrights Foundation mounted *Out of a Clear Blue Sky*, a program of four new James Purdy one-acts: "What

Is It, Zach?," "Now," "Adeline," and "Wonderful Happy Days."[118] Frank Geraci, an actor, directed eight players. James invited Virgil Thomson, who responded enthusiastically to one performance. John Wynne accompanied Purdy on the night that Tennessee Williams arrived drunk with his entourage and was "laughing the whole time, even during the serious parts," as was his wont during his own plays. "James was oversensitive to it."[119] As novelist Donald Windham remarked, "Tennessee's humor was frequently inexplicable." Kim Stanley, known for her roles in Williams plays, was seated right behind him. "Why Kim, fancy meeting you here," said Tennessee, who had not seen Stanley in years.[120]

Purdy shared Tennessee's positive remarks on "Now" with Ed Hefter, who became a donor to HB Playwrights. In October, Ed spoke on the phone to Tennessee, who said Purdy should "try his hand" with more "heterosexual individuals" as characters. "What do you think?" Hefter wondered. "Of course, the public appeal would be much greater." He wanted Purdy to focus on writing a play that might become a hit. "What do you think about concentrating on plays? I think Tenn feels the same interrelationships that exist amongst 'gays' exist among heterosexuals as well. Do you feel more comfortable writing about gays?" Ed acknowledged that were he a writer, he would, but cited Williams, Albee, and Wilde as "gay authors who wrote about heterosexuals. I hope you're not screaming to stop harping on Heteros. It's just that I want you to do a *Glass Menagerie* and get famous quickly."[121]

In 1979 and 1980, Purdy taught creative writing at New York University. He was probably low on funds since he swore he never wanted to return to the classroom. He told students to "write from their inner selves, because 'You don't know what you know.' If you write to please other people, you will not succeed."[122] When a student asked how he could become a better writer, Purdy answered, "Write what no one wants to hear."[123] Purdy, who also taught at Long Island University Brooklyn Center, avowed he did not "really like teaching much." Radio interviewer Don Swaim pressed: "But wasn't that exhilarating, working with all those young writers?" "No," Purdy laughed. In a 1982 interview, he was blunt: "I hate teaching. I like being with the students, and talking with them. But I hate teaching. I don't communicate that way."[124] Rumor had it James could be flirtatious with certain male students and Professor Joseph Skerrett Jr. heard that was why Purdy had to leave NYU.[125]

Gerald Busby, who like Thomson lived at the Chelsea Hotel, recalled Purdy at some of Thomson's parties of the late 1970s. By then he was outrageous, cracking jokes about everyone at the table, but no one got offended, at least not openly. Purdy's outrageousness was "part and parcel of his personality," Busby said. He would "run roughshod over people despite his charm" and was "very piercing—he could really insult people." He deployed "linguistic skill to make an impression," not caring what kind, seemingly with "no sense of correct behavior." He got people's attention, but did not seem to know how to stop. Even so, this was "part of his genius—his keen sense of immediacy and presence." His self-destructiveness was mostly brilliant: "it made you see him."

James and Virgil admired each other greatly, but openly mocked each other. Virgil had a longtime black servant from the South named Wendell Dorne, whom Virgil would summon by ringing a bell. Tall, handsome, "cheerful, courteous, and discreet," Wendell "served Virgil as cook extraordinaire," bartender, shopper, and masseur, biographer Anthony Tommasini writes. Wendell and Virgil were "cagey" about their relationship and most assumed "something was going on," but, "without explicitly forbidding it," Virgil made it clear this subject was not to be broached.[126] Purdy would "tune in" to their conversations. Later, James impersonated an aggrieved Wendell protesting, "I won't do no more niggering for you," Busby recalled.[127] His remarks or insults "always turned what was said into their most absurd conclusions" but they were "so astute and so funny that no one ever got angry. Mockery was his mode of expression, and it was startlingly spontaneous and surprising." Virgil was a "major target" of Purdy's roasts, as he was always "so sure about being right and speaking definitively on virtually all subjects."[128]

In winter 1979, Purdy's modern Sandman story, "Sleep Tight," appeared in *Antioch Review*. This horror, in which a wounded black burglar hides in a little boy's bedroom closet, was adapted into a short film by Kenneth Bowser that aired on Showtime in the 1980s and at festivals in Los Angeles and Berlin. "That wasn't too bad," Purdy judged.[129]

By the late 1970s, Purdy had attracted a circle of younger friends and admirers, for which he was grateful. However, it became clear that, amid the controversy over *Narrow Rooms*, Purdy's attention was diverted to writing obscure short plays and attending productions. His forte was fiction but his publishing career had faltered.

17

On Glory's Course

During the early 1980s, Purdy took customary long strolls through Brooklyn Botanical Gardens with his good friend, James Link, an aspiring young writer who had praised *Narrow Rooms* as Purdy's "most lavish, most awe-inspiring book" in the *SoHo Weekly News*. The Gardens had long been one of Purdy's favorite haunts, and he also enjoyed the walk to get there, which took nearly an hour. "Water drips off our umbrellas. Roses drip glistening in the drizzle, and everything is as green as it can be. Robins are pulling worms out of the lawn; otherwise we are alone, and New York seems a million miles away," Link wrote. Purdy came here nearly every day, year round, "to relax after writing."[1]

Purdy ushered in the 1980s decade by signing with Viking Press—after his near-miss with them in 1957. James worked with Corlies (Cork) M. Smith, who had edited *New World Writing* and had been with Viking since 1962. The downside was that Cork Smith was alcoholic, like many others in publishing, in Purdy's experience. In 1980, Viking issued *Dream Palaces*, a red omnibus holding *Malcolm*, *The Nephew*, and *63: Dream Palace*. In Edward Albee's foreword, which was also appended to paperback reissues, he confessed the "maggoty feelings of envy" he and others had felt when Purdy was showered with hosannas by Sitwell, Parker, Hughes, Williams, and others Purdy called the Choir Invisible of departed champions. James Link said "real literary events are the best kept secrets of them all. Viking ushered *Dream Palaces* into bookstores to less noise than a falling leaf: not one review in a major publication, no publicity, not even a book party." In the past, Purdy had won "rave reviews from the literary establishment," but now he was "generally ignored, or treated with contempt, and frequently castigated for his strongest work." Purdy remained an "underground writer, unofficial and unrecognized," his readers loyal but silent, unattuned to New York vogues.[2] Purdy continued working with his agents Gilbert Parker, assisted by Peter Franklin, and Ned Leavitt, assisted by Jo Lauria, at William Morris Agency.

In January 1980, Purdy was finishing up *Mourners Below*. He told Thom Gunn: "Every week a young actor I call The Gosling [Ed Gierke] comes and reads to me from it so that I can see where I am going. He laughs a lot while he reads, which must mean it is WORKING!"[3] He was thrilled to receive Gunn's *Games of Chance*, finding it "beautiful inside and out. I love these poems!" In the fall of 1980, Thom Gunn published "All Pretty Much Strangers," an astute review of the omnibus, in *The Threepenny Review*. "Purdy's prose style has an unsettling beauty, mixing idiomatic oddity with the more formal sugges-tiveness of poetry." Gunn cites a line in *63: Dream Palace* describing Fenton's eyes: "Those eyes looked dumb; Parkhurst saw them again, like maybe the eyes of the first murderer, dumb and innocent and getting to be mad." "Go back and try to change the diction of that last phrase, a phrase almost—like many of Purdy's verbal effects—between quotation marks, and you realize how the seeming awkwardness is a true felicity." Purdy was "deeply grateful" for Gunn's "beautiful and perceptive" review, which remains "one of the finest things written" on his work.[4]

In August, Purdy told Gordon Lish, now a fellow Viking author and still an editor at Knopf, that he would not be teaching creative writing at New York University that year because he was writing a new novel. He had just com-pleted the final draft of *Mourners Below*, but one could not stop him from writing. In September, he finished final revisions. "My tongue is hanging out with the heat and the book," he told Gunn. "I think my editor may have com-mitted hari-kari. Now everything is vacant and wide."[5]

Purdy never seemed inclined to travel back to Ohio but he corresponded with his brother Bob and sister-in-law Dorothy Purdy of Berea, Ohio. The brothers were not close, but Dorothy facilitated communication, taking the role of letter writer; James was encouraging of her writing letters and poems. James thanked them for "good letters" and was "happy to hear" about their activities; it was "wonderful news" her poems were being published. He was pleased to have heard from his nephew, David, and niece, Christine.[6] Bob called James yearly at Christmastime. James and Bob's family used to ex-change gifts through the mail, but one year, the gift Dorothy chose, a book by statesman Dag Hammarskjöld, prompted a dismissive comment from James, ending this custom.

Encouraged by Tennessee Williams and John Uecker, Purdy continued writing and publishing short plays that were performed. *New Directions* published "Clearing in the Forest." In 1980, Lord John Press of Northridge, California, published *Proud Flesh* in limited edition, with "Clearing in the Forest," "Strong," "Now," and "What Is It, Zach?" A note stated "Strong" had never been performed "except for a reading given by John Terry Uecker,[7]

Edward Charles Gierke, and Tennessee Williams." Purdy told an interviewer that a "very close friend" who is an actor, Williams, and he used to "go out together" for supper, and one night, "he read one of my plays ["Strong"] aloud to us in New York. Tennessee Williams read the part of the mother. He loved my dialogue."[8] Purdy enjoyed mimicking Williams, whom he called "the Bird": "that's mahte fahn dahlog."[9] Uecker said that Williams carried around a copy of *Children Is All*, containing "Cracks" and the title play, in his manuscript case for four years, unique as the only item he had not authored himself. Kim Stanley, known for her roles in Tennessee's plays, was looking for a producer to do "Children Is All"; she had wanted to play Edna for five years, but it was not in the cards.[10] In August 1981, August Moon, a summer arts-gathering hosted by the Iowa Theatre Lab in Catskill, New York, performed a program titled *Proud Flesh*, comprising "Clearing in the Forest," "Now," and "What Is It, Zach?", which they also put on in Baltimore. Purdy, who saw *Proud Flesh* in Baltimore with Jorma Sjoblom, was pleased that "half the audience in Baltimore was black, and they seemed to be able to accept the work more than white people."[11]

On March 17, 1981, Wendell Wilcox died, the lost friend in whom Purdy had expended so much time and thought over the decades. For years, Wilcox contended with alcoholism and cancer of the liver, along with poverty and loneliness following Esther's death in 1972, though he continued to make friends in North Carolina. "Wendell's going was not sad. Not in the least. Right up to the end he was charming strangers," artist August Becker told Sam Steward. A service was held in a Friends (Quaker) Meetinghouse. Incongruous in this staid setting, Gertrude's ex Frank Sandiford was there, "drunk, sentimental, imperious, theatrical," yet he and his wife "set the style somehow." Becker asked, "Did you know that Osborn Andreas once said his greatest ambition was to make Wendell famous by mentioning him in a footnote? Wendell sometimes had a rather violent effect on people." Purdy was one of them, and Wendell's death provided a certain release to him.[12]

In the spring of 1981, Purdy worked on a new novel that became *On Glory's Course*, and *Foment*, a full-length play. In March, he spent a week at Dartmouth College and read from his books. He liked "most of the people there very much" including English professor Donald Pease, who had published literary criticism on his work.[13] In May, James read at the University of Texas, impressing Austin writers and theater people, such as director and actor Doug Dyer. Novelist Edward Swift told Purdy he was "loved and admired" there. "Everyone at the University raves about your work."[14]

In 1981, *Second Coming*, a hip San Franciscan magazine published by the press of the same name founded by author A. D. Winans, published Purdy's transgressive story "Rapture." Gladys, a widow with a terminal disease, must find someone to care for her teenage son, Brice, a musician with long, golden locks. Kent, her "half-brother," returns from the service and finds himself attracted to his nephew, to the point of collecting golden hairs from his comb. After learning of this love, Gladys "now felt she could give up her son to someone who would cherish him as her bridegroom had cherished her."[15] "Rapture" closes with Kent and Brice fondling and embracing in bed as thunder booms, and in a final line, "rain fell in great white sheets against the house and the spattered windows"—suggesting a powerful ejaculation. Purdy again courted controversy with a taboo fantasy that literalized "uncle-nephew" references in gay slang. In 1981 *Second Coming* also published his "Adeline: A Short Play," which takes on the idealization of women. Edited by novelist Bradford Morrow, *Conjunctions* in 1982 reprinted that short play and "Wonderful Happy Days." The latter dramatizes the inevitable dissolution of the unity of two brothers, one wanted by the law, and their mother, who has been diagnosed with a terminal disease but does not yet know it.[16]

In June, Viking brought out *Mourners Below*, one of Purdy's most underrated books. The Midwestern novel was not a big seller, but produced an uptick of interest, positive reviews, and endorsements from writer friends, such as Barbara Probst Solomon and Paul Bowles, who called it Purdy's "best book to date."[17] Solomon, a memoirist and novelist, was known for covering Spain under the regime of Franco. *Mourners Below* earned praise from the *Philadelphia Inquirer* and *Publishers Weekly*. In the *New Republic*, Julia M. Klein said Purdy celebrates "bonds between brothers, between father and son, even as he underlines the near impossibility of intimacy. Creating a world where the supernatural merges with the real, he illuminates a reality whose core, if not its contours, matches our own." In July, novelist Jerome Charyn, who had positively reviewed *In a Shallow Grave*, analyzed and praised *Mourners Below* in the *New York Times Book Review*. "James Purdy is one of the very best writers we have. He exists in some strange limbo between adoration and neglect. His books are 'noticed,' but they are rarely celebrated the way they should be," perhaps because Purdy "doesn't play the peacock in his books or strut around with his talents. You have to peek under the feathers to catch the wildness of his prose." His agent Ned Leavitt was "so excited" about this praise; it felt like their efforts the previous year had been "thoroughly rewarded."[18]

Figure 17.1   Viking promotional photo of James Purdy by Thomas Victor for *Mourners Below*, 1981. Courtesy of Harriet M. Spurlin, estate of Thomas Victor.

To publicize his book, Purdy sat for interviews with the *Kansas City Star*, *Houston Chronicle*, the *Philadelphia Inquirer*, and author Gary Krist of *North Brooklyn News*. In June, Alabama native Christopher Cox, an assistant to Virgil Thomson, a lover of Edmund White, and a member of the Violet Quill writers group with White, interviewed James at home for the *SoHo News*.[19] Purdy closed his 1981 interview with Chris Cox with these reflective lines: "One of the things that fascinated me—even if I were not a writer—is 'Who is this person?' I'm not trying to play games. We really don't know who anybody is. We're mysteries. Life is so difficult and confusing, we don't have time to find out who we are. It's like being thrown into the ocean and having somebody ask you what stroke you're using; all you know is, you're just trying to get to land. We're so enmeshed with pain and doubt, we have no time for others. And yet, the older you get, the more you wonder about the people you've known. Who were they? At the same time, one of the most terrible things is to judge people by an absolute. Whitman said, 'I do not pity the wounded person, I become the wounded person.' If you're going to write about people, you can't judge them."[20]

In 1982, Penguin issued *Mourners Below* in paperback, but not until 1984 was the hardcover published in Britain, by Peter Owen. Novelist Francis

King in the *Spectator* praised the story's timeless quality, likening Purdy to
Ivy Compton-Burnett, a writer "similarly tragic and witty" and "obsessed
with the cruelties of family life." Like all Purdy novels, *Mourners Below* is
"disturbing and bewildering." He only "rarely received his due from his native America," even though he is a "writer of far greater originality and power
than Bellow, Roth, or Updike." That last statement gave Purdy a charge. Also
in 1984, the novel was published in French translation as *Les Inconsolés* by
Éditions Albin Michel, which in the 1970s published *Ce que raconta Jeremy*
and *Je suis vivant dans ma tombe* (I am Alive in My Grave, *In a Shallow
Grave*).[21]

Purdy continued to appreciate the friendship and support of Virgil
Thomson. In 1981 he enjoyed a "truly wonderful" party Thomson hosted
at Chanterelle, a French restaurant in SoHo straight out of Balzac. In 1982,
Purdy dined with Virgil and his partner Maurice at Ferrybank, in a lofty
nineteenth-century bank building near the Brooklyn Bridge that Purdy
loved. In 1983, Thomson supported Purdy's nomination for the MacArthur
"genius" fellowship. In Thomson's view, Purdy was not just a "great novelist" but the "very best" alive. As a stylist, he was matchless and had "contributed to American literature at least one legendary character, Malcolm."
Purdy's writing would endure and earn him a "permanent place in the history of American letters." The author whom Gore Vidal called "an authentic
American genius" did not receive the genius grant, however.[22]

Always skeptical of potential screenplay adaptations of his work, Purdy
turned down the proposal of producer Scott Rudin, who was not yet well
known, to adapt *63: Dream Palace* into a musical film. Purdy tongue-lashed
Rudin. *Palace* was "too important a property to be accorded the incommu-
nicative vague haphazard treatment you have given it. Evidently it is one out
of a thousand of your countless interests. Your sincerity is in question. Please
release the book from option."[23]

James threw himself into drafting *On Glory's Course*, a labor of love shot
through with ambivalence and humor. For this work, Purdy drew upon
his upbringing in Findlay in the 1920s and 1930s and his memory of Vera,
her stories, and her friends. For background, Purdy read novels of the period including Sherwood Anderson's underrated *Poor White* and Thornton
Wilder's *Heaven's My Destination*. In late December, Ned Leavitt enjoyed
reading the latest installment of *On Glory's Course*, which was "coming along
beautifully."[24]

The iconoclastic Baltimorean filmmaker and writer John Waters had become a dedicated fan. In 1982, Waters thanked him for sending *A Day After the Fair*; his favorites from the collection were the tragic title play, "Lily's Party," and "Some of These Days." John would be in New York soon and offered to take James out to dinner. In June, Waters wrote from Provincetown: "Just got to the part in *Jeremy's Version* where the bully freezes the kid's tongue to the fence and felt I could go no longer without dropping you a line." Waters invited Purdy to a 1983 Christmas party, adding, "Can't wait for your new book," and to a 1985 private cocktail party in the chapel at the Limelight club, on the site of a former Episcopal church.[25] Waters collected Purdy books, querying him about editions, and passed out copies to friends. In 1986, he told James: "I gave *Shallow Grave* to a few people for XMAS and I think I've turned them into Purdy addicts." In *Crackpot* (1987), Waters describes endlessly rearranging favorite books, sometimes kissing them: " 'Good morning James Purdy,' I chirp." In 1997, he told *Vanity Fair* that *Narrow Rooms* is a "starter book" he gives to "people of a certain type, to get them obsessed. They love it or hate it. In my circle of friends, *everybody* reads him." In 2015, Waters listed *Narrow Rooms* first among ten favorite books for the *New York Times Style Magazine*.[26]

Purdy's talent was transmitted via other media including music. In February, Richard Hundley's cantata based on Purdy poetry, "The Sea Is Swimming Tonight," premiered at Alice Tully Hall, performed by conductor Newell Jenkins and Clarion Music Society. Containing the original choral setting of "Waterbird," which became familiar in art song circles, it was a ten-movement, choral song cycle for mixed chorus, four soloists, and four-hand piano. *New York Daily News* reported it was an "instantaneous hit with the audience" as Hundley's style balanced the "sophisticated romance" of Rorem and the 'Plain talk' of Thomson."[27] This was the apogee of the Hundley-Purdy collaboration.

In April, Felice Picano, another member of the Violet Quill group and founder of Sea Horse Press, was quite impressed after hearing Purdy read for forty-five minutes straight from *Mourners Below*. "Although he is elderly and his voice quite low—and seems a bit hesitant at times—his work has mesmerizing cadences, and we were hypnotized." Picano approached Purdy afterward and asked if *Eustace Chisholm* was in the works for a reprint. Purdy said neither *Eustace* nor *Elijah Thrush* was in print and said Picano should call his agent. Sea Horse Press made an offer on *Eustace Chisholm and the*

Works that Purdy declined. Purdy next sent several stories and short plays intended for a collection before the concept shifted to only short plays. In December, Picano said he wanted to publish ten plays, but rejected a few of them for not meeting the "consistently high quality of the others." This verdict may have displeased Purdy, and ultimately, Sea Horse Press did not publish a Purdy book.[28]

Purdy was asked by the State Department to work for the United States Information Agency, to speak and travel through much of the remainder of 1982. Leaving in late June, Purdy toured Israel, Finland, and Germany. He did not know why USIS chose him. Vaguely, he told Richard Canning "one day they called from Israel" and asked him to visit; he apprised them he was not Jewish, which they knew. He had many readers in Israel, they said. "So I went. The young ones seemed to like my stories." He recited "Sleep Tight" and "Eventide" in Israel, and they responded "very deeply," especially to "Eventide." While being chauffeured, when they passed the town of Endor, Purdy referred to the Witch of Endor, a biblical medium (1 Samuel 28: 3–25), impressing the driver who said that "most gentiles who come here don't have the vaguest idea." Purdy replied: "I was brought up to read the Bible in Sunday school and was scolded if we didn't know everything."[29]

Finland was his favorite of the countries he toured. Among other locales, he visited Helsinki, where *Malcolm* had been published in Finnish translation in 1966, and found the Finns "beautiful, some resembling Norse gods. Also the lakes and green trees were wonderful," he told Gordon Lish. In Berlin, he met his German publisher, Albino Verlag, founded by Gerhard Hoffmann and Peter Schmittinger the year before, which specialized in German editions of works of gay literature by renowned international authors. Albino published *Enge Räume* (*Narrow Rooms*) that year, which was receiving good reviews.[30] They were very kind and fed him well. Admitting that publishing was not their main source of income, they offered to show him their other enterprise. It was a "glorious, old-fashioned ice-cream parlor in which young men read their poetry." At first, he wondered if it were "a house of ill-repute!"[31] There Purdy read from *Narrow Rooms*, followed by a German writer who read the same passage from *Enge Räume*. In 1984, Albino published a translation of *I Am Elijah Thrush* under the memorable title *Die Millionärin auf der Wendeltreppe Kannibalischer Beziehungen* (The Millionairess on the Spiral Staircase of Cannibalistic Relationships). In the 1990s they brought out a translation of *In a Shallow Grave* and reissued a translation of *Eustace Chisholm and the Works* originally published by Rowohlt in 1970. "My reception in these countries was enthusiastic beyond my expectations, and it was brought home to me that my stories reach some deep note in readers who are receptive and open."[32]

In 1982, *New Directions in Prose and Poetry* published a short play, "The Berry-Picker." "*They were the sweetest fruit I ever ate,*" Donovan recalls. "*And the cream. . . . Never before or after did I taste its equal.*"[33] This work evokes the berry-pickers found in the works of Purdy's predecessor, Sherwood Anderson. In January, to celebrate James Laughlin's contribution to literature as head of New Directions Publishing, Purdy, Anne Waldman, and Walter Abish gave readings at B. Dalton in Greenwich Village. From October through December, "The Berry-Picker," "What Is It, Zach?," and "True" were mounted by Night Shift, a group working in the Laight Again Club in the East Village, led by Australian director Lindzee Smith. Innovative Smith was "very intuitive, sensitive" but "strong too, which is good," so it was best to not interfere, Purdy thought. Flyers for the performance resembled those of DIY punk rock shows; also recalling punk venues, the club was "harrowing and uncomfortable." Sadistically, Purdy thought "people who wanted to see those plays should suffer. They shouldn't be too comfortable." If they cannot "suffer the discomfort of the place, they shouldn't be there." He attended nearly all performances, suffering a bad cold from sitting in the "damp cellar." Yet it was kind of wonderful since that theater "just seems like it's nowhere."[34] Bette Gordon adapted "What Is It, Zach?" into a short film.

In early 1983, James was suddenly drawn to Texas by Edward Albee's magnet. In February, Edward was at Southwestern University, a small private Methodist school near Austin. Drama professor Richard Hossalla, with a big budget at his disposal, invited his idol. Albee did a one-month residency, directing his flaccid adaptation of *Malcolm*. On January 15, Albee wrote Purdy, luring him with financial assistance. "The boys and girls seem very talented and the theatre is very nice. The cooperation of all involved leads me to believe we will have a splendid production. I wonder if you would like to come down and take a look at it at the end of February?"[35] So Purdy flew to Texas and worked alongside Albee. "He entrances you," senior Paige McDaniel said of Albee, who cast her as Madame Girard. "When I look at him, when I listen to him, I'm so much in awe, I cannot take my eyes off him." Albee was paid $20,000 (about $52,290 in 2020).[36]

So it was that Purdy was out of town on February 25 when Tennessee Williams died at the Hotel Elysée in New York after years of struggle with excesses of Seconal and alcohol. John Uecker, Tennessee's assistant, was in his own room of their shared suite. "When Tennessee died, I couldn't reach James," he said, which was odd and distressing.[37] In the morning, when Uecker found Tennessee's body on the floor next to his bed, a photocopied manuscript of Purdy's "Some of These Days" was on the bed, Uecker told biographer Lyle Leverich. At the top, Purdy had written lines by the English poet, Thomas Chatterton: "Water witches crowned with reeds [reytes] / Bear me to your lethal tide." The refrain of this "Minstrel's Song" goes, "My love is dead, / Gone to his death-bed, / All under the willow-tree."[38] Purdy attended a memorial service in New York and wrote an unpublished tribute to his long-time friend, who was only three years older than him. "Tennessee Williams' death is a deep personal loss to me. I greatly admired his use of the American language, the insight, the remarkable sympathy he had for his characters, his humor, his poetry. I also owe another debt of gratitude to him because he was one of the first American writers to be attracted to my fiction. He frequently attended productions of my plays and read the texts with care—always encouraging me to write more for the theater."[39]

Edited by Betsy Sussler, *BOMB* magazine in 1983 ran an interview with Purdy and published his outlandish "Mud Toe the Cannibal," an urban fairy tale of sorts that was loosely based on an experience of Richard Hundley ("songster Baby Bundy").[40] *The Antioch Review* was also interested, and fiction editor Nolan Miller wondered what Purdy would call this fantastic story: "A tall tale? A fairy tale for grown-ups? I can even see it as a book for grown up children with illustrations by, say, Sendak." *The Antioch Review*'s fiction special issue was called Mud Toe the Cannibal and Others.[41]

Through early 1983, Purdy continued drafting *On Glory's Course*, but found it difficult. Was it ever easy? As early as July 1982, he told Lish he was finishing it. To Bradford Morrow, he spoke of its origins. "I don't know when I've started a book. For example, *On Glory's Course*." He knew the heroine largely through his mother, only recalling her because Vera spoke of her so often. "I thought this would make a wonderful story but it was too far away from me, too removed from my actual memory. But it just started and I couldn't stop: I resisted it all the way through, the last fifty pages I thought I'd never see through." *On Glory's Course* is informed by Vera, her stories and friends, and his own experiences in Findlay, Purdy told Parker Sams, editor of the Findlay *Courier*. In this comic melodrama, Fonthill mirrors Findlay in 1930: residents of the fictional town also read *The Courier*, where for many years, heroine Adele Bevington had worked and written "brilliantly" as a reporter.[42] In *On Glory's Course*, Reverend Farquar had Adele Bevington

"dismissed from her post as chief librarian of the heavily endowed town library." She was "summoned before the trustees" years after her "disgrace,"
and accused of being "unfit to recommend reading material to the young,
or indeed the mature, readers of the library."[43] Purdy could not forget the
"horribly disfigured" World War I veterans he had seen as a boy on his way
to school, with "plates in their legs" and heads, and he put them in the novel.
"They've stayed with me."

In June 1983, Purdy reviewed galleys of *On Glory's Course* and answered
editorial queries. In November, his editor Cork Smith and Viking parted
ways, and Dan Weaver stepped in instead. During Purdy's tenure with Viking,
they fired his editors "one right after the other"; then, they gave him "this *boy*
editor" who "looked about twelve" and edited Stephen King.[44] "When Cork
Smith left, they lost all interest and fired the different editors" who helped
him with *Glory*. "So I ended up with this young preppy editor, Chuck Verrill,
who'd never heard of me."[45]

In July, *The Great City*, a program of three short plays, gained attention
from critics, who were sharply divided. Performed at The Theatre-Studio,
The Great City was presented by Ann Raychel in association with Gary
C. Walter and John Uecker. To the *New York Native* critic Jim O'Quinn, these
works were united by Purdy's "relentless focus on the existential primacy of
relationships, and his chilling insistence that within [them], love and hate,
torture and pleasure, are virtually simultaneous and inseparable." In *Back
Stage*, drama critic Victor Gluck praised Lucile Patton's acting but criticized
repetition and a thin plot in the script. Uecker adapted "Don't Call Me by
My Right Name" but Gluck found its story undeveloped and poorly staged.
Gluck's biggest disappointment was "What Is It, Zach?" which remained
"pregnant with unrealized possibilities." To Jim O'Quinn, however, "in a
few masterfully lean and powerful strokes," Purdy explores a "tenuous bond
between a disabled Vietnam veteran and the street kid he has taken in as
cook and companion." Gluck thought Michael Santoro was too old for the
role of the young cook, and since "the older man's need for the younger
man" was implicit in the text, "Mr. Uecker's performance lacked nuance
and menace." Au contraire, wrote O'Quinn—only Uecker and Santoro in
"Zach" approached "the level of intense interaction" the plays demanded.
When Purdy writes plays, he leaves "Welty country" and enters "realms
of Strindberg and Pinter: language is loaded to the breaking point, and
beyond that, chaos and violence" await. Purdy had a "drawerful" of short
plays and was working on a new full-length drama. Good news, O'Quinn

declared: "His voice in the theater is so strong and clear that it will be heard (we have good evidence) even through the static of flawed productions." *Village Voice* drama critic Michael Feingold concurred, calling Purdy's playwriting a "marvel of cogency and understated passion." Why had a playwright so gifted not gained a "stronger foothold" in the theater? "Oddly enough, Purdy's presence is so strong, the pleasure of hearing his words such a relief from the usual counterfeits, that the relative badness of the performance" hardly seemed to matter.[46]

One anecdote speaks volumes about how Purdy lived his life rarely satisfied. In 1983, producer Douglas Blair Turnbaugh presented a dramatized reading of Purdy works off-Broadway, at the Puerto Rican Travelling Theatre, with a "distinguished cast of Equity actors" including the veteran black actress Jane White. Purdy was dissatisfied with the male casting, however. "Whom do you want?" Turnbaugh asked. "James Dean and Marlon Brando."[47]

James did find some satisfaction in New York City life, notwithstanding its problems. The city was "decaying in many ways," its subways "dangerous and filthy." "I have to ride on them all the time, but every time I get on them, I think maybe it's my last ride."[48] "Despite New York's drawbacks, its pandemonium of crime, madness, filth, and noise, all finding their apotheosis in the hot seats from hell, the subways, I have found it the place where I can write undisturbed, and where I can communicate freely with other souls," he wrote in 1984. Edmund White wrote in *States of Desire* (1980) that in New York, a gay man must be smart and successful, but success "need not be monetary." Bookworms from the Midwest found it a curious reversal: "in the city, knowledge (or at least a reputation for having it) can carry a distinct social cachet." To say "he's very smart" is a "less ambiguous compliment in New York than in gay culture at large. Wisdom, of course, is less prized than savvy, but even so," New York's love of culture renders it "more suitable for older gays than most other places. The man of sixty who . . . publishes books will never be without his coterie in New York."[49]

In an unusual role reversal, in November, Gordon Lish sent Purdy his first novel, *Dear Mr. Capote*. The narrator, claiming to be a serial killer in search of a chronicler, addresses the immortalizer of the murderers of a rural Kansan family, somewhat recalling the scenario of *Cabot Wright Begins*. Purdy loved it since he could hear Lish's "voice so clearly in it." James mailed Lish some of his books to give to "kindred souls that might pass your way" and sent Valentine's Day cards to him during the 1980s.[50] Purdy mailed vintage Easter,

Valentine's, birthday, and Christmas cards to special friends during this period.

James Purdy showed no signs of slowing down in his work, but his younger brother Robert retired in 1983, culminating thirty-four years as a teacher, coach, and athletic program administrator. He was honored by several awards for his educational career and his civic leadership with the Kiwanis Club, and a high school gym was later named in his honor.[51] In 1984, Purdy told Findlay journalist Parker Sams that Bob had "never read more than a paragraph" of his work, and "if he read more he would be totally disgusted or bored to death. So you see how hard it is to get readers!"[52] He told Richard Hundley he thought Bob and Dorothy had never "read a book he had written" and would be "horrified if they read one."[53] Bob was not much of a reader in general, though he published a book with a New York press, *The Successful High School Athletic Program* (1973). Bob and Dorothy, who coauthored a collection of poetry with Nancy Spiegelberg, did not allow their children to read Uncle Jim's novels growing up because of what Dorothy called their "very controversial" content.[54] While their son Dave was growing up, he never heard anyone refer to Uncle Jim as gay.

In February 1984, Viking published *On Glory's Course*, perhaps Purdy's funniest book, though a plot summary would not betray the humor. Set in a small Midwestern city in 1930, the story focuses on a woman from a wealthy family who back in 1897 "had an illegitimate child" and her "life was ruined," her baby taken away, Purdy said. The story begins when she is forty-eight: her "adopted errand boy" gets a girl "in trouble," and "suddenly his baby, and this similar predicament, digs up her past life, which she thought she had kept a secret. Actually everybody knew about it all along. It's based on a true story," he told novelist Bradford Morrow.[55] "Mostly about Findlay and Gilboa," as Purdy revealed to Sams, the novel has an endearingly vintage cinematic, melodramatic flavor. "All the characters in it are based on real people, but the two young men, Ned and his brother, are composites of boys I knew, including myself." Adele Bevington is based on Nell Baker, for whom Purdy ran errands as a boy and who was Findlay's head librarian and journalist.[56]

American reception was divided. Critic Dan Cryer, a Findlay native who used to cut Vera Purdy's lawn as a boy, called it "another triumph by a genuinely moving storyteller." *Publishers Weekly* declared Purdy "a master of comic art as distinctive as P. G. Wodehouse but deeper toned." Novelist Carolyn See recommended it in the *Los Angeles Times*, saying it evoked memories of life before television. In the *New York Times*, however, novelist Robert

J. Seidman called it "longwinded and self-conscious," a stylistic failure in which all the characters "have trouble speaking their lines," despite offering funny moments.[57] A friend, the Greco-American artist Vassilis Voglis, who had been a close friend of Tennessee Williams, threw a party for the book at his place on East 21st Street. Representing Viking were Chuck Verrill and editor and novelist Gary Zebrun. Purdy had sent Zebrun a birthday card and his poem, "I Will Arrest the Bird That Has No Light," that was published in a very limited edition by Santa Susanna Press. Zebrun first met Purdy in 1975, when he was an undergraduate at Notre Dame.[58]

On Glory's Course found special appreciation among women. At Books & Co., Purdy read from the novel and Barbara Probst Solomon, a friend and champion, spoke. After the novel was published in Britain by Peter Owen in 1985, Edith Sitwell's biographer Victoria Glendinning compared Purdy to John Updike because both work on a mythological scale limning obscure American lives, but Updike "seems bleached in comparison." In fact, most novelists "seem colourless after Purdy." Several more women reviewers recommended the novel. In 2006, Paula Fox among many other writers was asked by the *New York Times Book Review* and the National Book Critics Circle to select the best work of American fiction since 1980. Her choice was *On Glory's Course* by James Purdy.[59]

In 1985, *On Glory's Course* was nominated for the PEN-Faulkner Award for Fiction. Purdy was asked to join PEN again in December 1984, at Norman Mailer's request.[60] In 1978, after being invited he had written the admissions committee, refusing vehemently, citing their past neglect. He denounced the *New York Times* and the *New York Review of Books* for propagating a literary establishment rife with cronyism and timeservers. Such writers and editors, who also dominated PEN, constituted an "incestuous closeted perpetual cocktail party." They abused their power while wringing their hands over the persecution of foreign writers and injustice abroad. Purdy would no more join PEN than a "Southern Black would reconsider and join the Klan," words calculated to wound.[61] Instead of *On Glory's Course*, Tobias Wolff's short novel *The Barracks Thief* was awarded the prize that year.

During this period, Purdy was writing "gay stories" appealing enough to be accepted by a magazine dubbed the "gay *New Yorker*"—*Christopher Street*, which published "Dawn" in February 1984. Patrick Merla, an editor at *Christopher Street* and its spinoff biweekly newspaper, *New York Native*, both published by Charles Ortleb, strongly supported Purdy. In "Dawn," a father travels from North Carolina to New York to retrieve his son after seeing a picture of him in the newspaper in his underwear—the young man was doing modeling work in the city while trying to break into acting. "Dawn" enjoyed an extended life, appearing in *The Faber Book of Gay Short Stories* (1991) and *Growing Up Gay/Growing Up Lesbian* (1993), which was innovative in being aimed at teenagers. In 1986, *Christopher Street* published "In This Corner . . ." another take on the contemporary gay story. It concerns a forty-two-year-old Wall Street businessman whose second wife has recently died; he falls in love with a homeless young man, who promptly disappears. It was based on a friend of his who had died, Purdy told Ohio State University librarian Jay Ladd. In 1988, it was reprinted in *Men on Men 2: Best New Gay Fiction*, showing Purdy was inevitably labeled a "gay writer" despite his vocal rejection of the tag.[62]

Purdy supported young gay novelists who reached out to him. One was Edward Swift of Austin, who in November 1984 interviewed him for *New York Native*. Purdy told Swift that when a marginalized group becomes absorbed into the mainstream, "you lose something very precious. In the gay movement, not all but many seem to think that if they can be accepted by the Great Society, they will reach the apogee of their dreams. But to me, I don't think I ever want to be accepted by the Great Majority. If they did accept us, they would accept us because our books are selling; they wouldn't care about what was in the books."[63]

The next year, Purdy assisted the Kiwi novelist Noel Virtue, who was living in London and working as a zookeeper to make ends meet. In November 1985, Noel Virtue, whose name and day job make him seem like a Purdy character, gratefully told his biggest hero: "Your words about my novel moved me to tears." He was trying to get *The Redemption of Elsden Bird* published, so Purdy showed this "powerful" and "terrifying" novel to William Morris. Intriguingly, Purdy shared that James Leo Herlihy, who stopped publishing in the early 1970s, had been "disruptive" over his plays. Though no more detail is known, one wonders if Herlihy bristled at the similarity between the scenario of "Now" and his novel *Midnight Cowboy*. Virtue replied consolingly that Herlihy had "produced very little work" and his final novel was "dreary."[64]

In July 1984, Purdy underwent surgery to remove a polyp on his right vocal cord and was unable to speak for some time.[65] Throat trouble and surgery dated back to the 1940s in the Army Air Corps. In August, Purdy was improving; he was allowed to speak, but he could not overtax his voice. His neighbor and friend Elaine Benton sent a get-well card: "I continue the throat healing dance with Chief Swallow Well, who silently joins me in this nightly ritual. He is a good dancer but does not tap as well as you."[66] In the early 1980s, Elaine Benton, the spouse of poet William Benton, became a valued helper, typing his manuscripts and reading them aloud to James. They became good friends, and beginning in 1983, they went on regular walks together.[67] Purdy, who loved cats but had no pet, got to spend time with her cat. As Purdy drafted his next novel, *In the Hollow of His Hand*, featuring Ojibwe characters and Indigenous themes, Benton assisted him and would tease his claim to Native ancestry. A campy dreamcatcher with pink feathers she gave him matches her tone. Elaine Benton became a co-dedicatee of Purdy's most Native novel.[68]

Purdy's claim of Native ancestry became more specific over the years. His first public claim of having Native ancestry through his great-grandmother arrived in a 1967 publisher bio. The next year, Purdy told Gordon Lish his "great-grandmother was said to be of American Indian origin." In the mid-1970s, he added the detail of the maternal line to his biography for *World Authors 1950–1970*. In 1984, Purdy was more specific in an autobiographical piece: Nettie was one-eighth Ojibwe. He identified with this ancestry. In 2008, he remarked that the Jewish critic Bettina Schwarzschild, who as "a child under Hitler" escaped with her family "by the skin of her teeth" to America, could not believe that an American wrote *Color of Darkness*. "I didn't tell her I was really an Indian."[69]

In September, Purdy moved to Eclectic, Alabama, a town of about a thousand souls near Montgomery, to continue recuperating. It served as another refuge. James was the guest of a young friend and admirer, David Granger Carr, a community college professor, writer, editor, and interior decorator. Purdy planned to stay until mid-October, when he would see his New York doctor for a follow-up. After that, he might possibly return to Alabama.[70] Carr, who responded to portions of the novel in manuscript, became a co-dedicatee of *In the Hollow of His Hand*.

Another young professor friend, Jack Collins, wrote from San Francisco in February 1985, saying it had been such a pleasure to spend another one of their "wonderful times together." He remembered each meeting with great clarity and gratitude. "Life always becomes suddenly magic when our paths cross. It feels sometimes like a reassuring chuckle. It also feels sometimes like an almost familial warmth. I think we have known each other for many centuries."[71] Jack Collins later acted as a go-between with Purdy and Bob Sharrard, editor at City Lights Publishers in San Francisco, and Purdy told Sharrard, "he is a wonderful man."[72] Likewise, Collins said that "James was a lifeline," a "wonderful friend" after his partner, Dr. Martin G. Cogan, a professor of medicine and research physiologist, was diagnosed with AIDS in 1990. Jack and James talked almost every Saturday until Cogan's death five years later. The last time Jack saw James was in New York on the street. James said, "look up in the sky." Jack did. When he looked back down, James was gone.[73]

In October 1985, James Link died of AIDS, plunging Purdy into melancholy. Purdy's companion was loyal and had even traveled to see his plays performed in "upper New York state." "I have been terribly upset over it, as he was one of my closest friends. He was only 30. I think he would have had a very fine career had he lived."[74] Tom Zulick believed that "if James were ever in love with someone, it would have been" Link, but he did not know Jorma Sjoblom. At Christmastime, Purdy was "missing James Link," and six months later, he still longed to see his departed friend. Recalling their "little excursions to the galleries and botanic gardens," he dedicated *In the Hollow of His Hand* to the memory of James Link.[75]

Purdy and Gordon Lish remained friends. "I am very happy you go on writing. I feel you are keeping me company in all this bleak city," Purdy wrote.[76] Lish responded to a 1985 Valentine's Day card by simply writing, "Yours is the largest heart."[77] Nevertheless, Lish said their friendship eventually fizzled because of Purdy's tendency to make jibes about Jewish publishers and critics. Purdy was convinced, Lish said, that "if it hadn't been for Jews, his success would've come sooner," and "Jews were interfering with his success." Lish's policy was that if someone uttered a disparagement, "to avoid embarrassment" he would "let the other party know" he was Jewish. Lish "kept putting Jim on notice that this was the case," but he seemingly "failed to recognize" this. So at some point, Lish stopped socializing with him. Jim was "certainly paranoid in the matter. But of course, he may not have been so paranoid at all. Who knows?" Regardless, "I liked Jim. I admired him and was fond of him" and "did for him all I could." Purdy was not so easy to help because had "a chip on his shoulder" and "a sense of his exception." The underrated fictionist finally remarked, "He's not had his due, but who has?"[78]

In May, Richard Hundley's eight-minute choral adaptation of Purdy's poem "Ball" premiered in Lakewood, near Cleveland, Ohio. The composer, who hailed from Cincinnati, was present, as were Bob and Dorothy Purdy. The Cleveland *Plain Dealer* said "Ball" was the standout, and the audience gave Hundley a standing ovation. "Ball" was superficially "just a fun piece"

Figure 17.2 James Purdy and John Uecker by Nan Goldin, December 1985. Courtesy of Nan Goldin.

about a "bunch of kids tossing and catching a ball" but the words and "ultimately, Hundley's music, seem to imply that there are deeper levels of significance to be plumbed"—such as its homoeroticism. To scholar Rainer J. Hanshe, "Ball" is a clear "instance of erotic transcendentalism."[79] Bob and Dorothy introduced themselves to Richard Hundley, who "liked them immediately." "We had a wonderful talk," Hundley said, and after returning to New York, he told James he had met these "lovely people" who "wonder why you don't keep in touch better with them." James simply replied, "If they read one of my books, they would have a horror stroke."[80]

Lakewood, Ohio, is the hometown of John Uecker, and he and Richard Hundley often did not see eye to eye. Both controversial figures and dramatic personalities, they were rivals for Purdy's attention and loyalty. Barry Horwitz found Hundley lovable, while Gerald Busby said he was "extremely neurotic, peculiar, rather unpleasant"—but "James loved that," since he adored eccentrics and drama. Botanist and Purdy aficionado Dennis Moore said there was not space for both Uecker and Hundley in the Purdy orbit.[81] Richard Hundley said that he and James "got along wonderfully until the last years, when he started writing more plays all the time under the influence

Figure 17.3 "James Purdy. Brooklyn Heights, NY," 1987, by Robert Giard. The Miriam and Ira D. Wallach Division of Art, Prints and Photographs, The New York Public Library. Courtesy of Jason Silin, estate of Robert Giard.

of his friendship with Uecker."[82] In 1992, Purdy wrote an emphatic defense of Uecker against Hundley's criticism. In a single-spaced letter, he accused Hundley, "known everywhere as a backbiter," of the "Mortal Sins" of jealousy and envy. "I have been upset and pained for several years now by your angry and vituperative attacks on John Uecker. You give him no credit as a director, and you fail to understand that through him I have found a new career in playwrighting." Hundley had ranted and raved "like a Madwoman" about Uecker's alleged failure to locate "talented young men as actors." That is because Hundley had never had to audition the "hundreds of actors who come looking for parts" in Purdy's plays, most of whom "have no ability."

Yet Hundley blamed Uecker for this. Furthermore, Hundley knew "nothing about the theater." Purdy turned the tables: for years, he had attended Hundley's concerts, only to hear singers who "poorly performed" his friend's "beautiful songs." "But I would never go around and tell people that your singers are no good because you do not know how to direct singers!" "Our friendship cannot continue until there is some change in your Attitude toward my work as a Playwright. But I know change is very difficult for you. You love comfort, pleasure, and you have spent more time with Anthony of London than composing. He has spoiled you." Purdy railed against his British producer friend Anthony Harvey, "born into wealth and privilege and helped by famous and wealthy screen stars. He never had to crawl as I have had to. And he never lifted a finger to help me when HE COULD HAVE." Harvey was ignorant of "how plays are written and produced in America." Purdy also addressed a poem to Hundley noting his debt: "To a Deadbeat."[83]

Perhaps John Uecker influenced the tone of that letter. As a result of their shared love of drama, James eventually cast John in the "role of daemon." John eventually became "the horrible thing James did," which was "clearly to James's delight." John fed a part of James, providing "scandal and horror," said Matthew Stadler, who was assigned *In the Hollow of His Hand* to review for *New York Native*. Stadler loved the book, so editor Patrick Merla said he and the author should meet, beginning a friendship. Stadler visited monthly during most of 1986 through 1988, and made several more visits after that period. In the midst of drama or confusion, he said, Purdy's admirers might wish for a tête-à-tête, for clarification. But James was "not interested in helping to clear things up—he wanted entanglement, drama, horror." Stadler, as others had been before him, was surprised to find himself a character in Purdian drama. Purdy was lovable, if at times a bit "wicked." To access Purdy, it became increasingly clear that one had to be approved by John Uecker. In time, Dennis Moore said, certain detractors even refused to utter John's name, referring to him only as "*that man.*"

In the Hollow of His Hand is Purdy's most Native American story. While drafting this picaresque, magical realist-inflected novel, Purdy said it was based on a story his grandmother had told him.[84] Set in the 1920s, the story opens in Yellow Brook, a small Midwestern town, possibly nodding to Yellow Springs, the home of *The Antioch Review*. Conflict arises with the reappearance of an Ojibwe man, Decatur, who fourteen years earlier had enjoyed a clandestine tryst with a laudanum-hazed Mrs. Eva Coultas. The result is fourteen year-old Chad Coultas, who was always treated as the progeny of

Lewis Coultas, a white man. Returning from the Great War, Decatur begins slowly but surely to claim his offspring. Decatur exemplifies a modernist type of Native protagonist, similar in some ways to the haunted returned veterans and other alienated heroes of canonical Native novels including John Joseph Mathews's *Sundown* (1934), N. Scott Momaday's *House Made of Dawn* (1968), and Leslie Marmon Silko's *Ceremony* (1977). Purdy's novel is at times reminiscent of Momaday's novel, with which he was familiar. *Hollow* is similar, in that Decatur, alienated from many traditions, struggles over his identity in the midst of white occupation of former Anishinaabe land. Nevertheless, Decatur voices resistance: "I belong here more than any of you do," he declares. "This is where I grew up. This is where my people used to be—all over this territory, the dry land and the water too."[85] The second half of the novel resembles *The Adventures of Huckleberry Finn*. Chad follows a surreal, winding journey north into "Indian country" that initiates him into both Ojibwe identity and manhood. Chad ultimately chooses his Indigenous heritage over that of his mother.

During the writing process of *In the Hollow of His Hand*, Purdy shared manuscripts, stories, and thoughts on Natives with his friend, novelist Paula Fox, Granger Carr, editor Betsy Sussler of *BOMB*, and two Dutchmen: Jan Erik Bouman, an intense Purdy fan, and Johan Polak, his Dutch publisher at Athenaeum-Polak & Van Gennep Press in Amsterdam, which had been publishing Purdy's books in translation since 1973. In March 1985, Carr wrote: "You know I am queer for this story, and as you guide it to perfection, passing it along to me, it's as if I held all the world's riches amidst a multitude of impoverished and neglected brethren." Although Jan Erik Bouman could be overzealous about Purdy, incurring criticism from Polak for quizzing the writer about "texts or their whereabouts," Dennis Moore said there was no "sweeter soul on the planet" than Jan Erik, whose name is in the titles of published Purdy poems.[86]

In October, Sam Steward replied to Bouman, who had inquired about his and James's lives in Chicago as young men. James and Sam had made up after a ten-year break in friendship after Purdy's objections to his portrayal in *Dear Sammy: Letters from Gertrude Stein and Alice B. Toklas* (1977). "James and I talk over the phone now about every other week," Sam told Bouman. "I enjoy hearing from him because it is quite like old times . . . and we gossip like a couple of ancient housewives over the back fence." Sam became smitten with Jan Erik: "I haven't simpatico'd with anyone in years as quickly as with you. You are a real refreshment, and I have a real affection for you. Is it love?

We'll see. It's pretty deep, anyway. Maybe it really is."[87] Purdy and Steward kept in touch until the latter's death on New Year's Eve, 1993.

Purdy, proud of his alleged trace of Ojibwe ancestry, did not have ties to any Native communities, only to individuals. He was friends with Maurice Kenny, a gay Mohawk poet. As co-editor of the *Contact / II* journal and press, Kenny published Purdy's poems in the journal and in *The Brooklyn Branding Parlors* (1986), a limited-edition chapbook of seven poems with artwork by Vassilis Voglis. When Kenny lived in Brooklyn Heights, he was introduced to Purdy by a mutual friend, Willard Motley, a closeted gay black author of a bestseller.[88] After their first meeting, Kenny and Purdy "bumped into each other at a secondhand bookstore and became friends."[89] Purdy told Kenny about his maternal line's claim of Ojibwe ancestry. Though usually skeptical of such claims, Kenny had "no doubt that James probably had blood." There is "no reason to doubt what he said about blood, or reason to disprove it." James was a "very honest man" and "insightful into himself and others."[90] Kenny, whose essay "Tinseled Bucks" (1975) inaugurated discourse on the "two-spirit" and Indigenous same-sex desire, was considered the elder statesman among gay Native writers and opened doors for later writers such as Muscogee author Craig S. Womack.[91] In Kenny's introduction to *On Second Thought*, he writes that his friend, writer Paddy Chayefsky, planning travel to Russia on a cultural exchange, asked Kenny's help in assembling a collection of superlative US writers. Along with O'Connor, Capote, and Faulkner, "certainly James Purdy's masterpiece, *Malcolm* was suggested." Showing his esteem for Purdy, in his preface to *Rain*, his story collection, Kenny regretted he "could never present these stories to James Purdy, Faulkner, Maugham, [or] Chekov, for either their pleasure or their critique." To Kenny, narrative was both a challenge and a "morning exercise" through which he purged poetry of the prosaic. Conversely, "James Purdy once confided that his morning exercise is to write poetry to rid his prose of lyric overture." Kenny and Purdy complemented one another nicely.[92]

Another connection to a Native writer is the Blackfoot and Gros Ventre poet and novelist James Welch, who was a fan of Purdy's work. Matthew Stadler recalled bringing up his admiration of Purdy in a 1995 conversation with Welch, who replied that he esteemed Purdy as an "authentically great writer." Purdy also knew a gay poet that he believed was Native, or pretended to believe was Native, James L. White. He told Gordon Lish: "I know an American Indian who writes quite well, and is mad. But reasonable. The only thing unreasonable about him is his name. Why don't you write him and ask him for a story; it will come with feathers, probably." He shared White's Utah address, adding, "(a Navaho Indian)." Born in Indianapolis in 1936, White taught poetry in Navajo Nation schools, and he created and directed the Navajo Folk Art Theater, but was not Diné. In an undated letter, James White asked Purdy, "May I send you anything from the Navajo? Clifton says you're interested in Indians. I'd love to send you something. When I find a copy of Momaday's *House Made of Dawn*, I'll drop it off to you."[93] That landmark novel joined Purdy's collection and its influence on *In the Hollow of His Hand* seems clear. White taught with Allen Ginsberg at Naropa in Boulder, Colorado, and edited *The First Skin Around Me* (1976), collecting Native writers and poets like Joy Harjo.

In the 1980s, Purdy connected to a much younger generation of creative gay men who were inspired by his visionary work. Matthew Stadler recalled James Purdy at a party around 1986 at the loft he shared with "four other young queers." Present were director Howard Brookner, "who was casting for a film version of *Eustace Chisholm* that he never made"; his partner, biographer and storywriter Brad Gooch, who had hipped Brookner to this writer who influenced him; writer and editor Chris Cox, who had interviewed Purdy; editor Patrick Merla, who published his work; poet Tim Dlugos; and probably, artist and writer, Joe Brainard.[94] Novelist Dennis Cooper wrote that his friend Tim Dlugos dated writer Bo Huston in the early 1980s, bonding over their "mutual love for James Purdy." Dlugos and Huston inspired Cooper to nearly adore Purdy's work rather than just respect it. Sadly, many of these talented men were victims of AIDS. Brookner died in 1989 after finishing a screenplay of *Eustace Chisholm*. Chris Cox and Tim Dlugos died in 1990, Bo Huston in 1993, and Joe Brainard a year later.[95] Part of the reason that Purdy's recognition slipped in the 1990s is that so many of his young champions were tragically taken away.

Purdy parted ways with Viking, as Chuck Verrill did not care for *In the Hollow of His Hand*. His agent Ned Leavitt dismissed the publisher, saying "Viking wasn't serious." Yet, had Cork Smith not been alcoholic, Purdy claimed, he "would've stayed there forever."[96] Levitt told Purdy to sign with a new press, Weidenfeld & Nicolson of New York, and they published *In the Hollow of His Hand* in the fall of 1986. The venerable British publisher's New York house was started by George Weidenfeld, a Zionist known for his London parties, and Ann Getty, the wife of oil billionaire Gordon Getty. As unlikely as it seems, these were the people behind Purdy's next publisher. Vice president and editor-in-chief John Herman, formerly senior editor at

Simon & Schuster, signed Purdy and included the novel on the imprint's list—a hodgepodge dominated by nonfiction titles on subjects ranging from real estate to princesses—not daring fiction like *In the Hollow of His Hand.*[97]

Giving an endorsement was Brooklyn novelist Paula Fox, the author of *Desperate Characters*. "There is no voice like Purdy's. It is a wonderful story—full of wonders. I love this book." Since 1959, Fox was a correspondent whose writing Purdy encouraged. She became a good friend and a dedicatee of *I Am Elijah Thrush*. Purdy believed Fox possessed "a very keen insight" as a writer. Also endorsing the book was composer and memoirist Ned Rorem, who read an advance copy "in one fell swoop." The novel cemented his long-standing opinion that Purdy was "one of the most necessary of American fiction writers: purposeful, energetic, madly original, with a good ear, and a profound sense of the tragic and comic in the lives of ordinary people—who are never ordinary."[98]

The book found many champions. In the *New York Times Book Review*, the Southern novelist Lee Smith called it a "grimly antic antipicaresque" that would vastly entertain, enrage, and baffle readers.[99] Overviewing Purdy's career, Vince Aletti in *The Village Voice Literary Supplement* said Purdy had crafted a "jolting, dizzying, loopy language, at once prim and profane, perfectly suited to his astonishing stories." Novelist and memoirist John Espey wrote in the *Los Angeles Times* that Purdy used his signature blend of "surface realism, hilarious burlesque and flashes of divine magic to explore two of his obsessive themes: the blood forces of generations and the mutual needs of a father and a son." Richard Dyer in the *Boston Globe* called it "a fable or parable that displays all of James Purdy's remarkable gifts," which include his "appealing American humor, wherein redemption lies."[100]

In the fall of 1987, Weidenfeld & Nicolson published *The Candles of Your Eyes and Thirteen Other Stories* and reissued *Malcolm* and *The Nephew* in attractive trade paperbacks. Author David R. Slavitt in the *Chicago Tribune* declared the "general level in this collection is very high—Himalayan in fact."[101] Matthew Stadler praised the collection in a thoughtful essay review for *New York Native*. *Candles* generally received mixed reviews but certain stories were singled out for praise. In 1988, Peter Owen published *In the Hollow of His Hand* and *The Candles of Your Eyes* in Britain. *The Sunday Times* praised the range and subtlety of the stories but found the novel thin and disjointed. In the *Times Literary Supplement*, novelist Andrew Rosenheim did not like either book, and seemed creeped out by the novel, which he called "quirky and perverse." Failing to turn a profit, in 1989 Weidenfeld & Nicolson purchased Grove from Barney Rosset and became Grove Weidenfeld. Though his new publisher had taken up Purdy's new and backlist work, he said, "Weidenfeld was not terribly supportive."[102]

In November 1987, City Lights editor Bob Sharrard reached out to ask if Purdy had anything new for their publications. James offered to send unpublished plays and the first chapter of a novel-in-progress abut New York, *Garments the Living Wear*. Sharrard liked the plays—which made Purdy very happy—and accepted "Souvenirs" for *City Lights Review*. Purdy sent some more recent plays, and "What Is It, Zach?" In 1988, City Lights reissued *In a Shallow Grave*, which had gone out of print, and Purdy loved the jacket.[103] Gay Men's Press (GMP) of London followed suit.

It seemed that James Purdy and Quentin Crisp were destined to meet at some point. In 1988, the witty English author and performer published "The Discreet Charm of Mr James Purdy" in the *European Gay Review*. In the six years Crisp had lived in New York, Purdy had sent him four books. Crisp was flattered and even read them, remarkable since his view of literature was "books are for writing, not for reading." Crisp lived just like a "character in any of Mr. Purdy's stories might live," which is probably why he was "so tightly drawn to them." "Some gay organization summoned" him to "one of those innumerable dim cellars with which the rock of Manhattan is riddled." On a tiny stage, he was seated between Purdy and Armistead Maupin, three decades Purdy's junior. The contrast was stark: "Mr Maupin was, as ever, pink and white, rounded, smiling, while Mr. Purdy was thin, infinitely dignified and minimally present." After Purdy read a "fabulous" story and was applauded by the "huddle of listeners gathered before him, he graciously acknowledged the ovation with a faint smile but no one could claim that he basked in it. I don't think he will ever 'stage a Callas.' In the body of world literature, I would say that Mr. Purdy is a recessive gene." He seemed shy but pleased to be "the subject of my worthless praise," Crisp wrote. When Purdy agreed that most of his protagonists are losers, adding, "because I'm one," Crisp understood more deeply the compassion running through his work. Purdy's art lies in his ability to make readers understand that the "oddities that his characters' privations force upon them are natural—even inevitable to them. If a friend is someone who tries to see our problems as they appear to us," then Purdy is "a friend of the disinherited." Readers "must surely marvel at his compassion for—nay, his identification with the victims of fate."[104]

In May 1988, James wrote a short tribute to his artist friend for the book *The Two Worlds of Vassilis Voglis* (1988), which also included four Purdy poems.[105] Like several other friends and acquaintances, Voglis contracted HIV in the late 1980s; he died in 1990. Over these years, Purdy attended numerous funerals of friends who died of AIDS. In the late 1980s, he attended AIDS banquets that the Quakers (Friends) hosted on Mondays for young patients. He told Matthew Stadler, "I went rather faithfully, but they died every week, and finally I felt I just couldn't go anymore. So I started a story about a 94 year-old man who'd been a lawyer who was going to these banquets until finally, the last time he'd went, there was just this 17 year-old boy left, and him. Neither of them AIDS patients. And it was a terrible moment for both of them. He said to the boy, 'when I was a young man, in nineteen-two, gay people were called 'twilight men.' That's as far as I've gotten."

Such harrowing circumstances informed the creation of *Garments the Living Wear*, a dark comedy of New York taking on wealth, patronage, the theater, Christianity, evangelism, sex, and HIV, referred to only as "the pest" or "the plague." Characters work through the "claustrophobia of aristocratic prostitution and artistic patronage," critic Andrew St George later wrote.[106] As the elderly financier Edward Hennings laments Manhattan's decline, Purdy's voice might be discerned. Hennings had seen New York when it was in flower, but in the time of developer Donald Trump and barely concealed mob influence on city politics, it was but a "collection of glass boxes, its government ruled largely by crooks, its citizens picked to the bone by insatiable landlords. The streets surrendered to roving packs of hoodlums, and uncollected garbage, derelicts asleep on the walks day and night as in New Delhi." Meanwhile, as Purdy wrote Paula Fox, "cackling old Ed Koch," the mayor, declared that "all is well from his buggery roost."[107]

In May 1988, Kenneth Bowser's film adaptation of *In a Shallow Grave* opened in New York, starring Michael Biehn (*The Terminator*) as Garnet Montrose. It received several positive notices, but also mixed and negative reviews. Visually the film is brilliant and Jonathan Sheffer's soundtrack is superb, but the film failed to effectively translate this strange and poignant work. "Nicely acted, handsome looking, and impenetrable," the movie "might be more tolerable on public television than at Cinema 1," Vincent Canby wrote in the *New York Times*.[108] The *Los Angeles Times* and *Newsday* praised it, but Douglas Turnbaugh in the *Advocate* was offended by its straightwashing: "Purdy is still the best kept secret of literate America. But this film will help keep him so. His name should be removed from this travesty. It is a deliberate distortion and, therefore, is best described as a fraud." Because of its gay undertones, the film was "sanitized" by cutting twenty-four minutes from the 1988 theatrical release.[109] Initially, Purdy said he liked it very much, it was a real achievement, and the director understood his work quite well.[110] But really, it "wasn't very good," Purdy later remarked. "It's beautifully done, but they were scared of the homosexuality. Still, I don't think the book is about that. There's a kind of loneliness that's like death, then someone comes along and touches you. That isn't homosexual. That brings you to life. That's what *In a Shallow Grave* is about: a young boy that brings you to life. If you want to call it homosexual, go ahead."[111] He later remarked, "Hollywood toned down all of the gay love story; it's just implied. They always want to water-down my stories to make them palatable."[112] The film was released on videocassette by Warner Brothers and the soundtrack was issued on a record. In 1990, the restored version was broadcast on *American Playhouse* on PBS, earning praise from the *Los Angeles Times*.

Also in May, *Enge Räume* (*Narrow Rooms*) was on trial in Germany, after its Berlin publisher, Albino, was charged with indecency by a women's group. The entire novel was read aloud in court, Purdy said, and he was warned not to enter Germany during the trial. He told Sharrard that "police censors" had impounded the book and "made it illegal to purchase," but later, the book was judged not pornographic and allowed to return to bookstore shelves. The judge said the plaintiff was wasting the court's time by bringing the work of a brilliant writer to trial.[113]

In June, Threshold Theater in Kingston, Ontario, presented *A Day After the Fair*. It was the play "American theater people said could never be done and should never be done. But now they've done it in Canada," Purdy said.[114] Jennie Punter wrote that "the play itself is a veritable anti-circus of violence, exploding emotions and sexual perversity that is initially quite repulsive, but ultimately true to human nature." It was true catharsis, partly because "actors weren't afraid to fully explore the ugly dimensions of their characters—and one was compelled to respond somehow." The production proved "theater can and should depict the bizarre and the grisly possibilities in human nature."[115]

Also a bit grisly, Purdy caught herpes in his eye, making reading and writing difficult. It made him averse to work for a time, but Elaine Benton helped him out a great deal. Six months later, he was still having problems with nerve endings.[116]

In December, City Lights accepted *Garments the Living Wear*, and paid him $3,000 (about $6,350 in 2020). Purdy had told Sharrard that *Enge Räume* had a "very strong jacket design" by Rainer Fetting, a "very fine artist" who had lived in Manhattan. Fetting's strikingly homoerotic "Kuss II" was thus selected for the cover of *Garments*. In February 1989, Purdy gratefully wrote: "I am overwhelmed to have a publisher that wants to please me. I've never had a publisher that wanted to do anything but screw me! (With a stone chisel of course.)"[117]

Purdy continued to invent black characters who speak in vernacular, and two powerful black actors starred in his short plays. In April 1989, *Sun of the Sleepless*, an evening of two one-acts directed by John Uecker, was performed at The Theater for the New City, featuring Laurence Fishburne and Sheila Dabney. If the only Purdy work you knew was *Souvenirs*, John Strausbaugh wrote in *New York Press*, "you could think Purdy was black."[118] "He's not Black!" Sheila Dabney exclaimed to the producer's assistant Victoria Linchong, on first catching sight of James Purdy.[119] "Laurence was great but Sheila was incandescent," Linchong wrote.[120] Only a teenager, Linchong "fell right into producing," which felt "weirdly natural." She met Uecker in 1988 during a Theater for the New City Thanksgiving dinner; they hit it off and, while visiting his Manhattan apartment, she examined his Purdy books, intrigued. Purdy thought the plays were "beautifully well done," especially "Souvenirs."[121] *Village Voice* critic Michael Feingold praised Purdy's delicacy that "makes his dialogue lilt and his action progress with the implacable slow grace of a minuet." *Heatstroke* is a "short erotic adagio for two white actors, *Souvenirs* a long elegiac movement for two black ones." The evening belonged to Sheila Dabney, as the tormented heroine of *Souvenirs*. Fishburne had the "big rhetorical speeches—all bloodshed and agony and black rage—but Dabney can make the single word *why* sound like a complete requiem mass and make the cross from couch to easy chair look like the end of the world."[122] In *American Theater*, critic John Yohalem wrote that *Heatstroke* presents a "chance meeting in tropical exile of two American outcasts, a guilt-ridden murderess and a dying faith healer with a violent past" who find in each other a "sort of salvation," but "circumstances conspire to frustrate their bond." By contrast, in *Souvenirs*, a black fugitive in rural Missouri searches for his "estranged and abandoned wife," hoping for "understanding and succor." Linchong saw *Souvenirs* several times: each time it ended and the lights came on, all the women in the audience "of one accord let out a huge sigh and slumped over in their chairs." Purdy thanked Paula Fox and her husband Martin Greenberg, an editor and literary critic, for coming to the plays. "I loved the black actors. The young director, John Uecker, sweated many a cold sweat trying to make *Heatstroke* work, but alas!"[123]

Purdy was working on a novel, *The Vorago*, and in 1989 he published an excerpt in *Christopher Street* and in the first issue of *Satchel*, a literary magazine. "Both Obadiah and Willie Son are *real* boys from Alabama!" he told bibliographer Jay Ladd. Obadiah Kerr is based on Granger Carr of Eclectic. Two outrageous pages in the "anonymous letters" style reference "The Black Cock Feather League."[124] Purdy had been mailing Granger Carr carefully wrapped volumes from Loeb's Classical Library and anonymous letters, "vaguely salacious tales reimagining" Granger and friends with "quasi biblical names," the language "formal to a campy degree and full of carefully wrought innuendo," author Michael Carroll wrote. But Purdy exclaimed: "Do you know what that idiot did? He left an iron going and burned down his cabin with my letters in it!" Purdy was "understandably" angry and hurt, but he "had a viper tongue." In a 1989 radio interview, Purdy said *The Vorago* [abyss] was about Brooklyn and Manhattan. In the published excerpt, Nathanael, a twenty-two-year-old poet, describes Maude and her son, who are Hungarian immigrants in Brooklyn, acrobats who are being tracked by the police, and Mother Machree, fabulously wealthy from real estate deals, who shelters "illegals" in her basement. After Nathanael lost his family in a fire, he tried to commit suicide by jumping from a building, but survived—and then inherited buildings. It is discovered he possesses a small rudimentary tail. In summer 1989, Purdy continued drafting *The Vorago* and completed plays, "tidying them up for the typist."[125]

In July, Purdy felt sad he was not up for travel to San Francisco to promote *Garments the Living Wear* for City Lights. He told Bob Sharrard he had "a kind of relapse" in health. He would do all he could to promote *Garments* by giving readings locally. Purdy's patron, possibly Ed Hefter, who was going to finance his trip, had died. "My friend who died of AIDS has been keeping me going financially for some years, and now I won't have anybody to give me a hand." In other news, a Dutch company purchased film rights to *In the Hollow of His Hand*, making a "very generous down payment." Since Weidenfeld had returned the rights to Purdy and his agent, he suggested that City Lights might want to acquire the paperback rights.[126] No film was ever made nor any paperback issued in the United States. Amid the late August swelter in New York, Purdy told Sharrard there was "lots of interest in *Garments the Living Wear*, but the U.S. is such a *dead* culture [so] who knows? The New York zombies have done a number on me for years! Still, there are some living souls about, even here." Having called New York

"Zombie City, USA" in 1981, Purdy now assessed: "it's even zombier, dirtier, it stinks more. It's more criminal. Nor without any real authority."[127]

Purdy discerned City Lights truly cared about him and *Garments the Living Wear*, not a particularly commercial book. In November, he thanked Bob Sharrard heartily for sending white roses; his reading at Manhattan's GayLesbian Center was "very successful! A great audience! And all the books were sold! Thanks for all you are doing." Purdy told *Out Week* that *Garments* had been rejected by ten publishers before City Lights acquired it.[128] Technically, Peter Owen were the first to publish it, in Britain a few months earlier. City Lights accepted Purdy's manuscripts as complete and did not make significant changes, Sharrard said. Purdy typically railed against publishers, but he praised City Lights: "I think they're my favorite publisher. Yes, I like them." He was like Dr. Seuss's Sam, who finally states, "Say! I like green eggs and ham! / I do, I like them, Sam-I-am." Purdy loved the beautiful, eye-catching design.[129] He asked Sharrard to send copies of *Garments the Living Wear* to the African American pianist and composer Bobby Short, actresses Jane Fonda and Carroll Baker (*Baby Doll*), and writer Fran Lebowitz, who thought he was "it." Spooky Vincent Price "might care to read" it; Purdy sent his Beverly Hills address. William S. Burroughs might like one: Purdy was told the Beat Generation icon liked his books. Gore Vidal should receive one. Purdy also sent personally inscribed copies to Price, Waters, Lebowitz, and Barbara Probst Solomon, who replied: "Though I love all of your novels, this one really gets to me." She "truly delighted in it, identified with it"—"simply fantastic!" Solomon was "wonderfully supportive," Purdy said.[130] Purdy also had a do-not-send list, topped by the *New York Times Book Review*, which he called "fiercely anti-homosexual" and "bigoted in general against anyone not in their stable of safe writers."[131]

Sometime in the late 1970s, Fran Lebowitz met for coffee with James at his invitation on Hudson Street in Manhattan and they became friends. "It was summertime, and he was wearing a seersucker suit," she recalled. "He was very old-fashioned in his manner, very courtly, very proper in his dress. It was very apparent to me that he had no money." She occasionally arranged readings for him, since this was the only way to encounter his store of unpublished work, but found he made no concessions to the audience. "He did not make any concessions, period. That, to me—in addition to the carrying of grudges—is the definition of character," Lebowitz said in her inimitable way.[132]

Garments the Living Wear was the second of only three novels Purdy set in New York, despite its being his home for nearly fifty years. Confronting the AIDS epidemic, the novel ends with the young evangelist Jonas Hakluyt disappearing in flames, "the consumption by fire burning from blood." Jared Wakeman said the flames did not originate from the garment he handed Jonas. "No! they came from his own blood, flesh, and bones! The fire was all from inside and on top of his flesh!" Purdy lost to AIDS "over fifty people" whom he had been "talking with," not always close friends.[133] The novel's cast includes a transgender character, Estrellita, the young Cuban partner of the elderly financier and crypto-Bolshevik Edward Hennings. In addition to Cora Naldi in *Malcolm* from thirty years before, who is indeterminate in race and gender, Purdy's genderbending portrayals were ahead of their time. Purdy told interviewer Don Swaim that the novel's characters are based on real people, and only one was upset. Along with Ed Hefter, the actress Jane Lawrence Smith was also a model; like Peggy Sawbridge, she was a widow hailing from Montana.[134] John Uecker inspired, at least in part, Jared Wakeman, "the Thespian."

As had been the case for many years in the reception of Purdy's new books, *Garments the Living Wear* was praised, if mostly by the already-converted. Purdy prized Quentin Crisp's review, which concludes: "A self-indulgent melancholy is everywhere, but this book is never for a moment dreary. On the contrary, it constantly entertains the reader with vivid descriptions of bizarre people and their misguided relationships in prose that is a mixture of wistful poetry and outrageous satire." Crisp, whom Purdy called "brilliant," also went to his plays. Literary critic Irving Malin, a consistent supporter, hailed the book.[135] The Southern literary scholar W. Kenneth Holditch applauded *Garments* in the *New Orleans Times-Picayune*. A "master at work," Purdy had been "neglected by the critical establishment, and, as a sad consequence, by many readers."[136] Holditch noted he is "a writer's writer": indeed, Gordon Lish was then teaching Purdy's stories in his popular seminars, shaping generations of writers. Holditch was blown away by *Eustace Chisholm*, which "shocked" him out of complacency, and he befriended Purdy after corresponding. He used to visit New York at Easter and, on Good Friday, would bring James hot cross buns to enjoy while they discussed Faulkner and Williams, both of whom Holditch had met. One time, though, Purdy offered a "shot of bourbon," which a "Mississippian never turns down." Purdy showed hospitality since "he was not much of a drinker." He was "so charming" and Kenneth felt "just awestruck," like an "uninformed teenager who had bumbled by accident into the presence of genius. He was wonderful to visit and talk to."[137]

Garments the Living Wear delves obliquely into Christian themes, commingling the sacred and the profane. In the *New York Times*, Bertha Harris claimed that Purdy had again "produced fiction that could easily pass (at least in part) as writings of a richly inspired prophet who's been disqualified from the realm of the sacred texts on the grounds of explicit sex and especially rowdy humor." Young and charismatic, Jonas Hakluyt is a chiseled street preacher, to whom Jesus once appeared in the "back room of an orgy parlor." Jesus also briefly appears unto Jared Wakeman, after he falls on the subway. As Jared is aided by Good Samaritans, the former atheist, whose partner, Des Cantrell, suffers from HIV, has an epiphany: "Jesus cured by means of the Holy Spirit," he hears himself saying to passersby, and he had read somewhere "the Good Shepherd often appears to atheists and infidels like himself." Regardless of what Jared "thought he believed or did not believe, love had claimed him, and would never from this time forth let him go."[138] When Purdy was asked if he was a religious man, he said he did not attend church, but continued: "Certainly I'm in touch with Jesus Christ and all those other people. But they're to me like living people, rather than gods. I can see Jesus in people in New York. Like in the Young Evangelist. And I see him in the derelicts that we, our government, allow to die in the streets." "Jesus and his disciples were so close, in touch with life, not with money or respectability or hypocrisy, that I see them in many of the derelicts and the poor." The Old Testament too is "one of the most influential books on a writer, if he's read it." Stadler later asked James if he was Christian. He replied, "My Christianity is unconnected with the church. The modern church is an agent of the state. I think Jesus was a total revolutionary." "The life of Christ was very interesting," Purdy told Richard Canning. "One wonders what was going on. I'm sure it wasn't any ordinary gay thing. But it certainly has that feeling."[139]

Purdy was getting at something important in his work, linked to his deep compassion for his characters, which is not often recognized. Purdy once wrote: "I have a Christian vision. When Jesus approached any human being, he didn't approach them from any category or pigeonhole, you know, he accepted the person totally. . . . Every human being was sacred, was to be taken seriously, was to be accepted in toto." That is what the writer must do. "You have to accept your characters completely. We all fall down in this sense: we judge other human beings, in such a totality, and gossip" but "when we really understand someone, you can't judge them anymore."[140]

18

Color of Darkness

The 1990s were not kind to Purdy. Advancing in age, he published fewer new books than in prior decades. Yet growing older had compensations. In *Garments the Living Wear*, Purdy writes: "The thing about being so old is that one is gratified and rewarded in taking in every detail about everything around one." If he published fewer novels, he still profusely created fiction, poetry, drama, letters, and drawings. Nevertheless, he slowly slipped under the radar of US literary culture. In 1998, the gay writer and critic Bruce Bawer opened a review with a rhetorical question: "What ever happened to James Purdy?" Early work had earned praise that established a "major stature" but Purdy had been "all but absent from the American literary scene for a decade or more"—despite publishing two novels plus collections in that time. The renewed attention he had enjoyed in the early 1980s had vanished. "America has forgotten me," he rued to his friend, novelist Matthew Stadler, but he was still hungry for recognition.[1]

Laughter helped him through this rough period. Stadler loved seeing his blue eyes fill with laughter that author John Strausbaugh called "bitterly merry." Purdy's core energy, Stadler said, was humor and "delight in the awful." His core action was "the moment when he erupts with laughter."[2] Likewise, the protagonist of *Cabot Wright Begins* is overcome by an orgasmic paroxysm of laughter near the end: "After all laughter is the greatest boon Nature has bestowed on miserable unjoyous man," we are told. "Meaning there is no meaning but the laughter of the moment made it almost worth while. That's all it's about. We was here, finally laughed."[3]

The continued support of John Uecker, a soldier on the dramatic front, meant a lot during the 1990s. In February 1990, he directed *'Til the Eagle Hollers*, two short plays, at Theater for the New City, working with production coordinator Victoria Linchong and actress Jane Smith. "She was divine," John said of Smith, who was also a friend of Tennessee Williams.[4] In both plays, a white woman struggles to regain trust and closeness with a wronged black woman. Obie Award winner Sheila Dabney and Jane Smith starred in "Scrap of Paper," adapted from the short story, a clash between a strong-willed servant and her flamboyant mistress. Dabney and Crystal Field, award-winning actress and the Theater's cofounder, played "Band Music," limning the dynamic between a wealthy widow and her former milliner. Praising Sheila Dabney, Michael Feingold likened Purdy's text to a "steady parade of phrases that tickle the ear and reverberate" the heart.[5] Edward Albee attended 'Til the Eagle Hollers on its last night, and Uecker, who had not seen him in ten years, encountered him after curtains closed.

"Hi, Edward, how are you?"

"I have a meeting with Crystal in ten minutes," Albee said coldly, staring, with no comment on the plays. Uecker walked away. Uecker was on Albee's "list of people to destroy," he said, so Albee went around falsely telling influential people like Field that he was a drunk, an addict, and not to be trusted.[6]

Spurred by Uecker, Purdy diligently wrote full plays throughout the early 1990s. In June 1990, he had recently completed Enduring Zeal and Ruthanna Elder. In Enduring Zeal, set in a small Midwestern village in 1920, inheritance comedy turns into tragedy.[7] Dan, age twenty-five, tells Glen, twenty-eight, that the travel he did in the navy wasn't real since sightseeing is just moonbeams and dreams. He articulates a Purdian credo: "I only got this place for home, run it down all you like. What else do we have but where we're from."[8] By 1991, prolific Purdy had completed the full-length plays Foment (begun in 1981), In the Night of Time, The Paradise Circus, and The Rivalry of Dolls.[9]

The latter three plays plus Enduring Zeal were collected as In the Night of Time and Four Other Plays in 1992 by Purdy's Dutch publisher, Athenaeum-Polak & Van Gennep, and dedicated to John Uecker. They are all set in a rural Midwestern deep past. In the Night of Time, set in a 1930s small town, explores creativity and gender. It presents Richard McColl, a forty-year-old dressmaker, who has sewn since he was a boy, but agonizes over whether dressmaking is proper work for a man. He seems to agree with society that it is "degrading for a man to sew," yet he is compelled to fulfill his calling: "if I didn't sew I would run crazy," his relation to sewing analogous to his creator's relation to writing. Richard sews with the "desperation of calling the dead back to earth," as he declares before bursting into tears at the end. In The Paradise Circus, Midwestern Gothic meets Christopher Marlowe and magic realism. Arthur sells his two sons to circus owner Giuseppe Onofrio for $10,000, and later turns to Alda, a dabbler in herbs and magic, reputedly a witch, for assistance in getting them back.[10]

In May 1991, the New York Public Library for the Performing Arts sponsored dramatic readings of four one-act plays that were published among many others in a special issue of *Antaeus*—cofounded by Paul Bowles and editor Daniel Halpern—including Purdy's "Heatstroke" and an Arthur Miller play. Actors included William Hurt, Nathan Lane, Marian Seldes, Mike Nussbaum, Patricia Hodges, and Paul Calderon.

Along with his plays, Purdy's poetry was gaining traction. He gave a reading at St. Marks Church in the Bowery for the Poetry Project. Purdy wrote a kind of poetry, like his stories, that was "bound to be ignored by the hidebound literary establishment. Many of them are like a child would write. And that's considered terrible." Gloria Vanderbilt called one day to express appreciation for the poem, and a surprised Purdy thought perhaps he had "gone mad."

"James, this is Gloria. Gloria Vanderbilt. I've just read your poems." She read some aloud to him. "I'm mad about them. Why weren't they published in America?"

"Well, one publisher said these are just like Mother Goose."

"Mother Goose is one of the greatest books ever written."[11] Sharing mutual friends and circles, Vanderbilt for decades was a friendly fan of Purdy's work, and paid him more than one visit, so perhaps he exaggerated his surprise. Purdy told Douglas Turnbaugh: "We sent my poems to American publishers, and they were about as interested as if we'd brought them a plate of cold vomit."[12]

In March 1990, Purdy flew to the Netherlands to promote *Collected Poems*, which synchronized with the Dutch translation of *Garments the Living Wear*, both published by Athenaeum-Polak & Van Gennep. The owner of the press, Mr. Ad ten Bosch, paid his expenses. He visited Jan Erik Bouman, a co-dedicatee of *Garments*. Bouman had told Purdy he lived "in a ballroom, surrounded by black tulips," which Purdy took to be metaphors, until he visited him in Holland, in a ballroom, where he grew black tulips.[13] Jan Erik Bouman "opened many doors" for him, Purdy said. "He got me to appear on television in the Netherlands, introduced me to a publisher that was very fond" of his writing, and published his poems in English there in small bibliophile editions.[14] Purdy and his books were very well received. He was interviewed on a TV talk show by host and author Adrián Van Dis and was told the exchange had at least one million viewers. Purdy expressed a queer theory: he did not believe in homosexuality or heterosexuality. Such terms were "invented by mechanists, psychologists, who have never understood human nature . . . there is no such thing." This was the only television appearance he ever did. Purdy's signing events at bookstores attracted crowds; in Amsterdam, readers queued into the street, and it took four hours to sign all the books.[15] Ad ten Bosch believed that Purdy was uniquely dedicated to his vision. "You cannot only support a writer when you're going to make money. You must support the work."[16]

Jan Erik Bouman paid visits to James in the late 1980s and 1990s. Bouman later told Dennis Moore of his "sparse journeys" to Brooklyn, which were "always an ordeal." His final visit was recorded poetically:

> The last time I went for seven days.
> I stayed in Brooklyn, Clarkstreet,
> with Elaine Benton (she did typework for James),
> and who died shortly after from cancer
> Though I was silent and tranquil,
> she seemed not prepared to have a guest,
> so I walked on eggs. I'm still thankful,
> for I couldn't afford anymore my old favorite,
> the Chelsea Hotel.
> James saw me that first afternoon,
> which was good. But the following days
> he did hide in bed and couldn't see me.
> The last day we met again.
> Then he told me that one hour would
> have been enough and that
> I should have known that.
> He said I was spoiled. That I expected
> him to take me out to expensive restaurants,
> which was of course nonsense and his
> own romantic wishful dreaming.
> Then I knew I was part of a fantasy,
> and not for real. More so I knew
> it was my last visit to Brooklyn, though
> I never talked about it anymore.
> I never cared for money,
> even when I ran out of it completely.
> So I always kept working for James.
> He is and will always be

A limited edition of Purdy's story *Brawith* was Bouman's "most beautiful Purdy production," but his own copy was "not even signed."

Purdy read poetry in Weill Recital Hall at Carnegie Hall accompanied by harp music composed and played by his friend Gerald Busby in December 1991. Purdy read "Faint Honey," "Do You Know Why I Am Sleepy?," "The Black Boy," "Men of Bangladesh," "My Greatest Pain," "Go He Must," "What the Young Stripper Said," and "Jan Erik, Alone."[17]

Along with an increased volume of poetry, Purdy created many free-hand line drawings recalling Cocteau or Picasso. In 1991, interest in them grew, and he produced a great number of them, sometimes using colorful markers.[18] In 1993, small galleries were starting to buy them. Drawing served as prewriting sometimes: "if I'm sort of puzzling over what to write, I begin to draw," he told Stadler.[19]

While Purdy created copious plays, poems, and drawings through the decade, he never forgot he was primarily a novelist. In October 1990, Purdy worked on a project that became *Out with the Stars*. The initial story, partly based on the lives of the late Virgil Thomson and Carl Van Vechten, also focused on the "traffic in flesh and souls of the illegal aliens" in New York, with "many other themes" to boot, Purdy apprised Bob Sharrard.[20] From *The Vorago*, Purdy seemed to export the topic of New York immigrants into his new project, but later abandoned it. Purdy continued to work on *The Vorago* well into the 1990s but never finished it.[21]

In June 1991, Purdy won the Bill Whitehead Award, named for the openly gay American editor and early champion of gay writers. The award, sponsored by a New York–based LGBTQ professional group, The Publishing Triangle, honored a writer whose lifetime achievement had "benefitted gay and lesbian readers" and awarded a thousand dollars. Instead of delivering the "usual hour-long, state-of-gay-publishing address," Purdy simply read a story. He had been surprised to receive their call. His friends told him not to accept it since "these people had never done a thing" for him, he claimed. "But, I needed the money." In spite of such recognition, Purdy insisted the gay establishment had "never really accepted" him. When asked about benefiting from gay readership, Purdy countered: "Too many gay readers have the appetite of very delicate ladies. The gay critics scream when they see a mouse, faint at the sight of blood. They don't really understand what I'm doing." Despite his books' relative lack of availability, they continued to inspire new generations of LGBTQ creatives.[22]

In late 1991, in Los Angeles, Black Sparrow Press, helmed by Purdy's ad-
mirer John Martin, published *63: Dream Palace: Selected Stories 1956–1987*
to return them to print. It collected the contents of *Color of Darkness* and
Children Is All, four stories from *The Candles of Your Eyes*, plus "In This
Corner . . ." from *Christopher Street*. This was a welcome collection, though
Black Sparrow might have been more inventive with the title, since *63: Dream
Palace* had already been used for three books. In the *Washington Post*, the gay
writer Richard McCann said that Purdy constructs a "meticulously gothic
and hallucinatory America," unsettling the reader by "dosing him with
mixtures of comedy and horror" and images "surreal and inscrutable." The
collection is a "strange but hugely impressive edifice" simultaneously "grotesque and beautiful, as strangely shaped and ultimately sacred as Gaudi's
modern but gargoyle-laden cathedral."[23]

He was also placing new stories exploring new terrain. In 1992, *Conjunctions*, edited by novelist Bradford Morrow, published "Kitty Blue," a whimsical
fairytale about a special cat owned by an opera singer that is kidnapped. Its
dedicatee, soprano Teresa Stratas, was a fan. In 1993, "Kitty Blue" was published
in limited edition in Utrecht, its design derived from a Purdy line drawing.
"He could talk about my cats all night," editor Donald Weise recalled.[24]

In January 1992, Ned Rorem asked Paul Bowles if he would second his
nomination of Purdy for the American Academy and Institute of Arts and
Letters. Later thanking Paul, Rorem noted that Joyce Carol Oates had refused
to second on the shaky grounds that "Purdy once gave her a bad review
[*sic*], and therefore 'might not be pleased' to have her recommend him." The
acclaimed and prolific writer whom Purdy called "Jessie Rolled Oats" was a
thorn in the side of some great gay writers. To Truman Capote, she was the
"most loathsome creature in America. To *see* her is to loathe her. To read
her is to absolutely vomit." Gore Vidal declared the "three saddest words in
the English language" were Joyce Carol Oates. A more gentlemanly Edmund
White broke the pattern, calling her his friend and muse.[25]

In London, the film director Derek Jarman, dealing with the effects of HIV
and its treatment, mulled over adapting *Narrow Rooms*, as he had for a long
time.[26] At the 1991 Sundance Festival, Jarman was embraced by a new circle
of US filmmakers, and suddenly, shooting an American story in America
seemed feasible.[27] In March 1992, Jarman was in New York for the opening
of his queered *Edward II* by Marlowe. Malcolm Leigh, a continuity editor,
hosted a party at the Chelsea Hotel, at which Purdy met Jarman. James "gave
his blessing" to the development of *Narrow Rooms* and Jarman grew more

serious. Curious, Purdy went to his friend Chester Page's place with Uecker to watch Jarman's *Caravaggio* on videocassette since Purdy did not own a VCR. In the summer of 1992, Jarman, suffering health problems, focused on *Narrow Rooms*, *Chroma: A Book of Colour* (1994), and *Wittgenstein* (1993). Jarman selected Keith Collins, his handsome longtime companion, to play Roy Sturtevant, the renderer, and asked him to help write the screenplay.[28] Consulting with Jarman, Collins labored on a first draft later revised by Ken Butler. Meanwhile, Jarman conferred with the production company, Working Title, which, represented by Antony Root, approached US producer Christine Vachon, linked to the New Queer Cinema. Sadly, Root left Working Title, which dropped the project. Jarman rapidly connected Vachon to Steve Clark-Hall, who had co-produced *Edward II* with Root. From August to September, Jarman was determined to move *Narrow Rooms* forward. On the same day he saw his doctor about failing eyesight, he called his agent to take out an option on Purdy's novel. In September, Channel 4's drama department got on board, offering development funding. Casting talks were reactivated; Jarman was determined Collins would play the renderer.[29] Later, Jarman learned Channel 4 was withdrawing. Given his dire health and Channel 4's heel-dragging, it could not have been that surprising; nevertheless, everyone else was surprised and disgusted. In May, Vachon and Clark-Hall had taken the project to Cannes, began establishing coproduction possibilities, and were in the midst of "approaching or considering a range of actors including Debbie Reynolds, Sissy Spacek, and Matt Dillon." In June 1993, Frances Welch reported that Jarman looked very delicate and fragile. "Yet the power of his deep voice and his depth of feeling belie this physical weakness. He is totally convincing when he interrupts our talk to speak to his producer (in the process of signing up Matt Dillon as the gay hero of his next film, *Narrow Rooms*)." Jarman vowed, "I *will* finish this film. Even if I have to do it from a bed and on a drip."[30] Suddenly, doom: Channel 4 was "dropping the film because Collins was neither well-known nor experienced enough" to carry the lead role. Collins "offered to step aside" but Jarman would not hear it. Emotions ran high, the result was hard to accept, but in retrospect, this "allowed escape from a project which, with the best will in the world, its director could never have hoped to complete," biographer Tony Peake writes.[31] In November, Purdy said he very much liked Jarman's work. "I like him and his friend Keith Collins, who takes good care of him. Keith said I was one of his heroes, which is nice because I always feel I am neglected." But "when Derek Jarman wants to film me, I realize people do know me, somewhere. And that I'm influencing people." Jarman died in February 1994.[32]

In March and April 1992, Theater for the New City staged *The Rivalry of Dolls*, directed by Uecker and produced by Linchong. The first full-length Purdy play to be produced domestically, it starred Kitty Crooks, Gordon McDonald, Crystal Field, William Alderson, Christine Langner, and Paul Anthony Stewart. In 1920, in Midwestern farm country, two sisters, Amelia and Sadie, and their aunt, Pauline Radwell, are split by their desperate, cruel, and tender competition for widowed Dr. Clyde Radwell.[33] *Village Voice* critic Vince Aletti, who had praised the novels, was unimpressed. "Deliberately stilted, unnaturalistic, and absurd," the play occasionally hit a "fizzy, outlandish patch" that felt like work by the Spanish film director Pedro Almodóvar, but "more often it flails and stalls like bad Tennessee Williams."[34] Gordon McDonald became a fan and friend, later helping with *Out with the Stars* by reading aloud the manuscript to Purdy, who dedicated the novel to him and Jane Lawrence Smith. In the fall, Purdy finished his family play, *Brice*, with Uecker's assistance and encouragement.[35]

In March, Purdy drafted "The White Blackbird," a wonderful "new fairy-tale," which in 1993 appeared in *Conjunctions*. Exploring anomaly and mystery, it was inspired by a story his grandmother told him entailing a mischievous bird attracted to shiny objects that became a jewel thief. He hoped to have a collection of tales published.[36]

In June 1993, Peter Owen published *Out with the Stars* in Britain, its first publication anywhere. Purdy was pleased with editor and manager Michael Levien's dedication to the art of writing. The British reviews were mixed. To novelist Jonathan Coe, while the novel is not his most polished, there is "fun to be had" as the story reaches a "pitch of high camp" buoyed by "superbly fruity" dialogue. Purdy could still be "truly bizarre and unpredictable." In *The Guardian*, the English gay novelist Philip Hensher quipped that "Purdy was exposed at too early an age to Ronald Firbank," and the novel suggests he had fallen into "the trap of a lot of writers who have a cult rather than a readership. With not much public to surprise, why bother being surprising? It's much easier to be extravagant." Seven months later, Purdy told his bookseller friend Robert Wilson that no American publisher had yet accepted *Out with the Stars*. "Too daring, says week-kneed tired Alfred Knopf (he turned down *Color of Darkness* and *Malcolm* on the grounds Mrs. Knopf thought ill of the books)."[37]

In October, Purdy told Jay Ladd he was in "very severe financial straits." Ladd, special collections librarian at Ohio State University, paid Purdy for letters and ephemera. Purdy asked for more money due to his nagging "accountant-overseer" who was unhappy with OSU—despite Purdy's previous string of thank-you notes for "generous checks," and having once said Ladd was paying him too much. Purdy later declared: "I must find another way to make a living as publishing and the theatre don't pay enough to keep a sparrow in birdseed." This situation improved in 1993, when Purdy became a client of Patricia (Patty) Moosbrugger of Curtis Brown Ltd. *The Antioch Review*, loyal Purdy publishers, soon accepted "Gertrude's Hand" and all subsequent submissions.[38]

Though he lacked an American publisher for his new novel and often felt overlooked, Purdy cherished the appreciation he received from his friend and neighbor, Chester Page, a pianist, bibliophile, and through his life, a "very cheerful and sympathetic" friend to lesbian and gay writers. Page had befriended two major poets who appreciated Purdy's work—Marianne Moore and Elizabeth Bishop—and was a confidant to author Djuna Barnes. On summer evenings, Chester and his partner, Swan Erikson, oft spotted Purdy on the promenade, sometimes with a young companion. Purdy seemed a formidable presence, not approachable, but around 1990 Page finally worked up the courage to introduce himself. When he did, he found James to be most friendly. Subsequently, when Page and Erikson ran into him, they stopped to share "delightful conversations" about his work and other topics, and when they spied the "evening star and the moon over New York harbor," they departed to their respective homes. Later, Chester would visit James at home. Purdy was "very happy to have Chester Page as a friend. He is a splendid and very kind man." He wished he had known Page earlier because "Brooklyn is a kind of spiritual wilderness. Except for the old mansions."[39]

In spring 1993, Chester Page and Swan Erikson accompanied Purdy to the ceremony where he was honored with the Morten Dauwen Zabel Fiction Award from the Academy of Arts and Letters. The prestigious award, which included $10,000, recognizes progressive, original, and experimental work and was named for the University of Chicago English professor who had been a prized colleague of Sam Steward's at Loyola. Present at the ceremony were painter Paul Cadmus, dancer Agnes de Mille, and Jacqueline Onassis, who was there to hear her friend Arthur Schlesinger Jr. deliver the address. "Over the years," the Academy stated, "James Purdy's polymorphous fictions have multiplied like a wing of surreal statuary: figures so intense they seem relieved of costume or background, but whose unrelenting singularity again and again melts into flesh-and-blood likenesses we recognize as our own."[40] Page said that some attendees were visibly interested in meeting this talented and mysterious man. Purdy, however, showed no interest in mingling with famous and influential people who might have helped him. Instead, he asked Chester to take him back to Brooklyn Heights, where Chester treated him to a late meal. Amid the praise, the contrarian was bitter about his difficulties getting his new work published.[41]

In late 1993, City Lights published *Out with the Stars* in the United States. In this arch tale of New York arts circa 1965, Cyril Vane is a photographer who had immortalized the great beauties of his period: first, Hollywood actresses of the silent era and, later, talented young black men. Cyril hid his craving for male youth from his wife, actress Madame Olga Petrovna, and after he dies, she is scandalized to learn the truth. Vane's contemporary, composer Abner Blossom, comes to possess a mysterious libretto based on Cyril's sub rosa life, and begins composing an opera. Madame Petrovna, to some a "harpy" and a "maenad," deploys all her powers to suppress it. Richard Hundley was the model for another composer, Val Sturgis: "I appear in the novel *Out with the Stars* which is based on Virgil Thomson, myself, and Carl Van Vechten and his wife," Fania Marinoff, the former silent film star.[42]

The novel's American critical reception was warmer than it had been in England. Edmund White, reviewing the novel as a roman à clef, declared Purdy had "never been lighter or more ebullient." Abner Blossom is clearly Virgil Thomson, "down to his Parisian past, his deafness, his snappishness and his residency" in a hotel like the Chelsea. But White did not know that Valentine Sturgis was based on Richard Hundley. Val Sturgis, White thought, is a hybrid of "Ned Rorem's talent with Coleman Dowell's Kentucky background, but Rorem, though Thomson's student, was always far more sophisticated and intelligent than Val (if equally lachrymose as the *Paris Diaries* reveal, when he was still drinking in the 1950s)." Likewise, Dowell was "more self-destructive and *sauvage* than Val, and Dowell never studied with Virgil but did write music before becoming a novelist." *Boston Globe* critic Richard Dyer thought Sturgis was a blend of Rorem and Purdy, "freshly arrived in New York" and photographed by Van Vechten. Though as White concludes, knowledge of Purdy's sources is not necessary: "If these keys are tossed aside and *Out with the Stars* is allowed to swing open on its own hinges, there is little to criticize and much to enjoy. Purdy's characters are larger than life, his pace is unflagging, his generosity of spirit overwhelming, the ambient kindness enviable."[43] Despite Edmund White's positive review, in which he hailed *Narrow Rooms* as Purdy's "best book," John Waters recorded in his preface to *The Complete Short Stories of James Purdy* that White said he was "allergic to James Purdy."[44] Nonetheless, White's connection to Thomson drew him to Purdy's *Stars*. To Richard Dyer, the campy atmosphere of the novel was that of Carl Van Vechten's 1920s novels; Purdy pays homage to the "vanished genre created by Thomas Love Peacock and polished to perfection by Ronald Firbank" in which Van Vechten wrote. As the latter described his own Wildean strategy, here Purdy treats "extremely serious themes as frivolously as possible." Purdy, writing with "an extraordinary, airy and effortless elegance of style," had created "such a gay book in both the ancient and modern senses of the word—deft, amusing, full of laughter sunlit and dark, and suffused with a gay sensibility." Paradoxically, Purdy was "one of America's most accomplished, honored and little-read novelists." In the *New York Times*, Queens College professor and gay novelist John Weir disagreed, however, finding its style "generic" and obfuscating. The novel shows that "high camp is just another masculine ploy, a means to remain unaffected by loss." In contrast, *Library Journal* discerned that "even while confronting and conflating racial and sexual stereotypes," Purdy had "never been funnier" than in this "dazzling gothic comedy." Critic Irving Malin concurred in *Contemporary Fiction*, calling Purdy "one of our best writers."[45]

To address Purdy's engagement of race and stereotype, the plot entails white artists—writers, photographers, and musicians—celebrating and borrowing from black culture. The novel therefore engages questions of "stereotype, fantasy, and prejudice," notes professor Christopher Lane, who interviewed Purdy. Characters struggle to form ethical relations to love, creativity, and composition "(in the example of the two operas), to representation and censorship (around Cyril Vane's photography), and finally, to race (for instance, the two menservants, Harlan Yost and Ezekiel Loomis)," which is perhaps the "most challenging and troubling dimension."[46] Black culture is exalted by white artists; nevertheless, the relationships between white principals and characters of color are vexed. Men of color are in positions of servitude, even if they are also lovers or friends, as is the case with Harlan Yost, a mixed-blood Ojibwe man who takes a major role in the novel's middle portion. Purdy raises questions of race, power, and patronage, and implicitly critiques white supremacy.

For his next project, Purdy's thoughts returned to Chicago and Gertrude Abercrombie, whose artistry, friendship, vivid personality, and jazzy milieu had profoundly affected him. He commenced the process of drafting a manuscript that eventually became *Gertrude of Stony Island*. He was still haunted by his old friend who died in 1977, perhaps feeling nagging guilt over not lending his portrait or appearing at her retrospective. After about forty pages, he lost track of his first-person narrator, but stories and voices kept moving in his head.[47]

Purdy struggled with the manuscript while working on short stories in various stages. He revised "Brawith," his gothic horror of a profoundly damaged veteran and his spectacular disintegration, which Uecker had dug out of Purdy's filing cabinet. Purdy thought he wrote "Brawith" back in 1970; therefore, Brawith is a predecessor to the Vietnam veteran Garnet Montrose of *In a Shallow Grave*. In 1994, *The Antioch Review* published "Brawith" and reprinted it in an anniversary issue. Five years later, Hugin & Munin of Utrecht published a limited-edition book of the story. These reprintings show its impact as one of Purdy's best stories. Also in 1994, another small Dutch press, Avalon, published a limited, linen-bound, slipcase edition of another story, "Reaching Rose," with both Dutch and English volumes. Poignantly, "Reaching Rose" introduces an elderly man who lingers in a phone booth inside a bar, pretending to talk to people. Recalling the narrative frame of "Daddy Wolf," it speaks volumes of Purdy's loneliness and isolation as he aged.

Further manifesting his widespread influence, in October 1993, a week-long Purdy homage was staged in Seattle, "Celebrating a Lifetime of Creative Work," organized by Matthew Stadler for the Rendezvous Reading Series. The mayor of Seattle even proclaimed a James Purdy Week. With Stadler's help, Purdy had selected a dozen of his drawings and as many portraits by Carl Van Vechten for a monthlong exhibition in the New City Theater Gallery. At New City Theater, Purdy was moved to tears by a reading of "Some of These Days" by a young actor, Eric Maas, which was bookended by a Fats Waller recording of the song that gave Purdy his title. Composer David Mahler presented an original composition setting Purdy's poetry to music. Stadler's adaptation of the story "Mr. Evening" was presented by a local cast starring Susan Ludlow. A panel comprising the gay poet and filmmaker James Broughton, photographer Mary Randlett, and Purdy discussed "Sustaining a Lifetime of Creativity."[48] A chipper, elderly Broughton said writers should be declared national treasures. Purdy retorted that would be awful, Stadler said.

Purdy recited his recently completed story, "Brawith." He was in his "mad prophet phase," Stadler said, his eyes darting around under uncontrollable eyebrows. He had physical magnetism; with an intense, terrific gaze, he faced the audience, which he likened to "one hundred eyes of tigers looking right at you." His words were considered, delivered slowly and carefully, and the cumulative effect was mesmerizing. Dennis Moore, a retired chemist and community garden activist, attended every event. As Purdy reached the stunning climax, he registered Dennis's awestruck expression. Purdy later told Moore, whom he met in Seattle, that at that moment, "I loved you"—giving Moore a cherished moment. Purdy knew that someone in the audience really understood.[49]

Moore was impressed by the large turnout of lesbians, an encouraging show of LGBTQ solidarity. The gay novelist Tom Spanbauer, who like Purdy had created Native American characters, read first; Purdy later praised Spanbauer's novel *The Man Who Fell in Love with the Moon* (1991) as a "new thing in gay writing." At Seattle Public Library, where an exhibit documenting Purdy's writing process was installed, he addressed a group of young writers from the city's public schools. When he uttered his advice to young writers— "You have to be ready to have your brains beaten out of you every minute of your life"—the students tuned in. An adult was talking to them honestly.[50]

Matthew Stadler, who interviewed Purdy at length for an intended article, wondered how he had supported himself over the years. "I'm helped by friends, often, and I've saved some money. I don't make enough from writing, never did. I've never gotten very much money from the publishers. It's like the feudal ages where the peasant was lucky to get one meal a day, while the lord of the manor ate everything. I draw, and people buy these drawings." He alluded to mysterious women who gave him a stipend or allowance and specified one. "I do have a patron, a former actress who helps me out. We took a taxi back to Brooklyn one evening and she handed me 'a little something,' which turned out to be a check for $10,000."[51] John Uecker said that Jane Smith once gave Purdy and him $10,000 dollars apiece.[52]

As though compelled, Purdy revisited the traumas of his career in conversation with Stadler and others. His play *Brice* comes to mind, when old Simeon remarks: "There is an old saying time heals all wounds. It's a bit wide off the mark." Or, as Purdy told Richard Canning, "When you're hit by a brick, your body knows it. You can forget it, but you're going to have a wound there."[53] With Stadler, Purdy rehearsed moments when he felt he had been betrayed by someone whom he supposed would treat him well. The fallout with Farrar, Straus & Giroux over Wilfrid Sheed's hatcheting of *Eustace Chisholm* was the most revisited trauma. Matthew was skeptical since Purdy's accounts were sometimes "overlaid with anti-Semitism" and "dislike of the literary establishment," which put him on guard, and he even remembered thinking, "it's too bad he's going crazy." But later, driven by curiosity, he would investigate a Purdy claim and find it was "verbatim true." Purdy increasingly grew to see the world as full of treachery and betrayal. This was part of Uecker's appeal to him, Stadler thought, since John often saw the world that way.[54]

Despite the honors he received from the gay community, Purdy remained ambivalent about 1990s gay literature and activism. In 1990, author George DeStefano in *Out Week* claimed that Purdy was a "partisan of gay liberation" who gave readings at A Different Light bookstore and the Lesbian and Gay Community Center, of which he was a member. Yet in the same piece, Purdy mocked the members of the "gay literary establishment" who had maligned *Eustace Chisholm* and *Narrow Rooms* for being violent and tragic as devotees of "moonglow, rainbows, and rectal anesthetics."[55] In 1992, Purdy declared: "The gays have never really helped me. I'm too strong for them. Of course, there are a lot of gays that like my work, but I guess you could call them The Silent Majority."[56] "I've had the most vicious reviews from gay people," Purdy told Richard Canning. "So many books treat being gay like you were finally able to join such a comfortable club. And: 'Of course my daddy's gay!' It's all such a lark. But for most of us, being gay was a very heavy burden. I think it still is. I don't think the world as it's constituted today is ever going to welcome gays and blacks." Even with civil rights, "they still treat blacks horribly. Just to say, 'We came out now and everything's all right!' It isn't. It's still very tragic to be gay." Over history, most gays suffered greatly, "burned at the stake" and "mistreated by the literary establishment."[57] Purdy told Christopher Lane the gay movement had become too mainstream and gay writers such as David Leavitt and he had little in common. Leavitt wanted gays to be "very nice people, not to have sex, and to be well-behaved bourgeoisie." Ironically, Leavitt, whom Purdy privately called "the Sugarplum Fairy," coedited *The Penguin Book of Gay Short Stories* and included "Some of These Days." Tom Zulick said Purdy "embraced the gay community, but he was never an activist." In 1994, he remarked on "big gay parades and carrying on" in New York to Stadler: "I don't feel gay or connected with it. I belong to another century. My struggles and many defeats and many triumphs belong to another sphere." A group dies the minute it becomes "media-oriented."[58] He hated to categorize himself, but he would "always be a revolutionary. Whatever is, is wrong." Such was his radically contrarian position. "I always have to be wrong to be right, but I'm used to that. You just have to not worry about what society thinks."[59] *Harvard Gay and Lesbian Review* published literary critic Reed Woodhouse's essay "James Purdy's Escape from the Wasteland." His final claim for Purdy's inclusion in the gay canon was that his authorial gayness had nothing to do with his subject, style, audience, or "even his own avowed homosexuality," but with his total, implicit message to LGBTQ readers: "Don't give in, and don't sell out. Don't believe what you read in the newspapers." Trust your passions, but "do not expect love to make you happy. Savor, and suffer, your abnormality."[60]

In 1995, Reed Woodhouse visited Purdy to prepare a second feature. He noted that Purdy's large single room, with its "spartan writing desk," simple bed, and bookshelves, felt "barracks-like" and likewise, Purdy seemed a "battered soldier or prize-fighter." Editor Don Weise recalled that in Purdy's little bathroom, he found a vintage touch, a bottle of olive oil and a shaving brush and cup. In some ways, it seemed like Purdy remained in another era, "like he was still living in the 1920s."[61] Purdy, "distinguished and ignored," had "trained himself to say what others won't allow themselves to think," Woodhouse wrote. Conversation is thus not for "the unwary or the disingenuous. He fits into no groups—whether sexual, intellectual, political, or artistic—and fiercely resists incorporation." Purdy again denied he was a "gay novelist" and likened the *New York Times Book Review* to *Pravda*, the Soviet communist party newspaper. "Enthusiastic praise of his works" he took as merely his due, and he did not conceal "his hunger for applause." Reed found him a "charming companion but not the least interested in making you like him," his discourse a "warrior's ostentation of wounds"—out of print books, vindictive reviewers, and poverty. Even so, in 1994, the *New York Press* declared him "Best New York Novelist," wagering that his work would still be read after "shifting sands of taste" had obliterated the "names of many currently hyped mediocrities."[62]

Dennis Moore of Seattle began corresponding with Purdy and flying to New York to visit him, becoming a part of his circle. With degrees in botany and chemistry, Moore had to halt an emerging research career in environmental chemistry after contracting AIDS. A botanist, he became an advocate of community gardening, which is how he was known at home. Though devoted to James's well-being, and the founder of the James Purdy Society, Moore was at times hurt by his association with Purdy and Uecker. In 1996, and not for the last time, Moore "actually left James's in tears," believing that he had "seen both sides" of stepping into Purdy's world. Moore noted a pattern in which young male devotees would be drawn in to the circle, but

Figure 18.1 Purdy's mantle, 236 Henry St., March 2009. Photo by the author.

eventually were denied access to James.[63] Over time, an emotionally sado-masochistic dynamic began to emerge.

In the winter of 1994, a young actor, Jason Hale, met John Uecker, leading to a special relationship with Purdy. A friend told Hale he must meet Uecker, which led to him participating in acting workshops organized by the Running Sun Theater Company. John Uecker "has a theater for my plays," Purdy informed Stadler, "run by the Franciscan Brothers." According to Uecker, it was funded by a few donors including Jane Smith and Uecker himself.[64] The workshops included readings of Purdy plays, which reached a new level of intensity when performed. Immediately, Uecker wanted Hale to meet Purdy. "Something about my look, my disposition, I was 22—he felt there was great casting opportunity for me." Hale met Purdy at his favorite local Italian restaurant, La Traviata on Montague Street. Uecker later employed Hale to help Purdy with daily tasks twice a week, and they bonded over Hale's having grown up in Allentown, just down the street from the apartment where Purdy had lived with Jorma. "We had things in common like jelly rolls, things made in Pennsylvania and Ohio. We talked about food a lot." James even remembered the shoe repair shop around the corner from

Jason's house. Jason cooked dishes like tilapia in Indian seasoning or brought favorites from Lassen & Hennigs: a turkey sandwich with raw onions, lettuce, and mayo on a Kaiser roll, and tiramisu for dessert. Hale read aloud from Purdy's new work, such as "No Stranger to Luke," as James lay in bed, eyes closed, sometimes asking Hale to mark a change. Later, when James needed a full-time caregiver, Jason still came just to provide companionship. Generous and warm, Purdy was unique, and one of the most open, honest people he had ever met. For visitors, he always donned jacket and tie. "It was a shock that he could write such awful books, awful in the sense of violence. You could never pull that from James, except when he talked about the writing establishment."[65]

Such close contact lent Hale insight into the dynamic between Purdy and Uecker, who had a "very special relationship." James showed great care for him; he would phone Jason and made him "promise that I would look after John." John and James "fought a lot and would go a week without talking, but they had a closeness about them that I saw was unbreakable. I never saw a relationship like that. It was almost like a father-son relationship, but not." At times, though, John seemed to be the father, while at other times, the expected dynamic was in place. It was also almost like a fraternal relationship.[66]

In 1995 and 1996, Purdy composed "Moe's Villa," a vivid novella drawing from his youth. In Findlay, from 1927 to 1930, George W. Moe managed The Villa confectionary—this was the original Moe's Villa that dispensed candy and ice cream, referenced at the beginning of *Mourners Below*.[67] But the second fictional Moe's Villa is more elaborate and less innocent, offering an illegal tavern and casino. Its proprietor, Moe Swearingen, who takes in teenage Rory Hawley and employs him, has Shawnee ancestry; Shawnee were commonly found in what is now Ohio.

In the fall of 1996, Purdy completed his first and second versions of "Moe's Villa." Valuing input from friends, he would have "young men come and read" new work aloud, and could thereby detect inessential material. "Moe's Villa" became popular in his circle. Like *In the Hollow of His Hand* but more subtly, "Moe's Villa" explores a theme of secreted Native paternity. Central to plot and symbol are the red "jewels" that had been given to Rory Hawley by his putative father, who is now deceased, which had been stashed away. Purdy sometimes awoke in the middle of the night, inspired to write. He didn't know how to end the tale. "But I dreamed it, where my mother told me, 'The jewels are candy.' I said, 'How ridiculous! That's unbelievable.' Well, it isn't believable. But you fall under the spell of the story and believe it." The answer to whether they are bona fide rubies, among other hints, suggests that the real "red" gift is Moe's paternal gift of Native blood to Rory Hawley.

In late 1996, Purdy tried to put together *Gertrude of Stony Island*, which did not easily cohere. He had written copious pages in the "anonymous letters" style, with much heightened humor, which were almost all cut later. The novel was pursued using that unconscious technique until a narrative focus was found, and John Uecker played a key role in the process. *Gertrude* needed a great deal of revision. "I got stuck in the mud with it. It was originally four hundred pages. A friend of mine helped me cut it down." Uecker described organizing and reorganizing several stacks of pages laid across Purdy's floor. "We hammered it out in the first-person style," Uecker said, stressing that he "didn't write a single line." Throughout his life, Purdy wrote thousands of "anonymous, anomalous letters of passion" defaming the recipient "by telling him the truth about himself." They were a "blowing off of steam," Purdy said. "But the novels sort of come out of it."[68]

In the spring of 1997, Peter Owen published *Gertrude of Stony Island Avenue* in Britain. Set in Chicago, the story is rendered via Greek myth—Demeter's descent into the underworld in pursuit of her daughter Persephone, lost to Hades. The novel centers on Gertrude's elderly mother, Carrie Kinsella, who goes on a quest to learn the truth about her daughter, a jazz-loving, sex-positive bohemian artist who has been dead for several years as the story opens. The plot recalls Alma's project to memorialize Cliff in *The Nephew*, contemplating the mystery of other lives. This publication was the world premiere of a novel by a writer who was considered major by many critics and whose works had once been widely reviewed in Britain, but there was apparently no British critical response. This suggests not only that Purdy's status slipped after the mostly negative response to *Out with the Stars* in England, but also that Peter Owen dropped the ball on promotion.

Contrastingly, at home, the weekly *New York Press* ran an issue in March 1997 celebrating James Purdy including an interview, essays, and an excerpt from *Gertrude of Stony Island Avenue* on the front page. Author and *New York Press* editor John Strausbaugh visited James at home for the feature, describing him as a "white-haired and delicate but not frail man now in his mid-70s"—though in fact he was eighty-two. His speech was vigorous: get him "cranked up about the piss-elegant bluenoses who've dissed his works over the decades," the "middlebrow gatekeepers of establishment culture," and he'll recite a favorite ditty with "a wicked spark in his eye": "Although your shit is finer than taffeta, few if any ladies are wearing it for hats." Strausbaugh expressed disbelief that this fine novel had not yet found a US publisher.[69]

Soon afterward, *Vanity Fair* ran a feature by Peter Theroux, who deplored the sad state of publishing when a master like James Purdy, an American treasure lauded by Tennessee Williams, could not find a home in the States for his latest imaginative work. Gore Vidal said Purdy had "no category. But then he has few peers." He had no constituency, not among academics or the gay establishment, whose position was that "fags are just like everyone else, only nicer. Well, not in James Purdy's books." As for "the hacks of academe," as Vidal called them, they "cannot deal with originality, particularly of style."[70] After reading Theroux's piece, Betty Kelly Sargent, an editor at the publisher William Morrow and Company, contacted Curtis Brown. But the agency was in the process of dropping Purdy, who was told there was no longer an agent there to represent his books.[71]

In June, John Uecker approached Harold Dennis Schmidt, who had his own literary agency and had been friendly with Purdy since the 1970s, to negotiate a deal with William Morrow and Company.[72] Uecker had apprised Schmidt that William Morrow "expressed interest in publishing" *Gertrude of Stony Island Avenue* and mailed him the manuscript. Schmidt liked it very much and told Purdy and Uecker he would be happy to represent Purdy. In turn, Purdy told Schmidt that for the first time in his career, he was going to be represented by someone "who knew and respected his work." Schmidt then worked to improve Purdy's situation. He persuaded Sargent to raise Purdy's advance from $7,500 to $10,000, and ironed out Canadian rights with Peter Owen, which sped up the publication window. Pleased, Purdy told him to accept the contract.[73]

A series of events then unfolded, which, to Schmidt, revealed that Uecker could step in and "totally take control of James's affairs."[74] In July 1997, Uecker "threw the first wrench into the proceedings." Uecker had been talking with International Creative Management about handling properties for film rights and an ICM book agent wanted to look at *Gertrude*. Schmidt rejoined it was "a little late to be shopping for literary agents" since he, with Purdy's blessing, had already closed the deal with William Morrow and Company. "A brouhaha ensued." Schmidt had made plans to see Purdy, but now Uecker forbade this. Purdy was instructed not to sign any agency contract until Uecker and his lawyer met Schmidt, who waited in vain for a call. Schmidt insisted that he and James should have a direct relationship—it was ridiculous for an agent to be forbidden from meeting his client. Purdy said he and John had squabbled over this, but gave Schmidt permission to come over to Brooklyn Heights. There James told Harold that "Uecker's quarreling had made him ill." Uecker had asked Purdy to meet with an ICM agent, but Purdy refused. Schmidt told Purdy he must "keep Uecker at bay" and prevent him from calling Sargent without consulting him, after which they had a "very cordial meeting" in which Purdy said that Curtis Brown had "let him go," and the agency would "probably be happy" to let go of the "foreign rights." Purdy authorized Schmidt to contact Dave Barbor, director of foreign rights at Curtis Brown, who was amenable. On July 7, Curtis Brown sent Schmidt a list of active foreign licenses, ten novels in five languages.[75] Schmidt was to represent the "old titles in the foreign market." The contract arrived from William Morrow and fine tuning ensued. Schmidt told Purdy he was sending the agreement and his standard letter, and mentioned that like most small agencies, the commission was 15 percent and the author would be charged for expenses such as postage and copies. Purdy "expressed no concerns."

On October 24, however, Schmidt received a fax saying Purdy was under a doctor's care; he had appointed attorney Julius Lang to decide all contractual arrangements. Lang called a couple days later, saying Purdy was being treated for a heart condition; he was "terribly upset" by the agency letter, since he had never agreed to such things and never would. When Schmidt asked what Purdy wanted changed, Lang declared it was too late for that: Purdy did not want to work with Schmidt anymore. Schmidt retorted, "it was too late for that: this was a done deal." Schmidt was barred, and he then just tried to collect his commission. In November, Julius Lang told Schmidt he was forbidden from talking to William Morrow. Furthermore, if he continued to hold himself out as Purdy's agent, there would be "serious repercussions." Schmidt was no longer representing Purdy, but only trying to get paid for the work he had done. He left a message with Lang telling him to stop threatening and pay up, and he called Purdy, who said he could not speak to him and he was under a doctor's care. Schmidt told Purdy to tell Lang to pay him; in his high-pitched voice, Purdy replied, "You'll get your money."[76] Schmidt hired a lawyer, Kenneth Norwich, to aid him, and he eventually received the $1,500 he was owed. This all went to pay his lawyer's fee, but this was a matter of principle. Reviewing this episode "brought back a lot of painful memories" of betrayal and feelings of outrage. "But I can also look back now and feel proud about the way I handled myself in refusing to give in to Uecker's attempt to erase me and my honorable efforts to be the kind of literary agent for James" that he said he "always wanted and never had."[77]

In March and April 1997, Purdy's full-length play *Foment* was "expertly performed" by the Running Sun Theater Company, guided by the Uecker-Linchong team, at Greenwich Street Theater. James became fond of actors Roman Marocco (Johnny) and Ricky Martin (the bartender). In a feature, John Strausbaugh, calling *Foment* a "highly melodramatic Nazarene retelling about a faith healer and his cult of destitute wild boys," wondered how critics would react. It was "partly an old-fashioned gangster yarn, partly a cautionary tale about today's religious cults and partly a retelling of the Christ story with a strong gay subtext."[78] Though Strausbaugh wondered what reviewers would think, it is not clear that anyone else but him reviewed the play in print. Although he was a Purdy supporter, in his review, he admitted *Foment* was "not for everyone. A Christlike faith healer in the 1930s gathers a following of down-and-out young men, including his own faithful John [the Baptist] (Johnny) and Judas (Judd), and meets the requisite tragic end. Typical of Purdy, it takes about a second for the air to become thick with foreboding, dread, and thwarted homoerotic fevers; add the uniquely lyrical-yet-gutsy poetics Purdy's characters speak," sounding like "Elizabethan gangsters" and the result is a "very strange, very intense theatrical experience you'll either love or hate."[79] *Foment* had premiered in 1992 at Ontario's Threshold Theater, which had previously debuted *A Day After the Fair*.[80] The production failed to draw critical attention. It seemingly also failed to reach its artistic goals, since around this time, Purdy asked John Uecker not to do any more of his plays. He chose to turn away from playwriting to refocus on fiction. Unlike all of Purdy's other produced plays and many unproduced ones, *Foment* was never published.

Victoria Linchong made weekly visits during this period, offering sustenance and company. Every Sunday, for around two years, she went out to Brooklyn Heights and bought a lunch for Purdy from Lassen & Hennigs. For an octogenarian, he was spry and made his way down the flights of winding wooden stairs without problem, opened the heavy front door, and kissed her hello. Her approach to Purdy was different from most others. She brought her son and a book or other object that might interest or inspire him. John Uecker worried she was tiring him and sometimes gave her "an earful," to no avail. She spent weeks reading aloud Howard Zinn's *A People's History of the United States*. She brought a Ouija board, which James refused to touch, but she and her son, then about six, used it. They got spooked when the planchette kept spelling "AMOS AMOS"—the name of the character resembling young James in *Eustace Chisholm and the Works*. Purdy falsely told at least one reference book writer that his middle name was Amos. A Ouija board appears in a later story, "Easy Street." Purdy would have an "entire pie waiting" for them, which she said was unnecessary, but always, there was pie: cherry, peach, or pumpkin (recalling "Lilly's Party"). After each ate a slice, James insisted she take it home, which her son loved. James called one day and told her not to come. Was pie a financial burden? Or maybe she "really *was* wearing him out?" Then, she and Uecker had a falling out, and she did not see Purdy again.[81] In 2013, Uecker and Linchong were reunited by a James Purdy Society panel at an American Literature Association meeting in Boston, sharing lunch with the author.

In November 1997, Purdy met the English scholar, Richard Canning, who visited him for an interview. Among many subjects, Purdy elaborated his criticism of US foreign policy. American culture and government had gone downhill since the Korean War. "We didn't understand what we were doing there. Then Vietnam has been a cancer on America" and drove people to drugs. He continued to take interest in Latin America and his country's involvement there. "I used to believe what the government said. Now I don't believe anything they say. What we've done in Guatemala, for instance. The CIA killed 200,000 people! We were behind that—maybe secretly. Also in El Salvador. We murdered Allende in Chile. We don't have anything to do with Cuba, yet we're in bed with communist China, which is a horrible country. So you feel hopeless, impotent, with government. It's now a government of the super-rich."[82] An astute scholar, Canning continued to write about Purdy, and this interview, leading Canning's book, *Gay Fiction Speaks*, was one of the most important Purdy ever did. It commenced a friendly relationship between them.

After all the drama surrounding its contract, in October 1998, William Morrow and Company published *Gertrude of Stony Island Avenue* in the United States. Irving Malin called the novel one of his best, noting Purdy had never received in his home country the critical attention he deserves.[83] Of course, he had rarely received such attention anywhere. *Kirkus Review* hailed it as a "rare triumph: as elegant in its simplicity of tone as it is moving in its purity of feeling, Purdy's work deserves to place its author in the first rank of contemporary writers."[84] In the *Washington Post*, Miranda Schwartz said that had Truman Capote and Edith Hamilton (*Mythology*) cowritten a novel, it might have resembled *Gertrude of Stony Island Avenue*. Readers who give Purdy a chance, Schwartz promised, will be "utterly taken in by this sophisticated, mellifluous novel." The gay writer and critic Bruce Bawer, hailing Purdy as a "singular American visionary" in the *New York Times*, said although the novel is somewhat puzzling, most readers with "lively minds will find the rewards of Purdy's art to be worth the effort." The avant-garde fiction writer Brian Evenson concluded "the value of Purdy's art is not primarily mimetic" but is found in his ability to transform the world in his vision, and in so doing, to cut through all that "obscures what it means to be human." At first very quiet, *Gertrude* "soon builds to a powerful pitch." This "first-rate read" proved that Purdy remained "vital, impressive, and necessary." In light of John Uecker's extensive editorial assistance, it is interesting Evenson discerns in this novel a "narrative voice decidedly different from that found in his other fiction."[85]

Brian Evenson, an imaginative novelist who sustained a decade-long correspondence with Purdy, views him as stylistically groundbreaking and severely underrated. A great stylist, Purdy "refused to keep writing the same book," so he lost an opportunity for "brand recognition" that some contemporaries enjoyed. Purdy "refused to pigeonhole himself" and "remained curious," forever "willing to try something new and go where his interests" carried him. Evenson is deeply inspired by Purdy's "ability to keep reinventing himself at the same time he was holding on to aspects of language and style that were so important." Purdy's manifest "pleasure of language" is "infectious."

Like many others, Evenson was introduced to Purdy's work by Gordon Lish, who edited one of his own books. In an interview and in his book on Raymond Carver, Evenson stresses the key role Lish played in spreading Purdy's influence, both explicitly, through teaching and recommending works, and implicitly, through his aggressive editing of several writers, not just Carver, using early Purdy stories as his guide "more than anyone else," as Lish told the *Paris Review*.[86] In 1992, Lish told Matthew Stadler, "I have around fifty writing students and every one of them reads Purdy. I make certain Purdy gets into their hands."[87] Therefore, Purdy is an uncredited cocreator of neo-minimalism, a dominant genre in US postmodern fiction.

Timed with the publication of *Gertrude of Stony Island Avenue*, *The Advocate*, the largest LGBTQ publication in America, sent novelist Robert Plunket to visit Purdy. He found Purdy was an "impeccably polite, neatly dressed man, thin as a rake, with big startled eyes." There was "something saintly about his persona—that is, until he opens his mouth. No saint was ever so tactless. Literature is holy ground to him, and woe to those who defile it." Purdy made hamburger out of "the establishment's sacred cows." James

Joyce was the "most boring writer in the world." Updike? "I hate him." 1950s classics *Lolita* and *The Catcher in the Rye* were the "golden turds of literature." Plunkett was optimistic about Purdy's enduring appeal, especially to a LGBTQ audience. Younger gay readers were discovering Purdy, with good reason: "His novels are timeless; even those set in an America that has long since disappeared are as relevant to the homosexual experience as anything being written today" and in his short stories, Purdy wrote overtly of contemporary gay experience.[88]

In fall 1998, Purdy worked on *All That Glitters*, another novel project that was never completed. Around this time, Purdy participated in an informal reading of "Dangerous Moonlight," a domestic one-act play in a rural setting, in which the husband Val Noble is a brutal Stanley Kowalski type. It was accompanied by "Down the Starry River," cowritten with John Uecker, which anticipates discussions of transgender identity and rights. Uecker said he wrote one scene because they were trying to get him into the Dramatists Guild. "River" focuses on Jack, a singer and drag performer who has an epiphany: he wants to wear dresses all the time, not only on stage. Jack is fired from his job at the Music Box club. The drama encircles black magic, curses, and spells to make time stand still.

In 1999, Chicago's Steppenwolf Theater Company staged director Jane Jones's adaptation of *In a Shallow Grave* after five months of workshopping. In 2001, her *Shallow Grave* was mounted by Book-It at Seattle Repertory Theater. Critic Joe Adcock wrote that Purdy's novel is obscure, but actor Stephen Hando took Garnet Montrose and created something lucid. Insightfully, he added: "Sometimes Purdy's obscurity reflects the impossibility in rural Virginia of dealing plainly with homosexual love. The characters flounder around in the veiled eroticism of Walt Whitman's Civil War writings. Wounds and illnesses allow men to touch and hold one another."[89] In a review, the lesbian novelist Rebecca Brown said Jane Jones wrote a "mature, nuanced, and very satisfying interpretation," and the production was a "valuable staging of an important and underappreciated American classic about the mystery of love and how it can redeem even the most wounded among us."[90]

Purdy's two novels published in the 1990s were not widely read or critically discussed, and at present remain neglected and due for rediscovery. Even when Purdy had been in vogue, however, he never had a bestseller, never enjoyed a big breakthrough. Nevertheless, as shown by film and stage adaptations of *In a Shallow Grave* and the opera made from *63: Dream Palace* by Hans-Jürgen von Bose, performed in Munich in 1990 and later shown on German television, Purdy's powerful stories inspired diverse and surprising forms and, most of all, found homes in the minds and hearts of a passionate group of readers.

19

The Acolytes

"Purdy's reputation has risen and fallen more than any other author still writing today," stated literary agent and editor Patrick Merla in 2000. As a new century drew near, younger writers were "eager to acknowledge their debt to this near-forgotten master." A prominent figure in the history of gay publishing, Merla edited three periodicals that featured, reviewed, and published Purdy's work: *Christopher Street*, *New York Native*, and *The James White Review*, named in honor of Purdy's poet friend who died in 1981. In 2000, Merla had *The James White Review* devote a special issue to James Purdy. It was guest-edited by novelist Matthew Stadler, who views the iconoclastic Purdy as a role model, and included an essay by him, a revealing interview between Purdy and the British scholar Richard Canning, several rare family photos, articles, and tributes.[1] The gay writers Scott Heim, Kevin Killian, Bruce Benderson, and Paul Lisicky paid homage, joined by Stacey Levine and Jonathan Letham, who had published *Motherless Brooklyn* the previous year. Kevin Killian noted a Promethean quality in his hero's work: "there's Aeschylus and then there's James Purdy." All of Killian's writing stemmed from Purdy's, he said. "He is to the novel what William Carlos Williams is to poetry—the seed, the source, the beginning of everything."[2]

Patrick Merla later reflected that Purdy "always had fierce advocates" who "went out of their way to help him," and surely the editor was among them. Purdy was fortunate to be surrounded by such "adoring acolytes." The writer and producer Douglas Blair Turnbaugh wondered at the tremendous output of anonymous letters that joins Purdy's published work. He learned from Purdy's example that "it need not be a tragedy if a writer lives for his writing, for if he takes such pleasure in it as James does, nothing else can compare." As for fringe benefits, James had "beautiful men clamoring to meet him, and love him. James did not write erotic poetry until late in his career, but now he relishes it." Despite Purdy's sustained anger at critics, his books were almost always well received, Merla remarked. Nonetheless, he remained "unsatisfied—that's the word for James Purdy." Purdy felt chronically wronged by publishers who failed to "promote his genius." He gained a reputation for being "very hard to work with" and was "infamous for turning on people." Merla cited Douglas Turnbaugh, who considered Purdy kin, as just one example. Likewise, Dennis Moore said Purdy "could switch on a dime."[3]

Despite his advanced age, Purdy was still writing, finishing past manuscripts with the encouragement of John Uecker as they planned a new Purdy collection. This collection would bring together the short stories that were published in magazines during the 1990s with the completed novella *Moe's Villa* that was a hit with his friends and admirers. Supplementing this material to fill out a book, Uecker helped Purdy comb through old story manuscripts in his filing cabinets. The best of them, such as "Easy Street," John "made" James revise or complete.

In this manner, they assembled an appealing collection full of the kind of Midwestern magic realism that Purdy was known for. But the stories also show that Purdy's imagination continued to expand as he ventured into new, more lighthearted areas. Nonetheless, Purdy's agent failed to find an American publisher, indicating the decline in his literary status. In 2000, *Moe's Villa & Other Stories* was published in Britain as a paperback original by Arcadia Books, a small independent press founded in 1996 by Gary Pulsifer, a gay American expatriate who for seven years had worked for Peter Owen, Purdy's prior British publisher. *Moe's Villa* had scant promotion, however, and British reviewers ignored it. Across the globe, in the *Courier-Mail* of Queensland, Australia, Graham Clark said the book offered "excellent reading" and the novella showed Purdy "at his best." Purdy "strips life to its barest essentials," then "lights the fuse." This is the only known review of the book's first edition.[4]

Contrasting the British non-reception, and despite the lack of US publication, in the weekly *New York Press*, editor and author John Strausbaugh celebrated Purdy's new British book. Purdy was writing a bit "more gently, if just as eccentrically" in his antiquated Midwestern terrains. What surprised Strausbaugh was Purdy's deft handling of "adult fairytales." The absence of this book in Purdy's home country was "nuts, but not unusual." *Moe's Villa* found no US publisher until 2004.[5]

The Antioch Review sustained their strong support and Purdy never complained of their editorial choices. In the summer of 2001, under the editorship of Robert Fogarty, the journal announced that Purdy, who had appeared in their 60th Anniversary Issue, was the first winner of the Lloyd Distinguished Fiction Award. In their winter 2001 issue, they ran "No

Stranger to Luke," which appeared in *Moe's Villa & Other Stories*. Drawing from an incident from Purdy's teenage years, this story centers on a mystery over money missing from the kitchen cabinet in Luke's home. Dan's resentment of what he perceives as Luke's and his mother's domestic bliss—even though they had to convert their fatherless home into boarding house—conveys a theme of the grass being greener on the other side of the fence. Late in life, Purdy recalled a "very handsome boy from Findlay," a "kleptomaniac" who used to visit when they were having supper. When his mother went to the kitchen and noticed something missing, she thought, "Daniel did that." In life and art, his name was Dan Schofield. "But she forgave and forgot, the end."[6] In 2002, *The Antioch Review* published the story "Easy Street," which somewhat recalls his early story "Eventide." The bustling activity of a movie filmed on location in New York disrupts the routine of Mother Green and Viola, two elderly black women living in a four-story brownstone, but they are befriended by a young actor with roots in the same part of Alabama as them. Then, a Ouija board adds some strangeness to the mix.

Hailing from Alabama, novelist and poet Kevin McGowin by late 2002 had served as Purdy's literary assistant on numerous playscripts. Purdy generously endorsed McGowin, who embraced the Internet as a publication medium, as "the Rabelais of his generation." In turn, McGowin said Purdy possessed the "most beautiful heart of any man" he ever knew. McGowin was a typewriter enthusiast and when he visited Purdy in 2002, he noted a busted Olivetti Lettera 32 on his desk. "I gave him mine." Purdy was not a Luddite but he preferred to compose on a typewriter and used them for his anonymous letters.[7]

In 2003, Dennis Moore flew to New York from Seattle to visit and was fascinated to watch Purdy work at close hand. Drafting *The Manse*, a novel project, James handed Dennis "freshly typed pages from each day" to read aloud to him. Purdy struggled with the dialect of black characters who had been imprisoned and was not sure if he could write it. Related to *The Manse*, he often spoke of a haunted building on Poplar Street, Brooklyn, that had been an orphans' home for boys, and included this on a literary walking tour he took his neighbor, Philip F. Clark, on in the 1970s. Moore noted that James was always in a good mood—if he had been out, if he had been to his favorite deli (Lassen & Hennigs), and if people in the neighborhood recognized or greeted him. Moore shared simple meals with him in his apartment. He gained insight into where "fact and fiction merge into one, in a world" that came to resemble a story. After returning to Seattle, Moore experienced an epiphany: James's "life is just like a Purdy story."[8]

Purdy's devotees were spread as far as Australia, and in his home country, he was again recognized by the academy after much scholarly neglect. In February 2003, Lindzee Smith directed *What Is It, Zach? and Daddy Wolf*, two offspring of his "long love affair with Purdy's writing," theater critic Kate Herbert wrote in the *Melbourne Sun*. Purdy's narrative threads encapsulated keen feelings of "deprivation, loneliness and loss."[9] In October, the first academic conference dedicated to Purdy took place at the University of Massachusetts Amherst, convened by Joseph T. Skerrett Jr. Purdy had not been a common subject of academic study since the mid-1970s, and these advocates sought to change this. The conference opened with a dramatic reading of Purdy's short play "Dangerous Moonlight" directed by Michael Bennett. Matthew Stadler and professors Christopher Lane, Martin Kich, and Don Adams all participated in the gathering. Purdy did not appear and expressed reservations about such scholarly events, but was interested to receive regular reports on the phone from his young actor friend, Roman Marocco.

Along with this show of academic interest, things were looking up on the publishing front. Donald Weise, senior editor with Carroll & Graf, signed James Purdy in a trade paperback deal, making his works available to a new generation. A key behind-the-scenes figure in gay publishing, Donald Weise worked with many esteemed gay authors including Gore Vidal, Edward Albee, John Rechy, Edmund White, Dennis Cooper, and Samuel R. Delaney. In August 2004, Carrol & Graf gave *Moe's Villa & Other Stories* a home in the United States, with cover endorsements by John Waters and Matthew Stadler. John Waters called *Moe's Villa* "as deep as the word eternity itself. Such stirring fairy tales for both the innocent and the depraved. Truly one of Purdy's best books." Stadler admired Purdy "above all other living writers" and *Moe's Villa* presents the gamut of "this astonishing writer's gift." What few reviews the book garnered were positive. In the *Lambda Book Report*, author Thom Nickels said Purdy, the possessor of "a strange and individual talent," tells tales of love and obsession in a simple style, resembling "twisted adult fairy tale versions of Thornton Wilder's *Our Town*." Art critic Donna Seaman said "Purdy's fables exert a strange fascination." *Publishers Weekly* said the collection is a "gratifying mix" brimming with jewels, songs, grandmothers, and wills—"the stuff of an old storyteller's magic." *Kirkus Reviews* declared these stories "amply justify Purdy's reputation as a cult hero who's slowly (and be-latedly) stepping into the light of day."[10]

Three more reissues with eye-catching cover designs ensued from Carroll & Graf. Beginning in November 2004, new readers met *Eustace Chisholm and the Works*. March 2005 brought the first ever US paperback of *The House of the Solitary Maggot*. July brought *Narrow Rooms* and December *Jeremy's Version*. The lives of these new editions were cut short due to publishing industry consolidations, however. In January 2007, Perseus Books Group purchased Avalon, the parent company of Carrol & Graf, and in May, they suddenly "terminated" the publisher founded in 1982, and these reissues fell out of print. Looking back, Don Weise wondered over "the magic of Purdy—he's an alien among his generation of the postwar years, where he's not a Beat, and he's not in that Capote-Vidal-Tennessee Williams circle—he's kind of out on his own, doing this outlaw fiction that I've never seen anything quite like."[11]

Working with Purdy, Donald Weise developed a "special fondness" for him unlike any he had felt for a writer. So it was that on two Christmas Eves, Don journeyed from the Upper West Side to Brooklyn Heights, bringing groceries and greetings, he writes in "Christmas with James Purdy." Weise said entering the apartment was like "a door opening to the past." The scene could have taken place three or four decades earlier. The radio often played classical music.[12] On first meeting Purdy, Weise was delighted to learn that a writer whose works could be "so withering and caustic and dark could personally be so warm and inviting." Slim and lightweight, Purdy was "ba-sically cooped up" in his studio apartment. "He seldom left home, even if he ran out of food, which is why groceries were appreciated." Weise sat with him, hearkening to stories from a half-century of writing, until Purdy's "de-voted friend and all-around literary champion, John Uecker, would arrive to spend Christmas with him." Uecker was Purdy's "conduit to the outside world, and he cared for his well-being as if Purdy were his own father. Better, probably."[13] Weise was given a key to the front door and visited regularly, rations in tow. Purdy would lay out cookies, but Weise never actually saw James eat at home, and there was scant evidence of meals having been pre-pared or consumed. Purdy made trips to Manhattan for doctor and den-tist appointments, and he went out for haircuts,[14] but otherwise, he mainly stayed inside, using binoculars to gaze out his window to the street below or perhaps into windows opposite. James was frail and physically feeble, but mentally keen and alert.

Regardless of the adoration he received from gay writers, Purdy still failed to understand why "anyone would call themselves a gay novelist," even though he "was in fact gay and a novelist who wrote prominently about gay subjects." Whether Purdy "adored or despised someone," Weise wrote, he was "such a fascinating raconteur—particularly if he *did* dislike someone—that I could've listened to him all night."[15] Purdy had "a coyness about him." He giggled, almost "like a little kid," which was endearing.[16]

In late 2004, Purdy, age ninety, continued to build "The Manse," which still had a ways to go. In late 2005, he said the story, alternately titled "Mrs. Harrington and the Manse," is about a rich small-town woman who wants to be a preacher and succeeds only too well.[17] Purdy again drew from Bowling Green matriarch Mrs. Belle Harrington, who reigned from her Victorian manse complete with trumpet vines. "The Manse" was never completed.

A British author, Martin Goodman, interviewed James in November 2004 and noted the effects of advanced age. "At 116 pounds, his nerves sustain as well as bedevil him." Purdy had just been released from the hospital with high blood pressure. George W. Bush had just been re-elected, an election Purdy found hard to take, having opposed the war in Iraq. America made Purdy nervous since it was "all lies" and "totally lost."[18]

In December, Michael Ehrhardt commenced a series of interviews. Despite Purdy's "crabapple appearance," he embodied "Old World politeness: tall and greyhound thin, with quick, playful blue eyes and a head of unruly silver hair" that sometimes resembled "the sprightly crest of an exotic bird." Because the building owner never installed an intercom or buzzer, Purdy had to wend his way down two tightly twisting flights of stairs to admit visitors. James seemed courtly in a cardigan, English-style boots, and a subtle scent of Pinaud cologne. An elegant herringbone hat sat on a hallway table. Inside the small studio apartment were displayed vintage lithographs of nineteenth-century pugilists and a photo of Edith Sitwell on the Federal-style mantelpiece, gazing out with the "imperious glance of Minerva." On the wall above hung an oil painting of a young man who could have been Malcolm: Purdy in his twenties, as seen by Gertrude Abercrombie in an uncharacteristically realistic work. In 2013, it was used on the cover of *The Complete Short Stories of James Purdy*, published by Norton/Liveright.[19] Purdy, a "gracious host who exudes Golden Age civility," rarely left his own neighborhood. The city had "become very daunting" and subways felt "very sinister."[20]

During Purdy's last decade, he developed a "circle of acolytes not best interested in promoting his reputation," Andrew Male wrote in *The Guardian*.

Figure 19.1 Purdy's dresser and hats. Photo by the author.

Richard Canning said such followers believed in "alchemy and secret genealogies." The Englishman would call Purdy's apartment but unknown persons would answer, saying James was not in, which was highly improbable. Some friends worried over him, but "he always loved being on the wrong side of the tracks."[21] Two acolytes, the emerging scholar John Hanshe and his friend, Pennsylvanian actor Roman Marocco, who played a role in Purdy's *Foment*, were during the early 2000s drawn more deeply into the Purdy circle. John Uecker had hired Marocco to assist Purdy in daily life. Roman was "really sweet" and loved Purdy, Dennis Moore said. Roman's mother Nancy liked James so much, she offered to move him into their home outside Pittsburgh, but James decided against it.[22] Of this time, during which Uecker saw Purdy less often than before, he wrote, "I'm not a caregiver with no other interests for ten years. I needed to save myself for the end. That's what people do. James was fully aware of this." So, he hired others to assist. "God I was getting into such trouble without a REAL agency. He wanted people he could be friends with and so I found them for him," but this led to "fallout."[23] Roman and James enjoyed talks over lunch, but Roman was apparently impractical. Mold grew "halfway up the refrigerator" and moths lived in the closet. Roman just ordered food, ate, and talked. Purdy was fond of him. "After paying for Roman," James "didn't want to hire anyone else for other things." James was happy, but his apartment got out of control. Moore's report to John of filthy conditions was used as a reason to fire Roman, which Moore regretted since it "broke James's heart."[24] Moore was only concerned that James have decent living conditions.

Through Roman Marocco, John Hanshe, a young intellectual and writer later styling himself as Rainer J. Hanshe, and Loretta Burns, a high school teacher, met and befriended Purdy. They visited, had long conversations, and James grew especially fond of Loretta, who taught his stories. Jason Hale said Hanshe became "pretty close with James but he started to get too close in a way that started to upset John." Hanshe tried "to become like an assistant to James like John Uecker, which is just impossible to do, but Hanshe seemed pretty determined to do it." "He was mirroring me," Uecker levied. Inevitably, there was a "big falling out" and James told Hanshe to stop visiting. Hale did not know if Uecker had requested that, but certainly James did not want anyone placing obstacles "in the way of his relationship with John."[25]

Hanshe decided he would organize a James Purdy tribute event to be hosted by The New School for Social Research. Though Hanshe was cut off from visiting, he seemed to be the "only mover" at this time promoting Purdy's career, said Bill Troop, a devoted friend. Hanshe had good intentions but his plan led to conflict. His strategy was to focus on celebrities—Edward Albee, Susan Sontag, and Gloria Vanderbilt. But, Uecker alleged, Hanshe and the New School did not properly approach Purdy about the event. Purdy felt such poor communication and failure to ask permission to perform his work were disrespectful. "I felt like I was a living ghost," Purdy said.[26] The New School sent four people to Purdy's agent, Uecker said, but no one phoned James or John, or "introduced themselves and spoke to him like a person. And artist." Instead, they treated him "like a child. Or not all there. This really hurt him. He wrote a letter to Gloria and she believed it. Albee didn't believe him."[27] Purdy was not a huge fan of the New School's socialist vibe to begin with, or their cavalier insistence that their plans were protected per fair use copyright law. The final straw, Uecker said, was an ad announcing a performance of a Purdy work, which provided legal grounds to halt the homage. In August 2004, Purdy wrote Vanderbilt in longhand:

> I am distraught over the Homage. The gentleman who initiated the Homage at no time got in touch with me about his plans to present my work to a

public performance! This same gentleman has been known to engage in un-professional activities. I am also worried that this same person may involve you and other friends of mine in activities about which I have no knowledge, and over which I did not give him permission or approval, and certainly I would never appear personally in such activities. I hope his speaking to you did not occur you to think I authorized him or to believe the so called Homage came from my knowledge or participation in his plans."[28]

Thus Hanshe went from being an acolyte to being excommunicated.

In Holland, another zealous acolyte was left out in the cold. In 2004, Jan Erik Bouman published *The Blue House: Forbidden Poems*, twenty-one uncollected Purdy poems in a very limited, numbered and signed edition, with his own Utrecht press, Hugin & Munin. The subtitle and Purdy's lack of response to this arcane book suggest that Bouman had not been granted formal permission to publish it, even though Purdy reluctantly signed them. In August 2005, Bouman had still received no reply from James to his letters about the book and his feelings were hurt. Jan Erik and James had once been very close, but now, Purdy's "hostile non reaction" almost blew him away. "The pain. Again I wrote a long letter without getting any answer. So it is quite dark now, between us." Moore was kind: "Most people will never know of your level of devotion to James. I want you to know I cherish our being in contact and that I will never forget about all you have done for James and his work." Jan Erik appreciated this since he was "consumed by a chronic depression" that made everything he did "very heavy."[29]

Purdy's mood improved in February 2005, when Gore Vidal published "James Purdy: The Novelist as Outlaw" in the *New York Times*, praising him and *Moe's Villa & Other Stories* and reviewing his career. Paul Theroux noted that in the 1970s and 1980s, Vidal corresponded with Paul Bowles about Purdy, who bears the "distinction of having shocked both writers—quite a feat."[30] In a memoir, *Point to Point Navigation*, Vidal pores over a stack of Purdy books on his desk, "wondering why so unique a writer has been so ignored." In 1978, he called Purdy "an authentic American genius." Now, he argued Purdy should not be ghettoized as a "gay writer" but rather "placed alongside William Faulkner." Shrewdly, unlike most critics, Vidal noted the evolution across Purdy's work. Although Purdy "never abandons for long his 'Malcolm' characters—those lost or losing golden ephebes at large in some alien city or sleepwalking through moon-crowned countryside—as he himself ages, he often deals with the old and their sometimes disconcerting wiles." Thus, Vidal, nearly eighty himself, found "Reaching Rose" the "finest and strangest" story in the collection.[31]

Purdy earned more recognition in November when he received the Mercantile Library's Clifton Fadiman Award for Excellence in Fiction—given to a great American novel that was overlooked or due for a revival—for *Eustace Chisholm and the Works*. He was nominated by Jonathan Franzen, who read the novel at Paula Fox's urging.[32] Donald Weise, who accompanied Purdy to the ceremony, said he shone that night. "I had never seen him more dapper or dashing in a tie, tan coat, and hat." He had never seen Purdy outside his apartment and did not know the last time he had left his neighborhood, so the "anticipation of the night ahead" as they "crossed the Manhattan Bridge into the City was almost out of *Sunset Boulevard*. Here was the elite New York literary establishment sending for one of its old, 'forgotten,' as the *Times* would have it, writers." At the Italian palazzo-style clubhouse of the Century Association, James seemed "taller than ever before."[33] Jonathan Franzen hymned the power of *Eustace*—reprinted as "Love Letters" in Franzen's essay collection *Farther Away*—and presented the award to James, who remained seated. Although Purdy seemed unaware of Franzen's high literary status, *The Corrections* later sat on his bookshelf. He was "flabbergasted" they chose to honor him for *Eustace Chisholm*, "of all things!" "The critics stoned me alive when it first came out. Some people didn't think I'd ever be published again." Purdy was quite moved when Franzen walked to the back of the dining room and crouched down by his chair to talk and pose for photos.[34]

Behind the scenes, trouble was brewing in the Purdy circle, and accusations of impropriety emerged. At a certain juncture, financial data in the files of the Running Sun Theater Company office became known to Dennis Moore, raising concerns and suspicions about John Uecker, who was managing Purdy's affairs. As it turned out, Purdy had a great deal of money in multiple accounts but he always "cried poormouth," as Thomson and Moore said.[35] Friends worried over how James ate and paid rent.[36] "James was playing me," said Moore, who had mailed the author drawing pads, believing him destitute. Purdy, who sometimes complained he could not pay rent, "acted poor when he had a million dollars."[37] Among other expenditures, Moore noticed a pattern of regular $600 withdrawals that eroded Purdy's savings. More than that, millions of dollars "evaporated in about a year's time," Moore claimed, probably an exaggeration. Uecker, disputing Moore's claims and credibility, said that Purdy never had more than $800,000 in the bank. Bill Troop says that Purdy at some point split his estate in half with John, and when he died, John was left with 1.5 million dollars in holdings. Moore's inquiries triggered his expulsion from the circle. "I was run out of New York City; I even thought of suicide."[38] He shared his concerns with others who had been close to Purdy. In August 2005, Moore told Hanshe: "I actually became part of *this* story—and guess I still am. Unfortunately it is one that breaks my heart, yet at the same time seems so natural, almost like destiny." Moore referred to a "long stream of bodies that precede us," the "emotionally damaged."[39] John Uecker charged that later, Richard Hundley, Dennis Moore and John Hanshe, supported by Edward Albee, tried to wrest control of the Purdy estate from him. Troop confirms that Moore tried "to cook something up" with Hundley to remove John from managing Purdy's affairs. But Bill understood that John was clearly James's designated partner, so he stopped supporting Dennis at this point. Before Moore died, he revealed that Hanshe had given him Albee's lawyer's name and phone number to use in case of emergency.[40]

After Moore reflected on his and others' experiences, he found "the 'mystery' had in some ways deepened. The edges I have glimpsed have really only given me some insight to James's artist vision." As he connected to an increasing number of people who had "known James and/or been a part of the choir visible," the mystery of Purdy only further grew. It was "an intoxicating world to be sure," but one he found "way too intense—where everything can change on a WORD—just like in a Purdy novel." Hearing the stories of Roman Marocco, Kevin McGowin, and Jan Erik Bouman allowed him "not to take any of it too personal—whether from James or John." He found it hard to keep a "proper perspective within this protracted dream." It was "all very strange" that he had so much contact with people who knew James but, for various reasons, were no longer in his life. Likewise, Matthew Stadler, who had devoted so much time and energy to understanding and promoting the work of James Purdy, was barred from seeing his friend and role model after 2003 because "John convinced him I was ungrateful or destructive, or something" else he was never sure of.[41]

One who remained on the inside of Purdy's circle was Bill Troop. During Purdy's later years, Troop in London took dictation over the telephone, recording some of Purdy's wild tales and satires. A photographer and writer who had also lived in Manhattan, he became a Purdy aficionado and visited him in the early 2000s. Troop's friends in England formed a coterie of Purdy advocates, evidencing the small but intense followings he had accrued internationally. The memoirist and peace activist Robin Prising and his life partner, poet William Leo Coakley, introduced Troop to Purdy's work; they had founded Helikon Press to publish British poets like Thom Gunn, who admired Purdy's writing. After many years of urging Troop to read Purdy, they mailed him a copy of *I Am Elijah Thrush*—and Bill was enraptured. He rang up Purdy and told him that with his book of *Elijah*, he had "extinguished all of twentieth century fiction." Naturally James liked that, Troop said, because he was a destroyer; he wanted the reader to find anything else deficient after reading him.[42]

Bill Troop did a lot of thinking about Purdy, his work, and his relation to John Uecker. James, the "child of a narcissistic mother," was "above all, a voyeur, of everything, at all times." The novel *In the Hollow of His Hand* indicates that Purdy wanted a son; Troop saw Uecker in the character of Chad Coultas, who is claimed by his Ojibwe father. John was the Jungian archetype *puer aeternus*, the eternal boy like Peter Pan. He was deeply frustrated and hurt by Purdy's stinginess in giving credit to those who had helped or influenced him, especially any living writer. This resentment came to a head in the mid-2000s, after Uecker had provided great assistance with Purdy's last two book manuscripts, *Gertrude of Stony Island Avenue* and *Moe's Villa & Other Stories*. "James would never give John credit," Troop said. "James was too narcissistic. He gave no credit." At other times, though, he "should have kept his mouth shut. James was his own worst enemy."[43]

Special recognition of John Uecker's loyalty came with the dedication in the US edition of *Moe's Villa & Other Stories*: "I would like to pay tribute to John Uecker, whose creative editorial support over many years has made this collection possible." Albeit this was done grudgingly, after Uecker's bibliophile friend John Wronoski told James that John deserved more acknowledgment than just a simple dedication.[44] A rare book dealer, Wronoski ("Duck") was hired by Uecker to review and catalog Purdy's manuscripts and letters. He and his partner, the transgressive artist Heide Hatry, would visit and Heide would keep Purdy company while Wronoski catalogued the papers. Purdy grew fond of Hatry, who recalled that he would become childlike at times, stretching out his legs and giggling. Nevertheless, in late 2005, Uecker's wound was ripped open when Hillel Italie interviewed Purdy at home for an AP feature. When asked if he had help with his books, Purdy said in front of Uecker that he did everything himself. Purdy's reply was not included in the story; nevertheless, Uecker was hurt and "shocked" that James would "lie so boldly." "After that, I wasn't around too much." "At a certain point," Moore said, "John didn't want to do the adult care."[45]

John Uecker therefore hired a young friend of his from Kansas to assist James. But personal and professional lines blurred. In 2008, Purdy told J. W. McCormack, neighbor and amanuensis, that "a young man from Kansas fell in with JT Uecker" and he "could not get enough of JT's beauty and cleverness." The Kansan became "one of the countless numbers of young gay men who inherited the terrible malady then so prevalent with those who thirsted for love at the expense of their own health. JT was then driven to accept the youth from Kansas who turned everything around and gave him the hex as thanks. Having the hex on both of them then, they decided without knowing it to be twins of evil."[46] Dennis Moore revealed, "John found out he had HIV and went crazy with drugs." Bill Troop corroborated that Uecker became a "crystal meth-head." John and his "errand boy" smoked meth and crack, and became habitues of New York's dark "underground nightlife," Moore claimed, recalling a night when Uecker took him to a "rough trade" bar where most patrons were decked out in leather from head to toe. Purdy's largesse funded drug binges and spending sprees. With a "craving for companionship," James was "ruinously generous," Troop remarked. Calling it "expenses for the office," Uecker and his young friend lived the "high life" on Purdy's dime, Moore charged.[47] Uecker questioned Moore's discernment, yet never questioned his love for James.

In early 2006, Purdy took a fall down the steep, winding stairs of his building. He assured friends he was fine. At some point, John used an agency to hire a young man from Haiti to provide more help, who was replaced by Jean, a woman of Jamaican origin. These were professional caregivers, as opposed to acolytes who tried to fill both professional and literary roles. Dennis said Jean took care of James, fed him well, and made sure he had quality food in the fridge. For a while, "James liked her" and "she came to love James."[48]

In 2007, there arrived a crisis in James Purdy's affairs, Troop and Moore said. His bank accounts were frozen and James called Moore complaining that he could not access his account, and his rent check bounced.[49]

In March 2008, Troop and his wife Elspeth Barker, a Scottish journalist and author of the novel O Caledonia (1991), flew to New York to spend a week and check in on Purdy's situation. They found things had returned to an even keel. Purdy was doing calisthenics under Uecker's direction and Troop noted his tallness as they waited for him to finish. Then James stretched out on his bed and Elspeth sat down next to him.

"I am The Lady of the Lake, James," she declared, alluding to Walter Scott's poem, holding out both hands to the elder writer.

"Oh, I know that. A bird visited me this morning and gave me the low-down on you. He's been watching you for some time now, day and night, and knows all you do," he replied cryptically. "A raven, black as your locks."

"What a daunting old seer," Elspeth said when they were back out on the street. "I almost expected him to speak Ancient Greek." Troop thought this was "the highest compliment she could pay."[50]

The writer J. W. McCormack, who lived around the corner on Montague Street, visited regularly in 2008 to take dictation from Purdy. McCormack also read to him and kept him company. "Frighteningly lucid, congenitally heteroclite, and partial to marigolds, Purdy was every bit the sweet melancholic Calvino recalled in his journals," McCormack wrote in *Tin House*. Brooklyn Heights had long since traded "temples to literary history for gentrified redundancy" but Purdy had not left his flat in years and seemed to believe he still lived on a "shady, criminal block." As amanuensis, McCormack's oddest and most secretive job was "mailing, and sometimes acting as proxy author of," anonymous letters. Purdy moreover dictated memoirs, sketches, and aperçus.[51] His favorite maxim: "To see you is to adore you, but to hold you is divine."[52] "I was so young that I didn't appreciate how strange and tender our acquaintance really was (he usually remembered who I was)," McCormack said, indicating Purdy's occasional memory issues then. "It was strange because on one hand, he was this ancient old man who thought the Jamaican caregiver was stealing from him, but on the other, it was James Fucking Purdy and he would snap to often times and rattle off these amazing remembrances and maxims." One time, McCormack read "Sleep Tight" to its author, who did not care for the story nor could he remember having written it. Physically, he was grotesque, with visible herpes, and "looked like a dead body," perhaps reminiscent of the wounded veteran Garnet Montrose in *In a Shallow Grave*. Yet McCormack understood he was "in the presence of genius."[53] When he read *In a Shallow Grave*, he was stunned because it mirrored his current scenario with Purdy: "I was reading my own life. It was exactly what I was doing."[54]

James's younger brother Robert L. Purdy died in November 2008 at age eighty-seven, a citizen much honored by his community of Berea, Ohio. Though Bob was the last member of James's immediate family, he and James had not been in close contact. Around 1990, James sent Bob a postcard replying to a genealogical query Bob had made as he researched their family background. Sadly, James and Bob, a high school athletic director, never developed a great brotherly love. His obituaries mentioned his many professional and civic honors—but not that he was survived by novelist James Purdy or predeceased by actor Richard Purdy.[55]

Drawing from his family background in the farm country of Ohio, Purdy's plays were collected in 2009 by Ivan R. Dee of Chicago. *Selected Plays*, his first American play collection, demonstrates his remarkable dramatic talent. Edward Albee gave an ambiguous blurb: "Purdy's plays have much of the exciting existentiality that infuses his novels and seem content to take drama to interesting places it does not always want to go." The plays were "developed, assembled, and edited" by John Uecker "in close association" with Purdy. Uecker credited the journalist and media producer Ian McGrady, J. W. McCormack, and acting coach Susan Aston for "additional editorial assistance." Early on, Northwestern University professor Christopher Lane and later, Bill Troop were uncredited editors. Drama critic Michael Feingold had written in 2000 that because Purdy's plays are unconventional and highly character-based, they remain "so many sleeping beauties, waiting for the prince of some future civilization to come and kiss them into theatrical life."[56] Debuting in print were *Brice*, Purdy's autobiographical family play that is his finest dramatic work, but was never produced, and *Where Quentin Goes*. At the end of the latter play, Endors tells Quentin: "Everything is change in this life. And change is very painful. The more we try to hold onto love, the more it seems to elude our grasp." More hopefully: "There is always something else waiting for us, Quentin, if we will only seek it." This collection, though poignant and historic, does not seem to have garnered any substantial reviews. In 2019, *The Paradise Circus* was finally given a production, at London's Playground Theatre, directed by Anthony Biggs and starring Sophie Ward, earning many compliments.

In November 2008, because of his weakening health, a decision was made that James would be moved from his apartment on Henry Street into the Lillian Booth Actors home of The Actors Fund, in Englewood, New Jersey. This was a difficult move since Purdy had lived at Henry Street for nearly fifty years and would have rather stayed put. Purdy started out living in his own apartment and was later moved to assisted living. It was a poor scenario in assisted living because his roommate could not speak, write, or move, so if something happened to James, he could not call for help or serve as a witness. Friends who came to visit, such as John Wronoski and J. W. McCormack, described the atmosphere as bleak and institutional.

In early March 2009, Purdy fell and fractured his hip and was placed in Englewood Hospital. John Uecker later blamed the doctor for the drugs he prescribed that affected his balance and accused a very tall and large assistant of clumsiness and negligence. Uecker alleged the assistant evasively told him that James "fell and might have sprained his arm," but he actually suffered "three big breaks in his leg. The guy sat on him."[57] J. W. McCormack visited him at this time, but Purdy confused him with, as he put it, "one of Uecker's crew of homosexual hustler freakazoids." James had a final phone call with Jorma Jules Sjoblom in Baltimore, in which they "declared their love for each other." Sjoblom had married a black Baltimorean woman and James was not happy he had turned his back on his gay identity for what seemed to him a marriage of convenience, but the love between them was eternal.[58]

On Friday the thirteenth of March 2009, James Purdy died at age ninety-four in Actor's Fund nursing home. In the last year of his life, J. W. McCormack said, "there was a verse that Master Purdy repeated," but he never asked from whence it derived. Later, he learned it was the final verse of Thomas Chatterton's "Minstrel's Song."[59] These were same lines Purdy had written on a copy of "Some of These Days" and given to Tennessee Williams, which was lying on the playwright's bed when his body was discovered by John Uecker.

Figure 19.2 James Purdy laughing during an interview in his apartment, August 2, 2005, by Bebeto Matthews. Courtesy of Associated Press.

> Water-witches, crowned with reytes,
> Bear me to your lethal tide.
> I die! I come! My true love waits. . . .
> Thus the damsel spake, and died.

"His attitude toward death was very casual," McCormack said. "He was ready to go anytime and envisioned it as a dirigible that would fly him away." He joked that Purdy probably "went to heaven bitching the whole way." Later, he mulled over what Purdy used to say: "Heaven is sending me somebody but I may not be here when they arrive."

"If I could have anything in this world," McCormack later wrote, "I wish I could spend just a few minutes with him in his prime. I saw flashes of brilliance and personality every day we spent together or talked on the phone, but I definitely understood that this was the last act."[60]

In 2005, Purdy was asked if he had enjoyed his life. He said: "I don't know about enjoy. I'd hate to live it over. Now there's all these problems with my health and no real money coming in. But I don't really care about that. I don't care that I'm not a money maker." That said, he had been fortunate to receive film option money, stock market tips, and patronage. He underscored his contrarian nature: "I don't think I'd like it if people liked me. I'd think that something had gone wrong."[61] Matthew Stadler likened Purdy to a high-stakes acrobat atop the highwire. He played the role of "the truth-teller, who is refused, a creation largely his own."[62] Back in 1960, Purdy was working through Edward Gibbon's six-volume *Decline and Fall of the Roman Empire* and he found that the footnotes, though challenging, were "most rewarding." He was encouraged by "the one where Gibbon says he has had a very happy life, for he has found his joy in his work."[63] Though happiness often eluded Purdy, he clearly found great joy in his work. Looking back, it might be said he was ultimately liberated to say and write whatever he saw fit. Although he was often displeased with how his work was published, promoted, or reviewed, he was fortunate to possess the freedom and the keen talent to reach so many people with his richly imaginative fiction, poems, plays, and letters.

"James is going to live on in his own funny way," remarked Donald Weise.

Acknowledgments

I am grateful to the following people who made this book possible.

My deep gratitude goes to Susan Ferber at Oxford University Press in New York for her longtime interest and belief in this project, her patience, her suggestions on structure, and for making countless improvements to the manuscript. Her specific queries prompted me to do additional research to fill in some gaps and cracks or to provide needed context. This book has benefitted greatly from her editorial guidance.

The Purdy family of northern Ohio, specifically James's sister-in-law, Dorothy Purdy, nephew John David (Dave) Purdy, and niece Christine Reese, have been generous in spending time and sharing memories and materials with me including a copy of Purdy's rare master's thesis. Many thanks to Dorothy and Dave for hosting me in 2009 and 2019. And thanks to Dave, especially for answering many follow-up questions. Sadly, I was not able to meet Robert (Bob) Purdy, James's younger brother, who died in 2008. James was not the only author in the Purdy family, as books published by Bob, Dorothy, and Dave demonstrate.

My most helpful contact throughout the project was John Uecker, partner and assistant to James, director of his plays, and a muse and catalyst of his drama and fiction. John passed away while this biography was in its final stages. John will always have my profound gratitude. Dating back to 2008, when I was completing my PhD dissertation on Purdy at the University of Oklahoma, John spent copious hours, even days, indefatigably talking with me on the phone and sometimes in person. Special occasions included American Literature Association meetings of the James Purdy Society, his hosting me at his apartment in Manhattan not long after Purdy's passing in 2009, and the burial ceremony of James Purdy ten years after his death, beside the grave of Dame Edith Sitwell in a small English village cemetery. The day after the mourners below laid his ashes to rest, John and I visited Purdy's site again after the others had left, a most cherished memory. I am also grateful to John in his role as the executor of the literary estate for granting permission to quote from Purdy's published and unpublished works and correspondence.

THE CHOIR INVISIBLE: I celebrate the memory of individuals who were, along with John Uecker, close with James Purdy, or tirelessly championed his work, with whom I spoke and who died during the writing process of this book. Chemist and librarian Jorma Jules Sjoblom, James's longtime partner and devoted lifelong friend, allowed me to interview him and spend time with him at his summer home in Ashtabula, Ohio. Richard Hundley, a composer of art songs who adapted many poems by his close friend, would ring me up and dramatically announce: "This, is Richard . . . *Hund*ley!" They also include my former jazz concert buddy, the much missed professor Joseph T. Skerrett; the Mohawk poet Maurice Kenny; Professor Jere Real; and Dennis Clay Moore of Seattle, who according to Uecker, "loved James the most." I spent time with Dennis at a number of events organized by the James Purdy Society, which he established and helped keep going, and we became friends. Paul W. Miller of Springfield, Ohio, a professor who published foundational biographical-critical articles, hosted me and shared insights. Professors Beth Casey, Wallace Pretzer, and Diane Pretzer of Bowling Green State University shared stories from their memories and local contacts.

In Purdy's hometown of Findlay, Ohio, Parker Chastaine Sams, former editor of the Findlay *Courier*, took an interest in Purdy's early biography. Thanks go to Parker for hosting me, showing me sites in Findlay, and sharing insights and materials, including articles, photos and letters from Purdy to him about his youth there.

I am grateful to many friends and supporters of James Purdy who took the time to speak to me in person, on the phone, or via videoconference. The gifted novelist Matthew Stadler, to whom Purdy was a role model and mentor, was most generous with his time, insights, and perspective as a literary artist. John Stewart Wynne, a writer and retired audiobook producer, has been most supportive and generous, as has his partner, Harold Dennis Schmidt, a literary agent. Professor Barry D. Horwitz and Michael Tillotson, a teacher, filled in gaps about Purdy's time in Berkeley. Chester Page, friend and neighbor to James in Brooklyn Heights, was enthusiastic and generous, helping to fill in the literary and cultural history of New York. Likewise, Professor Philip F. Clark, a neighbor of Purdy's in the 1970s, provided observations of James and John Uecker in their natural habitat. Tom Zulick lent insight into Purdy's spirituality. Bill Troop kindly hosted me in his London flat for an interview in 2019 and shared many insights then and over the telephone. Professor Jason Hale, who was a friend to James and John Uecker, and a student of John's, provided me with more understanding of their relationship. John Wronoski and his partner Heide Hatry gave me a glimpse into Purdy's last months living at home.

Writers, critics, agents, editors, and publishers helped me to understand Purdy within contexts and traditions of literary fiction, gay fiction, and the book trade. I am grateful to Gordon Lish, Katha Pollitt, Donald Weise, Patrick Merla, Jack Collins, Stephen D. Adams, Edmund White, Michael Carroll, David Breithaupt, Geoffrey Elborn, Brian Evenson, Jack Fritscher, Robert Sharrard, and W. Kenneth Holditch for their time and insights. Thanks to Professor Michael Nott for sharing documents about Purdy and poet Thom Gunn.

I am grateful to the composers Gerald Busby and Joseph Fennimore for sharing their witty anecdotes and insights about Purdy's links to the art music world, especially to the composers Virgil Thomson, Ned Rorem, Robert Helps, and Richard Hundley.

Shoutouts to some global 24-Hour Purdy People: Victoria Linchong, who produced Purdy's plays, promoted his work, and visited him; Dutch academic Looi Van Kessel, for carrying the Purdy torch to the next generation; and the brilliant English scholar Richard Canning, for his huge achievements in gay literary studies. All three attended Purdy's burial ceremony at Weedon Lois and the symposium at University of Northampton that Richard organized, as did Maria Cecilia Holt and Professor Charles Lock, who were key in arranging the ceremony with John Uecker and assisting the financing of Purdy's beautifully carved stone.

Special thanks go to the writer and editor J. W. McCormack, who was hired to transcribe material dictated by Purdy in 2008, for sharing the material and reflections on his experiences with Purdy going beyond his *Tin House* article.

I am especially grateful to David Kuebeck of Bowling Green, Ohio, who has done extensive research into *The Nephew* and its hometown roots. David has been kind and generous in supplying me with important pieces of data and photocopies of research and article draft material. A fellow Buckeye, David exemplifies what I think of as Ohio friendliness and pride of place.

Thanks to Megan Wheeler for photographing me.

I want to thank the dedicated librarians at the archives and special collections I visited over many years, and those who made duplications of documents for me, including the Harry Ransom Center at the University of Texas at Austin, the Beinecke Rare Book & Manuscript Library at Yale University, the Thompson Library at The Ohio State University, the Lilly Library at Indiana University Bloomington, Jerome Library at Bowling Green

State University, the University of Delaware, Temple University, University of Washington, Princeton University, the Bancroft Library at University of California, Berkeley, Kenneth Spencer Research Library at University of Kansas, Bizzell Library at the University of Oklahoma, Johnson Memorial Library in Hicksville, Ohio, and, at The New York Public Library, the Berg Collection and the Rare Book and Manuscript Library at the Stephen A. Schwarzman Building, and at the New York Library for the Performing Arts, the Music Division and the Billy Rose Theatre Division.

I wish to thank Dr. Roxanne Mountford, chair of the Department of English at University of Oklahoma for her support. Thanks to the Office of the Senior Vice President and Provost (then Kyle Harper) for the Presidential International Travel Fellowship that funded travel to England in 2019 for the burial ceremony. Enduring thanks to my University of Oklahoma dissertation committee of 2009: Timothy S. Murphy (chair), Ronald Schleifer, Craig S. Womack, Rita Keresztesi, and Julia Ehrhardt.

I thank the Andreas Foundation for a generous Research Grant in 2009.

Deep love and gratitude goes to my very own "Dibbs," Professor Pamela S. Stout, for her enduring support and editorial assistance.

I thank my family, who have listened to me talk about James Purdy for many years, especially my parents, Dr. Estel Eugene (Gene) Snyder and Christine Hadley Snyder of southwestern Ohio, for their longtime support. Thanks to Philip Snyder, plasma fusion scientist, and his wife, teacher Mary Snyder; and Timothy Snyder, author and Yale historian, for their support and conversation. Thanks especially to my sister-in-law, Marci Shore, author and Yale historian, for her insights into research and book publication. I thank my beloved daughters, Ivy and Cora, for their encouragement and patience.

Notes

Introduction

1. Purdy, "Remembrances/Memoir," in "Trick and Treat," dictated to J. W. McCormack, 2008.
2. Sitwell to Purdy, 20 Oct 1956, in *Edith Sitwell: Selected Letters*, ed. Lehmann and Parker, 206–7.
3. Sitwell to Purdy, 26 Nov 1956, in *Selected Letters of Edith Sitwell*, ed. Greene, 377–78.
4. Sitwell, "Under the Skin"; Sitwell to Sir Malcolm Bullock, 13 Oct 1959, *Selected Letters*, 241; Sitwell to Purdy, 28 July 1959, *Selected Letters*, 240 [blurb for *Malcolm*].
5. Max, "Carver Chronicles."
6. Baldanza, "James Purdy's Half-Orphans," 272; Qtd. in Schott, "James Purdy: American Dreams," 300.
7. Qtd. in Malin, "James (Otis) Purdy."
8. S. Adams, *James Purdy*, 113.
9. Lish, interview with Stadler, 9 April 1992, box 4, Article 1, MSP.
10. Television interview. Adriaan van Dis, Interviewer. *De IJsbreker*. Amsterdam: Dutch television, March 1990.
11. Purdy, "James Purdy," 304.
12. Sontag, "Laughter in the Dark," 5.
13. *On Glory's Course*, hardcover dust jacket.
14. Steiner, rev. of *Eustace Chisholm and the Works*, *Sunday Times*, qtd. in Purdy, "James Purdy," *Contemporary Authors Autobiography Series* [hereafter cited as *CAAS*], 303.
15. Tanner, "Birdsong," 609.
16. Michaud, "Strange, Unsettling Fiction of James Purdy."
17. Sjoblom, tel. interview, 25 May 2009.
18. Busby, tel. interview, 23 Feb 2020.
19. James Link, "James Purdy," 62.
20. Plunket, "The Visionary," 91.
21. Purdy, *Out with the Stars*, 147.
22. Reed, "The Greatest," *New York Times*, Nov 30, 1975.
23. Franzen, "Love Letters," 269.
24. Thanks to David Kuebeck of Bowling Green, Ohio, for pointing out Fremont's proximity to Clyde.
25. Would-be biographers have included professors Paul W. Miller, Dr. Larry Myers, and, after Purdy's death, Cory MacLauchlin.
26. Skerrett, "James Purdy and the Black Mask of Humanity," 81; Stadler, int. Purdy, b. 4. f. Art. 1, MSP.

27. Purdy, in Richard Canning, "James Purdy," *Gay Fiction Speaks: Conversations with Gay Novelists*, 32.

28. Weise, tel. interview, 1 Sep 2020.

29. Uecker, tel. interviews, 13 Oct, 26 Nov 2020.

Chapter 1

1. *Ojibwe* is also spelled Ojibwa, Ojibway, and another Anglicization is Chippewa; their Indigenous name is Anishinaabe. They reside across Ontario, Wisconsin, Minnesota, Michigan, and elsewhere. Around 1800, Ojibwe lived in northern Ohio.

2. Purdy, *Jeremy's Version*, 19.

3. Purdy, Autobiographical Statement, typescript, 1966, 1.3, HRC; Dorothy Purdy, personal interview, July 2009.

4. Woodhouse, "James Purdy (Re)visited," 17.

5. *Commemorative Historical and Biographical Record of Wood County, Ohio*, 187.

6. *Wood County*, 187.

7. Dorothy Purdy, personal interview, July 2009.

8. Purdy, Autobiographical Statement, typescript, 1.3, HRC; William Purdy to Purdy, 4 Oct 1965, Berg.

9. W. Purdy to Purdy, 10 Aug 1963, Berg.

10. W. Purdy to Purdy, 3 Sep 1959, Berg.

11. "Otis," *Tribune* [Hicksville, Ohio], Dec 24, 1908, 1.

12. *Commemorative Biographical Record of Northwestern Ohio*, 136–38.

13. Stadler, int. Purdy, 18 Mar 1992, b. 4, f. Art. 1, MSP.

14. "Cowhick," *Hicksville Tribune*, Oct 9, 1919, 2.

15. Shouf is alternately spelled Shoaf. Cowhick is pronounced "Co-wick."

16. "Cowhick," *Hicksville Tribune*, Oct 9, 1919, 2.

17. D. S. Cowhick's brother, O. F. Cowhick, lived in Cheyenne, Wyoming (*Hicksville News*, August 30, 1883); "Local Department," *Hicksville News*, July 13, 1882, 4.

18. *Hicksville News*, Jan 11, 1883, 4; July 12, 1883, 4.

19. *Hicksville News*, Apr 9, 1885, 4.

20. "Local and Miscellany," *Hicksville News*, Apr 23, 1885, 4; David McCullough, *The Wright Brothers* (New York: Simon & Schuster, 2015), 19-20.

21. "Otis," *Tribune* [Hicksville], Dec 24, 1908, 1.

22. *Commemorative Biographical Record*, 187.

23. "Cowhick," *Hicksville Tribune*, Oct 9, 1919, 2.

24. Purdy, "Fragments and Sayings," in "Trick and Treat," dictated to J. W. McCormack, 2008.

25. *Tribune* [Hicksville], June 26, 1913, 5; Otis, *Genealogical and Historical Memoir of the Otis Family in America*, 633; "Hicksville News," *Fort Wayne Daily News*, Nov 20, 1916, 11.

26. "Hicksville News," *Fort Wayne Sentinel*, Nov 6, 1918, 11; Lloyd and Barbara were divorced; he later married Elizabeth Daeblet.

27. Anderson, *Poor White*, 117–18.

28. US census, 1930, ancestry.com; "Ohio Oil Company," *American Oil & Gas Historical Society*, aoghs.org/stocks/ohio-oil-company/.

29. Humphrey, *Findlay*, 132, 86–100.

30. W. Purdy to Purdy, 19 Dec 1961, Berg.

31. US census, 1900, ancestry.com.

32. *Hicksville Centennial*, 27.

33. *Tribune* [Hicksville], Apr 18, 1907, 1.

34. "Masons Honor William Purdy with 50-Year Pin," *Defiance Crescent*, Jan 22, 1955, 2; *Defiance Democrat*, June 16, 1905, 2.

35. *Tribune*, July 11, 1907, 1.

36. *Tribune*, Jan 9, 1908, 1.

37. "Newsy Notes from the West End Town," *Defiance Democrat*, Dec 17, 1907.

38. *Defiance Crescent-News*, Jan 29, 1908, 2.

39. *Tribune*, Nov 5, 1908, 1; "Newsy News Notes from Hicksville," *Daily Crescent-News* [Defiance], Nov 11, 1908, 4.

40. "Newsy News Notes from Hicksville," *Daily Crescent-News*, Mar 4, 1909, 3.

41. *Tribune*, Dec 17, 1908, 4.

42. *Tribune*, July 15, 1909, 5.

43. *Defiance Democrat*, Aug 6, 1910, 6.

44. "Woman's Christian Temperance Union (Hicksville)," MMS 391, Bowling Green State University, Center for Archival Collections.

45. "Social," *Tribune*, Oct 28, 1911, 8.; "Hicksville News," *Fort Wayne Gazette*, May 19, 1916, 25.

46. "Mrs. J. K. Bauman Called by Death," Findlay *Courier*, Dec 15, 1962; Battershell, *Hicksville Centennial*, 26.

47. "Local and Personal," *Bryan Democrat*, June 28, 1910, 3; "Local News," *Democrat*, Sep 2, 1913: 4; "Personal Paragraphs," *Democrat*, Aug 20, 1912, 3.

48. "Daisy Viola Jones," *Nebraskana*, ed. Sara Baldwin and Robert Baldwin (Hebron, NE: 1932), 627.

49. *Tribune*, May 30, 1912; *Tribune*, Dec 18, 1913, 9.

50. "The New Bank," *Tribune*, Sep 12, 1912, 1.

51. *Tribune*, Sep 26, 1912, 1.

52. Battershell, *Hicksville Centennial*, 29; "Big Deal in Hicksville," *Fort Wayne Sentinel*, April 14, 1916, 8.

53. Baldanza, "Northern Gothic," 574; "Hicksville Plan O.K.'d," *Cincinnati Enquirer*, June 13, 1913, 3; "Ordinance no. 20," *Tribune*, July 31, 1913, 1.

54. "Letter to Public: Official Reply to Petitioners for Injunction," *Tribune* [Hicksville], June 26, 1913, 1; *Tribune*, May 21, 1914, 1.

55. Paul W. Miller, "James Purdy's Early Years in Ohio," 109.

56. Purdy, "Interview," int. by Morrow, 104.

57. "Worthy of Special Notice," *Fort Wayne News*, March 4, 1916, 18.

58. *Fort Wayne News*, April 10, 1916, 10.

59. "Hicksville News," *Fort Wayne Sentinel*, July 15, 1916, 5.

60. "Business Good," *Fort Wayne News,* March 16, 1917, 16; "Hicksville News," *Fort Wayne Gazette,* April 21, 1917, 11; "Hicksville News," *Fort Wayne Gazette,* Sep 8, 1917, 12; "Factory Men Reorganize their Plant on New Basis," *Fort Wayne Gazette,* Dec 18, 1918, 14.
61. "Suit at Hicksville May Open Political Graves," *Fort Wayne Sentinel,* Sep 11, 1918, 9.
62. "Bonds Placed and Street Improvements Will Go Right Along," *Tribune* [Hicksville], Sep 10, 1914, 1.
63. *Fort Wayne News,* June 24, 1919, 5; "Old Case Settled," *Fort Wayne Sentinel,* Mar 19, 1920, 12; "State Upholds Defiance Court," *Defiance Democrat,* Nov 26, 1921, 1.

Chapter 2

1. "Hicksville News," *Fort Wayne Sentinel,* April 23, 1919, 17; Heminger, *Across the Years in Findlay,* 190. Thanks to David Kuebeck for informing me of the Purdys' first two residences on Lima Street.
2. Heminger, *Across the Years in Findlay,* 105–6, 133, 138–40, 143, 192; Brown, *History of Hancock County,* 197; Humphrey, *Findlay,* 205–6, 112, 170, 185.
3. James Purdy, tel. conversations with the author, 30 April 2008, 14 May 2008.
4. Purdy, tel. conversation, 14 May 2008.
5. Jeanie Wiley Wolf, "50 Years Ago: Palm Sunday Tornados Left Devastation," *Courier* [Findlay], April 11, 2015.
6. Van Renterghem, *Findlay in Vintage Postcards,* 47.
7. Heminger, *Findlay,* 143.
8. Humphrey, *Findlay,* 154.
9. Connie Barton, "Gilboa Physician Still on the Job Some 65 Years and 1,500 Babies after Starting," Findlay *Republican Courier* [Date unknown], 1961, 1; David Breithaupt, personal interview, July 2, 2019.
10. Purdy to Parker Sams, 9 Feb 1985, Sams personal collection.
11. Purdy to Sams, 9 Aug 1984, Sams collection.
12. Barton, "Gilboa Physician"; Purdy, "Interview with James Purdy," int. Real, 27. Dr. Ray's tragic story became the basis of the play "Ruthanna Elder," which had been related briefly by wise old Dr. Ulric in the novel *Narrow Rooms.*
13. "Miss Nell Baker Dies at Gilboa," *Republican-Courier* [Findlay], Jan 14, 1936; Humphrey, *Findlay,* 154; Jenne Cairns, "Not Just Thursdays: How the Women's Clubs Impacted Findlay," lecture, Nov 5, 2020, Hancock Historical Society.
14. Humphrey, *Findlay,* 154.
15. Canning, *Gay Fiction Speaks,* 6–7.
16. "Sugar Beet Production in Northwestern Ohio."
17. Findlay High School yearbook, 1925, n.p.
18. Dorothy Purdy, personal interview, 2 July 2019.
19. David Purdy and Dorothy Purdy, interview, July 2009.
20. "James Purdy Interviewed by Don Swaim, 7 Dec 1989."

21. Purdy, "James Purdy," *CAAS*, 299–300.

22. Qtd. in Aletti, "American Gothic," 18. Ellipsis in original.

23. Canning, *Gay Fiction Speaks*, 28.

24. Heminger, *Findlay*, 83.

25. Purdy, "Interview with James Purdy," int. Gavron 1; Purdy, "Interview," int. Morrow, 97.

26. Purdy to Sams, 9 Feb 1985, collection of Sams.

27. Purdy, handwritten "Autobiographical Statement," 1.3, HRC.

28. Purdy, "Trick and Treat"; Sams, "Purdy's Latest Novel Set in His Hometown Findlay."

29. "Miss Ada Lee Coe Taken by Death," *Republican-Courier*, Jan 11, 1943.

30. "Hold Pupils Recital" [*sic*], *Morning Republican*, June 25, 1926, 6.

31. Parker Sams to Purdy, 2 Jan 1985, 3.27, OSU.3.

32. Troop, tel. interview, 18 Mar 2022; Purdy, "Interview," int. Morrow, 108.

33. Personal interview with Dorothy Purdy, David Purdy, and Christine Purdy, July 2009; "Gas Kills Banker," *Defiance Crescent*, Aug 14, 1930, 4.

34. Minniebelle Conley, "Purdy, Active in Business at 84, Praised at Meeting," *Bowling Green Sentinel*, Nov 14, 1961, 1.

35. Humphrey, *Findlay*, 206.

36. "Clues in Brutal Killing of Local Man Are Meager," *Morning Republican*, Jan 16, 1928, 1–2. Thanks to Parker Sams, retired journalist and editor, for sharing this article and others from microfilmed archives of Findlay newspapers.

37. "Pay Tribute to Ol' Sam," *Morning Republican*, Jan 16, 1928, 1–2; "Clues in Brutal Killing," *Morning Republican*, Jan 16, 1928, 1–2.

38. *Lima News* [Ohio], May 12, 1928, 2.

39. "Two Youths Admit Murder of Recluse," *Beacon Journal* [Akron], May 7, 1928, 7.

40. "Not Guilty Is Plea of Youths," *News-Journal* [Mansfield], May 13, 1928, 1; "Half Brothers Indicted for Murdering Man," *Tribune* [Coshocton], May 13, 1928.

41. "Convict Dead, Two at Large after Break," [Circleville] *Herald*, Nov 5, 1929, 1.

42. Purdy, "Out with James Purdy," int. Lane, 73; Purdy to Sams, 15 Dec 1984, collection of Sams.

43. U.S. census, 1930, Ohio, Fairfield County, Hocking Township, District 12.

44. Purdy, "Remembrances/Memoir," in "Trick and Treat"; Van Renterghem, *Findlay in Vintage Postcards*, 67.

45. Purdy, "James Purdy," int. Barron, 92.

46. Humphrey, *Findlay*, 206–7.

47. Purdy to Sams, 9 Feb 1985, Sams collection.

48. Purdy, "James Purdy," int. Northouse, 186.

49. Purdy to Sams, 24 Aug 1984, Sams collection.

50. Findlay High School yearbook, 1922, 16.

51. Sams, "James Purdy's Latest Novel."

52. Varble, "I Am James Purdy," 29; Parker Sams to Purdy, 2 Jan 1985, 3.27, OSU.3.

53. Miller, *Dictionary*, 421–22; Dorothy Purdy, personal interview, July 2, 2019.

54. "Divorce Is Granted," *Morning Republican*, Aug 29, 1930, 2.

55. Thanks to David Kuebeck for alerting me to Will's objection and the source: Judgement Entry, Aug 28, 1930, *Case #22498, Vera C. Purdy, Plaintiff vs William Purdy, Defendant*, Hancock County Court of Common Pleas.

56. "Matthew Paris and Dave Zimmer Interview James Purdy."

57. Purdy, "Trick and Treat," dictated to McCormack.

58. Purdy, *Jeremy's Version*, 63–64.

59. Purdy, "Trick and Treat."

60. Uecker, tel. interview, July 1, 2010.

61. David Purdy, tel. interview, 8 Jan 2019.

62. Purdy, "Trick and Treat."

63. Purdy to Parker Sams, 24 Aug 1984, Sams collection.

64. "Clubs of Senior High Assemble," *Morning Republican*, 30 Nov 1931, 10; Findlay High School yearbook, 1932, 63.

65. "Poetry Contest Winners Named," *Findlay Republican-Courier*, Apr 25, 1932; Purdy to Sams, 2 Jan 1985, Sams private collection.

Chapter 3

1. Purdy, "James Purdy," 299. Thanks go to David Kuebeck of Bowling Green for sharing financial data he found on William and Cora Purdy.

2. "Mrs. B. W. Purdy Was a Pioneer" [obit. Catherine Purdy], *Sentinel-Tribune* Oct 15, 1932, 1+.

3. Purdy to Baldanza, 18 Aug 1971, BGSU.

4. H. B. Williams, "An Appeal to Loyalty," *Bee Gee News*, June 7, 1933, 4; "College of Education and Human Development: Our History," Bowling Green State University, archived by Wayback Machine on Oct 11, 2011, web.archive.org/web/20111011155259/http://www.bgsu.edu/colleges/edhd/page80935.html.

5. Purdy, "Tragic America," 3, 9, 15.

6. "Centennial Perspectives: Unforgettable Faculty," *Archival Chronicle* [BGSU Libraries] 29, no. 1 (March 2010); "Collection Overview," Rea McCain Collection, Bowling Green State University Archives and Special Collections, https://lib.bgsu.edu/archives/repositories/4/resources/708.

7. "Bee Gee Players Present 'The Old Soak,'" *Bee Gee News*, Nov 14, 1934, 1.

8. "'St. Joan' Will Be Given Tonight," *Bee Gee News*, Jan 24, 1935, 1; "Bee Gee Players Give 'Joan of Arc,'" *Bee Gee News*, Feb 20, 1935, 5.

9. "Players Present 'Merchant of Venice,'" *Bee Gee News*, May 8, 1935, 1.

10. Email from Beth A. Casey to the author, 16 April 2009; Purdy, *Nephew*, 36–37, 47; Purdy, int. Lear, 72.

11. "Mrs. B. W. Purdy Was a Pioneer"; "Bowling Green," *Cincinnati Enquirer*, June 20, 1926, 90.

12. Diane Pretzer and Wally Pretzer, email to the author, 30 Apr 2009; Miller, "Limits of Realism," 87; Purdy, *Nephew*, 32; "Miss Baird Enjoys European Voyage," *Bee Gee News*, Oct 9, 1935, 4.

13. *Bee Gee News*, June 10, 1935, 32.

14. Purdy, notebook, Sep 1958–Aug 1959, 101, 38.6, HRC.

15. Purdy, Bowling Green transcript; *Bulletin of Bowling Green State College* 18, no. 2 (Feb 1932); *Bulletin* 19, no. 2 (Feb 1933); *Bulletin* 20, no. 2 (Feb 1934).

16. Charlotte Dunipace Shaw to Michael Sibbersen, 13 June 1990, courtesy of David Kuebeck.

17. *Nephew*, 51.

18. Purdy, "James Purdy," *CAAS*, 300; Purdy, "James Purdy," int. Link, 62.

19. Canning, *Gay Fiction Speaks*, 28.

20. Purdy, "James Purdy," *CAAS*, 300.

21. Sjoblom, telephone interview, 25 May 2009.

22. Baldanza to Dr. Hollis A. Moore Jr., 19 Oct 1970, BGSU; Christine Purdy Reese, personal interview, July 2009; Purdy, int. Lear, 72.

Chapter 4

1. University of Chicago to Fred B. Millet, 14 Oct 1957, b. 2, OSU.208. "James Otis Purdy attended ICU Autumn 1935–Autumn 1936. Took A.M. in English Spring 1937. Further work in English Autumn 1938; Autumn 1944–Spring 1945 in Spanish."

2. Ehrhardt, "Wizard of Id," 27.

3. Sandburg, "Chicago," *Poetry*, 1914.

4. Purdy, "James Purdy," *CAAS*, 299.

5. Miller, "James Purdy's Fiction as Shaped by the American Midwest," 150.

6. Samors and Dauber, *Entertaining Chicago*, 37–38, 41.

7. Peretti, *Jazz in American Culture*, 45, 106; Steward to Purdy, 1 July 1971, 1.11, OSU.171.

8. Miller, "James Purdy's Fiction," 150–51.

9. Huston, "Gertrude Abercrombie."

10. Ehrhardt, "James Purdy, 1914–2009."

11. Rorem, *Knowing When to Stop*, 102.

12. Abercrombie to Purdy, 1 Feb 1971, 44.14, HRC.

13. Paul W. Miller, personal interview, July 2009.

14. Purdy to Abercrombie, 17 Sep 1965, GAP.

15. Miller, "James Purdy's Fiction," 151.

16. Donald Gallup to Purdy, 4 Apr 1957, 2.40, JPP.

17. Moore, tel. interview, 21 May 2012.

18. Wilcox, "No One Ever Looks Up," 16–23.

19. Steward, *Lost Autobiography*, 97.

20. Drury, *Old Illinois Houses*, 147–149.

21. "Norman MacLeish," *Modernism in the New City: Chicago Artists, 1920–1950*, 2018, www.chicagomodern.org/artists/norman-macleish/.

22. Miller, interview, July 2009.

23. Uecker, tel. interview, 1 July 2010.
24. Weininger, "Introduction," n.p.
25. Burns and Dydo with Rice, eds., *Letters of Gertrude Stein & Thornton Wilder*, 100, 103, 293; Miller, "James Purdy's Fiction," 153.
26. Weininger, "Introduction."
27. Galanes, "Gertrude Stein," 359–60.
28. Miller, "James Purdy's Fiction," 153.
29. Wendell Wilcox Papers, finding aid, "Manuscripts 1933–1960" and "Printed Matter, Manuscripts 1935–1936," Princeton Library, findingaids.princeton.edu/collections/C0666/c0208.
30. Purdy, int. Frame, 21.
31. Wilder to Stein, 12 Apr, 25 June 1936; Abercrombie to Stein, 13 July 1936, *Letters of Gertrude Stein & Thornton Wilder*, 99–100, 103.
32. Steward, *Lost Autobiography*, 97.
33. Stein, *Everybody's Autobiography*, 268.
34. Stadler int. Purdy, 1993, b. 1, f. Art. 1, MSP.
35. Paul W. Miller, interview, July 2009.
36. Uecker, email to the author, 19 April 2012.
37. Wendell Wilcox Papers, finding aid, "Manuscripts 1933–1960" and "Printed Matter, Manuscripts 1935–1936," Princeton U. Library, findingaids.princeton.edu/collections/C0666/c0208; Wilcox, "Color of Darkness," 3.1, WWP; Wilcox, "Narrow Rooms," 17.6, WWP.
38. Purdy to Orme, 8 Oct 1964, 3.18, OSU.3.
39. This address was handwritten on Purdy's master's thesis, dated Dec 1936.
40. Purdy, tel. conversations with the author, 30 April, 14 May 2008.
41. Purdy, "Trick and Treat," 2008.
42. Purdy to W. C. Williams, 27 Aug 1956, 20.611, WCW; Mencken to Purdy, 7 July 1937, r. 52, H. L. Mencken papers, Manuscripts and Archives Division, New York Public Library.
43. Pearson, *The Sitwells*, 133.
44. *Malcolm*, 84.
45. White, *States of Desire*, 255–56.
46. Purdy, "Ronald Firbank: The End of the Decadent Tradition," 10, 38, 39, 42–43.
47. "Is Writing Novel," *Republican-Courier* [Findlay], July 22, 1937, 5; Uecker, tel. interview, 1 July 2010.
48. Rorem, *Knowing When to Stop*, 124.
49. Rorem, *Later Diaries*, 374.
50. Steward, *Chapters from an Autobiography*, 41.
51. Steward, Ledger Compiling Info from Stud File, 1941–1945, b. 32, SSP.
52. Steward to Bouman, 15 Aug 1988, b. 3, SSP; Purdy, *Eustace Chisholm*, 41.
53. U. of Chicago to Fred B. Millet, b. 2, f. n.n., OSU.208.
54. Purdy, "A Good Woman," 5–10; Purdy, "James Purdy," int. Link, 62.
55. Stephen D. Adams, *James Purdy*, 14, 15–16.
56. Edgar Lee Masters to Purdy, 11 Mar 1939, Berg.

Chapter 5

1. "Lights out for Richard Purdy," *Findlay Republican-Courier*, Dec 23, 1967.

2. "Play Reviews are Given for Group," *Republican Courier*, Dec 22, 1939, 2.

3. "Guild Play Set," *Republican Courier*, June 5, 1941, 8.

4. Sullivan, "Days of *The Phoenix*," 142; Purdy, Federal Security Agency, Experience and Appointment Record; Application for Federal Employment, Feb 1, 1943.

5. Purdy in Canning, *Gay Fiction*, 19.

6. Purdy, "James Purdy," int. Link, 62.

7. Norman MacLeish to Purdy, 24 Jan 1969, b. 16, HRC.

8. "James Purdy Interviewed by Don Swaim, 7 Dec 1989"; Purdy, Honorable Discharge from the Army of the United States, Dec 30, 1941.

9. Application for Federal Employment, February 1, 1943.

10. Purdy, int. Morrow, 105.

11. Bérubé, *Coming Out under Fire*, 101, 100, 104.

12. Purdy, "Out with James Purdy," int. Lane, 81–82.

13. Purdy's US Civil Service Commission form; Purdy, Honorable Discharge from the Army of the United States, Dec 30, 1941.

14. "William Purdy's Son's Book 'Best Kind of Original Genius,'" [Bowling Green] *Sentinel-Tribune* [date unknown], 1958, collection of Dorothy Purdy.

15. MacLeish to Purdy, 5 Jan 1967, b. 16, HRC.

16. MacLeish to Purdy, 5 Mar 1957, 3.69, JPP.

17. MacLeish to Purdy, postcard, n.d., ca. late Jan 1972, 16.4, HRC.

18. MacLeish to Purdy, 17 Jan 1972, 16.4, HRC.

19. MacLeish to Purdy, 25 Feb 1961, 3.69, JPP.

20. Federal Security Agency, Experience and Appointment Record.

21. Studebaker, "U.S. Office of Education," 64.

22. Application for Federal Employment, Feb 1, 1943.

23. US Government Manual—FSA, 1945.

24. FSA, Report of Efficiency Rating, Mar 31, 1944.

25. FSA, Experience and Appointment Record.

26. Studebaker, "U.S. Office of Education," 67.

27. Marguerite Schumann, "Bullfight Posters Help Keep Spanish Students Interested," [Appleton] *Post-Crescent*, Nov 22, 1951, 16.

28. Purdy, "PW Interviews," int. Dahlin, 13.

29. David Purdy, email to the author, July 29, 2020.

30. Purdy to Vera Purdy, p.m. 18 Sep 1944, courtesy of Dave Purdy.

31. Miller, "James Purdy's Gertrude," 34, 32; "Gertrude Abercrombie" [bio], Feb 3, 1976, series 1, GAP.

32. Becker, "Gertrude Abercrombie."

33. "Gertrude Abercrombie," Feb 3, 1976, 1., series 1, GAP.

34. Paul Masterson writes: "Priebe aficionados flutter on" over his bird paintings, but he should also be known for "paintings of black cultural personalities," and other black subjects, unusual for the time ("Remembering Wisconsin's Forgotten Gay Artist, Dudley Huppler," *Shepherd Express*, July 3, 2017). According to Robert Cozzolino in

Dudley Huppler: Drawings, Huppler, born in Muscoda, Wisconsin, was a "precocious, self-taught artist" who studied English at UW-Madison in the late 1930s, joining Marshall Glaziers' salon of "artsy black, white, gay and straight 'brilliant misfits.' He also met his 'best boyfriend,' Karl Priebe, shuttling frequently" to Milwaukee to see him. Around 1949, Huppler moved to New York City, where, through "art, ambition and natural gifts," he "penetrated the innermost circles of gay aristocracy," his work owned by Auden and Pound. Befriended by photographer George Platt Lynes, this "young parvenu was social gold." In 1955, he joined Warhol's entourage, collaborating with Andy while being catty about him in letters. All this, amid the "infamous Red and Lavender Scares under another Wisconsinite," Senator Joseph McCarthy. Eventually, Huppler returned to Wisconsin to teach English. His drawings then focused on male nudes. Huppler had a "powerful, almost devastating, personality."

35. Tyler Friedman, "Imaginative Realism of Karl Priebe," *Shepherd Express*, Nov 12, 2013.

36. As an art-critical term, "magic realism" was coined by Franz Rohr in 1925 in *Nach Expressionismus: Magischer Realismus*. In Buenos Aries, the term was soon applied to European writers, but it was not until the 1960s that it became widely known as a literary genre describing work of Latin American writers.

37. Purdy, *Malcolm*, 114.

38. Dizzy Gillespie, in *Gertrude Abercrombie: A Retrospective Exhibition*, n.p.

39. Duncan, "Heretics in the Heartland," 100.

40. Seaman, "Bebop Artist Gertrude Abercrombie," 130; Weininger, "Gertrude Abercrombie," 5.

41. Wakefield, *New York in the 50s*, 301.

42. Uecker, tel. interview, July 1, 2010; Weise, "Christmas with James Purdy."

43. *Malcolm*, 171.

44. Littleton, *Enter the Giants*, 197.

45. Miller, "James Purdy's Fiction," 151; Miller, personal interview.

46. *Malcolm*, 149.

47. O. Andreas to Cox, 176-70-45, 2.9, UW.

48. Uecker, tel. interview, 9 Oct 2009.

49. Lahr, *Tennessee Williams*, 9–15; Cassidy's review rpt. in Richard Christiansen, "A Tough Little Play, a Tough Little Review," *Chicago Tribune*, Jan 29, 1995.

50. Purdy, Autobiographical Statement, typescript, 1.3. HRC.

51. Purdy, int. Morrow, 105.

52. Desnoes to Purdy, 9 Mar 1965, 1.22, JPP.

53. Purdy, "Fragments and Sayings," in "Trick and Treat," 2008.

54. Cox, "James Purdy's Fighting Words."

55. Breithaupt, "Remembering James Purdy."

56. See Michael Moon, *A Small Boy and Others* (Duke University Press, 1998), 15-30.

57. "Richard Purdy Draws Praise of New York Drama Critics," *Findlay Republican-Courier*, Sep [n.d.], 1945.

58. Arthur Pollock, "Four Actors and Young Man Named Dan," *Brooklyn Eagle*, Sep 23, 1945, 25.

59. Purdy, "You Reach for Your Hat," *Prairie Schooner* 20 (spring 1946): 185–192.

60. Sams, "Purdy's Latest Novel"; Purdy, "You Reach for Your Hat," *Complete Short Stories*, 67.

61. Purdy, "Interview," int. Morrow, 105.

62. Purdy, "James Purdy," int. Northouse, 209.

63. Canning, *Gay Fiction Speaks*, 6–7, 22; Ehrhardt, "James Purdy, 1914–2009"; Purdy to Sams, 6 Aug, 9 Aug 1984, Sams personal collection.

64. Ellison, "Twentieth Century Fiction and the Black Mask of Humanity," 3; Skerrett Jr., "James Purdy and the Black Mask of Humanity," 81, 83, 88.

Chapter 6

1. "South American Is Honored," *Post-Crescent* [Appleton], Oct 24, 1946, 26.

2. Morrow, "Interview," 105–6.

3. Uecker, tel. interview, 13 June 2008; Geller, "WLB Biography," 572, 574.

4. Uecker, tel. interview, 18 Aug 2010.

5. John David Purdy [Dave], tel. interview, 8 Jan 2019.

6. Bruenig, 212.

7. Uecker, emails to the author, 30, 31 Aug 2010; "Pusey Tells Trustees of Changes at College," *Post-Crescent*, June 11, 1948, 12.

8. "Jorma J. Sjoblom" [obituary], *Star Beacon* [Ashtabula, Ohio], Oct 11, 2015.

9. Sjoblom, tel. interview, 25 May 2009.

10. Sjoblom, personal interview, July 17, 2009.

11. "Faculty Personal History Record," Jorma Jules Sjoblom, Lawrence College archives; Winks, *Cloak and Gown*, 345; Tom E. Mahl, *Espionage's Most Wanted* (Potomac, 2003), 229.

12. "Dr. John Bucklew Will Speak in Lecture Series," *Post-Crescent*, March 6, 1957, 17.

13. John Bucklew Collection, LU-ARC026, Lawrence U., Mudd Library.

14. G. H. Gabriel Jones Papers, 1942–1951, Lawrence U. Archives, archives.lawrence.edu/?p=collections/controlcard&id=463; Bucklew to Purdy, n.d., 1962, 8.7, HRC.

15. Purdy to Richard Purdy, 26 July 1947, private collection of David Purdy.

16. "James Purdy," *Contemporary Authors*, vol. 19, 389.

17. Stadler, int. Purdy, b. 4, f. Art. 1, MSP.

18. Purdy, "James Purdy," *CAAS*, 299.

19. Purdy to Peden, 7 Feb 1969, HRC.

20. Purdy to Powys, 1 Nov 1957, 4., JPP; New York, Passenger Lists, 1820–1957.

21. Purdy, "Fragments and Sayings," in "Trick and Treat."

22. Purdy to Richard Purdy, 26 July, 2 Aug 1947, private collection of David Purdy.

23. Morrow, "Interview," 109.

24. Stadler, "House of the Solitary Maggot," 93.

25. Ancestry.com. *New York, NY, Marriage License Indexes, 1907–1995* (Lehi, UT, 2017).

26. O. Andreas to E. G. Cox, Feb 28, 1948, 476-70-45, 2.8, UW.

27. Harold Knapik to Virginia Knapik, 4 Oct, 5 Oct 1953, Knapik mss; Janet Malcolm, "Gertrude Stein's War"; Edward M. Burns, email to the author, 22 Feb 2022.

28. Becker, "Gertrude Abercrombie."

29. Judith Ann Moriarty, rev. *Complete Short Stories of James Purdy*, *Shepherd Express*, Sep 23, 2013.

30. Jorma Sjoblom, personal interview, July 17, 2009.

31. James Auer, "Ex-Fox Cities Author Wins Acclaim for Book: J. O. Purdy's Stories, Plays Probe Love," Appleton *Post-Crescent*, Dec 2, 1962: C12.

32. "College Adds Oxford Graduate, Two Other Teachers to Its Staff," *Post-Crescent*, Sep 2, 1948, 20.

33. Marguerite Schumann, "Bullfight Posters Help Keep Spanish Students Interested," *Post-Crescent*, Nov 22, 1951, 16.

34. Sjoblom, personal interview, July 17, 2009; Diane Pretzer, email to the author, 30 April 2009.

35. Strassman to Purdy, 9 Jan 1949, 1.1, OSU.74.

36. Breunig, *Great and Good Work*, 216–17.

37. "Lawrence College Professors Will Teach, Travel and Study," *Post-Crescent*, June 16, 1949, 9.

38. Bucklew to Purdy, 20 Aug 1960, 8.7, HRC.

39. Purdy to Schott, Feb 6, 1964, courtesy of John Uecker.

40. "College Faculty Panel Opposes Aid to Franco Spain," *Post-Crescent*, Feb 18, 1950, 12; "College Spanish Club Will Stage Fiesta," *Post-Crescent*, May 10, 1950, 18; "Social Events on Agenda of Fellowships," *Post-Crescent*, April 15, 1951, 16.

41. Whitney, *Finks*, 15.

42. Saunders, *Cultural Cold War*, 83

43. "Richard Purdy," Internet Movie Database, www.imdb.com/name/nm1686156/.

44. Si Steinhauser, "Great Stage Stars Appear on TV 'Whodunit,'" *Pittsburgh Press*, Oct 4, 1951, 51.

45. "Findlay Actor Has Heavy Schedule," *Findlay Republican-Courier*, June 11, 1951, 14.

46. Purdy, "Remembrances/Memoir," in "Trick and Treat."

47. Henry T. Murdock, "Leueen MacGrath Stars in New Comedy at Locust," *Inquirer*, Dec 26, 1951, 47.

48. Varble, "I Am James Purdy," 28.

49. "Founder of Freshman Studies Passes Away at 94," *Lawrentian*, Nov 16, 2001.

50. Breunig, *Great and Good Work*, 228–29.

51. "Founder of Freshman Studies," *Lawrentian*, Nov 16, 2001.

52. "4 Lawrence Faculty Members, 12 Students Will Go to Europe," *Post-Crescent*, May 31, 1952, 10; "Lawrence Language Teachers Spent Summer Vacation in Europe," *Post-Crescent*, Oct 1, 1952, 18.

53. Spring, *Secret Historian*, 142–43; Purdy to Wendell and Esther Wilcox, 25 Aug 1952, 14.10, WWP.

54. Spring, 153; Purdy to Steward, May 19, 1972, 1.11, OSU.171.

55. Purdy to W. and E. Wilcox, 25 Aug 1952, 14.10, WWP.

56. Strausbaugh, "Pure Purdy," 41.

57. Purdy to Abercrombie, p.m. 14 Jan 1953, 5.d. Purdy n.d. and 1953–1973, microfilm #1432, GAP.

58. *U.S., Departing Passenger and Crew Lists, 1914–1966* (Provo, UT: Ancestry.com, 2016); Purdy to Gerald Brenan, 28 Oct 1970, 5.5, HRC; "James Purdy," *Contemporary Authors*, vol. 19, 386.

59. Purdy, "Fragments and Sayings," in "Trick and Treat"; Sjoblom, interview, July 17, 2009; "26 Lawrence Faculty Members, Students Will Visit in Europe," *Post-Crescent*, May 22, 1953, 13; "John Bucklew Dies; Professor at Lawrence," *Post-Crescent*, Apr 1, 1974, 21.

60. "Students Go All Out for Beaux Arts Ball," *Post-Crescent*, March 2, 1953, 26.

61. "Lawrence Houses Blaze of Light, Color for Homecoming Weekend," *Post-Crescent*, Oct 31, 1953, 12.

62. Breunig, 226–28.

63. "Ex-Yale Professor Accepts Duke University Presidency," *Lawrentian*, Nov 2, 1962, 1.

64. Knight, *Dancer and the Dance*, 97, 106, 96.

65. Purdy, Satires, 3.8, HRC.

66. Sjoblom, tel. interview, 25 May 2009.

67. Sjoblom, personal interview, 17 July 2009.

68. Purdy to Wendell and Esther Wilcox, p.m. 6 Apr 1955, 14.10, WWP; Purdy, liner note, *63: Dream Palace by James Purdy, Read by the Author* [LP set].

69. Morrow, "Interview," 106; Creeley, "Black Mountain Review," 512; Creeley to Purdy, 30 Mar, 25 June 1961, 17 Jan 1963, 1.18, JPP.

70. Personal interviews with Dorothy Purdy and David Purdy, July 2009, and 2 July 2019.

71. David Purdy, tel. interview, 11 June 2021.

72. "Five Teachers Complete Staff at Lawrence," *Post-Crescent*, Sep 10, 1955, 7.

73. Sjoblom, tel. interview, 25 May 2009.

74. Purdy, autobiographical statement, typescript, 1.3, HRC.

75. Stadler int. Purdy, b. 4, f. Art. 1, MSP.

76. *Indiana, Marriages, 1810–2001* (Provo: Ancestry.com, 2014).

77. Becker, "Gertrude Abercrombie," n.p.

78. "James Purdy Has Volume Published," *Post-Crescent*, Aug 3, 1956.

79. Sjoblom, tel. interview, 25 May 2009.

80. Purdy, "Interview," int. Morrow, 106.

81. Miller, "James Purdy's Fiction," 151.

82. Uecker, tel. interview, 30 Aug 2010; email to the author, 30 Aug 2010.

83. Uecker, tel. interview, 1 July 2010.

84. Uecker, tel. interview, 9 Jan 2013.

85. W. Wilcox to Purdy, p.m. 20 Sep 1969, 21.6, HRC.

86. Purdy to Abercrombie, 2 March 1971, GAP.

87. See Purdy to Strassman letters, 1.1, OSU.74.

Chapter 7

1. Jorma Sjoblom, tel. interview, 25 May 2009; *Bible*, Luke 24:13–35; "Company History—1940s," Air Products, https://www.airproducts.com/-/media/airproducts/files/en/42497_company_history.pdf.

2. "James Purdy Has Volume Published," *Post-Crescent*, Aug 3, 1956; Sjoblom, tel. interview, 25 May 2009; Peg, "Cream for Your Morning Coffee," *Republican-Courier*, Apr 27, 1957, 8.

3. "William Purdy's Son's Book 'Best Kind of Original Genius,'" [Bowling Green] *Sentinel-Tribune* [unknown], 1958, courtesy of Dorothy Purdy; William Purdy to Purdy, 30 July 1957, 27 Mar 1962, Berg.

4. Sjoblom, tel. interview, 25 May 2009.

5. Sjoblom, tel. interview, 23 June 2011.

6. John Bucklew to Purdy, 3 Oct 1959, 8.7, HRC.

7. Phil Sparrow [Sam Steward] to Purdy, JPP, 14 Jan, 31 Mar, p.m. 1 Apr 1957, 5.122, JPP.

8. Purdy, "Remembrances/Memoir," in "Trick and Treat."

9. Sjoblom, interview, 17 July 2009.

10. Sjoblom, tel. interview, 25 May 2009.

11. Edmund White, *City Boy*, 7.

12. Purdy, "Voyage of Discovery," int. Huizenga, 70.

13. Purdy, int. Northouse, 202.

14. Stadler, int. Purdy, b. 4, f. Art. 1, MSP.

15. W. C. Williams to Purdy, 7, 16 Sep, 15 Dec 1956, 9.219, JPP.

16. W. C. Williams to Purdy, 1 Sep 1960, 9.219, JPP.

17. Algren to Purdy, 19 Sep 1956, 1.3, JPP.

18. Wilder to Purdy, 8 Oct 1956, JPP, 9.217.

19. Elborn, *Edith Sitwell*, 227–28.

20. Salter, *Last Years of a Rebel*, 88.

21. Sitwell to Purdy, 20 Oct 1956, *Edith Sitwell: Selected Letters*, 206–7.

22. Elborn, *Edith Sitwell*, 228.

23. Qtd. by Purdy in Ehrhardt, "Wizard," 27; Purdy, "Conversation," int. Goodman.

24. Sitwell to Purdy, 26 Nov 1956, *Selected Letters of Edith Sitwell*, 377–78.

25. Whitney, *Finks*, 4, 34–35; Sitwell to Purdy, 4 Dec 1956, 4.117, JPP.

26. Sitwell to Lacerda, 1956, *Selected Letters*, 210.

27. Purdy, "James Purdy," *CAAS*, 303.

28. Sitwell to Purdy, 17 July 1957, 4.118, JPP; Purdy to Sitwell, July 1957, qtd. in Glendinning, *Edith Sitwell*, 323–24.

29. Purdy to Elborn, 5 June 1976, KU.

30. Van Vechten to Purdy, 9 Nov, 6 Dec 1956, 5.133, JPP; CVV to Purdy, n.d. 1957, 5.134, JPP.

31. Sjoblom, personal interview, 17 July 2009; "James Purdy Interviewed by Don Swaim, 25 June 1987."

32. Kellner, ed., *Letters of Carl Van Vechten*, xxvii.

33. Van Vechten to Purdy, 18 Nov 1956, *Letters of Carl Van Vechten*, 264–65.

34. Kellner, ed., *Letters of Carl Van Vechten*, 264, n1.

35. Van Vechten to Purdy, 9 Feb 1957, HRC, JPC, 21.3

36. Hughes, "Carl Van Vechten," 418.

37. Kellner, ed. *Letters of Carl Van Vechten*, 270, n2.

38. Purdy, int. Northouse, 199; "James Purdy Interviewed by Don Swaim, 25 June 1987."

39. Hughes to Purdy, 15 Nov 1956, 2.51, JPP.

40. Hughes to Purdy, 25 Jan 1957, 2.51, JPP.

41. Atkinson to Purdy, 19 Sep 1956, 1.3, JPP; Olivier to Purdy, 19 Dec 1956, 3.83, JPP; Sitwell to Purdy, 19 Jan 1957, 4.118, JPP.

42. Gish to Purdy, 14 Nov 1956, 2.42, JPP.

43. Purdy to Thomson, 24, 23 Oct 1956, VT. Brackets in original.

44. Thomson to Purdy, 21 Dec 1956, VT.

45. Purdy to Strassman, 26 Oct 1956, 1.1, OSU.74.

46. Sjoblom, interview, 17 July 2009; Purdy int. Stadler, b. 4, f. Art. 1, MSP.

47. Becker to Purdy, 12 Dec 1959, 1.4, JPP.

48. Purdy, *Malcolm*, 96–99.

49. Purdy, *Malcolm*, 104.

50. Purdy, *Malcolm*, 166–92.

51. Simone de Beauvoir to Purdy, 7 Nov 1956, 1.6, JPP.

52. Elizabeth Bishop to Purdy, 3 Dec 1956, 1.9, JPP.

53. Alice B. Toklas to Steward, 14 Sep 1957, in *Staying On Alone*, 349.

54. Steward, *Dear Sammy*, 222; Spring, *Secret Historian* 251.

55. Purdy to Steward, 29 Nov 1974, 1.11, OSU.171.

56. Marianne Moore to Purdy, 18 Sep 1956, 3.76, JPP; M. Moore qtd. in De Stephano, "Purdy Principle," 51.

57. Chester Page, tel. interview, 8 June 2021.

58. Page, *Memoirs*, 30–31.

59. Purdy, "Vendrá," encl., Purdy to Van Vechten, 22 Feb 1957, ser. 2, 12.279, JPP.

60. Jason Hale, videoconference interview with the author, 6 April 2021.

61. Purdy, "Interview" with Morrow, 107.

62. Malcolm Cowley to Purdy, 26 Nov 1956, 1.17, JPP; Kaiser, *Gay Metropolis*, 100.

63. Purdy to Toni Strassman, 5 Dec 1956, 1.1, OSU.74.

64. "Pascal Covici, Book Editor, Dies," *New York Times*, Oct 15, 1964.

65. Purdy, "Interview," int. Morrow, 102.

66. Purdy to Helen K. Taylor, copy to Giroux, 3 Mar 1963, FSG, b. 286, f. gen. corr.

67. Salter, *Last Years of a Rebel*, 88–89; Purdy to Sitwell, 11 Dec 1956, Sitwell to Purdy, 28 Dec 1956, 4.117, JPP.

68. Sitwell to Purdy, 28 Dec 1956, 4.117, JPP.

69. Purdy to Strassman, 8 Dec 1956; Strassman to Purdy, 8 Dec 1956, 1.1, OSU.74.

70. Purdy to MacGregor, 28 Dec 1956, b. 289, f. Reader, FSG; Shwartz, ed., *For the Love of Books*, 221.

71. Purdy to Strassman, 9 Dec 1956, 1.1, OSU.74.

72. Sitwell to Purdy, 26 Nov 1956, *Selected Letters*, ed. Greene, 377–78; Edwin McDowell, "Jenny Bradley Is Dead at 97," *New York Times*, June 11, 1983, 21.

73. T. Williams to Purdy, 16 Dec 1956, 9.214, 3.71, JPP.

74. T. Williams to Campbell, 5 Jan 1957, *Tennessee Williams' Letters to Donald Windham*, 292.

75. Jorma Sjoblom, interview, 17 July 2009; Purdy, "James Purdy," 303.

76. William Purdy to Purdy, 26 Dec 1956, Berg.

77. Baily, "Uneven, Rewarding Country of the Short Story," 491.
78. Norman Mailer to Purdy, 16 Oct 1956, p.m. 12 Feb 1957, JPP.
79. Purdy to Lish, 31 July 1971, b. 16, Lish mss.
80. "Cyrilly Abels," *New York Times*, Nov 9, 1975; Purdy, "You Reach for Your Wraps," *40 Best Stories from Mademoiselle 1935–60* (NY: Harper, 1960), 362–70.
81. Elborn, *Edith Sitwell*, 230; Goodman, "Conversation."
82. Van Vechten to Purdy, 14 Feb 1957, *Letters of Carl Van Vechten*, 270.
83. Guinness, *Blessings in Disguise*, 143.
84. Purdy, "Dame Edith Sitwell's Sad, Witty Farewell," 8.
85. Page, tel. interview, 8 June 2021; Page, email to the author, 11 June 2021.
86. Elborn, *Edith Sitwell*, 231.
87. Elborn, email to the author, 26 Mar 2021.
88. Coward to Purdy, 19 Mar 1957, 1.17, JPP; Elborn, *Edith Sitwell*, 231.
89. Burkhardt to Purdy, 22 Nov 1956, 1.14, JPP.
90. Angus Wilson to Purdy, 2 May, 8 Oct 1957, 9.215, JPP.
91. Purdy to Celia Simon-Ross, 5 August 1985, OSU.208.
92. Cheever, "Art of Fiction," 159.
93. Purdy, "About Jessie Mae," *Children Is All*, 32–34; Purdy, "About Jessie Mae," *New Yorker*, May 25, 1957, 87–92.
94. Qtd. in Nancy Franklin, "Lady with a Pencil," *New Yorker*, Feb 18, 1996, www.newyorker.com/magazine/1996/02/26/lady-with-a-pencil.
95. Ross, "Harold Ross's Vision for the *New Yorker*," American Studies at the University of Virginia, http://xroads.virginia.edu/~ug02/NewYorker/prospectus.html; Brooke Allen, rev. of *Early Novels and Stories* by William Maxwell, barnesandnoble.com, Jan 18, 2008.
96. "William J. Weatherby," *New York Times*, Aug 8, 1992; Weatherby, "Choler of Despair," 474.
97. Strassman to Maxwell, Apr 10, 1957; Maxwell to Strassman, 14 Mar, 15 Apr, 22 Apr 1957; Purdy to Maxwell, 25 Apr 1957, NYR.
98. Peden, *American Short Story*, 20.
99. Stadler, interview with Purdy, b. 1, f. Art. 1, MSP.
100. Sitwell to Purdy, 23 May 1957, 4.119, JPP.
101. Jo Thomas, "New, Uncensored Edition of Orwell," *New York Times*, Mar 8, 1986.
102. Gollancz, "Afterword."
103. Gollancz to Sitwell, 19 Mar 1957, copy in 4.118, JPP.
104. Purdy, "Introduction" to *Weymouth Sands* by Powys, 10; Sitwell to Purdy, 29 Sep 1957, 4.119, JPP; A. Wilson, *Observer*, 22 Dec 1957, 10; "New Fiction."
105. Hopkinson, "Life of the Damned."
106. Elborn, *Edith Sitwell*, 231.
107. Purdy, int. Northouse, 187–188.
108. Purdy to Strassman, 29 July 1957, 1.1, OSU.74.
109. Purdy to Jay Ladd, 7 Mar 1994, b. 1, OSU.208.
110. Powys, "Desperate Cry," [London] *Observer*, July 14, 1957, 11.
111. Purdy to Powys, 25 July, 14 Oct 1957, 4.101, JPP.

112. Sitwell, "Under the Skin."

113. Albee, Foreword, *Dream Palaces: Three Novels by James Purdy*, vii.

114. Van Vechten to Purdy, 6 July 1957, *Letters of Carl Van Vechten*, 270.

115. "Dolores Gray in 'Can-Can' Next at Municipal Opera," *St. Louis Post-Dispatch*, July 28, 1957, 79.

116. Dorothy Purdy, interview, July 2009.

117. Sjoblom, interview, 17 July 2009; "Lights Out for Richard Purdy [obituary]," *Findlay Republican-Courier*, Dec 23, 1967.

118. William Purdy to Purdy, 1 Feb 1958, Berg.

119. William Purdy to Purdy, May 20, July 24, 1958; May 19, 1959, Berg.

120. Richard Purdy to Purdy, 17 Aug 1959, Berg.

121. "Playhouse Hears Three Reviews," *Republican-Courier*, Jan 14, 1960, 3.

122. Purdy to Richard Purdy, n.d., Berg.

123. Purdy to Powys, July 14, 1957, 4.101, JPP.

124. Purdy to Powys, June 20, 1958, b. 4, JPP.

Chapter 8

1. The Pythian, Pythian.com; Purdy to Powys, 10 Aug 1957, 4.101, JPP.

2. Purdy to Powys, 14 Aug 1957, 4.101, JPP.

3. Purdy to Powys, 7 Dec 1957, 4.101, JPP.

4. Purdy to Powys, 12 Dec 1958, b. 4, JPP.

5. Purdy to Powys, 17 Sep 1957, 4.101, JPP.

6. "James Purdy," *CAAS*, 302.

7. Dowell, "At Home with Drosselmeier."

8. Sjoblom, tel. interviews, 25 May 2009, 23 June 2011.

9. Silverberg, "James Purdy," 50.

10. Van Vechten to Purdy, 23 Aug 1957, 6.141, JPP.

11. Van Vechten to Purdy, 31 Aug 1957, 6.141, JPP.

12. Macdonald, "Fictioneers," 76.

13. Sitwell to Purdy, 29 Sep 1957, 4.19, JPP.

14. Elborn, *Edith Sitwell*, 231.

15. Purdy to Powys, 17 Sep 1957, 4.101, JPP.

16. Carl Van Vechten to Purdy, 13 April 1957, *Letters of Carl Van Vechten*, 268.

17. Van Vechten to Purdy, p.m. 9, 19 Sep 1957, n.d., 6.143, JPP. Marilyn Monroe had two Purdy books in her collection, *Don't Call Me by My Right Name* and *Malcolm* ("The 430 Books in Marilyn Monroe's Library," *Open Culture*, 6 Oct 2014, www.opencult ure.com/2014/10/the-430-books-in-marilyn-monroes-library.html).

18. Purdy, "Love," encl., Purdy to Van Vechten, 14 Oct 1957, 12.272, JPP.

19. Purdy to Powys, 29 Mar 1957, b. 4, JPP.

20. Dowell, *Star-Bright Lie*, 129.

21. "Conversation with Coleman Dowell by John O'Brien."

22. Hayworth, *Fever Vision*, 60; White, *City Boy*, 255.

23. DuBois, "In and Out of Books."

24. Janis Londraville and Richard Londraville, *Most Beautiful Man in the World*, 197–98.

25. Purdy to Powys, 1 Nov 1957, JPP, 4.10, JPP.

26. Dowell, *A Star-Bright Lie*, 116.

27. Swan to Purdy, 29 Oct 1957, 4.101, JPP.

28. Swan to Purdy, 31 Oct 1957, 4.101, JPP.

29. Sjoblom, tel. interview, 25 May 2009.

30. Londraville and Londraville, 224–25.

31. Uecker, tel. interview, June 13, 2008.

32. Purdy, "Satires," 3.8, HRC.

33. Qtd in Stadler, untitled article draft, b. 4, f. Art. 1, MSP.

34. Purdy, int. Lear, 57.

35. T. Williams to Edwin Erbe [New Directions], n.d. ca. 1961, "Statement on Purdy," item #364434, Between the Covers Books, www.betweenthecovers.com/pages/books/364434/tennessee-williams-james-purdy/typescript-statement-on-purdy-blurb-for-children-is-all.

36. Purdy to Powys, 29 March 1958, b. 4, JPP.

37. Laughlin qtd. in Saunders, *Cultural Cold War*, 140.

38. Purdy, "Statement and Anonymous/Anomalous Letters," 175.

39. W. T. Scott, "Enter a Writer." A year later, W. T. Scott criticized *The Atlantic Book of British and American Poetry*, edited by Dame Edith Sitwell, prompting Sitwell to give him "a good slap" in a letter to the *American Review of Literature* that published his review. Sitwell wrote her friend, Father Caraman: "As a humanitarian, I am glad that Mr. Scott is not dead, I mean more dead than usual. I had thought he was. But I am also an eccentric. I prefer to be taught my job by someone in a position to do so. . . . By the way, who *is* Winfield Townley Scott?" (Pearson, *The Sitwells*, 462).

40. Peden, "And Never a Silver Lining"; Purdy to Strassman, 25 Nov 1957; "The Canker of Comedy," *Time*.

41. Paller, *Gentlemen Callers*, 214; Abelove, *Deep Gossip*, 67; Savran, *Communists, Cowboys, and Queers*, 4, 84–85; Van Vechten to Purdy, 13 Apr, 11 July 1957, *Letters of Carl Van Vechten*.

42. Porter qtd. In Purdy, "James Purdy," *CAAS*, 302.

43. Porter to Purdy, 15 Feb 1958, b. 3, JPP.

44. Sitwell to Purdy, JPP, 4.120.

45. "20 Awards in Arts Made by 2 Groups," *Washington Post*, April 30, 1958, D5; Cover bio of Purdy for *Children Is All* (London: Panther, 1972).

46. In mixed materials, 1.2, JPP.

47. Purdy to Powys, 20 June 1958, b. 4, JPP.

48. Beckett to Purdy, 8 Aug 1958, 1.4, JPP.

49. Purdy to R. Wilson, 16 April 1993, 1.3, UD.

50. Paul Nathan, "Rights and Permissions," *Publishers Weekly*, April 7, 1958, 66.

51. Purdy to Powys, 23 Feb 1958, b. 4, JPP.

52. Purdy to Powys, 29 Mar 1958, 18.3, HRC.

53. Strassman to Purdy, 16 April 1958, b. 1, OSU.74.

54. Kenneth Rexroth to Purdy, 26 Oct 1956, 4.108, JPP; Purdy to W. C. Williams, 20 May 1958, series 1, 20.611, WCW.

55. Purdy to Powys, 20 June 1958, b. 4, JPP.

56. Van Vechten to Purdy, 21 Oct 1956, 5.132, JPP.

57. Brad Gooch, *Flannery*, 220.

58. Newman to Strassman, 24 May 1957, NYR.

59. Strassman to Purdy, 28 Mar 1958, b. 1, OSU.74.

60. Polsgrove, *It Wasn't Pretty*, 52.

61. "Dorothy Parker on Books: Four Rousing Cheers," *Esquire* 50 (July 1958): 18, 20.

62. Parker to Purdy, 24 June 1958, 3.88, JPP; Purdy, "James Purdy," int. Barron, 92.

63. Gary Pulsifer, ed., *Paul Bowles by His Friends*, 92; Bowles, *Without Stopping*, 340.

64. Giroux to Purdy, 16 July 1958; Purdy to Giroux, 17 July 1958, b. 288, f. *Color of Darkness*, FSG.

65. Purdy to Laughlin, 24 July 1965, copy in b. 289, f. Reader, FSG.

66. Purdy int. Stadler, 18 Mar 1992, b. 1, f. Art. 1, MSP.

67. Purdy to Straus, 24 Sep 1969, FSG, b. 288, f. Eustace, gen., FSG.

68. Peden, *American Short Story*, 91.

69. Gottlieb, "Anatomy of a Publisher."

70. Kachka, *Hothouse*, 2–5, 11, 63; Uecker, tel. interview, 9 Jan 2013.

71. Purdy to Strassman, 17 Mar 1959, b. 1, OSU.74.

72. Purdy to Powys, 12 Dec 1958, b. 4, JPP.

73. Wakefield, *New York in the Fifties*, 154; Sjoblom, tel. interview, 25 May 2009.

74. Ryan, *When Brooklyn Was Queer*, 264–65; Barry Horwitz, tel. interview, 23 Aug 2019.

75. Chester Page, emails to the author, 14, 18 June 2021; Purdy to Sam and Sylvia Colton, 7 Oct 1963, collection of Page.

76. Strausbaugh, "Pure Purdy," 41.

77. Purdy, "Literary Ghosts Cling to Stone," 78.

78. Ryan, *When Brooklyn Was Queer*, 13–14, 143, 181–94.

79. Whitney, *Finks*, 36–37, 29, 83; James Purdy biography, OSU.208.

80. Even the initial financing of Farrar, Straus was linked to the CIA since $50,000 was invested by "playboys including Julius (Junkie) Fleischmann, the yeast and gin heir who ran the Farfield Foundation, a CIA dummy that funneled money to organizations like" the CCF, according to Ian Parker in the *New Yorker*.

81. Kachka, *Hothouse*, 50.

82. Kachka, *Hothouse*, 177–78.

83. Purdy to Giroux, March 15, 1959, b. 286, f. gen., FSG; Purdy, 1958–1959 notebook, 95, 119–20, 132–34, 143, 38.6, HRC.

84. Purdy, fragment, 3.5, HRC.

85. Powys to Purdy, June 20, 1959, b. 4, JPP.

86. Sitwell to Purdy, 22 Jan 1959, 4.120, JPP.

87. Newman to Purdy, 2, 16 Apr 1959; Purdy to Newman, 17 Apr 1959, b. 771, NYR.

88. Steward to Purdy, 22 Nov 1962, 5.122, JPP.

89. Podhoretz, *Making It*, 172.

90. Kachka, *Hothouse*, 67.

91. Whitney, *Finks*, 236; Warburg, *All Authors Are Equal*, 154.

92. Sitwell to Purdy, 4 Mar 1957, 4.118, JPP; Sitwell to Purdy, 29 Sep 1957, 4.119, JPP.

93. Farrar to Purdy, 24 Aug 1959; Purdy to Farrar, 26 Aug 1959, b. 288, f. *Malcolm*, gen., FSG.

94. Purdy to June Bové, 30 Aug 1959, b. 288, f. Malcolm, FSG.

95. Purdy to Elborn, 28 Sep 28, KU.

96. Angus Wilson to Purdy, May 29, 1959, 9.220, JPP.

97. Sitwell to Purdy, 20 June 1959, 44.13, HRC.

98. Warburg to Straus, 20 Sep 1966, b. 288, f. ECW, FSG; Warburg, *All Authors Are Equal*, 161–63.

99. Silverberg, "James Purdy," 50.

100. Ralph Ellison owned four Purdy books; his copy of *The Nephew* had been inscribed by Purdy to Saul Bellow, who passed it on to his friend, Ellison. "Ralph Ellison Collection, A Finding Aid," Rare Book and Special Collections, Library of Congress, 2016.

101. Lewis, "Recent Fiction: Picaro and Pilgrim," 152.

102. Lewis, "Baffling, Perverse, Demonic, Original."

103. Hicks, rev. of *Malcolm*.

104. Purdy, "Purdy's Purge."

105. Peden, "Mystery of the Missing Kin," 29; Peden, "Short Fiction vs. Long," 17–18; Peden, "Pilgrimage to Destruction."

106. Purdy to Robert de Ruig, 30 Apr 1971, 6.11, HRC.

107. Purdy, "Penthouse Interview," int. Barron, 8; Purdy, "James Purdy: An Interview," int. Profit, 131.

108. Hellman to Purdy, 25 Sep 1959, 2.49, JPP.

109. "James Purdy says He Doesn't Exist," 7.

110. Segal, "Under the Dust Cover."

111. Giroux to Purdy, 30 Nov 1959, b. 289, f. Nephew, gen, FSG.

112. Giroux to Purdy, 14 Jan 1960, b. 289, f. Nephew, gen, FSG.

113. Parker, rev. *Malcolm*.

114. Silverberg, "Purdy," 50.

115. Parker, rev. of *Malcolm*.

116. Purdy to Powys, 7 Dec 1959, b. 4, JPP; Purdy, "James Purdy," int. Northouse, 190–91; Purdy, in Shwartz, ed., *For the Love of Books*, 221; Purdy, typescript list of favorite stories given to David Breithaupt.

117. Purdy to Powys, 26 Nov 1960, b. 4, JPP.

118. Purdy to Powys, 10 Dec 1960, b. 4, JPP. Decades later, Peter Weller performed "Daddy Wolf" in *James Purdy and the Works*, an Ensemble Studio Theatre production.

119. Calvino, *Hermit in Paris*, 28, 33–34.

120. Podhoretz, *Making It*, 87–88, 219–20.

121. Calvino, 26, 45, 48–49.

122. Bonino, "Einaudi Primer," 10; Ladd, *James Purdy*, 58, 61, 63–64, 66–67.

123. "Kidnapping, Theft," *Daily News-Journal* [Murfreesboro, TN], Oct 3, 1932, 1.

124. Purdy to Orme, 14 Mar 1960, 4.15, OSU.3.

125. M. Andreas to Purdy, 19 June 1962, 1.2, JPP.

126. Purdy to Orme, 1 Oct 1964, 2.12, OSU.3.

127. Bowles to Purdy, 15 Jan 1959, 1.10, JPP.

128. Thomson to Purdy, March 1, 1960, 5.128, JPP.

129. "Matthew Paris and Dave Zimmer Interview James Purdy."

130. Purdy to Powys, 1 Mar 1960, b. 4, JPP.

131. Harry Hansen, "Most Creative Writing Prizes Go to New Yorkers," *Chicago Daily Tribune*, 20 Mar 1960, C5.

132. Saunders, *Cultural Cold War*, 139, 142, 238. James Angleton's name is familiar to researchers of the assassination of President John F. Kennedy.

133. Pearson to Purdy, 12 Mar 1960, 3.91, JPP; Winks, *Cloak and Gown*, 311, 317.

134. Pearson to Purdy, 17 Apr 1960, 3.91, JPP; "Lawrence College Psychology Teacher's Book Published," *Post-Crescent*, Dec 15, 1960, 26. Given Norman Holmes Pearson's intelligence role, it is not surprising that he let Purdy know he was monitoring his statements on Fidel Castro and Cuba: "Was interested to see you were stepping out for Castro in the press." Which press item Pearson refers to is unknown. In December, to Powys, Purdy said he admired Castro for "taking away all that property the Americans owned, and giving it back to the Cubans, where it really belonged."

135. Purdy to Dick [FSG], 1 Feb 1967, b. 288, f. ECW, subs., FSG; "James Purdy," *Contemporary Authors*, New Revision series, 389–95; Saunders, *Cultural Cold War*, 260, 144.

136. James Baldwin to Purdy, March 9, 1960, 1.4, JPP.

137. Purdy, "Merry-Go-Round Horses and Carousel," 299; Aiken to Purdy, 1 Apr 1960, 1.3, JPP.

138. Conrad Aiken to Purdy, 1 Apr 1960, 1.3, JPP.

139. Purdy to Powys, 18 Feb 1960, b. 4, JPP.

140. Daiches, rev. of *Malcolm* qtd. on *The Nephew* (FSC) dust jacket; Daiches, introduction to *Malcolm*, x; "New Fiction," *Times* (London), April 28, 1960, 17.

141. William Purdy to Purdy, June 20, 1960, Berg; David Purdy, personal interviews, July 2009, July 2, 2019.

Chapter 9

1. Van Vechten to D. Gallup, 29 Aug 1960, *Letters of Carl Van Vechten*, 276.

2. Thom Gunn, "All Pretty Much Strangers," 8.

3. *News from New Directions*, Feb 11, 1958, 1.4, OSU.74.

4. W. C. Williams to Purdy, 13 Sep 1960, 20.611, WCW.

5. Purdy to W. C. Williams, 14 Sep 1960, 20.611, WCW.

6. Purdy to Powys, 13 Aug 1960, b. 4, JPP.

7. Atkinson to Purdy, 23 Sep 1960, 1.3, JPP.

8. Bowles to Purdy, 7 Sep 60, 1.10, JPP.

9. Merrill to Purdy, 22 Dec 1959, 17 Feb 1961, 3.74, JPP.

10. Warren to Purdy, 9 Nov 1960, 9.216, JPP.

11. Southern, "New Trends and Old Hats," 381; *Nephew*, 96–99, 381.

12. Purdy to Southern, 6 Dec 1959, 25 Jan 1960, 26 Oct 1961, 2 Jan 1962, b. 287, f. CWB, FSG.

13. Schott, "Life Seen Through Haze of Gossip."

14. Vera Purdy to Purdy, 17 Sep 1960, 36.1, HRC [removed from p. 216 of *Jeremy's Version* notebook].

15. Paula Diamond to Purdy, May 6, 1960, b. 288, f. Color of Darkness, FSG.

16. Rust Hills to Roger Straus, 5 Jan 1961, FSG, b. 289, f. gen., FSG.

17. Purdy to Powys, 27 Oct 1960, b. 4, JPP.

18. Purdy to Powys, 26 Nov 1960, b. 4, JPP.

19. Gallup to Purdy, 19 Dec 1960, 2.40, JPP.

20. Nolan Miller to FSC, 16 Oct 1960; Robert Giroux to Miller, 19 Oct 1960, b. 286, f. gen. corr., FSG.

21. Joan Didion, "Edge of the Precipice," 315–16.

22. Paul W. Miller, "Limits of Realism," 85, 84.

23. Frank Baldanza to Dr. Hollis A. Moore Jr., 19 Oct 1970, BGSU.

24. Diane Pretzer and Wallace L. Pretzer, email to the author, 30 Apr 2009.

25. W. Purdy to Purdy, 4 Feb 1961, Berg.

26. "Purdy's Novel, Brilliant or Not?" *B-G News*, March 7, 1961, 2.

27. *Nephew*, 52.

28. *Nephew*, 51–56.

29. Diane and Wally Pretzer, email to the author, 30 April 2009; Charlotte Dunipace Shaw to Michael Sibberson, 13 June 1990, courtesy David Kuebeck, Bowling Green, Ohio.

30. Paul W. Miller, "Limits of Realism," 90.

31. *Nephew*, 92–93.

32. Pretzer and Pretzer, email to the author, 30 Apr 2009; Shaw to Sibbersen, 13 June 1990, courtesy of David Kuebeck.

33. "Dr. Nordheim, 74, Dead; Was Professor Emeritus," *Daily Sentinel-Tribune*, July 24, 1961, 2; *Nephew*, 54.

34. Purdy to Giroux, 16 Jan 1961, b. 288, f. Malcolm, gen., FSG.

35. *The Nephew* (London: Secker & Warburg, 1961), dust jacket.

36. Sitwell to Purdy, 18 Oct 1960, 44.13, HRC.

37. J. Davenport, "Masterpiece from America."

38. Purdy to Powys, 25 March 1961, b. 4, JPP.

39. Purdy to Powys, 2 Feb 1961, b. 4, JPP; Sjoblom, interview, 17 July 2009.

40. Purdy to Powys, 6 Feb 1961, b. 4, JPP.

41. Purdy to Solotaroff, 20 Mar 1961, 3.17, TS.

42. Purdy to Powys, 25 Mar 1961, b. 4, JPP.

43. Paller, *Gentlemen Callers*, 120–21.

44. Bergler to Purdy, 23 Aug 1956, 1.7, JPP.

45. Purdy to Powys, June 1, 1961, b. 4, JPP.

46. Bowles to Purdy, 3 Oct 1961, 1.10, JPP.

47. Sitwell to Purdy, 28 July 1959, *Selected Letters*, ed. Lehmann and Parker, 241.

48. Southern, "No Stranger to Excess," *Paris Review*, Dec 17, 2015.

49. Matthiessen int. with Charlie Rose, May 27, 2008, charlierose.com/videos/15312.

50. "Founding Editors," *Paris Review*, www.theparisreview.org/about/founding-editors.

51. abe.com listing, Derringer Books, Woodbridge, Connecticut, accessed April 6, 2017.

52. Van Vechten, postcard to Duval, 13 Jun 1961, NYPL, CVV collection, 1911–1964, corr.

53. See Wilford, "Playing the CIA's Tune? The 'New Leader' and the Cultural Cold War."

54. Gore Vidal, "Some Memories of the Glorious Bird," 1131.

55. Sundel, "Limp-Wrist School," 25–26.

56. See JPP, box 1, folders 11–13.

57. Capote to Lyndon, 4 July 1961, *Too Brief a Treat*, 321–22.

58. T. Williams to Windham, 23 Mar 1949, *Tennessee Williams' Letters to Donald Windham*, 323–24.

59. Van Vechten to Campbell, 27 Dec 1960, *Letters of Carl Van Vechten*, 278.

60. Purdy to Powys, July 8, 1961, b. 4, JPP.

61. Purdy to Powys, 8 Oct 1961, b. 4, JPP.

62. Jorma Sjoblom Curriculum Vitae, 1968, courtesy Sjoblom; Sjoblom, tel. interview, 25 May 2009.

63. Vera (Purdy) Bauman to Purdy, 20 Oct 1961, 1.4, JPP; William Purdy to Purdy, 26 Dec 1961, Berg.

64. William Purdy to Purdy, 4 Feb, 1961, Berg.

65. William Purdy to Purdy, 20 Oct 1961, Berg.

66. Ruth Ford to Purdy, 3 May 1961, 31 Oct 1961, 2.36, JPP.

67. Dennis Hevesi, "Ruth Ford, Film and Stage Actress, Dies at 98," *NYT*, Aug 14, 2009.

68. FSC memo, 2 Nov 1961, FSG, b. 289, f. Other works.

69. Martin Goodman, "Precognition, the Writer and James Purdy," *So You Want to Be a Writer*, June 21, 2006, http://martingoodman.com/soyouwanttobeawriter/2006/06/precognition-writer-and-james-purdy.html.

70. Purdy to Giroux, 26 Nov 1961, b. 287, f. CWB, subsidiary, FSG.

71. Purdy to Terry Southern, 2 Jan 1962, Berg.

72. Purdy in Canning, *Gay Fiction Speaks*, 5.

73. Margaret Drabble, *Angus Wilson*, 273; Purdy qtd. in "Talking About Angus Wilson," 120.

74. Purdy to Straus, 16 Feb 1962, b. 288, f. Malcolm, FSG.

75. Desnoes to Purdy, 24 Sep 1961, 1.22, JPP.

76. Beals to Purdy, May 8, 1962, 1.6, JPP.

77. W. Purdy to Purdy, 26 June 1962, Berg.

78. W. Purdy to Purdy, 27 Mar, 19, 26 June, 15 Nov 1962, Berg.

79. Purdy to James Leo Herlihy, n.d., 15 Mar 1962, Catalog of George Houle, Los Angeles.

80. Nin, *Diary of Anaïs Nin*, Vol. 6, 296; Herlihy to Purdy, p.m. 6 Mar, 15 Feb 1963, 2.47, JPP.

81. John Bucklew to Purdy, 20 June 1962, 8.7, HRC.

82. Bucklew to Purdy, 4 Oct 1962, 8.7, HRC.

83. Bucklew to Purdy, 28 Nov 1970, 8.7, HRC.

84. Purdy to Virgil Thomson, 27 June 1962, 75.29, VT.

85. Thomson qtd. in Stein, *Edie*, 248.

86. Wittke, "Vignettes of His Life and Times"; Tippins, *Inside the Dream Palace*, 101–2.

87. Purdy to Baldanza, 25 Aug 1971, BGSU.

88. Cryer in *Good Roots*, 62–63.

89. Purdy to Paula Diamond, n.d. [ca. Mar 1962], b. 289, f. Nephew, FSG.

90. James Oliver to Purdy, 24 Oct 1962, 1.5, JPP.

91. Purdy, "James Purdy," int. Northouse, 195.

92. Purdy to Powys, 11 Nov 1961, box 4, JPP.

93. Polsgrove, *It Wasn't Pretty*, 82.

94. Purdy to Straus, 22 Feb 1965, b. 286, f. gen. corr., FSG.

95. Purdy to Laughlin, July 24, 1965, copy in b. 289, f. Reader, FSG.

96. Thomson to Purdy, 22 Oct 1962, VT.

97. Alfred Chester qtd. in "Former Lawrence Teacher to Have Book Published," *Post-Crescent*, Nov 13, 1962, 15.

98. Hassan, "Of Anguish and Incongruity," 29; Horchler, "Impending Revelations," 395.

99. Dorothy Purdy, interview, July 2, 2019.

100. Sitwell, "Purdy: 'The Marrow of Form.'"

101. Phil Sparrow [Steward] to Purdy, 22 Nov 1962, 5.122, JPP.

Chapter 10

1. Jorma Sjoblom, tel. interview, May 25, 2009.

2. David Purdy, tel. interview, 8 Jan 2019.

3. Purdy to John Cowper Powys, 26 Feb 1963, b. 4, JPP.

4. William Purdy to Purdy, 13 Mar 1963; Richard Purdy to Purdy, 24 Mar 1965, Berg.

5. Schwarzschild to Purdy, 31 Jan 1963, b. 19, HRC.

6. Purdy to Giroux, 18 May 1963, 4 Dec 1962, b. 287, f. Cabot Wright Begins, FSG; Kachka, *Hothouse*, 9, 60.

7. Purdy to Powys, 26 Feb 1963, b. 4, JPP.

8. Giroux to Phelps, 1 Feb 1963, b. 287, f. CWB, FSG.

9. Giroux to Purdy, 5 Feb 1963, b. 287, f. CWB, FSG.

10. W. Purdy to Purdy, 13 Mar, 12 June, 10 Aug 1963, Berg.

11. W. Purdy to Purdy, 22 Sep 22, 1963, Berg.

12. Pearson to Purdy, April 23, 1963, 22.4, HRC.

13. Robert Penn Warren to Purdy, 11, 15 Feb 1963, b. 289. f. Other works, FSG.

14. Harry Hansen, "New Review Medium Finds an Ideal Backer," *Chicago Tribune*, May 26, 1963, 15.

15. Straus to Gordon N. Ray, 4 Mar 1962, b. 286, f. gen. corr., FSG.

16. Purdy, "Trick and Treat."

17. Hundley, "Ready All the Time," int. Hanshe, 169.

18. Richard Hundley, tel. interview, 30 Aug 2009.

19. Hundley, "Ready," int. Hanshe, 169.

20. Hundley, tel. interview, 30 Aug 2009.

21. Celluci, "Songs by Richard Hundley," 73.

22. Hundley, tel. interview, 30 Aug 2009.

23. Purdy to Abercrombie, 23 May 1971, GAP.

24. Hundley, tel. interview, 30 Aug 2009.

25. J. Malcolm, "Gertrude Stein's War."

26. Purdy, Satires, 3.8, HRC.

27. Purdy to Warburg, July 7, 1963, copy in b. 287, f. gen. corr., FSG; Ladd, *James Purdy*, 135-37; Jocelyn Brooke, "New Fiction," *The Listener* 70 (15 Aug 1963): 249.

28. Terrence McNally to John Farrar, 23 Aug 1963, encl., Farrar to Purdy, 29 Aug 1963, b. 286, f. gen. corr., FSG.

29. McNally, *The Play of Malcolm*, 40.9, McNally papers, HRC; Frontain in McNally, *Muse of Fire*, 127.

30. Albee, "Foreword," vii.

31. Heide, "Carousing in the Village"; Galanes, "Conversation with Terrence McNally."

32. *Every Act of Life*; Gussow, *Albee*, 107–9.

33. Turnbaugh, "James Purdy: Playwright," 75.

34. Lewis Funke, "News of the Rialto," *New York Times*, Dec 2, 1962.

35. Rorem, *Later Diaries*, 71.

36. *Cracks* program, Performing Arts Library, Billy Rose Theater Division, New York Public Library.

37. Donald Kirkley, "Birth and Death of a Drama," *Baltimore Sun*, Dec 7, 1963, 263.

38. Candace Womble, "*Color of Darkness Continues*," *New York Amsterdam News*, Oct 26, 1963, 15; Leonard Harris, "Evening with Purdy Worthwhile," Oct 1, 1963, [unknown], OSU.74.

39. Funke, "Purdy's 'Color of Darkness'"; Womble, "*Color of Darkness*"; "New York Play Based on James Purdy Works," *Post-Crescent*, Oct 4, 1963, 24; Harris, "Evening."

40. Purdy to Laughlin, 8 Dec 1969, 6.9, HRC.

41. Sjoblom, tel. interview, 25 May 2009; Rorem, *Later Diaries*, 74; Vanderbilt to Purdy, 19 Nov 1963, 9.210, JPP.

42. Purdy to Thomson, 1 Nov 1963, 75.29, VT.

43. Sjoblom, tel. interview, 25 May 2009; Purdy, "Literary Ghosts Cling to Stone," 78.

44. Ryan, *When Brooklyn Was Queer*, 268.

45. Robert C. Doty, "Growth of Overt Homosexuality in City Provokes Wide Concern," *New York Times*, Dec 17, 1963.

46. Christine (Purdy) Reese, personal interview, July 2009.

47. Purdy, "Penthouse Interview," int. Barron, 91.

48. Data courtesy David Kuebeck.

49. Geller, "WLB Biography," 572.

50. Schott, "James Purdy: American Dreams," 300.

51. Purdy to Thomson, July 23, 1964, VT.

52. Purdy to Orme, 1 Sep 1964, 2.17, OSU.3.

53. Diamond, FSG memo, 9 Apr 1964, b. 287, f. CWB—subs., FSG.

54. "Biographical Note," John L. Brown papers finding aid, Georgetown U. Archival Resources, https://findingaids.library.georgetown.edu/repositories/15/resources/10065.

55. John L. Brown to Straus, 25 Aug, 8 Sep, 1964, b. 287, f. CWB, FSG.

56. Purdy to Straus, 19 Sep 1964, b. 287, f. CWB, FSG.

57. Warburg to Phelps, 17 Sep 1964, copy in b. 287, f. CWB—Foreign, FSG.

58. Bowles [blurb for FSG], b. 286, f. gen. corr., FSG.

59. Purdy, "Interview," int. Morrow, 103.

60. Van Vechten to Van Dyke, 20 Oct 1964, *Letters of CVV*, 292.

61. Prescott, "Waste of a Small Talent," *New York Times*, Oct 19, 1964, 31.

62. Qtd. in Polsgrove, *It Wasn't Pretty*, 84.

63. Qtd. in Weatherby, "Choler of Despair," 474.

64. Peter S. Prescott to Farrar, 30 Oct 1964; Farrar to P. S. Prescott, 3 Nov 1964, b. 287, f. CWB, gen. corr., FSG.

65. Solotaroff, "Stud Farm for Horselaughs," 3.

66. Purdy to Solotaroff, Oct 29, 1964, 3.17, TS.

67. "James Purdy Says He Doesn't Exist," 1, 7.

68. Cromie, "Cromie Looks at Authors and Books."

69. Sontag, "Laughter in the Dark, 5.

70. Purdy, Satires, n.d., 3.8, HRC.

71. Purdy quoted in Varble, "I Am James Purdy," 29; Kachka, *Hothouse*, 150, 146, 148; Moser, *Sontag*, 213–14.

72. Tanner, *City of Words*, 85; Newman, "Beyond Omniscience," 47, 50. Newman revised this material for a landmark book, *The Post-Modern Aura: The Act of Fiction in an Age of Inflation* (1985).

73. Hawkes, "John Hawkes: An Interview," 143.

74. Stadler, "Theater of Real Speech," 12.

75. Purdy, "Dame Edith Sitwell's Sad, Witty Farewell."

76. Purdy to Elborn, 29 Apr 1978, qtd. in Elborn, *Edith Sitwell*, 231–232.

77. Purdy, "Carl Van Vechten," *Collected Poems*, 38.

78. Purdy to Giroux, 18 Jan 1965, b. 287, f. CWB, FSG.

79. Purdy to Orme, 26 Jan 1965, 2.20, OSU.3.

80. Davis, "New Mood," 22.

81. Purdy to Straus, 22 Feb 1965; Straus to Purdy, 23 Feb 1965, b. 286, f. gen. corr., FSG.

82. Purdy to Giroux, 6 Mar 1965, b. 289, f. poems, FSG; Purdy to Straus, 28 Mar 1965, b. 286, f. gen. corr., FSG

83. Purdy to Giroux, March 21, 1965, b. 286, f. gen. corr., FSG.

84. Thomson to Purdy, May 5, 1965, VT; White, *City Boy*, 253; Thomson to Purdy, May 31, 1965, VT.

85. Schaap, "Behind the Lines."

86. JT, FSG Memo, 17 June 1965, b. 287, f. CWB, FSG.

87. Angus Wilson, "Horror Game."
88. Furbank, "Opting Out," 80–81.
89. Farley Clinton, "Books in Brief," *National Review* 17 (4 May 1965): 387; Stephen Donadio, "The In Way Out," *Partisan Review* 32 (spring 1965): 299–302.
90. E. C. Kaiser to Lila Karpf, 27 Mar 1969, b. 287, f. CWB, subs., FSG.
91. Purdy to Straus, 10, 13 Sep 1966, b. 287, f., gen. corr., FSG.
92. MacGregor to Purdy, 13 July 1965; Purdy to MacGregor, 15 July 1965, copy in b. 289, f. Reader, FSG.
93. Purdy to Laughlin, 24 July 1965, copy in FSG, b. 289, f. Reader 1965–1966, FSG.
94. Purdy to Straus, 4 Sep 4, 1965; Straus to Moss, 14 Sep 1965; Moss to Straus, 21 Sep 1965, b. 286, f. gen. corr., FSG.
95. John Stewart Wynne, tel. interview, August 18, 2020.
96. Purdy to Abercrombie, 17 Sep 1965, GAP; Seaman, *Identity Unknown*, 76–77; Purdy in Canning, *Gay Fiction Speaks*, 27.
97. Page, *Memoirs of a Charmed Life in New York*, 67–69, 72, 168. Thanks go to Chester Page for generously giving me the two canceled checks.
98. Cora Purdy to Purdy, n.d. [1965], 18.3, HRC.
99. Skerrett to Purdy, 21 Sep 1965, copy in b. 287, f. CWB, FSG.
100. Peter L. Redmond to Purdy, 12 Aug 1970, 18.6, HRC.
101. *Bible*, Isaiah 48:22.
102. Purdy to Giroux, 4 Jan 1966, copy in 6.3, HRC.

Chapter 11

1. Rorem to Purdy, 15 Jan 1965, 18.8, HRC.
2. Rorem, *Later Diaries*, 77.
3. Flanagan qtd. in Gussow, *Albee*, 228.
4. Rorem, 15 Oct 1965 entry, *Later Diaries*, 152–53.
5. Mel Gussow, *Edward Albee*, 248–49.
6. Gussow, 270.
7. Gussow, 248.
8. Richard L. Coe, "One on the Aisle," *Washington Post*, Jan 14, 1966, B7.
9. Gussow, 19.
10. Wiese, tel. interview, 4 June 2019.
11. Purdy to Giroux, n.d. [ca. Dec 1965], b. 288, f. ECW, FSG.
12. John McCarten, "Innocent Astray," *New Yorker* 41 (Jan 22, 1966): 74.
13. "Speech, Theatre and Dance," *Choice* 3 (Sept 1966): 534.
14. Betty Flynn, "Critic-Free Public Is All Albee Asks," *Washington Post*, Mar 26, 1967, H1.
15. Purdy, "James Purdy's Notes on Edward Albee's Adaptation of *Malcolm* to the Stage," notes on mimeo playscript, 18 Aug 1965, 4.4, HRC.
16. Uecker, tel. interview, September 20, 2020.

17. Purdy, "Interview with James Purdy," int. Lear, 62.

18. Canning, *Gay Fiction Speaks*, 24.

19. Purdy, "James Purdy's Notes" on playscript, 4.4, HRC.

20. Goodman, "Conversation with James Purdy"; Purdy, "Notes," 4.4, HRC.

21. Purdy, Untitled article re: Albee's dramatization of Malcolm, 1.2, HRC.

22. Purdy, int. Profit, 129.

23. Purdy, "Notes," 18 Aug 1965, 4.4, HRC.

24. Purdy may have borrowed Melba's name from Nellie Melba, an Australian operatic soprano famous at the turn of the century. She liked to eat, apparently, as she is the namesake for Melba Toast, Peach Melba, and two other dishes.

25. Purdy, "Notes," 4.4, HRC; "Play Needs 3 Treadmills, 17 Stagehands," *Los Angeles Times*, Dec 28, 1965, D9; Louis Calta, "*Malcolm* Cast Meets Director," *New York Times*, Nov 24, 1965, 35.

26. Brustein, "Albee's Allegory of Innocence," 36.

27. Kauffmann, "Capote in Kansas," rev. of *In Cold Blood*, *New Republic*, Jan 22, 1966; Windham, *Lost Friendships*, 80.

28. Qtd. in Gussow, *Albee*, 249.

29. Purdy, Untitled article intended for *Life*, 1.2, HRC.

30. Giroux to MN, 12 Jan 1966, b. 288, f. Malcolm, FSG.

31. Purdy to Giroux, 24 Oct 1967, FSG, b. 287, f. gen. corr.

32. Purdy to Albee, Oct 22, 1967, 5.4, HRC.

33. Albee to Purdy, Oct 26, 1966, 7.4, HRC.

34. Albee to Purdy, 22 Aug 2005, courtesy Uecker.

35. Albee to Bill Flanagan, March 1966, qtd. in Gussow, *Edward Albee*, 251.

36. Purdy to Giroux, 13 Dec 1965, b. 289. f. Reader, FSG.

37. Hyman, "Conviction of Opinion," 19–20.

38. Purdy to Straus, 24 Apr, 11 May 1966, b. 287, f. gen., FSG.

39. Purdy to Giroux, 9 July, 13 July 1966, b. 288, f. ECW, FSG.

Chapter 12

1. Purdy to Robert Giroux, 5 Sept 1966; Giroux to Purdy, 6 Sept 1966, b. 288, f. Eustace Chisholm and the Works (hereafter ECW), FSG.

2. Fredric Warburg to Giroux, 13 Sept 1966, b. 288, f. ECW, FSG.

3. Warburg to Giroux, 20 Sept 1966, b. 288, f. ECW, FSG.

4. Giroux to Warburg, 23 Sept 1966, b. 288, f. ECW, FSG.

5. Jack Phelps to Warburg, 10 Nov 1966, b. 288, f. ECW, FSG.

6. Purdy to Giroux, 7 Dec 1966, b. 288, f. ECW, FSG.

7. Giroux to Phelps, 14 Nov 1966, b. 288, f. ECW, FSG.

8. Norman MacLeish to Purdy, 5 Jan 1967, b. 16, HRC.

9. Purdy to Frank Purdy, 10 Jan 1967, 6.10, HRC.

10. MacLeish to Purdy, 12 Apr 1967, b. 16, HRC; John Bucklew to Purdy, 11 Apr 1967, 8.7, HRC.

11. Thanks go to David Kuebeck of Bowling Green for sharing this financial data.

12. MacLeish to Purdy, 5 Jan 1967, b. 16, HRC.

13. Purdy, int. Profit, 125.

14. Purdy, "James Purdy," *CAAS*, 303.

15. Purdy, "I Am James Purdy," int. Varble, 29.

16. MacLeish to Purdy, 19 Jan 1967, b. 16, HRC.

17. Purdy, int. Northouse, 201.

18. Gore Vidal, "Rabbit's Own Burrow," 259; Philip F. Clark, tel. interview, 28 Mar 2019.

19. Roger Straus to Purdy, 2 Mar 1967; John Farrar to Purdy, 18 May 1967, b. 288, f. ECW, FSG.

20. Virgil Thomson to Purdy, n.d. [early 1967], copy in b. 288, f. ECW—gen., FSG; Ned Rorem to Purdy, 25 June 1967, 18.8, HRC; Bowles to Purdy, 1 June 1967, *In Touch*, 402.

21. Wetzsteon, "Making It the Hard Way"; Wilson, "Purdy Pushes Comedy Past Blackness."

22. Qtd. in FSG memo, n.d. [spring 1967], b. 288, f. ECW, FSG; George Steiner, rev. of *Eustace Chisholm*, *Sunday Times* [date unknown].

23. Qtd. in Kaiser, *Gay Metropolis*, 160.

24. Wilfrid Sheed, "An Alleged Love Story."

25. Sheed, "Heterosexual Backlash," 289–90, 292.

26. Purdy to Baldanza, 25 Aug 1971, 5.5, HRC.

27. Purdy, int. Northouse, 188.

28. Matthew Stadler, Skype interview, 15 June 2019.

29. Ian Parker, "Showboat"; Warren French to Straus, 9 May 1967, Straus to French, 11 May 1967, b. 288, f. ECW, gen, FSG.

30. Nelson Algren, "It's a Gay and Dreary Life," 67–68; Purdy, "Out with James Purdy," int. Lane, 81.

31. Donald Weise, "Christmas with James Purdy."

32. Donna Seaman, *Identity Unknown*, 82.

33. Saunders, *Cultural Cold War*, 144; Purdy to Giroux, 24 June 1967, b. 287, f. gen. corr., FSG.

34. James Lindroth, rev. of *Eustace*, 21; Purdy to Giroux, 8 July 1967, b. 287, f. gen. cor., FSG.

35. Purdy to Anthony Harvey, 6 Aug 1967, b. 14, f. 3, HRC.

36. Purdy acknowledges Andreas Brown's "generous help" in Purdy, *CAAS*, 302, n 9.

37. Purdy, "Scrap of Paper," *NDPP* 20 (1968): 34–44.

38. John Martin to Robert Giroux, 14 Sep 1967, b. 290, f. SMCV, FSG.

39. Purdy to Straus, 6 Aug 1967, b. 288, f. ECW—gen. corr., FSG.

40. Purdy to Straus, 24 Sep 1969, FSG, b. 288, f. ECW, FSG.

41. Purdy to "Dick" [FSG], Feb 23, 1968, FSG, b. 288, f. ECW.

42. Eliot Fremont-Smith, "Diddy Did It—Or Did He?" Rev. of *Death Kit* by Susan Sontag, *New York Times*, Aug 18, 1967, 31+.

43. Moser, *Sontag*, 213.

44. Straus to Purdy, n.d. [fall 1969], b. 288, f. ECW, FSG.

45. Stadler, Skype interview with the author, June 15, 2019.

46. Purdy to Straus, 6 Aug 1967, b. 288, f. ECW, FSG.

47. Purdy to Straus, 16 Aug 1967, b. 290, f. Sleepers in Moon-Crowned Valleys (hereafter SMCV), FSG.

48. Purdy to Straus, 26 Aug 1967, b. 287, f. gen. corr., FSG.

49. Paul Bowles to James Leo Herlihy, 4 Sept 4, 1967, in Bowles, *In Touch*.

50. Purdy to Giroux, 24 Sept 1967; Purdy telegram to Straus, 26 Sept 1967, b. 290. f. SMCV, FSG.

51. Susan Sontag "came out" as bisexual in 1995.

52. Purdy to Giroux, 10 Oct 1967, copy in 6.3, HRC.

53. Purdy to Phelps, 24 Oct 1967, b. 287, f. gen. corr., FSG; Purdy to Giroux, 24 Oct 1967, b. 287, f. gen. corr., FSG; Purdy to Giroux, n.d. Nov 1967, b. 290, f. SMCV, FSG.

54. "Price-Fixing Figure Found Shot to Death," *Chicago Tribune*, Oct 5, 1967, 24; Dept. of Justice, press release, 1 June 1967.

55. *Malcolm*, 73.

56. Osborn Andreas directed Pentron from 1961 through 1965; they started losing money in 1961, and their deficit plunged to $1.7 million by 1965. Osborn resigned that year after feuding with the man who succeeded him as president and Pentron recovered.

57. Vincent Butler, "4 Chicagoans Named in Stock Rigging Indictment," *Chicago Tribune*, 2 June 1967, D9; "Stock Scandal, '67 Style," *Newsweek*, June 12, 1967, 71; "Price-Fixing Figure."

58. Butler, "4 Chicagoans Named."

59. See Giancana and Giancana, *Double Cross* (New York: Warner, 1992).

60. Abercrombie to Purdy, 16 Feb 1968, 7.4, HRC.

61. Purdy to Laughlin, 27 Sep 1967, 6.9, HRC.

62. Purdy to Giroux, 7 Nov 1967, copy in 6.3, HRC.

63. Purdy to Thomson, 1 Sep 1968, VT.

64. Purdy to Thomson, 1 Dec 1968, VT.

65. Pearson to Purdy, n.d., encl. copy in Purdy to Giroux, 15 Oct 1968, b. 289, f. other works.

66. Purdy, "Mr. Evening," *New Directions* 23 (1971): 14–21; Purdy to Laughlin, 9 June 1969, 6.3, HRC.

67. Purdy to Laughlin, 16 May 1969, HRC, 6.9; Purdy to Lish, July 17, 1969, b. 16, Lish mss.

68. Purdy to Gallup, 9 Nov 1967, copy to Giroux, FSG, b. 287, Purdy, gen. corr.

69. Purdy, int. Lear, 73; Chupack, *James Purdy*, 103–4, 106, 20.

70. Purdy to Giroux, 28 Dec 1967, copy in 6.3, HRC.

71. Hundley, tel. interview, 30 Aug 2009.

72. David Purdy, Christine Reese, and Dorothy Purdy, personal interview, July 2009.

73. Purdy to Frank A. Purdy, 10 Jan 1968, 6.10, HRC; Purdy to Steward, 29 May 1971, 1.11, OSU.171.

74. "Matthew Paris and Dave Zimmer Interview James Purdy."

75. Purdy to Straus, 27 Feb 1968; 2 Mar 1968, b. 288, f. ECW, pub sub, FSG.

76. Lila Karpf to Paul Kresh, 29 Jan 1968, b. 287, f. gen. corr., FSG; Purdy to Giroux, 25 July 1968, b. 290, f. SMCV, FSG.

77. Purdy to Giroux, 17 Jan, 19 Nov 1968, b. 290. f. SMCV, FSG.

78. Truman Capote, qtd. in Inge, ed., *Conversations with Capote*, 158; Vidal qtd. in Frederic Raphael, "What Makes Norman Run?," *New York Times*, Jan 7, 1968; Roth, "Play That Dare Not Speak Its Name," *New York Review of Books*, Feb 25, 1965.

79. Epstein qtd. in Kaiser, *Gay Metropolis*, 224, 218.

80. Mailer, "Up the Family Tree," 175.

81. Moser, *Sontag*, 217.

82. Kostelanetz, *End of Intelligent Writing*, 51.

83. Tom Zulick, tel. interview, 29 June 2019.

84. Gordon Lish int. by Matthew Stadler, 9 April 1992, b. 4, f. Purdy Art. 1, MSP.

85. Lila Karpf to Lish, 15 May 1968, b. 288, f. Daddy Wolf, FSG; Purdy to Lish, 24 July, 28 Oct 1968, b. 16, Lish mss.

86. Purdy to Lish, 2 Dec 1969, b. 16, Lish mss.

87. Leavitt and Holditch, *World of Tennessee Williams*, 52; Devlin, ed., *Conversations with Tennessee Williams*, 204, 335–36.

88. Purdy to Laughlin, 11 Apr 1968, 3.80, JPP.

89. John Lahr, *Tennessee Williams*, 485.

90. Straus to Purdy, 3 Sept 1968, b. 290. f. Sleepers in Moon-Crowned Valleys [hereafter cited as SMCV], FSG.

91. Purdy to Giroux, 19 Nov, 10 Dec 1968, copy in 6.3, HRC.

92. Margaret Nicholson to Purdy, 9 Dec 1968, b. 290, f. SMCV, FSG.

93. Giroux to Purdy, 24 Jan 1969, b. 290 f. SMCV, FSG.

94. Purdy to Straus, 5 Dec 1968, b. 290 f. SMCV, FSG.

95. Purdy to James Laughlin, 8 Dec 1969, 6.9, HRC.

96. Purdy to Giroux, 25 Jan 1969, b. 290, f. SMCV, FSG.

97. Giroux to Purdy, 31 Jan 1969, b. 290, f. SMCV, FSG.

98. Purdy to Giroux, 1 Feb 1969, b. 290, f. SMCV, FSG.

99. Giroux to Purdy, 7 Feb 1969; Purdy to Straus, 8 Mar 1969; Straus to Purdy, 11 Mar 1969, b. 290, f. SMCV, FSG.

100. Purdy to Thomson, 11 Apr 1969, VT.

101. Tommasini, *Virgil Thomson*, 469.

102. Purdy to Thomson, 28 May 1969, VT; Tommasini, *Virgil Thomson*, 552, 553.

Chapter 13

1. Kachka, *Hothouse*, 113; Purdy to Angus Wilson, 13 June 1969, 7.2, HRC; Hills, "Structure of the American Literary Establishment."

2. Purdy to A. Wilson, 13 June, 22 June 1969, 7.2, HRC.

3. Straus to Purdy, 23 July 1969, b. 287, f. gen.; Purdy to Straus, 25 July 1969, b. 290, f. Sleepers in Moon-Crowned Valleys (hereafter SMCV), FSG.

4. Purdy to Paula Fox, 20 June 1970, 4.4, OSU.3.

5. Purdy, int. Northouse, 195; Purdy, int. Swaim, 1987.

6. Purdy, "I Am James Purdy," int. Varble, 28.

7. Saunders, *Cultural Cold War*, 285; "Militant Liberty," *Wikipedia*, en.wikipedia.org/wiki/Militant_Liberty:_A_Program_of_Evaluation_and_Assessment_of_Freedom.

8. Parker to Robert Giroux, 21 Nov 1969; Giroux to Gilbert Parker, 25 Nov 1969, b. 287, f. Cabot Wright Begins, FSG.

9. Purdy to Giroux, 30 Oct 1970, copy in 6.3, HRC.

10. Purdy to Giroux, 22 Nov 1969, 20 Jan 1970, b. 287, f. gen. corr., FSG.

11. Spring, *Secret Historian*, 344–45, 385.

12. "Robert Helps (1928-2001): A Timeline," Robert Helps Web Monument, helpsweb. free.fr/Composer/introduction.php?page = timeline.

13. Barry Horwitz, email to the author, 21 Aug 2019, tel. interview, 23 Aug 2019.

14. Gerald Busby, tel. interview, 23 Feb 2020.

15. Joseph Fennimore, email to the author, 18 May 2020.

16. James Baldwin, "Geraldine Page: Bird of Light," *Show*, February 1962; Photos by Steve Shapiro, gettyimages.com; "History," Torn Page Studios, www.tornpagestudios.org/history.

17. "On the Rebound," *Complete Short Stories*, 296, 299, 300.

18. Susan Dominus, "Rip Torn Won't Go Gentle Into That Good Night," *New York Times Magazine*, May 7, 2006.

19. Karpf to Robie Macauley [*Playboy*], 15 Aug 1968, b. 289, f. Other works, FSG; Lish to Purdy, 26 Nov 1969, 11.5, HRC.

20. Purdy to Giroux, 23 June 1969, b. 290, f. SMCV, FSG; Purdy to Fox, 20 June, 12 Aug 1970, 4.4., OSU.3; Purdy to A. Wilson, 22 June 1969, 7.2, HRC.

21. Thomson to Purdy, 19 July 1970, 5.128, JPP.

22. Purdy to Thomson, 24 June 1971, 75.29, VT.

23. Inscribed *Gloria Vanderbilt Book of Collage*, Charvat Collection of American Literature, Thompson Library, The Ohio State University.

24. Frank Baldanza, "Telephone conversation with James Purdy, Sept 13, 1971" notes, BGSU.

25. Paul Bowles, Doubleday press release, b. 3, OSU.208.

26. Frank Daniel, "Purdy Opens Trio."

27. Lindroth, rev. of *Jeremy's Version*; Wolff, "Stung Ventricles," 122–23.

28. Symons, "The Other Island," *Sunday Times*, June 8, 1971, 32; Glendinning, *Edith Sitwell*, 93, 251, 355.

29. Norman Shrapnel, "Plain and Fancy," *Guardian*, June 3, 1971, 15; David Williams, "Fiction," *The Times*, June 3, 1971, 12; "Keeping It in the Family," *Times Literary Supplement* (4 June 1971): 637.

30. Lish to Purdy, 15 Oct 1970, 11.5, HRC; Purdy to Baldanza, 25 Aug, 3 Dec 1971, 5.5, HRC.

31. Purdy to Baldanza, 25 Aug, 1971, BGSU.

32. Trevillion, "James Purdy: Balance of Cruelty and Wit," 57.

33. Rosen, *Cold Eye, Warm Heart*, 329–330.

34. Polsgrove, *It Wasn't Pretty*, 246.
35. Purdy to Lish, 11, 12, 14 Oct 1970, b. 16., Lish mss.
36. Max, "Carver Chronicles."
37. Polsgrove, *It Wasn't Pretty*, 243.
38. Polsgrove, *Pretty,* 246–47; Purdy to Harvey, 30 Oct 1970, 14.3, HRC; Purdy to Lish, 17 Oct 1970, 15 Mar 1971, b. 16, Lish mss.; Lish to Purdy, 15 Dec 1970, 16 Feb 1971, HRC, 11.5.
39. Purdy to Straus, 3 Dec 1970, b. 287, f. gen. corr., FSG.
40. Purdy to William J. Weatherby, 7 July 1973, b. 287, f. gen. corr., FSG.
41. Ned Rorem to Purdy, 25 Feb 1971, 4.107, JPP; Rorem, *Later Diaries*, 356; Purdy to Lish, 1 Mar 1971, Lish mss.; Taylor, "A Note from James Purdy."
42. Ed Hefter to Purdy, 28 Sep, 12 Oct, 1969, 14.5, HRC.
43. Kolin, "Tenn and the Banana Queen"; Hefter to Purdy, 4 Jan 1978, 65.2, HRC; Uecker, tel. interview, 19 Nov 2020, 27 Feb 2021.
44. John Uecker, tel. interviews, 18 Sep, 19 Sep 2020.
45. Purdy, *Garments the Living Wear*, 12, 100, 132.
46. Purdy to Abercrombie, Easter Card, n.d. Apr 1971, 11 May 1971; GAP.
47. Hefter to Purdy, 17 Dec 1971, 14.5, HRC.
48. Hefter to Purdy, 6 Jan 1972, 46.4, HRC.
49. Hefter to Purdy, 1962, 2.48, JPP; Purdy to Abercrombie, 8 June 1976, GAP.
50. Purdy to Steward, 29 May 1971; Steward to Purdy, 1 July 1971, 1.11, OSU.171.

Chapter 14

1. *I Am Elijah Thrush*, 33; Purdy to Sandy Richardson, 10 June 1971, TU [Richardson penciled his reply on Purdy's letter].
2. Richard Hundley, tel. interview, 16 Oct 2009.
3. Jorma Sjoblom to Purdy, May 18, 1972, 5.121, JPP.
4. Purdy to Gertrude Abercrombie, 24 May 1972, GAP.
5. Jackson, *Gwendolyn Brooks*, 28–29.
6. "Oral History Interview with John Carlis, 1968 Sep," int. Henri Ghent, *Smithsonian Archives of American Art*, www.aaa.si.edu/collections/interviews/oral-history-interv iew-john-carlis-11456#transcript.
7. Purdy to Abercrombie, June 8, 1976, GAP. Purdy later said he based Albert Peggs on a black man he knew who lived in a little place on Wall Street who became "very angry when the book was published," and in a piece for *New York*, he remarked that many pages were inspired by his friendship with "some of the black waiters" at Gage & Tollner (Lear, "Interview," 58; Purdy, "Literary Ghosts," 78).
8. Purdy to Gordon Lish, 12 June 1971, b. 16, Lish mss.
9. S. D. Adams, *James Purdy*, 142; Lish to Purdy, 25 June 1971, 11.6, HRC.
10. Purdy to Lish, 12 June, 6 July, 7 July 1971, b. 16, Lish mss.
11. Purdy to Giroux, July 6, 1971, b. 287, f. gen., FSG.

12. Giroux to Purdy, 28 July 1971; Purdy to Giroux, 29 July 1971; b. 287, Purdy, gen., FSG.

13. Purdy to Richardson, 4 Aug 1971, TU.

14. Hundley, "Ready," 173, 174.

15. Purdy to Abercrombie, 23 May 1971, GAP.

16. "Vocal Quartets Premiere Click at Ram Island," *Evening Express* [Portland, ME], 28 July 1971.

17. Photocopy enclosure, Richard Hundley to the author, 20 Sept 2009; Hundley, "Ready," 164.

18. Giroux to Purdy, 3 Dec 1971, b. 287, f. gen., FSG.

19. Purdy to Baldanza, 28 Sept 1971, BGSU; Purdy, "I Am Elijah Thrush" MS., b. 69, Lish mss.

20. Purdy to Baldanza, 3 Dec 3, 1971, BGSU.

21. Purdy qtd. in Malin, "James (Otis) Purdy"; Varble, "I Am James Purdy," 28.

22. Purdy qtd. in Jay Ladd, *James Purdy*, 17.

23. Abercrombie to Purdy, 16 Jan 1972, 46.1, HRC.

24. Purdy to Abercrombie, 13 Mar 1972, GAP.

25. Purdy, "CA Interview," *Contemporary Authors* 19, 393; Purdy to Sjoblom, 4 Mar 1972, 6.12, HRC.

26. Purdy to Sam Steward, 8 Mar 1972, 1.11, OSU.171.

27. Purdy to Tanner, 23 Feb 1972, 7.1, HRC.

28. Purdy to Sjoblom, 4 Mar 1972, 6.12, HRC.

29. John Uecker, tel. interview, November 26, 2020; Williams, *Small Craft Warnings*, 174.

30. Purdy, int. Northouse, 194.

31. Purdy to Steward, 19 May 1972, 1.11, OSU.171.

32. Paul Bowles to Purdy, 1 May 1972, 1.10, JPP.

33. Purdy, int. Real, 28.

34. Matthiessen, *American Renaissance*, 250.

35. S. Adams, *James Purdy*, 8, 130-31.

36. Norman MacLeish to Purdy, 10 May 1972, 3.69, JPP.

37. MacLeish to Purdy, 13 Jan 1971, 7 Jan 1972, 16.4, HRC.

38. Purdy to Sonny Rollins, 20 May 1972, 47.2, HRC.

39. Purdy, int. Matthew Stadler, 18 Mar 1992, b. 4, f. Art. 1, MSP.

40. Purdy to Giroux, 22 Nov 1969; 20 Jan 1970, b. 287, f. gen. corr., FSG.

41. Purdy, notebook, 34.1, HRC.

42. Purdy to Abercrombie, 24 May 1972, GAP.

43. Purdy to Abercrombie, n.d., ca. Sep 1972, GAP; Purdy to Fox, 25 Aug 1972, 4.5, OSU.3.

44. Graver, rev. of *I Am Elijah Thrush*, *New York Times*, July 2, 1972; "Briefly Noted: Fiction," *New Yorker* 48 (May 27, 1972): 114-15.

45. Purdy to Richardson, 22 July 1972, 4 Aug 1972, TU.

46. Purdy to Emily Varkala and Meta Evans, 5 Aug 1972, TU.

47. Purdy to Lish, 20 June, 22 July, 28 July 1972, b. 16, Lish mss.

48. Francis King, "Exotic Cast"; "Golden Suction," rev. of *Elijah Thrush*, *TLS*, 3 Nov 1972, 1305; Jim Hunter, "Success," rev. of *Elijah Thrush*, *The Listener* 88 (19 Oct 1972): 513; Auberon Waugh, "Faecal Felicities," *Spectator* 229 (21 Oct 1972): 626-27.

49. Purdy to Richardson, 12 Oct 1972, TU.

50. Purdy to Richardson, 8 Dec 1972, TU.

51. David J. Getsy, "Gutter Art: Stephen Varble and Genderqueer Performance on the Streets of 1970s New York," September 8, 2016, Leslie Lohman Museum of Gay and Lesbian Art, vimeo.com/182807556.

52. Purdy, int. Northouse, 196.

53. Ibid., 194.

54. Doubleday press release, Jan 5, 1973, TU.

Chapter 15

1. Purdy to Frank Baldanza, 27 July 1974, BGSU.

2. Jere Real, tel. interview, July 6, 2012; Purdy, "Interview," int. Real, 25.

3. Purdy to Richardson, 16 Jan 1973, TU.

4. Purdy to Richardson, 8 Mar 1973, TU.

5. Purdy to Thomson, 19 Mar 1973, 75.29, VT.

6. Purdy in Canning, *Gay Fiction Speaks*, 34.

7. Joyce Carol Oates, "Notions Good and Bad."

8. Purdy to Lish, 15 Mar 1971, b. 16, Lish mss. No published review by Oates of *I am Elijah Thrush* can be found.

9. Oates to Purdy, 6 Apr 1973, 50.1, HRC; Purdy to Oates, 10 Apr 1973, 50.1, HRC.

10. Purdy to Richardson, 9 May 1973, TU; Purdy int. Stadler, 18 March 1992, b. 4, f. Art. 1, MSP.

11. Weatherby to Purdy, 11 June 1973, b. 287, gen., FSG.

12. Purdy to Weatherby, 19 Aug 1973, b. 287, gen., FSG.

13. Purdy to Jo Ann (Doubleday), 23 Nov 1973, TU.

14. Purdy to Richardson, 26 Oct 1974, TU.

15. Purdy in Canning, *Gay Fiction*, 27–28.

16. Bowles to Halpern, 3 April 1973, in Bowles, *In Touch*, 446.

17. Lish to Purdy, 16 Feb 1974, b. 16, Lish mss.

18. "John Bucklew Dies; Professor at Lawrence," *Post-Crescent*, April 1, 1974, 21; "John Bucklew," *Lawrentian*, April 5, 1974, 3; "LU Lecture Is about Ethics in Psychotherapy," *Post-Crescent*, Feb 26, 1976.

19. Steward to Patricia Snoke, 17 June 1974, 1.11, OSU.171.

20. Purdy, int. Northouse, 200.

21. Purdy, "Penthouse Interview," int. Fred Barron, 89, 90.

22. Ibid., 92, 89.

23. Ibid., 91.

24. Purdy, "Voyage of Discovery," int. Chris Huizenga, 72.

25. Purdy, int. Barron, 91.

26. Purdy, int. Northouse, 200.

27. Purdy to Richardson, 26 Oct 1974, TU.

28. Giroux to Purdy, 25 Nov 1974, b. 287, f. gen., FSG.
29. Purdy in Canning, *Gay Fiction*, 29.
30. Purdy to Elborn, 28 Sep 1976, KU.
31. Michael Ehrhardt, "Wizard of Id," 27.
32. Purdy in Canning, *Gay Fiction*, 29.
33. Purdy int. Matthew Stadler, 18 Mar 1992, b. 1, f. Art. 1; Edmund White, email to the author, 15 Dec 2020; Stadler, Skype interview, 15 June 2019.
34. Strausbaugh, "Pure Purdy," 42.
35. Purdy to Paula Fox, 25 Aug 1972, 4.5, OSU.3.
36. Martin, "Skeletons in a Midwestern Closet."
37. Steward, "Comments on James Purdy's Novel *The House of the Solitary Maggot*," b. 287, f. gen. corr., FSG; Anderson, "Purdy: Endurance, a Family Theme"; Warren French, rev. of *The House of the Solitary Maggot*, 93
38. Purdy to Richardson, 14 Aug 1974, TU; Stadler, int. Purdy, 18 Mar 1992, b. 4, f. Art. 1, MSP.
39. Purdy to Frank Baldanza, 18 Oct 1974, BGSU.
40. Purdy to Richardson, 26 Oct 1974, TU.
41. Purdy, in Robert Wilson, ed., *Phoenix Book Shop*, n.p.
42. Purdy to Richardson, 3 Nov 1974, TU; David Means qtd. in Graves, "Brilliant but Little-Known James Purdy."
43. Purdy to Richardson, 23 Nov 1974, TU.
44. Joseph Fennimore, email to the author, 18 May 2020.
45. Gordon Lish, tel. interview, 2 June 2019.
46. Purdy to Lish, 13 Mar 1974, b. 16, Lish mss.
47. Purdy to Lish, 14, 17 Oct 1974, b. 16, Lish mss.
48. Purdy to Lish, 14 Oct 1974, b. 16, Lish mss.
49. Purdy to Baldanza, 9 Nov 1974, BGSU.
50. Martin, rev. of *A Day After the Fair*.
51. Purdy to Richardson, 1, 11 Dec 1974, TU.
52. Stadler, int. Purdy, 18 Mar 1992, MSP, Beinecke, b. 4, f. Art. 1.
53. Ned Rorem to Paul Bowles, 6 Jan 1975, in Rorem, *Wings of Friendship*, 87–88.

Chapter 16

1. Stephen D. Adams, *James Purdy*, 142.
2. "On the Alamo," annotated by Purdy, UD.
3. *Bible*, KJV, Isaiah 53:3, 53:5; Purdy, "Voyage of Discovery," int. Huizenga, 72.
4. Purdy, *In a Shallow Grave*, 132.
5. Adams, *James Purdy*, 147.
6. Gary Zebrun, "SLF—Preparation with Imagination," *Observer* [Notre Dame U.], Feb 27, 1975, 5; Andy Praschak, "Backstage Glimpses of a Festival," *Observer*, Mar 3, 1975, 5.

7. Purdy to Steward, 6, 27 May 1975, 1.11, OSU.171.

8. Purdy to Baldanza, 24 July 1975, BGSU; Purdy to Paula Fox, 15 Aug 1975, 4.5, OSU.3.

9. Horwitz, tel. interview, 23 Aug 2019; Purdy to Fox, 15 June, 15 Aug 1975, 4.5, OSU.3.

10. Horwitz, tel. interview, 23 Aug 2019.

11. Michael Tillotson, tel. interview, May 24, 2020.

12. Stephen D. Adams, email to the author, Sep 22, 2020.

13. Lear, "Interview," 73.

14. Spring, *Secret Historian*, 370–71.

15. Barry David Horwitz, email to the author, 21 Aug 2019.

16. Copy owned by Marvin Granland as of 2020, Abebooks.com.

17. Wilcox to Abercrombie, p.m. 26 Aug 1975, ser. 5.g. Wendell Wilcox, GAP.

18. Gayle Rubin, "James (Jim) Kane," *Leather Hall of Fame*, leatherhalloffame.com/inductees-list/30-james-jim-kane.html.

19. Purdy to Sam Steward, 13 Nov 1975, 11 Jan 1976, 1.11, OSU.171.

20. Purdy to Fox, 15 Aug 1975, 4.5, OSU.3; Bachardy, "James Purdy"; Purdy to Steward, 21 Jan 1977, 1.11, OSU.171.

21. Purdy to Fox, 15 Aug 1975, 4.5.

22. Purdy to Fox, 15 Aug 1975, 4.5, OSU.3; Purdy to Steward, 13 Nov 1975, 1.11, OSU.171.

23. Purdy to Abercrombie, 12 Mar 1976, GAP.

24. Busby, tel. interview, 23 Feb 2020.

25. "Matthew Paris and Dave Zimmer Interview James Purdy."

26. Chuck Taylor, "Heights History: Promenade Restaurant on Montague Street," *Brooklyn Heights Blog*, Mar 26, 2012.

27. John Wynne, tel. interview, 22 Sep 2020; Purdy to Fox, 15 June 1975, 4.5, OSU.3.

28. "Music by Joseph Fennimore" Program, b. 4, OSU.208; Raymond Ericson, "Fennimore Plays Own Works," *New York Times*, Oct 3, 1975; Fennimore, email to the author, May 18, 2020.

29. John Uecker, Skype interview, 24 June 2020; Tom Zulick, tel. interview, 29 June 2019; Purdy to Matthew Stadler, 24 Apr 1991, b. 5, f. letters 2, MSP.

30. Purdy in Canning, *Gay Fiction*, 12.

31. Jerome Charyn, "In a Shallow Grave," 2–3.

32. Davis, "Quest for Love"; Weigel, "There's More to Death."

33. Edmund White, *My Lives*, 301; Clark, tel. interview, 28 Mar 2019.

34. Edward Albee wanted John Uecker too as a boyfriend, he said, and to that end, his producer, Richard Barr, acting as a relationship broker, invited John over to his apartment. Uecker assumed Barr was hosting a party but he was the only guest. Barr, "blasted" on alcohol, proposed that John become Edward's lover. When Uecker declined, Barr was surprised and replied, "I'm sorry. I feel so sorry for you." After that, Uecker believed that he was ever after a target of Albee's mind games.

35. John Uecker, tel. interviews, 13 June 2008, 1 Jan 2013, 18 Feb, 2 Mar, 11 Mar, 20 Mar, 24 Mar, 31 Mar 2021.

36. Barry Horwitz, tel. interview, 23 Aug 2019.

37. Gerald Busby, tel. interview, 23 Feb 2020.

38. John Strausbaugh, "Pure Purdy," 42.

39. Purdy to Abercrombie, 8 June 1976, GAP.

40. Purdy, int. Northouse, 191–92

41. Purdy, int. Northouse, 195.

42. Purdy to Steward, 13 Nov 1975, 11 Jan 1976, 1.11, OSU.171.

43. Purdy, "Voyage of Discovery," int. Huizenga, 72.

44. All News WEAN, "Final Play," qtd. in Hohman, "Final Straw," 96.

45. Huizenga, "Purdy," 72.

46. Purdy to Steward, 1, 11 July, 17 Sep 1976, 1.12, OSU.171.

47. Horwitz, tel. interview with the author, 23 Aug 2019, email to the author, 21 Aug 2019; Purdy to Steward, 10 Aug 1991, b. 3, SSP.

48. Purdy to Elborn, 15 June, 28 Sept 1976, KU.

49. Steven Winn, "Old Friend Profiles Young Playwright," *SF Chronicle*, Oct 22, 1995.

50. Tillotson, tel. interview, 24 May 2020.

51. Purdy to Elborn, 28 Sep 1976, KU.

52. Purdy to Robert Fox, 18 Mar 1977, 1.4, OSU.3.

53. Purdy, int. Profit, 126.

54. Purdy, int. Northouse, 205.

55. Purdy, *True*, *NDPP* 28 (1974): 77–98.

56. Purdy to Thomson, 21 Apr 1977, VT.

57. Miller, "James Purdy's Gertrude," 33.

58. Wilcox, in Gertrude Abercrombie Retrospective Exhibition Catalog, n.p.

59. Purdy, int. Northouse, 201, 205.

60. Purdy to Straus, Western Union Mailgram, 13 July 1977, FSG, b. 287, f. gen. corr.

61. Purdy, int. Northouse, 185.

62. Ibid., 209–210.

63. Ibid., 208.

64. Purdy to Elborn, 8 Feb 1977, KU.

65. Purdy, int. Northouse, 186–87, 210–11.

66. Martin, rev. of *A Day After the Fair*; Purdy to Lish, 25 Feb 1973, b. 16, Lish mss.

67. O'Brien, "Purdy, Privately Printed."

68. "Margaret Cho Provides Further Evidence of San Francisco's Magic," *SF Bay Times*, Oct 2015; Michael Flanagan, "History of LGBT Bookstores in the Castro," *Bay Area Reporter*, July 17, 2016; *SF Sentinel*, Sep 24, 1977; Gunn to Tanner, 21 Jan 1978, 2.5, TG.

69. Purdy, "James Purdy," int. Link, 62.

70. Strausbaugh, "Pure Purdy," 42; Canning, *Gay Fiction*, 27.

71. Uecker, phone interview, 10 Jan 2013.

72. Dennis Moore, tel. interviews, 21 May 2012, 25 Aug, 31 Oct 2020; Jack Fritscher, email to the author, 16 Aug 2019.

73. Purdy to Robert Fox, 29 Sep 1977, 1.4, OSU.3.

74. Wynne, text message to the author, 5 April 2021.

75. Stephen D. Adams, email to the author, 22 Sep 2020.

76. Purdy to Gunn, 3 Jan 1978, 1.50, TG; Gunn to Purdy, 16 Jan 1979, 67.6, HRC.

77. Gunn to Tanner, 23 Feb 1978, 1.50, TG.

78. Collins to Purdy, 24 Feb, 18 July, 7 Oct 1978, HRC, 64.5; Purdy to Gunn 18 Dec 1978, 1.50, TG.

79. Purdy to Alec Wilder, 14 Feb 1978, 64.1, HRC.

80. Purdy to Ladd, 16 Dec 1977, b. 4, OSU.208; Purdy to Fox, 4 Feb 1977, 4.5, OSU.3.

81. Purdy, "Notes on Recognition," 69.

82. Canning, *Gay Fiction*, 18.

83. Purdy, int. Real, 27.

84. Zulick, tel. interview, June 29, 2020.

85. Uecker, tel. interview, 1 Dec 2020, 27 Feb 2021.

86. Hundley, tel. interview, 30 Aug 2009.

87. Wynne, tel. interview, 22 Sep 2020.

88. Edwin McDowell, "Donald Fine Is Dismissed as Arbor House Publisher," *New York Times*, Oct 26, 1983, C28.

89. Arbor House release, b. 1, OSU.208; Stephen D. Adams, email to the author, 22 Sep 2020; Christopher Cox, "Fighting Words."

90. Purdy, int. Allen Frame, 20.

91. Purdy to Lish, March 8, 1978, b. 16, Lish mss.

92. Purdy to Adams, 14 May 1978, summary in email to the author, 22 Sep 2020.

93. Katha Pollitt, "Ovid and the Boys."

94. Purdy, "Afterword" to "Sleep Tight," 35.

95. Cox, "Fighting Words."

96. Purdy to Elborn, 5 May, 17 May 1978, KU.

97. Purdy to Ladd, 9 Oct 1980, b. 1, OSU.208.

98. Stephen D. Adams, *Homosexual as Hero*, 65; S. D. Adams, email to the author, 22 Sep 2020; Purdy to Ladd, 9 Oct 1980, b. 1, OSU.208.

99. Jack Collins to Purdy, July 18, 1978, HRC, 64.5; Purdy to Mr. Inman, 17 Oct 1978, b. 27, AR; John Waters, *Mr. Know-It-All*, 280.

100. John Wynne, tel. interview, 27 Aug 2020.

101. Katha Pollitt, email to the author, 3 Oct 2020.

102. Wynne, tel. interview, 22 Sep 2020.

103. Waters, *Role Models*, 40.

104. Wynne, tel. interview, 22 Sep 2020.

105. S. Adams to Purdy, 13 July, 16 Aug 1978, 64.2, HRC.

106. Wynne, tel. interview, 27 Aug 2020.

107. Purdy to Adams, 29 Nov 1978, summary, Adams to the author, 22 Sep 2020.

108. Purdy to Adams, 21 July 1978 [from Provincetown], summary, Adams to the author, 22 Sep 2020.

109. Uecker, tel. interview, 27 Feb, 13 Apr 2021; Purdy to Elborn, flyer with note, p.m. July 1978, KU.

110. Purdy, "Fantasies *Are* the Truth," 34.

111. Collins, "James Purdy's New Novel," rev. of *Narrow Rooms*, *SF Sentinel*, July 14, 1978.

112. Collins to Purdy, 18 July, 7 Oct 1978, HRC, 64.5.

113. Thom Gunn, diary entry, 23 Nov 1979, 2.39, TG; Gunn to Douglas Chambers, 23 Dec 1979, TG.

114. Purdy, int. Northouse, 201, 188.
115. Purdy, "Interview with James Purdy," int. Real, 9.
116. Klein, rev. of *Mourners Below*, 39.
117. Purdy, int. Real, 26.
118. The short play "Adeline" is a different narrative from the posthumously published story "Adeline."
119. Purdy to Thomson, 21 Sep 1979, 75.29, VT; Wynne, tel. interview, 27 Aug 2020.
120. Windham, *Lost Friendships*, 167; Uecker, tel. interview, 25 Nov 2020.
121. Hefter to Purdy, p.m. 10, p.m. 16 Oct 1979, HRC, 68.1.
122. Purdy to Lish, 6 Aug 1980, b. 16, Lish mss.; Ehrhardt, "Wizard," 27.
123. Linchong, "Goodbye, James Purdy."
124. Purdy, int. Morrow, 107.
125. Purdy, int. Lear, 59; Skerrett Jr., in conversation with the author, May 2013.
126. Tommasini, *Virgil Thomson*, 468.
127. Busby, tel. interview, 23 Feb 2020.
128. Busby, email to the author, 14 May 2020.
129. Purdy to N. Miller, 21 Aug 1978, b. 27, AR; Purdy to Sams, 9 Feb 1985, collection of Sams; Turnbaugh, "James Purdy: Playwright," 75.

Chapter 17

1. James Link, "Consuming Love"; Link, "James Purdy," 62.
2. Link, "James Purdy," 62.
3. Purdy to Gunn, 21 Jan 1980, 1.50, TG.
4. Gunn, "All Pretty Much Strangers," 7; Purdy to Gunn, 5 Sep 1980, 1.50, TG.
5. Purdy to Lish, 6 Aug 1980, b. 16, Lish mss; Gunn to Purdy, 5 Sep 1980, 1.50, TG.
6. Dorothy Purdy, personal interview, Berea, Ohio, July 2, 2019; Purdy to Robert and Dorothy Purdy, n.d., card postmarked 21 Dec 1980, collection of Dorothy Purdy.
7. Uecker's full name is Terry John Uecker.
8. Lear, "Interview," 62.
9. Uecker, "Introduction," xi; Purdy, int. Morrow, 110.
10. Purdy to Lish, 20 May 1982, b. 16, Lish mss.
11. *August Moon: A Summer Arts Gathering, August 10-31, 1981* (Catskill, NY: Iowa Theater Lab, 1981); Christopher Cox, "James Purdy's Fighting Words."
12. Ancestry.com; Spring, *Secret Historian*, 371; August Becker to Steward, 29 Mar 1981, b. 1, SSP.
13. Purdy to Jerry Frasier, 3, 16, 23 Mar 1981, 13 Apr 1981, Berg.
14. *Austin Daily Texan*, May 4, 1981, 2; Edward Swift to Purdy, 21 May 1984, 22 Jan 1985, 3.27, OSU.3.
15. Purdy, "Rapture," *Complete Stories*, 369.
16. Purdy, "Adeline: A Short Play," *Second Coming* 10, nos. 1–2 (1981): 6–20.
17. Leigh Butler to Kathryn Court, Viking Press Memo, 10 July 1981, HRC, 73.3.

18. Klein, rev. of *Mourners Below*; Charyn, "Unloved and Angry"; Leavitt to Purdy, July 27, 1981, 73.5, HRC.

19. Viking Press Memo, HRC, 73.3.

20. Cox, "James Purdy's Fighting Words."

21. Francis King, "Particle of Genius."

22. Purdy to Thomson, 6 Dec 1981, 23 Oct 1982, VT; Thomson to Samuel Grupper, 21 Dec 1983, VT.

23. Purdy to Scott Rudin, 4 Dec 1981, 70.6, HRC.

24. Ned Leavitt to Purdy, 21 Dec 1981, 73.5, HRC.

25. Waters to Purdy, 21 Jan, 2 June 1982, 12 Dec 1983, 29 Nov 1985, HRC.

26. Waters, *Crackpot*, 59; Waters to Purdy, 7 Jan 1986, 3.29, OSU.3; Qtd. in Theroux, "Shocking Mr. Purdy," 116; Waters, "My 10 Favorite Books," *New York Times Style Magazine*, Nov 20, 2015.

27. Bill Zakariasen, "Water Music by Hundley," New York *Daily News*, Feb 5, 1982, 15.

28. Picano, "Felice Picano Diaries"; Picano to Purdy, 4 Dec 1984, 1.11, OSU.3.

29. Purdy, "Remembrances/Memoir."

30. Purdy to Lish, 10 June, 4 July, 26 July 1982, b. 16, Lish mss; "Albino Verlag," Wikipedia.

31. Purdy in Canning, *Gay Fiction Speaks*, 3–4.

32. Purdy, *Contemporary Authors*, 391.

33. Purdy, "The Berry-Picker," 163.

34. Purdy, "James Purdy Interview," int. Frame, 20, 21.

35. Albee to Purdy, 15 Jan 1982, courtesy of John Uecker.

36. Kathryn Baker, "Noted Playwright Visits Southwestern University," *Santa Cruz Sentinel*, 27 Feb 1983, C4.

37. Uecker, tel. interviews, 8, 9, Jan 2013.

38. Leverich, *Tom*, 2; Lahr, *Tennessee*, 586.

39. Purdy, "Tennessee Williams (eulogy)," 44.5, HRC.

40. Hundley, tel. interview, 30 Aug 2009.

41. Nolan Miller to Purdy, 12 July, 26 July, 1983, b. 27, AR.

42. Purdy, *On Glory's Course*, 312.

43. Ibid., 5, 4.

44. Purdy to Smith, 15 June 1983, 76.10, HRC; Charles McGrath, "Corlies Smith, Editor of All-Star Authors, Dies at 75," *New York Times*, Nov 24, 2004; Stadler, int. Purdy, b. 4, f. Art. 1, MSP.

45. Stadler, int. Purdy, b. 4, f. Arti. 1, MSP.

46. Gluck, "Great City," 56; O'Quinn, "Chaos beyond Language"; Feingold, "Purdy as a Picture."

47. Turnbaugh, "James Purdy: Playwright," 75.

48. Purdy, "*CA* Interview," 393.

49. White, *States of Desire*, 271–72.

50. Purdy to Lish, 19, 30 Nov 1983, p.m. 8 Feb, 18 April, 1984, b. 16, Lish mss.

51. "Robert L. Purdy: Wrote the Book on High School Athletics," (Cleveland) *Plain Dealer*, Nov 18, 2008.

52. Purdy to Sams, 15 Dec 1984, Sams personal collection.

53. Hundley, tel. interview, 20 Aug 2009.

54. Dorothy Purdy, personal interview, July 2009.

55. Purdy, "Interview," int. Morrow, 103.

56. "Miss Nell Baker Dies at Gilboa," *Republican-Courier*, Jan 14, 1936.

57. Cryer, "Readers Have Yet to Find Purdy"; Seidman, "War between Mothers and Sons"; Carolyn See, "What It Was Like BT."

58. Invitation in b. 1, f. 1, EB; Zebrun to Purdy, 9 Feb 1984, HRC, 76.10; Andy Praschak, "Backstage Glimpses of a Festival," *Observer* [Notre Dame U.], March 3, 1975, 5.

59. Glendinning, "Reassuring Sense of Sin"; Ladd, *James Purdy*, 198–202; Sara Nelson, "Literary Recount," *Publishers Weekly*, June 5, 2006, 6.

60. Anne Hollander of PEN to Purdy, 7 Dec 1984, 1.6, OSU.3.

61. Purdy to PEN, qtd. in Rollyson and Paddock, *Susan Sontag*, 240–41.

62. Purdy to Ladd, May 4, 1986, b. 1, OSU.208.

63. Swift, "Too Gay to Be Gay," 37, 39.

64. Hugh Hebert, "Dangers of Unsafe Sects," *Guardian*, April 22, 1987, 9; Virtue to Purdy, 28 Oct, 23 Nov, 30 Dec 1985, 3.29, OSU.3; Purdy, "*CA* Interview," 393.

65. Purdy to Sams, 11 Sep 1984, Sams private collection.

66. Elaine Benton to Purdy, n.d. 1984, 3.30, OSU.3.

67. Ken Lopez, bookseller, Catalog 161, 2013; Purdy to Benton, 19 Apr 1984, 1.1, EB.

68. Purdy to Ladd, 9 Aug 1984, b. 4, OSU.208.

69. Purdy, "Biography" [for FSG to give to Avon], b. 288, f., Eustace Chisholm, FSG; Purdy to Lish, n.d., p.m. 11 Dec 1968, b. 16, Lish mss; "James Purdy," *World Authors 1950–1970*, 1172; Purdy, "James Purdy," *Contemporary Authors Autobiography Series* [hereafter cited as *CAAS*], 299; Purdy, "Trick and Treat," 2008.

70. Purdy to Parker Sams, 11 Sep 1984, Sams collection.

71. Collins to Purdy, 26 Feb 1985, 1.3, OSU.3.

72. Purdy to Sharrard, 15 Feb 1989, UCB.

73. Jack Collins, tel. interview, 17 Aug 2019.

74. Purdy to Jay Ladd, 1 Nov 1985, b. 1, OSU.208.

75. Purdy to Ladd, 19 Dec 1985; 21 May 1986, b. 1, OSU.208; Tom Zulick, tel. interview, June 29, 2020.

76. Purdy to Lish, 23 Nov 1984, b. 16, Lish mss.

77. Lish to Purdy, 13 Feb 1985, b. 16, Lish mss.

78. Gordon Lish, tel. interview, 2 June 2019.

79. Robert Finn, "Richard Hundley, Non-conformist," (Cleveland) *Plain Dealer*, June 3, 1985; Hanshe, "Introduction," 166.

80. Richard Hundley, tel. interview, 30 Aug 2009.

81. Gerald Busby, tel. interview, 23 Feb 2020; Dennis Moore, tel. interviews, 21 Dec 2012, 19 Dec 2016, 1 Nov 2020; Chester Page, tel. interview, 8 June 2021.

82. Hundley, tel. interview, 16 Oct 2009.

83. Purdy to Hundley, May 1992, 65.3, RH; Purdy, "To a Deadbeat," 4.2, HRC.

84. Purdy to Stephen D. Adams, 10 Jan 1984, summary in email attachment to the author, 22 Sep 2020.

85. Purdy, *In the Hollow of His Hand*, 32.

86. Kerr [Carr] to Purdy, Mar 1985, 1.8, OSU.3; J. E. Bouman to Purdy, 16 July 1986, 1.2, OSU.3; Polak to Purdy, 6 Nov 1986, 1.2, OSU.3.

87. Steward to Bouman, 30 Oct 1987, b. 3, SSP.

88. Purdy, "James Purdy," int. Northouse, 198; Kenny, tel. interview, 17 May 2009.

89. Kenny, *On Second Thought*, 39, 37–38.

90. Maurice Kenny, tel. interviews, 4, 17 May 2009.

91. Kenny, "Tinseled Bucks," 15–17.

92. Kenny, *Rain*, 9–10.

93. J. White to Purdy, n.d., 21.5, HRC.

94. Stadler, Email to the author, 2 June 2019.

95. Cooper, "Tribute," 44; Rev. "Zombie OO" by Gooch, *Kirkus Reviews*, June 15, 2000; Gooch, *Smash Cut*, 64, 66, 110, 131, 132.

96. Stadler, interview with Purdy, b. 4, f. Art. 1, MSP.

97. Gigi Mahon, "Lord on the Fly: Peripatetic Publisher George Weidenfeld," *New York*, Feb 24, 1986, 41.

98. Purdy, int. Gavron, 4; Enclosure, John Herman to Purdy, 25 June 1986, 3.29, OSU.3.

99. Lee Smith, "Kidnapped by Everyone," 15.

100. Aletti, "American Gothic," 18–19; Espey, Review; Dyer, "American Odyssey."

101. Slavitt, "James Purdy's Wacky but Elegant Love Stories," 5.

102. Purdy interview with Stadler, 18 Mar 1992, b. 1, f. Art. 1, MSP; Stadler, "Shameless Reality"; Andrew Rosenheim, "Figuring Out the Father," Rev. of *In the Hollow of His Hand* and *Candles of Your Eyes*, *Times Literary Supplement* (19 Feb 1988), 186.

103. Purdy to Sharrard, 24 Nov 1987, 20 Jan 1988, 20 Sep 1988, UCB.

104. Crisp, "Discreet Charm of Mr Purdy," 18, 20, 21, 23.

105. Purdy, "Vassilis Voglis," 14, 46–53.

106. St George, "People to Avoid."

107. Purdy, *Garments the Living Wear*, 38; See Pileggi, "Mob and the Machine"; Purdy to Fox, 19 Feb 1986, OSU.3.

108. Canby, "Recluse Woos Widow in *In a Shallow Grave*."

109. Ladd, *James Purdy*, 213, 216; Turnbaugh, "Buried Wonder," 67–69; McCuller, [liner notes] *In a Shallow Grave* Soundtrack CD.

110. Malanowski, "Previews: Michael Biehn and James Purdy," 21.

111. Canning, *Gay Fiction*, 36.

112. Ehrhardt, "Wizard," 27.

113. Turnbaugh, "Fighting for His Words," 82; Purdy to Sharrard, 4 Jan 1989, UCB.

114. Purdy, int. Gavron, 7.

115. Jennie Punter, *Whig Standard* [Kingston, Ontario], June 1–11, 1988.

116. "James Purdy Interviewed by Don Swaim, 7 Dec 1989."

117. Collins, tel. interview, 17 Aug 2019; Purdy to Sharrard, 15 Feb 1989, UCB.

118. Strausbaugh, "Pure Purdy," 41.

119. Linchong, James Purdy Society panel, American Literature Association, May 2013, Boston.

120. Linchong, "Goodbye, James Purdy."

121. Purdy to Sharrard, 9 Apr 1989, UCB.

122. Feingold, "Waking Dreams," 81–82.

123. Yohalem, "Outlaw on Outlaws," 8; Purdy to Fox, 10 April 1989, 4.9, OSU.3.

124. Purdy to Ladd, 4 Oct 1989, b. 1, OSU.208.

125. Michael Carroll, 16 Dec 2020, Facebook message to the author; Purdy to Sharrard, 30 Aug 1989, UCB.

126. Purdy to Sharrard, 6 July 1989, UCB.

127. Purdy to Sharrard, 30 Aug 1989, UCB; Purdy, int. Gavron, 9.

128. Purdy to Sharrard, 25 Feb, 15 Nov 1989, UCB; DeStefano, "Purdy Principle," 51.

129. Dr. Seuss, *Green Eggs and Ham* (New York: Random House, 1960), 59; Purdy, audio int. Don Swaim, 1989; Purdy to Sharrard, 15 Aug, 22 Aug 1989, UCB.

130. Purdy to Sharrard, 20 July, 8 Aug 1989, UCB; Solomon qtd. in Purdy to Sharrard, 4 Aug 1989, UCB; Stadler int. with Purdy, b. 4, f. Article 1, MSP.

131. Purdy to Sharrard, 30 July 1989, UCB.

132. Lebowitz qtd. in Graves, "Brilliant but Little-Known James Purdy."

133. Purdy, *Garments the Living Wear*, 139; Purdy in Canning, *Gay Fiction*, 32.

134. Uecker, *Memento Mori*, V, jamespurdy.org/generic.php?id = 9; Uecker, tel. interview, 19 Nov 2020.

135. Crisp, "Entertaining Melancholy," rev. of *Garments*, [unknown], 1989; Malin, rev. of *Garments*, 327.

136. Kenneth Holditch, "Stylish Originals."

137. Holditch, tel. interview, 26 May 2021.

138. Harris, "Pest Can't Get Them Down"; Purdy, *Garments*, 84–85.

139. Purdy, *Wired for Books* audio int. Swaim, 1989; Stadler, int. Purdy, b. 4, f. Art. 1, MSP; Purdy in Canning, *Gay Fiction*, 18.

140. Purdy, "Christian Vision in My Work," 1.3, HRC.

Chapter 18

1. Purdy, *Garments the Living Wear*, 148; Bruce Bawer, "Sensuous Woman."

2. Matthew Stadler, Skype int., 8 June 2019; John Strausbaugh, "Pure Purdy," 41.

3. Purdy, *Cabot Wright Begins*, 213.

4. John Uecker, tel. interview, 27 Feb 2021.

5. Michael Feingold, "Half Nelson," 87–88; *'Til the Eagle Hollers* program, encl., Purdy to Sharrard, 1990; *New York* magazine, January 25, 1990, 83.

6. Uecker, tel. interviews, 15 Dec 2020, 10 Jan 2021.

7. Feingold, "Basic Questions: James Purdy's Plays," 41.

8. Purdy, *Enduring Zeal*, 84.

9. Purdy to Robert Sharrard, 11 Jan 1991, UCB.

10. Purdy, *In the Night of Time*, 244; Purdy, *Paradise Circus*, 164.

11. Purdy in Canning, *Gay Fiction Speaks*, 35.

12. Turnbaugh, "Fighting for His Words," 82.

13. Turnbaugh, "A.K.A. Adonis Whiteacre," 35.

14. Purdy, "Remembrances/Memoir."

15. De Stefano, "Purdy Principle," 51; Strausbaugh, "Pure," 42.

16. Purdy to Sharrard, 10 Apr 1990, UCB; "John Polak," "Ad ten Bosch," "Athenaeum-Polak & Van Gennep," *Wikipedia* (Dutch); Stadler, "James Purdy Article," b. 4, f. Art. 1, MSP.

17. "Nieuwsbrief 884: James Purdy," antiquariaat Fokas Holtuis, https://fokas.nl/2020/01/24/nieuwsbrief-884-james-purdy/.

18. Purdy to Sharrard, 4 Jan 1991, UCB.

19. Purdy to R. Wilson, 30 Jan 1993, 1.3, UD; Stadler, int. Purdy, b. 4, f. Art. 1, MSP.

20. Purdy to Sharrard, 19 Oct 1990, UCB.

21. De Stefano, "Purdy Principle," 51.

22. Ira Silverberg, "James Purdy," 52

23. Richard McCann, "Lives of Quiet Desperation."

24. Donald Weise, tel. interview with the author, 4 Jun 2019.

25. Grobel, *Conversations with Capote*, 140–41; Rorem, *Wings of Friendship*, 205; Wolcott, "Gored Again"; White, *My Lives*, 355, "Acknowledgments."

26. Purdy, int. Frame, 21. Nine years earlier, the German gay rights activist and controversial filmmaker Rosa von Praunheim had hoped to film it, but Purdy was "terrified" of what he "might do with it."

27. Tony Peake, *Derek Jarman*, 493.

28. Ibid., 495, 500–1.

29. Ibid., 507.

30. Jarman qtd. in Frances Welch, "Me and My God: Unbelieving, but with All the Trimmings," London *Sunday Telegraph*, June 6, 1993.

31. Peake, *Jarman*, 524–25.

32. Purdy, "Out with James Purdy," int. Lane, 88.

33. *New York*, April 13, 1992, 93.

34. Purdy, *Rivalry of Dolls*, 131; Aletti, "Fogged In."

35. Purdy to Stadler, 26 June, 16 Oct 1992, b. 5, f. letters, MSP.

36. Purdy to Stadler, 25 Mar 1992, b. 5, f. Art. 3, MSP.

37. Coe, rev. *Out with the Stars*, 22–23; Hensher, "Drama in Dressing Gowns"; Purdy to R. Wilson, 30 Jan 1993, 1.3, UD.

38. Purdy to Ladd, 19 Oct 1992, b.1, OSU.208; Purdy to Ladd, 7 Mar 1994, b. 2, OSU.208; Moosbrugger to Fogarty, 26 Feb 1993, b. 27, AR.

39. Purdy to Robert A. Wilson, 30 Jan, 16 Apr, 1993, UD.

40. Chester Page, *Memoirs of a Charmed Life in New York*, 168–69; Spring, *Secret Historian*, 38-40; Academy of Arts and Letters, b. 1, OSU.208.

41. Page, tel. interview, 8 June 2021.

42. Richard Hundley, notes, 9 April 1998, 65.3, RH.

43. Edmund White, "Fame, the Greatest Aphrodisiac," 208.

44. Jack Collins visited Edmund White in the early 1980s, and when White learned that Collins was also visiting Purdy, he snapped, "he gets away with writing things like that. How could you?"

45. Dyer, "Purdy Recreates a Gay, Surreal Old Time"; B. Kenney, rev. *Out with the Stars*, 128; Malin, rev. *Out with the Stars*, 208; Weir, "Everything Was Purpler Then."

46. Purdy, "Out with James Purdy," int. Lane, 76.

47. Purdy, "Out," int. Lane, 75; Purdy, int. Stadler, b. 4, f. Article 1, MSP.

48. Lyke, "Honors for an Outcast."

49. Dennis Moore, tel. interview, 25 Aug 2020.

50. Matthew Stadler, Skype interview, 8 June 2019.

51. Stadler, int. Purdy, 18 Mar 1992, b. 4, f. Art. 1, MSP; Stadler, Skype interview, 8 June 2019.

52. Uecker, tel. interview, 27 Feb 2021.

53. Purdy, *Brice*, II.7, in *Selected Plays*, 78; Purdy in Canning, *Gay Fiction*, 9.

54. Stadler, Skype interview, 8 June 2019.

55. De Stefano, "Purdy Principle," 52.

56. Silverberg, "James Purdy," 50.

57. Purdy in Canning, *Gay Fiction*, 8.

58. Zulick, tel. interview, 29 Jun 2019; Purdy to Stadler, 27 June 1994, box 5, f. letters 2, MSP; Michael Carroll, Facebook messages to the author, 16 Aug 2019, 16 Dec 2020 [on Purdy's nickname for Leavitt].

59. Purdy, "Out," int. Christopher Lane, 87, 89, 88.

60. Woodhouse, "James Purdy's Escape from the Wasteland," 24, 26.

61. Donald Weise, tel. interview, 4 June 2019.

62. Woodhouse, "James Purdy (Re)visited," 16; "New York Novelist," *New York Press*, Sep 21–27, 1994.

63. Email from Moore to Hanshe, 31 Aug 2005, courtesy Moore; "Dennis Clay Moore," *Seattle Times*, December 1, 2020, obituaries.seattletimes.com/obituary/dennis-moore-1081047218.

64. Purdy to Stadler, 27 June 1994, b. 5, f. letters 2, MSP; Uecker, tel. interview, 11 Mar 2021.

65. In 2021, Jason Hale is chair of the Theatre Department at Bilkent University–Faculty of Music and Performing Arts in Ankara, Turkey. He brought in John Uecker as a guest acting teacher, who was "wonderful with the students." John says he "learned a lot about acting from working with Tennessee and James." In turn, Hale said he "couldn't be a director today" had he not worked with Uecker and Purdy.

66. Jason Hale, video interview, 6 Apr 2021.

67. Bauman, *Divided by a River*.

68. Purdy in Canning, *Gay Fiction*; 28–29; Uecker, tel. interview, 20 Feb 2009; Purdy, int. Morrow, 97.

69. John Strausbaugh, "Pure Purdy," 41.

70. Paul Theroux, "The Shocking Mr. Purdy," 116.

71. Harold Dennis Schmidt, tel. interview, 29 Sep 2020; Schmidt to Kenneth P. Norwick, Esq., 25 Nov 1997, email encl., Schmidt to the author, 30 Sep 2020.

72. Purdy to Schmidt, 13 Oct 1994, email encl., Schmidt to the author, 30 Sep 2020.

73. Schmidt to Norwick, 25 Nov 1997, email encl. to the author, 30 Sep 2020.

74. Schmidt, email to the author, 30 Sep 2020.

75. Douglas Stewart to Schmidt, fax, 7 July 1997.
76. Schmidt to Norwick, 25 Nov 1997.
77. Schmidt, email to the author, 30 Sep 2020.
78. Strausbaugh, "Pure Purdy," 42.
79. Strausbaugh, "Foment."
80. "Eclectic Revives Bent at Alumnae," *Toronto Star*, Nov 5, 1992, E4.
81. Linchong, "Goodbye, James Purdy."
82. Purdy in Canning, *Gay Fiction*, 12–13.
83. Malin, rev. of *Gertrude of Stony Island Avenue*, 20.
84. Rev. of *Gertrude of Stony Island Avenue*, *Kirkus Reviews*, July 15, 1998.
85. Schwartz, rev. of *Gertrude*; Bawer, "Sensuous Woman," 8; Evenson, rev. of *Gertrude*, 169.
86. Brian Evenson, tel. interview, 1 Apr 2021; Evenson, *Raymond Carver's What We Talk About*, 116–17; Lish, "Art of Editing No. 2," 206.
87. Gordon Lish, int. by Stadler, 9 Apr 1992, b. 4, Purdy Art. 1, MSP.
88. Plunket, "Visionary," 91.
89. Joe Adcock, "Acting the Bright Spot in Murky 'Shallow Grave,'" *Seattle Post-Intelligencer*, 11 June 2001, E3.
90. Rebecca Brown, "Dark Beautiful Wounds," *The Stranger* [Seattle], 14 June 2001.

Chapter 19

1. Richard Canning's interview with Purdy was also published later that year in Canning's excellent *Gay Fiction Speaks*.
2. Patrick Merla, "From the Editor," 4; Merla, "Tributes," 42–43.
3. Merla, tel. interview, June 3, 2019; Douglas Turnbaugh, "A.K.A. Adonis Whiteacre," 30; Dennis Moore, tel. interview, 25 Aug 2020.
4. Amanda Hopkinson, "Gary Pulsifer obituary," *Guardian*, 6 April 2016; Graham Clark, rev. of *Moe's Villa*.
5. John Strausbaugh, "Clever Cats and Opaque Snakes," 24; John Uecker, tel. interviews, 12 Sep 2012, 8 Sep 2020.
6. Purdy, "Fragments and Sayings," in "Trick and Treat."
7. McGowin, "Why I Still Use a Manual Typewriter"; Moore, tel. interviews, 25, 26 Aug 2020; "Contributors," *Oyster Boy* 16, www.oysterboyreview.org/issue/16/contribut ors.html; McGowin, *Benny Poda Trilogy*, www.levee67.org/mcgowin/.
8. Philip F. Clark, tel. interview, 28 March 2019; Moore, tel. interviews, 28 Dec 2012; 31 Oct 2020.
9. Kate Herbert, "Intimate Fun in the Big Apple," *Melbourne Sun*, Feb 3, 2003, 72.
10. *Kirkus Reviews* 72, no. 7 (September 1, 2001): 831.
11. Donald Weise, tel. interview, 4 June 2019.
12. Weise, tel. interview, 1 Sep 2020.
13. Weise, "Christmas with James Purdy."

14. Weise, tel. interview, 1 Sep 2020.

15. Weise, "Christmas."

16. Weise, tel. interview, 1 Sep 2020.

17. Italie, "Cult Author James Purdy."

18. Purdy, "Conversation," int. Goodman.

19. Ehrhardt, "James Purdy, 1914–2009," 9.

20. Ehrhardt, "Wizard," 26, 31.

21. Andrew Male, "I'm Not a Gay Writer, I'm a Monster."

22. Uecker, tel. interviews, 18 Aug 2010, 18 Sep 2020, 5 July 2021.

23. Uecker, email to the author, 22 Apr 2011.

24. Moore, tel. interview, 25 Aug 2020.

25. Hale, video interview, 6 Apr 2021; Uecker, tel. interview, 9 Jan 2013.

26. Moore, tel. interview, 3 Nov 2020.

27. Uecker, email to the author, 22 Apr 2011.

28. Purdy to Vanderbilt, 9 Aug 2004, email attachment, Uecker to the author, 24 Dec 2012.

29. Email, Dennis Moore to Jan Erik Bouman, 30 Aug 2005; Email, Bouman to Moore, 31 Aug 2005, shared with the author by Moore; Moore, tel. interview, 21 Dec 2012.

30. Theroux, "Shocking Mr. Purdy," 116.

31. Gore Vidal, *Point to Point Navigation*, 35; Vidal, "Novelist as Outlaw."

32. Italie, "Cult Author James Purdy."

33. Weise, "Christmas with James Purdy."

34. Franzen, "Love Letters"; Ehrhardt, "Wizard," 26; Weise, tel. interview, 1 Sep 2020.

35. Thomson qtd. by Hundley, tel. interview, 30 Aug 2009.

36. Linchong, "Goodbye."

37. Moore, tel. interview, 28 Dec 2012.

38. Moore, tel. interview, 19 Dec 2016; Troop, tel. interview, 18 Mar 2022.

39. Email from Dennis Moore to John Hanshe, 31 Aug 2005, courtesy of Moore; Moore, tel. interview, 28 Dec 2012.

40. Uecker, tel. interview, 29 April 2021; Troop, tel. interview, 18 Mar 2022; Moore, tel. interview, 25 Aug 2020.

41. Stadler, email to the author, May 20, 2019.

42. "Troop Call-Up for Elspeth," [London] *Evening Standard*, Dec 21, 2007; Bill Troop, "Robin Prising."

43. Bill Troop, personal interview, London, 15 Mar 2019; Troop, tel. interview, 18 Mar 2022. Troop discarded his earlier theory that John Uecker was a symbolic son after he realized that Purdy had effectively transformed Uecker into his brother Richard— the addict actor. By withholding from John the credit he craved, James drove him to drugs and other self-destructive behaviors.

44. John Wronoski and Heide Hatry, video interview, 20 March 2021.

45. Italie, "Cult Writer Not Forgotten," 11 Dec 2005; Uecker, tel. interview, 18 Feb 2021; Moore, tel. interview, 25 Aug 2020.

46. Purdy, "Trick and Treat," 2008.

47. Troop, interview, 15 Mar 2019; Moore, tel. interviews, 25 Aug, 31 Oct 2020.

48. Moore, tel. interview, 31 Oct 2020.

49. Moore, tel. interviews, 19 Dec 2016, 25 Aug 2020.

50. Troop, interview, 15 Mar 2019; Troop, unpublished memoir, email encl. to the author, 26 March 2022.

51. McCormack, "On James Purdy," 155, 157, 156.

52. Purdy, "Fragments and Sayings," in "Trick and Treat."

53. McCormack, tel. interview, 27 Mar 2021.

54. McCormack, email to the author, 23 Mar 2021; McCormack, tel. interview, 27 Mar 2021.

55. Wally Guenther, "Robert L. Purdy, Wrote the Book on High School Athletics," Nov 18, 2008, cleveland.com.

56. Troop, tel. interview, 18 Mar 2022; Pat Vaughan Tremmel, "Lane Named Pearce Miller Professor in Literature," *Northwestern*, August 16, 2007, https://www.north western.edu/newscenter/stories/2007/08/Pearce-MIller-Professor.html;   Feingold, "Basic Questions," 42.

57. Uecker, tel. interview, April 29, 2021.

58. Jorma Sjoblom, personal interview, 17 July 2009.

59. McCormack, emails to the author, 23 Mar, 26 Mar 2021.

60. McCormack, email to the author, 23 Mar 2021.

61. Purdy, "Conversation," int. Goodman.

62. Matthew Stadler, video interview, 8 June 2019. Stadler's metaphor recalls Lawrence Ferlinghetti's poem "Constantly Risking Absurdity."

63. Purdy to Powys, 21 April 1960, b. 4, JPP.

Select Bibliography

Archives and Special Collections

[AR] Antioch Review mss. Lilly Library, Indiana University, Bloomington, Indiana.

[Berg] James Purdy papers. Uncatalogued. New York Public Library, Henry W. and Albert A. Berg Collection of English and American Literature, Stephen A. Schwarzman Building.

[BGSU] Correspondence [to] Frank Baldanza 1970–1975. Center for Archival Collections, Bowling Green State University, Bowling Green, Ohio.

Billy Rose Theatre Division, New York Public Library for the Performing Arts.

John Bucklew Collection. Mudd Library, Lawrence University, Appleton, Wisconsin.

[EB] Elaine Benton papers related to James Purdy. YCAL MSS 416. Beinecke Rare Book & Manuscript Library, Yale University, New Haven, Connecticut.

[FSG] Farrar, Straus & Giroux, Inc. Manuscripts and Archives Division, New York Public Library.

[GAP] Gertrude Abercrombie Papers, 1888–1977. Microfilm Roll 1429. Series 1, Biographical material. Archives of American Art, Smithsonian Institution.

[HRC] James Purdy Papers. MS-3353. Harry Ransom Center, University of Texas, Austin.

[JPP] James Purdy papers. YCAL MSS 44. Yale Collection of American Literature. Beinecke Rare Book & Manuscript Library, Yale University.

Knapik mss. Lilly Library, Indiana University.

[KU] [James Purdy] Letters to Geoffrey Elborn. MS302. Kenneth Spencer Research Library, University of Kansas.

Lawrence College Archives. Faculty records. Mudd Library, Lawrence University, Appleton, Wisconsin.

Lish mss. 1951–2017. Lilly Library, Indiana University.

[MSP] Matthew Stadler papers. GEN MSS 843. Beinecke Rare Book & Manuscript Library, Yale University.

[NYR] New Yorker records. Editorial Correspondence—Fiction. Manuscripts and Archives Division, New York Public Library.

[OSU.171] Melvon L. Ankeny Collection on Samuel Steward. SPEC.RARE.0171. Rare Books & Manuscripts Library, Ohio State University.

[OSU.208] The James Purdy collection, ca. 1950–1996 [Jay Ladd]. SPEC.RARE.0208. Rare Books & Manuscripts Library, Ohio State University.

[OSU.3] James Purdy Papers. CMS.0003. Rare Books & Manuscripts Library, Ohio State University.

[OSU.74] James Purdy Collection, 1948–1973 [Toni Strassman Collection]. CMS.0074. Rare Books & Manuscripts Library, Ohio State University.

[RH] Richard Hundley papers. Music Division, New York Public Library.

[SSP] Samuel Steward Papers. GEN MSS 987. Beinecke Rare Book and Manuscript Library, Yale University.

[TG] Thom Gunn Papers. 2006/235. Bancroft Library, University of California Berkeley.
[TS] Ted Solotaroff Papers. Manuscripts and Archives Division, The New York Public Library.
[TU] James Purdy Papers, 1971–74. SCRC 146. 1 folder. Temple University Libraries Special Collections, Philadelphia.
[UCB] James Purdy letters and manuscripts to Robert Sharrard, 1987–1994. Bancroft Library, University of California Berkeley.
[UD] Robert A. Wilson Collection related to James Purdy. 370. Series I. Special Collections, Morris Library, University of Delaware.
[UW] Edward Godfrey Cox papers, 1910–1961. Special Collections, University of Washington Libraries.
[VT] The Virgil Thomson Collection. Series 3. MSS 29. James Purdy, 1956–1983. Box 29/75, folder 29. Irving S. Gilmore Music Library of Yale University.
[WCW] William Carlos Williams papers. YCAL MSS 116. Series 1. Beinecke Rare Book & Manuscript Library, Yale University.
[WWP] Wendell Wilcox Papers, 1930–1960. CO666. Special Collections, Princeton University Libraries.

Interviews and Correspondence with the Author

Stephen D. Adams. Email, 22 Sep 2020.
David Breithaupt. Interview, Columbus, Ohio, 2 July 2019.
Gerald Busby. Email, 14 May 2020; telephone interview, 23 Feb 2020.
Michael Carroll. Facebook direct messages, 16 Aug 2019, 16 Dec 2020.
Beth A. Casey. Email, 16 Apr 2009.
Philip F. Clark. Telephone interview, 28 Mar 2019.
Jack Collins. Telephone interview, 17 Aug 2019.
Geoffrey Elborn. Email to the author, 26 Mar 2021.
Brian Evenson. Telephone interview, 1 Apr 2021.
Joseph Fennimore. Email, 18 May 2020.
Jack Fritscher. Email, 16 Aug 2019.
Jason Hale. Video interview, 6 Apr 2021.
Kenneth Holditch. Telephone interview, 26 May 2021.
Barry David Horwitz. Email, 21 Aug 2019. Telephone interview, 23 Aug 2019.
Richard Hundley. Telephone interviews, 20, 30 Aug, 16 Oct 2009.
Maurice Kenny. Telephone interviews, 4, 17 May 2009.
Gordon Lish. Telephone interview, 2 June 2019.
J. W. McCormack. Emails, 23, 26, Mar 2021. Telephone interview, 27 Mar 2021.
Patrick Merla. Telephone interview, 3 June 2019.
Paul W. Miller. Interview, Miller's home, Springfield, Ohio, July 2009.
Dennis Moore. Telephone interviews, 21 May, 21, 28 Dec 2012, 16, 19 Dec 2016, 25 Aug, 31 Oct, 1, 3 Nov 2020.
Michael Nott. Email, 10 July 2020.
Chester Page. Telephone interview, 8 June 2021. Emails, 12, 14, 18 June 2021.
Katha Pollitt. Email, 3 Oct 2020.
Diane Pretzer and Wallace L. Pretzer (Wally). Email, 30 Apr 2009.
David Purdy. Telephone interviews, 8 Jan 2019, 11 June 2021.

David Purdy and Dorothy Purdy. Interview, Berea, Ohio, 2 July 2019.

David Purdy, Christine (Purdy) Reese, and Dorothy Purdy. Interview, Berea, Ohio, July 2009.

James Purdy. Telephone conversations, 30 Apr, 14 May 2008.

Jere Real. Telephone interview, 6 July 2012.

Harold Dennis Schmidt. Telephone interviews, 26, 29 Sep 2020. Email, 30 Sep 2020.

Jorma Sjoblom. Interview, 17 July 2009, Ashtabula, Ohio. Telephone interviews, 25 May 2009, 23 June 2011.

Matthew Stadler. Email, 2 June 2019. Video interview, 8, 15 June 2019.

James Michael Tillotson. Telephone interview, 24 May 2020.

Bill Troop. Interview, Troop's home, Earl's Court, London, 15 Mar 2019; Telephone interview, 18 Mar 2022; Email 26 Mar 2022.

John Uecker, Emails, 30, 31 Aug 2010, 22 Apr 2011, 3 Jan, 19 Apr 2012. Skype interview, 24 June 2020. Telephone interviews, 13 June 2008, 20 Feb, 9 Oct 2009, 1 July, 18, 30 Aug 2010, 12 Sep 2012, 8, 9, 10 Jan 2013, 18 Feb, 8, 18, 19 Sep, 13, 22 Oct, 19, 25 Nov, 1, 15 Dec 2020, 4, 9, 10 Jan, 18, 27 Feb, 2, 11, 20, 24, 31 Mar, 13 Apr, 5 July 2021.

Donald Weise. Telephone interviews, 4 June 2019, 1 Sep 2020.

Edmund White. Email to the author, 15 Dec 2020.

John Wronoski and Heide Hatry. Video interview, 20 Mar 2021.

John Stewart Wynne. Telephone interviews, 18, 27 Aug 2020, 22 Sep 2020. Text message, 5 Apr 2021.

Thomas Zulick. Telephone interview, 29 June 2019.

Select Works by James Purdy

Arranged Chronologically

Books

Novels

Malcolm. New York: Farrar, Straus & Cudahy, 1959.

The Nephew. New York: Farrar, Straus & Cudahy, 1960.

Cabot Wright Begins. New York: Farrar, Straus & Giroux, 1964.

Eustace Chisholm and the Works. New York: Farrar, Straus & Giroux, 1967.

Jeremy's Version. Garden City, NY: Doubleday, 1970.

I Am Elijah Thrush. Garden City, NY: Doubleday, 1972.

The House of the Solitary Maggot. Garden City, NY: Doubleday, 1974.

In a Shallow Grave. New York: Arbor House, 1975.

Narrow Rooms. New York: Arbor House, 1978.

Narrow Rooms. Surrey, England: Ram/Black Sheep, 1980. [definitive edition, per Purdy]

Mourners Below. New York: Viking, 1981.

On Glory's Course. New York: Viking, 1984.

In the Hollow of His Hand. New York: Weidenfeld & Nicolson, 1986.

Garments the Living Wear. San Francisco: City Lights, 1989.

Out with the Stars. San Francisco: City Lights, 1993.

Gertrude of Stony Island Avenue. London: Peter Owen, 1997.

Gertrude of Stony Island Avenue. New York: William Morrow, 1998.

Story and Play Collections and Novellas

Don't Call Me by My Right Name and Other Stories. New York: William-Frederick, 1956. [privately published]

63: Dream Palace. New York: William-Frederick, 1956. [novella, privately published]

63: Dream Palace: A Novella and Nine Stories. London: Gollancz, 1957.

Color of Darkness. New York: New Directions, 1957. [novella *63: Dream Palace* and eleven stories]

Children Is All. New York: New Directions, 1962. [short plays "Children Is All" and "Cracks" and ten stories]

A Day After the Fair: A Collection of Plays and Short Stories. New York: Note of Hand, 1977. [privately published]

Two Plays. Dallas: New London, 1979. ["True" and "A Day After the Fair."]

Proud Flesh. Northridge, CA: Lord John, 1980. [short plays: "Strong," "Clearing in the Forest," "Now," "What Is It, Zach?"]

The Candles of Your Eyes and Thirteen Other Stories. New York: Weidenfeld & Nicolson, 1987.

63: Dream Palace: Selected Stories 1956–1987. Santa Rosa, CA: Black Sparrow, 1991.

In the Night of Time and Four Other Plays. Amsterdam: Athenaeum-Polak & Van Gennep, 1992. [Also *Ruthanna Elder, Enduring Zeal, The Rivalry of Dolls, The Paradise Circus*]

Moe's Villa & Other Stories. London: Arcadia, 2000.

Moe's Villa & Other Stories. New York: Carroll & Graf, 2004.

Selected Plays. Chicago: Ivan R. Dee, 2009.

The Complete Short Stories of James Purdy. Introduction by John Waters. New York: Norton/ Liveright, 2013.

Poetry Collections

The Running Sun. New York: James Purdy, 1971.

Sunshine Is an Only Child: Poems. New York: Aloe, 1973.

The Brooklyn Branding Parlors. New York: Contact/II, 1986.

Collected Poems. Amsterdam: Athenaeum-Polak & Van Gennep, 1990.

The Blue House: Forbidden Poems. Utrecht: Hugin & Munin, 2004.

In Periodicals

Stories

"A Good Woman." *Creative Writing* 1 (Jan–Feb 1939): 5–10.

"You Reach for Your Hat." *Prairie Schooner* 20 (spring 1946): 185–192.

"Sound of Talking." *Black Mountain Review*, issue 5 (summer 1955): 153–164.

"Don't Call Me by My Right Name." *New Directions in Prose and Poetry* 16 (1957): 46–53.

"You Reach for Your Wraps." *Mademoiselle*, Mar 1957, 104–5.

"About Jessie Mae." *New Yorker*, May 25, 1957, 87–92.

"Cutting Edge." *Evergreen Review* 1, no. 1 (1957): 99–109.

"You May Safely Gaze." *High*, June 1958, 8–10, 56–57.

"Home by Dark." *Harper's Bazaar* 91 (June 1958): 89, 110–111.

"Night and Day." *Esquire* 50 (July 1958): 108–112.

"The Lesson." *Texas Quarterly* 1 (winter 1958): 72–79.

"Everything Under the Sun." *Partisan Review* 26 (summer 1959): 363–370.

"Goodnight Sweetheart." *Esquire* 54 (Oct 1960): 106-108.

"Daddy Wolf." *New World Writing* 17, edited by Stewart Richardson and Corlies M. Smith, 151–160. Philadelphia: J. Lippincott, 1960.

"Sermon." *New Directions in Prose and Poetry* 17 (1961): 188–191.

"Scrap of Paper." *Evergreen Review* 11 (Aug 1967): 23–25, 81–82.

"Mr. Evening." *Harper's Bazaar* 101 (Sep 1968): 168+.

"Success Story." *New York Times*, June 6, 1971: BR24.

"Summer Tidings." *Esquire* 82 (Dec 1974): 186–87, 232–38.

"Some of These Days." *New Directions in Prose and Poetry* 31 (1975): 53–62.

"Short Papa." *The Antioch Review* 34 (summer 1976): 420–27.

"Sleep Tight." *The Antioch Review* 37 (winter 1979): 27–35.

"Rapture." *Second Coming* 10, nos. 1–2 (1981).

"Mud Toe the Cannibal." *BOMB* 7 (1983): 34–35.

"Dawn." *Christopher Street* 8, no. 1 (Feb 1984).

"In This Corner . . ." *Christopher Street* 9, no. 7 (Sep 1986).

"The Vorago: A Chapter from a Novel in Progress." *Christopher Street* 12, no. 7 (Sep 1989): 18–21.

"The Vorago." *Satchel* 1 (1989): 47–56.

"The White Blackbird." *Conjunctions* 20 (1993): 104–26.

"Brawith." *Antioch Review* 52, no. 2 (spring 1994): 199–208.

"No Stranger to Luke." *Antioch Review* 59, no. 1 (winter 2001): 13–25.

Plays

"Cracks." *Cosmopolitan* 153 (Aug 1962): 64–69.

"Children Is All." *Mademoiselle* 56 (Nov 1962): 108–9, 164–173, 184–186.

"Mr. Cough Syrup and the Phantom Sex." *December* 8, no. 1 (1966): 175–77.

"Q & A." *Esquire* 79 (May 1973): 134, 232.

"True" and "Wedding Finger." *New Directions in Prose and Poetry* 28 (1974): 77–98.

"A Day after the Fair." *Texas Arts Journal* 1 (1977): 51–77.

"The Berry-Picker." *New Directions in Prose and Poetry* 45 (1982): 157–165.

"Adeline" and "Wonderful Happy Days." *Conjunctions* 2 (spring/summer 1982): 60–83.

"Heatstroke." *Dirty Bum* 1 (fall 1987): 14–26.

"Souvenirs." *City Lights Review* 2 (1988): 64–70.

"Band Music." *City Lights Review* 9 (1990): 103–113.

Poems

"Four Poems." *Botteghe Oscure* 23 (1959): 299–302. ["Merry-Go-Round Horses and Carousel," "An Ode to Godwin Dwight," "Vendrá," and "What"]

"The Lovely Listless Wind Has Sighed," "Whenever You Pee," and "Carl Van Vechten." *December* 9, nos. 2/3 (1967): 100.

"Jan Erik." *Exquisite Corpse* 7 (Jan/May 1989): 15.

"8 Poems." *Contact/II* 9 (summer/fall 1989): 45. ["White Yellow Orange," "In a Deep Slumber," "Fighting in a Wood," "Blossoms," "Untitled," "From Rivers, and from the Earth Itself," "White Sheep," and "Men of Bangladesh"]

Essays, Articles, Letters, Reviews

"The Correspondence of James Purdy and John Cowper Powys, 1956–1963." Edited by Michael Ballin and Charles Lock. *The Powys Journal* 23 (2013): 13–114.

"Purdy's Purge." *Saturday Review*, Nov 14, 1959, 31.

"Dame Edith Sitwell's Sad, Witty Farewell." Review of *Taken Care Of* by Edith Sitwell. *Life*, Apr 30, 1965, 8.

"*Malcolm*, Mr. Cough Syrup and the American People." *Harvard Review* 100 (Mar 1966): 21.

Liner note, *63: Dream Palace by James Purdy, Read by the Author* [LP box set]. Spoken Arts, JP-4, 1968.

"Notes on Recognition." *Nimrod* 22 (spring/summer 1978): 69.

"Afterword" to "Sleep Tight." *Antioch Review* 37 (winter 1979): 35.

"The Anonymous / Anomalous Letters of Passion: The Saga of S. Vireo." *New Directions in Prose and Poetry* 38 (1979): 23–35.

"James Purdy on Denton Welch." *Little Caesar* 12 (1981): 31.

"A Statement [on James Laughlin] and Anonymous/Anomalous Letters." *Conjunctions* 1 (winter 1981/82): 175–85.

"Introduction" *Weymouth Sands* by John Cowper Powys, 7–10.. New York: Harper & Row, 1984.

"James Purdy." In *Contemporary Authors Autobiography Series, Volume 1*, edited by Dedria Bryfonski, 299–305. Detroit: Gale, 1984.

"Literary Ghosts Cling to Stone." *Newsday*, Sep 12, 1986, 78.

"Lunacy among the Teacups." Review of *Lillian's Story* by Kate Grenville, *New York Times*, Sep 6, 1986.

"Vassilis Voglis." In *Two Worlds of Vassilis Voglis*. New York: Saurus, 1988.

Published Interviews

"Penthouse Interview: James Purdy." Interview by Fred Barron. *Penthouse*, July 1974, 89–93.

"James Purdy: A Voyage of Discovery." Interview by Chris Huizenga. *After Dark*, July 1976, 72.

"Matthew Paris and Dave Zimmer Interview James Purdy." Nov 18, 1976. New York Public Radio. https://www.wnyc.org/story/james-purdy/.

"James Purdy: An Interview." Interview by Marie Claude-Profit. *Hyperion: On the Future of Aesthetics* 6, no. 1 (Mar 12, 2011): 123–42. [Rpt. of 1977 interview]

"James Purdy." Interview by Cameron Northouse. *Conversations with Writers II*, Vol. 3. Detroit: Gale, 1978. 183–211.

"Interview with James Purdy." Interview by Jere Real. *Blueboy*, Oct 1978, 25–28.

"PW Interviews: James Purdy." Interview by Robert Dahlin. *Publishers Weekly* 219 (June 1981): 12–14.

"An Interview with James Purdy." Interview by Bradford Morrow. *Conjunctions* 3 (autumn 1982): 97–111.

"James Purdy Interview." Interview by Allen Frame. *Bomb*, no. 5 (1983): 20–21.

"James Purdy: Fantasies *Are* the Truth." Interview by Larry Myers. *Christopher Street* 9, no. 10 (Dec 1986): 34–35.

"*CA* Interview." Interview by Jean W. Ross. In *Contemporary Authors*, New Revision Series, vol. 19, 391–393. Detroit: Gale, 1986.

"James Purdy Interviewed by Don Swaim, 25 June 1987." *Wired for Books*. Ohio University Libraries Digital Archival Collections, https://media.library.ohio.edu/digital/collect ion/donswaim/id/3995/rec/2.

"James Purdy Interviewed by Don Swaim, 7 Dec 1989." *Wired for Books*. Ohio University Libraries Digital Archival Collections, https://media.library.ohio.edu/digital/collect ion/donswaim/id/942/rec/3.

"An Interview with James Purdy." Interview by Donald J. Gavron. *Art Mag* 11 (spring/ summer 1989): 1–9.

"Interview with James Purdy." Interview by Patricia Lear. *StoryQuarterly* 26 (1989): 55–76.

Television interview. Adriaan van Dis, Interviewer. *De IJsbreker*. Amsterdam: Dutch television, Mar 1990. DVD compiled by Jan Erik Bouman, 2004.

"Out with James Purdy: An Interview." Interview with Christopher Lane. *Critique* 40, no. 1 (fall 1998): 71–89. [interview on Nov 27, 1993]

"James Purdy." In *Gay Fiction Speaks: Conversations with Gay Novelists*, by Richard Canning, 1–39. New York: Columbia University Press: 2000. [interview on Nov 5, 1997]

"A Conversation with James Purdy." Interview with Martin Goodman. MartinGoodman. com, April 28, 2005, martingoodman.com/archived_site/writing280405.htm.

Unpublished

"Tragic America." Introduction to Literature undergraduate thesis. Jan 1933. Bowling Green State University. [Collection of David Purdy]

"Ronald Firbank: The End of the Decadent Tradition." Master's thesis, University of Chicago. Dec 1936. [Collection of David Purdy]

"Cuban Mocking-Bird." [poem] Enclosure, Purdy to Van Vechten, p.m. 28 Mar 1957. Box 12, folder 275, series 2, JPP.

"The Christian Vision in My Work." n.d. Box 1, folder 3, HRC.

Interview with Matthew Stadler. 18 Mar 1992. Box 1, folder Article 1, MSP.

"Trick and Treat." Dictated to J. W. McCormack, 2008, email attachment to the author, 23 Mar 2021. [includes "Fragments and Sayings" and "Remembrances/Memoir"]

Other Books and Articles

Abelove, Henry. *Deep Gossip*. Minneapolis: University of Minnesota Press, 2003.

Adams, Stephen D. *The Homosexual as Hero in Contemporary Fiction*. New York: Barnes & Noble, 1980.

Adams, Stephen D. *James Purdy*. New York: Barnes & Noble, 1976.

Albee, Edward. "Foreword." In *Dream Palaces: Three Novels by James Purdy*, vii–ix. New York: Viking, 1980.

Albee, Edward. "James Purdy." In *Stretching My Mind*, 43–46. New York: Carroll & Graf, 2006.

Aletti, Vince. "American Gothic: James Purdy's Divine Madness." *Voice Literary Supplement* 48 (Sep 1986): 18–19.

Aletti, Vince. "Fogged In." Review of *The Rivalry of Dolls. Village Voice* 37 (Apr 14, 1992).

Algren, Nelson. "It's a Gay and Dreary Life." Review of *Eustace Chisholm and the Works. Critic*, Aug–Sep 1967, 67–68.

Allentown PA Bicentennial–Lehigh Country Sesquicentennial 1962 Commemorative Book: Allentown, 1762–1987, a 225 Year History, Vol. II: 1921–1987. Lehigh County Historical Society, 1987.

Anderson, Elliott. "Purdy: Endurance, a Family Theme." Review of *The House of the Solitary Maggot*. *Chicago Tribune*, Oct 20, 1974, F8.

Anderson, Sherwood. *Horses and Men*. New York: Huebsch, 1923.

Anderson, Sherwood. *Poor White*. Cleveland: Belt, 2018 [1920].

Anderson, Sherwood. *Winesburg, Ohio*. New York: Penguin, 1992 [1919].

Bachardy, Don. "James Purdy." Pencil and ink wash on paper, 29″ × 23″, 1975. Rpt. in *The James White Review* 17, no. 1 (Winter 2000): 3.

Baily, Anthony. "The Uneven, Rewarding Country of the Short Story." Review of *Don't Call Me by My Right Name and Other Stories*. *Commonweal*, Feb 8, 1957, 491.

Baldanza, Frank. "James Purdy's Half-Orphans." *The Centennial Review* 18, no. 3 (summer 1974): 255–72.

Baldanza, Frank. "Northern Gothic." *Southern Review* 10, no. 3 (July 1974): 566–82.

Battershell, James R., Jr. *Hicksville Centennial: It's Such a Nice Place*, compiled and edited by Battershell and James Meyers. Hicksville, OH, 1975.

Bauman, Pat. *Divided by a River: A History of Downtown Findlay, Now and Then*. [Findlay, OH]: Allegra, 2007.

Bawer, Bruce. "The Sensuous Woman." Review of *Gertrude of Stony Island Avenue*. *New York Times*, Aug 30, 1998.

Beck, Warren. "An Absorbed Commitment to a Restricted Vision." Review of *Children Is All*. *Chicago Daily Tribune*, Nov 18, 1962, E6.

Becker, August. "Gertrude Abercrombie." *Apartamento* 22, Nov 1, 2018.

Bernard, Emily. *Carl Van Vechten and the Harlem Renaissance*. New Haven, CT: Yale University Press, 2012.

Bérubé, Allan. *Coming Out under Fire: Th e History of Gay Men and Women in World War Two*. New York: Plume, 1991.

Bonino, Guido Davico. "The Einaudi Primer." Translated by Yvonne Freccero. *Massachusetts Review* 54, no. 4 (winter 2013): 612–23.

Bowles, Paul. *In Touch: The Letters of Paul Bowles*. Edited by Jeffrey Miller. New York: Farrar, Straus & Giroux, 1994.

Bowles, Paul. *Without Stopping: A Memoir*. New York: Harper, 1999 [1972].

Breithaupt, David. "Remembering James Purdy Esquire." *The Nervous Breakdown*, Mar 16, 2009. http://www.thenervousbreakdown.com/dbreithaupt/2009/03/remember ing-james-purdy-esquire/.

Breunig, Charles. *A Great and Good Work: A History of Lawrence University 1847–1964* Appleton, WI: Lawrence University Press.

Brown, Robert C. *History of Hancock County*. Chicago: Warner, Beers, 1886.

Brustein, Robert. "Albee's Allegory of Innocence." *New Republic* 154 (Jan 29, 1966): 34, 36.

Burns, Edward M., and Ulla E. Dydo with William Rice, eds. *Letters of Gertrude Stein & Thornton Wilder*. New Haven: Yale University Press, 1996.

Calvino, Italo. *Hermit in Paris: Autobiographical Writings*. New York: Vintage, 2004.

Canby, Vincent. "Recluse Woos Widow in *In a Shallow Grave*." *New York Times*, May 6, 1988.

"Canker of Comedy." Review of *Color of Darkness*. *Time*, Dec 9, 1957, 114.

Canning, Richard. *Gay Fiction Speaks: Conversations with Gay Novelists*. New York: Columbia University Press, 2000.

Canning, Richard. *Hear Us Out: Conversations with Gay Novelists*. New York: Columbia University Press, 2003, 291.

Canning, Richard. "Notes toward a Biography of Ronald Firbank." *James White Review* 17, no. 4 (2000): 5+.

Capote, Truman. *Too Brief a Treat: The Letters of Truman Capote*. Edited by Gerald Clarke. New York: Random House, 2004.

Carlis, John. "Oral History Interview with John Carlis, 1968 September." Interview by Henri Ghent. *Smithsonian Archives of American Art*. www.aaa.si.edu/collections/int erviews/oral-history-interview-john-carlis-11456#transcript.

Celluci, Lisa A. "An Examination of Selected Songs by Richard Hundley." DMA diss., University of Cincinnati, 2000.

Charyn, Jerome. "In a Shallow Grave." *New York Times Book Review*, Feb 8, 1976, 2–3.

Charyn, Jerome. "Unloved and Angry." Review of *Mourners Below*. *New York Times Book Review*, July 26, 1981, 8.

Cheever, John. "Art of Fiction." In *Paris Review Interviews*, vol. 3, 142–67. New York: Picador, 2008.

Chupack, Henry. *James Purdy*. Twayne's United States Authors Series. Boston: Twayne, 1975.

Coe, Jonathan. Review of *Out with the Stars*. *London Review of Books*, July 23, 1992, 22–23.

Collins, Jack. "James Purdy's New Novel." Review of *Narrow Rooms*. *San Francisco Sentinel*, July 14, 1978.

Commemorative Biographical Record of Northwestern Ohio: Including the Counties of Defiance, Henry, Williams, and Fulton. Chicago: J. H. Beers, 1899.

Commemorative Historical and Biographical Record of Wood County, Ohio. Chicago: J. H. Beers, 1897.

Cooper, Dennis. "Tribute." *James White Review* 17, no. 1 (winter 2000): 44.

Corber, Robert J. *Homosexuality in Cold War America*. Durham, NC: Duke University Press, 1997.

Cox, Christopher. "James Purdy's Fighting Words." *SoHo News*, July 22, 1981.

Cozzolino, Robert. *Dudley Huppler: Drawings*. Madison: University of Wisconsin Press, 2003.

Creeley, Robert. "Black Mountain Review." In *Collected Essays of Robert Creeley*, 505–15. Berkeley: University of California Press, 1989.

Crisp, Quentin. "The Discreet Charm of Mr Purdy." *European Gay Review* 3 (1988): 18–23.

Cromie, Robert. "Cromie Looks at Authors and Books." *Chicago Tribune*, Nov 11, 1964, D3.

Cryer, Dan. "Preacher's Kid." In Lisa Watts, ed., *Good Roots: Writers Reflect on Growing Up in Ohio*, edited by Lisa Watts, 57–68. Columbus: Ohio University Press, 2006.

Cryer, Dan. "Readers Have Yet to Find Purdy." Review of *On Glory's Course*. L.A. Times–Washington Post News Service, [spring] 1984.

Daiches, David. Introduction to *Malcolm* by Purdy, ix–xxi. New York: Noonday, 1963.

Daniel, Frank. "Purdy Opens Trio." Review of *Jeremy's Version*. *Atlanta Journal and Constitution*, Oct 11, 1970, 9–D.

Davenport, Guy. Review of *Jeremy's Version*. *New York Times*, Nov 15, 1970, BR3.

Davenport, John. "A Masterpiece from America." Review of *The Nephew*. [London] *Observer*, Mar 19, 1961.

Davis, Douglas M. "'The New Mood': An Obsession with the Absurd." *National Observer*, Feb 15, 1965, 22.

Davis, Hope Hale. "A Quest for Love." Review of *In a Shallow Grave*. *The New Leader*, May 24, 1976, 14.

De Stefano, George. "The Purdy Principle." *Out Week*, June 13, 1990, 51.

Devlin, Albert J., ed. *Conversations with Tennessee Williams*. Jackson: University Press of Mississippi, 1986.

Didion, Joan. "The Edge of the Precipice." *National Review*, Nov 19, 1960, 315–16.

Doty, Robert C. "Growth of Overt Homosexuality in City Provokes Wide Concern." *New York Times*, Dec 17, 1963.

Drury, John. *Old Illinois Houses*. Chicago: University of Chicago Press, 1977.

Dowell, Coleman. "At Home with Drosselmeier." *BOMB*, Oct 1, 1984.

Dowell, Coleman. "A Conversation with Coleman Dowell by John O'Brien." *Review of Contemporary Fiction* 2, no. 3 (fall 1982).

Dowell, Coleman. *A Star-Bright Lie*. Normal, IL: Dalkey Archive, 1993.

Drabble, Margaret. *Angus Wilson: A Biography*. New York: St. Martin's, 1995.

DuBois, William. "In and Out of Books." *New York Times*, Oct 6, 1957, 280.

Duncan, Michael. "Heretics in the Heartland." *Art in America*, Feb 2006, 100.

Dyer, Richard. "An American Odyssey, Twain Style." Review of *In the Hollow of His Hand*. *Boston Globe*, Jan 6, 1987.

Dyer, Richard. "Purdy Recreates a Gay, Surreal Old Time." Review of *Out with the Stars*. *Boston Globe*, Feb 11, 1994: A22.

Ehrhardt, Michael. "James Purdy, 1914–2009, a Personal Remembrance." *Gay & Lesbian Review Worldwide* 16, no. 3 (May 1, 2009), https://glreview.org/article/article-547/.

Ehrhardt, Michael. "Wizard of Id: An Interview with the 'Outlaw of Fiction,' James Purdy." *Gay City News*, Jan 12–18, 2006, 26–27, 31.

Elborn, Geoffrey. *Edith Sitwell: A Biography*. Garden City, NY: Doubleday, 1981.

Ellison, Ralph. "Twentieth Century Fiction and the Black Mask of Humanity." *Confluence* 2, no. 3 (Dec 1953): 3–21.

Espey, John. Review of *In the Hollow of His Hand*. *Los Angeles Times*, Oct 5, 1986, BR8.

Evenson, Brian. *Raymond Carver's What We Talk About When We Talk About Love: Bookmarked*. New York: Ig, 2018.

Evenson, Brian. Review of *Gertrude of Stony Island Avenue*. *Review of Contemporary Fiction* 19, no. 3 (fall 1999): 169.

Feingold, Michael. "The Basic Questions: James Purdy's Plays." *James White Review* 17, no. 1 (winter 2000): 41–42.

Feingold, Michael. "Half Nelson." *Village Voice*, Feb 27, 1990, 87–88.

Feingold, Michael. "Purdy as a Picture." Review of *The Great City*. *Village Voice*, July 11, 1983.

Feingold, Michael. "Waking Dreams." Review of *Sun of the Sleepless*. *Village Voice*, Apr 4, 1989, 81–82.

Flanagan, Michael. "The History of LGBT Bookstores in the Castro." *Bay Area Reporter*, July 17, 2016.

Franzen, Jonathan. "Love Letters." In *Farther Away*, 263–69. New York: Farrar, Straus & Giroux, 2018.

French, Warren. "James Purdy." In *Research Guide to Biography & Criticism*, Vol. 6, 657–662. 1991.

French, Warren. *J. D. Salinger*. Twayne's United States Authors Series. Boston: Twayne, 1963.

French, Warren. Review of *The House of the Solitary Maggot*. *The Great Lakes Review* 1, no. 2 (winter 1975): 88–93.

Furbank, P. N. "Opting Out." Review of *Cabot Wright Begins*. *Encounter* 25 (Oct 1965): 80–84.

Galanes, Philip. "A Conversation with Terrence McNally, the Bard of American Theater." *New York Times Style Magazine*, Apr 10, 2010.

Galanes, Philip. "Gertrude Stein: Letters to a Friend." *Paris Review* 100 (summer–fall 1986): 359–78.

Geller, Evelyn. "WLB Biography: James Purdy." *Wilson Library Bulletin* 38 (Mar 1964): 572–74.

Gertrude Abercrombie Retrospective Exhibition Catalog. Chicago: Hyde Park Art Center, 1977.

Giancana, Sam, and Chuck Giancana. *Double Cross*. New York: Warner, 1992.

Glendinning, Victoria. *Edith Sitwell: A Unicorn among Lions*. New York: Knopf, 1981.

Glendinning, Victoria. "Reassuring Sense of Sin." Review of *On Glory's Course*. *The Sunday Times*, Feb 10, 1985.

Gluck, Victor. "The Great City." *Back Stage*, July 29, 1983, 56.

Gollancz, Victor. "Afterword." In George Orwell, *Down and Out in Paris and London*, 190. New York: Penguin, 1982 [1933].

Gooch, Brad. *Flannery: A Life of Flannery O'Connor*. New York: Little, Brown, 2009.

Gooch, Brad. *Smash Cut: A Memoir of Howard & Art & the '70s & the '80s*. New York: Harper, 2015.

Gottlieb, Robert. "Anatomy of a Publisher: The story of Farrar, Straus & Giroux." Review of *Hothouse* by Kachka, *New Yorker*, Aug 5, 2013, https://www.newyorker.com/magazine/2013/08/12/anatomy-of-a-publisher.

Greene, Richard. Introduction to *Selected Letters of Edith Sitwell*, edited by Greene. London: Virago, 1997.

Grimes, William. (AP). "A Fabulist Haunting the Fringes." *New York Times*, Aug 26, 2013.

Grobel, Lawrence. *Conversations with Capote*. New York: Signet, 1988.

Guinness, Alec. *Blessings in Disguise*. New York, Knopf, 1986.

Gunn, Thom. "All Pretty Much Strangers." Review of *Dream Palaces*. *Threepenny Review* 3 (autumn 1980): 7–8.

Gussow, Mel. *Edward Albee: A Singular Journey*. New York: Simon & Schuster, 1999.

Hanshe, Rainer J. "Introduction" to "Ready All the Time like Gunpowder: An Interview with Richard Hundley." *Hyperion* 6, no. 1 (Mar 2011): 161–68.

Harris, Bertha. "The Pest Can't Get Them Down." Review of *Garments the Living Wear*. *New York Times*, Oct 29, 1989, BR13.

Hassan, Ihab. "Of Anguish and Incongruity." Review of *Children Is All*. *Saturday Review*, Nov 17, 1962, 29.

Hawkes, John and John J. Enck. "John Hawkes: An Interview." *Wisconsin Studies in Contemporary Literature* 6, no. 2 (Summer 1965): 141–155.

Hayworth, Eugene. *Fever Vision: The Life and Works of Coleman Dowell*. Champaign, IL: Dalkey Archive, 2007.

Heide, Robert. "Carousing in the Village with Terrence and Edward." *WestView News*, May 3, 2020.

Heminger, R. L. *Across the Years in Findlay and Hancock County*. Findlay, OH: Republican-Courier, 1965.

Hensher, Philip. "Drama in Dressing Gowns." Review of *Out with the Stars*. *The Guardian*, July 30, 1992, 27.

Hicks, Granville. Review of *Malcolm*. *Saturday Review*, Sep 26, 1959, 15.

Hills, L. Rust. "The Structure of the American Literary Establishment." *Esquire*, July 1963, 40–43.

Hohman, Valleri J. "The Final Straw: Producing James Purdy at the Trinity Square Rep." *Theatre History Studies* 29 (2009): 95–102.

Holditch, Kenneth. "Stylish Originals." Review of *Garments the Living Wear*. New Orleans *Times-Picayune*, Mar 4, 1990, F11–12.

Hopkinson, Tom. "The Life of the Damned." Review of *63: Dream Palace*. [London] *Observer*, June 30, 1957, 12.

Horchler, Richard. "Impending Revelations." Review of *Children Is All*. *Commonweal* 77, no. 15 (Jan 4, 1963): 393, 395.

Hughes, Langston. "Carl Van Vechten: An Appreciation." In *Collected Works of Langston Hughes*, Vol. 9, 418–20. Columbia: University of Missouri Press, 2001.

Huizenga, Chris. "James Purdy: A Voyage of Discovery." *After Dark*, July 1976, 70–73.

Humphrey, William D. *Findlay: The Story of a Community*. Findlay, OH: Findlay Printing, 1961.

Hundley, Richard. "Ready All the Time like Gunpowder." Interview with Rainer J. Hanshe. *Hyperion* 6, no. 1 (Mar 2011): 159-85.

Huston, Carol J. "Gertrude Abercrombie (1909–1977): Midwestern Surrealist." Sullivan Goss Gallery, www.sullivangoss.com/gertrude_abercrombie/.

Hyman, Stanley Edgar. "The Conviction of Opinion." Review of *Cabot Wright Begins*. *New Leader* 47 (23 Nov 1964): 19–20.

Hyman, Stanley Edgar. *Standards: A Chronicle of Books for Our Time*. New York: Horizon, 1966.

Inge, M. Thomas. *Truman Capote: Conversations*. Jackson: University Press of Mississippi, 1987.

Italie, Hillel. "Cult Author James Purdy Starting to Gain Recognition." *Associated Press*, Dec 5, 2005.

Jackson, Angela. *A Surprised Queenhood in the New Black Sun: The Life and Legacy of Gwendolyn Brooks*. Boston: Beacon Press, 2017.

"James Purdy." *Contemporary Authors*, New Revision Series, Vol. 19, 389–95. Detroit: Gale, 1987.

"James Purdy." *World Authors 1950–1970*, ed. John Wakeman, 1172–75. New York: H. W. Wilson, 1975.

"James Purdy Says He Doesn't Exist because 'I Am Not Sophisticated in a Cultured Jewish–New Yorker Way.'" *Books* 1, no. 9 (Oct 1964): 1, 7.

The James White Review 17, no. 1 (Winter 2000). [James Purdy special issue.]

Kachka, Boris. *Hothouse: The Art of Survival and the Survival of Art at America's Most Celebrated Publishing House*. New York: Simon & Schuster, 2013.

Kaiser, Charles. *The Gay Metropolis: The Landmark History of Gay Life in America*. New York: Grove, 2019.

Kaplan, David. *Tennessee Williams in Provincetown*. East Brunswick, NJ: Hansen, 2007.

Kaufman, Jeff, dir. *Terrence McNally: Every Act of Life*. Floating World, 2018.

Kauffmann, Stanley. "Homosexual Drama and Its Disguises." *New York Times*, Jan 23, 1966.

Kauffmann, Stanley. "Theater: Edward Albee's 'Malcolm.'" *New York Times*, Jan 12, 1966.

Kellner, Bruce, ed. *Letters of Carl Van Vechten*. New Haven, CT: Yale University Press, 1987.

Kenney, Brian. Review of *Out with the Stars*. *Library Journal* 118 (Oct 1993): 128.

Kenny, Maurice. "Introduction: A Memoir." In *On Second Thought: A Compilation*, 1-63. Norman: University of Oklahoma Press, 1995.

Kenny, Maurice. *Rain and Other Fictions: Stories*. Buffalo: White Pine, 1989.

Kenny, Maurice. "Tinseled Bucks: A Historical Study in Indian Homosexuality." *Gay Sunshine* 26/27 (winter 1975–1976): 15–17.

King, Francis. "Exotic Cast." Review of *I Am Elijah Thrush*. Sunday *Telegraph*, Oct 22, 1972.

King, Francis. "Particle of Genius." Review of *Mourners Below*. *Spectator*, May 19, 1984, 31.

Klein, Julia M. Review of *Mourners Below*. *New Republic* 185, no. 3 (July 1981): 39.

Knight, Douglas M. *The Dancer and the Dance: One Man's Chronicle 1938–2001*. New York: Separate Star, 2001.

Kolin, Philip C. "Tenn and the Banana Queen: The Correspondence of Tennessee Williams and Marion Black Vaccaro." *Tennessee Williams Annual Review*, 2006. http://www.tennesseewilliamsstudies.org/journal/work.php?ID=72.

Kostelanetz, Richard. *The End of Intelligent Writing: Literary Politics in America*. New York: Sheed and Ward, 1974.

Ladd, Jay. *James Purdy: A Bibliography*. Columbus: Ohio State University Libraries, 1999.

Lahr, John. *Tennessee Williams: Mad Pilgrimage of the Flesh*. New York: W. W. Norton, 2014.

Leavitt, Richard Freeman, and Kenneth Holditch. *The World of Tennessee Williams*. East Brunswick, NJ: Hansen, 2011.

Leverich, Lyle. *Tom: The Unknown Tennessee Williams*. New York: W. W. Norton, 1995.

Lewis, R. W. B. "Baffling, Perverse, Demonic, Original." Review of *Malcolm*. *New York Herald Tribune*, Oct 11, 1959, 5.

Lewis, R. W. B. "Recent Fiction: Picaro and Pilgrim." In *A Time of Harvest: American Literature, 1910–1960*, edited by Robert E. Spiller, 144–53. New York: Hill and Wang, 1962.

Lewisohn, Ludwig. *Expression in America*. New York: Harper & Brothers, 1932.

Linchong, Victoria. "Goodbye, James Purdy." *A Hard Way to Make an Easy Living*, Mar 13, 2009. hardwayeasyliving.blogspot.com/2009/03/goodbye-james-purdy.html.

Lindroth, James R. Review of *Eustace Chisholm and the Works*. *America* 117 (July 1, 1967): 20–21.

Lindroth, James R. Review of *Jeremy's Version*. *America* 124 (Feb 27, 1971): 211.

Link, James. "Consuming Love." Review of *Narrow Rooms*. *SoHo Weekly News*, May 25, 1978, 51.

Link, James. "James Purdy." *Interview* 11, nos. 6–7 (June/July 1981): 62–63.

Lish, Gordon. "The Art of Editing No. 2." With Christian Lorentzen. *Paris Review* 215 (winter 2015): 195–217.

Littleton, Humphrey. *The Best of Jazz II: Enter the Giants 1931–1944*. London: Unwin, 1984.

Londraville, Janis, and Richard Londraville. *The Most Beautiful Man in the World*. Lincoln: University of Nebraska Press, 2008.

Lyke, M. L. "Honors for an Outcast: James Purdy's Work Has Outlasted Critics." *Seattle Post-Intelligencer*, Oct 12, 1993, C1.

Macdonald, Dwight. "Fictioneers." Review of *63: Dream Palace: A Novella and Nine Stories*. *Encounter* 9 (Sep 1957): 76–79.

Mailer, Norman. "Evaluations: Quick and Expensive Comments on the Talent in the Room." In *Advertisements for Myself*, 463–73. New York: Putnam, 1959.

Mailer, Norman. "Up the Family Tree." Review of *Making It* by Podhoretz. In *Existential Errands*, 157–79. New York: Signet, 1973.

Malanowski, Jamie. "Previews: Michael Biehn and James Purdy." *Interview* 18 (Apr 1988): 21.

Malcolm, Janet. "Gertrude Stein's War." *New Yorker*, June 2, 2003. https://www.newyorker.com/magazine/2003/06/02/gertrude-steins-war.

Male, Andrew. "I'm Not a Gay Writer, I'm a Monster." *The Guardian*, Mar 11, 2019.

Malin, Irving. "James (Otis) Purdy." In *Contemporary Novelists*, 3rd ed., edited by James Vinson. New York: St. Martin's, 1982.

Malin, Irving. Review of *Garments the Living Wear*. *Contemporary Fiction* 10, no. 1 (spring 1990): 327.

Malin, Irving. Review of *Gertrude of Stony Island*. *Hollins Critic* 37, no. 1 (Feb 2000): 20.

Malin, Irving. Review of *Out with the Stars*. *Review of Contemporary Fiction* 14, no. 2 (summer 1994): 208.

Martin, James M. "Of Greater Love and Sacrifices." Review of *In a Shallow Grave*. *Los Angeles Times*, Mar 7, 1976, P4.

Martin, James M. "A Potpourri of Prose from James Purdy." Review of *A Day after the Fair*. *Los Angeles Times*, Dec 18, 1977, 30.

Martin, James M. "Skeletons in a Midwestern Closet." Review of *The House of the Solitary Maggot*. *Los Angeles Times*, Nov 18, 1974.

Matthiessen, F. O. *American Renaissance: Art and Expression in the Age of Emerson and Whitman*. New York: Oxford University Press, 1941.

Max, D. T. "The Carver Chronicles." *New York Times*, Aug 9, 1998, SM34.

McCann, Richard. "Lives of Quiet Desperation." Review of *63: Dream Palace, Selected Stories 1956–1987*. *Washington Post*, Jan 12, 1992, 3+.

McCormack, J. W. "On James Purdy." *Tin House* 14, no. 1 (fall 2012): 155–58.

McCuller, Jerry. Liner notes. *In a Shallow Grave* Soundtrack. Varèse Saraband CD, 2008.

McGowin, Kevin. "Why I Still Use a Manual Typewriter." *Classic Typewriter Page: Typewriter Tributes*, n.d., site.xavier.edu/polt/typewriters/mcgowin2.html.

McNally, Terrence. *Muse of Fire: Reflections on Theater*. Edited by Raymond-Jean Frontain. Vancouver: Fairleigh Dickinson University Press, 2020.

McNally, Terrence. *The Play of Malcolm*. Dated summer 1964. Box 40, folder 9, McNally Papers, Harry Ransom Center, University of Texas.

McNamara, Eugene. "The Post-Modern American Novel." *Queen's Quarterly* 64, no. 2 (1962): 265–75.

Merla, Patrick. "From the Editor" and "Tributes." *James White Review* 17, no. 1 (winter 2000): 4, 42–43.

Michaud, Jon. "The Strange, Unsettling Fiction of James Purdy." *New Yorker*, 21 July 2015. https://www.newyorker.com/books/page-turner/the-strange-unsettling-fiction-of-james-purdy.

Miller, Paul W. "James (Otis) Purdy." In *Dictionary of Midwestern Literature*, edited by Philip A. Greasley, 421–23. Bloomington: Indiana University Press, 2001.

Miller, Paul W. "James Purdy's Early Years in Ohio and His Early Short Stories." *MidAmerica* 11 (1984): 108–16.

Miller, Paul W. "James Purdy's Fiction as Shaped by the American Midwest: The Chicago Novels." In *American Literature in Belgium*, *Costerus* new series, vols. 66–67, 149–61. 1988.

Miller, Paul W. "James Purdy's *Gertrude* (1997): A Visit to Chicago Painter Gertrude Abercrombie (1909–1977) in Hades." *Midwest Miscellany* 27 (fall 1999): 26–35.

Miller, Paul W. "The Limits of Realism in James Purdy's First Ohio Novel, *The Nephew*." *MidAmerica* 12 (1985): 83–96.

Moser, Benjamin. *Sontag: Her Life and Work*. New York: Ecco, 2019.

"New Fiction." Review of *63: Dream Palace*. London *Times*, July 4, 1957, 13.

Newman, Charles. "Beyond Omniscience: Notes toward a Future for the Novel." *TriQuarterly* 10 (fall 1967): 37–52.

Newman, Charles. *The Post-Modern Aura: The Act of Fiction in an Age of Inflation*. Evanston, IL: Northwestern University Press, 1985.

Nicolson, Nigel. "The Face Behind the Façade." Review of *Edith Sitwell* by Glendinning, and *Edith Sitwell* by Elborn, *Washington Post*, June 7, 1981, 5.

Nin, Anaïs. *Diary of Anaïs Nin, Volume Six, 1955–1966*. New York: Harvest/HBJ, 1977.

Oates, Joyce Carol. "Notions Good and Bad." Review of *Cabot Wright Begins*. *Kenyon Review* 27 (winter 1965): 175–180.

O'Brien, John. "Purdy, Privately Printed." Review of *A Day After the Fair*. *Chicago Daily News*, Nov 19–20, 1977, 22.

O'Quinn, Jim. "The Chaos beyond Language." Review of *The Great City*. *New York Native*, Aug 15–28, 1983.

Otis, William A. *A Genealogical and Historical Memoir of the Otis Family in America*. Chicago: Schulkins, 1924.

Page, Chester. *Memoirs of a Charmed Life in New York*. Bloomington, IN: iUniverse, 2007.

Paller, Michael. *Gentlemen Callers: Tennessee Williams, Homosexuality, and Mid-Twentieth-Century Broadway Drama*. New York: Palgrave, 2005.

Parker, Dorothy. "Dorothy Parker on Books: Four Rousing Cheers." Review of *Color of Darkness*. *Esquire* 50 (July 1958): 18, 20.

Parker, Dorothy. Review of *Malcolm*. *Esquire*, Dec 1959, 105.

Parker, Ian. "Showboat: Roger Straus and His Flair for Selling Literature." *New Yorker*, Apr 8, 2002. www.newyorker.com/magazine/2002/04/08/showboat.

Peake, Tony. *Derek Jarman: A Biography*. Minneapolis: University of Minnesota Press, 2011.

Pearson, John. *The Sitwells: A Family's Biography*. New York: Harcourt Brace Jovanovich, 1979.

Peden, William. *The American Short Story: Front Line in the National Defense of Literature*. Boston: Houghton Mifflin, 1964.

Peden, William. "And Never a Silver Lining." Review of *Color of Darkness*. *New York Times*, Dec 29, 1957, 126.

Peden, William. "Mystery of the Missing Kin." Review of *The Nephew*. *Saturday Review*, Nov 26, 1960, 29.

Peden, William. "Pilgrimage to Destruction." Review of *Malcolm*. *New York Times*, Sep 27, 1959, BR5.

Peden, William. "Short Fiction vs. Long." *Saturday Review*, Jan 25, 1958, 17–18.

Peretti, Burton W. *Jazz in American Culture*. Chicago: Ivan R. Dee, 1997.

Picano, Felice. "Felice Picano Diaries: Spring 1982." Edited by Kevin Stone Fries. *Lodestar Quarterly* 1 (spring 2002). https://lodestarquarterly.com/work/8/.

Pileggi, Nicholas. "The Mob and the Machine." *New York*, May 5, 1986, nymag.com/news/features/crime/46610/.

Plunket, Robert. "The Visionary." *The Advocate*, Oct 13, 1998, 91.

Podhoretz, Norman. *Making It*. New York: New York Review Books, 2017 [1967].

Pollitt, Kate. "Ovid and the Boys." Review of *Narrow Rooms*. *New York Times*, Apr 23, 1978, BR3.

Polsgrove, Carole. *It Wasn't Pretty Folks, but Didn't We Have Fun? Esquire in the Sixties*. New York: W. W. Norton, 1995.

Powys, John Cowper. "Desperate Cry." [London] *Observer*, July 14, 1957, 11.

Prescott, Orville. "The Waste of a Small Talent." Review of *Cabot Wright Begins*. *New York Times*, Oct 19, 1964, 31.

Profit, Marie-Claude. *James Purdy: Les cauchemars de papier*. Paris: Belin, 1998.

Pulsifer, Gary, ed. *Paul Bowles by His Friends*. London: Peter Owen, 1992.

Purdy, Dorothy, and Nancy Spiegelberg. *Fanfare: A Celebration of Belief*. Portland, OR: Multnomah, 1981.

Purdy, John David. *Dads Are Special, Too*. Wheaton, IL: Tyndale House, 1985.

Purdy, Robert L. *The Successful High School Athletic Program*. West Nyack, NY: Parker, 1973.

Rollyson, Carl, and Lisa Paddock. *Susan Sontag: The Making of an Icon*. New York: W. W. Norton, 2000.

Rorem, Ned. *Knowing When to Stop: A Memoir*. New York: Simon & Schuster, 1994.

Rorem, Ned. *The Later Diaries of Ned Rorem, 1961–1972*. Boston: Da Capo, 2000.

Rorem, Ned. *Wings of Friendship: Selected Letters, 1944–2003*. Berkeley, CA: Counterpoint, 2005.

Rosen, Gerald. *Cold Eye, Warm Heart: A Novelist's Search for Meaning*. N.p.: Calm Unity Press, 2009.

Ryan, Hugh. *When Brooklyn Was Queer*. New York: St. Martin's, 2019.

St George, Andrew. "People to Avoid Like the Plague: 'Garments the Living Wear.'" *Independent*, May 27, 1989, 31.

Salter, Elizabeth. *The Last Years of a Rebel: A Memoir of Edith Sitwell*. Boston: Houghton Mifflin, 1967.

Samors, Neal, and Bob Dauber. *Entertaining Chicago*. Chicago: Chicago's Books, 2019.

Sams, Parker C. "Purdy's Latest Novel Set in His Hometown Findlay." *The Courier*, Sep 12, 1984.

Saunders, Frances Stonor. *The Cultural Cold War: The CIA and the World of Arts and Letters*. New York: New Press, 2000.

Savran, David. *Communists, Cowboys, and Queers: The Politics of Masculinity in the Work of Arthur Miller and Tennessee Williams*. Minneapolis: University of Minnesota Press, 1992.

Schaap, Dick. "Behind the Lines: The Unloved One." *New York Herald Tribune Book Week*, May 9, 1965.

Schott, Webster. "James Purdy: American Dreams." *The Nation*, Mar 23, 1964, 300.

Schott, Webster. "Life Seen through Haze of Gossip." Review of *The Nephew*. *Kansas City Star*, Nov 5, 1960.

Schwartz, Miranda. Review of *Gertrude of Stony Island Avenue*. *Washington Post*, Dec 20, 1998, X06.

Schwarzschild, Bettina. *The Not-Right House: Essays on James Purdy*. Columbia: University of Missouri Press, 1968.

Scott, Winfield Townley. "Enter a Writer, Talented and Intense." Review of *Color of Darkness*. *New York Herald Tribune Book Review*, Dec 29, 1957, 3.

Seaman, Donna. "Bebop Artist Gertrude Abercrombie." *Art in Chicago: A History from the Fire to Now*, edited by Maggie Taft, Robert Cozzolino, Judith Russi Kirsher, and Erin Hogan, 130. Chicago: University of Chicago Press, 2018.

Seaman, Donna. *Identity Unknown: Rediscovering Seven American Women Artists.* New York: Bloomsbury, 2017.

See, Carolyn. "What It Was Like BT (Before Television)." Review of *On Glory's Course. Los Angeles Times*, Mar 24, 1984, F6.

Segal, Lee. "Under the Dust Cover." *Louisville Courier-Journal*, Oct 4, 1959, 72.

Seidman, Robert J. "War between Mothers and Sons." Review of *On Glory's Course. New York Times Book Review*, Feb 26, 1984.

Sheed, Wilfred. "An Alleged Love Story." Review of *Eustace Chisholm and the Works. New York Times*, May 21, 1967, BR4.

Sheed, Wilfred. "The Stage: Heterosexual Backlash." *Commonweal*, May 1965, 289–92.

Shwartz, Ronald B., ed. *For the Love of Books.* New York: Grosset/Putnam, 1999.

Silverberg, Ira. "James Purdy: A Prophet Unhonored." *Gay Times*, June 1992, 50, 52–53.

Sitwell, Edith. *Edith Sitwell: Selected Letters.* Edited by John Lehmann and Derek Parker. London: Macmillan, 1970.

Sitwell, Edith. "Purdy: 'The Marrow of Form.'" Review of *Children Is All. New York Herald Tribune Book Review*, Nov 18, 1962, 6.

Sitwell, Edith. *Selected Letters of Edith Sitwell.* Edited by Richard Greene. London: Virago, 1997.

Sitwell, Edith. "Under the Skin." Review of *63: Dream Palace. Times Literary Supplement*, July 19, 1957, 437.

Skerrett, Joseph Taylor, Jr. "James Purdy and the Black Mask of Humanity." *MELUS* 6, no. 2 (summer 1979): 79–89.

Slavitt, David R. "James Purdy's Wacky but Elegant Love stories." *Chicago Tribune—Books*, 5 July 1987, 5.

Smith, Lee. "Kidnapped by Everyone." Review of *In the Hollow of His Hand. New York Times Book Review*, Oct 19, 1986, 15.

Snyder, Michael. "Becoming James Purdy: The 'New' Stories in *The Complete Short Stories of James Purdy.*" *MidAmerica, the Yearbook of the Society for the Study of Midwestern Literature* 44 (2017): 111–30.

Snyder, Michael. "Mixedblood Metaphors: Allegories of Native America in the Fiction of James Purdy." PhD diss., University of Oklahoma, 2009.

Snyder, Michael. "'Original Stock' in America: James Purdy's Native American Desire in *Eustace Chisholm and the Works.*" *Critique: Studies in Contemporary Fiction* 52, no. 2 (2011): 176–97.

Solotaroff, Theodore. *The Red Hot Vacuum and Other Pieces on the Writing of the Sixties.* New York: Atheneum, 1970.

Solotaroff, Theodore. "A Stud Farm for Horselaughs." Review of *Cabot Wright Begins, New York Herald Tribune Book Week*, Oct 18, 1964, 3.

Sontag, Susan. "Laughter in the Dark." Review of *Cabot Wright Begins. New York Times Book Review*, Oct 25, 1964, 5.

Southern, Terry. "New Trends and Old Hats." Review of *The Nephew. The Nation*, Nov 19, 1960, 380–82.

Southern, Terry. "No Stranger to Excess." *Paris Review*, Dec 17, 2015. https://www.theparisreview.org/blog/2015/12/17/no-stranger-to-excess/.

Spring, Justin. *Secret Historian: Professor, Tattoo Artist, and Sexual Renegade.* New York: Farrar, Straus & Giroux, 2010.

Stadler, Matthew. "The House of the Solitary Maggot." *Nest*, winter 1998–1999, 92–96.

Stadler, Matthew. "A Shameless Reality." Review of *The Candles of Your Eyes*. *New York Native*, May 18, 1987, 29.

Stadler, Matthew. "The Theater of Real Speech." *James White Review* 17, no. 1 (winter 2000): 6–12.

Stein, Gertrude. *Everybody's Autobiography*. New York: Random House, 1937.

Stein, Jean. *Edie: An American Biography*. Edited by Stein and George Plimpton. New York: Dell, 1983.

Steward, Samuel M. *Chapters from an Autobiography*. San Francisco: Grey Fox, 1981.

Steward, Samuel. *Lost Autobiography of Samuel Steward*. Edited by Jeremy Mulderig. Chicago: University of Chicago Press, 2018.

Steward, Samuel, ed. *Dear Sammy: Letters from Gertrude Stein and Alice B. Toklas with a Memoir by Samuel M. Steward*. Boston: Houghton Mifflin, 1977.

Strausbaugh, John. "Clever Cats and Opaque Snakes." *New York Press*, Nov 22–28, 2000, 24.

Strausbaugh, John. "Foment." *New York Press*, Apr 2–8, 1997.

Strausbaugh, John. "Pure Purdy." *New York Press*, Mar 19–25, 1997, 41–42.

Studebaker, John W. "The United States Office of Education." *ANNALS of the American Academy of Political and Social Science* 235 (1944): 62–68.

"Sugar Beet Production in Northwestern Ohio." *Bulletin of the Agricultural College Extension Service, Ohio State University*, no. 102, Nov 1930.

Sullivan, Alvin. "Days of *The Phoenix*." *Journal of Modern Literature* 2, no. 1 (Sep 1971): 137–43.

Sundel, Alfred. "The Limp-Wrist School." Review of *Color of Darkness*. *New Leader*, June 19, 1961, 25–26.

Swift, Edward. "Too Gay to Be Gay." *New York Native*, Nov 5–18, 1984, 37, 39.

"Talking about Angus Wilson." *Twentieth Century Literature* 29, no. 2 (summer 1983): 115–41.

Tanner, Tony. "Birdsong." *Partisan Review* 39 (fall 1972): 609–14.

Tanner, Tony. "Frames without Pictures." In *City of Words: American Fictions 1950s–1970*, 85–108. New York: Harper & Row. 1971.

Taylor, Robert. "A Note from James Purdy Cheers Up 'Wicked Witch' Actress Margaret Hamilton." *Harry Ransom Center Magazine*, Jan 20, 2015.

Theroux, Paul. "The Shocking Mr. Purdy." *Vanity Fair*, June 1997, 116.

Tippins, Sherill. *Inside the Dream Palace: The Life and Times of New York's Legendary Chelsea Hotel*. New York: Houghton Mifflin Harcourt, 2015.

Toklas, Alice B. *Staying On Alone: Letters of Alice B. Toklas*. Edited by Edward Burns. New York: W. W. Norton, 1982.

Tommasini, Anthony. *Virgil Thomson: Composer on the Aisle*. New York: W. W. Norton, 1997.

Trevillion, David. "James Purdy: A Balance of Cruelty and Wit." *Soho Weekly News*, Nov 17, 1977, 57–58.

Turnbaugh, Douglas Blair. "A.K.A. Adonis Whiteacre: Anonymous, Anomalous Letters from James Purdy." *James White Review* 17, no. 1 (winter 2000): 30–35.

Turnbaugh, Douglas. "A Buried Wonder." *Advocate*, May 24, 1988, 67–69.

Turnbaugh, Douglas. "Fighting for His Words." *Advocate*, Oct 9, 1990, 82.

Turnbaugh, Douglas Blair. "James Purdy: Playwright." *PAJ: A Journal of Performance and Art* 20, no. 2 (1998): 73–75.

United States Government Manual—Federal Security Agency, 1945.

Uecker, John. *Memento Mori*. jamespurdy.org.

Uecker, John. "Two Visionaries." Introduction to *Selected Plays of James Purdy*, ix–xii. Chicago: Ivan R. Dee, 2009.

Van Renterghem, Eric. *Findlay in Vintage Postcards*. Chicago: Arcadia, 2001.

Varble, Stephen. "I Am James Purdy." *Andy Warhol's Interview*, Dec 1972, 28–29.

Vidal, Gore. "The *Fag Rag* Interview." By John Mitzel, Steven Abbott, and the Gay Study Group, spring 1974. In *Conversations with Gore Vidal*, edited by Richard Peabody and Lucinda Ebersole, 16–35. Jackson: University Press of Mississippi, 2005.

Vidal, Gore. "James Purdy: The Novelist as Outlaw." *New York Times*, Feb 27, 2005. https://www.nytimes.com/2005/02/27/books/review/james-purdy-the-novelist-as-outlaw.html.

Vidal, Gore. *Point to Point Navigation: A Memoir 1964 to 2006*. New York: Doubleday: 2006.

Vidal, Gore. "Rabbit's Own Burrow." In *Selected Essays of Gore Vidal*, ed. Jay Parini, 239–63. New York: Doubleday, 2008.

Vidal, Gore. "Some Memories of the Glorious Bird and an Earlier Self." In *United States: Essays 1952–1992*, 1131–48. New York: Random House, 1993.

Wakefield, Dan. *Going All the Way*. New York: Delacorte, 1970.

Wakefield, Dan. *New York in the 50s*. New York: St. Martin's Griffin, 1992.

Warburg, Fredric. *All Authors Are Equal: The Publishing Life of Fredric Warburg, 1936–1971*. London: Hutchinson, 1973.

Warren, Paul [Frank Sandiford]. *Next Time Is for Life*. New York: Dell, 1953.

Waters, John. *Crackpot: The Obsessions of John Waters*. New York: Vintage, 1987.

Waters, John. *Mr. Know It All: The Tarnished Wisdom of a Filth Elder*. New York: Farrar, Straus & Giroux, 2019.

Waters, John. "My 10 Favorite Books." *New York Times Style Magazine*, Nov 20, 2015.

Waters, John. *Role Models*. New York: Farrar, Straus & Giroux, 2009.

Weatherby, William. "The Choler of Despair." *Times Literary Supplement*, June 10, 1965, 474.

Weininger, Susan. "Gertrude Abercrombie." In *Gertrude Abercrombie: An Exhibition*, 9–39. Springfield: Illinois State Museum, 1991.

Weininger, Susan. "Introduction." In *Gertrude Abercrombie and Friends*, n.p. Springfield: Illinois State Museum, 1983.

Weir, John. "Everything Was Purpler Then." Review of *Out with the Stars*. *New York Times*, Jan 16, 1994, BR24.

Weise, Donald. "Christmas with James Purdy." *Lambda Literary*, Dec 9, 2013, www.lambdaliterary.org/2013/12/christmas-with-james-purdy/.

Wetzsteon, Ross. "Making It the Hard Way." Review of *Eustace Chisholm*. *Book Week*, May 28, 1967.

White, Edmund. *City Boy*. New York: Bloomsbury, 2009.

White, Edmund. "Fame, the Greatest Aphrodisiac." Review of *Out with the Stars*. *LAMBDA Book Report* 4, no. 2 (Jan/Feb 1994): 208+.

White, Edmund. *My Lives*. New York: HarperCollins, 2006.

White, Edmund. *States of Desire: Travels in Gay America*. New York: Dutton, 1983.

White, Edward. *The Tastemaker: Carl Van Vechten and the Birth of Modern America*. New York: Farrar, Straus & Giroux, 2014.

Whitney, Joel. *Finks: How the CIA Tricked the World's Best Writers*. New York: OR Books, 2016.

Whittaker, Rick. *The First Time I Met Frank O'Hara: Reading Gay American Writers.* New York: Four Walls Eight Windows, 2003.

Wilcox, Wendell. *Everything Is Quite All Right.* New York: Bernard Ackerman, 1945.

Wilcox, Wendell. "No One Ever Looks Up." *Creative Writing* 1, no. 8 (Oct 1939): 16–23.

Wilford, Hugh. "Playing the CIA's Tune? The 'New Leader' and the Cultural Cold War." *Diplomatic History* 27, no. 1 (Jan 2003): 15–34.

Williams, Tennessee. *One Arm and Other Stories.* New York: New Directions, 1948.

Williams, Tennessee. *Small Craft Warnings.* New York: New Directions, 1972.

Wilson, Angus. "The Horror Game." Review of *Cabot Wright Begins. The Observer* [London], May 30, 1965.

Wilson, Angus. "Purdy Pushes Comedy Past Blackness." Review of *Eustace Chisholm and the Works. Life,* June 2, 1967, 8.

Wilson, Bob, ed. [Robert A.]. *The Phoenix Book Shop: A Nest of Memories.* Candia, NH: John LeBow, 1997.

Windham, Donald. *Lost Friendships: A Memoir of Truman Capote, Tennessee Williams, and Others.* New York: William Morrow, 1987.

Windham, Donald, ed. *Tennessee Williams' Letters to Donald Windham 1940–1965.* New York: Holt, Rinehart & Winston, 1977.

Winks, Robin W. *Cloak and Gown: Scholars in the Secret War, 1939–1961.* 2nd ed. New Haven, CT: Yale University Press, 1996.

Wittke, Paul. "Vignettes of His Life and Times." *Virgil Thomson: American Composer and Author.* www.virgilthomson.org/about/vignettes#new-york.

Wolcott, James. "Gored Again." *Vanity Fair,* Feb 10, 2015. https://www.vanityfair.com/culture/2015/02/gored-again.

Wolfe, Geoffrey. "Stung Ventricles." Review of *Jeremy's Version. Newsweek* 76 (Oct 12, 1970): 122–23.

Woodhouse, Reed. "James Purdy (Re)visited." *Harvard Gay & Lesbian Review* 2 (spring 1995): 16–17.

Woodhouse, Reed. "James Purdy's Escape from the Wasteland." *Harvard Gay & Lesbian Review* 1, no. 3 (summer 1994): 24–26.

Woods, Gregory. *A History of Gay Literature: The Male Tradition.* New Haven, CT: Yale University Press, 1998.

Yohalem, John. "An Outlaw on Outlaws." *American Theatre,* Apr 1989, 8.

Index